No. 9704
$27.90

HOW TO DESIGN & BUILD ENERGY–EFFICIENT FIREPLACES & CHIMNEYS

BY JOSEPH D. FALCONE

HOMEOWNER'S GUIDE TO SAVING ENERGY

REVISED EDITION

BY BILLY L. PRICE & JAMES T. PRICE

FIRST EDITION

FIRST PRINTING

Printed in the United States of America

Library of Congress Cataloging in Publication Data

Falcone, Joseph D
How to design & build energy-efficient fireplaces & chimneys, Homeowner's guide to saving-energy—revised edition.

Includes index.
1. Fireplaces—Design and construction—Amateur's manuals. 2. Chimneys—Design and construction—Amateur's manuals. 3. Dwellings—Energy construction—Amateurs' manuals. I. Price, Billy L.
Homeowner-s guide to saving energy, 1980.
II. Title.
TH7425.F35 697'.1 80-21245
ISBN 0-8306-9694-6

No. 1197
$13.95

HOW TO DESIGN & BUILD ENERGY-EFFICIENT FIREPLACES & CHIMNEYS

BY
JOSEPH D. FALCONE

TAB TAB BOOKS Inc.
BLUE RIDGE SUMMIT, PA. 17214

FIRST EDITION

FIRST PRINTING

Library of Congress Cataloging in Publication Data

Falcone, Joseph D
How to design & build energy-efficient fireplaces & chimneys.

Includes index.
1. Fireplaces—Amateurs' manuals. 2. Chimneys
—Amateurs' manuals. I. Title.
TH7425.F34 697'.1 80-19898
ISBN 0-8306-9716-0
ISBN 0-8306-1197-5 (pbk.)

Preface

Since the beginning of time, the discovery of fire has both performed miracles and danger to mankind. This great miracle means power, comfort and progress.

Conservationists and environmentalists are concerned about depleting our forests because of the influx of wood-burning heating equipment. Wood is a renewable resource and some generally agree that our forests are going to waste by not using the wood. Surveys report that our forests are capable of yielding enough fuel wood to heat at least half the homes in the country. This requires careful forest management practices. Wood burning is as much an art as it is a science and, as a primary heat source, it is a way of life unto itself.

Because of the energy crisis, people are seeking other means of heat. There are two reasons for this. One is to have standby heat during a power shutoff, and the second reason is to supplement the heating system to conserve fuel. Many people are turning to coal and wood burning stoves and fireplaces for heat; yet, not many are aware of the danger in using such equipment. Safety depends on knowing how to select, install, operate and maintain a solid fuel heating system. This book will explain the selection, installation, use and maintenance of coal and wood burning equipment.

Fireplaces, prefabricated units, open Franklin stoves, etc., are considered as free burners. They have no control of combustion air. These result in low efficiency, perhaps around 8 to 10 percent.

There are times when a free burner type unit will result in a net heat loss creating a larger fuel heating bill.

Wood stoves and fireplaces are not inherently dangerous; most fires could have been avoided by common sense safety measures. Safety is not an exciting subject, but it does deserve attention because life could depend on it. Trial and error is not the way. It must be right the first time because there may not be a second time.

Even if safety guidelines have been followed, this is no guarantee of danger-free operation. The wood burning equipment must be maintained and inspected periodically. Don't allow a dangerous situation to begin. Prepare a fire plan of escape. Provide practical drills to acquaint everyone in the house what to do to escape in the event of a fire. Only when everything possible to insure safety has been done should there be a feeling of safety and confidence.

Joseph D. Falcone, A.I.A.

Contents

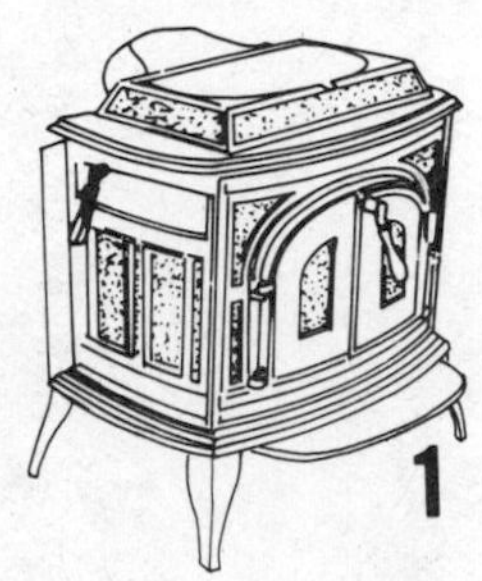

1

The Facts On Chimneys And Fireplaces

Chimneys, fireplaces and mantels are the main ingredients of good architecture, all of which came to us from our forefathers from other lands. Probably the first fireplace indoors consisted of an open fire on the ground with a hole in the roof to allow smoke to escape, or through cracks or voids in the walls. The first chimney was built of wood consisting of framework, interlocked with twigs and covered with mud. Another method was to interweave small logs and surface with mud. One advantage to the primitive fireplace was that the smoke under the roof discouraged rodents and insects from nesting or living there.

Eventually fireplaces were moved against an outside wall, probably to integrate the chimney/fireplace with the wall. Chimneys were exteneded above the roof to minimize the danger of sparks igniting the thatched roof.

Several questions must be answered before any planning is begun. Where is the fireplace to be built? What is the function? What size should it be? What style will best suit your needs? What is the cost? What are the restrictions based on building and zoning laws?

The secret of a good successful fireplace and chimney is proper planning and building. If not pre-built, it may cause dangerous fires resulting in loss of life, property, and/or serious injury. Begin with a copy of your local building code which can be obtained from the town or city hall office of the building inspector. This publication is the building law of the community and is the beginning toward planning.

Fig. 1-1. This fireplace will add beauty and charm to any room (courtesy of Majestic Company).

Fireplaces can be built in about any room in your home, offering you comfort, relaxation and attraction and creating a focal point of attention and open, inviting hospitality. Aesthetic design possibilities are unlimited ranging from built-in and free standing to prefabricated units, all of which are based on proper dimensions and proportion for successful operation and safety (Figs. 1-1 through 1-18).

Fireplace location within a room is a vital consideration. (Figs. 1-19 and 1-20). The size is determined by a generally accepted rule of thumb by adding the length of the room to the width resulting in the firebox dimension width in inches: 12′ + 15′ + 27″.

Fig. 1-2. A built-in fireplace unit (courtesy of Majestic Company).

Fig. 1-3. Fireplace location within a room is important (courtesy of Majestic Company).

The location is best served by placing the firebox opening on the shorter room dimension. A room measuring 12′ × 15′ would best be heated by placing the fireplace on the 12′ wall dimension.

The principal function of the fireplace is three-fold: to permit complete combustion of fuel, to allow a chimney to draw smoke completely and to radiate heat.

The warm, cozy fireplace is perhaps one of the largest single sources of energy waste (Fig. 1-21). Even while the fire is burning, it pulls more heat up and out through the chimney than it replaces, and pulls cold air into the house through cracks in the windows, doors and walls. Don't try to save money by not installing a damper. Even when closed, heated air will escape through the chimney.

Each fireplace must have a separate flue. The stack or chimney should contain all the flues. A flue is a separate chimney

Fig. 1-4. This unit rests nicely on floor tile (courtesy of Majestic Company).

Fig. 1-5. This handsome mantel design is made with a 5½" return to fit over a brick fireplace.

reserved only for one fire. Several flues may be built into a single stack, with one flue for every fire. Fireplaces can be built flush with the wall or projecting into the room.

FIREPLACE PROBLEMS

Following are several reasons why fireplaces might smoke:

- Want of air.
- Too large an opening in flue size.
- Chimney too short.
- More than one fireplace in same room competing with each other for air or draft.
- Locating a door on the same wall as a fireplace, with the door open, air skirted by the fireplace and through the door choking the fireplace because of insufficient draft or air.
- Strong winds blowing over a chimney overpowering the pressure within the chimney. Don't expect a fireplace to work properly if constructed of irregular jagged walls. The inside should be smooth to give the smoke a chance to flow or glide into the chimney.

A cozy open fire on a cold day may prove to be costly because you are robbing the house of heat generated from the heating system which is lost up through the chimney. A fire must consume a great amount of air in order to burn properly, and this air must

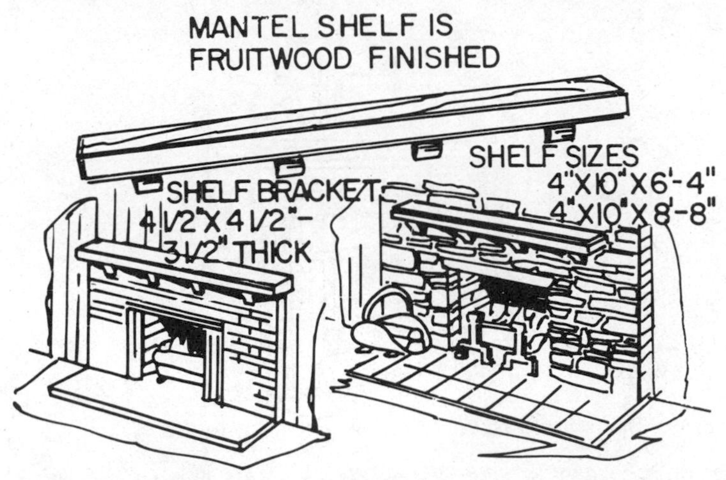

Fig. 1-6. The rough textured wood of the mantel shelf blends well with the rustic surroundings of the family room or den. This mantel shelf can be installed on the face of the fireplace wall with brackets or recessed into brick.

enter the house through the outside which is the cold air you have already heated through your heating system. This air movement creates a vacuum. This vacuum must be filled with new cold air starting the cycle all over again (Fig. 1-22).

One solution to this air flow problem is to install a duct from the outside directly to the fireplace hearth. A second solution

Fig. 1-7. One of the most popular mantels for both traditional and contemporary homes.

Fig. 1-8. The mantel is particularly adapted to modern interiors.

would be to open a window just a crack, preferably on an adjacent wall (Fig. 1-23).

Air enters the fireplace through the outside combustion air duct leading from the outside and is introduced into the combustion area through the vertical slots just behind the fire screen on either side. Since this air enters readily, almost no room air (which you have already paid to heat) is used for combustion, without creating any room drafts. The air that goes up the chimney is air from the outside. Outside air intakes can be closed when fireplace is not in use.

Fig. 1-9. This beautiful Georgian design is typical of those found in historic and colorful homes.

Fig. 1-10. A distinguished design in a decorative colonial mantel.

The system takes air from the room through intakes near the floor and heats it in an enclosed chamber around the firebox, and reintroduces it to the room through outlets above the fireplace. Outlets are provided for ducting heated air directly into as many as three rooms with optional blowers available for more heat distribution. Even a conventional fireplace draws cold outside air into your home. The thermostat connected to your central heating system reads the resulting drop in room temperature. In an effort to maintain this temperature setting, the thermostat turns on the central heating unit, making it produce heat just to catch up to the thermostat setting.

Fig. 1-11. The beauty of hip raised panels was selected by designers in the creation of this mantel.

Fig. 1-12. A note of provincial styling is expressed in this mantel design.

STRUCTURAL CONSIDERATIONS

The successful building of a fireplace is not a mystery; it is proper proportions and dimensions. The main factors affecting performance are:

- Fuel combustion.
- Proper draft for emitting smoke.

Fig. 1-13. This fireplace is part of an attractive setting.

- Maximum heat radiation.
- Structural safeness.

The fireplace should be given a prominent position in the room, away from traffic areas. The size of the firebox should be proportioned to the room. A fireplace width 28″ to 36″ would be adequate for a room of 250 square feet. A raised hearth may pose a danger of someone tripping over it, but it does bring the opening nearer to the eye and makes the fireplace seem larger. An inside chimney has better draft than in outside chimney because the masonry retains the heat longer which aids better draft.

A *hood* should be provided at the top of a chimney if it cannot be built high enough above a ridge to prevent the wind deflection

Fig. 1-14. An elegant looking fireplace.

Fig. 1-15. Here's a good place to lie down and relax, close to a beautiful fireplace.

from the roof. An extension of flue lining, chimney, or pre-built metal chimney may also be used to extend the height of a chimney. The chimney is probably the heaviest part of the building and must be properly supported by a foundation and footing. Concrete is recommended for this footing and must be designed to distribute the load over a wide area, enough to prevent cracking of walls and possible collapse of chimney. The footing should extend at least 6″ beyond the chimney walls on all sides and should be 12″ thick. If the footing for the chimney is outside the building, it must be below the frost line. Chimneys must be built from the ground up, independent and divorced from the building, or they can rest on the building, or they can rest on the building foundation or basement wall if the walls are 12″ thick and have a footing. Consult your local building code.

There are many devices that will make your fireplace a more efficient wood burner. These vary from special andirons and folding glass doors to wood stoves that replace fireplaces. Unless you live in an area where wood is fairly inexpensive, it will not pay you to invest in a fireplace as a replacement for gas, oil or electric heat. If on the other hand the fireplace is not used as a primary heat source, but only as a once in a while novelty, you may want to justify the added fuel cost for the pleasure derived from it. A few simple precautions will help keep down the heat loss make the flue airtight, and keep the damper closed when the fireplace is not in use. Normally, an open damper has the same effect on your fuel bill as a hole in the wall twice the size of the damper.

Fireplaces are only about one-third as efficient as a stove or circulator heater. However, a well designed and built fireplace can provide additional heat in mild climates and enhance the appearance and comfort of the room.

Fig. 1-16. An attractive stone fireplace.

Fig. 1-17. A fireplace near the dining area.

OPEN FIRE MECHANICS

The mechanics of an open fire are simple. Hot air rises and every cubic foot of heated air going up the chimney must be replaced from the outside by cold air. This cold air is drawn in through door, window and wall cracks. Warm air is attracted to cold air. When a door is opened, the cold air does not come in. The warm air goes out. If your house could be built airtight, you could not have an open fire because the fireplace would not draw and the smoke would fill your house instead of going up the chimney. The simple fact that the fireplace draws is proof that outside air is getting into your house.

Heat from the fireplace radiates from the fire brick lining, inside the firebox, which is heated by the fire. The heat could radiate long after the fire is extinguished. For this reason, the size of the fireplace opening or fire box should be in proportion to the room size. If the air temperature coming into the house from the outside is 50°F., the fire from the fireplace simply cannot heat the amount of cooler cubic feet of air leaking in from the outside.

In this situation, the heated air within the house generated from the mechanical heating system is lost through the open flue of the fireplace, which in turn will increase your heating bill. This free flow of air from the outside and out the chimney not only carries the heat with it, but also will cause the wood to burn rapidly. Doors on the fireplace will stop some warm air leaving the room, but they will also restrict the warm air radiating from the firebox into the room.

Heat is radiated into the room from the hot fire brick inside the firebox. If a hot burning hardwood is used such as oak, maple or hickory, the fire brick will generate a higher temperature and give off more heat. These hardwoods burn more slowly and consume less air. The rate of feeding a fire is also important. Once a hot bed of ashes has been created, add a medium to large size log at a rate that will maintain the hot bed. If the fire slows down or dies, fuel will be wasted in starting it up again to make it hot.

FIREPLACE SIZE

Proper fireplace size is in proportion to room size and location. If too small, little heating comfort will be felt. If too large, the room becomes overheated.

Fig. 1-18. Curl up with a good book next to a fireplace.

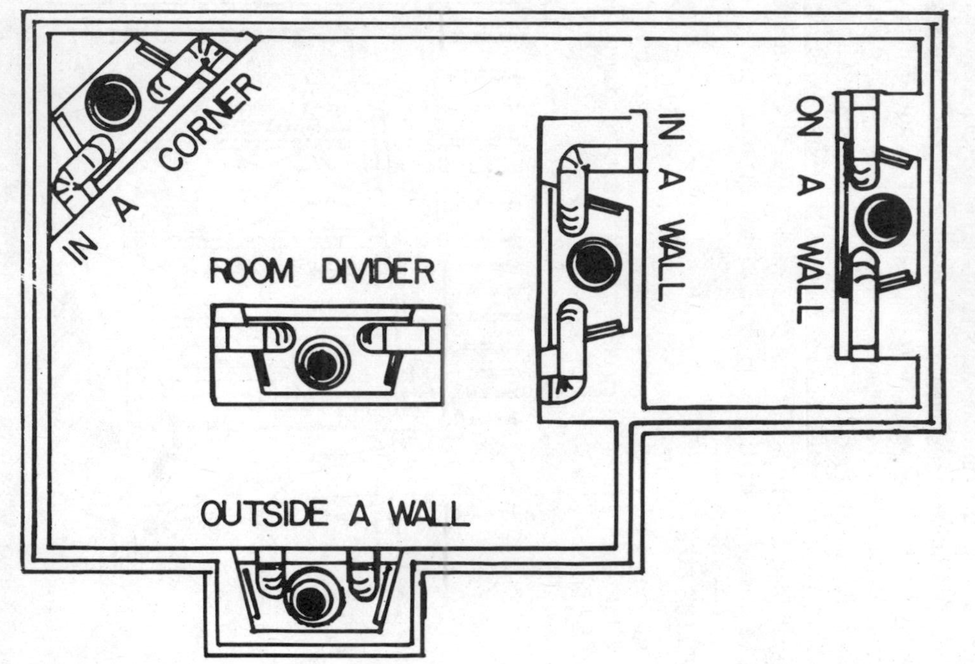

Fig. 1.19. Suggested fireplace locations.

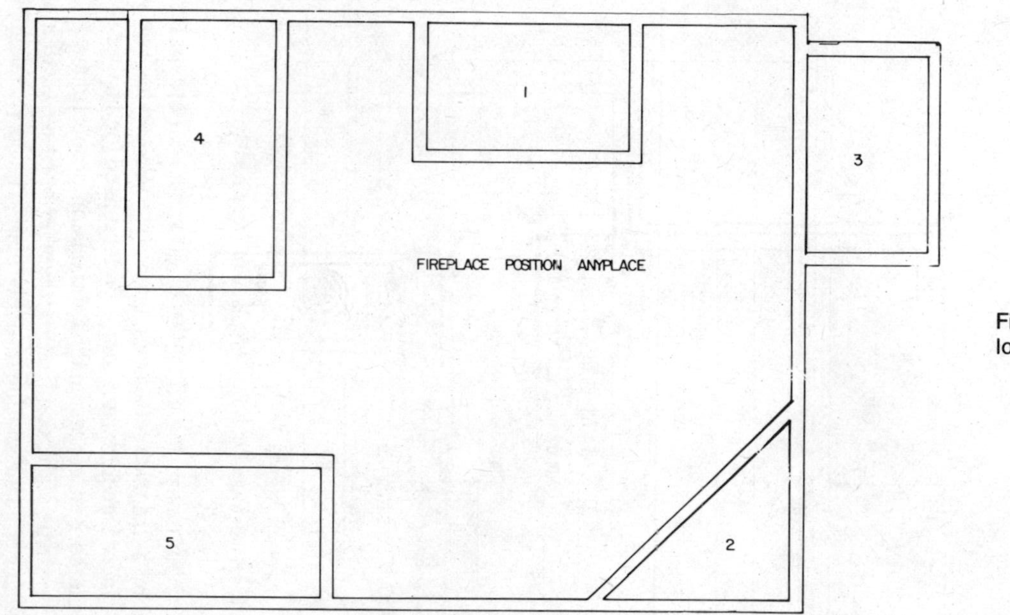

Fig. 1-20. More possible fireplace locations.

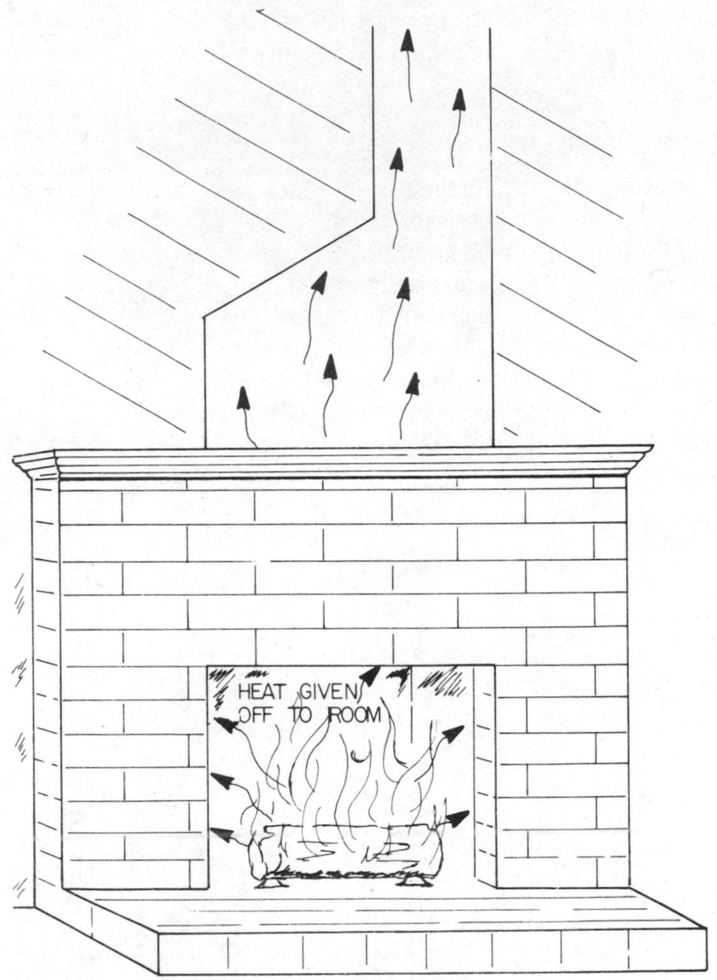

Fig. 1-21. An illustration of how a fireplace radiates heat.

A room measuring 15′ × 20′ or 300 square feet will be best served by a fireplace measuring from 30″ to 36″ wide. The width may be increased for larger rooms or decreased for smaller rooms, using the correct corresponding dimension proportions.

The shape of the combustion chamber or firebox will indicate the amount of heat radiating into the room. The correct shapes and slopes direct the heat into the room and the smoke up the chimney. It is advisable not to alter these dimensions becuase they have been time tested with many years of experience. The combustion chamber or firebox should be lined with fire brick laid with fireclay mortar.

TYPES OF FIREPLACES

Fireplaces are identified as single faced, two-faced, three-faced, open-faced and prefabricated. A Type 1 conventional fireplace generally requires a conventional throat damper (Fig. 1-24). If the fireplace has an unusually high opening or unusually deep opening, a multi-opening damper may be required.

A Type 2 through fireplace is the most popular type of multi-opening fireplace. It has a large variety of applications and is used to give a view of the fire from two different rooms (Fig. 1-25). It is sometimes used as a room divider. The Type 3 corner fireplace has

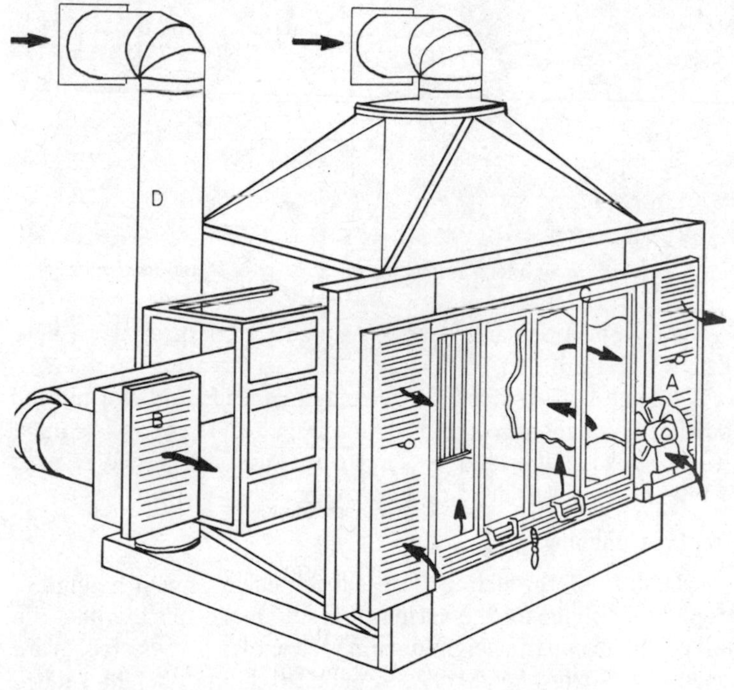

Fig. 1-22. Proper air flow within a fireplace.

Fig. 1-23. Outside air intake is important (courtesy of Martin Industries).

various applications and is very adaptable to different type floor plans (Fig. 1-26).

A Type 4 open sides fireplace may be used for either a midwall location or a diagonal corner location (Fig. 1-27). Type 5 is similar to Type 4 except it is elongated in shape (Fig. 1-28). It may be used at the end of a wall dividing two rooms.

Fireplace Openings

Tables 1-1 through 1-5 are suggested maximum heights of fireplace openings for the various sizes of the rectangular flue tile lining. The maximum height openings as shown in these tables are based on a chimney height of 20′. For an 18′ chimney height, reduce the heights in the tables by 1″. For a 16′ high chimney, reduce the size by 2″ and for a 14′ high chimney by 4″. The height of the chimney is measured from the throat level. The lower the chimney, the less the draft. During construction, leave the damper valve open. It is less likely to get jammed by falling mortar and the masonry will cure better. Try the damper to make sure it opens wide and closes tight. It may be necessary to clean out fallen mortar in order to obtain a tight closure. Do not build a fire in the fireplace for several days. Allow time for the masonry to dry and cure thoroughly or it will crack.

The back flange of the damper must be protected from intense heat by being fully supported by the masonry. At the same time, the damper should not be built in solidly at the ends but given freedom to expand with heat.

A Type 6 three-way fireplace juts out farther into the room, forming a short dividing wall (Fig. 1-29 and 1-30). It is somewhat prone to allow smoke to escape if drafts are present. This style will

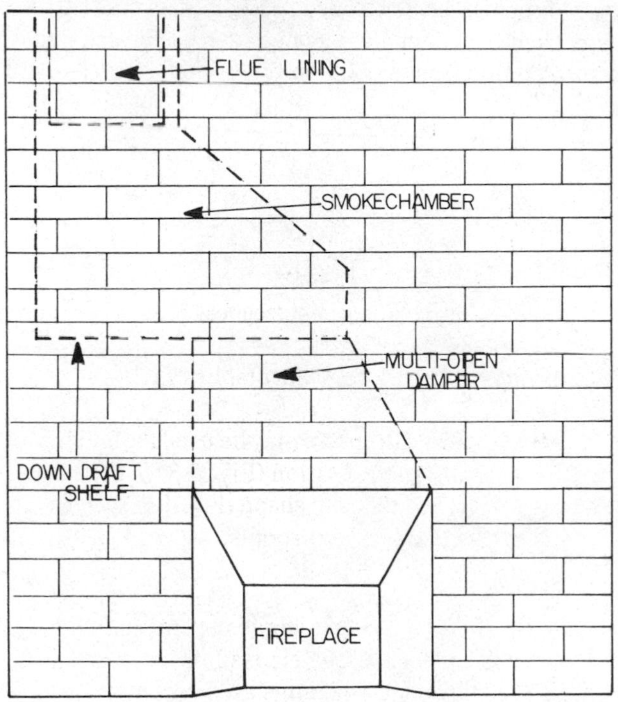

Fig. 1-24. A Type 1 conventional fireplace with one side open only.

Table 1-1. Information regarding Type 1 fireplaces (courtesy of Vestal Manufacturing).

Hearth Size	Maximum Height of Opening for Flue Tile Sizes			
Width x Depth	8-1/2" x 13"	13" x 13"	13" x 18"	18" x 18"
30" x 20"	32"	42"	52"	
33" x 24"	29"	38"	46"	
36" x 24"	26"	35"	45"	55"
42" x 24"	25"	34"	44"	54"
48" x 28"	20"	30"	38"	46"

bring the fire toward the center of the family circle with no one out of view of the fire (Table 1-6 and 1-7).

The chimney and fireplace in Fig. 1-31 is a free-standing structure not used for support of any part of the house. The single-faced fireplace is the most popular type and least difficult to build. It is also the most trouble free, if properly constructed. The two-faced fireplace is open front and back. It serves two rooms and is mostly used as a room divider, between dining and living room. A three-faced fireplace is open on three sides, usually both faces

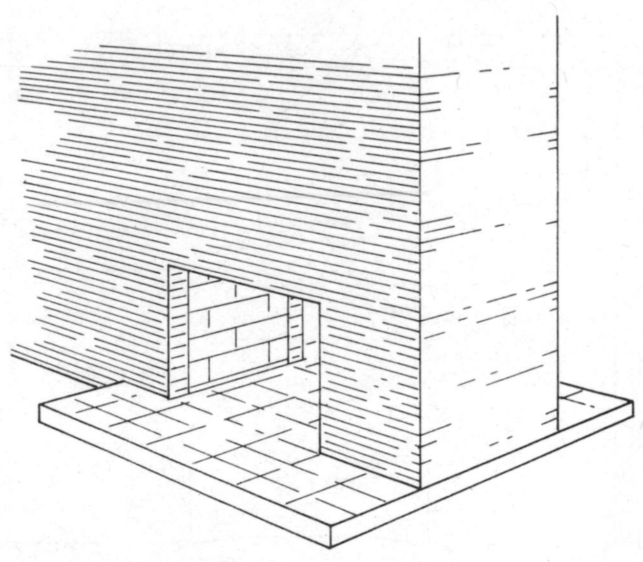

Fig. 1-25. A Type 2 through fireplace with two long sides open.

Table 1-2. Facts on Type 2 Fireplaces (courtesy of Vestal Manufacturing).

Width x Depth Hearth Size	Maximum Height of Opening for Flue Tile Sizes				
	13″ x 13″	13″ x 18″	18″ x 18″	20″ x 24″	24″ x 24″
30″ x 24″	22″	31″	41″		
33″ x 28″	20″	29″	37″		
36″ x 28″	17″	26″	32″		
42″ x 28″		25″	31″	38″	
48″ x 32″		20″	28″	34″	40″

and one end. It could add interest and is ideal serving three rooms at the same time. An open-faced fireplace has all sides open with no walls.

The depth of the fireplace should be about two-third the height of the opening. A 30″ high fireplace would have a 20″ depth from face to rear wall of the firebox. The flue area should be one-tenth the area of the firebox. If the chimney is less than 15′ in height, the flue size should be one-eighth the area. The height of the chimney is measured from the throat to the top of the chimney.

The back width of the fireplace is usually 6″ to 8″ narrower than the front. This helps to guide the smoke and gases to the rear. A vertical backwall of 14″ high tapers toward the upper section or

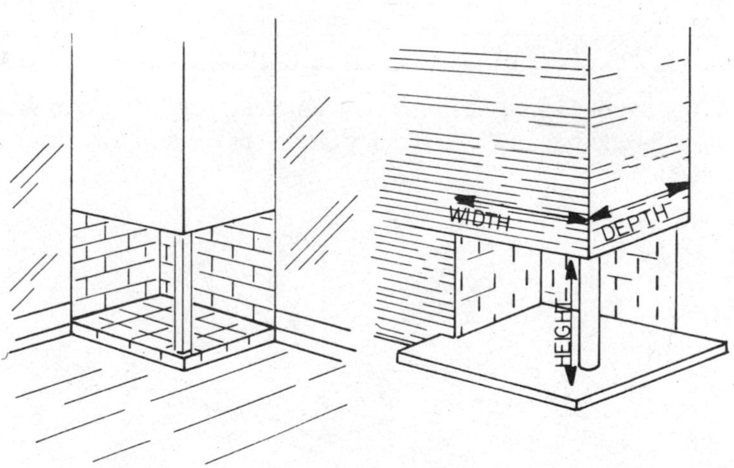

Fig. 1-26. A Type 3 projecting corner fireplace with one long side, and one short side open.

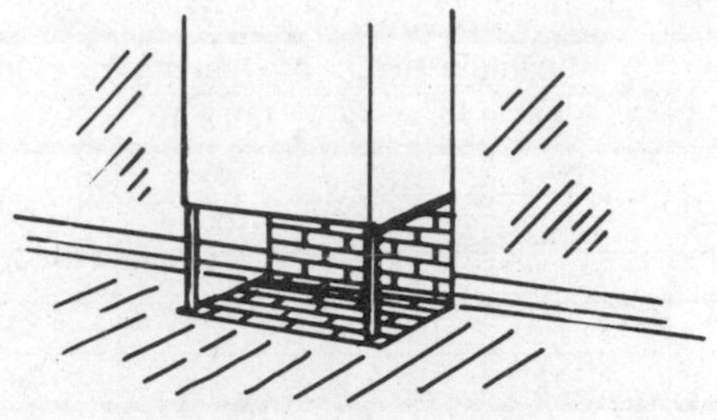

Fig. 1-27. A Type 4 fireplace has one long side, and two short sides open.

throat. The throat area is about one-fourth to one-third times the area of the flue.

The smoke shelf prevents back drafts. The height of shelf should be about 8″ above the top of the fireplace opening. Be sure

Table 1-3. Things You Need to Know About Type 3 Fireplaces (courtesy of Vestal Manufacturing).

Hearth Size	Maximum Height of Opening for Flue Tile Sizes			
Width x Depth	13″ x 13″	13″ x 18″	18″ x 18″	20″ x 24″
34″ x 20″	27″	36″	46″	
37″ x 24″	23″	32″	42″	
40″ x 24″	22″	31″	39″	
46″ x 24″	20″	28″	38″	46″
52″ x 28″	17″	25″	34″	42″

to concave the smoke shelf to retain rain that may enter from the top of the open chimney. A chimney cap will prevent rain and snow from entering.

Fig. 1-28. A Type 5 fireplace has two long sides, with one short side open.

Table 1-4. Information on Type 4 Fireplaces (courtesy of Vestal Manufacturing).

Hearth Size Width x Depth	Maximum Height of Opening for Flue Tile Sizes				
	13″ x 13″	13″ x 18″	18″ x 18″	20″ x 24″	24″ x 24″
38″ x 20″		27″	37″		
41″ x 24″		24″	33″	40″	
44″ x 24″		23″	31″	37″	
50″ x 24″		21″	29″	36″	42″
56″ x 24″		20″	27″	33″	38″

A steel angle called a *lintel* is used to support the brick above the firebox opening. This angle should be 8″ longer than the firebox opening width and should be supported on each end by the walls.

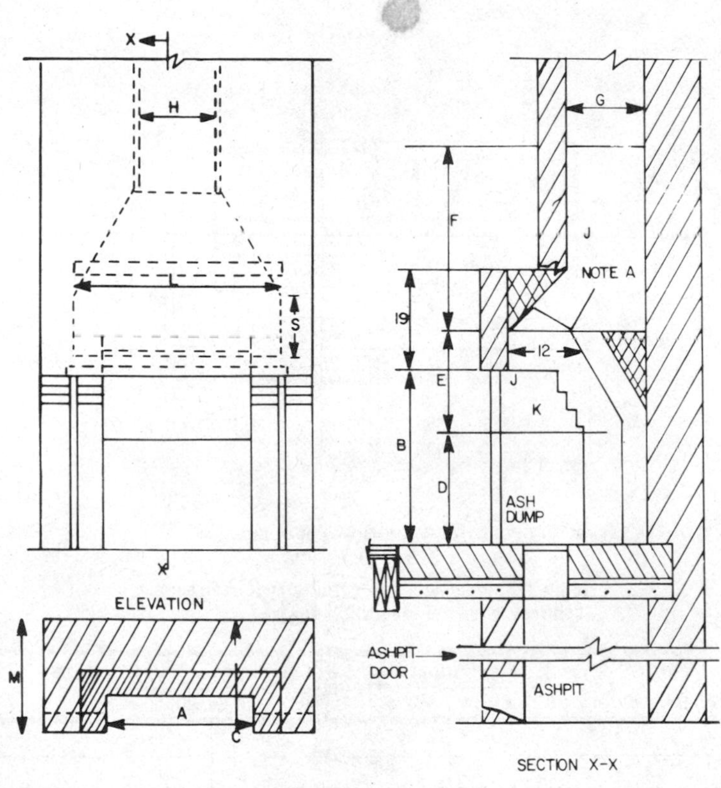

Fig. 1-29. A Type 6 three-way fireplace juts out into the room, forming a short dividing wall.

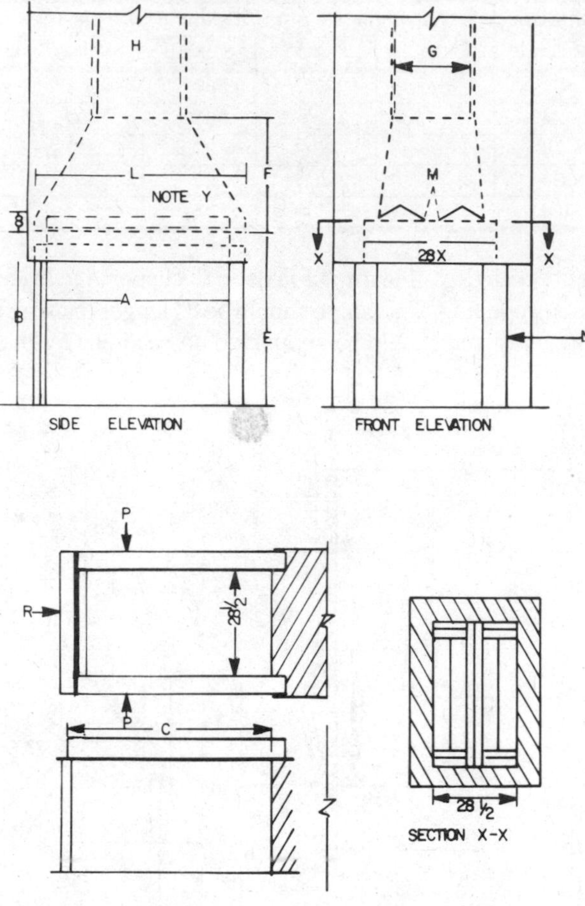

Fig. 1-30. Elevation details for a three-way fireplace.

Table 1-5. Dimensions Regarding Type 5 Fireplaces (courtesy of Vestal Manufacturing).

Hearth Size Width x Depth	Maximum Height of Opening for Flue Tile Sizes				
	13″ x 13″	13″ x 18″	18″ x 18″	20″ x 24″	24″ x 24″
34″ x 24″		23″	31″		
37″ x 28″		19″	28″	35″	
40″ x 28″			27″	34″	
46″ x 28″			25″	33″	38″
52″ x 32″			22″	27″	33″

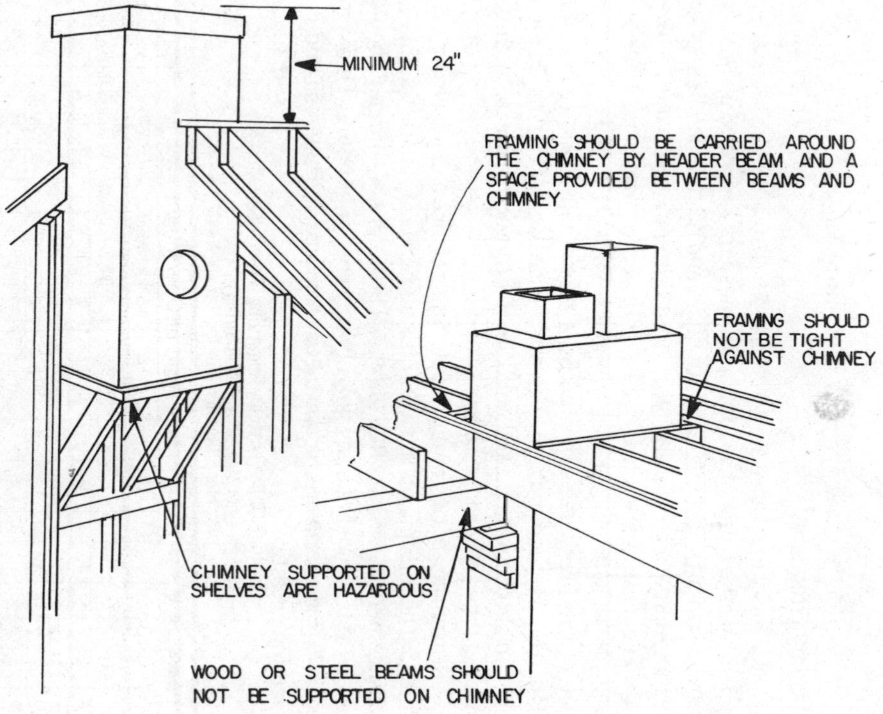

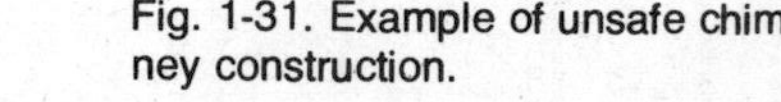
MINIMUM 24"
FRAMING SHOULD BE CARRIED AROUND THE CHIMNEY BY HEADER BEAM AND A SPACE PROVIDED BETWEEN BEAMS AND CHIMNEY
FRAMING SHOULD NOT BE TIGHT AGAINST CHIMNEY
CHIMNEY SUPPORTED ON SHELVES ARE HAZARDOUS
WOOD OR STEEL BEAMS SHOULD NOT BE SUPPORTED ON CHIMNEY

Fig. 1-31. Example of unsafe chimney construction.

Table 1-6. Dimensions for Three-Way Fireplaces.

						Old Flue Size		New Flue Size						
A	B	C	D	E	F	G	H	G	H	L	M	Ash-Pit Door	Plate Lintel K	Corner Post height
28	26-1/2	20	14	18	27	13	13	12	16	36	20	12 x 8	11 x 16	26-1/2
32	26-1/2	20	14	18	32	13	13	16	16	40	20	12 x 8	11 x 16	26-1/2
36	26-1/2	20	14	18	32	13	18	16	16	44	20	12 x 8	11 x 16	26-1/2
40	39	20	14	21	35	13	18	18	16	48	20	12 x 8	11 x 16	29
48	29	20	14	21	40	13	18	18	20	36	20	12 x 8	11 x 16	29

*Angle Sizes: A—3 x 3 x 3/16"; B—3-1/2 x 3 x 1/4".

Note A—The back flange of the damper must be protected from intense heat by being fully supported by the masonry. At the same time, the damper should not be built in solidly at the ends but given freedom to expand with heat.

Generally the size of the angle has one leg of 5", another leg of 3 ½" and a thickness of 5/16".

Masonry Fireplaces

Masonry fireplaces are built in several stages. The foundation supporting the chimney is first built. Masonry is carried up leaving provisions for the ashpit, cleanout doors and related flue linings for heating units, incinerators, gas, fired hot domestic water, etc.

The entire firebox is built of firebrick which is a special heat-resistant brick. The hearth should extend at least 16" from the face of the fireplace supported by a reinforced concrete floor or slab. The purpose of the hearth is to guard against flying sparks. The finish of the hearth should be of fireproof material such as brick, stone or ceramic tile.

Fireplaces of two or more openings require a much larger flue lining. The design of the chimney depends upon the number, arrangement and size of flue linings. The height of chimney should extend at least 3' above any neighboring roof or building. This is to avoid any draft current down the flues. Separate flues should be used for each fire.

Table 1-7. More Dimensions for Three-Way Fireplaces.

					Old Flue Size		New Flue Size					
A	B	C	E	F	G	H	G	H	L	Post Height (2 required) N	Drilled Angle (2 required) P	Special Welded Tee Section R
28	26-1/2	32	32	24	18	18	16	20	36	26-1/2	36	34
32	26-1/2	36	32	27	18	18	20	20	40	26-1/2	40	34
36	26-1/2	40	32	32	18	18	20	20	44	26-1/2	44	34
40	26-1/2	44	32	35	18	18	20	20	48	26-1/2	48	34
48	26-1/2	52	32	35	20	20	20	24	56	26-1/2	56	34

Part of the cost of fireplaces is due to the supporting structure ncessary to carry the weight. With the advent of prefabricated or pre-built units, the cost is much lower.

Conventional fireplace design uses room air for combustion, which must be replaced. This lowers the air pressure within the room, drawing cold air through cracks and crevices.

Chimneys are generally constructed of masonry units supported on a foundation. It must be structurally safe and capable of producing sufficient draft for the fireplace to carry away the fuel burning gases. Lightweight prefabricated chimneys do not require concrete foundations. These must be approved by Underwriters' Laboratory. Improved heating efficiency and correct fireplace proportioning can be obtained by installing factory made circulating fireplaces. The size of the chimney will dpened upon the number of flues.

Fireplaces are at best poor heaters. The volatile gases are drawn up the chimney before they adequately release their energy to the surrounding room. The draft created by the fire draws room air up the chimney along with the burning gases, sometimes resulting in a net heat loss for the whole house. Additional heat is lost if the damper is left open after the fire dies out. A typical masonry fireplace averages about 10 percent efficiency.

FIREPLACE MODIFICATIONS

Modifications to a fireplace can include a metal-lined heat exchanger that allows room air to be heated and be remitted out the top of the unit. By adding tightly fitted glass doors and outside air vents, the performance of a fireplace can be more than doubled.

Hollow tube grates can be placed in the fireplace to extract additional heat from the fire. With a blower, or by natural convection, a significant amount of energy can be extracted from the fire. Manufacturers claim heat gain of 5,000 to 50,000 British thermal unit (BTU)/hours from these devices.

A conventional stove can be adapted to a fireplace in any number of ways. A tight fitting metal or asbestos sheet can be installed in place of the damper or a covering for the fireplace can be fitted over the opening. An opening can be cut into the chimney over the damper and the stove pipe installed there. In any case, the object is not to allow warm room air to escape up the chimney.

If both heat and beauty are your objectives, another solution exists. Buy a combination unit. The typical Franklin stove is an example of this style, although there are many high efficiency stove/fireplaces on the market today. A Franklin stove is about 25 percent efficient with the doors open and about 30 percent efficient with the doors closed. The airtight combination units are about 30 percent efficient with the doors open and about 50 percent with them closed.

The atmosphere of an open fire is by far the most important reason people buy or install fireplaces. The fireplace is not an efficient heating device, even with extensive modifications. Except for supplemental or emergency usage, the fireplace is best left to being a pleasant experience.

MASONRY CHIMNEYS

A masonry chimney must be supported on a solid concrete pad or footing and never on a wooden support. As a general rule, the footing size should be 1′ larger in dimensions than the overall chimney size. If the chimney is on an outside wall, the concrete footing must be built below the frost line. If inside, the top of the footing can be level with the floor, but in either case, no less than 12″ thick and reinforced with ½″ diameter steel rods placed 8″ apart in both directions. Place about 2″ up from the bottom.

In areas subjected to earthquakes, masonry chimneys should be anchored to the wood frame building at each floor and roof more than 6′ above the ground. Use two steel straps secured to the chimney vertically, reinforced and fastened to the structural framework of the building, providing the unsupported depth of the chimney above the topmost anchor does not exceed 3′ (Fig. 1-32).

BRICK

If a brick chimney is added to a house already built, every effort should be made to match the existing brick, if any. If there is no brick existing, the range of color, size and texture is varied. The brick should be selected before construction is begun.

Brick is one of the oldest building materials available, dating back more than 5,000 years. The method laying brick is pretty much the same now as then.

Types of Brick

There are several types of brick used for specific purposes. The common brick are used for fillers usually not exposed. An example would be an 8″ thick brick wall made up of two thicknesses of 4″ each. The course behind the finish brick would be a common brick. These are the least expensive brick.

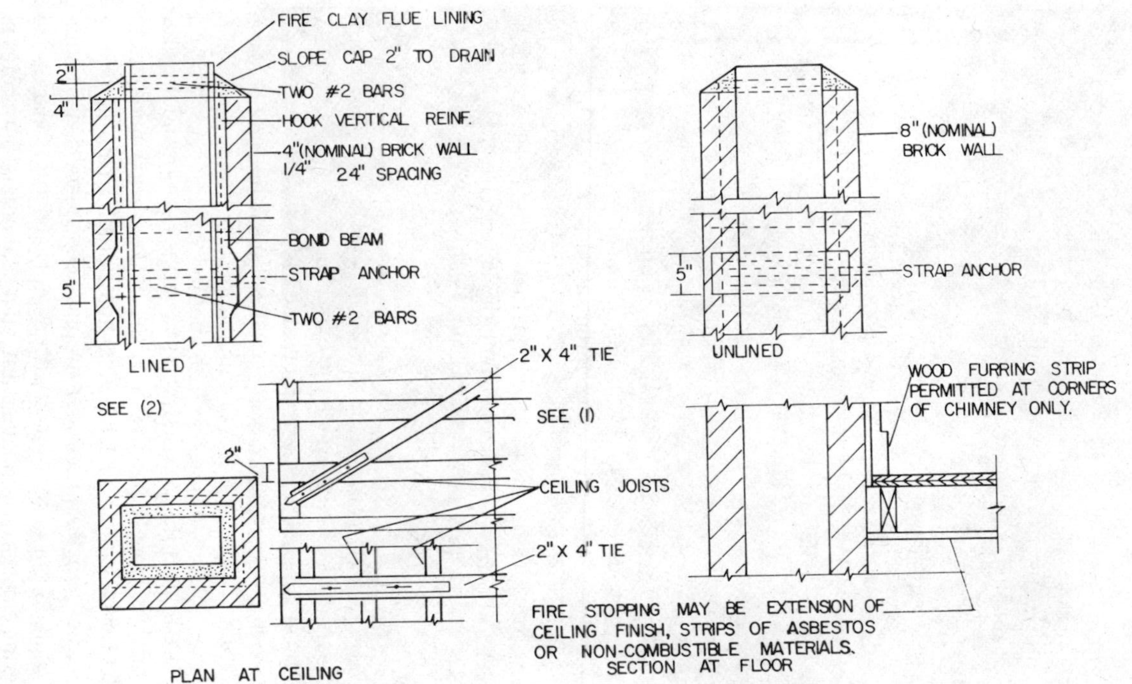

Fig. 1-32. Reinforcement plans for a chimney.

Fig. 1-33. Improper fireplace design can be dangerous (courtesy of Martin Industries).

Face brick is the exposed wall and varies in color and texture. This brick is more expensive than the backup or common brick.

"A house without a hearth is no home at all." This quote may be true; nevertheless, improper fireplace design and construction can result in burns to your children, dog and rug. Sparks and scattering embers can smudge paint, ruin ceilings and burn holes in your clothes, or even burn the entire house down. If for these reasons and no other, you must give proper thought and dimen-

Fig. 1-34. Brick is one of the oldest building materials (courtesy of Martin Industries).

sions to your fireplace. Freedom from sparks and efficiency of operation depend upon them (Figs. 1-33, 1-34 and 1-35).

Repair and Maintenance

Properly constructed brick walls are remarkably free of costly repair and maintenance. When required, the repair of existing walls is often more difficult and costly than proper construction of new work. Care in the selection and use of mortar, wetting brick, adequate flashing and tooling of joints will add only a small amount to the initial cost, but will insure a low maintenance throughout the life of the wall.

Where the mortar joints have softened or disintegrated, or large cracks are noted, it will be readily apparent that protective measures must be taken to correct or prevent leaky walls or structural weakness. This is done by cutting out all loose or disintegrated material for a depth of at least ½″ and repointing or filling with proper mortar. If the work is being done to correct leakage, all joints should be cut out in the affected area as it may be very difficult in some cases to determine the defective joints by visual inspection. If no leakage has been noted and the repointing is being done as maintenance work, it is necessary to remove only the defective mortar.

When cutting is completed all dust and loose material must be removed by brushing or, preferably, with a water jet. If water is used in cleaning the dust from the joints, no additional wetting may be required. The repointing should not follow immediately after the joints are washed. Little if any wetting will be necessary when the walls are constructed of low absorption brick.

Mortar for tuck pointing should never be denser than the original mortar. It should be preferably pre-hydrated by mixing one hour to two hours before using. Only a portion of the required mixing water is sufficient to produce a damp mass of such consistency that it will retain its form when pressed into a ball with the hands, but will not flow under the trowel. The mortar should then be allowed to stand for a period not not less than one hour nor more than two hours, after which it is thoroughly remixed with the addition of sufficient water to produce satisfactory workability. This greatly improves the workability and much of the initial shrinkage is eliminated. The mortar should then be packed in tightly in thin layers and finally tooled to a smooth compact concave surface.

When the mortar cracks and openings are small, a two coat

Fig. 1-35. This well-laid brick fireplace is an attractive addition to a home (courtesy of Martin Industries).

application cement-sand grout brushed vigorously into the mortar joints will provide an effective waterproofing method. A typical recommendation is to mix by volume 1 part portland cement, 1/4 part limestone flour, powdered flint or hydrated lime and 1 part sand passing a No. 30 sieve. The joints should be thoroughly wetted before applying the grout.

The omission of flashing or the incorrect placement of flashing is often responsible for serious masonry problems. Unflashed brick generally result in leakage or, at least, disfigured walls caused by efflorescence. The proper solution is an expensive repair job which requires removing the brick and placing suitable flashing around and under it. When continuous flashing is required in existing walls, it can be placed by removing alternate brick sections in widths up to 2 or 3′. After the flashing is placed and masonry properly aged, the immediate section can be removed and the flashing completed.

Improper caulking is often responsible for water leakage. The omission of caulking is easily corrected by filling all cracks with a good elastic caulking compound by means of a pressure gun. On the other hand, if the original caulking has cracked, peeled or separated, it should be removed and replaced with new caulking compound. Unless proper pressure is used, only a thin film of caulking compound will be placed. Even with good material, this will soon become ineffective. Thin films should be removed and properly replaced before serious damage results.

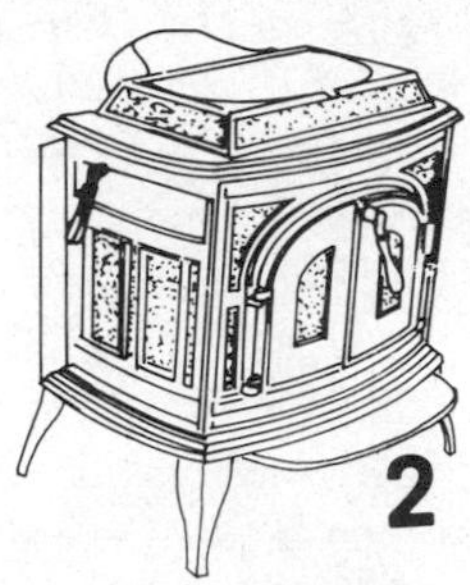

2

Foundations

Because of the heavier weight of a chimney compared to the adjoining walls, common in residential construction, a larger and heavier footing is required underneath the chimney. The foundation is generally poured of concrete, and is required for residences with or without a basement. It is a good idea to reinforce the foundation slab with steel. Reinforcing steel rods or reinforced concrete wire mesh should be used and put in place approximately half way up in the foundation slab (Fig. 2-1). If the chimney is on an exterior wall, the foundation must extend well below the frost line. The depth frost penetration and the bearing capacity of different soils vary with the locality. The foundation should extend at least 6″ outside the dimensions of the chimney walls. Pour the foundation slab level and allow to cure before starting the masonry work.

Do not build a foundation or footing on ground that has been filled. Dig down to virgin soil for proper loading (Table 2-1 through 2-9). The minimum depth for exterior foundations below virgin soils should be below the frost line. When soil freezes, it lifts upward and everything resting on the soil moves with it (Fig. 2-2). This is one of several causes of building failure. Foundation inside the buildings need by only the depth of the footing.

Footings or foundations are usually built of concrete placed in a form of proper size to support the chimney. The footing size is determined by the load bearing capacity of the soil and the weight of the chimney placed upon it. Local condition of soils can be established by the office of the building inspector. The minimum

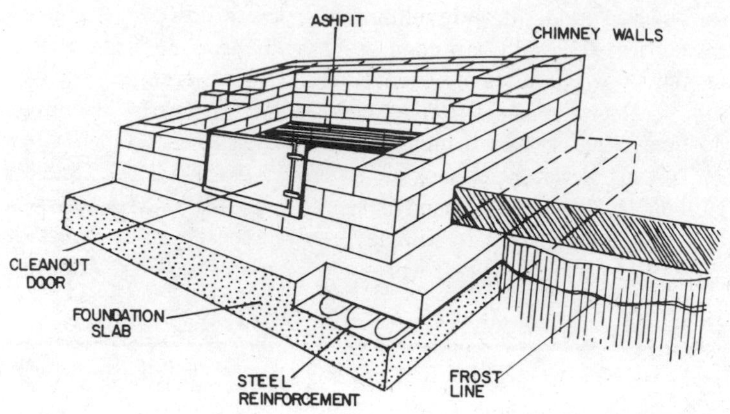

Fig. 2-1. A fireplace foundation.

size and footing should be 12″ deep and 6″ larger than the chimney on all sides. When excavating, if the soil is firm enough to prevent the walls from caving in, no wood forms are necessary. If not, forms of 2″ × 12″ must be built to conform to the footing size.

FOOTINGS

Poured concrete footings are most commonly used for foundations. Footings, properly sized and constructed, prevent settling or cracking of chimney walls. Footings must be completely level, and must extend at least 12″ below the frost line and at least 6″ into undistrubed soil. These requirements dictate the depth at which you place the footings. Do not place foundations on black top soil. Do not pour concrete if the temperature is expected to go below 40°F within the first week after pour, unless extensive measures are taken to protect the concrete against freezing. In moderate or negligible weathering areas, this is not a problem (Fig. 2-3).

Excavation

Make preliminary excavation for a perimeter footing. The amount of excavation may vary, depending upon site conditions. Allow adequate working space and excavate about 24″ beyond the outside footing line. If excavation is dug beyond the designed depth, do not fill with earth. Fill with concrete. Dig the footing trench to required depth. Install forms of ½″ plywood or 2″ × 12″ framing stock supported by 2″ × 4″ stakes driven into the soil about 24″ apart (Fig. 2-4).

These stakes should be driven below the top of the formboards to facilitate leveling the concrete. Prepare and place the concrete. If ready-mix concrete is available, order a mix with at least 2000 psi (pounds per square inch), 28-day strength. You may mix your own on the site using a 1:3:5 mix (1 part by volume of portland cement, 3 parts clean sand and 5 parts gravel). Use about 5½ gallons of water per sack of cement if wet sand is used and 6½ gallons per sack if dry sand is used (Table 2-1). Mix concrete thoroughly and place in thin layers. Spade and tamp concrete carefully between pours to prevent air pockets. Top of footing

Table 2-1. Excavation Factors.

Depth	Cubic Yards per Square Foot
2″	.006
4″	.012
6″	.018
8″	.025
10″	.031
1′ - 0″	.037
1′ - 6″	.056
2′ - 0″	.074
2′ - 6″	.093
3′ - 0″	.111
3′ - 6″	.130
4′ - 0″	.148
4′ - 6″	.167
5′ - 0″	.185
5′ - 6″	.204
6′ - 0″	.222
6′ - 6″	.241
7′ - 0″	.259
7′ - 6″	.278
8′ - 0″	.296
8′ - 6″	.314
9′ - 0″	.332
9′ - 6″	.350
10′ - 0″	.369

Example: Assume an excavation 24 ft. x 30 ft. and 6 ft. deep. 24 x 30 = 720. In the table the 6 ft. depth has a factor of .222 (the number of cu. yd. in an excavation 1 ft. square and 6 ft. deep) 720 x .222 = 159.84 Cu. Yds.

Table 2-2. Hourly Dragline Handling Capacity in Cubic Yards.

(Based on "short boom" operation)									
	Dragline Bucket Sizes in Cubic Yards								
Class of Material	3/8	1/2	3/4	1	1-1/4	1-1/2	1-3/4	2	2-1/2
Moist Loom or Sandy Clay	70	95	130	160	195	220	245	265	305
Sand and Gravel	65	90	125	155	185	210	235	255	295
Good Common Earth	55	75	105	135	165	190	210	230	265
Clay, Hard, Tough	35	55	90	110	135	160	180	195	230
Clay, Wet and Sticky	20	30	55	75	95	110	130	145	175

Conditions: 1. Cu. Yds. bank measurement per hour. 2. Suitable depth of cut for maximum effect. 3. Continuous loading with full bucket.4.90° Swing. 5. All materials loaded into hauling units.

should be smooth and level all around. Cure concrete and strip forms. In warm weather, leave forms in place for three day, sprinkling daily with water so concrete will not dry too quickly. In cold weather, leave forms in place 7 days; in cold weather (below 40°F) don't pour. Accurately locate outside wall corners by using a plumb bob.

Pouring and Curing Concrete

Place the forms in the excavation and check for levelness and squareness. Before concrete is poured into the form, place ½" diameter steel reinforcing rods spaced 8" apart in both directions. Build the reinforcing in the form of a mat, using wire to tie the rods together (Tables 2-11 and 2-12). Pour about 2" concrete into the form; then place the reinforcing rods into the concrete. Finish pouring the concrete to proper dimension. Do not pour concrete in freezing temperature.

Table 2-3. Hourly Shovel Handling Capacities in Cubic Yards.

	Shovel Dipper Sizes in Cubic Yards								
Class of Material	3/8	1/2	3/4	1	1-1/4	1-1/2	1-3/4	2	2-1/2
Moist Loam or Sandy Clay	85	115	165	205	250	285	320	355	405
Sand and Gravel	80	110	155	200	230	270	300	330	390
Good Common Earth	70	95	135	175	210	240	270	300	350
Clay, Hard, Tough	50	75	110	145	180	210	235	265	310
Rock, Well Blasted	40	60	95	125	155	180	205	230	275
Common, with Rocks and Roots	30	50	80	105	130	155	180	200	245
Clay, Wet and Sticky	25	40	70	95	120	145	165	185	230
Rock, Poorly Blasted	15	25	50	75	95	115	140	160	195

Conditions: 1. Cu. Yds. bank measurement per hour.2.Suitable depth of cut for maximum effect. 3. Continuous loading with full dipper. 4. 90° swing, grade level loading. 5.All materials loaded into hauling units.

Fig. 2-2. Extreme frost penetration within the continental United States in inches.

Table 2-4. Trench Excavations with Cubic Yard Content per 100 Lineal Feet.

Depth in Inches	Trench Width in Inches						
	12	18	24	30	36	42	48
6	1.9	2.8	3.7	4.6	5.6	6.6	7.4
12	3.7	5.6	7.4	9.3	11.1	13.0	14.8
18	5.6	8.3	11.1	13.9	16.7	19.4	22.3
24	7.4	11.1	14.8	18.5	22.2	26.0	29.6
30	9.3	13.8	18.5	23.2	27.8	32.4	37.0
36	11.1	16.6	22.2	27.8	33.3	38.9	44.5
42	13.0	19.4	25.9	32.4	38.9	45.4	52.0
48	14.8	22.2	29.6	37.0	44.5	52.0	59.2
54	16.7	25.0	33.3	41.6	50.0	58.4	66.7
60	18.6	27.8	37.0	46.3	55.5	64.9	74.1

The base of concrete footings supporting the chimney should be located below the frost line. Where footings are to be placed in an excatation below the water table or ground water level, the water should be removed by pumping until the concrete footings are cured.

Foundations should be designed to resist frost action and to safely support all loads. No foundations should be placed on frozen soil and no concrete should be poured during freezing temperatures. No foundation should be placed on fill soil unless properly compacted. Masonry work should begin at the footing, never from wood platforms or metal supports.

If the fireplace is on an outside wall, the house foundation may be used for the fireplace. Again, the size of the chimney depends upon the number, arrangement and size of flue linings.

The initial curing of concrete takes place almost immediately and should be kept continuously moist for at least seven days. One

Table 2-5. Weights of Earth.

Type of Earth	Lb. per Cu. Yd.		Cu. Yd. per Ton
	Packed	Loose	Loose
Dry Loam	2,700	2,160	.92
Moist Loam	2,700	2,430	.83
Mud	3,240	. . .	.62
Gravel	2,970	2,700	.74
Sand	3,240	2,700	.74
Shale	4,320	2,700	.74

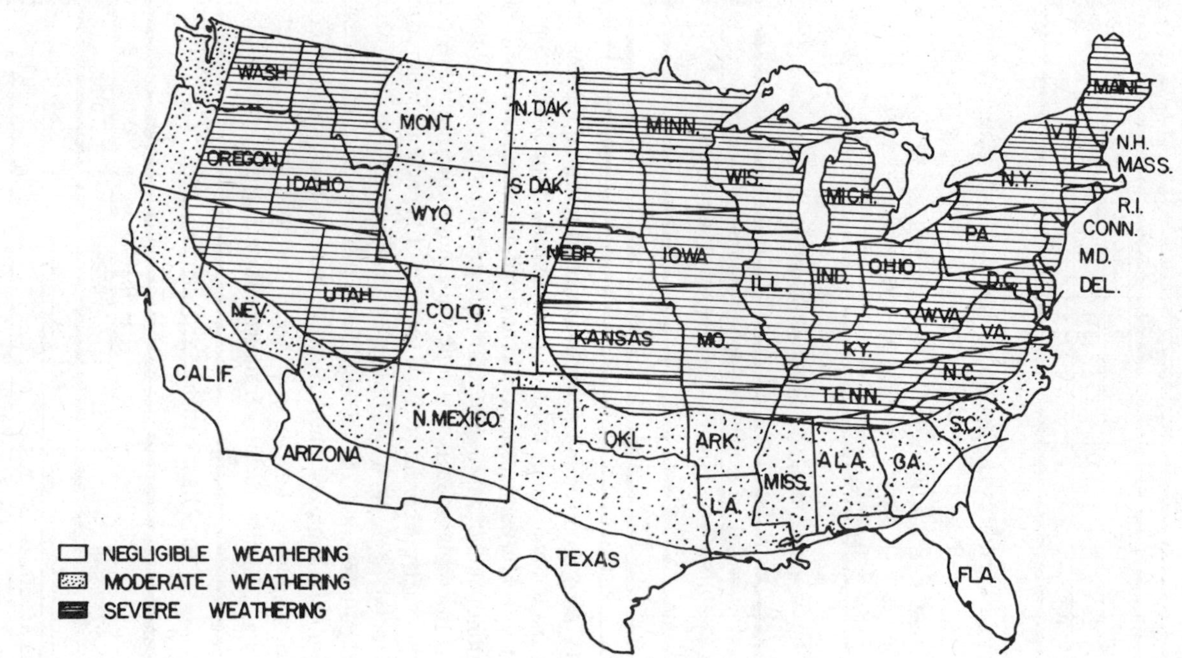

Fig. 2-3. Weathering areas within the United States.

Table 2-6. Machine Backfilling Information.

Type of Soil	Machine-hours Per 100 Cubic Yards.	
	Backfiller	Excavator
Heavy Soil or Clay	5	6
Medium Soil	3-1/2	4
Loam, Sand or Gravel	3	3-1/2

of several methods can be used to do this: sprinkling, mat or fabric kept wet or wet sand. Temperatures must be kept above 50°F. during this stage. Plastic shrinkage cracking is a term used to describe cracks. Allow a least three days for the concrete to cure, keeping it wet by hosing.

Table 2-7. Trenching Machine Excavating Information.

Width of Cut	Hours per 100 Cubic Yards			
	Medium Soil	Heavy Soil or Clay	Stiff Clay	Loam, Sand or Gravel
10 in.	8	11	14	7

The care required in the construction of footings and foundations of chimneys cannot be over emphasized. If the foundation is not laid correctly on firm ground, cracks will develop in the walls of the chimney and it will be very difficult to make the walls watertight. If the foundation is not square, if the dimensions are not followed exactly according to plan, and if the top of the foundation is not according to grade, it will have a direct effect on all that follows.

Frozen ground expands and tends to rise above its normal elevation, settling back when the frost is out of the ground. When the ground moves, everything attached to it will also move, causing serious damage to the structure. In order to overcome this

Table 2-8. Backfilling and Tamping Facts.

Type of Soil	Hours Labor Per 100 Cu. Yd.	
	Backfilling	Tamping
Heavy Soil or Clay	66	132
Ordinary Medium Soil	50	100
Sand or Loam	40	80
Hard Pan	70	140

Table 2-9. Hand Excavating Statistics.

Type of Soil	Hours Labor Per 100 Cubic Yard Dry	Wet	Plowed or Loosened	Trenches	Piers
Heavy Soil or Clay	222	333	106	416	435
Medium Soil	124	250	83	322	344
Sand or Loam	89	124	80	182	196
Hard Pan	250	400	118	500	526

problem, the footings must extend below the frost line. The depth is determined locally and usually extends 3 or 4′ to 6′ in some parts of the country.

FORMS

When forms fail, the time spent in erecting them is lost and much material is wasted. Loads on a foundation form are generally considered as hydraulic loadings that result in lateral pressure. The concrete acts as though it were in a liguid state pushing sideways against the forms. If the forms are not properly constructed and braced, this action will break the forms. In building forms, some of the things to keep in mind arc thc weight of the

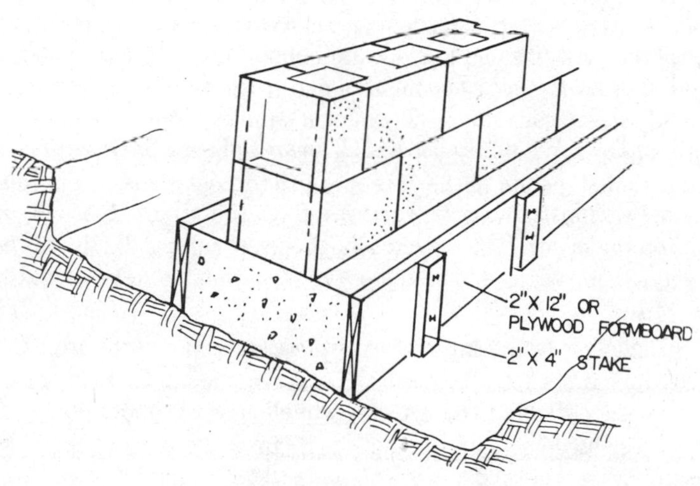

Fig. 2-4. Concrete block or brick foundation.

concrete, the rate of pour, the temperature of the surrounding air and the temperature of the concrete in addition to the method of placement. The weight of the concrete is determined by the specification of the mix. The rate of pour may be slow enough so that the concrete will begin to set, reducing the pressure on the forms. A low rate of pour would be from 1 to 2′ per hour. If ready mixed concrete is delivered, the rate of pour may increase to 3 or 4′ per hour or more.

Temperature is also important in form design and construction. The setting of concrete is somewhat delayed at lower temperatures, and the formwork must be made to take the additional strain, caused by the fact that the concrete remains liquid for a longer time. Ordinarily concrete should have a temperature of between 50 and 70°F. when placed in forms. The surface of tthe forms are generally wood stock of 2″ thick and properly braced by driving wooden stakes into the ground against the outside surface of the forms.

Chimneys built on steep slopes or rugged terrain should be rough graded before the excavation is laid out. Topsoil should be removed and piled where it will not interfere with construction of the chimney. This can be used for the finish grade after the project is completed. The size and shape of the excavation depends upon the design of the footing or foundation. Footings must be wide enough to spread the load over sufficient area so there is no possibility of settlement. Excavate beyond the dimensions of the footing about 1′ to allow enough room to work in setting the forms. Usually the excavation required for a chimney is little enough to excavate by hand, otherwise a back hoe may be used. Drive stakes and establish points of the corners of the foundations. Loose dirt and debris must always be removed from the ground that will be located under a footing, even though the resulting depth will be greater than required. The top of the form must be level with the top of the footing.

Usually most of the concrete can be poured directly from the ready-mix truck into the forms. To move the concrete to other areas not accessible to the truck, a wheelbarrow is generally used. Concrete should be placed as near to its final position of deposit as possible. To avoid separattion or segregation of the ingredients in the concrete, it should not be placed in large quantities at a given point and allowed to run or be worked over a long distance. Concrete should be placed in forms promptly after mixing. In

Table 2-10. Materials Required for 1 Cubic Yard of Mortar and Concrete.

	3/4" Gravel			1" Stone Dust Out			2-1/2" Stone Dust Out			2-1/2" Stone Most Small Stone Out		
Mixture	Barrels Cement	Cubic Yard Sand	Cubic Yard Stone	Barrels Cement	Cubic Yard Sand	Cubic Yard Stone	Barrels Cement	Cubic Yard Sand	Cubic Yard Stone	Barrels Cement	Cubic Yard Sand	Cubic Yard Stone
Mortar												
1:1-1/2	3.61	0.80	Using	very	fine	sand	3.87	0.86		Using	coarse	sand
1:2	3.02	0.90	"	"	"	"	3.21	0.95		"	"	"
1:2-1/2	2.60	0.96	"	"	"	"	2.74	1.01		"	"	"
1:3	2.28	1.01	"	"	"	"	2.39	1.06		"	"	"
Concrete												
1:1:2	2.30	0.35	0.74	2.57	0.39	0.78	2.63	0.40	0.80	2.72	0.41	0.83
1:1-1/2:3	1.71	0.39	0.78	1.85	0.42	0.84	1.90	0.43	0.87	1.96	0.45	0.89
1:1-3/4:2-3/4	1.75	0.43	0.75	1.85	0.47	0.80	1.93	0.46	0.84	2.00	0.48	0.85
1:2:3	1.54	0.47	0.73	1.70	0.52	0.77	1.73	0.53	0.79	1.78	0.54	0.81
1:2:3-1/2	1.44	0.44	0.77	1.57	0.48	0.83	1.61	0.42	0.85	1.66	0.50	0.88
1:2:4	1.34	0.41	0.81	1.46	0.44	0.89	1.48	0.45	0.90	1.53	0.47	0.93
1:2-1/2:4	1.24	0.47	0.75	1.35	0.52	0.82	1.38	0.53	0.84	1.42	0.54	0.87
1:2-1/2:4-1/2	1.16	0.44	0.80	1.27	0.48	0.87	1.29	0.42	0.88	1.33	0.51	0.91
1:2-1/2:5	1.10	0.42	0.83	1.19	0.46	0.91	1.21	0.46	0.92	1.26	0.48	0.96
1:3:4	1.15	0.52	0.72	1.26	0.58	0.77	1.28	0.58	0.78	1.32	0.60	0.80
1:3:5	1.03	0.47	0.78	1.11	0.51	0.85	1.14	0.52	0.87	1.17	0.54	0.89
1:3:6	0.99	0.42	0.84	1.01	0.46	0.92	1.02	0.47	0.93	1.06	0.48	0.97

general it should be placed in the form in horizontal layers of uniform thickness of about 6″ thick.

As the concrete is placed, it is spaded or vibrated enough to compact it thoroughly and produce a dense mass. Working the concrete next to the walls of the forms tends to produce a smooth surface, free from honeycombing along the form face. This practice is important if the concrete foundation is to be exposed and not completely buried below ground. A spade or piece of wood may be used for this purpose. The large aggregates or stone are forced away from the form face and any air that may have been trapped along the form face is released, creating a smooth finish.

CONCRETE

The definition of concrete is an artificial conglomerate stone made by uniting cement and water into a paste and mixing into this paste a fine material, such as sand, and a coarser material such as broken stone, gravel, slag or cinders. Upon the hardening of the paste the entire mass becomes like a solid stone. Mass concrete was employed by the Egyptians and the Romans, but the use of steel reinforcing did not begin until the nineteenth century.

Because of its composition, concrete has great compressive strength but little ability to withstand tension such as used in a floor or footing. Steel bars, rods or mesh fabric are consequently incorporated in those parts of the concrete members in which it is required that tensile stresses be resisted. Concrete may be divided into two classes: mass concrete, where weight of bulk is required and where to a large degree only compressive stresses are present; and reinforced concrete, where it is necessary to introduce steel to counteract the tensile stresses caused by the nature of the material.

The chemically active element of concrete is the cement. It becomes hydrated, is united chemically and physically with the water and binds the sand, stone or other coarse material together. Broken stone cinders or slag are chemically inert and are classed as aggregates. The material under ¼″ in diameter is called fine aggregate and generally refers to sand. All material over ¼″ in diameter is called coarse aggregate and includes the broken stone, cinders, etc. Any crushed rock or slag or any clean hard natural gravel may be used as coarse aggregate. Granite, traprock or hard limestone are used for this purpose. They are crushed and screened to size so the aggregate are graded by sieve passing. Rocks containing iron pyrites forming sulfuric acid should not be used.

Table 2-11. Areas of Steel Reinforcement per Foot Width of Slab.

Size of Bar	Spacing of Bars in Inches																		
	3	3-1/2	4	4-1/2	5	5-1/2	6	6-1/2	7	7-1/2	8	8-1/2	9	9-1/2	10	10-1/2	11	11-1/2	12
	Area of Steel in Square Inches																		
#2	0.20	0.17	0.15	0.13	0.12	0.11	0.10	0.09	0.08	0.08	0.07	0.07	0.07	0.06	0.06	0.06	0.05	0.05	0.05
#3	0.44	0.38	0.33	0.29	0.26	0.24	0.22	0.20	0.19	0.18	0.17	0.16	0.15	0.14	0.13	0.13	0.12	0.11	0.11
#4	0.80	0.69	0.60	0.53	0.48	0.44	0.40	0.37	0.34	0.32	0.30	0.28	0.27	0.25	0.24	0.23	0.22	0.21	0.20
#5	1.24	1.06	0.93	0.82	0.74	0.67	0.62	0.57	0.49	0.46	0.49	0.43	0.41	0.39	0.37	0.35	0.33	0.32	0.31
#6	1.76	1.51	1.32	1.17	1.05	0.96	0.88	0.81	0.75	0.70	0.66	0.62	0.58	0.55	0.52	0.50	0.48	0.46	0.44
#7	2.40	2.06	1.80	1.60	1.44	1.31	1.20	1.11	1.03	0.96	0.90	0.85	0.80	0.76	0.72	0.69	0.66	0.63	0.60
#8	3.16	2.71	2.37	2.10	1.89	1.72	1.58	1.45	1.35	1.26	1.18	1.11	1.05	0.99	0.94	0.90	0.86	0.82	0.79
#9	4.00	3.43	3.00	2.67	2.40	2.18	2.00	1.85	1.72	1.60	1.50	1.41	1.33	1.26	1.20	1.14	1.09	1.04	1.00
#10	5.08	4.35	3.81	3.38	3.04	2.77	2.54	2.34	2.17	2.03	1.90	1.79	1.69	1.60	1.52	1.45	1.38	1.32	1.27
#11	6.24	5.35	4.68	4.16	3.74	3.40	3.12	2.88	2.67	2.50	2.34	2.20	2.08	1.97	1.87	1.78	1.70	1.63	1.56

There seems to be little preference between crushed stone and gravel. More tampering may be required with crushed stone and gravel may not yield as much concrete per bag of cement. The placing of large stone will require less concrete to fill the forms. Be sure concrete is placed between the stone.

Admixtures

Chemicals are added to concrete during or immediately before mixing to retard or accelerate the time of initial set, increase its durability and water retardant qualities, improve its workability and harden its surface. Many of the compounds contain calcium chloride, hydrated lime and kaolin. Hydrated lime and kaolin make the concrete more workable and reduce the amount of water. Calcium chloride and calcium oxychloride are used to hasten the set. Retarders are sometimes used during hot weather so that concrete may be moved from the mixer to the forms before initial setting takes place. Always use admixtures with manufacturers recommendations, if used at all. Do not use admixes to correct any faulty mixing of concrete.

Water

If too much water is used in the mixing of concrete, it will produce an inferior mix. If water raises to the top when the concrete is spaded or tamped, it is a sign of too much water. This will cause a thin, milky layer containing cement and other fine particles called *laitance* to appear on the surface. These layers are a sign of weakness in the mix and are subject to failure upon exposure of the weather. Excess water also makes the mix porous and greatly reduces the strength and durability. The water used should be clean and free from oil, acid, alkali, organic matter an other foreign substances. Never use sea water in mixing concrete.

Proportioning concrete means adding ingredients to form a workable and economical mixture with a maximum density and the desired strength. A method used in the past is known as arbitrary proportioning. It specifies a ratio of cement, sand and water with coarse aggregates without reference to their function or to the amount of water used in the mix. The most common mix for the average job is 1 part cement to 6 parts combined aggregates with a maximum water-cement ratio of 7½ gallons of water for each 94 pound sack of cement. The 1:6 mix may be 1:2:4 or 1:2½:3½ with the latter being more satisfactory.

Table 2-12. Sizes, Areas, Perimeters and Weights of Deformed Reinforcing bars.

Number of Bars		Size of Deformed Bars									
		#2	#3	#4	#5	#6	#7	#8	#9	#10	#11
1	A	0.05	0.11	0.20	0.31	0.44	0.60	0.79	1.00	1.27	1.56
	o	0.786	1.178	1.571	1.963	2.356	2.749	3.142	3.544	3.990	4.430
	W	0.167	0.376	0.668	1.043	1.502	2.044	2.670	3.40	4.303	5.313
2	ΣA	0.10	0.22	0.40	0.62	0.88	1.20	1.58	2.00	2.54	3.12
	Σo	1.57	2.36	3.14	3.93	4.71	5.50	6.28	7.09	7.98	8.86
	ΣW	0.33	0.75	1.34	2.09	3.00	4.09	5.34	6.80	8.61	10.63
3	ΣA	0.15	0.33	0.60	0.93	1.32	1.80	2.37	3.00	3.81	4.68
	Σo	2.36	3.53	4.71	5.89	7.07	8.25	9.43	10.63	11.97	13.29
	ΣW	0.50	1.12	2.00	3.13	4.51	6.13	8.01	10.20	12.91	15.94
4	ΣA	0.20	0.44	0.80	1.24	1.75	2.41	3.16	4.00	5.08	6.24
	Σo	3.14	4.71	6.28	7.85	9.42	11.00	12.57	14.18	15.96	17.72
	ΣW	0.67	1.50	2.67	4.17	6.01	8.18	10.68	13.60	17.21	21.25
$12a_s$		0.60	1.32	2.40	3.72	5.28	7.20	9.48	12.00	15.24	18.72

INSTRUCTIONS FOR USE — Perimeters are based on the properties of plain round bars of equal weight and may be used in design for perimeters of deformed bars.

Cross sectional areas (A or ΣA) of bars are given in sq. in.

Perimeters (o or Σo) are given in inches.

Weights (W or ΣW) are given in lb. per foot of length.

The last line gives values of $12a_s$ for use in the formula:

$$\text{Spacing of bars in slab (in inches)} = \frac{12a_s}{A_s}$$

in which $12a_s$ = cross sectional area of 12 slab bars of size used.

A_s = cross sectional area per foot width of slab required.

Areas, perimeters, and weights of groups of more than four bars may be easily obtained from the table by simple additions or multiplications.

Rod Size (in.)	Area (sq in)	Weights (lb per ft)
1/4	.05	1.67
3/8	.11	.376
1/2	.20	.668
5/8	.31	1.043

NOTES — Maximum pitch to be not greater than one-sixth of core diameter; the clear spacing between wires not greater than 3 inches. (See "Building Code Requirements for Reinforced Concrete" of American Concrete Institute.)

Pitches not shown for smaller core diameters must be checked by above rule to determine minimum spacing.

Pitches less than 1-5/8 inches not recommended.

Pitch variation by 1/4-inch intervals recommended.

Mixing Concrete

Concrete is best mixed by a mechanical mixer. These may be hired or rented from a local dealer. They are driven by gasoline or electricity. The ingredients should be carefully measured and thoroughly mixed. The mixers consist of drums or barrels rotated and provided on the inside with paddles or scoops which thoroughly raise, cut and stir the materials as the container revolves. The drum types are discharged through spouts and the barrel types by tilting the barrel. Small, medium or large size mixers containing 2 cubic feet to 4 cubic yards are available.

The materials may be measured by volume or weight, but in either case allowances must be made for the amount of water carried by the aggregates since water increases both weight and bulk. The specified amount of water must be carefully maintained. Some mixers are equipped with water measuring devices and, when set, will not allow any more water in the mix than preset measurement. One minute is generally allowed for mixing each batch of cubic yard or less. Every effort should be made to hold the same amount of ingredients for subsequent mixes. This will assure the same strength for the entire amount of concrete required to complete the project.

If for any reason a mechanical mixer is not available, the mix should be placed in a tight wood or metal box. The dry cement and sand are first shoveled or hoed together until the mixture assumes a uniform color. The coarse aggregate and the water are then added and the whole mass repeatedly shoveled over and over until it becomes the same color and is homogeneous in composition.

In most cities, central mixing plants have ready mixed concrete. This is transported to the project in watertight dumping trucks or in trucks with large revolving drums which prevent separation of the aggregates during transit. The concrete may be completely mixed, including the water, before leaving the plant, or it may be mixed dry before starting and the water added during transit. The distance or time required to reach the job site will determine which method is used. Ready-mixed concrete offers greater convenience and economy in addition to less work. It results in better concrete because the mix is controlled. No more than 1½ hours should pass between adding cement and discharging mix into forms. The mixing should begin not more than 30 minutes after the cement has been added to the aggregate.

Testing Concrete

The test given to concrete for strength is the compression test. Specimens are taken from the ready-mix truck and put into a cylinder made of nonporous material, usually heavy paper. These cylinders are about 6″ in diameter and about 12″ long. When the cylinder is full with a sample of the concrete, it is rodded with 25 stokes of a ⅝″ rod, 24″ long. The surface of the cylinder is leveled with a trowel, left to stand for 24 hours and taken to a laboratory and cured in a moist atmosphere at 70°F. After 28 days the specimen is put into a machine until crushed. A reading is taken at the time of failure or crushing and the amount of compression is recorded.

Transporting Concrete

It is important that after mixing concrete, it should be placed in the form as quickly as possible with a minimum of separation of its ingredients. When the concrete is mixed at the site of construction, the mixer should be in a central position convenient for loading and unloading. A drop of more than 4′ should be avoided in placing concrete into the forms. A longer fall will tend to separate the ingredients. Masses of concrete should not be allowed to accumulate at the mouth of the chute to be spread later by shoveling. Sufficient tampering is necessary to make the concrete firm and dense without air holes. Since the chemical processes in the hardening of concrete are dependent upon warmth and moisture, it is important to know that concrete deposited in cold or freezing weather will set very slowly and may never attain its normal strength. The most favorable temperatures for hardening are considered to be between 50 and 70°F for at least three days or above 50°F for at least five days for normal cement. These temperatures are not difficult to maintain with modern methods of construction.

The water, sand and aggregates are heated before mixing. Generally it is not necessary to heat the aggregates above 50°F. The remaining heat is provided by the water, which should not be higher than 175°F at the time of mixing. After depositing concrete, it should be protected with canvas, building paper, wet sand or straw. The use of alcohol, glycerine or other antifreeze compounds are not recommended. The amount necessary to prevent freezing is so great that it will affect the strength of the concrete. Calcium chloride is acceptable if used in quantities not exceeding 2 pounds per bag of cement. Concrete should never be poured on frozen ground.

Hardening Concrete

Regardless of the care taken in mixing and placing, first quality concrete can be obtained only when proper provisions are taken in curing. The hardening of concrete is caused by the chemical action between the water and the cement. This hardening continues indefinitely as long as moisture is present and the temperature is favorable. The initial set does not begin until two or three hours after the concrete has been mixed. During this time moisture evaporates, especially on the exposed surface. The result is that unless provisions are made to prevent loss of moisture, the concrete will craze. Concrete should be protected for a period of seven days.

To prevent the loss of moisture during curing, several methods may be employed. The concrete may be covered with burlap kept wet or with building paper with edges pasted down. Another method is to cover the concrete with a 1″ layer of wet sand or sawdust. Still another method is to sprinkle water.

Hold to accurate dimensions when building forms. They should be rigid and strong enough to support the weight of the concrete with no deformation. Spruce and pine are generally used for formwork. Hemlock has a tendency to stain the concrete and should not be used when concrete is exposed. Green or partially seasoned lumber is preferable since dry lumber will expand when wet. Wood forms should be thoroughly wet before concrete is poured. There are no exact rules concerning the length of time the forms should remain in place. Obviously they should not be removed until the concrete is strong enough to support its own weight. The minimum length of time is two days. For practical purposes we may assume that concrete attains its desired strength at the end of 28 days.

Hot Weather Concreting

Following are precautions to be used in hot weather concreting:

- Have all material and tools ready before any work is started. Start late in the afternoon and schedule work with the least delay.
- Soak the ground with water where concrete is to be placed.
- Once concrete has been thoroughly mixed, place it immediately into the forms.

- Place temporary burlap water soaked covering over the concrete.
- Start curing as soon as the surface is hard enough to resist marring or damage. Keep constantly wet to avoid alternate wetting and drying during the curing stage and continue curing for at least seven days.

Defects, Causes and Remedies

Scaling occurs when the surface of hardened concrete breaks away from the slab. It is caused by rapid surface drying due to hot sun or drying winds. Another possible cause is premature floating and troweling due to excess amount of surface water. As a remedy, apply fog or spray and cover with burlap after finishing. Keep damp while curing for several days. Remove excess surface water by evaporation.

Dusting is the appearance of powdered material on the surface. It is caused by excess of clay or silt in the concrete mix, premature floating and troweling with excess water and no curing or inadequate curing. Prevent this occurrence by using clean and well-graded aggregates. Remove excess water before finishing. Remember, proper time in curing is essential.

3

Chimney and Fireplace Construction

For many years brick sizes were relatively standard, with only three generally available: standard, roman and norman. The sizes varied only slightly. This situation no longer exists. Brick are now available in many sizes ranging in thickness from a nominal 3 to 8″ and even 10 and 12″. Height ranges from 2 to 8″ and lengths up to 16″. Consequently, it has become more important, when buying and using brick, to avoid misunderstandings.

BRICK SIZES

The size of brick units shown in Table 3-1 and Fig. 3-1 are most typical of those currently being produced by the industry. However, few manufacturers produce all of the sizes shown; also, other-sizes are produced by some manufacturers, the dimensions of which will vary from those shown. For this reason, it is recommended that you consult with the manufacturer or distributor in your area before proceeding with a design incorporating a specific brick size that may not be readily available in your particular locality.

The nomenclature indicated, although typical, is also not completely standard throughout the industry. Except for the Standard, Roman and Norman sizes, individual manufacturers may have their own nomenclature for certain sizes listed, or may have adopted the name for a size with different dimensions. Except for the non-modular "standard," "oversize" and 3″ units, most brick are produced in modular sizes. The nominal dimensions of modular brick are equal to the manufactured dimensions plus the thickness of the mortar joint for which the unit is designed. In general, the joint thickness used with brick are ⅜″ or ½″.

The actual manufactured dimensions of the brick may vary, of course, from the specified dimensions by not more than the permissible tolerances for variation in dimensions as prescribed the industry. The designed manufactured heights for the standard brick and all modular brick are designed to be laid three courses to 8″.

BRICK POSITIONING AND COURSING

Most brick are laid as "stretchers," so that the longer of the face dimension is horizontal. See Figs. 3-2 through 3-18. Figure 3-2 also illustrates terms applied to other brick positions as placed in the wall. The shaded areas indicate the surface of the brick that are exposed.

Table 3-2 and 3-3 contain vertical coursing dimensions for both non-modular and modular brick. For the non-modular brick in Table 3-2, vertical coursing dimensions are dhown for both ⅜″ and ½″ mortar joints. In both tables the bricks are assumed to be positioned in the wall as stretchers.

LIME, GYPSUM AND CEMENT

The three most widely used materials for masonry work are lime, gypsum and cement. Following is a summary of each:

- **Gypsum.** Sulfate of lime. $CaSo_4 + 2H_2O$. Burned above 212 or 400°F. Low heat. Does not slake. Hardens by reabsorption of water and crystallization.
- **Common lime.** Pure limestone. Carbonate of lime. $CaCO_3$. Burned to 1600°F. Low heat. Slakes.
- **Magnesia limestone.** $CaCO_3 + MaCO_3$. Hardens by reabsorption of carbon dioxide.
- **Hydrated lime.** Stone composed of lime, silica and alumina. Burned to 1600°F. Low heat. Sets under water. Slakes.
- **Portland cement.** Artificial mixture of limestone and clay-like materials containing silica and alumina. Burned to fusion at 2700 to 3000°F. High heat. Sets under water. Does not slake. Hardens by formation of new chemical compounds and crystallization.

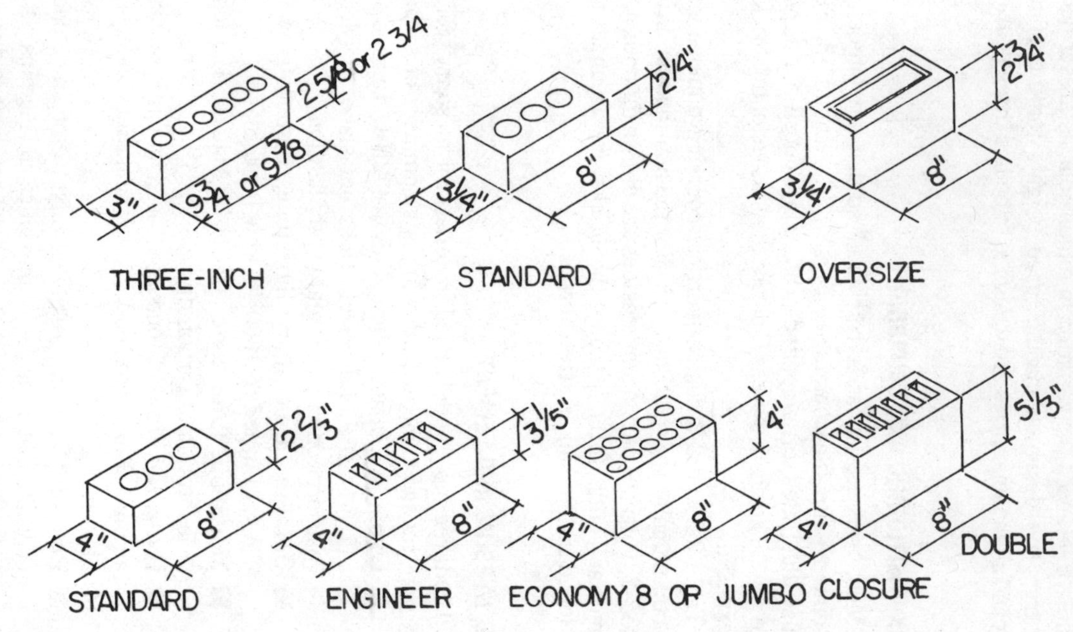
2 5/8 or 2 3/4
3"
9 3/4 or 9 5/8
THREE-INCH
2 1/4"
3 1/4"
8"
STANDARD
2 3/4"
3 1/4"
8"
OVERSIZE
2 2/3"
4"
8"
STANDARD
3 1/5"
4"
8"
ENGINEER
4"
4"
8"
ECONOMY 8 OR JUMBO CLOSURE
5 1/3"
4"
8"
DOUBLE

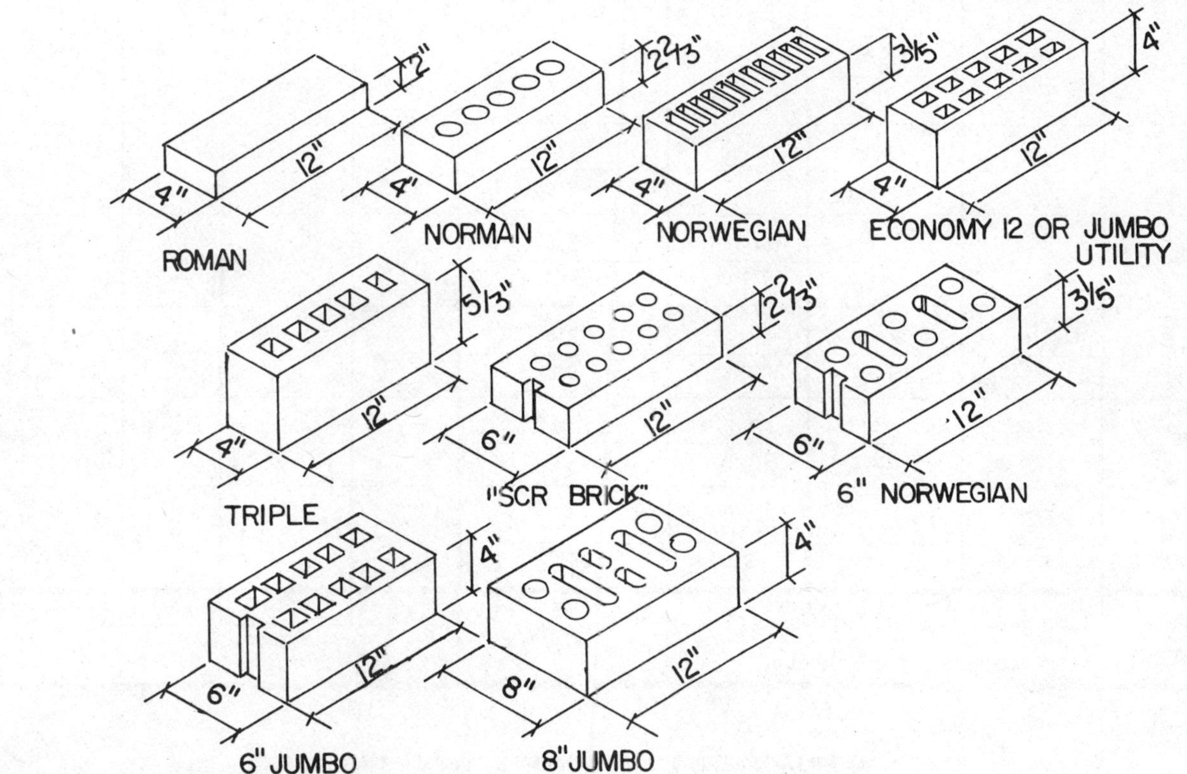

Fig. 3-1. Actual dimensions for non-modular brick and nominal dimensions for modular brick.

Table 3-1. Sizes of Modular Brick (courtesy of Structural Clay Products Institute).

Unit Designation	Nominal Dimensions, in			Joint Thickness in.	Manufactured Dimensions in.			Modular Coursing in.
	t	h	l		t	h	l	
Standard Modular	4	2-2/3	8	3/8	3-5/8	2-1/4	7-5/8	3C = 8
				1/2	3-1/2	2-1/4	7-1/2	
Engineer	4	3-1/5	8	3/8	3-5/8	2-13/16	7-5/8	5C = 16
				1/2	3-1/2	2-11/16	7-1/2	
Economy 8 or Jumbo Closure	4	4	8	3/8	3-5/8	3-5/8	7-5/8	1C = 4
				1/2	3-1/2	3-1/2	7-1/2	
Double	4	5-1/3	8	3/8	3-5/8	4-15/16	7-5/8	3C = 16
				1/2	3-1/2	4-13/16	7-1/2	
Roman	4	2	12	3/8	3-5/8	1-5/8	11-5/8	2C = 4
				1/2	3-1/2	1-1/2	11-1/2	

Norman	4	2-2/3	12	3/8	3-5/8	2-1/4	11-5/8	3C = 8
				1/2	3-1/2	2-1/4	11-1/2	
Norwegian	4	3-1/5	12	3/8	3-5/8	2-13/16	11-5/8	5C = 16
				1/2	3-1/2	2-11/16	11-1/2	
Economy 12 or Jumbo Utility	4	4	12	3/8	3-5/8	3-5/8	11-5/8	1C = 4
				1/2	3-1/2	3-1/2	11-1/2	
Triple	4	5-1/3	12	3/8	3-5/8	4-15/16	11-5/8	3C = 16
				1/2	3-1/2	4-13/16	11-1/2	
SCR brick[2]	6	2-2/3	12	3/8	5-5/8	2-1/4	11-5/8	3C = 8
				1/2	5-1/2	2-1/4	11-1/2	
6-in. Norwegian	6	3-1/5	12	3/8	5-5/8	2-13/16	11-5/8	5C = 16
				1/2	5-1/2	2-11/16	11-1/2	
6-in. Jumbo	6	4	12	3/8	5-5/8	3-5/8	11-5/8	1C = 4
				1/2	5-1/2	3-1/2	11-1/2	
8-in. Jumbo	8	4	12	3/8	7-5/8	3-5/8	11-5/8	1C = 4
				1/2	7-1/2	3-1/2	11-1/2	

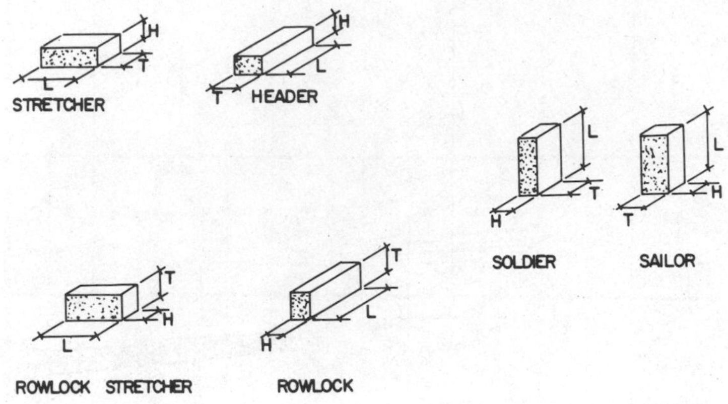

Fig. 3-2. Example of brick positions in a wall.

BONDS AND PATTERNS IN BRICKWORK

Frequently, bonds such as English or Flemish, or variations of these, may be used to create patterns in the face of the wall. However, in the strict sense of the term, pattern refers to change or color used in the face. Therefore it may be possible to secure many patterns using the same bond. Patterns also may be produced

Fig. 3-3. Spread a uniform bed or mortar over only a few brick. Furrow only lightly, if at all. Place plenty of mortar on the end of the brick to be placed. Brick is then shoved into place so that mortar is squeezed out of the top of the head joint.

Fig. 3-4 After placing, mortar squeezed out of a bed joint is cut off to prevent staining the wall.

Fig. 3-5. When placing closures, place plenty of mortar on ends of brick in place and on ends of brick to be placed. Shove the closure into place without disturbing brick on either side.

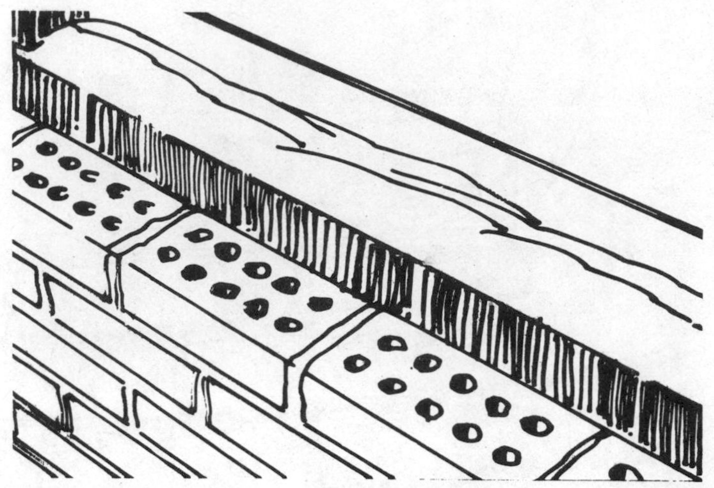

Fig. 3-6. In cavity wall construction, mortar droppings should not be permitted to fall into the cavity. An aid in preventing this is to bevel the bed joint away from the cavity.

by the method of handling the mortar joint or by projecting or recessing certain brick from the plane of the wall, thus creating a distinctive wall texture that is not solely dependent upon the texture of the individual brick.

Fig. 3-7. When a mortar joint becomes thumbprint hard, tool with a steel jointer slightly larger than the mortar joint.

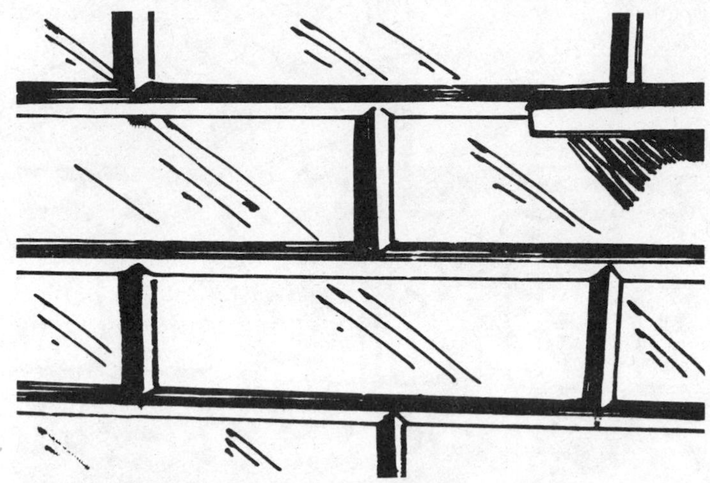

Fig. 3-8. Concave or V joints have best weather resistance.

There are five basic bonds commonly used which create patterns. These are the running, common, Flemish, English and stack bonds (Figs. 3-19 and 3-20).

Running bond. This is the simplest bond consisting of all stretchers. Since there are no headers in this bond, metal ties are

Fig. 3-9. A wall can be capped with a brick rowlock course.

Fig. 3-10. It is essential that all vertical joints be completely filled when a wall is capped with a brick rowlock course.

usually used. Running bond is used largely in cavity wall construction and veneered walls of brick.

Common bond. This is a variation of running bond with a course of full headers at regular intervals. These headers provide

Fig. 3-11. In metal-tied walls, a parge coat between wythes is the barrier to moisture penetration. Parging may be applied to either backup or facing units.

Fig. 3-12. In either case, excess mortar squeezed out of the joints should be cut off and 1/4 to 3/8″ of mortar trowelled on.

structural bonding as well as pattern. Header courses usually appear at every fifth, sixth or seventh course. In laying out any bond pattern, it is important that the corners be started correctly. For common bond, a three-quarter brick should start each way

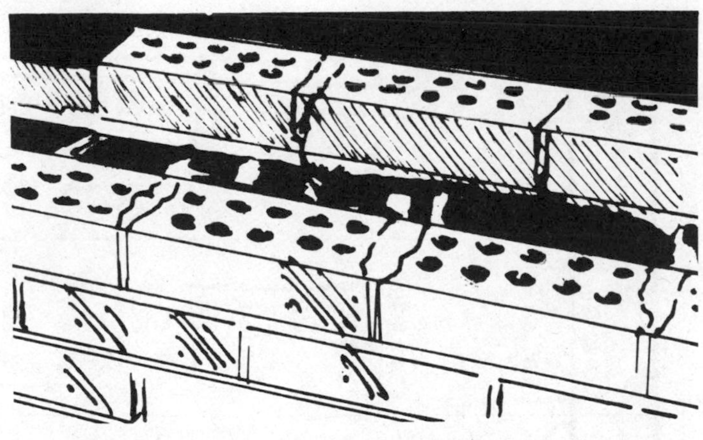

Fig. 3-13. When brick are laid on a beveled bed joint, a minimum of mortar is squeezed out of the joint. Brick (A)—beveled joint. Brick (B)—conventional joint.

Table 3-2. Vertical Coursing Table for Non-Modular Brick (courtesy of Structural Clay Products Institute).

No. of Courses	2-1/4 in. High Units		2-5/8 in. High Units		2-3/4 in. High Units	
	3/8" Joint	1/2" Joint	3/8" Joint	1/2" Joint	3/8" Joint	1/2" Joint
1	0' 2-5/8"	0' 2-3/4"	0' 3"	0' 3-1/8"	0' 3-1/8"	0' 3-1/4"
2	0' 5-1/4"	0' 5-1/2"	0' 6"	0' 6-1/4"	0' 6-1/4"	0' 6-1/2"
3	0' 7-7/8"	0' 8-1/4"	0' 9"	0' 9-3/8"	0' 9-3/8"	0' 9-3/4"
4	0' 10-1/2"	0' 11"	1' 0"	1' 0-1/2"	1' 0-1/2"	1' 1"
5	1' 1-1/8"	1' 1-3/4"	1' 3"	1' 3-5/8"	1' 3-5/8"	1' 4-1/4"
6	1' 3-3/4"	1' 4-1/2"	1' 6"	1' 6-3/4"	1' 6-3/4"	1' 7-1/2"
7	1' 6-3/8"	1' 7-1/4"	1' 9"	1' 9-7/8"	1' 9-7/8"	1' 10-3/4"
8	1' 9"	1' 10"	2' 0"	2' 1"	2' 1"	2' 2"
9	1' 11-5/8"	2' 0-3/4"	2' 3"	2' 4-1/8"	2' 4-1/8"	2' 5-1/4"
10	2' 2-1/4"	2' 3-1/2"	2' 6"	2' 7-1/4"	2' 7-1/4"	2' 8-1/2"
11	2' 4-7/8"	2' 6-1/4"	2' 9"	2' 10-3/8"	2' 10-3/8"	2' 11-3/4"
12	2' 7-1/2"	2' 9"	3' 0"	3' 1-1/2"	3' 1-1/2"	3' 3"
13	2' 10-1/8"	2' 11-3/4"	3' 3"	3' 4-5/8"	3' 4-5/8"	3' 6-1/4"
14	3' 0-3/4"	3' 2-1/3"	3' 6"	3' 7-3/4"	3' 7-3/4"	3' 9-1/2"
15	3' 3-3/8"	3' 5-1/4"	3' 9"	3' 10-7/8"	3' 10-7/8"	4' 0-3/4"
16	3' 6"	3' 8"	4' 0"	4' 2"	4' 2"	4' 4"
17	3' 8-5/8"	3' 10-3/4"	4' 3"	4' 5-1/8"	4' 5-1/8"	4' 7-1/4"
18	3' 11-1/4"	4' 1-1/2"	4' 6"	4' 8-1/4"	4' 8-1/4"	4' 10-1/2"
19	4' 1-7/8"	4' 4-1/4"	4' 9"	4' 11-3/8"	4' 11-3/8"	5' 1-3/4"
20	4' 4-1/2"	4' 7"	5' 0"	5' 2-1/2"	5' 2-1/2"	5' 5"
21	4' 7-1/8"	4' 9-3/4"	5' 3"	5' 5-5/8"	5' 5-5/8"	5' 8-1/4"
22	4' 9-3/4"	5' 0-1/2"	5' 6"	5' 8-3/4"	5' 8-3/4"	5' 11-1/2"

23	5′ 0-3/8″	5′ 3-1/4″		5′ 9″	5′ 11-7/8″		5′ 11-7/8″	6′ 2-3/4″
24	5′ 3″	5′ 6″		6′ 0″	6′ 3″		6′ 3″	6′ 6″
25	5′ 5-5/8″	5′ 8-3/4″		6′ 3″	6′ 6-1/8″		6′ 6-1/8″	6′ 9-1/4″
26	5′ 8-1/4″	5′ 11-1/2″		6′ 6″	6′ 9-1/4″		6′ 9-1/4″	7′ 0-1/2″
27	5′ 10-7/8″	6′ 2-1/4″		6′ 9″	7′ 0-3/8″		7′ 0-3/8″	7′ 3-3/4″
28	6′ 1-1/2″	6′ 5″		7′ 0″	7′ 3-1/2″		7′ 3-1/2″	7′ 7″
29	6′ 4-1/8″	6′ 7-3/4″		7′ 3″	7′ 6-5/8″		7′ 6-5/8″	7′ 10-1/4″
30	6′ 6-3/4″	6′ 10-1/2″		7′ 6″	7′ 9-3/4″		7′ 9-3/4″	8′ 1-1/2″
31	6′ 9-3/8″	7′ 1-1/4″		7′ 9″	8′ 0-7/8″		8′ 0-7/8″	8′ 4-3/4″
32	7′ 0″	7′ 4″		8′ 0″	8′ 4″		8′ 4″	8′ 8″
33	7′ 2-5/8″	7′ 6-3/4″		8′ 3″	8′ 7-1/8″		8′ 7-1/8″	8′ 11-1/4″
34	7′ 5-1/4″	7′ 9-1/4″		8′ 6″	8′ 10-1/4″		8′ 10-1/4″	9′ 2-1/2″
35	7′ 7-7/8″	8′ 0-1/4″		8′ 9″	9′ 1-3/8″		9′ 1-3/8″	9′ 5-3/4″
36	7′ 10-1/2″	8′ 3″		9′ 0″	9′ 4-1/2″		9′ 4-1/2″	9′ 9″
37	8′ 1-1/8″	8′ 5-3/4″		9′ 3″	9′ 7-5/8″		9′ 7-5/8″	10′ 0-1/4″
38	8′ 3-3/4″	8′ 8-1/2″		9′ 6″	9′ 10-3/4″		9′ 10-3/4″	10′ 3-1/2″
39	8′ 6-3/8″	8′ 11-1/4″		9′ 9″	10′ 1-7/8″		10′ 1-7/8″	10′ 6-3/4″
40	8′ 9″	9′ 2″		10′ 0″	10′ 5″		10′ 5″	10′ 10″
41	8′ 11-5/8″	9′ 4-3/4″		10′ 3″	10′ 8-1/8″		10′ 8-1/8″	11′ 1-1/4″
42	9′ 2-1/4″	9′ 7-1/2″		10′ 6″	10′ 11-1/4″		10′ 11-1/4″	11′ 4-1/2″
43	9′ 4-7/8″	9′ 10-1/4″		10′ 9″	11′ 2-3/8″		11′ 2-3/8″	11′ 7-3/4″
44	9′ 7-1/2″	10′ 1″		11′ 0″	11′ 5-1/2″		11′ 5-1/2″	11′ 11″
45	9′ 10-1/8″	10′ 3-3/4″		11′ 3″	11′ 8-5/8″		11′ 8-5/8″	12′ 2-1/4″
46	10′ 0-3/4″	10′ 6-1/2″		11′ 6″	11′ 11-3/4″		11′ 11-3/4″	12′ 5-1/2″
47	10′ 3-3/8″	10′ 9-1/4″		11′ 9″	12′ 2-7/8″		12′ 2-7/8″	12′ 8-3/4″
48	10′ 6″	11′ 0″		12′ 0″	12′ 6″		12′ 6″	13′ 0″
49	10′ 8-5/8″	11′ 2-3/4″		12′ 3″	12′ 9-1/8″		12′ 9-1/8″	13′ 3-1/4″
50	10′ 11-1/4″	11′ 5-1/2″		12′ 6″	13′ 0-1/4″		13′ 0-1/4″	13′ 6-1/2″
100	21′ 10-1/2″	22′ 11″		25′ 0″	26′ 0-1/2″		26′ 0-1/2″	27′ 1″

Fig. 3-14. The mortar squeezed from the joints on the cavity side may be plastered on to the units. This same procedure may be used for laying exterior wythes of reinforced brick walls. Mortar droppings should not be permitted in grout core.

from the corner at the header course. Common bond may be varied by using a Flemish header course.

Flemish bond. The bond consists of alternate stretchers and headers at each course, with the headers in alternate courses

Fig. 3-15. Cavity wall metal ties are embedded in bed joints as units are laid.

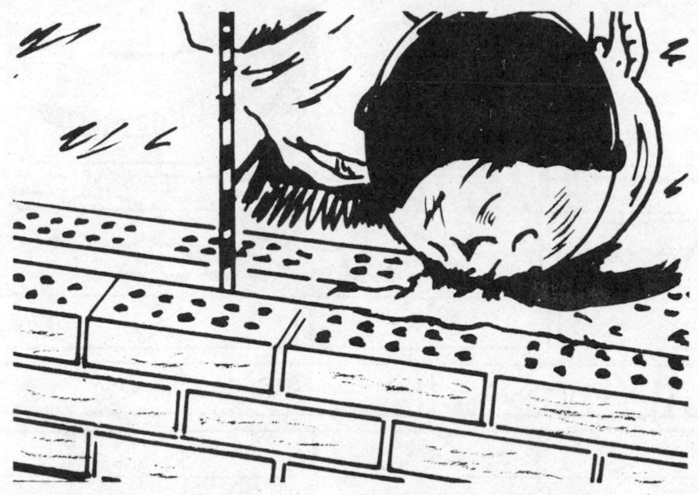

Fig. 3-16. In reinforced masonry, vertical steel should be placed before masonry is laid. Grout should be mixed with sufficient water to cause it to pour readily.

centered over the stretchers in the intervening courses. Where the headers are not used for structural bonding, they may be obtained by using half brick called "clipped" or "snap" headers. Flemish bond may vary by increasing the number of stretchers between

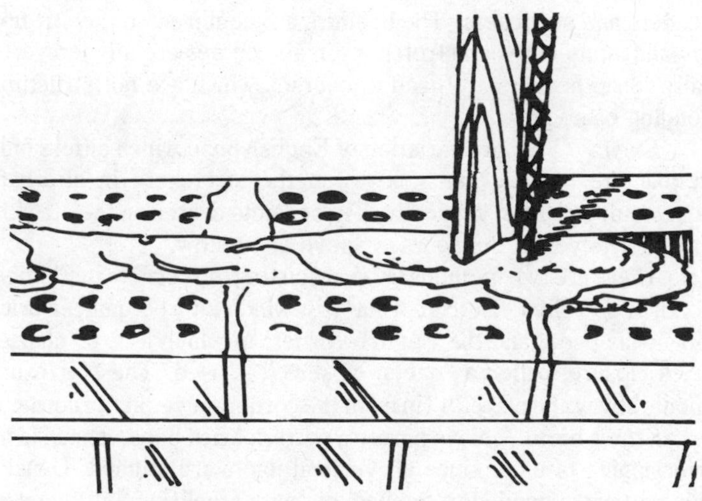

Fig. 3-17. After grout is poured, it should be puddled to consolidate it.

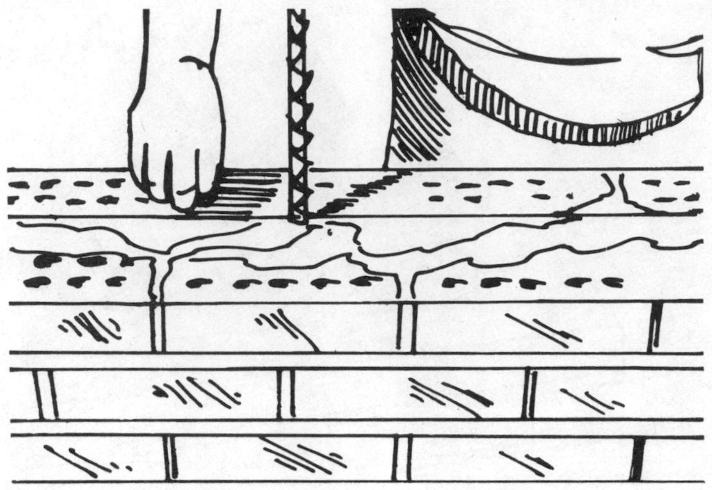

Fig. 3-18. Horizontal steel may be placed in grout core as wall is built.

headers in each course. If there are three stretchers alternating with a header, it is known as *garden wall* bond. If there are two stretchers between headers, it is designated as *double stretcher garden wall* bond. Garden wall bond may also be laid with four or even five stretchers between the headers.

English bond. This is composed of alternate courses of headers and stretchers. The headers are centered on the stretchers and joints between stretchers in all courses are aligned vertically. Snap headers are used in courses which are not structural bonding courses.

English Cross is a variation of English bond which differs only in that the vertical joints between the stretchers in alternate courses do not align vertically. These joints center on the stretchers themselves in the courses above and below.

There are two methods used in starting the corners in Flemish bond: A so-called "Dutch corner", in which a three-quarter brick closure is used, and the English corner, in which a 2″ or quarter brick closure, called a "queen closure," is used. The 2″ closure should always be placed 4″ in from the corner, never at the corner.

Stack bond. This is purely a pattern brick bond. There is no overlapping of units since all vertical joints are aligned. Usually this pattern is bonded to the backing with steel ties, but when 8″ bonder units are available, they may be used. In large wall areas and in load bearing construction, it is advisable to reinforce the wall with steel reinforcing placed in the horizontal mortar joints. In stack bond it is imperative that prematched or dimensionally accurate brick units be used if the vertical alignment of the head joints is to be maintained.

MORTAR JOINTS

Mortar joint finishes fall into two classes: *troweled* and *tooled* joints. In the troweled joint, the excess mortar is simply cut off (struck) with a trowel and finished with the trowel. For the tooled

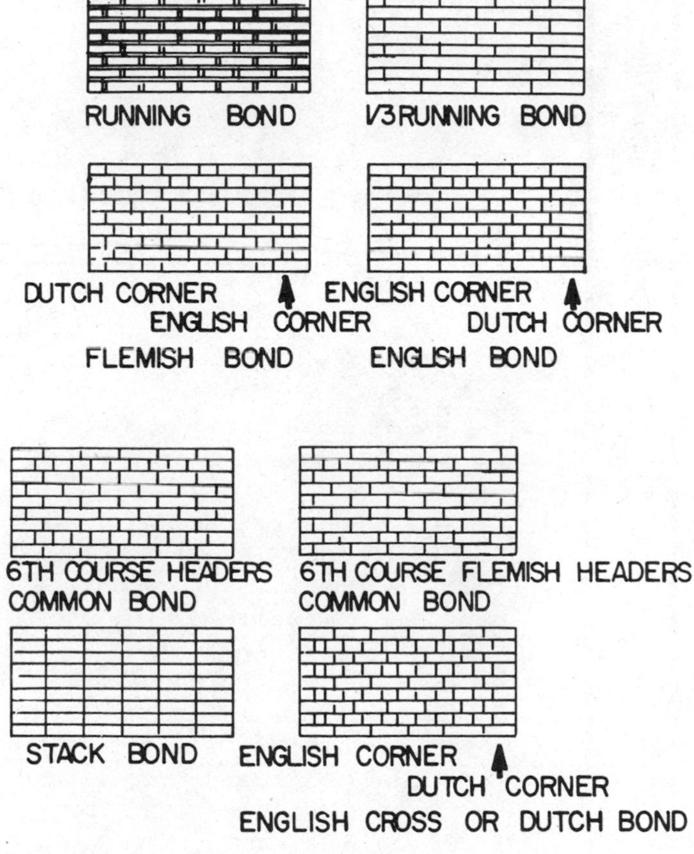

Fig. 3-19. Traditional pattern bonds.

Table 3-3. Vertical Coursing Table for Modular Brick (courtesy of Structural Clay Products Institute).

No. of Courses	Nominal Height (h) of Unit				
	2″	2-2/3″	3-1/5″	4″	5-1/3″
1	0′ 2″	0′ 2-11/16″	0′ 3-3/16″	0′ 4″	0′ 5-5/16″
2	0′ 4″	0′ 5-5/16″	0′ 6-3/8″	0′ 8″	0′ 10-11/16″
3	0′ 6″	0′ 8″	0′ 9-5/8″	1′ 0″	1′ 4″
4	0′ 8″	0′ 10-11/16″	1′ 0-13/16″	1′ 4″	1′ 9-5/16″
5	0′ 10″	1′ 1-5/16″	1′ 4″	1′ 8″	2′ 2-11/16″
6	1′ 0″	1′ 4″	1′ 7-3/16″	2′ 0″	2′ 8″
7	1′ 2″	1′ 6-11/16″	1′ 10-3/8″	2′ 4″	3′ 1-5/16″
8	1′ 4″	1′ 9-5/16″	2′ 1-5/8″	2′ 8″	3′ 6-11/16″
9	1′ 6″	2′ 0″	2′ 4-13/16″	3′ 0″	4′ 0″
10	1′ 8″	2′ 2-11/16″	2′ 8″	3′ 4″	4′ 5-5/16″
11	1′ 10″	2′ 5-5/16″	2′ 11-3/16″	3′ 8″	4′ 10-11/16″
12	2′ 0″	2′ 8″	3′ 2-3/8″	4′ 0″	5′ 4″
13	2′ 2″	2′ 10-11/16″	3′ 5-5/8″	4′ 4″	5′ 9-5/16″
14	2′ 4″	3′ 1-5/16″	3′ 8-13/16″	4′ 8″	6′ 2-11/16″
15	2′ 6″	3′ 4″	4′ 0″	5′ 0″	6′ 8″
16	2′ 8″	3′ 6-11/16″	4′ 3-3/16″	5′ 4″	7′ 1-5/16″
17	2′ 10″	3′ 9-5/16″	4′ 6-3/8″	5′ 8″	7′ 6-11/16″
18	3′ 0″	4′ 0″	4′ 9-5/8″	6′ 0″	8′ 0″
19	3′ 2″	4′ 2-11/16″	5′ 0-13/16″	6′ 4″	8′ 5-5/16″
20	3′ 4″	4′ 5-5/16″	5′ 4″	6′ 8″	8′ 10-11/16″
21	3′ 6″	4′ 8″	5′ 7-3/16″	7′ 0″	9′ 4″
22	3′ 8″	4′ 10-11/16″	5′ 10-3/8″	7′ 4″	9′ 9-5/16″
23	3′ 10″	5′ 1-5/16″	6′ 1-5/8″	7′ 8″	10′ 2-11/16″
24	4′ 0″	5′ 4″	6′ 4-13/16″	8′ 0″	10′ 8″
25	4′ 2″	5′ 6-11/16″	6′ 8″	8′ 4″	11′ 1-5/16″

26	4′ 4″	5′ 9-5/16″	6′ 11-3/16″	8′ 8″	11′ 6-11/16″
27	4′ 6″	6′ 0″	7′ 2-3/8″	9′ 0″	12′ 0″
28	4′ 8″	6′ 2-11/16″	7′ 5-5/8″	9′ 4″	12′ 5-5/16″
29	4′ 10″	6′ 5-5/16″	7′ 8-13/16″	9′ 8″	12′ 10-11/16″
30	5′ 0″	6′ 8″	8′ 0″	10′ 0″	13′ 4″
31	5′ 2″	6′ 10-11/16″	8′ 3-3/16″	10′ 4″	13′ 9-5/16″
32	5′ 4″	7′ 1-5/16″	8′ 6-3/8″	10′ 8″	14′ 2-11/16″
33	5′ 6″	7′ 4″	8′ 9-5/8″	11′ 0″	14′ 8″
34	5′ 8″	7′ 6-11/16″	9′ 0-13/16″	11′ 4″	15′ 1-5/16″
35	5′ 10″	7′ 9-5/16″	9′ 4″	11′ 8″	15′ 6-11/16″
36	6′ 0″	8′ 0″	9′ 7-3/16″	12′ 0″	16′ 0″
37	6′ 2″	8′ 2-11/16″	9′ 10-3/8″	12′ 4″	16′ 5-5/16″
38	6′ 4″	8′ 5-5/16″	10′ 1-5/8″	12′ 8″	16′ 10-11/16″
39	6′ 6″	8′ 8″	10′ 4-13/16″	13′ 0″	17′ 4″
40	6′ 8″	8′ 10-11/16″	10′ 8″	13′ 4″	17′ 9-5/16″
41	6′ 10″	9′ 1-5/16″	10′ 11-3/16″	13′ 8″	18′ 2-11/16″
42	7′ 0″	9′ 4″	11′ 2-3/8″	14′ 0″	18′ 8″
43	7′ 2″	9′ 6-11/16″	11′ 5-5/8″	14′ 4″	19′ 1-5/16″
44	7′ 4″	9′ 9-5/16″	11′ 8-13/16″	14′ 8″	19′ 6-11/16″
45	7′ 6″	10′ 0″	12′ 0″	15′ 0″	20′ 0″
46	7′ 8″	10′ 2-11/16″	12′ 3-3/16″	15′ 4″	20′ 5-5/16″
47	7′ 10″	10′ 5-5/16″	12′ 6-3/8″	15′ 8″	20′ 10-11/16″
48	8′ 0″	10′ 8″	12′ 9-5/8″	16′ 0″	21′ 4″
49	8′ 2″	10′ 10-11/16″	13′ 0-13/16″	16′ 4″	21′ 9-5/16″
50	8′ 4″	11′ 1-5/16″	13′ 4″	16′ 8″	22′ 2-11/16″
100	16′ 8″	22′ 2-11/16″	26′ 8″	33′ 4″	44′ 5-5/16″

Brick positioned in wall as stretchers.

For convenience in using table, nominal 1/3″, 2/3″ and 1/5″ heights of units have been changed to nearest 1/16″. Vertical dimensions are from bottom of mortar joint to bottom of mortar joint.

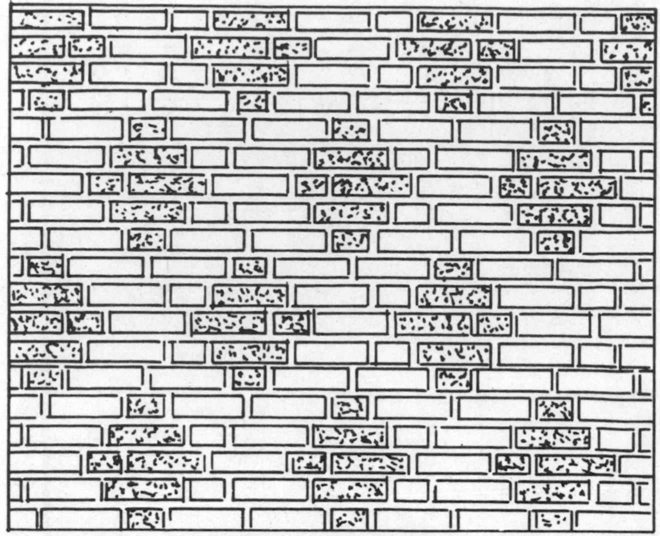

DOUBLE STRETCHER GARDEN WALL BOND WITH UNITS IN DIAGONAL LINES

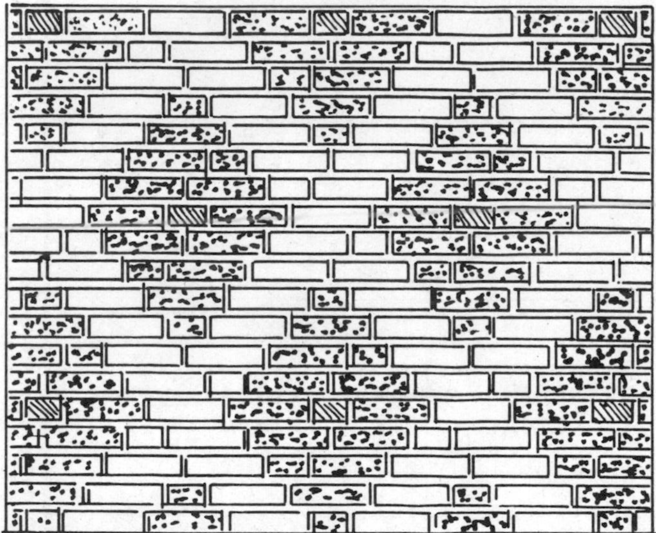

GARDEN WALL BOND WITH UNITS IN DOVETAIL FASHION

Fig. 3-20. Examples of garden wall bonds.

joint, a special tool other than a trowel is used to compress and shape the mortar in the joint. See Fig. 3-21 for typical cross section joints used in good brickwork.

Concave Joint And V-Shaped Joint. These joints are normally kept quite small and are formed by the use of a steel jointing tool. These joints are very effective in resisting rain penetration and are recommended for use in areas subjected to heavy rains and high winds.

Weathered Joint. This joint requires care as it must be worked from below. However, it is the best of the troweled joints as it is compacted and sheds water readily.

Struck Joint. This is a common joint in ordinary brickwork. This is an easy joint to strike with a trowl. Some compaction occurs, but the small ledge does not shed water readily, resulting in a less watertight joint.

Rough Cut or Flush Joint. This is the simplist joint, since it is made by holding the edge of the trowel flat against the brick and cutting in any direction. This produces a joint with a small hairline crack where the mortar is pulled away from the brick by the cutting action. This joint is not always watertight.

Raked Joint. This is made by removing the surface of the mortar, while it is still soft. While the moint may be compacted, it is difficult to make it weathertight, and is not recommended where heavy rain, high wind or freezing is likely to occur. This joint produces marked shadows and tends to darken the overall appearance of the wall.

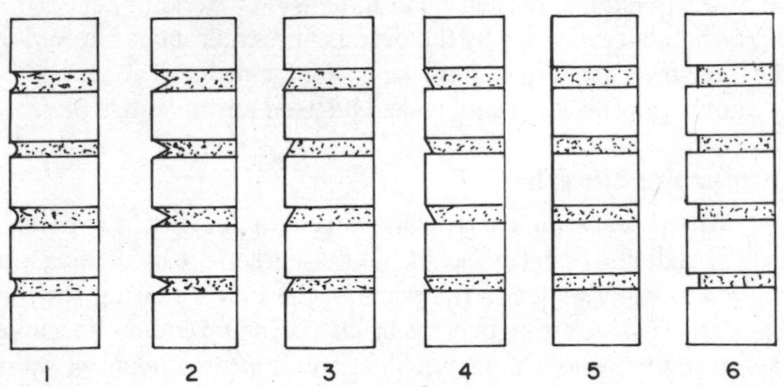

Fig. 3-21. Mortar joints.

Colored Mortar. To enhance the patterns in masonry, colored mortars may be successfully used. Two methods are commonly used: the entire mortar joint may be colored or, where a tooled joint is used, *tuck pointing* is the best method. In this technique, the entire wall is completed with a 1″ deep raked joint and the colored mortar is carefully filled in later.

BRICK PROPERTIES

As with other types of construction, the performance and durability of brick depend upon the quality of the materials—brick, mortar, grout and sand—of which the construction is composed, the workmnaship and methods of construction and the design. In considering mortar and grout, which are bonding agents and are relied upon to produce a homogeneous construction, it will be found that their performance is affected not only by the properties of these materials but often to an equal degree by the properties of the brick with which they are combined. For this reason, care should be used in selected quality material. High strength mortars do not develop a good bond with all brick. Smooth brick develop slightly lower bonds than rough brick.

Clays and shales used in the manufacture of brick make it impossible to establish a uniform material. The resultant product will reflect the variations of the natural clays. The properties of brick which have been found to have the most effect upon the design, performance and durability are size, strength, water absorption and the bonding between the mortar and the brick.

Standard sizes have been adopted by the industry which can be laid economically without excessive cutting. Few manufacturers produce all sizes and shapes. It is suggested you check the size in your area. Nominal masonry unit dimensions are joint center line dimension but may vary by the permissible tolerances allowed by the industry. Standard joint thickness for facing brick are ⅜″ or ½″ but not both. The same joint should be used for the entire project.

Compressive Strength

When measuring compressive strength of brick, it is defined as the maximum resistance of the unit to a gradually increasing load applied at right angles to the plane of the unit's bearing surface. The compressive strength of the brick has an important effect upon the strength of the wall in combination with the amount of water used in the mortar mix. The raw materials used for the production of brick are representative of the clays and shales used in current production. Manufacturers are improving method of production and manufacture by using modern ways, of firing. This will increase the density of the brick reducing the absorption and increasing the compressive strength.

Water Absorption and Texture

The pores or small openings in brick serve as capillaries which tend to draw water into the unit. For this reason, brick should be wet before laying so as not to dry out the mortar resulting in a bad bond.

The surface effect or appearance of the brick, apart from color, is the texture. This results from the process of manufacturing, such as a smooth surface which is produced by extruding the clay column through a steel die, or the sand finish texture obtained in the mud process when the molds are lubricated with sand. Other textures are produced by mechanical means to obtain desired effects and range from very course, produced by scratching and rolling the clay column, to very fine, where the die skin is removed by wire cutting.

Texture which affects the performance of brick is the surface in contact with mortar and grout. These surfaces will usually be smooth, scored, combed or roughened.

Smooth Surface. It is not altered or marked in manufacture but left as a plane surface formed by the die or mold.

Scored Finish Face Surface. It is grooved as it comes from the die to give increased bond for mortar.

Combed Finish Face Surface. The surface is altered by more or less parallel scratches or scarfs in manufacture to give increased bond for mortar.

Roughened Finish Face Surface. This is entirely broken by mechanical means, such as wire cutting or wire brushing, to give increased bond for mortar.

Durability

The weathering action that has the greatest effect on most building material is alternate freezing and thawing in the presence of moisture. This is practically the only action of weathering that has any significant effect upon brick. Any well burned brick will resist the action of freezing and thawing over a long period of time and from a structural standpoint may be considered most durable.

The most important property of mortar affecting the performance of brick is the ability to form a strong and durable bond with the brick. A good workable mortar is essential to good workmanship. Water retentivity of mortars is affected by the ingredients. Mortar flow has an important effect on mortar strength and bond between mortar and brick.

In most brick structures, mortar strength is of secondary importance to bond strength, workability and water retention. As would be expected, increased flows which produce increased water-cement ratios are associated with decreased strength. The time between spreading a mortar joint on one brick and placing a brick on the joint will affect the flow of the mortar when it comes in contact with the top brick, especially if the mortar is spread on a brick of relatively high suction. This time should be reduced to a minimum. Loss of water from the mortar after mixing will decrease through evaporation and will affect the flow and reduce the bond strength.

Wind Force

The most common cause of force or load on brick walls is wind. The force varies from place to place and in most cases walls have been engineered to resist this force without failure. There are locations where very great wind force must be resisted. This will require special design factors in building chimneys. Recommendations can be made from the local office of the building inspector.

Damage to chimneys by wind is extensive. Building codes set a minimum standard of design to make the structures safe from wind force damage or collapse. There are several reasons for this:

- High wind velocities or pressure drops strike certain areas.
- Chimneys become weak from age, disrepair or rot in their resistance to normal maximum wind force.
- Faulty design or construction.
- Chimneys built beyond the limits of local laws or codes.

It is possible to design and construct chimneys to withstand wind of even tornado or cyclone intensity, but this requires careful attention to the laws of aerodynamics and detail of design.

SPECIFICATIONS IN THE CONSTRUCTION CONTRACT

When work is done by masons on a contract basis (other than owner), certain recommendations must be followed to avoid possible trouble and legal action by either party. Following are recommended specifications which should be considered as part of the construction contract:

- Furnish all labor, materials, service, equipment and appliances required to complete the masonry work.
- Build into masonry all bolts, anchors, nailing blocks and inserts necessary to construct the work.
- Build in all doors, vents and conduits necessary to construct the work.
- Furnish sample of all brick and lay a sample wall for approval of owner.
- Clean masonry and remove surplus material and waste.
- Provide all concrete work including furnishings and placing of anchor bolts and steel dowels in concrete.
- Furnish and install bolts and metal attachments.
- Furnish and place all structural steel.

GENERAL REQUIREMENTS

Face brick shall conform to the requirements of ASTM (American Society of Testing Material) specifications. The color and texture shall be as selected by the owner.

Mortar and mortar materials shall conform to the requirements of the property specifications of ASTM. The consistency of mortar shall be adjusted to form a solid bond between mortar and brick. If mortary begins to stiffen due to evaporation or absorption of a part of the mixing water, the mortar shall be retempered by adding water and remixing. mortar and grout shall not be used after it has begun to set.

All mortar shall be stored under cover in a dry place. Brick shall be stacked on a platform in a dry place. During freezing weather, all material shall be protected with tarpaulins or other suitable covering. At the time of laying, all brick shall be clean and free from ice or other coatings. Reinforcement shall be free from the elements and, before placing, should be free from loose rust.

Wetting Brick

All brick having absorption rates in excess of ¾ ounce per minute shall be wetted sufficiently so that the rate of absorption when laid does not exceed this amount. The units shall be wetted from three to four hours before they are used, and the method shall be such as to insure that each is uniformly wetted. All units shall be free from water adhering to their surfaces when they are placed in the wall. During freezing weather, units that require wetting shall be sprinkled with warm water just before laying.

Protection of Work

During erection all walls shall be kept dry by covering at the end of each day or shutdown period with a canvas or waterproof paper. Partially completed walls not being worked on shall be similarly protected at all times. Covering shall overhang at least 2′ on each side of the wall.

Freezing Weather

No masonry shall be laid when the temperature of the outside air is below 40°F. unless suitable means are provided to heat the masonry materials and protect the completed work from freezing. Protection shall consist of heating the masonry materials to at least 40°F. and maintaining an air temperature above 40°F. on both sides of the masonry for a period of at least 48 hours.

Joining of Work and Bonding

Where fresh masonry joins masonry that is partially set or totally set, the exposed surface of the set masonry shall be cleaned, roughened, and lightly wet so as to obtain the best possbile bond with the new work. All loose brick and mortar shall be removed.

If it becomes necessary for construction purposes to "stop off" a horizontal run of masonry, this shall be done only by racking back one half brick length in each course and, if grout is used, stopping grout 4″ back of the rack. Toothing shall not be permitted except upon written approval of the owner. When grouting is stopped for one hour or longer, the grout shall be stopped 1½″ below the top of the last course grouted except at the finishing course.

Brick shall be laid in the bond selected by the owner. In unexposed masonry, all vertical joints shall be bonded by at least 2″. All walls shall be bonded each course at corners and intersections and shall be bonded or anchored to connecting work.

Jointing and Built-In Work

When the mortar has become thumbprint hard, all exposed joints shall be tooled with a round or other approved jointer. The jointer shall be slightly larger than the width of the mortar joint so that a complete contact is made along the edges of units, compressing and sealing the surface of the joint. Exterior joints below grade shall be trowel-pointed and other joints shall be flush cut.

The masonry contractor shall build in all louvers, cleanout doors, etc. He shall supply all such accessories.

Caulking

All outside perimeter joints adjoining other material with masonry shall be ¼″, nor more than ⅜″ wide, and shall be cleaned out to a uniform depth of at least ¾″ and filled solidly with an approvided elastic caulking compound forced into place with a pressure gun. Caulking compound shall be elastic and waterproof and shall gradually form a thin, tough skin on exposed surfaces while remaining plastic indefinitely beneath the surface. It shall not be affected by long exposure to extremes of outside temperature.

Pointing and Cleaning

At the completion of the work, all holes or defective mortar joints in exposed masonry shall be pointed and, where necessary, defective joints shall be cut out and repointed. Exposed masonry shall be protected against staining from wall covering or other sources, and excess mortar shall be wiped off the surface as the work progresses. At the completion of the work, all exposed masonry shall be thoroughly cleaned. If stiff brushes and water do not suffice, the surface shall be thoroughly wetted with clear water and then scrubbed with a solution of not more than 1 part hydrochloric (muriatic) acid to 9 parts water, followed immediately by a thorough rinsing with clear water. If masonry is cleaned with an acid solution, all metal parts shall be thoroughly protected.

Type A-1 or A-2 mortar shall be used for all masonry in contact with earth. Type A-1, A-2 or B mortar shall be used for all other exposed masonry.

Workmanship

All masonry shall be laid plumb and true to lines. Brick shall be laid with full mortar joints. Mortar beds shall be spread smooth or only slightly furrowed. The ends of brick shall be buttered with sufficient mortar to fill the end joints. The vertical longitudinal joint in solid brick walls shall be completely filled by parging, pouring the vertical joint full of grout or by shoving. Closure shall be rocked into plase with the head joints thrown against the two adjacent bricks in place. All collar joints in exterior brick shall be completely filled with mortar by parging. In laying brick, the mason shall avoid overplumbing and pounding of the corners to fit stretcher units after being set in position. Where an adjustment must be made after the mortar has started to harden, the mortar shall be removed and replaced with fresh mortar.

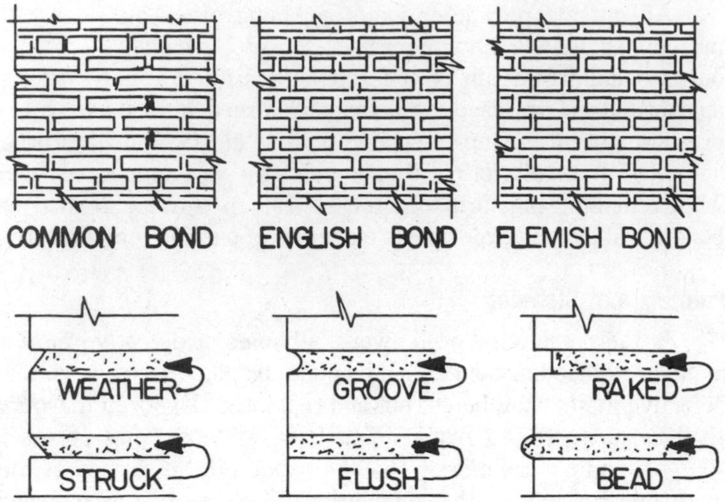

Fig. 3-22. Examples of bonds and brick coursing.

Brick shall be bonded with headers or metal ties. When bonded with headers, not less than 4 percent of the wall surface shall be composed with headers extending not less than 4″ into the wall. The distance between adjacent bonders shall not exceed 24″ either vertically or horizontally.

Anchorage

When intersecting walls are carried up, the perpendicular joint shall be regularly toothed or blocked with 8″ maximum offsets and the joints provided with metal anchors having a minimum cross section or ¼″ by 1½″ with ends bent up at least 2″ or with cross pins.

MASONRY UNITS

There are many kinds of brick and block available for fireplace and chimney construction. The exterior face should be what is called a *face brick*. These are manufactured in a variety of colors and textures and are the most expensive. The backup brick, which is not seen, can be what is called common brick, concrete brick or concrete block. All units are pretty much standard in dimension . Concrete block are all 16″ long, 8″ high and 2″, 4″, 6″, 8″ and 12″ wide. If the total wall thickness is 8″, use a 4″ thick block, or a

Table 3-4. Brick and Mortar Quantities for Chimneys.

All units laid with 1/2-in. joints; quantities based on use of standard (non-modular) brick 2-1/4 x 3-3/4 x 8. The two-flue chimneys have no brick separating the flues.

	One 8-1/2" x 8-1/2" Flue				Two 8-1/2" x 8-1/2" Flues				One 8-1/2" x 13" Flue				Two 8-1/2" x 13" Flues			
Height of Chimney in feet	Number of brick required	Cubic feet mortar required for brick	No. of 8 x 16 x 16 chimney blocks required if used	Cubic feet mortar required for blocks	Number of brick required	Cubic feet mortar required for brick	No. of 8 x 4 x 16 chimney blocks required if used	Cubic feet mortar required for blocks	Number of brick required	Cubic feet mortar required for brick	No. of 8 x 16 x 20 chimney blocks required if used	Cubic feet mortar required for blocks	Number of brick required	Cubic feet mortar required for brick	No. of 8 x 4 x 16 chimney blocks required if used	Cubic feet mortar required for blocks
1	27	.486	1-1/2	.12	36	.61	6	.17	31.5	.58	1-1/2	.14	45	.81	7-1/2	.23
2	54	.98	3	.18	72	1.23	12	.34	63	1.14	3	.21	90	1.62	15	.45
3	81	1.46	4-1/2	.30	108	1.84	18	.51	95	1.71	4-1/2	.35	135	2.43	22-1/2	.68
4	108	1.95	6	.36	144	2.45	24	.68	126	2.27	6	.42	180	3.24	30	.9
5	135	2.43	9	.54	180	3.06	30	.85	158	2.85	9	.56	225	4.05	37-1/2	1.12
6	162	2.92	9	.54	216	3.68	36	1.02	180	3.4	9	.56	270	4.86	45	1.35
7	189	3.40	12	.72	252	4.29	42	1.19	221	3.98	12	.84	315	5.67	52-1/2	1.58
8	216	3.80	12	.72	288	4.9	48	1.36	252	4.54	12	.84	360	6.48	60	1.8
9	243	4.38	15	.90	324	5.5	54	1.53	284	5.11	15	1.05	405	7.29	67-1/2	2.03
10	270	4.85	15	.90	360	6.12	60	1.7	315	5.57	15	1.05	450	8.1	75	2.25
15	405	7.29	23	1.38	540	9.18	90	2.55	473	8.52	23	1.61	675	12.15	112-1/2	3.38
20	540	9.72	30	1.8	720	12.24	120	3.4	630	11.34	30	2.1	900	16.2	150	4.5
25	675	12.15	38	2.28	900	15.3	150	4.25	788	14.19	38	2.66	1125	20.25	187-1/2	5.63
20	810	14.58	45	2.7	1080	18.36	180	5.10	945	17	45	3.15	1350	24.3	225	6.75
Note: 31'8" is the average height of a bungalow or 1-1/2-story house																
31'-8"	855	15.39	48	2.88	1140	19.38	180	5.4	998	17.96	48	3.36	1425	25.65	237-1/2	7.13
Note: 38'0" is the average height of a 2-story house																
38'-0"	1026	18.46	57	3.42	1368	3326	228	6.46	1197	21.54	57	4.0	1710	30.78	285	8.55

Table 3-5. Fire Brick Estimating.

Following data based on use of standard 2-1/2 x 4-1/2 x 9-in. size of fire-brick. From 400 to 600 lb. of high-temperature cement of fireclay are sufficient to lay 1,000 straight brick.

1 sq. ft. 2-1/2" thick wall requires 3.58 brick
1 sq ft. 4-1/2" wall requires 6.31 brick
1 sq. ft. 9" wall requires approx. 14 brick
1 sq. ft. 13-1/2" wall requires approx. 21 brick
1 cu ft. of fire-brickwork requires 17 brick
1 cu ft. of fire-brickwork weighs 125-140 lb.

common or concrete brick with a 4" (standard) face brick. If a building has brick existing, use the same color, texture and jointing. If no brick is existing, a brick, joint, color and texture must be chosen Tables 3-4, 3-5, 3-6 3-7 and Fig. 3-22.

Before any masonry work is begun, a story pole must be made. This is a straight wooden pole made from 1" × 3" stock measuring about 10′ long. A straight piece of wood furring should do. Select a piece free from knots or other defects because this pole will last until the job is completed. Lay out the masonry coursing units on the pole. Use a rule, measure up from the bottom of the pole and mark off all the courses with a pencil. Using the square, draw straight lines across the wide part of the story pole and mark every course (Fig. 3-23). If there is a masonry wall existing, use the coursing to mark the story pole to afford the same coursing on the new wall. If no brick wall exists, measure the height of the brick plus the masonry joint which will consist of a course, and mark off the courses on the pole. Number the courses after marking. With this system, all courses will be the same dimension. Use the story pole at every course to set the line. Store the pole in a dry place to prevent warping or bowing out of shape.

Tools and Use

- Trowels used for spreading the mortar.
- Mason hammer used to cut brick or block.
- Plumb level used for leveling masonry courses.
- Folding rule used for brick and block layout.
- Brick set chisel used for cutting masonry units clean.
- Lines used to align each course.
- Brush used to do finsihing touches on masonry.
- Steel square used for squaring corners.
- Jointers used to finish mortar joints (Fig. 3-24)

Cold Weather Recommendations

- Construction materials should be received, stored and protected to prevent water from entering the material.
- Frozen sand and wet masonry units must be thawed. Masonry units below 20°F. must be heated above the temperature without overheating.
- Mortar ingredients should be heated to produce temperatures between 40°F. and 120°F. Every effort should be made to produce consecutive batches of mortar with the

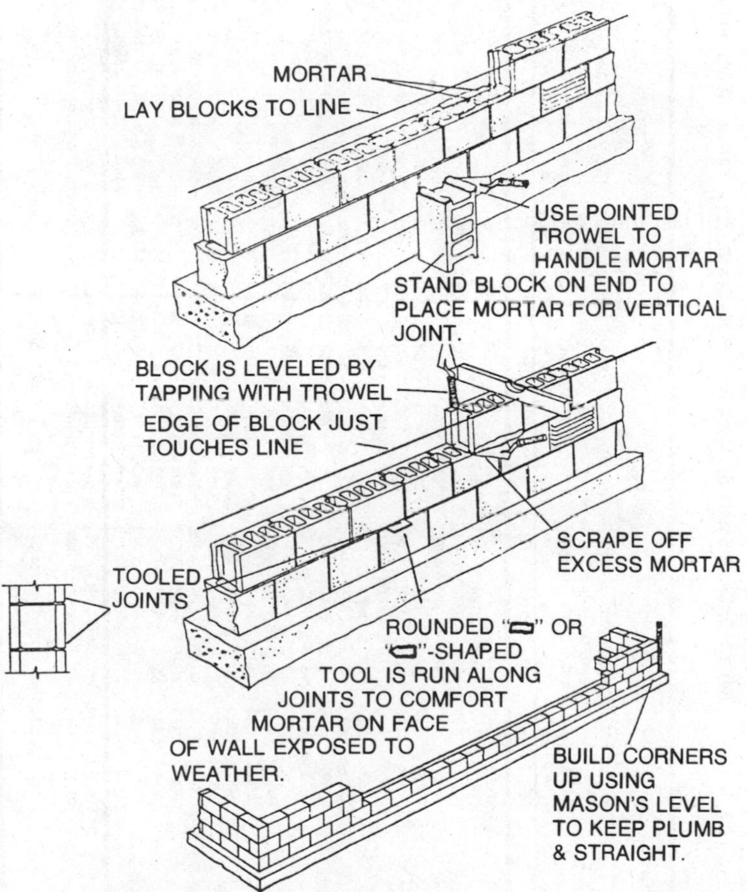

Fig. 3-23. Details on building masonry walls (courtesy of American Plywood Association).

Table 3-6. Quantities of Standard (Non-Modular) Brick for Various Bonds and Joint Thickness.

Sq. Ft. of Wall	RUNNING — Face Brick	RUNNING — Backing Brick in 8" Wall	RUNNING — Backing Brick in 12" Wall	COMMON Header Course Every 7th Course — Face Brick	COMMON — Backing Brick in 8" Wall	COMMON — Backing Brick in 12" Wall	ENGLISH AND ENGLISH CROSS* Full Headers Every 6th Course — Face Brick	ENGLISH — Backing Brick in 8" Wall	ENGLISH — Backing Brick in 12" Wall	FLEMISH Full Headers Every 5th Course — Face Brick	FLEMISH — Backing Brick in 8" Wall	FLEMISH — Backing Brick in 12" Wall	DOUBLE HEADERS Alternating with Stretchers Every 5th Course — Face Brick	DOUBLE HEADERS — Backing Brick in 8" Wall	DOUBLE HEADERS — Backing Brick in 12" Wall	Sq. Ft. of Wall
1	6.16	6.16	12.32	7.04	5.28	11.44	7.19	5.13	11.29	6.57	5.75	11.91	6.78	5.54	11.70	1
5	31	31	62	36	27	58	36	26	57	33	29	60	34	28	59	5
10	62	62	124	71	53	115	72	52	113	66	58	120	68	56	117	10
20	124	124	248	141	106	229	144	103	226	132	115	239	136	111	234	20
30	185	185	370	212	159	344	216	154	339	198	173	358	204	167	351	30
40	247	247	494	282	212	458	288	206	452	263	230	477	272	222	468	40
50	308	308	616	352	264	572	360	257	565	329	288	596	339	277	585	50
60	370	370	740	423	317	687	432	308	675	395	345	715	407	333	702	60
70	432	432	864	493	370	801	504	360	791	460	403	834	475	388	819	70
80	493	493	986	564	423	916	576	411	904	526	460	953	543	444	936	80
90	555	555	1110	634	476	1030	648	462	1017	592	518	1072	611	499	1053	90
100	616	616	1232	704	528	1144	719	513	1129	657	575	1191	678	554	1170	100
200	1232	1232	2464	1408	1056	2288	1438	1026	2258	1314	1150	2382	1356	1108	2340	200
300	1848	1848	3696	2110	1584	3432	2157	1539	3387	1971	1725	3573	2034	1662	3510	300
400	2464	2464	4928	2816	2112	4576	2876	2052	4516	2628	2300	4764	2712	2216	4680	400
500	3080	3080	6160	3520	2640	5720	3595	2565	5645	3285	2875	5955	3390	2770	5850	500
600	3696	3696	7392	4224	3168	6864	4314	3078	6774	3942	3450	7146	4068	3324	7020	600
700	4312	4312	8624	4928	3696	8010	5033	3591	7903	4599	4025	8337	4746	3878	8190	700
800	4928	4928	9856	5632	4224	9152	5752	4104	9032	5256	4600	9528	5424	4432	9360	800
900	5544	5544	11088	6336	4752	10296	6471	4617	10161	5913	5175	10719	6102	4986	10530	900
1000	6160	6160	12320	7040	5980	11440	7190	5130	11290	6570	5750	11910	6780	5540	11700	1000
2000	12320	12320	24640	14080	10560	22880	14380	10260	22580	13140	11500	23820	13560	11080	23400	2000

*The quantities in this column also apply to common brick with headers in every sixth course.

For other than 1/2" joints, the following percentages must be added to or subtracted from above results:

Add: for 1/8" joint, 21%; for 1/4" joint, 14%; for 3/8" joint, 7%.

Subtract: for 5/8" joint, 5%; for 3/4" joint, 10%; for 7/8" joint, 15%; for 1" joint, 20%.

Table 3-7. Brick Selection Chart.

Material	Types	Grades[2]	Where to use	Advantages	Disadvantages	Remarks
Brick....	Common	SW, MW, NW	Back up, bearing piers and walls receiving paint or other finish.	Strong, durable, non-combustible, low-maintenance under normal conditions. Pleasing appearance in wide range of natural colors.	Fairly high cost. May stain or effloresce. Darkens in industrial atmosphere.	Brick may be glazed to provide varied colors and impervious, low-maintenance surface. Face brick may be used only where the additional cost can be justified.
	Face.....	SW, MW, NW	Exposed wall surfaces where superior appearance is important.			
	Fire......	NW..........	Fireplaces, chimney cores, refractories.			

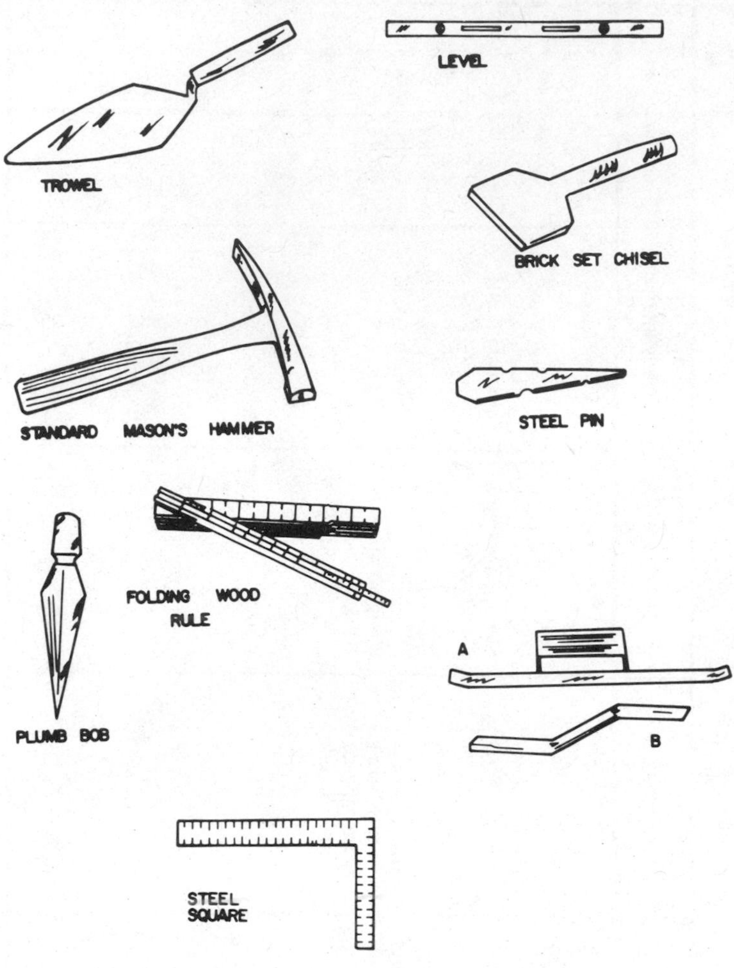

Fig. 3-24. Tools for fireplace construction.

same temperature falling within this range. The mortar temperature after mixing and before use should be above 40°F., maintained by portable heaters under the mortar board or by frequent mixing of mortar batches. Heated mortar boards should not become excessively hot (greater than 120°).

- During below normal temperatures, masonry units should be placed only on frozen free foundations.

Table 3-8. Cold Weather Masonry Construction and Protection Recommendations.

Work Day Temperature	Construction Requirement	Protection Requirement
Above 40 F	Normal masonry procedures.	Cover walls with plastic or canvas at end of work day to prevent water entering masonry.
40 F - 32 F	Heat mixing water to produce mortar temperatures between 40 F - 120 F.	Cover walls and materials to prevent wetting and freezing. Covers should be plastic or canvas.
32 F - 25 F	Heat mixing water and sand to produce mortar temperatures between 40 F - 120 F.	With wind velocities over 15 mph provide windbreaks during the work day and cover walls and materials at the end of the work day to prevent wetting and freezing. Maintain masonry above freezing for 16 hours using auxiliary heat or insulated blankets.
25 F - 20 F	Mortar on boards should be maintained above 40 F.	
20 F - 0 F and below	Heat mixing water and sand to produce mortar temperatures between 40 F - 120 F.	Provide enclosures and supply sufficient heat to maintain masonry enclosure above 32 F for 24 hours.

Masonry should never be placed on a snow or ice covered surface because of the danger of movement when the base thaws and the possibility of very little bond being developed between the mortar and the supporting surface.

- At the end of the day, the top surface of all masonry should be protected to prevent moisture such as rain, snow or sleet from entering the masonry wall. This protection must cover the top surface and should extend a minimum of 24″ down all sides of the wall (Table 3-8).

FIREPLACE BUILDING

There are several items which constitute good fireplace trouble free construction: size and shape of firebox, flue lining size and smoke shelf. See Tables 3-9 through 3-11 and Figs. 3-25 and 3-26.

Allow the chimney footing to cure for a few days before any masonry is started. Use caution and care in setting the masonry walls making all lines level, true and plumb. Install each section of flue lining in place ahead of the walls, using them as a guide for building the walls. Be sure the joints of the flue linings are tight, bedded in mortar. Flush the inside mortar joint of the flue lining to

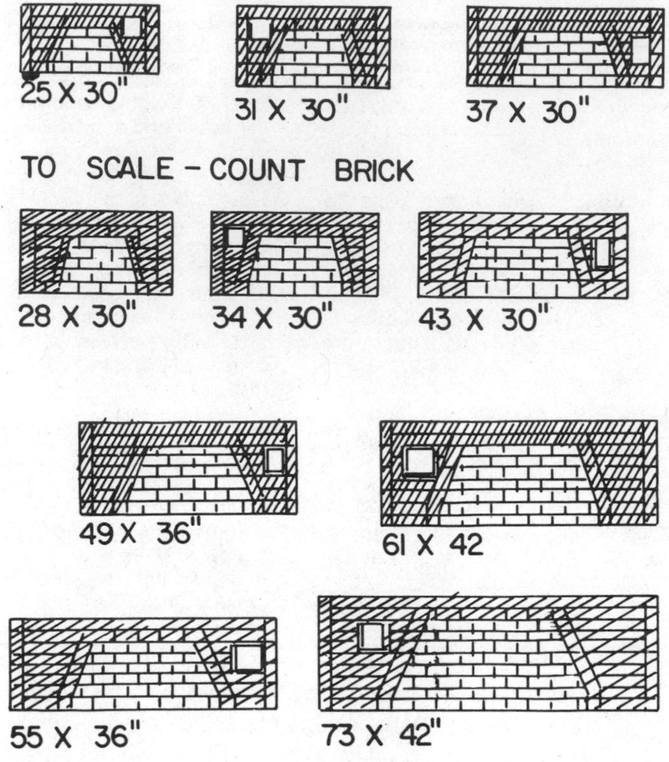

Fig. 3-25. Hearth plans and brick layout.

afford a smooth surface. Where pipes or bends are necessary, they should be formed by cutting and mitering the flue linings to secure a tight joint. The angle and the offset should be limited to about 60°. The center line of the offset should not fall beyond the center line of the wall below. This system of bending or offset is called *corbeling* (extend inward or outward). Corbeling should not exceed 1" projection in each course of brick or block.

Openings in the floor, ceiling or roof should be prepared before the chimney and fireplace are built. Flashing is used around the chimney to seal the space between the brick and the roof to prevent leaks. This flashing should be of corrosion resistant metal such as aluminum, copper or lead. The flashing is built into the joints of the brick and is extended down the roof, lapped under and over the roof covering.

Ashpit

The hollow space below the hearth into which ashes fall and are stored is called the *ashpit*. The ashes must be removed periodically through the ashpit door. The ashes fall through a pivoted metal door located in the hearth. (Fig. 3-27).

Cleanout Door

Accumulation of soot on the inside wall of the flue lining can be the cause of a chimney fire. To minimize this possibility, a space for this soot to accumulate must be provided along with a cleanout cast iron door for removal of soot. Provide a floor at the base of the chimney with concrete or masonry and install a cast iron cleanout door to fit snugly and kept tightly closed. Each flue should have a separate cleanout and not interconnected. (Fig. 3-28).

These units are ready for installation in a variety of sizes; 12" wide and 8" high should be adequate for residential chimneys. Be sure to have a tight joint around the frame so as not to interfere with proper chimney draft. Cast iron is recommended for cleanout doors, and the frame is held in place by inserting a wire or nails through the holes in the flange of the door frame, held in place by the mortar joint. Every flue lining should have a cleanout door.

It is necessary to provide an opening into the ashpit as a means to remove the accumulation of ashes. The door should be made of metal and closed tightly. Doors made of long lasting cast iron have much more resistance than steel doors to the acidic condition found in ashes and to the elements.

Ash Dump

A pivoted door made of metal located flush with the firebox floor is the *ash dump*. This allows the ashes to be dropped into the

Table 3-9. Typical Fireplace Proportions for Various Damper Sizes.

Damper Size	25 x 30	28 x 30	31 x 30	34 x 30
Foundation Size Approx.	51 x 25	54 x 30	56 x 30	60 x 30
Width of Opening	25"	26-28"	29-31"	32-34"
Height of Opening	24-30"	24-30"	24-30"	24-30"
Depth of Opening	16-18"	18-24"	18-24"	18-24"
Flue Tile Size	8-1/2 x 8-1/2	8-1/2 x 13	8-1/2 x 13	8-1/2 x 13

Damper Size	37 x 30	43 x 30	49 x 36	55 x 36	61 x 42	73 x 42
Foundation Size Approx.	72 x 30	76 x 30	81 x 34	98 x 34	102 x 38	124 x 42
Width of Opening	35-37"	38-43"	44-49"	50-55"	56-61"	67-73"
Height of Opening	24-30"	24-30"	30-36"	30-26"	36-42"	36-42"
Depth of Opening	18-24"	18-24"	22-28"	22-28"	28-36"	28-36"
Flue Tile Size	13 x 13	13 x 13	13 x 18	13 x 18	18 x 18	18 x 18

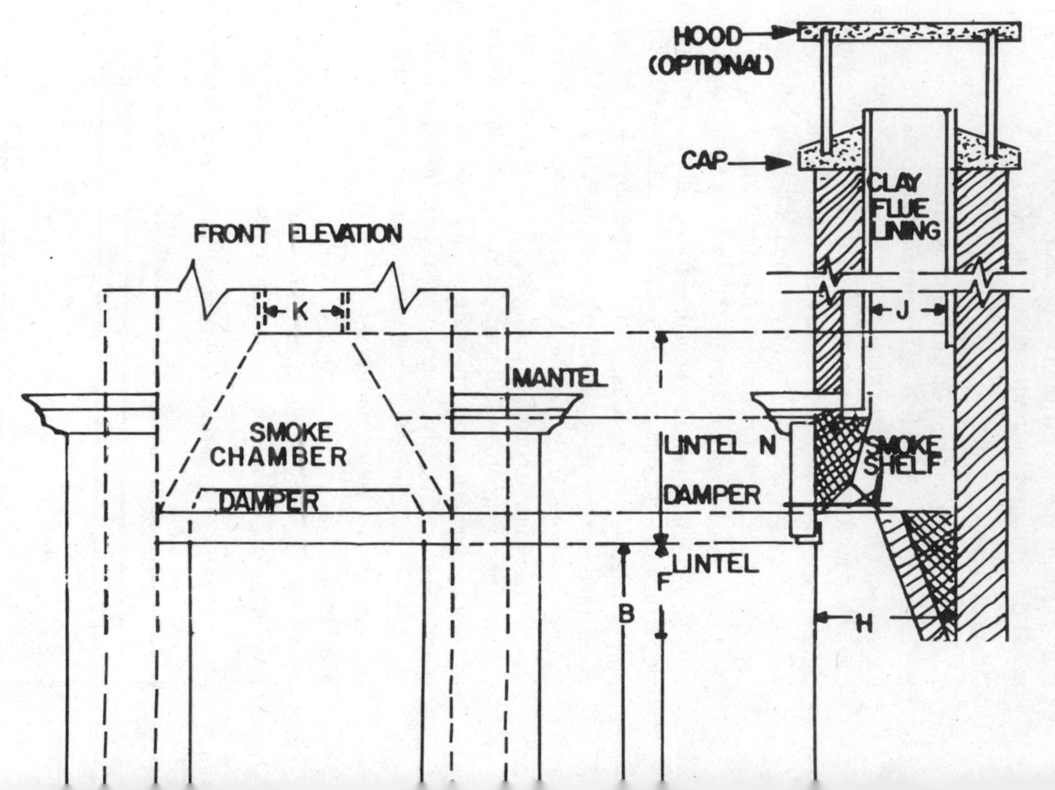
FRONT ELEVATION
K
SMOKE CHAMBER
DAMPER
MANTEL
HOOD (OPTIONAL)
CAP
CLAY FLUE LINING
J
LINTEL N
SMOKE SHELF
DAMPER
LINTEL F
B
H

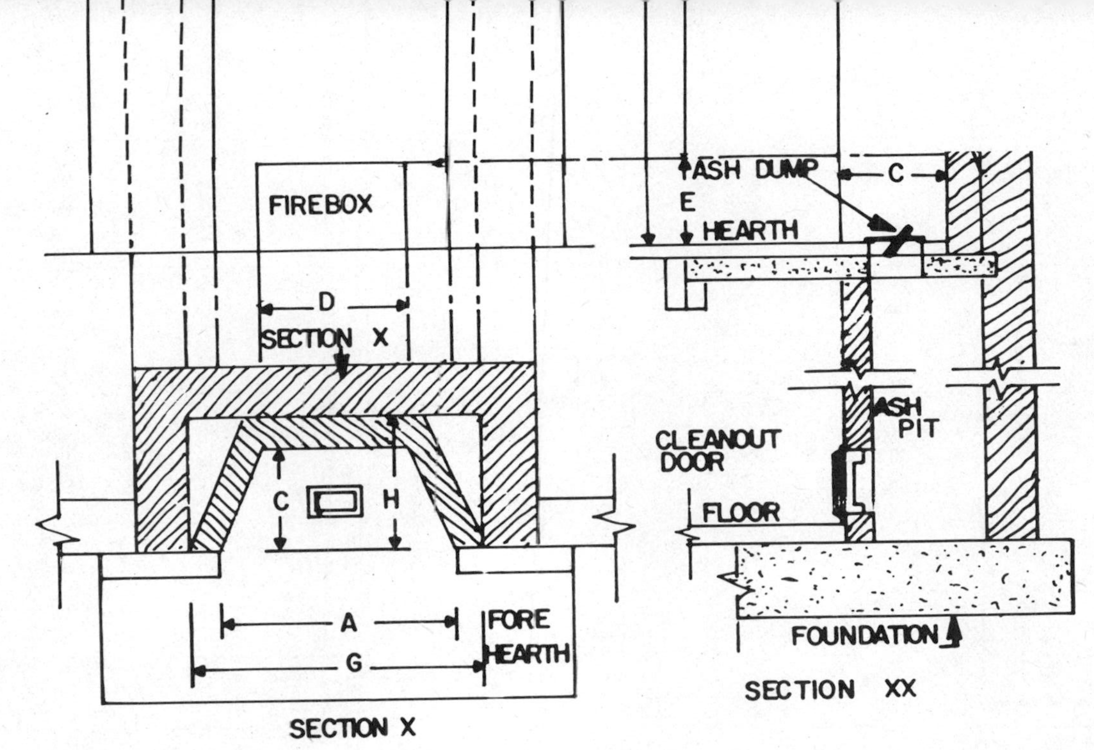

Fig. 3-26. Details and general principles of fireplace construction.

Table 3-10. Area of Fireplace Openings.

Width 22″ 1′ 10″	Width 24″ 2′ 0″	Width 26″ 2′ 2″	Width 28″ 2′ 4″	Height	Width 30″ 2′ 6″	Width 32″ 2′ 8″	Width 34″ 2′ 10″	Width 36″ 3′ 0″
Square Feet					Square Feet			
3.67	4.00	4.33	4.67	24″ = 2′ 0″	5.00	5.33	5.67	6.00
3.82	4.17	4.51	4.86	25″ = 2′ 1″	5.21	5.56	5.90	6.25
3.97	4.33	4.69	5.06	26″ = 2′ 2″	5.42	5.78	6.14	6.50
4.12	4.50	4.87	5.25	27″ = 2′ 3″	5.62	6.00	6.37	6.75
4.28	4.67	5.05	5.44	28″ = 2′ 4″	5.83	6.22	6.61	7.00
4.43	4.83	5.24	5.64	29″ = 2′ 5″	6.04	6.44	6.85	7.25
4.58	5.00	5.42	5.83	30″ = 2′ 6″	6.25	6.67	7.08	7.50
4.74	5.17	5.60	6.03	31″ = 2′ 7″	6.46	6.89	7.32	7.75
4.89	5.33	5.78	6.22	32″ = 2′ 8″	6.67	7.11	7.55	8.00
5.04	5.50	5.96	6.42	33″ = 2′ 9″	6.87	7.33	7.79	8.25
5.19	5.67	6.14	6.61	34″ = 2′ 10″	7.08	7.55	8.03	8.50
5.35	5.83	6.32	6.80	35″ = 2′ 11″	7.29	7.78	8.26	8.75
5.50	6.00	6.50	7.00	36″ = 3′ 0″	7.50	8.00	8.50	9.00
5.65	6.17	6.68	7.19	37″ = 3′ 1″	7.71	8.22	8.73	9.25
5.80	6.33	6.86	7.39	38″ = 3′ 2″	7.91	8.44	8.97	9.50
5.96	6.50	7.04	7.58	39″ = 3′ 3″	8.12	8.66	9.21	9.75
6.11	6.67	7.22	7.78	40″ = 3′ 4″	8.33	8.89	9.44	10.00
6.26	6.83	7.40	7.97	41″ = 3′ 5″	8.54	9.11	9.68	10.25
6.42	7.00	7.58	8.16	42″ = 3′ 6″	8.75	9.33	9.91	10.50
6.57	7.17	7.76	8.36	43″ = 3′ 7″	8.96	9.55	10.15	10.75
6.72	7.33	7.94	8.55	44″ = 3′ 8″	9.16	9.77	10.39	11.00
6.87	7.50	8.12	8.75	45″ = 3′ 9″	9.37	10.00	10.62	11.25

7.03	7.67	8.30	8.94	46″ = 3′ 10″	9.58	10.22	10.86	11.50
7.18	7.83	8.40	9.14	47″ = 3′ 11″	9.79	10.44	11.09	11.75
7.33	8.00	8.66	9.33	48″ = 4′ 0″	10.00	10.66	11.33	12.00
7.48	8.17	8.84	9.52	49″ = 4′ 1″	10.21	10.88	11.57	12.25
7.64	8.33	9.02	9.72	50″ = 4′ 2″	10.41	11.11	11.80	12.50
7.79	8.50	9.20	9.91	51″ = 4′ 3″	10.62	11.33	12.04	12.75
7.94	8.66	9.38	10.11	52″ = 4′ 4″	10.83	11.55	12.27	13.00
8.00	8.83	9.56	10.30	53″ = 4′ 5″	11.04	11.77	12.51	13.25
8.25	9.00	9.75	10.50	54″ = 4′ 6″	11.25	11.99	12.75	13.50
8.40	9.16	9.93	10.69	55″ = 4′ 7″	11.45	12.22	12.98	13.75
8.55	9.33	10.11	10.88	56″ = 4′ 8″	11.66	12.44	13.22	14.00
8.71	9.50	10.29	11.06	57″ = 4′ 9″	11.87	12.66	13.45	14.25
8.86	9.66	10.47	11.27	58″ = 4′ 10″	12.08	12.88	13.69	14.50
9.01	9.83	10.65	11.47	59″ = 4′ 11″	12.29	13.10	13.93	14.75
9.16	10.00	10.83	11.66	60″ = 5′ 0″	12.50	13.33	14.16	15.00
9.32	10.16	11.01	11.86	61″ = 5′ 1″	12.70	13.55	14.40	15.25
9.47	10.33	11.19	12.05	62″ = 5′ 2″	12.91	13.77	14.63	15.50
9.62	10.50	11.37	12.24	63″ = 5′ 3″	13.12	13.99	14.87	15.75
9.77	10.66	11.55	12.44	64″ = 5′ 4″	13.33	14.21	15.11	16.00
9.93	10.83	11.73	12.63	65″ = 5′ 5″	13.54	14.44	15.34	16.25
10.08	11.00	11.91	12.83	66″ = 5′ 6″	13.74	14.66	15.58	16.50
3	11.16	12.09	13.02	67″ = 5′ 7″	13.95	14.88	15.81	16.75
10.39	11.33	12.27	13.22	68″ = 5′ 8″	14.16	15.10	16.05	17.00
10.54	11.50	12.45	13.41	69″ = 5′ 9″	14.37	15.32	16.29	17.25
10.69	11.66	12.63	13.60	70″ = 5′ 10″	14.58	15.55	16.52	17.50
10.84	11.83	12.81	13.80	71″ = 5′ 11″	14.79	15.77	16.76	17.75
11.00	12.00	13.00	14.00	72″ = 6′ 0″	15.00	16.00	17.00	18.00

To find the number of square feet contained in an opening 24″ x 30″ read in the 24″ column opposite the 30″ figure in the center column. This equals 5.00.

Table 3-11. Standard Size Fireplace Dimensions in Inches (Courtesy of Vestal Manufacturing).

Finished Fireplace Opening						Rough Dimensions			Flue Lining Size: Old Rectangular	Flue Lining Size: New Modular
A	B	C	D	E	F	G	H	I	J x K	J x K
24	24	16	11	14	15	32	20	19	8-1/2 x 13	8 x 12
30	29	16	17	14	20	38	20	24	8-1/2 x 13	12 x 12
33	29	16	20	14	20	41	20	24	13 x 13	12 x 16
36	29	16	23	14	21	44	20	27	13 x 13	12 x 16
42	32	16	29	14	23	50	20	32	13 x 13	16 x 16
48	32	18	34	14	23	56	22	37	13 x 18	16 x 16
54	36	20	37	16	26	62	24	44	13 x 18	16 x 20
60	38	22	42	16	28	68	26	45	18 x 18	16 x 20
72	40	22	54	16	29	80	26	54	20 x 20	20 x 24

ashpit below. The ash dump is exposed to the heat from the fire. It is known in fact that cast iron has much more resistance to heat than steel. For permanence, the ash dump should be made of cast iron (Fig. 3-29).

Ash Cady

In some homes, design features do not permit the construction of an ashpit. This is especially true of homes designed on slab, without a basement. If design does not permit an ashpit, the ash cady can easily be installed in the fireplace hearth during construction. The *ash cady* is a real convenience for removal of ashes. Simply sweep or shovel ashes through the top grating of cast iron, into the galvanized removal pail below. To remove the ashes, the grating is lifted aside and the pail is lifted out by the bail. (Fig. 3-30).

Hearth

The part of the fireplace on which the fire is laid is called the hearth. The forehearth is the area outside the fireplace opening. It is important that the hearth be wholly supported by the chimney. This prevents cracking in case unequal settlement occurs. The forehearth should be supported by the chimney but in many designs this is not practical. The usual practice is to pour a rough concrete slab reinforced with ½″ reinforcing steel rods. The soundest construction provides a continuous slab to serve as a base for both

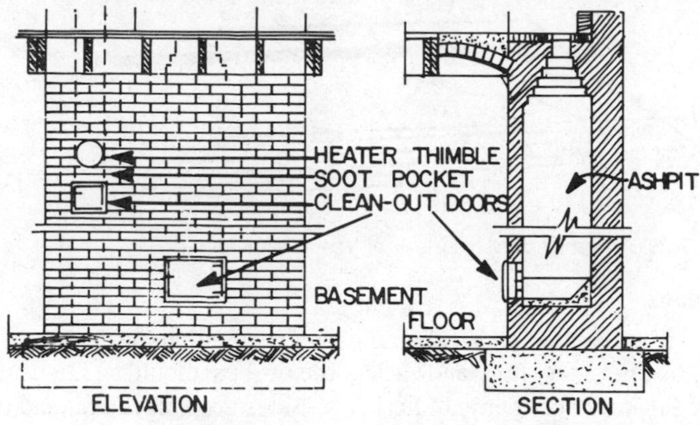

Fig. 3-27. An ashpit for a fireplace should be of tight masonry and should be provided with a tight fitting iron cleanout door and frame 10″ high and 12″ wide.

hearth and forehearth. The ash dump or the pit door is installed in the rough hearth slab at the time of pouring the concrete. The finished hearth surface of brick, tile or any other fireproof finish building material is then applied over the rough base slab. The fireplace hearth can also be formed by arching the brick or using wood forms, filling the arch or forms with reinforced concrete to the established level, bearing in mind the thickness of the finish material and the concrete base (Figs. 3-31 and 3-32).

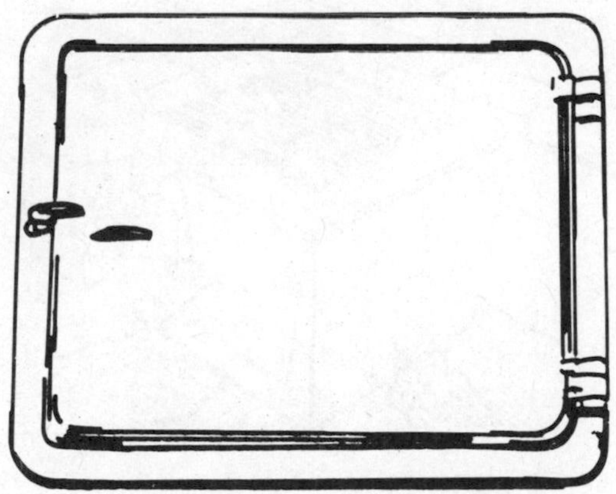

Fig. 3-28. A cleanout door (courtesy of Vestal Manufacturing).

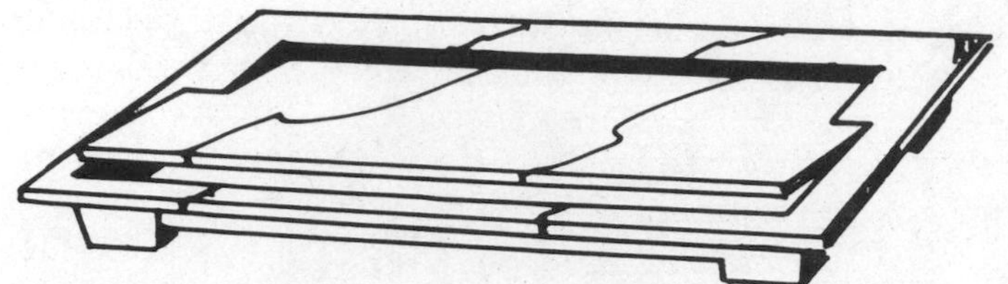

Fig. 3-29. An ashpit door (courtesy of Vestal Manufacturing).

Firebox

The chamber which contains the fire is called the *firebox* (Fig. 3-33). The sides, floor and back of the firebox should be lined with one thickness or course of firebrick. Sides are splayed in, and the back wall sloped to reflect a maximum of heat into the room. The splayed sides make the back of the fireplace narrower than the front opening, and gives the fireplace a reflector shape. This splay should be approximately 3″ to 4″ to the foot in depth. Curving the back of the firebox should be avoided. The best plan is to build the back wall plumb for three to five courses of firebrick and then start the back wall forward on an angle that will bring the fire brick back wall up under the entire rear flange of the throat damper.

Fireplace Opening

Correct proportioning of the fireplace opening has a great deal to do with how well the fireplace will function (Fig. 3-34). The size

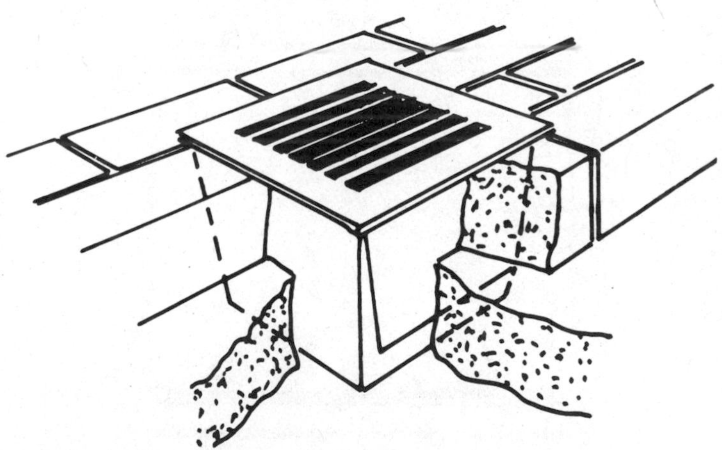

Fig. 3-30. An ash cady (courtesy of Vestal Manufacturing).

of the opening also determines the correct size of the flue lining to use. The total area of the fireplace opening is found by multiplying the finished open width by the finished open height. The result will be square inches. The generally accepted rule for a conventional fireplace (one side only open) is that the cross sectional area of the flue lining be one-twelfth or greater than the area of the fireplace opening. For modern design fireplaces, (two or more open sides), the cross sectional area of each open side must be calculated and all open sides added together. The cross section area of the flue should be one-tenth or greater than the total area of all open sides for this type fireplace.

There are no arbitrary rules controlling the depth of the fireplace or the height of the opening. These two do have a relationship and should be correctly proportioned. In general, the wider the opening, the greater the depth and height. If the fireplace is designed primarily to burn hardwood logs, some find it desirable to increase the front to back depth by 3″ to 6″.

The combustion chamber or firebox should be lined with 4″ firebrick set in fireclay mortar. It is shaped to reflect heat into the room and lead smoke and gases into the throat with velocity and out through the chimney. If the fireplace is deeper than necessary, heat will be lost through the chimney and less will be radiated into the room.

The damper is used to prevent heat loss when the fireplace is not in use. It is the same length as the width of the firebox face

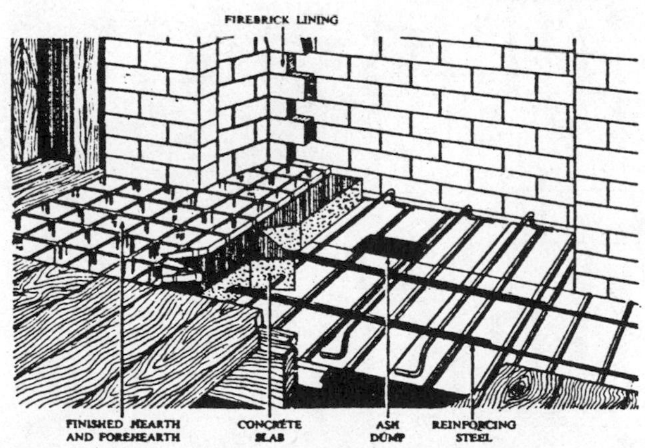

Fig. 3-31. Details of hearth construction (courtesy of Vestal Manufacturing).

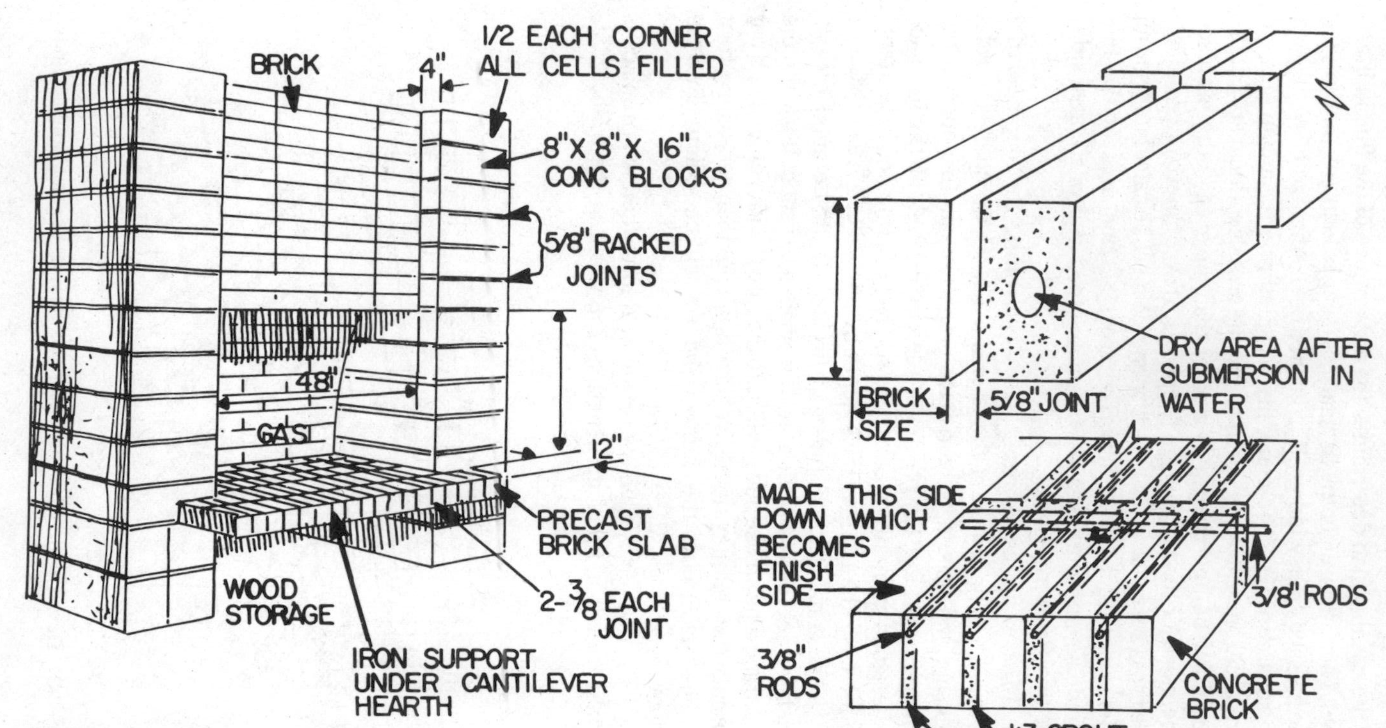
BRICK
4"
1/2 EACH CORNER
ALL CELLS FILLED
8" X 8" X 16"
CONC BLOCKS
5/8" RACKED
JOINTS
48"
GAS
12"
PRECAST
BRICK SLAB
2-3/8 EACH
JOINT
WOOD
STORAGE
IRON SUPPORT
UNDER CANTILEVER
HEARTH
BRICK
SIZE
5/8" JOINT
DRY AREA AFTER
SUBMERSION IN
WATER
MADE THIS SIDE
DOWN WHICH
BECOMES
FINISH
SIDE
3/8" RODS
3/8"
RODS
CONCRETE
BRICK
1:3 GROUT

Fig. 3-32. A cantilevered hearth.

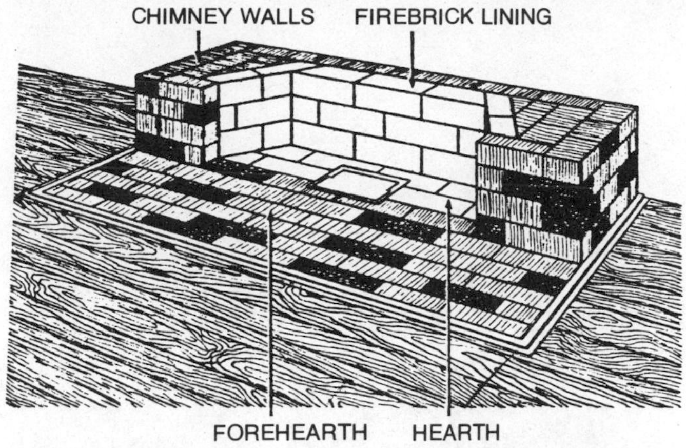

Fig. 3-33. Example of a firebox (courtesy of Vestal Manufacturing).

placed about 6″ to 8″ above the top of the opening. Dampers are made of steel and cast iron, rotary or poker type operation. The damper location establishes the height of the smoke shelf, which is directly under the flue lining.

The hearth is supported with a 4″ thick concrete floor reinforced with ½″ steel rods placed about midpoint in the slab thickness and spaced about 8″ apart in the short dimension. If an ash

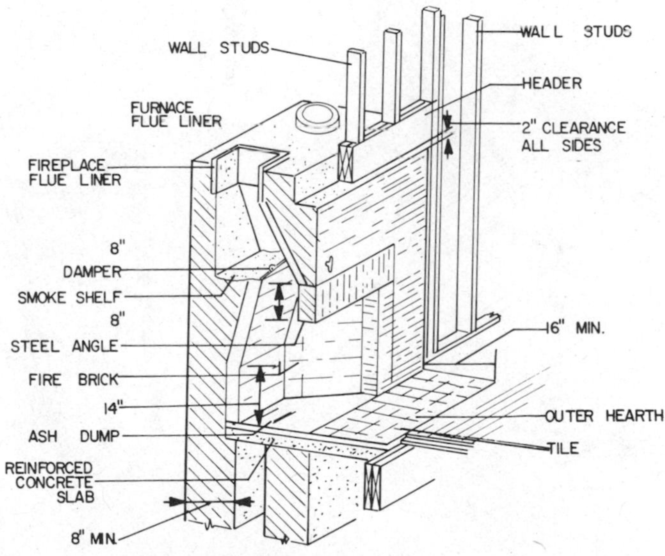

Fig. 3-34. Typical firebox detail.

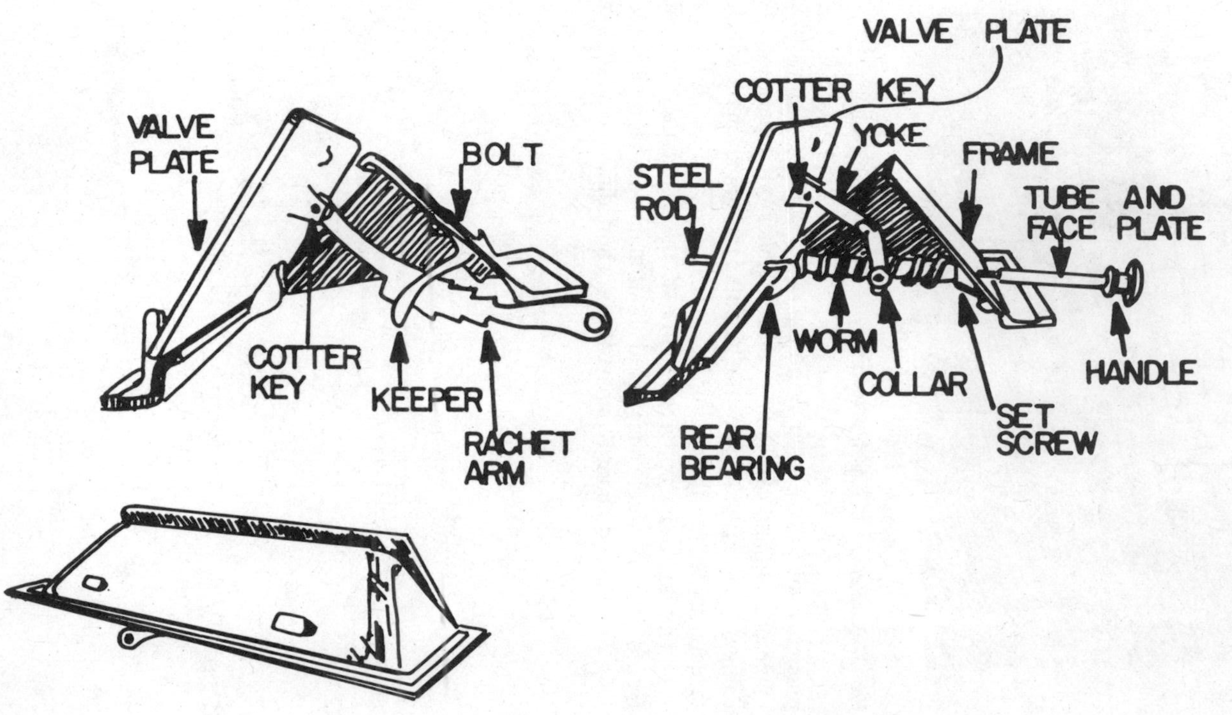
VALVE PLATE
BOLT
COTTER KEY
KEEPER
RACHET ARM
VALVE PLATE
COTTER KEY
YOKE
FRAME
STEEL ROD
TUBE AND FACE PLATE
WORM
COLLAR
HANDLE
SET SCREW
REAR BEARING

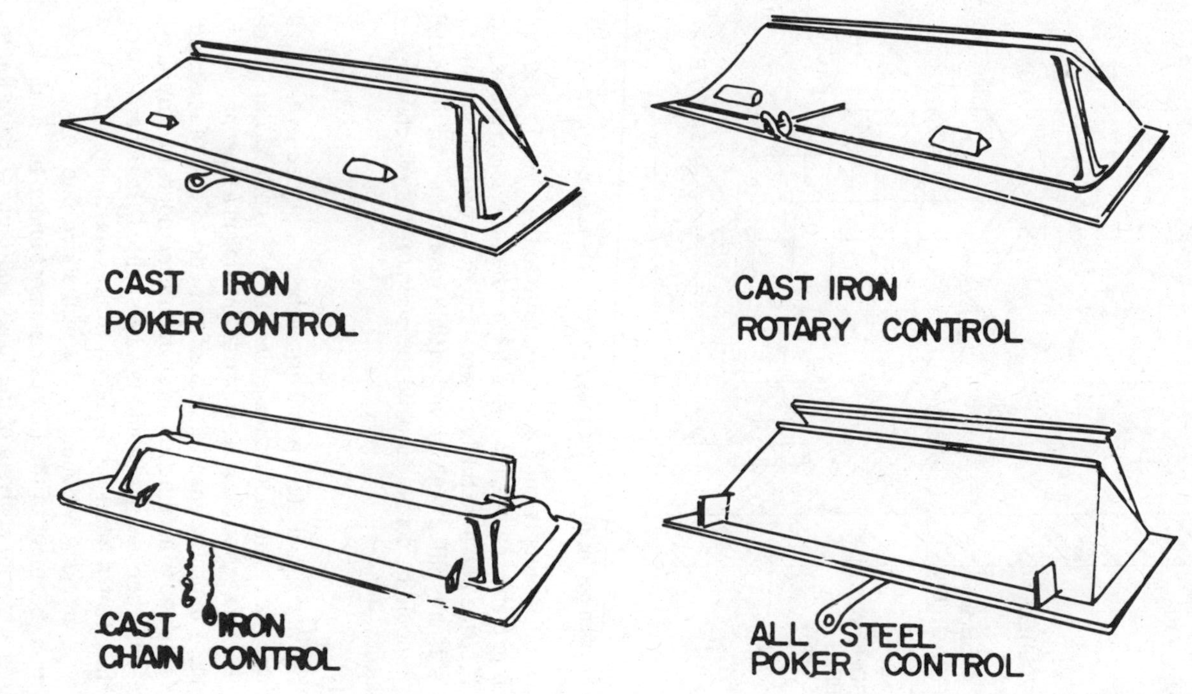

Fig. 3-35. Fireplace throat dampers.

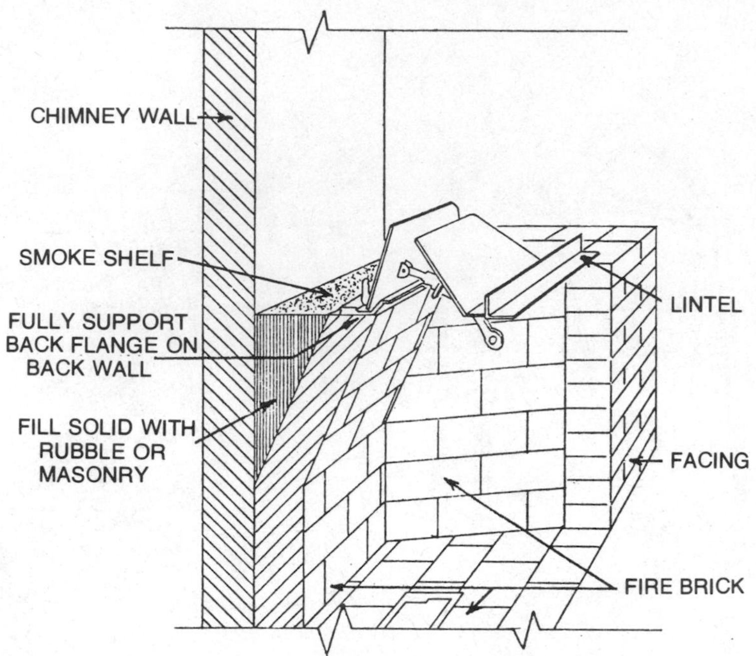

Fig. 3-36. Damper installation (courtesy of Vestal Manufacturing).

dump is used, simply build a wooden form to the size of the ashpit door frame and remove the wood form when the concrete is set. The 2" space between the brickwork and the wood framing members is usually filled with incombustible insulation. All joists and rafters should be doubled around the perimeter of the chimney or fireplace.

Lintels

The horizontal steel members or beams placed over a wall opening to carry the superimposed load above is called a *lintel*. The type of lintel section chosen to span an opening in a masonry wall is dependent upon the span (distance from end to end of opening). Lintels are important functions of structural members in a fireplace. Therefore, their design should not be slighted. It is particularly important that a lintel be designed to prevent the possibility of structural cracks developing in the wall above due to excessive deflection (bending) of the lintel or support under the load. This requires a careful analysis of the loads and their distribution together with the application of the proper formulas in determining the stresses developed.

Damper

The rate of burning, the amount of air or draft control, and the efficiency of the fire is controlled by the *damper*. Turning the damper down or in a closed position will result in a slow burning fire. Because of low temperatures, the fire is unburned and a great amount of heat is lost. With the damper wide open, the fire burns hotter, but the heat generated is lost up the chimney. It seems either way that there is a loss. At best, a compromise in a happy medium position between open and closed seems to be the best position. This will require some experimenting for the best damper position (Figs. 3-35, 3-36 and 3-37).

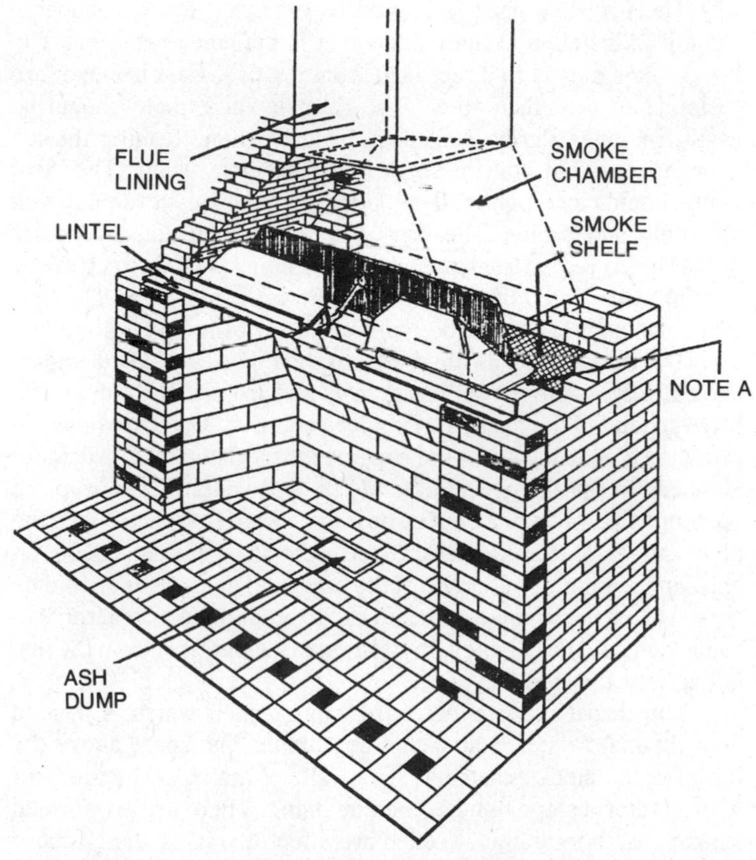

Fig. 3-37. Do not fill the ends of the damper in solidly with masonry. Leave room for expansion from the heat (courtesy of Vestal Manufacturing).

Throat or Smoke Shelf

The *throat* is the part of the fireplace just above the fireplace opening and serves to connect the firebox with the smoke chamber. Proper shaping of the throat is the most critical part of the fireplace. A properly designed fireplace damper relieves the mason the responsibility of designing the important throat. The throat should be long and narrow to make the fire burn evenly across the back wall. The throat should have a large area of cross section and a long shape, and should have smooth side walls with as little friction as possbile for smoke drawing up the chimney. The damper also allows the draft to be shut off during non-use periods, conserving other sources of heat or air conditioning. It also permits regulation of draft when the fireplace is in use.

The fireplace damper should be designed for permanence. Once it is installed in the chimney, it is difficult to replace. The damper is exposed to direct heat from the fire. Cast iron is more resistant to heat than steel. The damper valve plate should be easily removed during construction, and when cleaning the accumulation of soot from the smoke shelf after long usage. The valve plate should close tightly. The operating mechanism should work smoothly and easily. The back flange of the fireplace damper should be protected from intense heat by being placed directly over and fully supported by the back wall firebrick masonry. The fireplace damper should not be built solidly at each end.

The throat controls the draft and should be carefully designed and built. It should not be less than 4″ and preferably 8″ above the highest point of the top of the fireplace opening. The back slopes to the same height and forms the support for the damper. The damper is placed in the throat and extends the full width of the fireplace opening. The valve plate opens upward toward the back. When the plate is open, it forms a barrier to stop the down draft and deflect it back up the chimney along with the smoke. The damper should be closed when the fireplace is not in use to prevent heat loss from the room going up the chimney, in addition to keeping dirt from the flue falling into the firebox.

The throat is installed in the smoke shelf which is located directly under the bottom of the flue lining. The space above the throat is the smoke chamber. The walls of the chamber are built with a uniform slope to meet the flue lining. There are pre-formed smoke chambers of metal which are effective giving the chamber its proper shape and smooth surfaces to help to simplify brick laying (Figs. 3-38 and 3-39).

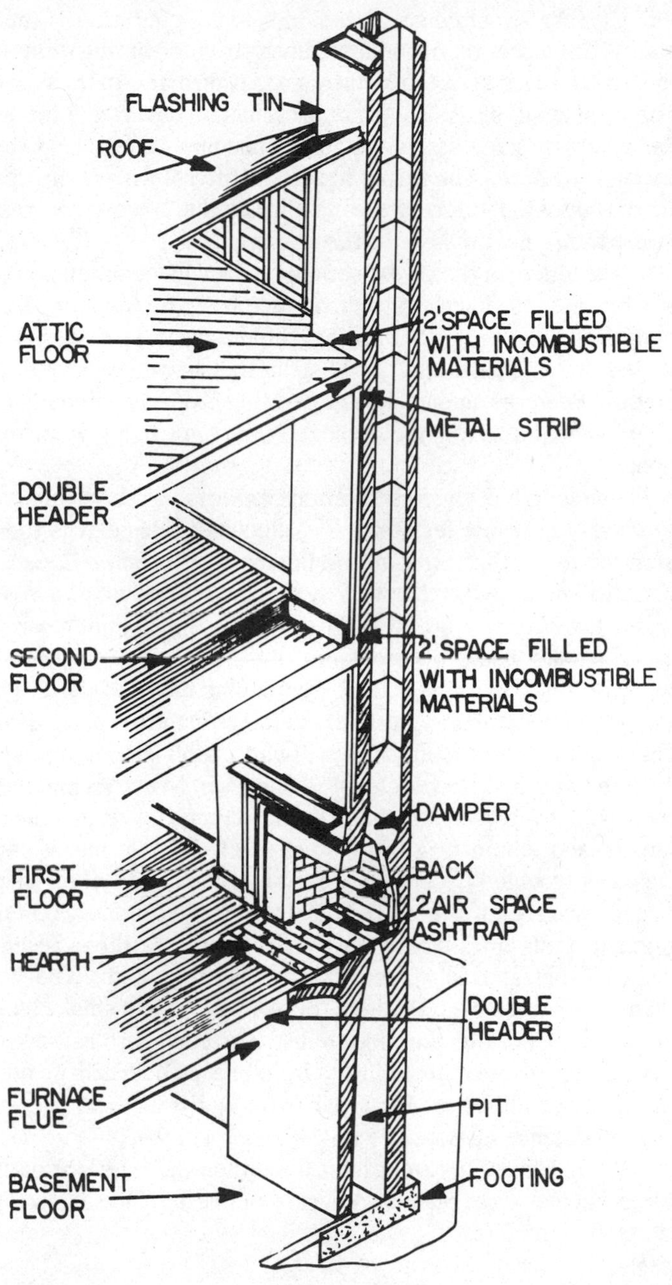

Fig. 3-38. A properly built built fireplace and chimney.

Correct throat construction adds to the operation of the fireplace. The direction of the air coming from down the chimney is reversed when it strikes the throat and is directed up the chimney. The rapid upward passage of hot air creates a downward current on the opposite side, but not strong enough to interfere with the upward pressure. The throat increases the velocity of the upward air movement. If there were no throat, the downward pressure would force the smoke into the room.

The length of the throat should be the widest dimension of the firebox opening. Part of the throat is formed by the damper. The front flange allows it to sit against the masonry. The rear flange is sloped to conform to the combustion chamber or rear wall of the firebox. Be sure the damper is operating properly when installed. There should be a slight clearance at the ends to allow for expansion.

The length of the smoke shelf is as wide as the firebox. The depth should be not less than 4″. The smoke chamber is the area from the top of the throat to the beginning of the flue lining. This space will hold smoke temporarily if a gust of wind blows across the top of the chimney blocking the draft. If the chamber were not there, smoke would fill the room.

The smoke shelf is made by extending the back wall firebrick lining forward until it meets the rear flange of the fireplace damper. The depth for the smoke shelf will vary, depending on the size of the flue lining and the depth of the fireplace. Many fireplaces have been built by placing the flue lining directly over the fireplace damper and eliminating the smoke shelf. This is one of several causes of troubled fireplace operations. The smoke shelf helps to turn the wind coming down the flue back up the chimney. It helps to eliminate puffs of wind entering the fireplace and to keep accumulations of soot and ash from coming into the room. The smoke chamber extends from the level of the damper and smoke shelf up to the bottom of the clay flue lining. The enclosure narrows as it extends up to the flue lining. The slope of both sides must be identical and all walls should be trowelled smooth to present as little resistance as possible to the rising smoke.

If you want to prevent heat loss when the fireplace is not in use, a damper is a necessity. A screen or glass front will add to your safety and comfort.

Mantel

The *mantel* is a decorative part of the fireplace with no function except aesthetics. It should be compatible with the style or design of the house. All wood parts of the mantel should be at least 8″ away from the firebox at the sides, and at least 12″ away from the firebox at the top. A mantel can be purchased pre-assembled, requiring simple installation. Very often no mantel is used, but instead the finish brick is the finished face of the fireplace.

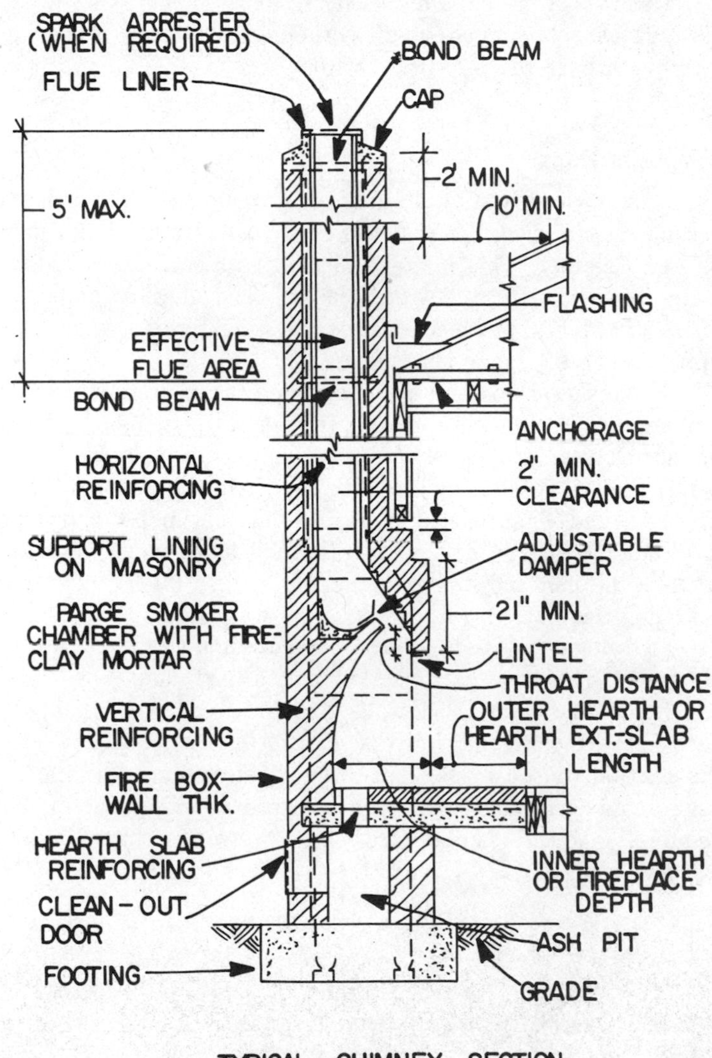

Fig. 3-39. Detail of a masonry chimney.

CORBELING

Whenever a chimney is to change direction, size or shape, the process is called *corbeling*. Several rules must be followed if corbeling is used:

- Do not corbel from the wall more than 6″.
- Do not corbel a wall less than 12″ thick.
- Do not project a brick course more than 1″.
- Do not begin or end the corbeling to within 6″ of passing through the roof (Fig. 3-40).

Composite Walls

When two separate walls are built forming one wall, such as a backup and face wall, this is called a composite wall and they must be tied together. This is accomplished with wall ties. Another method is to bond the wall with a header. When using a combination of brick and block, one block course will equal three brick courses in height, each totaling about 8″ high.

Expansion and contraction of masonry caused by moisture and temperature change will cause movement of the members, creating shrinkage. This appears as a hairline crack or cracks in the joints. For this reason, care must be used in laying masonry, being sure a full bed of mortar surrounds the entire perimeter of the unit. If the unit has to be readjusted after the mortar has begun to harden, remove the unit and mortar and apply a fresh mix of mortar in resetting the unit.

In trying two walls together, metal ties must be used to form a solid wall. This is accomplished by a variety of metal ties, any of which will do the job. Brick walls sometimes fail from wind pressure and earthquake shock. Brick and mortar are not able to resist the tension caused by bending from these actions. Placing the reinforcing horizontally will help to counteract this problem. The reinforcing should also be used where there is a change in wall thickness and at "L", "T" and "U"-shaped chimneys (Fig. 3-41).

Brick Arches

When brick arches are to be built, the arch curvature is formed with wooden forms which must be strong enough to temporarily support the arch. Once the mortar has set, the wood form may be removed (Fig. 3-42).

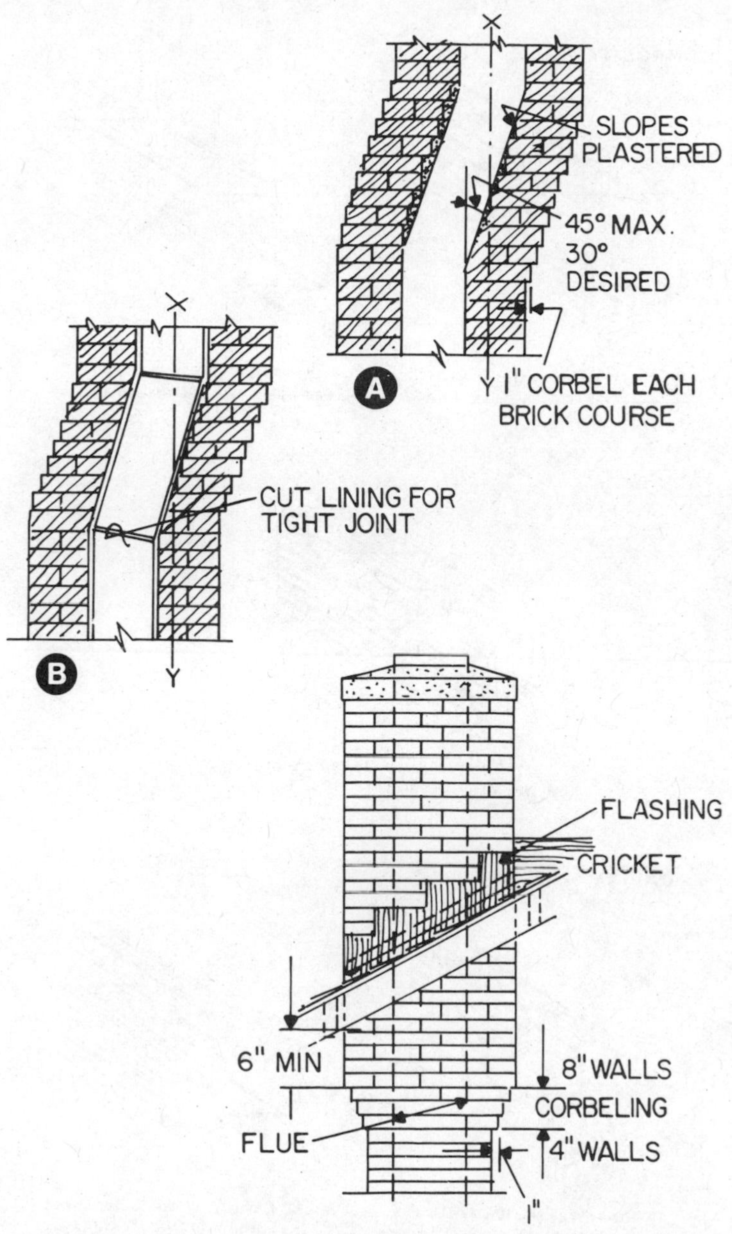

Fig. 3-40. (A). Start the offset of the left wall of an unlined flue two brick courses higher than the right wall so that the area of the sloping section will not be reduced after plastering. (B). Method of cutting lining to make a tight joint. (C). Corbeling of chimney to provide 8″ walls for the section exposed to the weather.

COMPOSITE WALLS

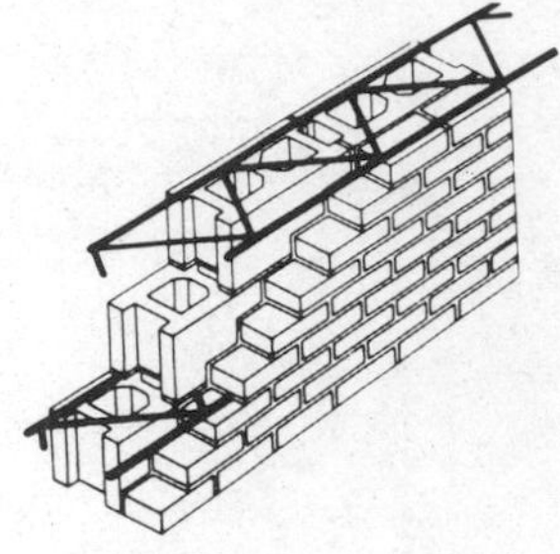

12″ Tied Wall No. 12 Dur-O-waL 16″ c. to c.

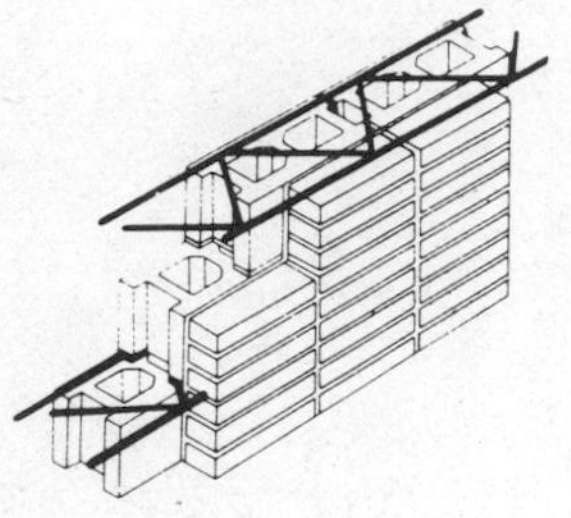

12″ Tied Wall with Stack Bond Facing No. 12 Dur-O-waL 16″ c. to c.

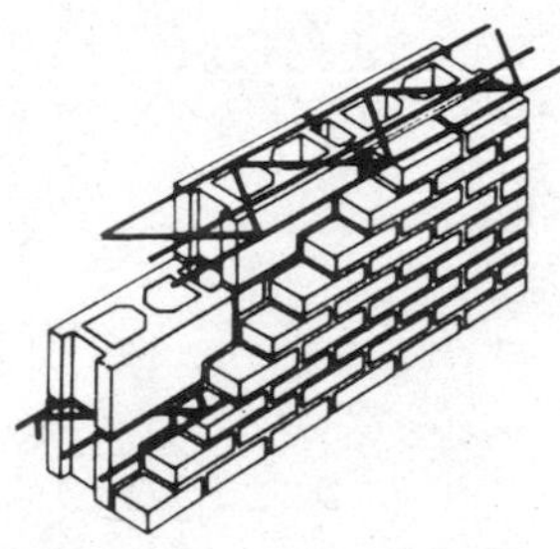

12″ Tied Wall Stack Bond Backup No. 12 Dur-O-waL Trirod 16″ c. to c.

CAVITY WALLS

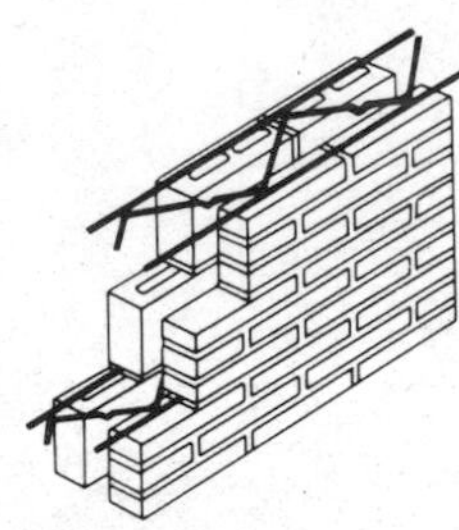

10″ Cavity Wall No. 10 Dur-O-waL With Drip 16″ c. to c.

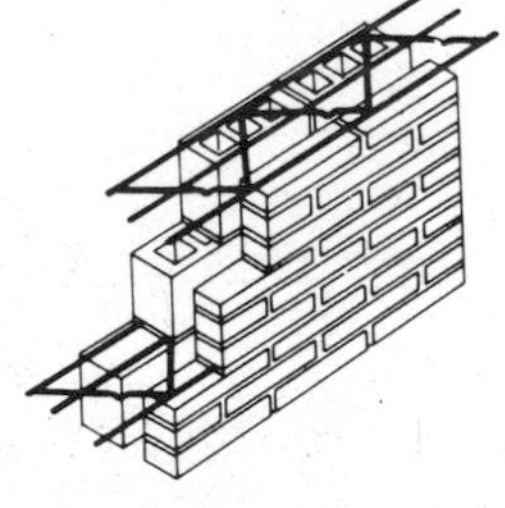

12″ Cavity Wall No. 12 Dur-O-waL Trirod with Drip 16″ c. to c.

Fig. 3-41. Composite walls, cavity walls and single wythe walls (courtesy of Dur-O-Wal).

SINGLE WYTHE WALLS

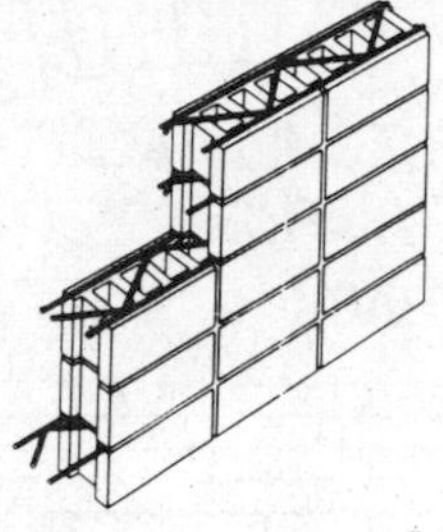

Stack Bond Load Bearing Walls. Dur-O-waL—8″ c. to c. Top 3 Courses. 16″ c. to c. Remainder of Wall. Non Load Bearing Walls. Dur-O-waL—16″ c. to c.

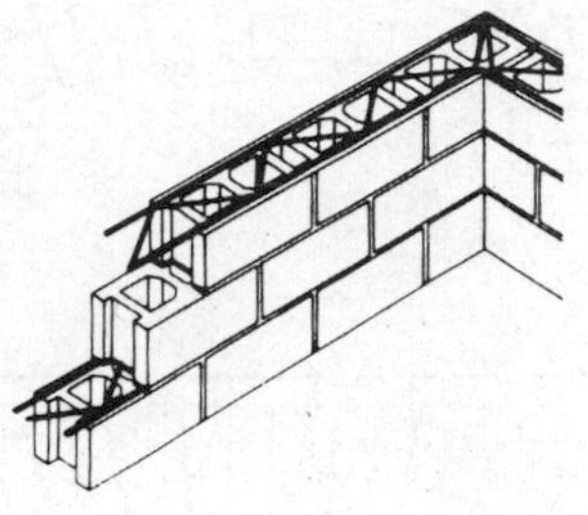

8″ Wall showing Corner No. 8 Dur-O-waL 16″ c. to c.

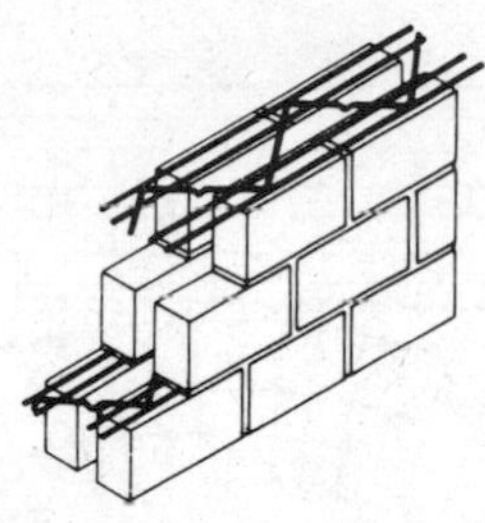

10″ Cavity Wall No. 10 Dur-O-waL Double With Drip 16″ c. to c.

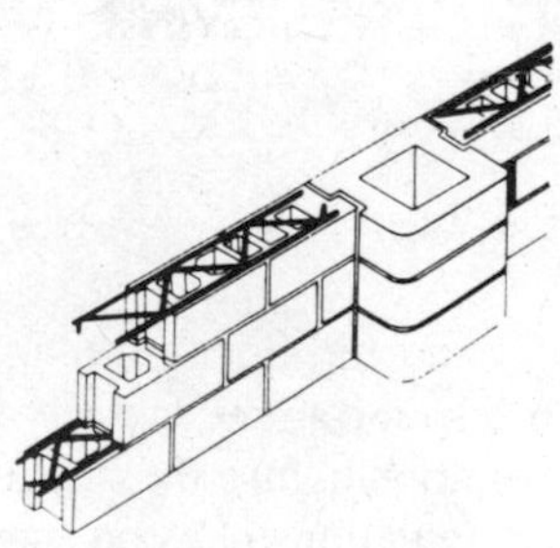

8″ Wall with Pilaster No. 8 Dur-O-waL 16″ c. to c.

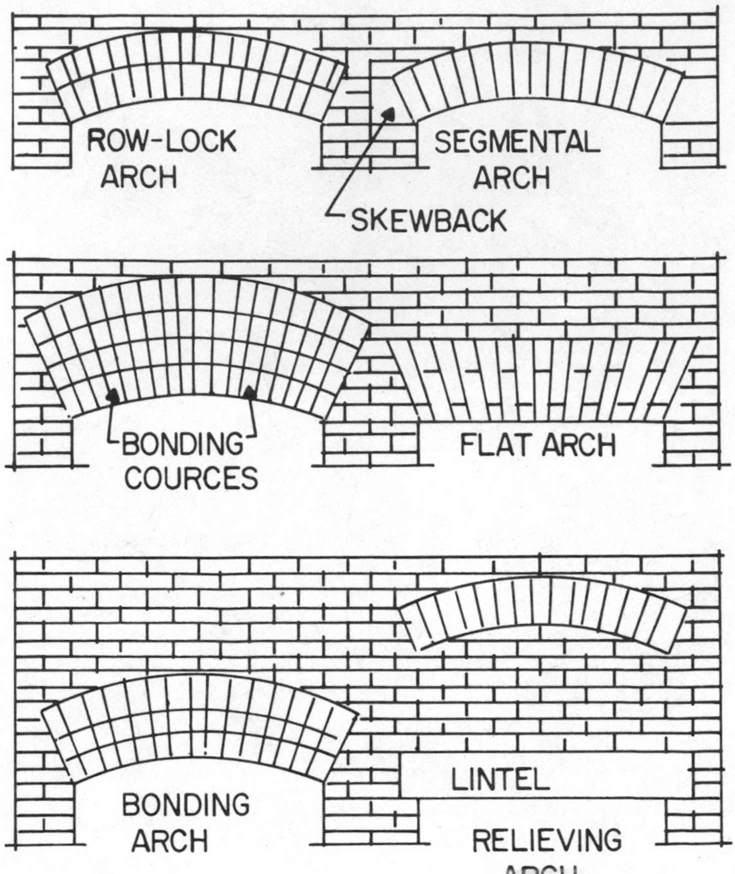

Fig. 3-42. Brick arches.

Insulation

Fill the space between the wall and the floor framing with incombustible material. Do not use brick mortar or concrete. Fiber glass insulation is best. Place the insulation before the finish floor is laid which will help prevent the accumulations of wood shavings (Fig. 3-43 and 3-44).

Chimney Height

When the height of the chimney walls does not exceed 35′, the walls should be at least 8″ thick. The greater the difference in temperature between inside and outside of the chimney, the better the draft. The chimney top should be 2′ above the ridge or a wall

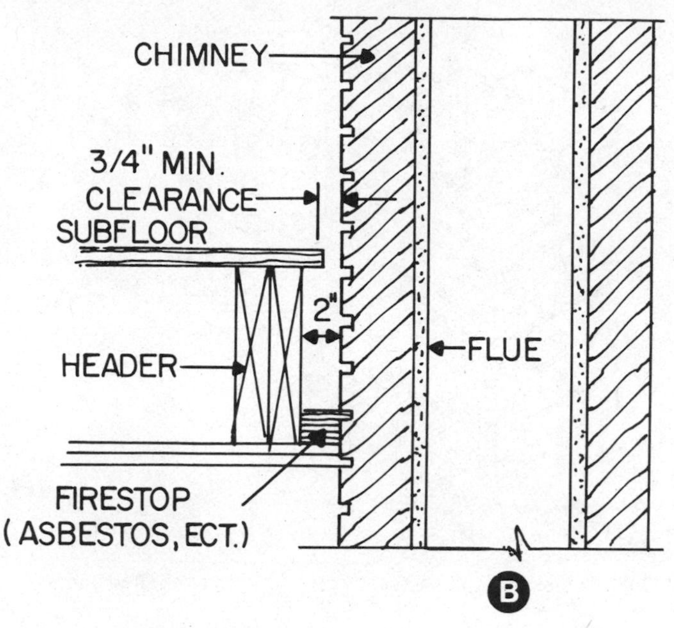

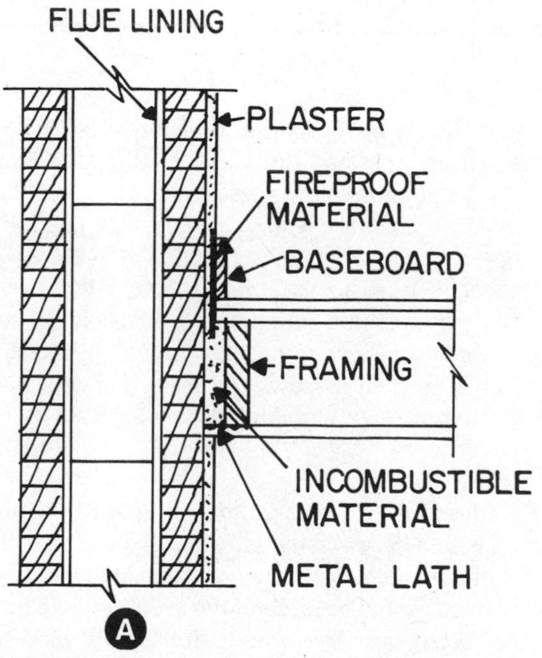

Fig. 3-43. (A). Clearances for wood construction. (B) Method of insulating wood floor joists and baseboard at a chimney.

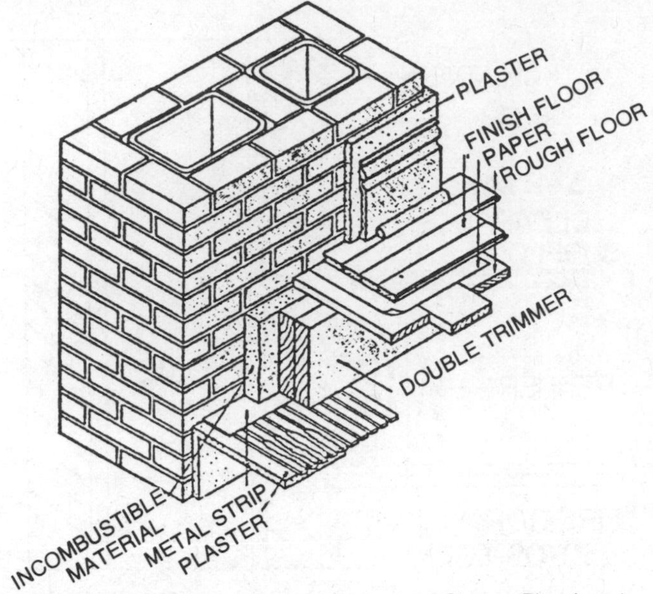

Fig. 3-44. Fire-stopping at chimney (courtesy of Simons Broadman).

that is within 10′. Flat or low pitched roofs should extend at least 2′ above the highest point of the roof (Figs. 3-45 and 3-46).

Flashing

Chimneys must be flashed and counterflashed to seal the space between the roof and the chimney (Fig. 3-47). When the chimney is located on the roof slope, a cricket or saddle is built. Metals used for flashing are lead, copper or aluminum (Fig. 3-48). Flashing made of aluminum is subject to attack by the caustic alkalis present in fresh unhardened mortar. Although dry, seasoned mortar will not affect aluminum. Corrosion can occur if the adjacent mortar becomes wet; therefore, aluminum will be unsatisfactory as a flashing unless there is a coating of ashphalt, zinc chromate primer or other suitable means (Tables 3-12 and 3-13).

Chimney Saddle

The purpose of a chimney *saddle* or *cricket* is to shed water away from the area between the chimney and the roof. The frame work of 2 × 4s, can be built on the ground, nailed into position and put in position on roof. The pitch of the saddle should be the same pitch as the roof. Cover the frame with ½″ plywood sheathing, building paper and roofing to match existing roof. Flash the valleys of the saddle (Fig. 3-49).

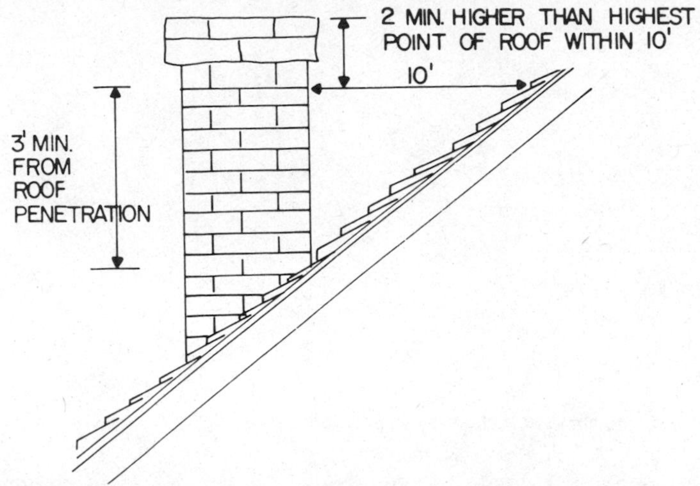

Fig. 3-45. Chimney height detail.

On sloping roofs, a chimney saddle should be installed at the upper side of the chimney, 30″ or more in width. Carefully seal the saddle with flashing at the intersection of roof and saddle (Fig. 3-50).

Chimney Cap

There are several methods of finishing the top of the chimney. The flue lining should extend at least 4″ above the cap or top course

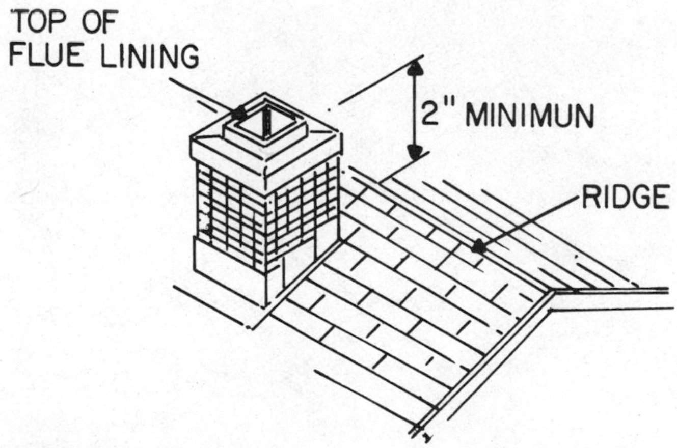

Fig. 3-46. Minimum chimney height.

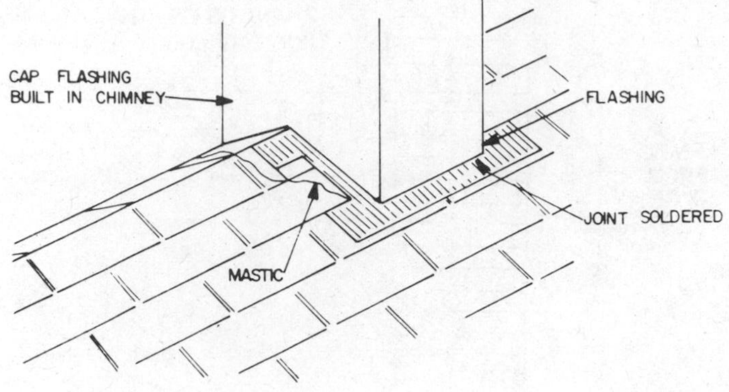

Fig. 3-47. Flashing at a chimney located on a roof ridge.

of masonry and should be surrounded by at least 2" of cement mortar (Fig. 3-51). The mortar is finished with a slope to direct air currents upward and to drain water away from the flue. Hoods are used to keep rain and snow out of chimneys and to prevent down drafts. If the hood covers more than one flue, it should be divided by wythes or brick courses, so that each flue has a separate section. Spark arresters will reduce the possibility of flying embers starting fires on roofs or in wooded areas. They should be built of rust-resistant material and should have mesh or screen openings not

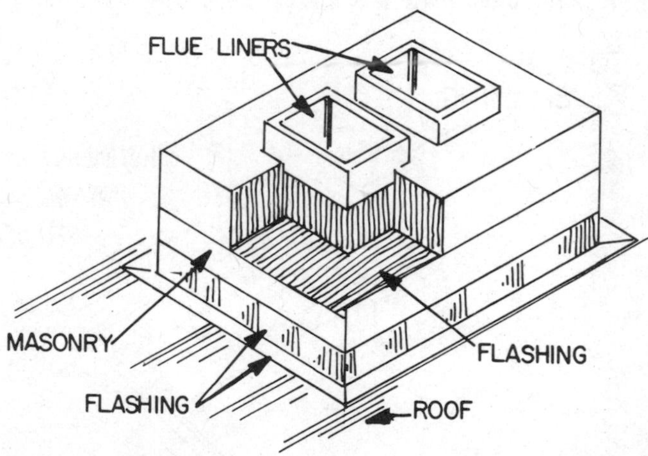

Fig. 3-48. Chimenys must be flashed to seal the opening between the roof and the chimney.

Table 3-12. Sheet Metal Uses for Flashing

	Materials								
	Aluminum		Copper	Galv. Iron or Steel		Sheet Lead	Stainless Steel	Terne Plate	Zinc-Copper Alloy
	Minimum			Minimum Gage					
	Thickness	Tensile Strength	Minimum Thickness	1.25 oz.	1.50 oz.	Minimum Weight	Minimum Thickness	Min. Gage	Minimum Thickness
Use	in.	psi	in.	ga.	ga.	psf	in.	ga.	in.
Areaways	—	—	—	16	18	—	—	—	—
Flashing									
exposed	.019	16,000	.020	26	28	2.5	.015	30	.020
concealed	.015	14,000	.012	28	30	1.5	.010	30	.012
head	.024	16,000	.020	28	28	—	.015	30	.020

Table 3-13. Sheet Metal Materials Shown in Column A Should Be Isolated from Materials Shown in Column B.

Column A	Column B	Minimum Protection
Copper	Other metallic materials except lead	Coating of asphalt or other suitable means
Galvanized Iron or Steel	Other metallic materials except zinc	Same as above
Stainless steel	Other metallic materials	Same as above
Terne Plate	Other metallic materials	Same as above
Zinc Copper Alloy	Copper or high-copper alloys	Same as above
Aluminum (1)	Other metallic materials except zinc	Coating of asphalt, zinc chromate primer or other suitable means

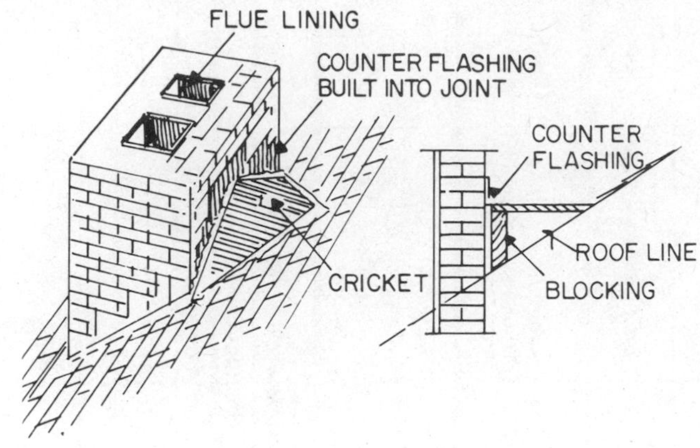

Fig. 3-49. Construction of a cricket behind a chimney.

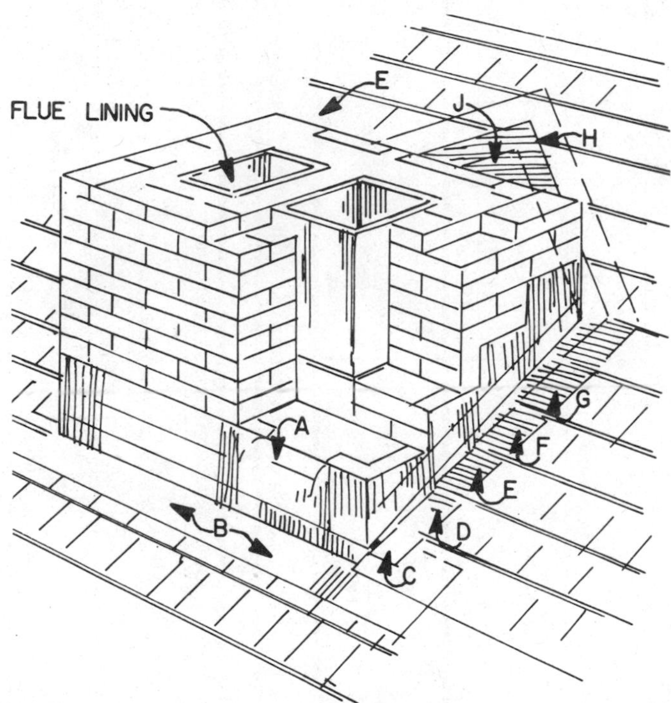

Fig. 3-50. Flashing at a chimney located on the slope of a roof. Sheet metal (h) over cricket (j) extends at least 4″ under the shingles (k) and is counterflashed at (L) in the joint. Base flashings (b, c, d and e) and cap flashings (a, f and g) lap over the base flashings to provide watertight construction. A full bed of mortar should be provided where cap flashing is inserted in joints.

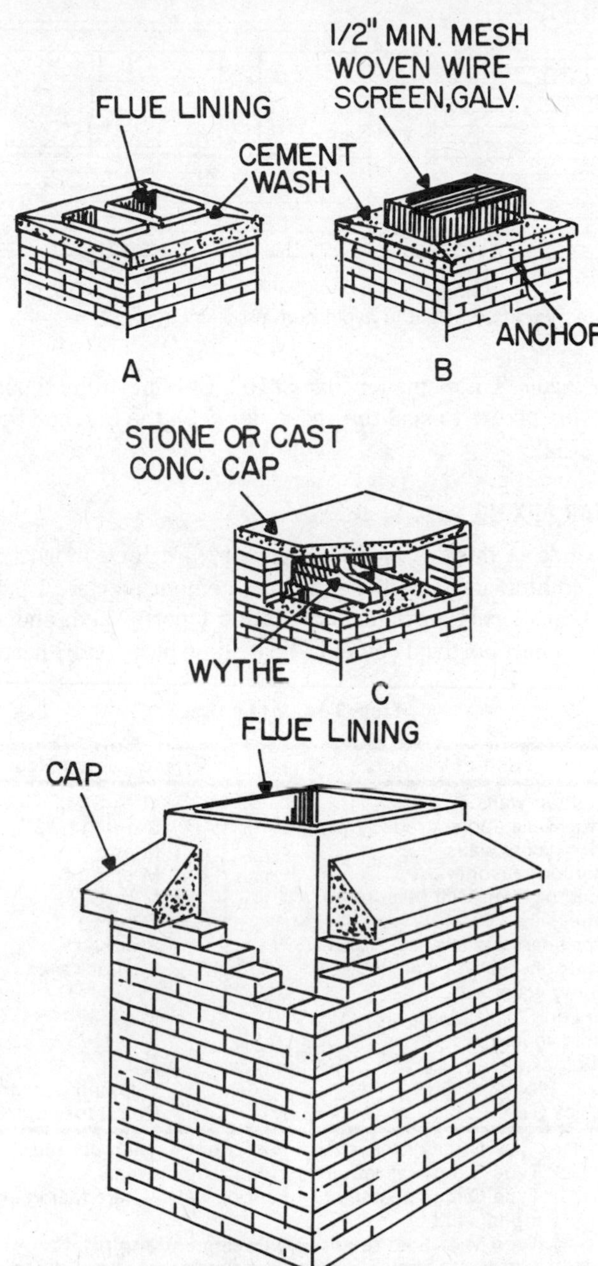

Fig. 3-51. (A). Method of finishing top of chimney; flue lining extends 4″ above cap. (B). Spark arrester of bird screen. (C). A hood to keep out rain.

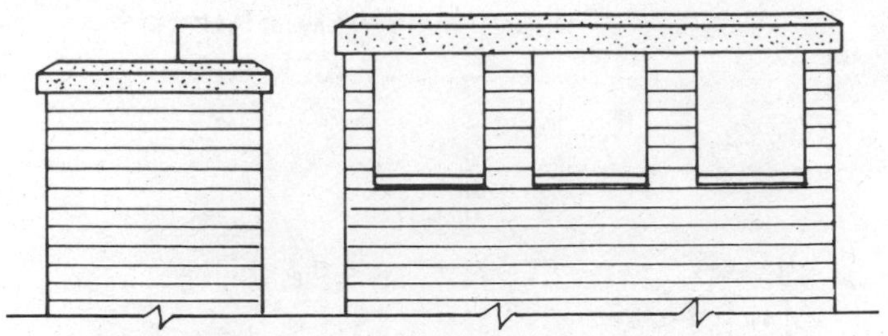

Fig. 3-52. Vary flue height to avoid draft problems.

larger than ⅝″, nor smaller than 5/16″. Chimney tops should have a cap of concrete to seal the space between the flue and the brick (Fig. 3-52).

MORTAR MIXING

Kinds of mortar used for masonry are lime mortar, 1 part hydrated lime and 3 parts sand; lime cement mortar, 1 part hydrated lime, 1 part portland cement and 6 parts sand; and cement mortar, 1 part portland cement ¼ part lime putty and 3 parts sand.

Table 3-14. Mortar Uses.

Kind of Masonry	Type of Mortar Required (6)
Foundation walls or piers	M or S (1)
Exterior walls above grade	S or N (2) (3)
Exterior cavity walls	M or S
Reinforced masonry	M or S (4)
Grouted or filled Cell Masonry	M or S (4)
Chimneys	S or N
Interior bearing walls	S or N
Interior non-bearing walls	S, N or O
Retaining walls	M
Sewers and manholes	M
Ceramic veneer	S or N (5)
Glass block	N
Gypsum block	Gypsum mortar
Fire brick	Refractory mortar

Notes: (1) Type N may be used with solid units when parged.
(2) Type S may be required in high wind areas.
(3) Type O may be used for exterior walls where facing and backing is solid units.
(4) Type M or S as required by design strength.
(5) Aggregate shall not exceed 4 times the portland cement content.
(6) Mortar shall comply with ASTM C-270 requirements for unreinforced masonry and ASTM C 476 for reinforced masonry.

Table 3-15. Grade Requirements for Clay or Shale Brick.

Use	Weathering Region		
	Negligible	Moderate	Severe
In vertical surfaces:			
In contact with earth	MW	SW	SW
Not in contact w/earth......	MW	MW	MW
In horizontal surfaces:			
In contact with earth	SW	SW	SW
Not in contact w/earth......	MW	SW	SW

Portland cement mortar is used only below grade. Lime putty added to cement mortar makes the mix more workable and increases its watertightness (Table 3-14 through 3-17). Do not use frozen materials in mixing mortar. Do not use cement which contains hard knots or lumps. Mortar for firebrick and flue linings should be fireclay mortar (Table 3-18 and 3-19).

It is very important that the sand and water be clean. Use a mortar box for mixing. Begin with the sand using a standard dirt shovel. Put half the amount of sand needed in the mortar mixing box. Spread the desired amount of portland cement and lime over the sand. Add the remaining sand over the cement and lime. Dry mix thoroughly the entire batch with a hoe or shovel, pulling the mix to one side of the mortar box, then the other. When thoroughly dry mixed, add a little water at a time to one end of the mortar box and draw the dry mix into the water slowly. Keep adding water until the entire mix is of a working consistency.

Do not mix any more than you use before the mix begins to set. A good test is to pick up a small amount of mortar and snap it onto a trowel with a quick downward fling of the wrist. Turn the trowel upside down. If the mortar remains on the blade of the trowel, it is still of a working consistency. Do not mix in freezing

Table 3-16. Grade Requirements for Sand-Lime brick.

Grade	Use
MW	Exterior walls in moderate and negligible weathering areas and where exposed to temperature below freezing but unlikely to be saturated with water. May be used in foundations or below finish grade in negligible weathering areas.
SW	Walls exposed to temperature below freezing in presence of moisture and for foundations or below finish grade in moderate and severe weathering areas. Required for exterior walls in severe weathering areas.

Table 3-17. Mortar Mix by Volume

Mortar Type	Portland Cement or Portland Blast Furnace Slag Cement	For Type, see Figure 3-26 Masonry Cement	Hydrated Lime or Lime Putty (2)	Aggregates (3)
M	1	1 (Type II)	—	Not less than 2-1/4 and not more than three times the sum of the volumes of the cement and lime used.
	1	—	1/4	
S	1/2	1 (Type II)	—	
	1	—	over 1/4 to 1/2	
N	—	1 (Type II)	—	
	1	—	over 1/2 to 1-1/4	
O	—	1 (Type I or II)	—	
	1	—	over 1-1/4 to 2-1/2	

Notes: (1) Proportions by volume.
(2) Quicklime, ASTM C-5 except that lime shall contain not more than 8 percent magnesium oxide (M_gO). Quicklime should be used in plant mixing operations only and shall be thoroughly slaked before mixing.
(3) Measured in a damp loose condition.

weather. In lieu of hand mixing, pre-mixed bagged mortar can be purchased requiring only water to be added.

Always wear safety glasses when using mortar. If mortar is accidently splashed into the eyes, do not rub them. Wash the eyes immediately with clean water and see a doctor as soon as possible.

Before applying mortar to the wall, dry set the brick or block for proper spacing to achieve equal joints throughout. Leave them in position and lay one unit at a time so as not to lose the spacing. All courses must be laid to a line which acts as a guide in laying the brick straight and level. Use the story pole described earlier to establish the courses. The line can be set secured at the very ends of the wall, working up each succeeding course. Wrap the line around a dry brick and set at both ends of the wall, aligning the line so that it is on the outer top edge of the brick and is level. Lay each brick according to the line as a guide. Be sure to lay mortar on the line, holding the brick to gain proper height. Be sure the line is taut at all times. Spread mortar on the wall with a trowel without disturbing the line. Lay the brick on the bed of mortar with proper face out. Press brick into position with the line. You will find mortar oozing out of the joint. Simply wipe it clean with the trowel edge and place the excess mortar on the wall. Brick must be not only in alignment with the line but also level. It may be necessary to tap the brick level using the handle of the trowel. Once the brick is in contact with the mortar, do not remove it without reapplying the mortar, or the seal will be broken. Don't use bricks that are chipped or broken. Be sure to check the wall for vertical plumbness as well as horizontal level, using the mason's level.

A full bed or mortar must be used on all brick. Apply mortar to the end of the succeeding brick before laying the next brick. The principle used in laying brick also apply to laying block and stone. In estimating the number of brick required to complete the job, figure about seven brick per square feet of wall surface.

The wall of the chimney should be a minimum of 8" thick, or two bricks wide. Build the walls up to the hearth, or floor, of the firebox. Allow space for the firebox fire brick, which should be built along with the wall. The hearth can be built later, but be sure to allow a shelf in the brick to support one end of the hearth. Allow for the ashpit door. Continue building the firebox and the walls using the correct slope and dimensions. When the wall of the firebox is reached, install the angle or lintel to support the wall above the opening. Continue the walls following the correct dimensions to the damper. Install the damper which will sit on the brick wall on the two ends of the back. The front wall is built over the damper wall following the slope of the damper. The rear wall terminates at the damper location to preface for the smoke shelf.

The rear inside wall of the chimney is in alignment with the flue lining above the smoke shelf. Continue the sloped wall established by the damper until it meets the required outside flue lining dimension, projecting on brick course around the perimeter of the chimney to support the first course of flue lining. From that point in, the walls surrounding the flue lining should be at least 8' thick. Where the chimney is not visible, common brick or concrete brick or block may be used instead of face brick or stone.

Carry the chimney to the required height working the flue lining or linings together with the walls providing for flashing in the joints of the masonry at the roof level. The hearth can now be built using temporary wood forms, supported on one end at the recess provided earlier in the brick wall, and the other end by the double header of the floor joists. Decide the level of the hearth and

Table 3-18. Mortar Proportioning.

The following mortar proportions are by volume and are for mixing with sufficient water for a minimum period of 3 min., to produce desired workability, in a drum-type batch mixer (hand mixing may be permitted with approval of purchaser outlining hand mixing procedure:

Mortar Type	Parts by Volume of Portland Cement	Parts by Volume of Masonry Cement	Parts by Volume of Hydrated Lime or Lime Putty	Aggregate, Measured in a Damp, Loose Condition
M.....	1	1 (type II)	—	Not less than 2-1/4 and not more than 3 times the sum of the volumes of the cements and lime used.
	1	—	1/4	
S.....	1/2	(type II)	—	
	1	—	over 1/4 to 1/2	
N.....	—	1 (type II)	—	
	1	—	over 1/2 to 1-1/4	
O.....	—	1 (type II)	—	
	1	—	over 1-1/4 to 2-1/2	
K.....	1	—	over 2-1/2 to 4	

NOTE: Quantities of materials for types A-1, B and C are shown in opposite column. Source: ASTM, C270-54T.

QUANTITIES OF MATERIALS FOR LIME-PUTTY MASONRY MORTARS

LUMP QUICKLIME
(70 Cu. Ft. Lime Putty per Ton of Lump Quicklime)

Proportions by Volume			Quantity of Materials Required: For one cubic yard of mortar			Quantity of Materials Required: To lay 1000 brick (17 cu. ft.)		
Cement	Lime Putty	Sand	Cement Bags	Lime Lbs.	Sand Cu. Yd.	Cement Bags	Lime Lbs.	Sand Cu. Yd.
0	1	3	0	257	1	0	162	.63
1	3	12	2-1/4	193	1	1.42	121-1/2	.63
1	2	9	3	171-1/2	1	1.89	108	.63
1	1-1/2	7-1/2	3.6	154	1	2.27	97	.63
1	1	6	4-1/2	128-1/2	1	2.83	81	.63
1	1/2	4-1/2	6	86	1	3.78	54	.63
1	0	3	9	0	1	5.67	0	.63
1	*10%	3	9	26	1	5.67	16	.63
1	*15%	3	9	39	1	5.67	24	.63

Table 3-18. Mortar Proportioning.

Pulverized Quicklime
(80 Cu. Ft. Lime Putty per Ton of Pulverized Quicklime)

Proportions by Volume			Quantity of Materials Required: For one cubic yard of mortar			To lay 1000 brick (17 cu. ft.)		
Cement	Lime Putty	Sand	Cement Bags	Lime Lbs.	Sand Cu. Yd.	Cement Bags	Lime Lbs.	Sand Cu. Yd.
0	1	3	0	225	1	0	142	.63
1	3	12	2-1/4	169	1	1.42	106	.63
1	2	9	3	150	1	1.89	94-1/2	.63
1	1-1/2	7-1/2	3.6	135	1	2.27	85	.63
1	1	6	4-1/2	112-1/2	1	2.83	71	.63
1	1/2	4-1/2	6	75	1	3.78	47	.63
1	0	3	9	0	1	5.67	0	.63
1	*10%	3	9	22-1/2	1	5.67	14	.63
1	*15%	3	9	34	1	5.67	21	.63

Hydrated Lime
(46 Cu. Ft. Lime Putty per Ton of Hydrated Lime)

Proportions by Volume			Quantity of Materials Required: For one cubic yard of mortar			To lay 1000 brick (17 cu. ft.)		
Cement	Lime Putty	Sand	Cement Bags	Lime Lbs.	Sand Cu. Yd.	Cement Bags	Lime Lbs.	Sand Cu. Yd.
0	1	3	0	391	1	0	246	.63
1	3	12	2-1/4	293-1/2	1	1.42	185	.63
1	2	9	3	261	1	1.89	164	.63
1	1-1/2	7-1/2	3.6	235	1	2.27	148	.63
1	1	6	4-1/2	195-1/2	1	2.83	123	.63
1	1/2	4-1/2	6	130-1/2	1	3.78	82	.63
1	0	3	9	0	1	5.67	0	.63
1	*10%	3	9	39	1	5.67	25	.63
1	*15%	3	9	59	1	5.67	37	.63

*Based on Volume of Cement Required.
No allowance for waste.

subtract the thickness of the finished hearth material to establish the level of the concrete slab. The slab should be 4″ minimum thickness with ½″ diameter steel rods for reinforcing. When the concrete slab is completely installed, finish the hearth. If no mantel is used, the fact of the fireplace should be of marble, stone or face brick. If the mantel is used, the portion of the wall covered by the mantel can be of common brick or less expensive units of masonry. The side face walls of the fireplace should be no less than 12″ wide. Thus, the surface of the wall that will receive the mantel (usually pre-assembled) will be ready for installtion.

Table 3-19. Quantities of Materials for Various Masonry Mortars.

The following mixes are classified according to the volume proportions of Portland cement, hydrated lime and sand. Cement is assumed as one bag equal to one cu. ft. and weighing 94 lb. Hydrated lime is assumed as one bag equal to one cu. ft. and weighing 40 lb. per cu. ft., and 50 lb. to the bag. Sand has been based on average conditions, in which a cubic foot of loose, damp sand, as normally used in construction contains approximately 80 lb. of dry sand.

Type M Mortar: 1-0.25-3 Mix

Cu. Ft. of Mortar	Weight			Volume		
	Cem.	Hyd. Lime	Sand	Cem.	Hyd. Lime	Sand
	lb.	lb.	lb.	Sack	Sack	Cu. Ft.
1	28	3	71	0.3	0.06	0.92
2	56	6	147	0.6	0.12	1.8
3	85	9	221	0.9	0.18	2.8
4	113	12	294	1.2	0.24	3.7
5	141	15	368	1.5	0.30	4.6
6	169	18	442	1.8	0.36	5.5
7	197	21	515	2.1	0.42	6.4
8	226	24	583	2.4	0.48	7.4
9	254	27	682	2.7	0.54	8.3
10	282	30	736	3.0	0.6	9.2
20	564	60	1472	6.0	1.2	18.4
27	761	81	1987	8.1	1.6	24.8
30	846	90	2208	9.0	1.8	27.6
40	1128	120	2944	12	2.4	36.8
50	1410	150	3680	15	3.0	46
60	1692	180	4416	16	3.6	55
70	1974	210	5152	21	4.2	64
80	2256	240	5888	24	4.8	74
90	2538	270	6624	27	5.4	83
100	2820	300	7360	30	6.0	92

Type S Mortar: 1-1-6 Mix

Cu. Ft. of Mortar	Weight			Volume		
	Cem.	Hyd. Lime	Sand	Cem.	Hyd. Lime	Sand
	lb.	lb.	lb.	Sack	Sack	Cu.Ft.
1	15.3	6.5	78.	0.16	0.13	1
2	31	13	157	0.3	0.3	2
3	46	20	235	0.5	0.4	3
4	61	26	314	0.7	0.5	3.9
5	76	33	392	0.8	0.7	4.9
6	92	39	470	1.0	0.8	5.9
7	107	46	549	1.1	0.9	6.9
8	122	52	627	1.3	1.0	7.9
9	138	59	706	1.5	1.2	8.8
10	153	65	784	1.63	1.3	9.8
20	306	130	1568	3.3	2.6	19.7
27	413	176	2117	4.4	3.5	26.5
30	459	195	2352	4.9	3.9	29.5

Table 3-19. Quantities of Materials for Various Masonry Mortars.

40	611	260	3136	6.5	5.2	39.3
50	764	325	3920	8.2	6.5	49.2
60	917	390	4704	9.8	7.8	59.0
70	1070	455	5488	11.4	9.1	68.8
80	1223	520	6272	13.0	10.4	78.6
90	1375	585	7056	14.7	11.7	88.5
100	1528	650	7840	16.3	13	98.3

Type O Mortar: 1-2-9 Mix

Cu. Ft. of Mortar	Weight			Volume		
	Cem.	Hyd. Lime	Sand	Cem.	Hyd. Lime	Sand
	ib.	lb.	lb.	Sack	Sack	Cu. Ft.
1	10.3	8.75	79.2	0.11	0.18	1
2	21	18	158	0.2	0.4	2
3	31	26	238	0.3	0.5	3
4	41	35	317	0.4	0.7	4
5	52	44	396	0.6	0.9	5
6	62	53	475	0.7	1.1	5.9
7	72	61	554	0.8	1.2	6.9
8	83	70	634	0.9	1.4	7.9
9	93	79	713	1.0	1.6	8.9
10	103	87.5	792	1.1	1.75	9.9
20	207	175	1584	2.2	3.5	19.8
27	279	236	2138	3.0	4.7	26.7
30	310	263	2376	3.3	5.3	29.7
40	414	350	3168	4.4	7.0	39.6
50	517	438	3960	5.5	8.8	49.5
60	620	525	4752	6.6	10.5	59.4
70	724	613	5544	7.7	12.3	69.3
80	827	700	6336	8.8	14.0	79.2
90	931	788	7128	9.9	15.8	89.1
100	1034	875	7920	11	17.5	99

The ash dump consists of a metal frame with a pivoted door. If no ashpit is installed or ash cady, cover the firebox floor to contain the ashes until ready to remove. The firebox floor is sometimes recessed about 1″ below the hearth to help contain the ashes.

Flue linings should start not less than 8″ below the intake or 8″ from the throat of the fireplace. When two ore more flues are contained in the same chimney, they should be separated with a 4″ brick wall.

STONE MASONRY

Stone laying is a creative task that can be developed. The secret is to "size" up the shape of the stone to fit into the wall with a minimum of cutting (Fig. 3-53). Stone arches, like brick arches,

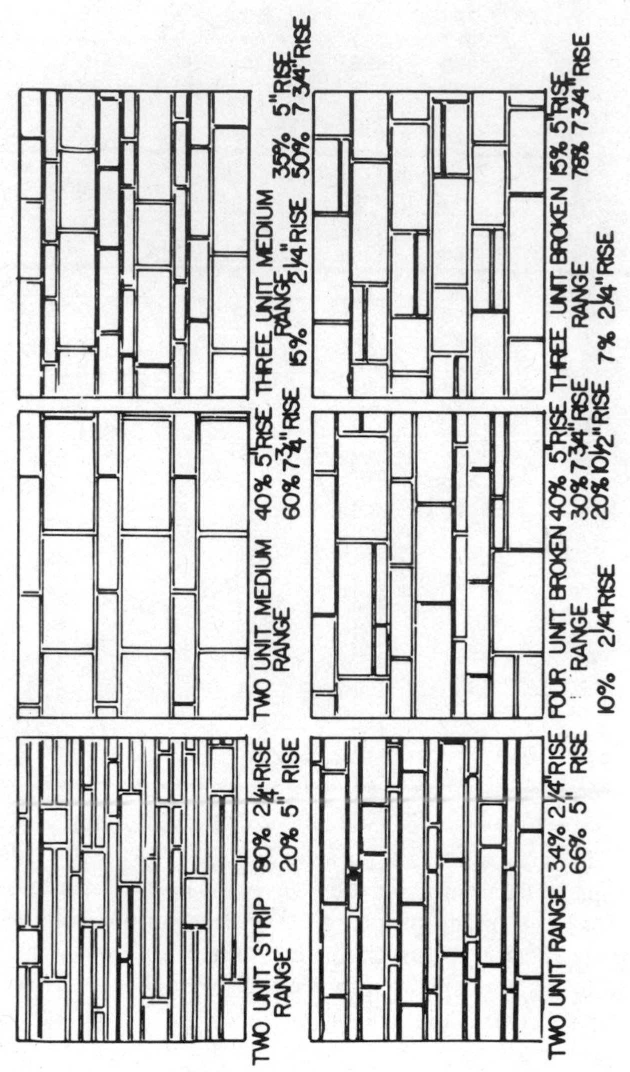
TWO UNIT STRIP RANGE
80% 2¼" RISE
20% 5" RISE
TWO UNIT MEDIUM RANGE
40% 5" RISE
60% 7¾" RISE
THREE UNIT MEDIUM RANGE
15% 2¼" RISE
35% 5" RISE
50% 7 3/4" RISE
TWO UNIT RANGE
34% 2 1/4" RISE
66% 5" RISE
FOUR UNIT BROKEN RANGE
10% 2¼" RISE
40% 5" RISE
30% 7 3/4" RISE
20% 10½" RISE
THREE UNIT BROKEN RANGE
7% 2¼" RISE
15% 5" RISE
78% 7 3/4" RISE

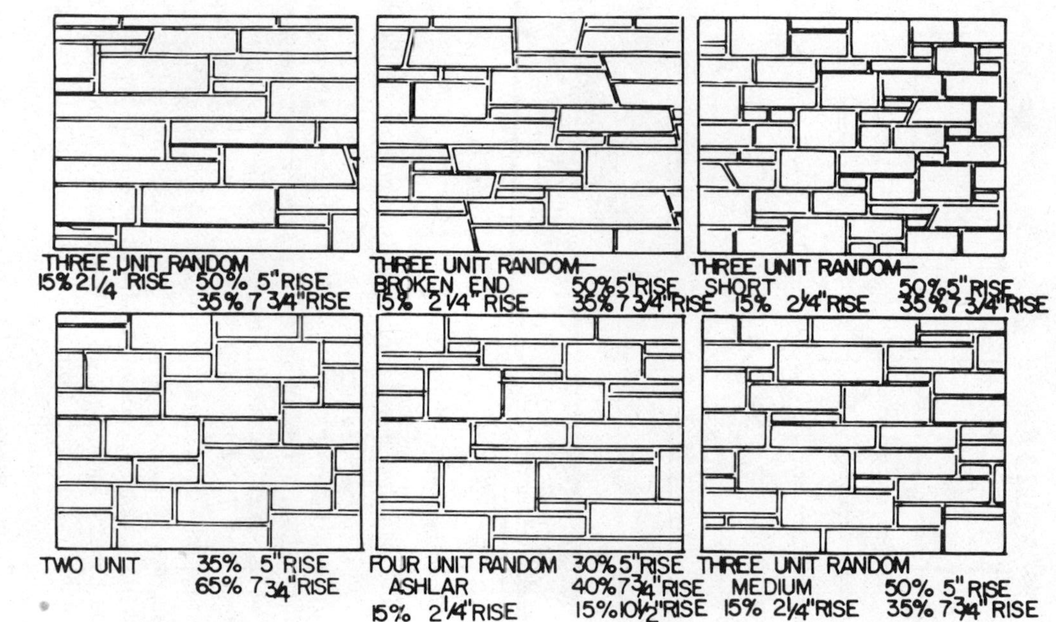

Fig. 3-53. Stone patterns and proportions.

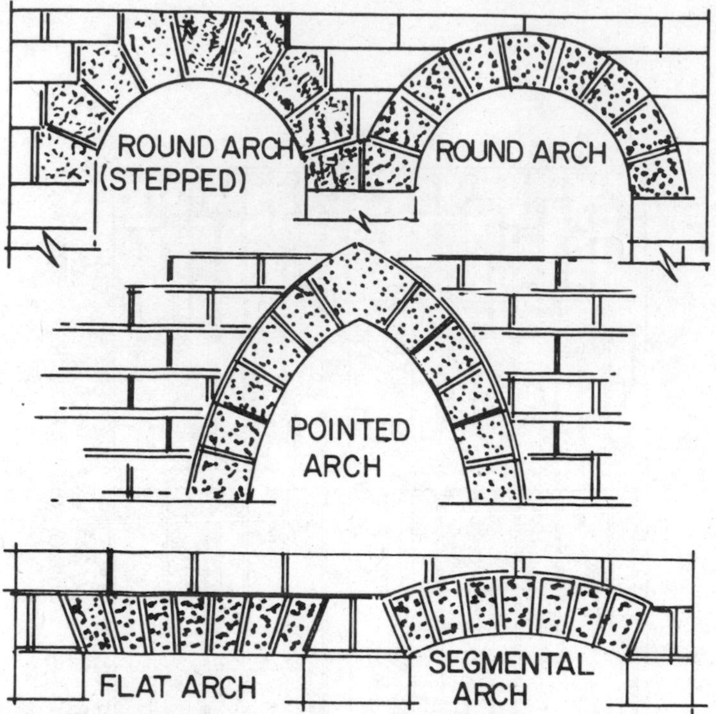

Fig. 3-54. Stone arches.

must be formed with wood temporarily to conform to the desired shape of the arch (Fig. 3-54).

A stone wall is not perfectly plumb, but instead is in alignment from projection to projection of each stone. Each stone should be laid on its widest surface for best weight distribution and better bonding. Try not to lay stone held in position by stone chips. Be sure the stone is clean of foreign material for proper handling and holding power. Larger stones should be used in the lower part of the wall, gradually becoming smaller towards the top. This is for proper balance and weight distribution. Large stones may be used occasionally as bonding stones. The mortar joint should not exceed 2′ because the joint will shrink away from the stone causing hairline cracks. Do not attempt to fill a large amount of mortar behind a stone until the wall has set; otherwise the mortar will collapse or fall out of place. If a stone has to be reset after placing, remove it completely and reset it in a fresh bed of mortar.

If stone must be cut for proper fit, use a face hammer and stone chisel. Be sure to wear safety glasses to guard against flying stone chips. The mortar mix for stone masonry is similar to brick and block masonry.

Rubble stone is a term used for fieldstone of irregular size and shape. Squared stone usually are cut to have flat surfaces on the stone. Of the two, squared stone are much easier to install. Never cut stone on a hard surface such as concrete, because the concrete is too hard to absorb the blow. The stone might break in the wrong places or crumble. A wooden platform has give and simplifies the cutting job.

Stone masonry should be at least 4″ thick backed at least with a 4″ masonry wall. Wall reinforcing is done by using an 8″ thick stone locked into the brick wall every other course, or by using corrugated metal ties built into the joints of the brick every 24″ apart horizontally and vertically. These ties are bent and locked into the stone joint bonding the wall.

Stone joints should have a full bed of mortar. Sometimes the stone are laid upon thin chips of wood. The thickness of the mortar joint supports the weight of the stone until the mortar has set. Remove the wood chips and fill the space with mortar. Mortar is kept 1″ back from the edge of the stone face for pointing later. Cleaning of stone is done with muriatic acid similar to brick.

Fig. 3-55. Old Chicago style of brick (courtesy of Z-Brick Company).

Fig. 3-56. Inca used style of brick (courtesy of Z-Brick Company).

SURFACE VENEER FINISHES

There are many products on the market that can be surface applied to simulate a stone or brick finish. These products can be used for interior and exterior finish. Materials are fireproof and the end result is climactic and eye catching. The problem is that they are made to look like the original which makes it difficult for the untrained eye to tell the difference (Figs. 3-55 through 3-63).

Use And Application

Simulated brick and stone are nonstructural wall surface coverings, suitable for both interior and exterior installation. They can be applied over almost any type of sound surface with a *minimum* of preparation. They do not require any special foundation supports, footings or fastenings. Do not use units for fire brick application.

After application, units must be sealed for ease of cleaning and to prevent moisture penetration. They must be protected from direct rain and free from moisture for 48 hour after installation. Do not use muriatic acid, ammonia or bleach for cleaning. No special equipment, parts, accessories or devices are required to apply this

Fig. 3-57. Inca white style of brick (courtesy of Z-Brick Company).

Fig. 3-58. Inca red style of brick (courtesy of Z-Brick Company).

Fig. 3-59. Country rustic smoke style of brick (courtesy of Z-Brick Company).

material. Regular tools are all that is necessary. Spacing of mortar joints should be gauged to match the panels (Figs. 3-64, 3-65 and 3-66).

Installation

Spread a layer of adhesive approximately 1/16″ thick over a sound surface. The individual units of panels are placed in position and firmly pressed into the adhesive, squeezing surplus into the mortar line areas. The adhesive mortar is smoothed to seal all edges of the panel. Working time for the adhesive mortar is about 30 minutes and a strong set is achieved within 2 hours. Units are easily scored and snapped to fit to size, or may be cut with a masonry saw. Corners may be mitered or butted.

On painted or sealed masonry surfaces, wire mesh lath is applied with concrete nails to support a scratch coat. When applying over wood or drywall, a moisture barrier of 15 pound felt paper should be applied before installing the lath. Apply the scratch coat of mortar over 2.5 pound metal lath, ½″ to ¾″ thick. Before the

Fig. 3-60. Country rustic red style of brick (courtesy of Z-Brick Company).

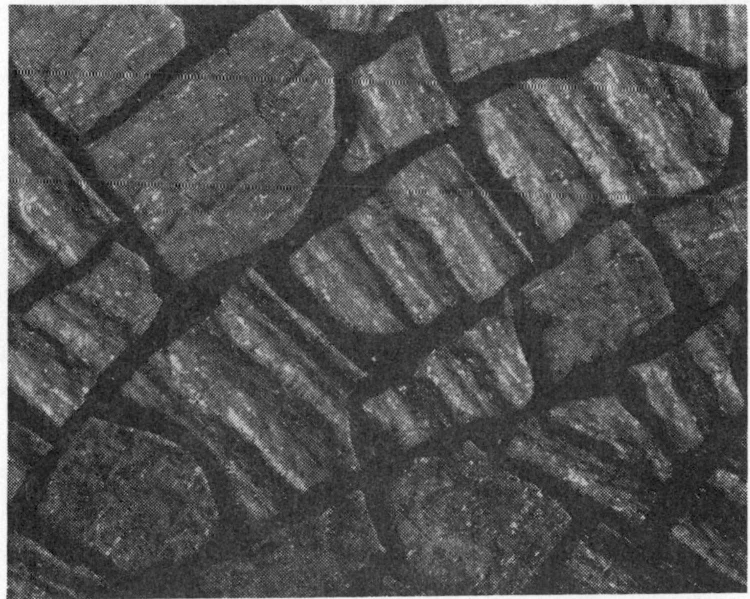

Fig. 3-61. Country rustic harbor gray style of brick (courtesy of Z-Brick Company).

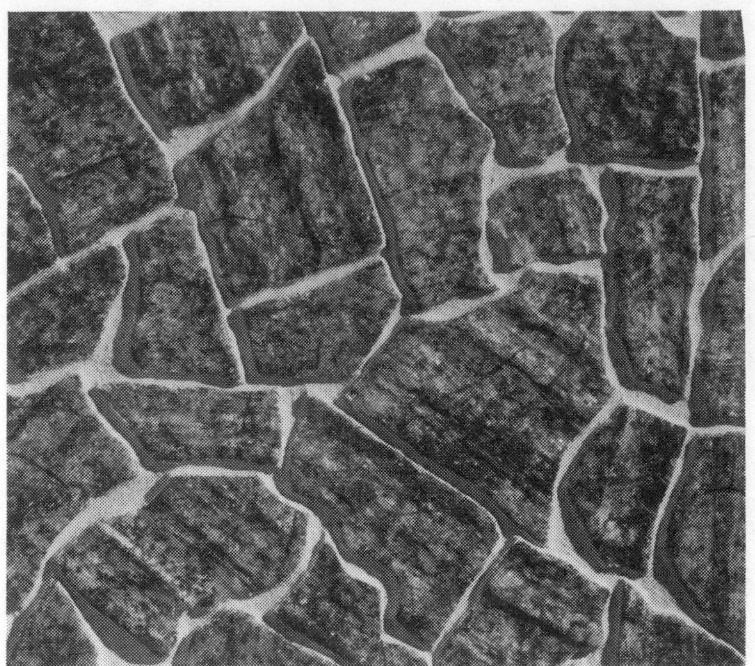

Fig. 3-62. Brown fieldstone (courtesy of Z-Brick Company).

mortar sets, scratch the surface to leave a ribbed pattern to afford better bond. Allow the scratch coat to dry for at least 48 hours before applying the veneered panels (Fig. 3-67). Remove several slabs from the pallet (Fig. 3-68). In breaking the stone, strike the slab firmly with an axe or hammer to break into random pieces (Fig. 3-69). Save the small pieces for filling in where necessary. Lay the stone on the ground or floor to make selection easier. This product is real stone cut into very thin slabs. Prepare a mortar mix of 1 part portland cement and 1 part sand, adding enough water to make a a working consistency. Butter the ribbed side of the stone (Fig. 3-70). Beginning at the top and working your way down, place the pieces into place by rotating in position to get a good bond (Fig. 3-71). Fill a grout bag with mortar and squeeze into the joints around the stone (Fig. 3-72). Point the joints for a natural finished look. At the end of the day's work, brush the stone to clean mortar from the surface (Fig. 3-73). After completion, seal the panels with masonry sealer.

Open wood studs spaced 16″ on center shall be covered with building paper. For exterior application, apply No. 18 gauge, 1″

Fig. 3-63. White fieldstone (courtesy of Z-Brick Company).

Fig. 3-64. An attractive simulated stone chimney (courtesy of Stucco Stone of California).

Fig. 3-65. Space mortar joints properly (courtesy of Stucco Stone of California).

woven wire mesh with galvanized nails spaced 6″ apart. The nails shall be of sufficient length to provide a 1″ penetration into the studs. Apply ½″ plaster scratch coat over the wire mesh to provide a rigid backing for the veneer.

Allow the plaster to cure for at least 48 hours before applying the veneer. For interior application, plywood or plasterboard

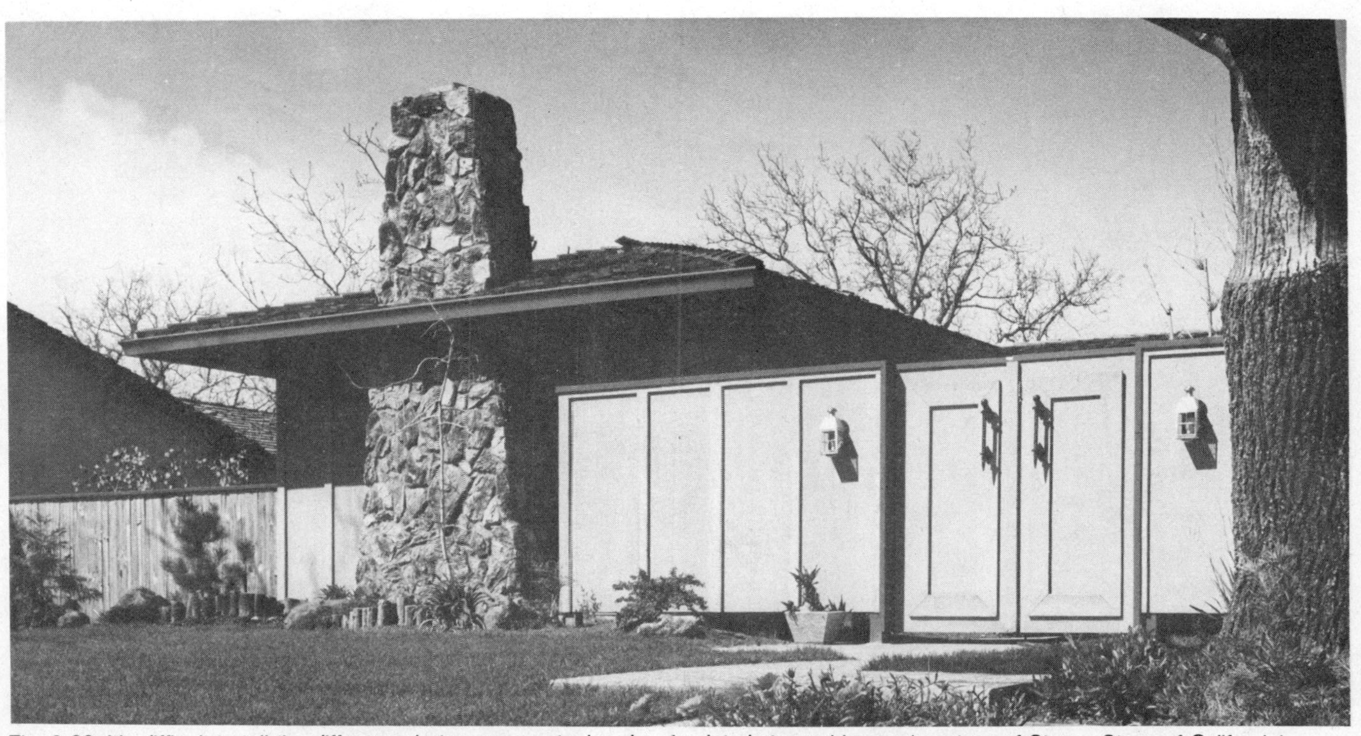

Fig. 3-66. It's difficult to tell the difference between an actual and a simulated stone chimney (courtesy of Stucco Stone of California).

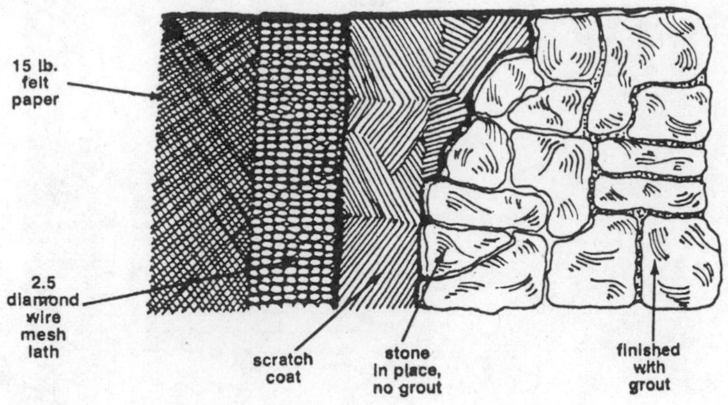

Fig. 3-67. Allow the scratch coat to dry before applying veneered panels (courtesy of Universal Stone Company).

(drywall) may be used as a base for the veneer. The mortar bed shall be applied to the wall or the back of the panel of a thickness not less than ½″. Press the panel firmly in place to allow the mortar to squeeze out around the perimeter of the panel. The veneer may also be applied to a masonry wall but the surface must be clean. Wet down the wall before application. At the end of the day's work, the entire wall should be broomed or bristle-brushed to remove any excess mortar from the face of the stone. Do not wet down the

Fig. 3-68. Remove several slabs from the pallet (courtesy of Universal Stone Company).

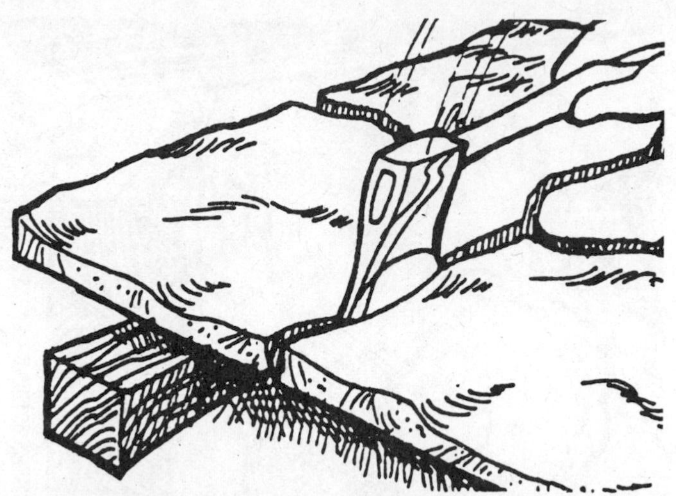

Fig. 3-69. Break the slab into pieces (courtesy of Universal Stone Company).

finished wall for at least 48 hours to allow the mortar to set. If used on an exterior masonry wall, the wall must first be waterproofed with a masonry sealer. The veneer shall be shaped and fitted so that the width of the mortar joints are held to a minimum and the joints shall be allowed to become firm before pointing.

Another veneer product made of molded polyster resin reinforced with fiber glass provides a timeless beauty of masonry and a

Fig. 3-70. Butter the ribbed side of the stone (courtesy of Universal Stone Company).

Fig. 3-71. Put the pieces into place (courtesy of Universal Stone Company).

versatile, lightweight, durable and easy to install building material. It can add a bold an dramatic effect to any fireplace facing or chimney. These panels are avialable in 4′ × 8′, interior or exterior use. They can be installed flat or on curved walls. The look, texture and contour of real brick, stone or wood has been reproduced to give a very dramatic effect.

Pointing

Pointing is done when the exterior and interior face brick or stone is completed. The voids at the joints are filled with mortar made of 1 part non-staining waterproof portland cement, 1 part lime putty and 3 parts white sand. The joint finish is accomplished with a small trowel, squeezed in the joint and rubbed smooth with a jointer to a flat or concave surface.

Smoke Test

After the mortar has hardened and all appliances connected, a smoke test should be made in each flue. Build a small smokey fire at the bottom of the flue. While the smoke is escaping through the chimney, cover the top tightly. If smoke rises through another flue, somewhere there is a leak which must be sealed. Repairing a leak is difficult, which makes it doubly important that work is done carefully initially. Soot accumulations inside a flue present a dangerous situation because a chimney fire could begin, causing danger from sparks igniting the roof covering and even the chimney itself. The easiest method of cleaning a chimney is to fill a burlap bag with rags and a few rocks to weight it down. Tie a rope to the bag and brush it along the walls of the flue lining from the top. Be sure to provide proper covering below because it is a messy job.

Some fireplaces are for show only and seldom used. If you are faced with one of these, the chimney must be thoroughly inspected using the smoke test method. Some chimneys have walls too thin and built without flue linings. Clearances from combustible structural members should be checked. Inspect the damper (if there is one) to see that it is working properly.

Efflorescence

A white deposit of water soluble upon the surface of a masonry wall is called *efflorescence*. This is caused by the chemicals in the mortar mix. There are several ways to reduce this problem: use clean water when mixing mortar; keep brick, sand and other building materials covered at all times; cover the wall after building until the mortar sets; or form a good bond between the unit and the mortar at the joint.

Efflorescence can be removed by washing with water. If this fails, use a diluted solution of 1 part muriatic acid to 9 parts water using a bristle brush and rinse thoroughly after cleaning. These stains are an indication that water is getting into the walls some-

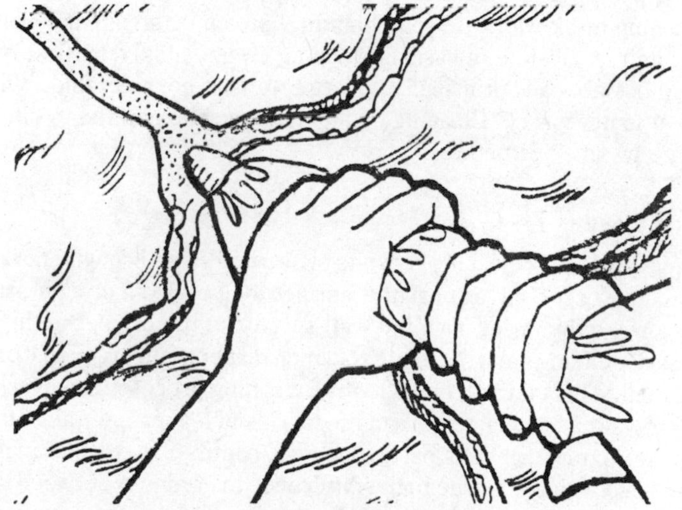

Fig. 3-72. Fill a grout bag with mortar and squeeze into the joints around the stone (courtesy of Universal stone Company).

where, probably because care was not exercised in a full, tight mortar joint, or a faulty flashing installation.

The cause of the staining should be corrected. Muriatic acid will remove the stain.

CLEANING OLD WALLS

Processes used in cleaning depend upon the materials to be cleaned and the nature and chemical composition of the spots or stains to be removed. Cleaning brick is no exception to this rule. The problem is further complicated by the fact that brick structures consist of two materials, the clay in the brick and the mortar which holds them in place, each of which has different characteristics. Many cleaning compounds to which clay products are entirely impervious have a damaging effect upon mortar.

Texture and absorption of the brick and the nature of the material or stain to be removed also determine to a very great extent the results which may be obtained with various cleaning methods. Proper cleaning methods will restore brick to its original appearance.

High absorption or rough textured brick are more difficult to clean. If the staining material has penetrated into the pores of the brick, it frequently cannot be removed without removing a part of the brick itself, thus destroying the original texture and resulting in an appearance different from the original. Principal methods of cleaning brick walls are sand blasting, steam or steam and water jet, and application of various cleaning compounds. The first two methods are used principally on large walls as considerable equipment is necessary. Cleaning compounds may be applied to either large or small structures.

Sand Blasting

This type of cleaning consists of blowing sand through a nozzle by compressed air against the surface to be cleaned. The sand removes a thin layer from the wall surface of the brick, the thickness depending upon the depth to which dirt or stain may penetrate the wall. This method is an effective cleaning process; however, it destroys the original texture of the brick and leaves the wall with a coarse texture which is particularly susceptible to the accumulation of soot and dirt. Due to the difference in hardness between the brick and the mortar joint, sand blasting may do serious damage to the joints.

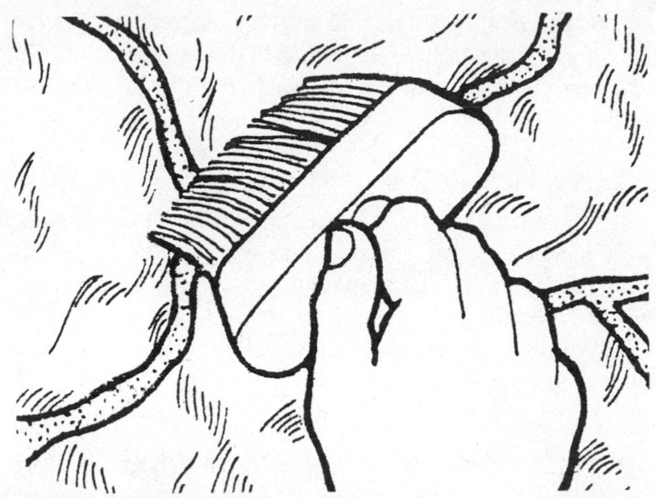

Fig. 3-73. Brush the stone to clean mortar from the surface (courtesy of Universal Stone Company).

If sand blasting is used, it will frequently be necessary to repoint the mortar joints after the surface has been cleaned. The application of a colorless waterproofing compound to the roughened surface will tend to make the walls self-cleansing, and will prevent the rapid soiling of the surface from smoke and dust particles in the air. Sand blasting should never be used on glazed units having special surfaces or textures.

Steam or Steam and Water Jets

This method cleaning consists of washing the wall with a steam or steam and water jet under pressure. It is effective in removing soot and dirt which accumulates on a wall over a period of time. Best results are obtained when it is used on low absorption brick; however, it also has been used with fair success on high absorption or rough textured brick. It is not effective in removing stains which penetrate into the pores, nor in removing such substances as mortar or paint.

Frequently an alkaline such as sodium carbonate, sodium bicarbonate or trisodium phosphate is added to the cleaning water when the cleaning is done by the jet method. Chemically these compounds are known as salts, and, while they aid materially in the cleaning action, some of the salt will be retained in the brick and will appear later on the face of the wall in the form of efflorescence. The amount of the salt retained by the brick can be materially reduced by thoroughly wetting the surface with clean water before the cleaning solution is applied. The wall should be washed with an abundance of clean water after cleaning to remove the salt from the surface.

Application of Cleaning Compound

This method is applicable to structures of all sizes and is probably used to a greater extent than any of the other methods. Most cleaning solutions contain compounds which, if absorbed by the brick, will subsequently appear on the face of the wall in the form of efflorescence. For this reason the surface to be cleaned should be thoroughly wetted with clean water before the cleaning solution is applied. Following are some stain removal tips.

- **Paint**. For fresh paint apply a commercial paint remover, or a solution of trisodium phosphate in water—2 pounds of trisodium phosphate to 1 gallon of water. Allow to stand and remove paint with scraper and wire brush. Wash with clean water. For very old dry paint, organic solvents similar to the above may not be effective, in which case the paint must be removed by sand blasting or scrubbing with steel wool.
- **Iron Stains**. Mix 7 parts lime-free glycerine with a solution of 1 part sodium citrate in 6 parts lukewarm water, and mix with whiting or *kieselguhr* to make a thick paste. Apply paste to stain with a trowel, and scrape off when dried out. Repeat until the stain has disappeared and wash thoroughly with clean water.
- **Tobacco Stains**. Dissolve 2 pounds phosphate in 5 quarts of water. In a separate container make a smooth stiff paste of 12 ounces of chloride of lime in water. Pour the former onto the paste and stir thoroughly. When the lime has settled, draw off the clear liquid and dilute with equal parts of water. Make a stiff paste of this with powdered talc and apply in the same way as described for iron stains.
- **Smoke Stains**. Make smooth stiff paste of trichlorethylene and powdered talc and apply as described above. Cover with glass or pan to prevent rapid evaporation. If a slight stain is left after several applications, wash thoroughly and then use the method described under tobacco stains. Precautions should be

taken to ventilate a closed space in which trichlorethylene is used, as the fumes are harmful.

- **Copper or Bronze Stains**. Mix together, in the dry form, 1 part of ammonium chloride (sal ammoniac) and 4 parts of powdered talc. Add amonia water and stir until a thick paste is obtained. Place this over the stain and leave until dry. When working on polished marble, use a wooden stick to scrape off the paste. An old stain of this kind may require several applications. Sometimes aluminum chloride is used in the above procedure instead of the sal ammoniac.
- **Oil Stains**. Make a paste of a solution of 1 pound of trisodium phosphate to 1 gallon of water and whiting which may be obtained at any paint store. Spread this paste in a layer about ½″ thick over the surface to be cleaned and leave until it dries.
- **Coal Smoke Stains**. Scrape with powdered pumice and wire brush.

Proper Use of Cleaning Agents

When the brick work or stone work is completed, it should be cleaned with 10 percent muriatic (hydrochloric) acid and water. Scrub with a hard bristle brush until all stains are removed, followed by a clean water washing and rinsing, an added protection to remove the acid completely.

Care in laying the masonry units will help reduce the cleaning. Cut off the mortar excess clean without smearing the wall. Striking the joints too soon causes unnecessary smearing. If the bricks are too wet when laying, the mortar will not absorb properly and the joints will bleed, causing a stain. Mixing the mortar to proper consistency will help reduce stain, causing smearing.

When using a cleaning agent two common mistakes are made. Manufacturer's instructions on the use of a product are ignored, which can result in too strong a mix, causing possible permanent burn damage. Covering too large an area causes improper rinsing. This practice could cause acid burns.

Minerals in certain kinds of brick will react with some cleaning agents, especially acids. Dark colored brick are most apt to stain. Try a sample cleaning in an inconspicuous place first. When using acids, be certain to wear a hat, rubber apron and rubber gloves, and especially important, safety glasses.

The only tool required is a piece of brick to remove and scrape mortar by rubbing the spot with the brick, a water hose for rinsing, and a wooden or plastic (not metal) bucket with a good stiff bristle brush for scrubbing.

Using a solution of hydrochloric (muriatic) acid, a hardware store item, and following manufacturer's recommendations, prepare the mix. Pour the acid into the water. Do not pour the water into the acid. If instructions are not given, *do not mix more than one part acid with 9 parts clear water*.

- Dry clean the walls by removing large particles of mortar (it may be necessary to use the chisel or wire brush) by rubbing with the piece of brick.
- Pre-soak the wall with water to remove loose dirt.
- Scrub with a wood-handled fiber brush (do not dip wire brush or scrapers into acid solution).
- Keep all masonry below the area being cleaned-soaked with water flushed free of acid. If acid scum is permitted to dry, it may be impossible to remove the stain caused by acid.
- Scrub the wall but not the joints.
- Clean a small area at a time, not more than 10 by 20 square feet.
- Rinse the cleaned area thoroughly.

CLEANING FIREPLACES

Keeping fireplaces clean requires a routine of dusting and vacuuming to stay ahead. Stains caused by smoke and soot can be controlled by wiping with ammonia, water and a sponge. Dry with a soft cloth to remove any possible ammonia stains. Do not dust mop marble because the dust particles and grit may scratch the surface. The firebox can be wet mopped and scrubbed to remove fire stains.

Grease stains can be removed from masonry by using a petroleum solution such as lighter fluid (be careful, because it is flammable or a clothes cleaning solution. A *poultice* should be applied after removing the stain by mixing*fuller's earth* (drug store item) with distilled water (rain water) into a stiff mud. Apply over the stain about ½″ thick. This solution will absorb the grease within 24 hours. All that is necessary after applying the mix is to brush dry the area. An alternate solution is made with ammonia water and a commercial dry cleaning powder containing tetracholor-oethylene or perchlor-oethylene. Hydrogen peroxide is another active cleaning agent mixed as a poultice.

The early fireplaces were of a soft brick, made from a porous clay. In order to make brick less porous, they were dipped in red ochre mixed with water or milk. Sometimes a mixture of black lead and soap was applied to attain a glossy surface to shed off the stain-causing elements. Another solution to reduce the absorption of brick was to rub lamp oil into the surface. Often, the brick was painted to avoid this problem. It was not unusual to find a zinc sheet above the ash line to reflect the heat.

REPAIRING MASONRY

Masonry breakdown is caused by rain, snow, temperature changes, and faulty material and workmanship. The secret is to prevent water from getting into the mortar joints. Redoing old mortar joints is called *repointing*. The old joints should be cut out to a depth of at least ½″ using hammer and chisel, taking care not to damage the face of the brick, block or stone. Remove any broken units at this point. After cutting out, remove all loose material with a brush. Mix fresh mortar following previous instructions.

Dampen the mortar joints to be repointed with a brush and water before filling the joint. Do not use too much water; just dampen. Tuck the mortar into the joints tightly, using a pointing tool matching the size of the joint.

One of the problems of repointing and repairing a chimney is getting to it. Sometimes building a scaffold is more work than the actual repairing. Scaffolding can be built of 2″ × 4″ legs tied (not nailed) to the roof or chimney with rope. Protect the roof against puncture or damage by covering the working area with plywood sheets. Working on a roof and making chimney repairs is extremely hazardous, and all safety precautions must be employed.

Cracking of masonry walls occur in may different ways. Most often cracks are caused by expansion and contraction of the wall. These movements are due to extreme temperature change. This action is called *thermal movement*. Do not make repairs immediately as cracks occur because movement may still be actual. Wait about one year after the cracking is detected to give the action enough time to settle down. Another source is by improper foundation design or inadequate soil bearing properties. If either of these are the cause of cracking, there is not much that can be done to prevent the problem. Eventually, a settling position will be reached. Then make the repairs.

CHIMNEY MAINTENANCE

Chimneys should be inspected every year for defects. Look for loose or fallen brick, cracked or broken flue linings, excessive soot accumulations and creosote.

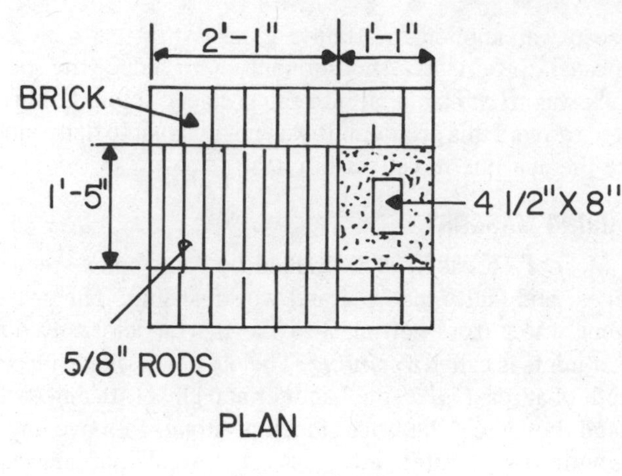

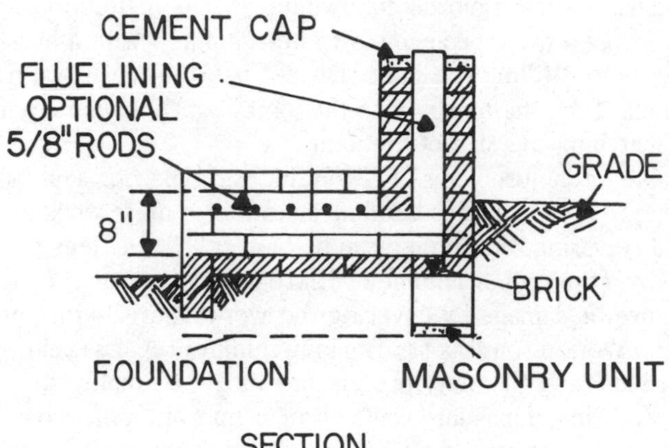

Fig. 3-74. An outdoor fireplace of modest design.

This can be accomplished by lowering an electric light from the top into the flue and, in the case of a fireplace, by shining a light through the damper. Check the joints of the masonry by scraping away loose mortar and repointing. If it is not possible to reach the defect, remove the chimney down to the area to be repaired and rebuild.

Chemical soot remover is not recommended. it can be responsible for fires and possible explosions.

Creosote is difficult to remove. The only safe method is to scrape it away from the walls with a blade, bring careful not to weaken any mortar joints or damage the flue lining.

OUTDOOR FIREPLACES

Designs for outdoor fireplace range from a simple makeshift unit to an elaborate structure. Built-in features such as ovens, cranes, grilles, storage compartments, sinks, and benches add to the function and appearance (Figs. 3-74 through 3-77).

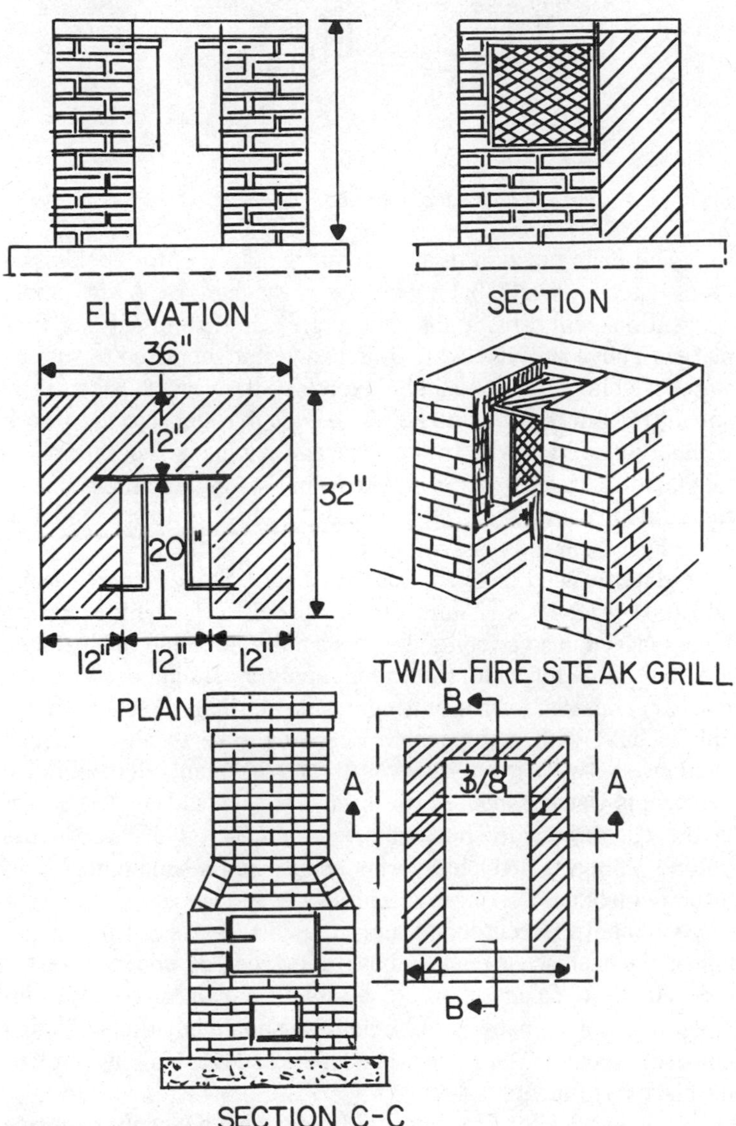

Fig. 3-75. Outdoor fireplace details.

Fig. 3-76. Example of an outdoor fireplace.

The main function of an outdoor fireplace is for cooking all types of food, usually, but not always, with charcoal. A few simple suggestions will provide for a more pleasant use of outdoor fireplaces. They should be well drained and not subjected to surface water puddling. Care should be exercised to provide shade. They should be built near the kitchen with enough room around to work without interfering with traffic. Prevailing wind is another important factor in order to avoid smoke from blowing into the house or the outdoor eating area. Don't build too close to low lying trees since heat from the fire will affect them.

Material used should be sound and hard. Stone is more readily adopted because it is a natural outdoor product. Pre-built ovens can be purchased in a variety of designs and sizes. Some of these uits are removable for winter storage, simply by sliding out from the masonry construction and storing indoors until the next season. If a unit is built with a removable oven, be sure to allow enough clearance between the masonry walls and the oven wall to allow for expansion. Usually about 3/16″ on each side should do. The height of the cooking grille should be between 24″ × 30″ above the ground. All parts and accessories should be on hand before construction begins.

Chimneys for outdoor fireplace as a rule are not necessary unless the fireplace is enclosed by a patio roof, or wood is used for fuel. Another exception would be using the fireplace as an incinerator. If a chimney is to be built, it should be at least 7′ high above the ground. The same procedure is used for building outdoor fireplaces as indoors.

Accessories for fireplaces will determine how your fireplace will look. These can harmonize, emphasize or deemphasize the fireplace. The most important accessory is a properly fitted screen (Figs. 3-78 through 3-82).

STARTING FIREPLACE FIRES

The first fire in a masonry fireplace should be a small one to help cure the mortar with several normal succeeding fires. Be sure the damper is open when the fireplace is in use and closed when not in use. Should you forget to open the damper when using the fireplace, you'll soon know about it and it won't happen again.

If the fireplace does not get adequate air, it will pull air down from the chimney filling the room with smoke. Sometimes opening the window a crack will help supply enough air. Split and seasoned hardwoods are recommended for fire wood. Scrap lumber can cause dangerous sparks. Fires should always be elevated from the firebox floor with grating or andirons which will insure air flow around the fire bed for proper combustion.

Crumbled newspaper is placed on the bed of the grate covered with a criss-cross of small kindling sticks topped by logs. The largest log should be placed at the rear of the firebox and a split log beside it with a space between. The third log is placed on top of these two. An open sheet of newspaper set on fire placed on top of the pile of logs will warm up the flue and help to establish good draft. While this is burning, light the kindling under the logs, draw the screen and sit back and relax.

In the event of a chimney fire, first call the fire department. Most chimney fires die out harmlessly if the chimney is sound and tight. Next, suffocate the fire by holding a wet blanket in front of the fireplace (Fig. 3-83). Hold it tightly because the draft may tend to pull the blanket into the fireplace. Do not use water to extinguish a chimney fire. Wet down the roof with a garden hose.

Fig. 3-77. A door for an outdoor fireplace.

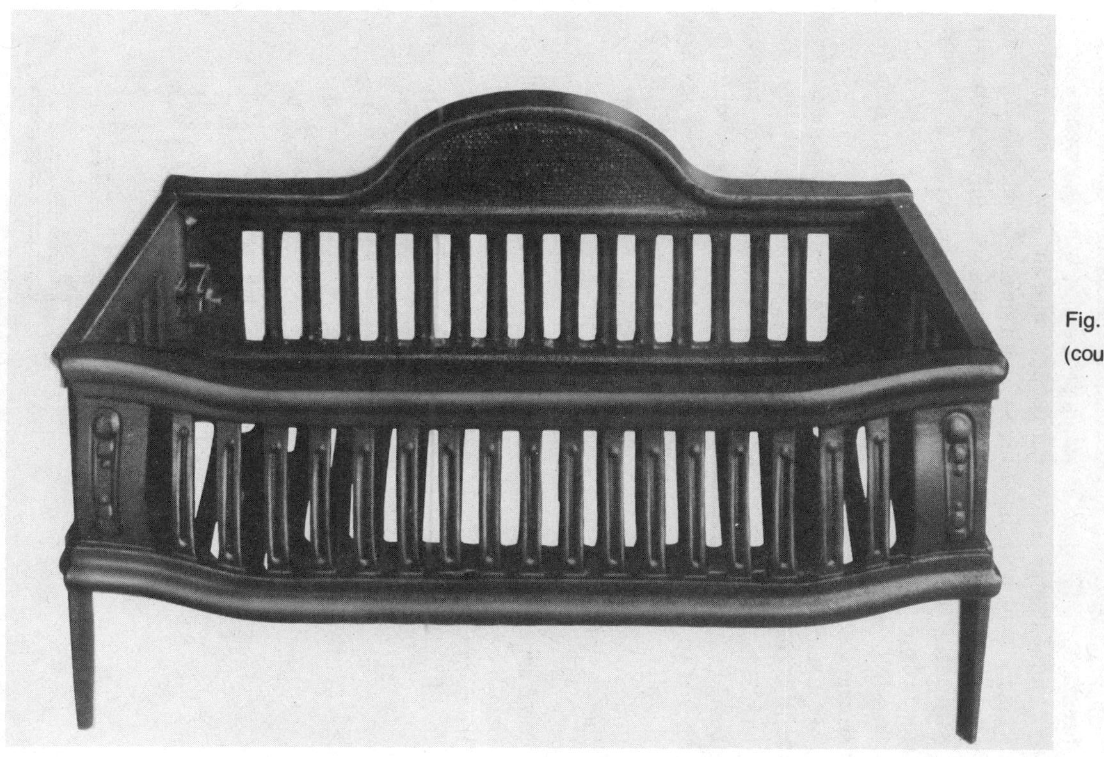

Fig. 3-78. A fireplace grating (courtesy of Martin Industries).

PAINTING BRICK

Although some brick walls require protective coatings to impart color and help in resisting rain penetration, brick requires no painting or surface treatment. Brick walls are generally selected because, among other characteristics, they have integral and durable color and, when properly constructed are resistant to rain penetration.

Brick walls may be painted both to increase light reflection and for decorative purposes. Most paint authorities agree that, once painted, exterior brick will require repainting every three to five years.

It is often erroneously assumed that brick walls that are to be painted can be built with less durable materials and, in some instances, with less than extreme care in workmanship than would normally be used for unpainted walls of brick. This is not the case. When a brick wall is to be painted, the selection of materials, both brick and mortar, and the workmanship used in constructing

Fig. 3-79. Andirons are metal supports for firewood used on a hearth (courtesy of Martin Industries).

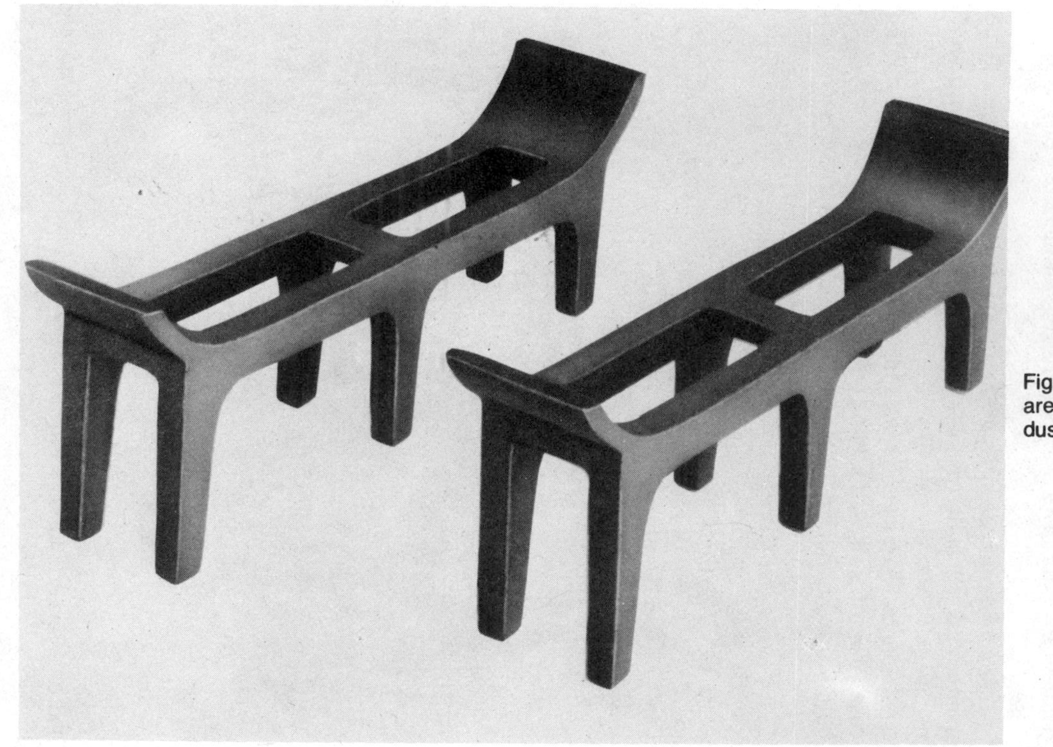

Fig. 3-80. Accessories like andirons are important (courtesy of Martin Industries).

Fig. 3-81. Another fireplace grating (courtesy of Martin Industries).

the wall should all be of the highest quality, at least as good in quality as when the walls are to be left exposed. Every care should be taken to see that joints are properly filled with mortar to avoid the entrance of moisture into the wall. It may become trapped behind the paint and cause problems. Every care should be taken to see that there are no efflorescing materials in the wall, either in the mortar, brick or backup. Efflorescence beneath the paint film can cause problems also.

In walls of brick to be painted, do not use a lower grade of brick than would be used for unpainted brick walls. It may be acceptable to use brick which are durable but differ in color in a wall to be painted. Care should be taken that the brick have similar absorption and suction characteristics, so that the paint applied will adhere to all the surfaces and have a uniform appearance. Paint for application to brick should be durable, easy to apply and have good adhesive qualities. It should be porous if applied on the exterior wall permitting the wall to breathe and preventing trapping of free moisture behind the paint film.

Paint Problems

Of primary concern should be the composition of the surface of the wall to be painted. A primer coat of paint may be necessary where unusual or severe weather conditions exist. The chemical property of brick may have a significant effect on paint durability and performance in the alkalinity of the brick. Brick are normally neutral but are set in mortars which are chemically basic. Paint products, which are based on drying oils, may be attacked by free alkali and the oils can become saponified. To prevent this, an alkaline-resistant primer is recommended.

The deposit of water-soluble salts on the surface of brick walls, efflorescence, is another factor that can hamper the performance of painted masonry. Efflorescence, which is present on the surface, should be removed and, once removed, the surface should be observed for reoccurrence prior to being painted. Water and moisture in a brick wall will generally hamper the satisfactory performance of the painted surface. Moisture may enter masonry walls in any of several ways: through the pores of the brick, through incompletely bonded or only partially filled mortar joints, through incomplete caulked joints and improperly installed flashing or where flashing has been omitted. In general, brick surfaces should be dry for painting (Table 3-20).

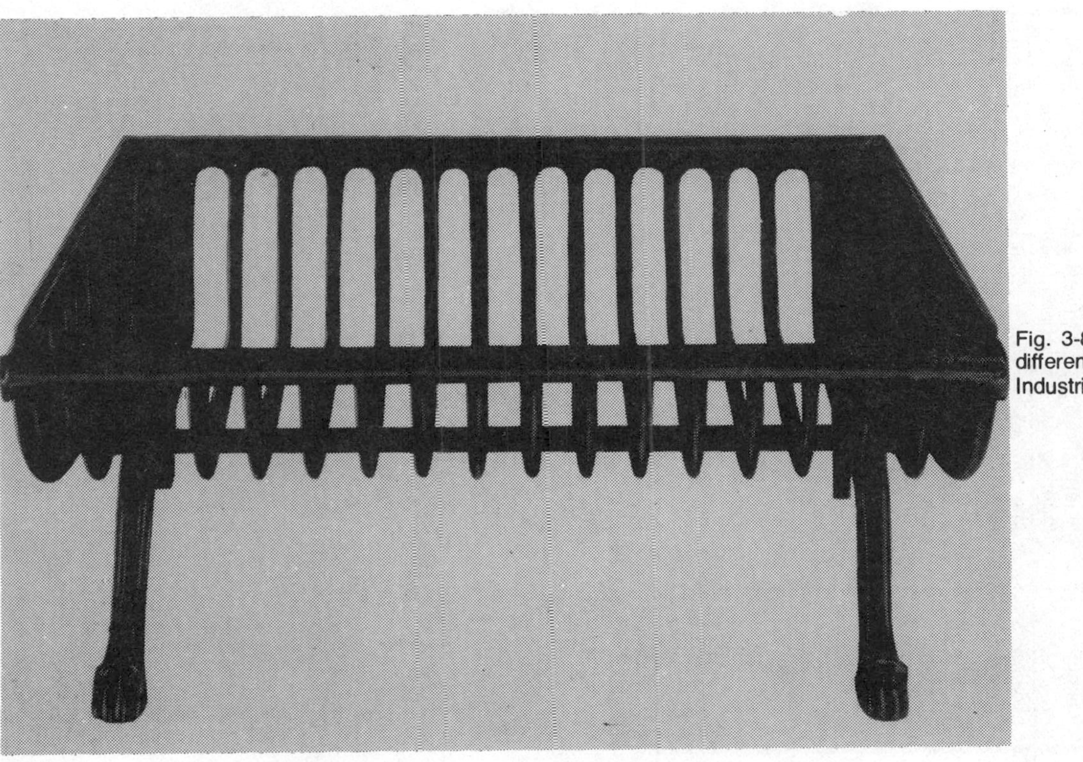

Fig. 3-82. Gratings come in many different designs (courtesy of Martin Industries).

Table 3-20. Types of Paint Failures (courtesy of Structural Clay Products Institute).

Defect	Description
Alligatoring	Wrinkling of the paint surface, caused by paint coats of different hardnesses
Bleeding	The working up of a stain into succeeding coats, imparting a discoloration to the newly applied coat
Blistering	Bubbles resulting from moisture trapped behind an impermeable paint film
Chalking	Powdering at or just beneath a paint surface. Slight chalking may be normal due to weathering
Checking	A defect in organic paints, manifested by slight breaks in the film surface
Erosion	Wearing away by weathering
Excessive Paint Buildup	Result of applying too much paint or coats which are too thick
Flaking	Detachment of small pieces
Map Cracking	Breaks in a paint surface extending entirely through the paint film, usually caused by shrinkage
Mildew	Fungus growth sometimes found feeding on paint or particles adhering to the surface in damp places, generally black or gray in color.
Peeling	A partial detachment of paint
Scaling	An advanced form of flaking

Surface Preparation

The surface must be properly prepared because each coat is the foundation for all future coats. Success or failure depends largely upon surface preparation. Thoroughly examine all surfaces to determine the required preparation. Previously painted surfaces often require the greatest effort. Before painting, remove all loose matter. Take special care when cleaning surfaces for emulsion paints and primers. They are nonpenetrating and require cleaner surfaces than solvent-based paints. Some paints can or should be applied to damp surfaces. Others must not. Be sure to follow directions carefully.

New Walls

As a rule, new brick walls are seldom painted. It is difficult to justify the added cost for initial and future painting. There are, however, precautions that must be taken if the wall is to be painted. Do not wash new brick walls with acid cleaning solutions. Acid reactions can result in paint failure. Use alkali-resistant paints. If low-alkali portland cement is not used in the mortar, it may be

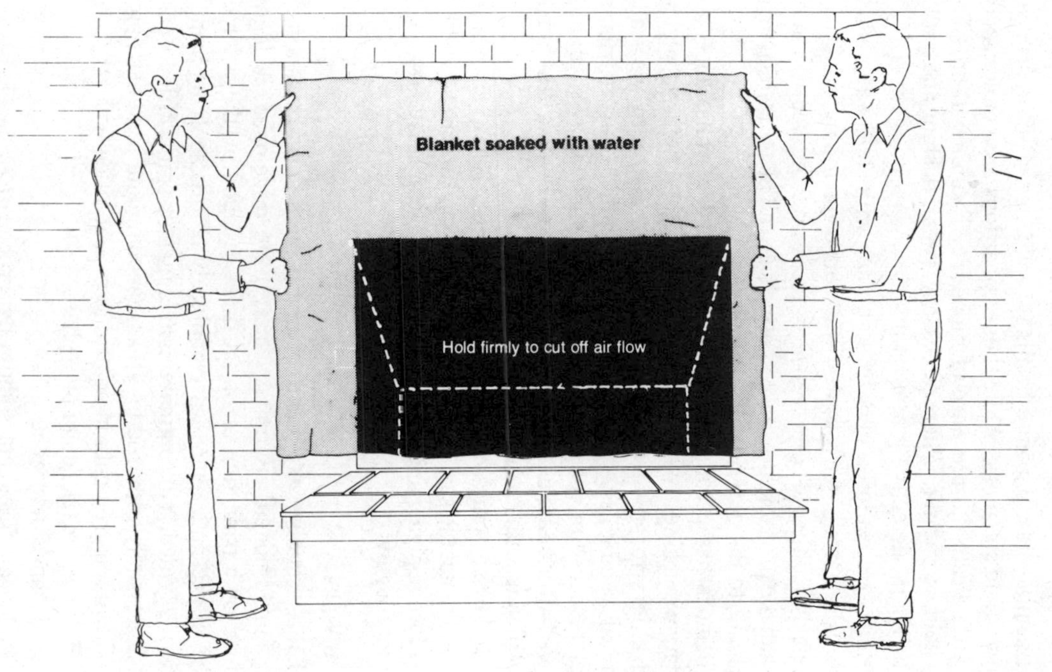

Fig. 3-83. Procedure for suffocating a chimney fire.

necessary to neutralize the wall to reduce the possibility of alkali-caused failures. Zinc chloride or zinc sulfate solution, 2 to 3½ pounds per gallon of water, is often used for this purpose.

Existing Walls

Examine older unpainted walls for evidence of efflorescence, mildew, mold and moss. While these conditions are not common, they all indicate the presence of moisture. Examine all possible entry points for water. Where necessary, repair flashing and caulking, tuckpoint defective mortar joints.

Remove all efflorescence by scrubbing with clear water and a stiff brush. A wall which has efflorescence for a long time may present difficulties. The presence of moisture, the deposition of salts and the probable presence of alkalis are all factors which may contribute to the deterioration of paints.

If moss has accumulated on damp, shaded walls, apply an ordinary weed killer. Wet the wall with clear water before applying weed killers to prevent them from being drawn into the wall. Chemical weed killers may contain solubles which can contribute to efflorescence or react unfavorably with paint. They should be removed after being used by scrubbing the wall with a stiff brush while rinsing with clear water.

Mildew seldom occurs on unpainted brick. However, where present, treat it the same as on painted surfaces. Be sure to wet the wall before applying any cleaning solution. Clean small areas and rinse thoroughly.

Painted Walls

These require extensive preparation before repainting. Under humid conditions, mildew may have developed. Mildew may feed on a paint film or on particles trapped by the painted surface. If present, remove it completely before applying paint, otherwise, growth will continue, damaging new paint. Mildew has been successfully removed by steam cleaning and sand blasting. The following ingredients in solution are also effective:

- 3 ounces trisodium phosphate.
- 1 ounce detergent.
- 1 quart 5 percent sodium hyperchlorite.
- 3 quarts warm water, or enough to make one gallon of solution. See Table 3-21.

Use this solution to remove mildew and dirt. Scrub with a medium soft brush until the surface is clean. Then rinse thoroughly

Table 3-21. Sources of Cleaning and Masking Agents (courtesy of Structural Clay Products Institute).

Agent	Supply Source
1. Aluminum Chloride	Pharmacist.
2. Ammonia Water	Supermarket. Household ammonia water.
3. Ammonium Chloride	Pharmacist. Salt-like substance.
4. Ammonium Sulfamate	Nursery and garden stores. Past use was as a base for weed killers. Not now readily available. Substitute any brand weed killer solution.
5. Acetic Acid (80%)	Commercial and scientific chemical supply firms.
6. Hydrochloric Acid	Hardware stores. Muriatic acid is generally available in 18° and 20° Baumé solutions.
7. Hydrogen Peroxide (30–35%)	Some commercial and scientific chemical supply firms.
8. Kieselguhr	Commercial, scientific chemical and swimming pool supply firms. Diatomaceous earth.
9. Lime-free glycerine	Drug stores. Used as a hand lotion base.
10. Linseed Oil	Hardware and paint stores.
11. Paraffin Oil	Hardware stores.
12. Powdered Pumice	Hardware stores. A sanding or polishing material.
13. Sodium Citrate	Pharmacist. Appears like enlarged salt granules.
14. Sodium Hydroxide (Caustic Soda)	Supermarket. Available in brand name substances such as Drano.
15. Sodium Hydrosulphite	Pharmacist or photographic stores. A white salt or "hypo" of photographic fixing agent.
16. Talc	Drug stores. Inert powder available as "purified talc." Bathroom talcum powder may be substituted.
17. Tricloroethylene	Commercial/scientific chemical supply firms and possibly some service stations or supermarkets. A highly refined solvent for dry cleaning purposes.
18. Trisodium Phosphate	Paint stores, some hardware stores, supermarkets. Strong base type powdered cleaning material sold under brand names. Also available in brand name substance such as Calgon.
19. Varsol	Service Stations. A refined solvent by the brand name Varsol.
20. Whiting	Paint manufacturers, possibly some large paint stores. A powdered chalk. Substitute kitchen flour, if purchase is difficult.

with fresh water. For small areas, use an ordinary household cleanser. Scrub with a medium soft brush and then rinse thoroughly. Use masonry paints containing a mildewcide to help prevent molds from recurring.

Remove all peeled, cracked, flaked or blistered paint by scraping, wire brushing or sand blasting. In some instances, old paint may be burned off, but this should be done by skilled labor. Like efflorescence, paint blistering is caused by water within the wall. Search for the water's source and take the necessary corrective measures to keep water out of the wall. If alligatoring exists, remove the entire finish. There is no other means of correction.

If slight chalking has occured, brush the surface thoroughly. However, if chalking is deep, remove by scrubbing with a stiff fiber brush and a solution of trisodium phosphate and water. Rinse the surface thoroughly. Use a penetrating primer to improve adhesion of the final coat.

Excessive paint buildup results from too many coats or thick coats of paint. Where it occurs, remove all paint and treat as a new surface. Completely remove cement-based paints before repainting with other types. An exception to this rule its the use of cement-based paints as primers which will be covered by another paint within a relatively short time. If the wall will be painted with another cement-based paint, wire brushing and scrubbing will do the job (Table 3-22).

Masonry Paints

Because all paints have distinct properties and surfaces vary considerably, even the most experienced painter should carefully examine a surface before making recommendations. The following will generally indicate the proper use of masonry paints.

Cement-Based Paints

For many years, cement-based paints have been satisfactory coatings for brick. They achieved popularity because they have relatively good adherence and tendency to make a wall less permeable to free water. Cement-based paints are permeable, permitting the wall to breathe. Their main components are portland cement, lime and pigments. Additives, binders and sands may be added.

Although cement-based paints are more difficult to apply than other types, good surface protection results when properly applied. While they are not complete waterstops, cement-based paints help to seal and fill porous areas, excluding large amounts of

Table 3-22. Cleaning Guide for New Masonry (courtesy of Structural Clay Products Institute).

Brick Category	Cleaning Method	Remarks
Red and Red Flashed	Bucket and Brush Hand Cleaning High Pressure Water Sandblasting	Hydrochloric acid solutions, proprietary compounds, and emulsifying agents may be used. *Smooth Texture:* Mortar stains and smears are generally easier to remove; less surface area exposed; easier to presoak and rinse; unbroken surface, thus more likely to display poor rinsing, acid staining, poor removal of mortar smears. *Rough Texture:* Mortar and dirt tend to penetrate deep into textures; additional area for water and acid absorption; essential to use pressurized water during rinsing.
Red, Heavy Sand Finish	Bucket and Brush Hand Cleaning High Pressure Water	Clean with plain water and scrub brush, or *lightly* applied high pressure and plain water. Excessive mortar stains may require use of cleaning solutions. *Sandblasting is not recommended.*
Light Colored Units, White, Tan, Buff, Gray, Specks, Pink, Brown and Black	Bucket and Brush Hand Cleaning High Pressure Water Sandblasting	*Do not use muriatic acid!!* Clean with plain water, detergents, emulsifying agents, or suitable proprietary compounds. Manganese colored brick units tend to react to muriatic acid solutions and stain. Light colored brick are more susceptible to "acid burn" and stains, compared to darker units.
Same as Light Colored Units, etc., plus Sand Finish	Bucket and Brush Hand Cleaning High Pressure Water	Lightly apply either method. (See notes for light colored units, etc.) *Sandblasting is not recommended.*
Glazed Brick	Bucket and Brush Hand Cleaning	Wipe glazed surface with soft cloth within a few minutes of laying units. Use soft sponge or brush plus ample water supply for final washing. Use detergents where necessary and acid solutions only for *very difficult mortar* stain. For dilution rate, see Step 1d, *Select the Proper Solution*, under Bucket and Brush Hand Washing. Do not use acid on salt glazed or metallic glazed brick. Do not use abrasive powders.
Colored Mortars	Method is generally controlled by the brick unit	Many manufacturers of colored mortars do not recommend chemical cleaning solutions. Most acids tend to bleach colored mortars. Mild detergent solutions are generally recommended.

free water. White and light colors tend to be most satisfactory. It is difficult to obtain a uniform coating with darker shades. Lighter colors tend to become translucent when wet and dark colors become darker. Colors return to normal as the wall surface dries. Cement-based paints can provide a good base for other paints applied within a relatively short time.

The following procedure for applying paint on a properly prepared surface generally applies:

- Cure new brick walls for approximately one month before applying cement-based paints.
- Dampen wall surfaces thoroughly by spraying with water.
- Cement-based paints are packaged in powdered form. Their components begin to hydrate upon contact with water. Mix immediately prior to application.
- Apply heavy coats with a stiff brush, allowing at least 24 hours between coats.
- During this time, keep the wall damp by spraying with water.
- Apply additional coats in a like manner.
- Keep the final coat damp for several days to properly cure.

Water-Thinned Emulsion Paints

These are commonly referred to as latex paints and are relatively easy to apply. Water-thinned paints may be brushed, rolled or sprayed. However, brush application is preferred, especially on coarse textured brick. Emulsion paints dry quickly, have no odor and present no fire hazard. They may be applied to damp surfaces, permitting painting shortly after a rain or on walls damp with condensation.

As a group, these paints are alkali-resistant. Hence, neutralizing washes and curing periods are not usually necessary before painting. Water emulsion paints possess high water vapor permeability and are known to have performed well on brick.

Emulsion paints will not adhere well to moderately chalky surfaces. If possible, repainting should be done before the previous coat chalks. Specially formulated latex paints are available containing emulsified oils or emulsified alkyds which facilitate wetting of chalky surfaces. This property enables the paint to bond the chalk together and to the substrate.

The principle water-thinned emulsion paints are *butadiene-styrene, vinly, acrylic, alkyd and multicolored lacquers.*

Butadiene-Styrene Paints. These relatively low cost rubber- based latex paints develop water resistance more slowly than vinyl or acrylic emulsions. They are most satisfactory in light tints as chalking rate may be excessive in deep colors.

Vinyl Paints. Polyvinyl acetate emulsion paints dry faster, have improved color retention and a more uniform, lower sheen than rubber-based latex paints.

Acrylic Emulsion Paints. These have excellent color retention, permit recoating in 30 minutes or less and have good alkali resistance. Acrylics have high resistance to water spotting and may be scrubbed easily.

Alkyd Emulsion Paints. These are related to solvent-thinned alkyd types, but have all the general characteristics of latex paints. They do have more penetration than most water-thinned emulsions, achieving better adhesion on chalky surfaces. Compared to other emulsion paints, these are rather slow to dry, have more odor, are not as resistant to alkalis and have poorer color retention. Under normal exposure conditions, alkyd emulsions can serve as a finished coat over a suitable primer.

Multicolored Lacquers. A specialized paint group is applied only by spray gun. The finished film appears as a base color with separate dots or particles of contrasting colors. These paints will cover many surface defects and irregularities. They must be applied over a base coat of another type for example polyvinyl acetate or acrylic emulsion paints.

Fill Coats

These are base coats for exterior brick painting. They are similar in composition, application and uses to cement-based paints. Fill coats contain an emulsion paint in place of some water, giving improved adhesion and a tougher film than unmodified cement paints. Fill coats have greater water retention, giving the cement a better chance to cure. This is particularly valuable in arid areas where it is difficult to keep the painted surface moist during the curing period.

Solvent-Thinned Paints

The five major solvent-thinned paints are *oil-based, alkyd* (synthetic resin), *synthetic rubber, chlorinated rubber* and *epoxy*. Oil-based and alkyd paints are not recommended for exterior masonry. Solvent-thinned paints should be applied only to completely dry, clean surfaces. They produce relatively nonporous films and should be used only on interior masonry walls not susceptible to moisture penetration. The exceptions to this are special purpose paints such as synthetic rubber, chloriinated rubber and epoxy paints.

Oil-based paints have been used for many years. They are relatively nonporous and recommended for interior use only. Although several coats may be required for unifrom color and good appearance, they bind well to porous masonry. As with most solvent-based paints, they have good penetration on relatively chalky surfaces but are highly susceptible to alkalis. New brick walls must be thoroughly neutralized to avoid saponification. Available in a wide color range, oil-based paints are moderately easy to apply. Several days of drying may be required between coats.

Alkyd paints are similar to oil-based paints in most general characteristics. They may have slightly less penetration, resulting in somewhat better color uniformity at the cost of adhering power. Alkyd paints are more difficult to brush, dry faster and give harder film than oil-based paints. These, too, are nonpermeable and are recommended for interior use only.

Synthetic rubber and chlorinated rubber paints have excellent penetration and good adhesion to previously painted, moderately chalky surfaces as well as new surfaces. They are reported to be more resistant to efflorescence and are good in alkali resistance. They may be applied directly to alkaline masonry surfaces, but are more difficult to brush on than oil paints. Darker colored synthetic rubber paints lack color uniformity. Both types have high resistance to corrosive fumes and chemicals. For this reason, they are often specified for industrial applications. Both types require very strong solvents, a fire hazard which may prove undesirable.

Epoxy paints are of synthetic resins composed of two parts, a resin base and a liquid base activator. They must be used within a relatively short time after mixing. Epoxies can be applied over alkaline surfaces, have very good adhering power and good corrosion and fume resistance. Some types chalk excessively if used outdoors. Epoxies are relatively expensive and somewhat difficult to apply.

High-Build Paint Coatings

These are generally used on interiors to give the effect of glazed brick. Some coatings are based on two-component urethane polyesters and epoxies. Others are of an emulsion-based coat with

Table 3-23. Dampness of Walls and Choice of Paint (courtesy of Structural Clay Products Institute).

Relative Humidity in Equilibrium With Surface, Per Cent	Wall Condition	Electrical or Hygrometric Meter Indicator (not microwave meter)	Recommendation
100	Wet (with obvious moisture at wall surface)	Red Zone	Chances of failure high. Postpone painting if possible. If postponement is not feasible, wipe dry and use special types of paint[1] suitable under adverse conditions.
100	Wet (no obvious water at wall surface)	Usually Red Zone	Painting is best postponed. If essential, use: (1) White cement paint (2) Special types of paint[1]
90–75	Drying	Usually Amber Zone	As above. Other porous paints give reasonable chances of success. As surface becomes drier, range may be progressively increased to include: (1) Most emulsion paints (2) Special types of permeable flat oil paints
Less than 75	Dry	Usually Green Zone	No restrictions

[1]Some manufacturers offer special porous, highly pigmented emulsion paints which may give somewhat better results in very adverse conditions where delay is not acceptable.

acrylic lacquer. These paint systems usually include fillers to smooth out surface irregularities.

Other Coatings

Heavily applied coatings of the so-called breathing type are available with either a water or solvent base. They are composed of asbestos fiber and sand, and applied thickly to hide minor surface imperfections. The presence of moisture on the surface of a wall will not harm the latex type. Lower application temperatures of 35°F. on the other hand are less damaging to the solvent type. For both types, adhesion is mostly mechanical because of low binder and high pigment content. Some coatings require special primers to insure adhesion. Although these coatings are reported to have good performance on brick, they tend to show stains where water runoff occurs.

They are capable of allowing passage of water vapor, but cannot transmit large quanitites of water that may enter through construction defects. Failure may occur as a result of freezing of water accumulation behind the film.

Painting Near Unpainted Brick

When a self-cleaning paint is used, unfortunately self-cleaning is achieved through chalking. The theory is that rain will wash away chalked paint, constantly exposing a fresh paint surface. The theory works well, but too often no provision is made to keep chalk-contained rain water away from other surfaces. The result is more unsightly than dirty paint. Avoid this problem by choosing nonchalking paints and by providing a means of draining water away from wall surfaces (Table 3-23).

4

Flue Linings

The flue lining is a clay lining inside the chimney through which smoke and gases from the fire are directed to the open air. The correct size flue is measured by the cross-sectional area. When warm air rises through the flue, it moves in spirals and uses the center of the flue. If the flue lining is round, there is little resistance. If, however, the flue lining is squared or rectangular, there are cold spots. Soot accumulates in the areas of the corners of the flue lining which could possibly render the total area of such a flue in a circle equal to the smallest dimension of the flue. The size of the flue linings for wood burning stoves are recommended by the manufacturer.

INSTALLATION

The flue lining size for fireplaces is generally equal to one-tenth the area of the firebox. For example, a 42″ wide and 30″ high fireplace opening has an area of 1,260 square inches; one-tenth of 1,260 = 126 square inches of effective area flue size (Tables 4-1 and 4-2). If the chimney is more than 20′ high, a larger flue lining must be used. Use the next larger size. If between 20′ and 30′ high, the flue area should be one-twentieth the area of the firebox. If it is more than 30′ high above the hearth, the flue area should be one-twelfth the firebox area. For example, a fireplace opening of 4′ wide and 2′ 6″ high with a chimney height not above 25′ would have

Table 4-1. Modular and Non-Modular Flue Liners.

Area (inside net)	Dimension	outside	Shell Thickness	Length Available (standard)
Modular—Rectangular or Square (note: Nominal dimensions given—subtract 1/2" both width and depth for actual size)				
15 sq. in.	4" x 8"		1/2"	2'-0"
20 " "	4" x 12"		5/8"	2'-0"
27 " "	4" x 16"		3/4"	2'-0"
35 " "	8" x 8"		5/8"	2'-0"
57 " "	8" x 12"		3/4"	2'-0"
74 " "	8" x 16"		7/8"	2'-0"
87 " "	12" x 12"		7/8"	2'-0"
120 " "	12" x 16"		1 "	2'-0"
162 " "	16" x 16"		1-1/8"	2'-0"
208 " "	16" x 20"		1-1/4"	2'-0"
262 " "	20" x 20"		1-3/8"	2'-0"
320 " "	20" x 24"		1-1/2"	2'-0"
385 " "	24" x 24"		1-5/8"	2'-0"
Non-Modular—Rectangular or Square				
21.63 sq. in.	4-1/2 x 8-1/2"		5/8"	2'-0"
36.25 " "	4-1/2 x 13 "		5/8"	2'-0"
50.63 " "	8-1/2" x 8-1/2"		5/8"	2'-0"
78.57 " "	8-1/2" x 13 "		3/4"	2'-0"
107.75 " "	8-1/2" x 18 "		7/8"	2'-0"
124.63 " "	13 " x 13 "		7/8"	2'-0"
168 " "	13 " x 18 "		7/8"	2'-0"
232 " "	18 " x 18 "		1-1/8"	2'-0"
279 " "	20 " x 20 "		1-3/8"	2'-0"
337.5 " "	20 " x 24 "		1-1/2"	2'-0"
420 " "	24 " x 24 "		1-1/2"	2'-0"
Non-Modular—Round Flue Tile				
	Outside Dimension	Inside Dimension		
26 sq. in.	7-1/4" dia.	6" dia.	5/8"	2'-0"
47 " "	9-1/2" "	8" "	3/4"	2'-0"
74.5 " "	11-3/4" "	10" "	7/8"	2'-0"
108 " "	1'- 2 " "	1'-0" "	1 "	2'-0"
171 " "	1'- 5-1/4" "	1'-3" "	1-1/8"	2'-0"
240 " "	1'-10-3/4" "	1'-8" "	1-3/8"	2'-0"
298 " "	1'-10-3/4" "	1'-8" "	1-3/8"	2'-0"
433 " "	2'- 3-1/4" "	2'-0" "	1-5/8"	2'-0"
551 " "	2'- 7 " "	2'-3" "	2	2'-6"
683 " "	2'-10-1/4" "	2'-6" "	2-1/8"	2'-6"
829 " "	3'- 1-1/2" "	2'-9" "	2-1/4"	2'-6"
989 " "	3'- 5 " "	3'-0" "	2-1/2"	2'-6"

Table 4-2. The Net Inside Cross Section Area in Square Inches for the Three Common Kinds of Clay Flue Lining. A Convenient Guide for Determining Flue Capacities When Designing Fireplaces (courtesy of Vestal Manufacturing).

Table: For Area of Clay Flue Linings (Inside Minimum Net Area Square Inches)

Standard Rectangular		Modular Rectangular		Round	
Outside Dimensions	Net Inside Area Sq. In.	Nominal Outside Dimen.	Net Inside Area Sq. In.	Inside Diameter	Net Inside Area Sq. In.
8-1/2" x 8-1/2"	52.5	8" x 8"	35	6"	28.27
8-1/2" x 13"	80.5	8" x 12"	57	8"	50.26
8-1/2" x 17-3/4"	109.6	8" x 16"	74	10"	78.54.
13" x 13"	126.5	12" x 12"	87	12"	113
13" x 17-3/4"	182.8	12" x 16"	120	15"	176.7
18" x 18"	248	16" x 16"	162	18"	254
20" x 20"	298	16" x 20"	208	21"	346
20" x 24"	416	20" x 20"	262	24"	452
24" x 24"	441	20" x 24"	320	27"	572
		24" x 24"	385	30"	706

an area of 1,440 square inches; consequently, the flue area should be 1,440 divided by 10= 144 square inches inside area.

A 13″ × 13″ flue has an area of 124.63 square inches, which is not large enough. The next flue size is 13″ × 17″ or 180.88 square inches, 16″ × 16″ which has 162 square inches or a round flue, 15″ in diameter with 176.7 square inches.

Because smoke rises in a circular or swirling motion, a round flue lining is considered to be more effective than a square or rectangular flue. Flues should have 8″ of masonry around them except when two or more flues are used. Then the wall between the flues can be 4″ thick (Fig. 4-1). Some text books will recommend 4″ walls of masonry around the flue with the lining used to stiffen the chimney structurally. This practice is not recommended because the chimney must be totally and completely separated and self supported. It must be completely divorced from the house structure.

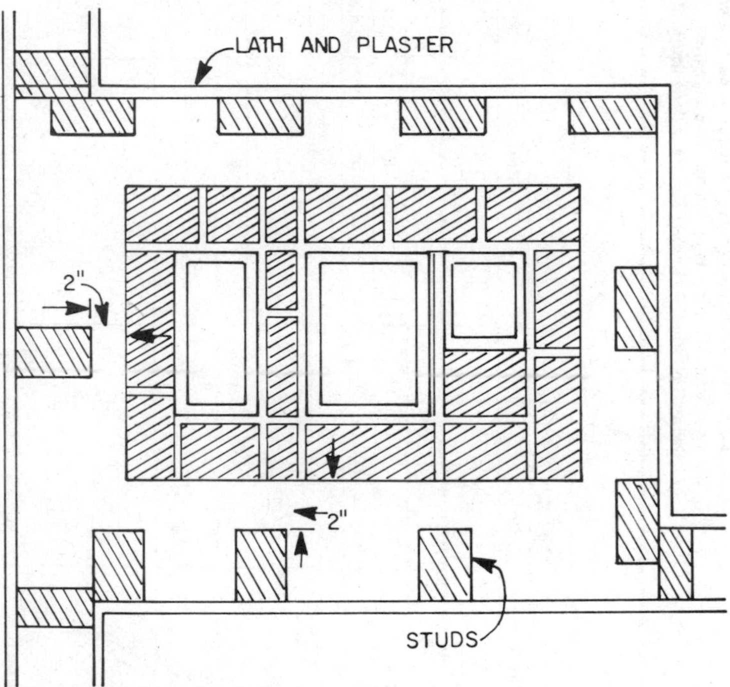

Fig. 4-1. Chimney plan showing proper arrangement of three flues. Bond division wall with sidewalls by staggering the joints of successive courses. Wood framing should be at least 2″ from brickwork.

There should be a separate flue for every fire in order to attain the maximum draft. Using a common flue for more than one fire may cause serious problems in draft. When direction of the flue changes, the angle should be no greater than 45°. Sharp turns create trouble spots by collecting soot and dirt thereby restricting the effective area of the flue.

The high velocity built up in the throat is dependent upon the flue lining size and the chimney height. The size of flues are designed to be enclosed by an even number of brick. An 8″ × 8″ flue will require six standard brick for each course. An 8″ × 12″ flue will require seven brick to enclose the flue. If more than one flue is contained within the same chimney, it should be separated by a brick wall of at least one brick thick (Fig. 4-2).

Flue linings should be installed far enough ahead of the masonry walls to allow for careful bedding of mortar at the joints, which will afford a tight smooth joint. The linings are supported by the brick by simply projecting the brick enough to support the first flue lining section, which should begin at least 8″ below the thimble used for connecting the smoke or vent pipe. In fireplaces, the flue lining begins at the top of the throat and in both cases extends to the top of the chimney.

Flue linings are made in 24″ lengths in the following sizes: 8″ × 8″, 8″ × 12″, 12″ × 12″, 12″ × 16″ and up to 20″ × 20″. The same area can be had in round flues. The wall thickness of the flue linings vary from 5/8″ thick to 1 3/8″ thick, depending upon the size. Flue linings should be installed with care, one on top of the other with a full bed of mortar between and the joint carefully flushed on the inside to avoid any rough spots. The outside of the flue lining should have the brick placed close and tight with mortar between, leaving no voids.

Flue linings can easily be cut with a mason chisel and hammer. Place the lining on a solid base or floor, fill the lining with sand and carefully score the cut mark with the hammer and chisel around the perimeter. Repeat the blows lightly, working around the mark until the lining breaks. You should have a smooth, even cut. The minimum brick wall surrounding flue linings should be 8″. If more than one flue is installed in the same chimney, a 4″ brick wall separating the flues will be sufficient. Stagger the joints of the flue linings, if more than one is installed. Check to see that they are not cracked or broken before installing.

At the bottom of all flue linings should be a cleanout door to remove soot and accumulations from the chimney. The size of the

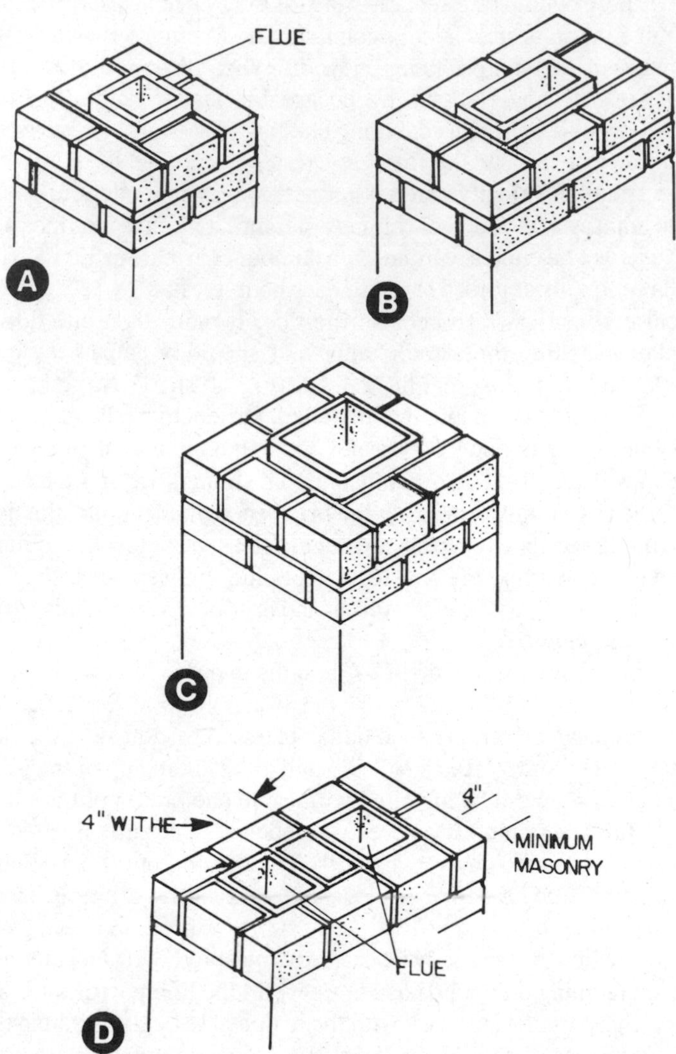

Fig. 4-2. Brick and flue combinations. (A). 8 × 8″ flue lining. (B). 8 × 12″ flue lining. (C). 12 × 12″ flue lining. (D). Two 8 × 8″ flue linings.

cleanout door is generally 8″ × 12″ made of cast iron built into the wall.

The custom of using clay flue linings has now become almost universal. Building codes in many localities require clay flue lining for their fire safety code. It is good construction practice to carry the flue lining 3′ to 4′ above the chimney cap.

CHIMNEY CAP

The brick, stone or other masonry material used to construct the chimney should be capped at the top with mortar or concrete. Concrete is preferred. The cap keeps the weather from penetrating any cracks in the masonry and reduces chimney maintenance. The surface of the cap should slope downward from the flue linings to the outer edges to provide proper drainage.

Sometimes a hood is used to prevent rain and snow from falling down the flue. It serves also as a spark arrester and helps to keep out birds, bats and other flying animals. It helps to eliminate drafts and wind puffs from blowing down the flue. If a hood is constructed, the area of the hood must exceed the area of the flue lining (Fig. 4-3). The chimney top or cap offer design possibilities compatible with the house design. If tops are used, be sure not to reduce the flue area.

No cutting of the flue should be done after the flue is in place. It will probably shatter from the blow and fall out of place. Flue linings are available with openings to receive the smoke pipe

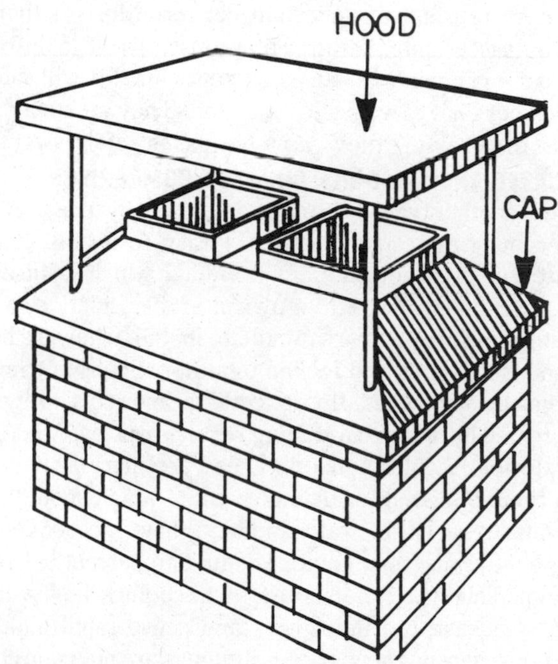

Fig. 4-3. Example of a chimney hood.

connection. If the opening has to be cut, use the method described before the lining is installed. When more than one flue lining is used in the same chimney, extend them to different heights.

The best safeguard against rain and snow from entering the chimney top is to build a solid cap of stone or reinforced concrete. If of stone, bluestone is best about 2″ or 3″ thick; if of concrete, build a slab of concrete about 4″ thick on the ground and place it on top of the chimney after curing. Don't forget to reinforce the concrete with steel rods. In installing the cap, extend the corners of the chimney above the height of the walls about 16″ to 24″, leaving all sides open, and place the cap on the extended corners with mortar. Use wire mesh screening on top of the flue linings to keep out animals.

A good mortar to use in setting flue linings in masonry is 1 part portland cement, 1 part hydrated lime and 6 parts clean sand measured by volume. Enough water should be used to make the mix a working consistency. Smoke test the chimney before connecting any apparatus or lighting any fires. Build a fire of paper, straw or tar paper at the base of the flue and check for smoke leaks while the column of dense smoke is ascending. Block up all leaks immediately.

Chimneys present an uncertain danger. Most of them are concealed or inaccessible. Yet they play a critical role in the overall safety of your equipment. Be sure that your chimney will safely do its job. Chimneys have two basic functions. They create a draft to bring air to the fire, and they carry hot gases safely away.

PREFABRICATED AND MASONRY CHIMNEY COMPARISON

There is another type of chimney other than the masonry type. This is becoming more popular and is easy to install. It is the prefabricated or pre-built chimney of metal which is insulated. Prefabricated chimneys have their own internal insulation and they allow greater flexibility and are simple to install. They are built in sections and are twisted and locked together. Special fittings are sold for going through walls, floors, ceilings and roofs. Only those listed and tested by a national testing service, such as Underwriters Laboratories, should be used. These are more heavily insulated than the type listed for use as "vents" which should not be used as chimneys. Triple wall chimneys have no conventional insulation, but they use an ingenious natural air current to keep the chimney cool. This type is so successful at cooling, however, that it tends to condense the flue gases and cause rapid buildup of creosote. Consquently, these triple chimneys are not good choices for use with wood stoves.

Masonry chimneys are more costly to construct, but they have other benefits that they may outweigh their additional cost against pre-built chimneys. This is one of the reasons why in colonial New England, it was common practice to build houses with large center chimneys. These inside masonry chimneys increase the net efficiency of the heating system by up to 15 percent due to heat "leaking" from the chimney into the house. In addition to being more attractive, masonry chimneys also tend to be more durable because they are more resistant to corrosion and will last the life of the house.

CHIMNEY INSPECTION

Most of us will not be installing a new chimney for our stove; we will be using an old one. Perhaps we can be sure about the safety of a newly installed chimney because we can check it during construction, but we have no such luxury with an old chimney. We have no way of knowing the quality of the initial installation, and it is difficult to check its durability over time. Thes best way is to get the opinion of an expert. Ask the local fire department to make an inspection. Generally they will welcome the chance to advise you of danger spots and avoid a fire alarm call. A competent mason may be able to point out defects, and the local building inspector can advise you about compliance with building codes.

There are also some things you can check for. First look for a flue lining. Not all old chimneys have one, but their proven safety makes them essential. Look up or down the chimney with a flashlight. The flue should look smooth and uniform.

Scrape its surface and you will find that it is much harder than brick. If you do not have a liner, one must be installed in the old chimney or the chimney must be completely rebuilt. The flue tiles are brittle and they sometimes crack. You must be sure that the liner is in good condition. Hot gases and creosote cannot escape the flue prematurely and start a fire. Visually check for cracks; then perform the smoke test described earlier. This will force the smoke through any cracks or holes. Leaks must be repaired or the chimney should not be used. Next, check for loose mortar by scraping between the bricks. If the mortar crumbles easily, you will need to have the bricks repointed and repaired by scraping out the old mortar, removing the damaged bricks and making the repair with new mortar and bricks, a most difficult job.

Following are a list of things not to do:

- Don't use a masonry chimney that is supported by brackets or shelves. Not only is this a building code violation, and a danger, but the brackets may weaken and the entire chimney may fall while in use.
- Don't use a chimney that is used to support a structural part of framing of the house. Heat conducted to the framing may eventually start a fire. For interior chimneys, a full 2″ of clearanace between the chimney and any combustible material is required. An exterior chimney may have contact with exterior siding.
- Don't connect more than one appliance to a single flue. Backdrafts may force carbon monoxide into your home. A fireplace flue may be used for a stove only if the fireplace opening is closed off by a non-combustible material.
- Don't use snap in covers to close unused smoke pipe inlets. A chimney fire can easily pop them out. Fill the hole with masonry or tile built up to the same thickness as the chimney.
- Don't use a chimney whose flue is not at least 25 percent larger than the proper stovepipe for your stove. This will help prevent backdrafts.

The final area for inspection is chimney height. A chimney should extend at least 3′ above flat roofs. On pitched roofs, the chimney should be 2′ higher than any point within 10′ away to prevent downdrafts and fires from sparks. It is a relatively simple task for a mason to extend a chimney that does not meet these minimum safety requirements.

CLEANING CHIMNEYS

Chemical cleaners can be used to break down creosote, but do not rely on these as your sole cleaning method. These are best used frequently before creosote becomes too thick. Eventually every chimney will require manual cleaning. There are commercial chimney sweeps who will do the job for you, but it is simple enough to do it yourself. If you neglect the job now, you probably won't think of it again until trouble starts. You may not have enough time without closing down the heating system to do the job. The wood burning stove has resulted in a rapid growth of the chimney sweeping business. Where you may have had trouble finding one in the past, you may not have trouble finding one now. If this is your choice for getting the chimney cleaned, shop around. Don't look for the best price, but instead look for the best job. Having the job done right in the first place will save you money and trouble later. It may even save your life as well as your home. A bad job will give you a false sense of security. When you find the chimney sweep, find out what is included in the cleaning (Fig. 4-4). A good sweep will climb up on the roof and inspect the chimney inside and out from top to bottom. He should also give you a list descirbing the condition of your chimney after he has finished his job. The National Fire Protection Association recommends cleaning the chimney every year.

A reputable chimney sweep will go on the roof to inspect the chimney. Do not be content with a visual examination from the fireplace upward. Strong lights must be needed to properly inspect the chimney. A flashlight alone will not do the job properly. The flue lining must be inspected from above and below with this light. A good sweep will remove the damper, clean the smoke shelf and replace the damper, trying it to be sure it is in working order. In addition to cleaning the chimney, he should clean all stovepipes, grates, andirons and the firebox as well as the chimney.

Should you decide to do the job yourself, you will need special wire brushes (Fig. 4-5). These brushes come in a variety of sizes to fit your flue lining. Be sure to get the correct size.

If the brush is too small, it won't get to the walls of the lining. If it's too large, it may get stuck in the chimney lining. Know the size of the flue lining before buying the brush. There are several ways to use the brush. Working from below, you may push the brush up using connecting flexible poles attached to the brush. Working from the roof, you may hang a weight, about 25 pounds, from the bottom of the brush which will run it through the lining. From the other end, fasten a strong rope, working the brush back and forth or up and down. If the flue has sharp bends, this method may be difficult and dangerous because the weight might damage the flue lining. This works best on straight flues. If the flue has turns, a better and safer method is to tie ropes to both ends of the brush. With a helper, work the brush up and down by each person pulling on the rope.

If you have a stove, take it apart, including the stovepipe. Carry it outdoors and clean each part with an ordinary wire brush. If the parts of the stove look worn or burned out, replace them. While up on the roof, check the flashing around the seal and the chimney cap. Repair the cracks immediately; otherwise they will get worse. While there, check the brick joints. Remove the damper plate and

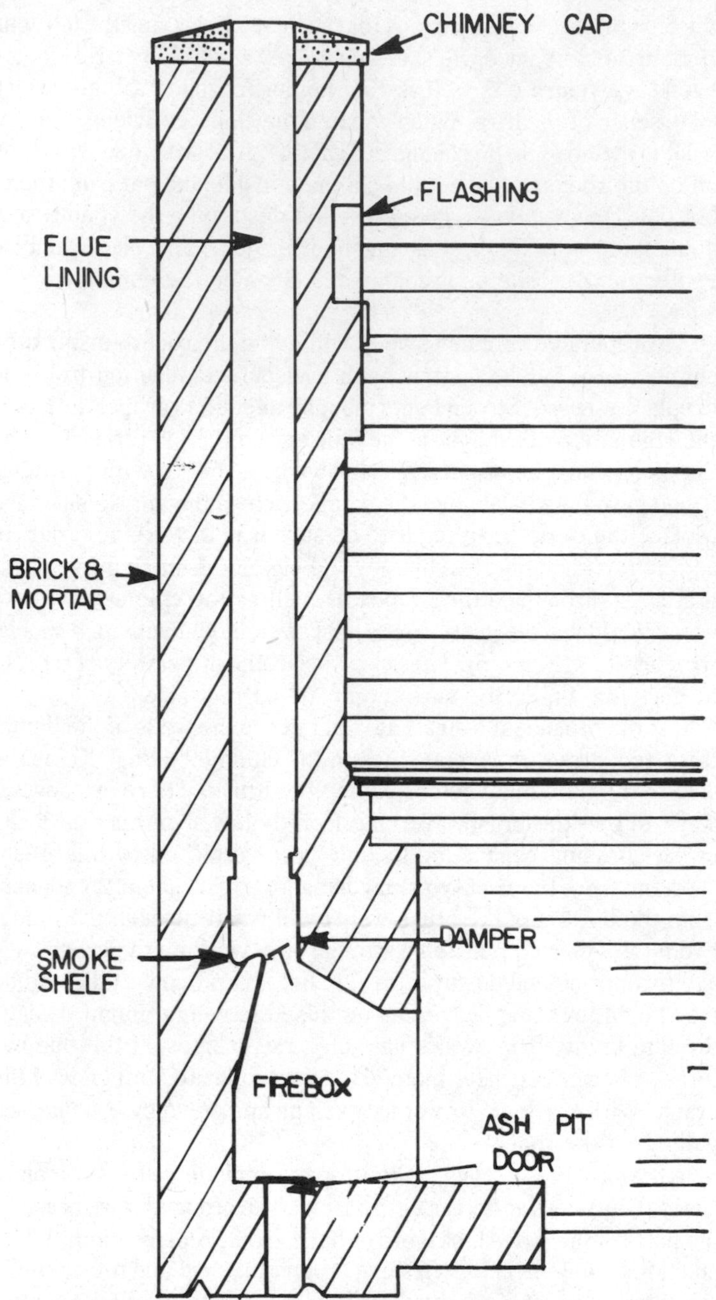

Fig. 4-4. Areas of a chimney requiring inspection.

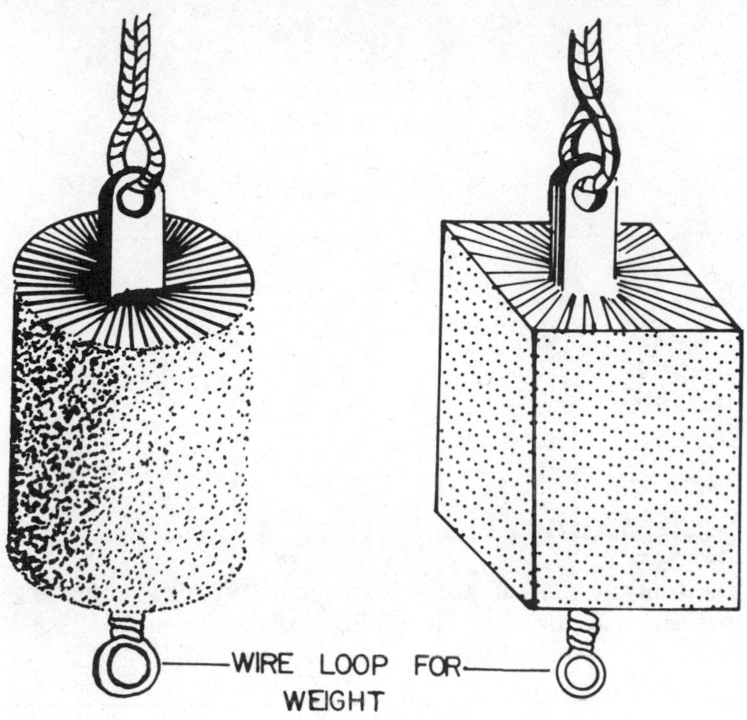

Fig. 4-5. Flue cleaning brushes.

(normally held by a pin or bolt) sweep debris off the smoke shelf. When you remove the damper plate, debris will fall. Work carefully to avoid any undue mess and wear safety glasses and a dust mask. Look at the debris carefully for chunks of broken lining or brick. If you see anything unusual, it may mean further repairs. Don't be alarmed if you see chunks of dried mortar. This was probably caused by the mason spilling mortar during construction of the chimney. Do not vacuum this debris, pick it up and put it in a disposable bag.

5

Scaffolding

Two separate elements are separated into scaffolding; supporting members and platforms. The former may consist either of wood construction or of built up sectional steel tubing, while the platform or staging is generally 2″ × 10″ wood planking for all types.

During the past decade, tubular steel sections have been extensively used for exterior and interior scaffolding. They are especially practical for construction where the fire hazard from flammable scaffolding must be processed with chemicals to render it fire resistant.

TYPES OF SCAFFOLDS

The various types of scaffold generally used for masonry work include the following:

- **Horse Scaffolds**. These consist of trestles of horses generally 4 to 5′ high and approximately 4′ long. Plank platform or staging supported by the horses are not less than 2″ thick.
- **Single Pole Scaffolds**. A single row of posts or uprights set not to exceed 5′ from the wall and spaced out not more than 7′ apart. Minimum post sizes are in Table 5-1.

  All posts should be thoroughly braced diagonally and connected horizontally with stringer and ledger members. Logs, nominal size 4″ × 4″, to carry the plank platform are supported on a ledger at the outer end, and in

Table 5-1. Minimum Post Sizes.

Minimum Post Sizes	
Height	Size
Up to 24 feet	3″ x 4″
24 to 40 feet	4″ x 4″
Over 40 feet	4″ x 6″

a wall recess on the inside. At the completion of the wall the recesses are filled in as the scaffolding is removed.

- **Built-Up Scaffolds**. These consist of a double row of posts or uprights—the inner row set as near the wall as practical. Minimum post sizes, allowable heights and longitudinal spacing are similar to the requirements for single pole scaffolds.
- **Suspended Scaffolds**. These are generally recommended for walls more than five stories high. These are constructed of structural steel skeleton framing.
- **Swinging Scaffolds**. Consisting of a platform at least 30″ wide, these are suspended with steel wire cables from overhead steel beam outriggers. The platform may be raised or lowered by means of a windlass.
- **Square Scaffolds**. Framed wood squares or jacks are used in supporting a plank platform in a manner similar to horses or testle scaffolding.
- **Tubular Pole Scaffolds**. Recommended for heights up to 200 ′, these are made from galvanized steel tubing fastened together with steel couples or other approved locking devices.

TEMPORARY STAGING

As the construction of the chimney rises above reach, a temporary scaffold or staging must be built. Several types may be built, borrowed or rented. Portable metal scaffolds may be rented and easily assembled, made up of prefabricated frames and crossbracing. A safety factor of not less than four times the load is required. Use extreme care in erections to be certain the base is on firm ground, level and plumb.

Other metal scaffolding supports are wedged in place where bricks have been left out. When the staging is dismantled the left out brick is installed. This type is called a single pole scaffold. As the construction work of the chimney rises above ground level, scaffolding must be built or installed. Although they are only temporary structures, they must be designed to carry the load of men and material and provide maximum safety. Several kinds of scaffold are available or can be built, depending on the height of the chimney. In addition, safety codes in localities must be met. Rented or leased prefabricated metal frame type scaffold offer the best type (Fig. 5-1). These are portable and can be safely, easily and quickly assembed to almost any height.

Care must be used in erecting the scaffold so that it rests firmly on a base and is kept plumb and level. Wood scaffolds are also generally used and built as a temporary structure following the same safety rules. Scaffolds are generally classified as light trade pole and used by carpenters, painters and others. The heavy trade scaffold is used by tradesmen who use heavy loads or material such as brick. Light trade scaffolds must be designed to carry a working load of at least 25 pounds per square foot, and heavy trade scaffolds must support a load of at least 75 pounds per square foot.

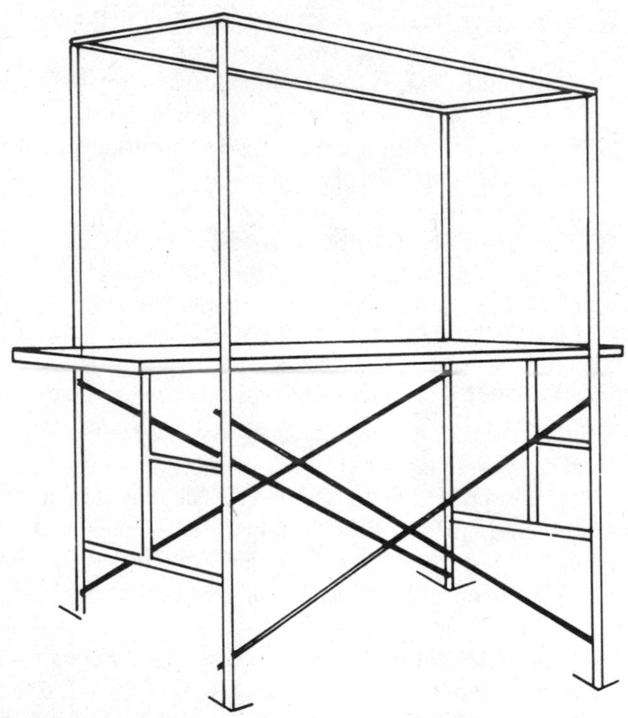

Fig. 5-1. A portable scaffold.

SAFETY PRACTICES

A double pole scaffold is a free standing unit with four legs. The working platform of the scaffold should be of 2″ plank laid tightly together and not less than two planks wide (16″ to 24″). The ends overhanging the scaffold should not be more than 6″. Regardless of the type of scaffolding used, it should be kept at a distance of 3″ to 4″ away from the wall to prevent bumping or damaging the wall. It is important that scaffolds be assembled or built before work is begun. They should be secured and anchored every 20′ in height to prevent toppling toward or away from the wall. This is easily done on most structures. Whenever scaffolding cannot be secured to an adjacent structure, it must not exceed three or four times the narrowest base dimensions of the scaffold, unless secured by guy wires. One set of guy wires should be placed at the four corners. Following are safe scaffolding practices which should be studied for safety:

—All lumber used in scaffolds should be of good quality, reasonably straight grained and free from weakening knots and other defects.

—Be sure the scaffold is built or assembled using the principals of design and safe loads which various members can carry.

—Special lumber for scaffold use should be painted green on the end so it can be distinguished from other miscellaneous lumber.

—Scaffold bracing should always be installed in triangular fashion.

—When it becomes necessary to extend the scaffold upright, cleats not less than 4′ long should be nailed on two adjacent sides of the upright at the joint.

—Planks for flooring should be of uniform thickness. They should extend at least 6″ and not more than 12″ past the center of the next support.

—Scaffolds more than 6′ above ground should have substantial handrails and toe boards installed approximately 42″ high and toe boards not less than 5½″ high. If the lower edge of the railing is more than 34″ above the scaffold floor, an intermediate rail should be installed.

—Install a wire screen of not more than ⅜″ mesh between the top railing and the toeboard.

—If work is carried on above the men on a lower level, the scaffold should have overhead protection or a roof of light construction, heavy canvas or heavy wire mesh.

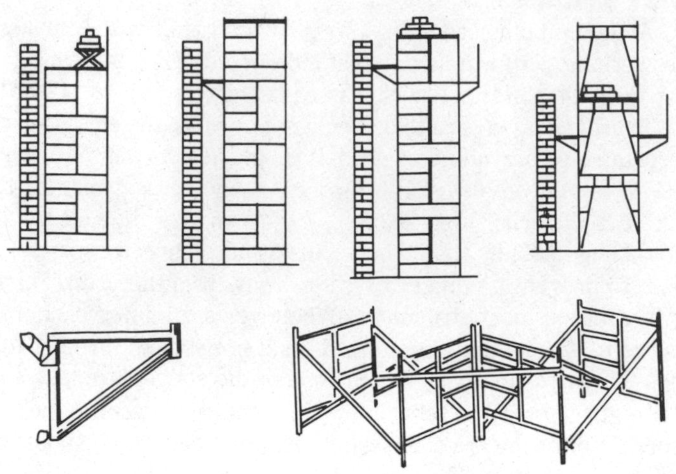

Fig. 5-2. Panel arrangement and platform extenders of scaffolding.

—Do not work on a scaffold outside during a storm or high wind.

—Clean scaffolds of all rubbish, tools, buckets, etc., at the end of each day's work. They should not be left on any scaffold when workers leave the job. In winter, snow and ice should be removed from the scaffold before work is started. The platform may be sprinkled with sand or ashes to prevent slipping.

—One or more safe means of access such as stairs or ladders should be provided to reach each level of the scaffold. If a ladder is used, it should be fastened at the top and bottom so it cannot tip or slip.

—Scaffold members should be fenced in or otherwise protected so vehicles cannot strike or dump material against them.

—Hoisting engineers should be warned not to allow swing loads to strike or catch the scaffold.

—Do not jump or allow anything to fall on the scaffold.

—Do not pass under a scaffold.

—Follow local load codes in constructing scaffolding.

—Provide adequate pads or sills under scaffold posts.

—Plumb and level each section or platform.

—Guard against power lines. Consult local power service company if power lines interfere.

—Never use boxes or any unstable base to gain additional height (Fig. 5-2).

6

Pre-Built Units

Prefabricated metal fireplaces are becoming more popular in a greater number of sizes, dimension and shapes. Some are wall-mounted and some are free-standing. Don't confuse these models with the metal firebox type. The metal firebox type takes the place of firebrick and requires walls to be built around it. The prefabricated type is packaged and need only to be installed ready for use. No masonry work is necessary. It is ideal for summer cottages or basements.

There are several types of preformed steel fireplaces on the market. The include the combustion chamber, damper and smoke chamber. You can set one on the hearth and build the walls around it (Fig. 6-1 and Tables 6-1, 6-2 and 6-3).

Metal firebox liners of one piece steel include the combustion chamber, smoke dome and also, in instances, the angle or lintel which supports the face brick. No fire brick is necessary with these self contained units. Merely set the steel box on a masonry hearth and enclose it with brick and stone (Fig. 6-2).

Pre-built self-contained units should have a nationally recognized testing laboratory label. Usually they consist of a fire chamber, a roof assembly and one or more chimney sections. Be sure to follow manufacturers' recommendations for installation (Fig. 6-3).

The chimney sections should be installed to provide the required clearance from combustible materials. Sections which ex-

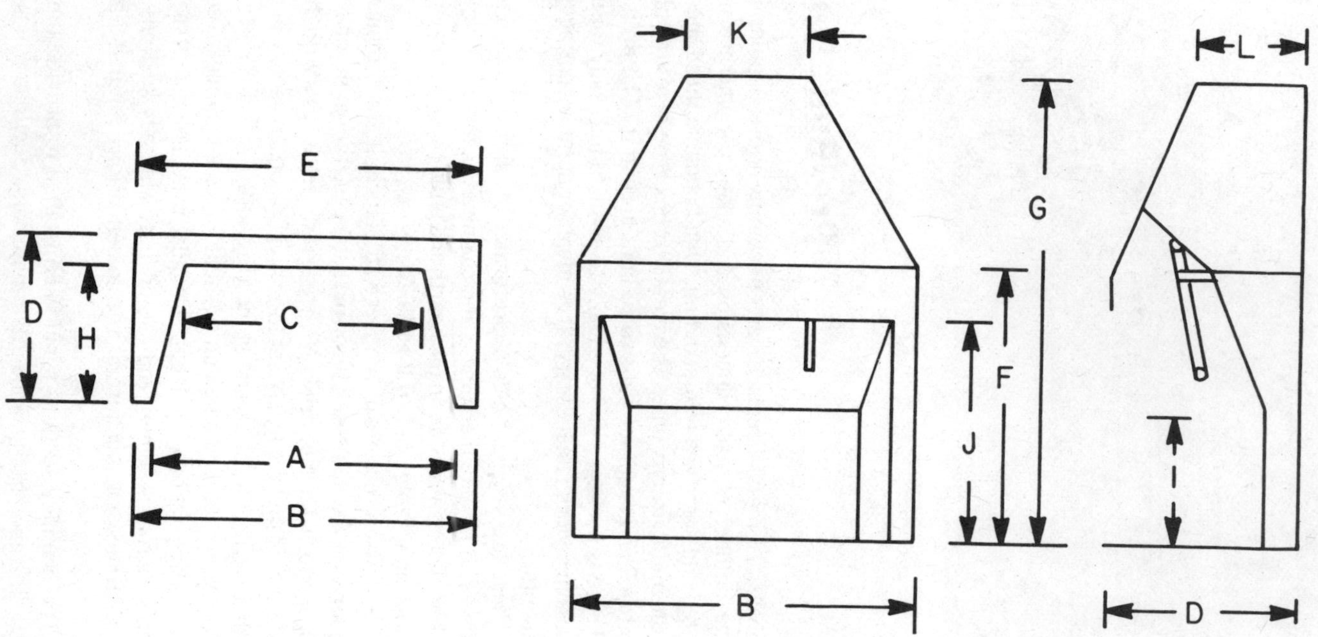

Fig. 6-1. Units of a circulator fireplace. See Table 1-1 for unit dimensions.

Table 6-1. Unit Sizes (courtesy of Vestal Manufacturing).

Finished Opening		Fuel Capacity	Shipping Weight
Width	Height		
28″	24″	Up to 24″	195
32″	26″	Up to 28″	237
36″	28″	Up to 32″	275
40″	30″	Up to 36″	335
48″	32″	Up to 42″	420

Table 6-2. Unit Dimensions in Inches (courtesy of Vestal Manufacturing).

A	B	C	D	E	F	G	H	I	J	K	L
30	34	22-1/4	18-1/2	34	30	46-1/4	15-1/4	14	25	11-3/4	7-3/4
34	38	24-1/4	19-3/4	38	32	49-3/4	16-1/2	14	27	11-1/2	11-1/2
38	42	28-1/4	21-1/4	42	35	53-3/4	17-1/2	16	29-1/4	11-1/2	11-1/2
42	47	31-1/4	23-1/4	47	38	58-1/4	19-1/4	16	32	16-1/2	11-1/2
50	56	39-1/4	25-1/4	56	40-1/4	62-3/4	20-1/4	17	34	16-1/2	11-1/2

Table 6-3. Chimney Flue Sizes (courtesy of Vestal Manufacturing).

For Chimneys over 20′ High			For Chimneys 16′ to 20′ High		
Standard Flue	Modular Flue	Round Flue	Standard Flue	Modular Flue	Round Flue
8-1/2 x 13″	12″ x 12″	10″	8-1/2″ x 13″	12″ x 12″	10″
8-1/2″ x 13″	12″ x 12″	10″	13″ x 13″	12″ x 16″	12″
13″ x 13″	12″ x 16″	12″	13″ x 13″	12″ x 16″	12″
13″ x 13″	12″ x 16″	12″	13″ x 13″	16″ x 16″	15″
13″ x 18″	16″ x 16″	15″	13″ x 18″	16″ x 20″	15″

Outside dimensions shown for standard and modular flues—inside dimensions for round flues. Chimney height is measured from hearth.
NOTE: Dimensions shown are actual measurements. Be sure to allow 1/2″ to 1″ space for glass wool insulation for heat expansion between all points of the Circulator and the masonry.

tend through floors, walls and roof are to be enclosed to avoid contact with combustible material and damage to the chimney.

Hearth extension should project at least 18″ in front of and at least 8″ beyond the sides of the fireplace opening. It should be built of fireproof material.

The heating capacity of a factory built firebox is increased because the construction consists of double walls within which the

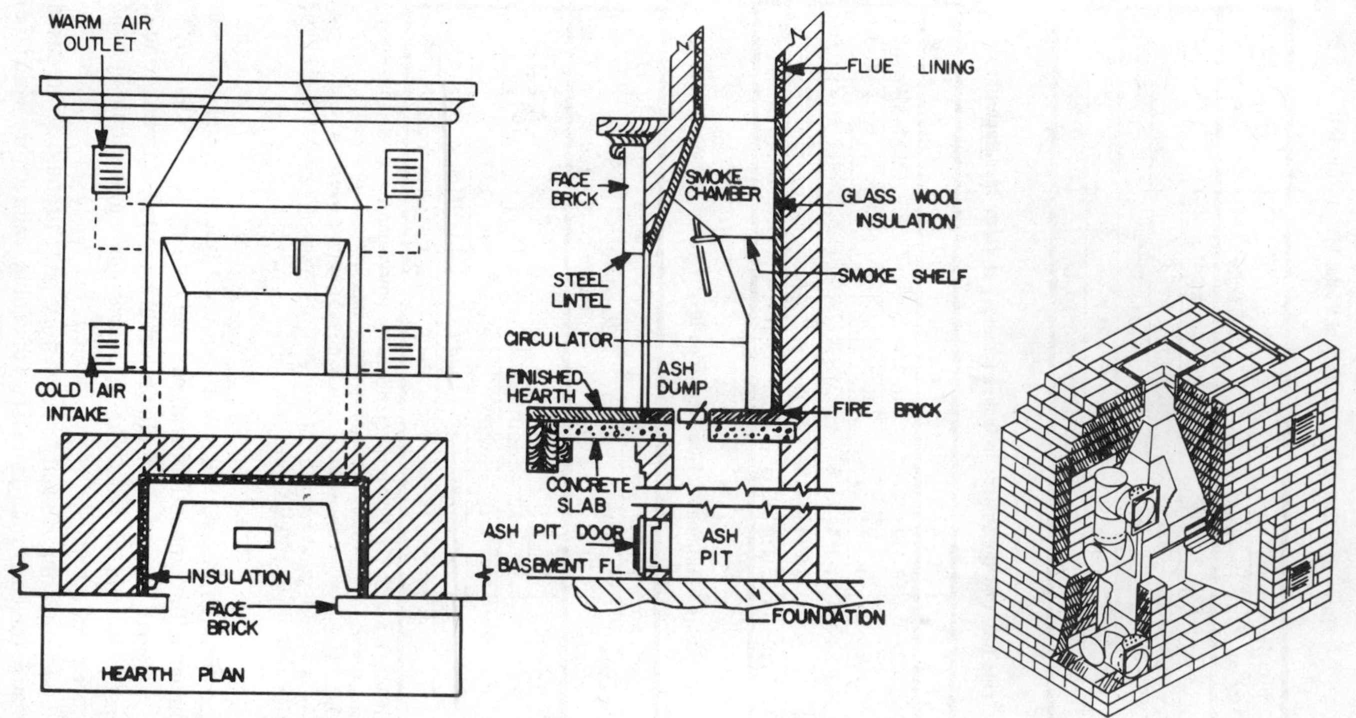

Fig. 6-2. A typical construction detail.

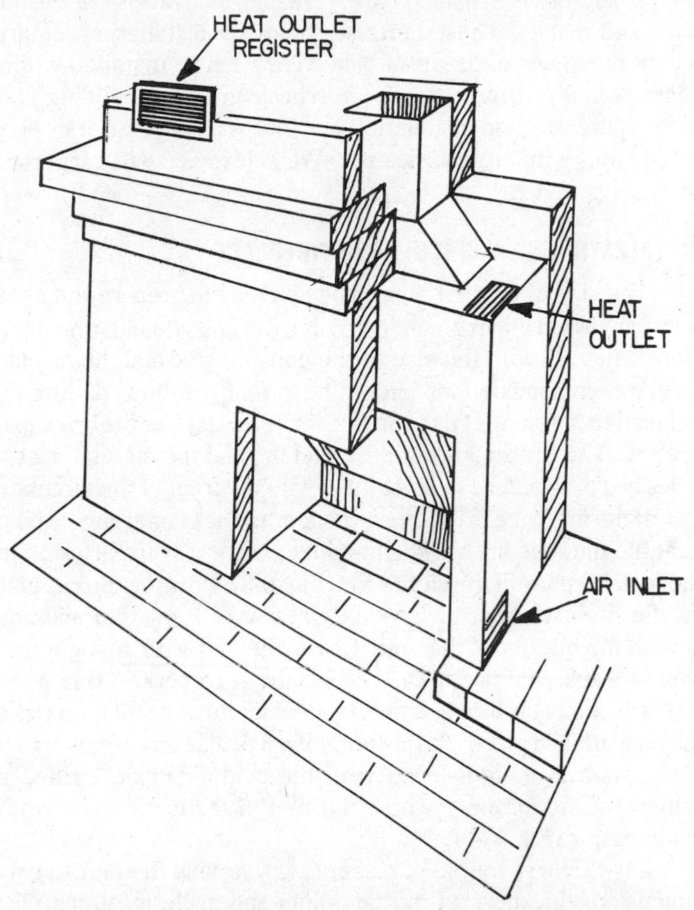

Fig. 6-3. A modified fireplace. Air is drawn through inlet A from the room being heated. It is heated by contact with the metal sides and back of the fireplace, rises and is discharged through outlet B. Inlets and outlets are connected to registers which may be located at the front or ends of the fireplace or on the wall of an adjacent or second-story room.

the air is heated. Cold air enters the space at the bottom and pushes the hot air out the top, repeating the cycle.

To install, simply place the unit in position and build the walls around it on the outside. The unit should not be used to support any brick or masonry. Follow manufacturers' installation recommendations. Some models will require insulating material placed around the unit.

Ready made fireplaces are available in a variety of designs, sizes and shapes. These units are ready for installation requiring only a chimney and fireproof base. They can be installed within a short period of time. Be sure to check the local building codes before purchase and installation and follow manufacturers' recommendations without modification. Wall clearance will vary from 5′ to 3′ (Figs. 6-4 through 6-7).

INSTALLATION OF A CIRCULATOR FIREPLACE

The size of the unit should be selected to prepare the necessary foundation dimensions to receive the unit. Foundation dimensions will vary with the size of the unit selected and the manufacturer's recommendations should be carefully followed. After the foundation is completed to the firebox level, lay the firebrick in the firebox. The firebrick should extend beyond the circulator at the sides and back and be at least flush with the front of the circulator.

If the fireplace is to have an ashpit, the ash dump should be put in at the time the firebrick is installed. Do not lay firebrick up into the metal firebox of the circulator (Fig. 6-8). Position the circulator on the firebrick hearth. Unpack glass wool insulation and apply around the bottom of the unit. Cover the unit with a single thickness of insulation, taking care especially at corners. A thin watery mixture of mortar brushed on the steel circulator will help to hold the insulation in place. At this point if particular care is given to the glass wool insulation, location of the cold air intake grille, and gauging of the masonry work, the rest of the installation will be made easier (Fig. 6-9).

Lay the first course of masonry dry around the unit to check dimension, thickness of mortar joints and grille locations. Take care to prevent the masonry from touching the unit at any point. The finished width of the fireplace opening should be about 1″ or 2″ less than the width on each side of the circulator opening, making a concealed joint between the circulator and the masonry. Due to heat expansion, mortar will not stay in this concealed joint. See Fig. 6-10

Plan the location of the cold air intake grilles. Air must not pass directly from the cold air inlet to the hot air inlet. The air must be circulated through the unit. Air passages should be finished smoothly to speed air flow and prevent heat loss. Sometimes it is desirable to locate grilles beyond the chimney masonry; if such is the case, use sheet metal ducts for the inlet and insulated sheet metal ducts for the warm air outlet. If electric fan grilles are to be

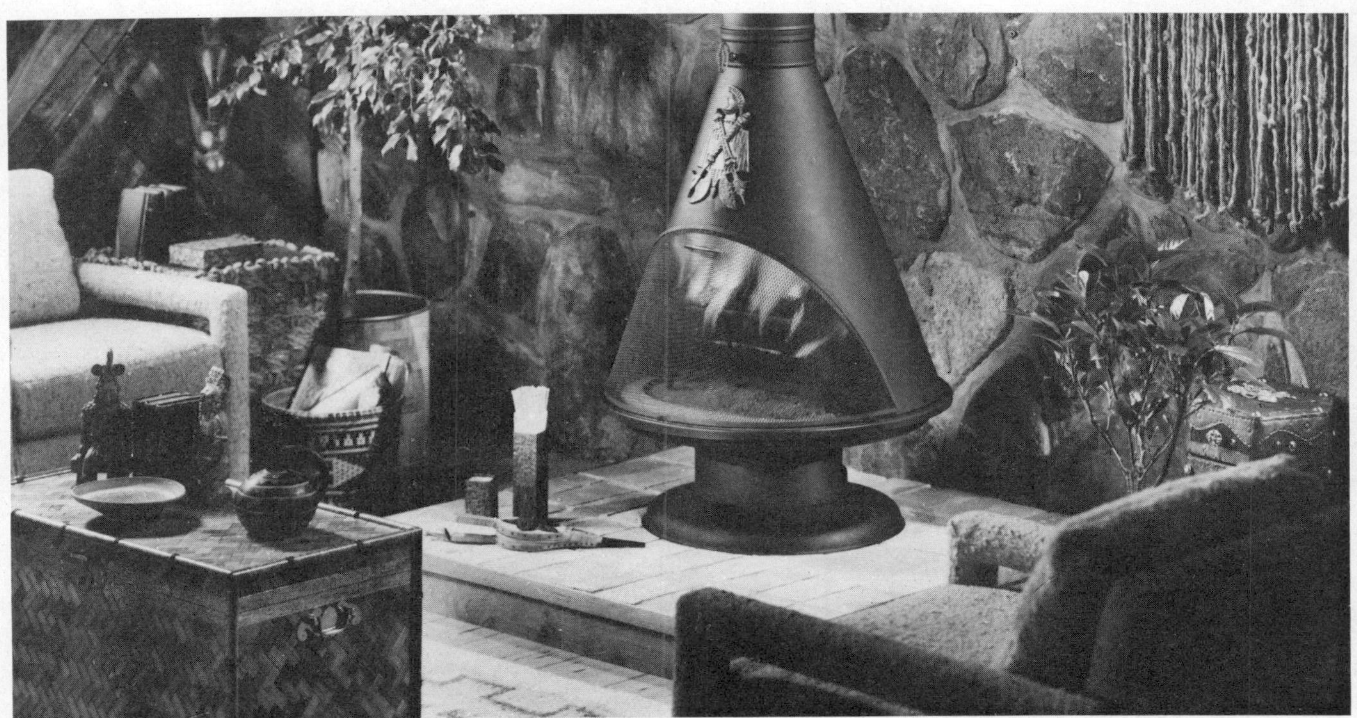

Fig. 6-4. Pre-built units come in all kinds of sizes and shapes (courtesy of Metalbestos Systems).

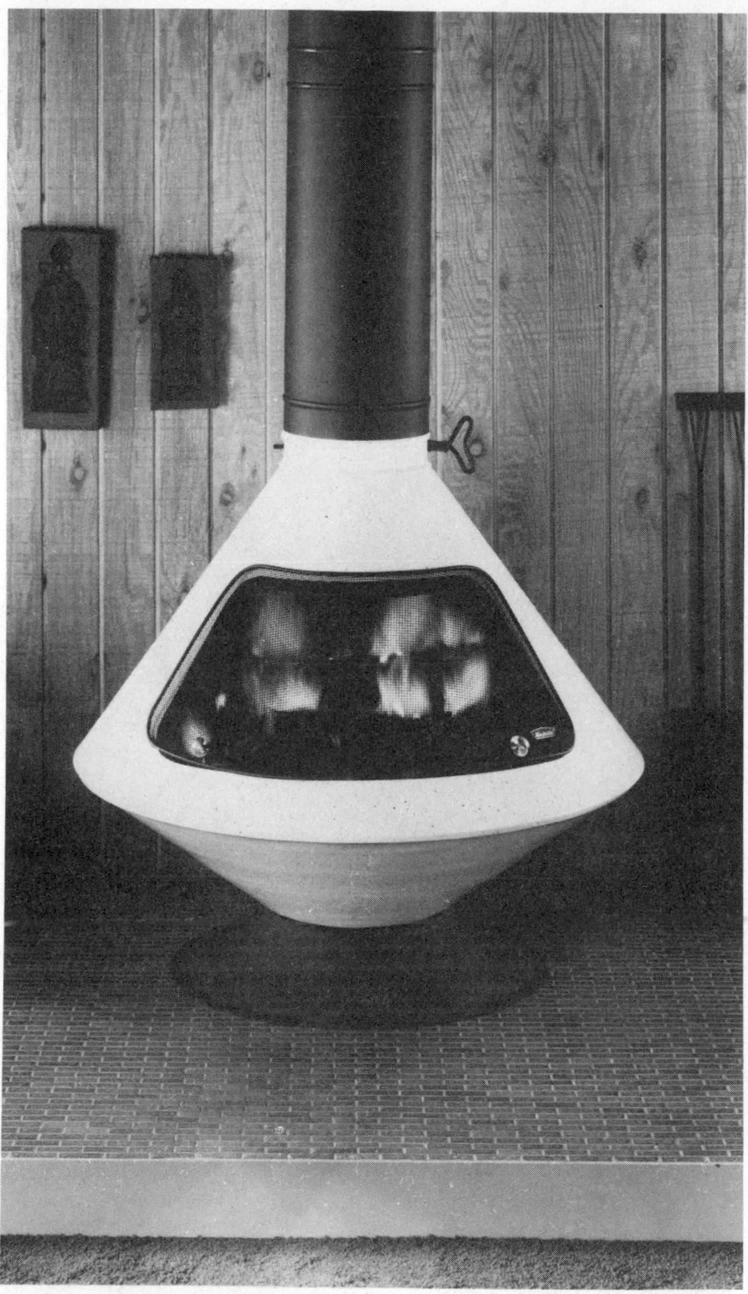

Fig. 6-5. This unit requires a chimney and fireproof base (courtesy of Majestic Company).

Fig. 6-6. Follow manufacturers' instructions when installing pre-built units (courtesy of Martin Industries).

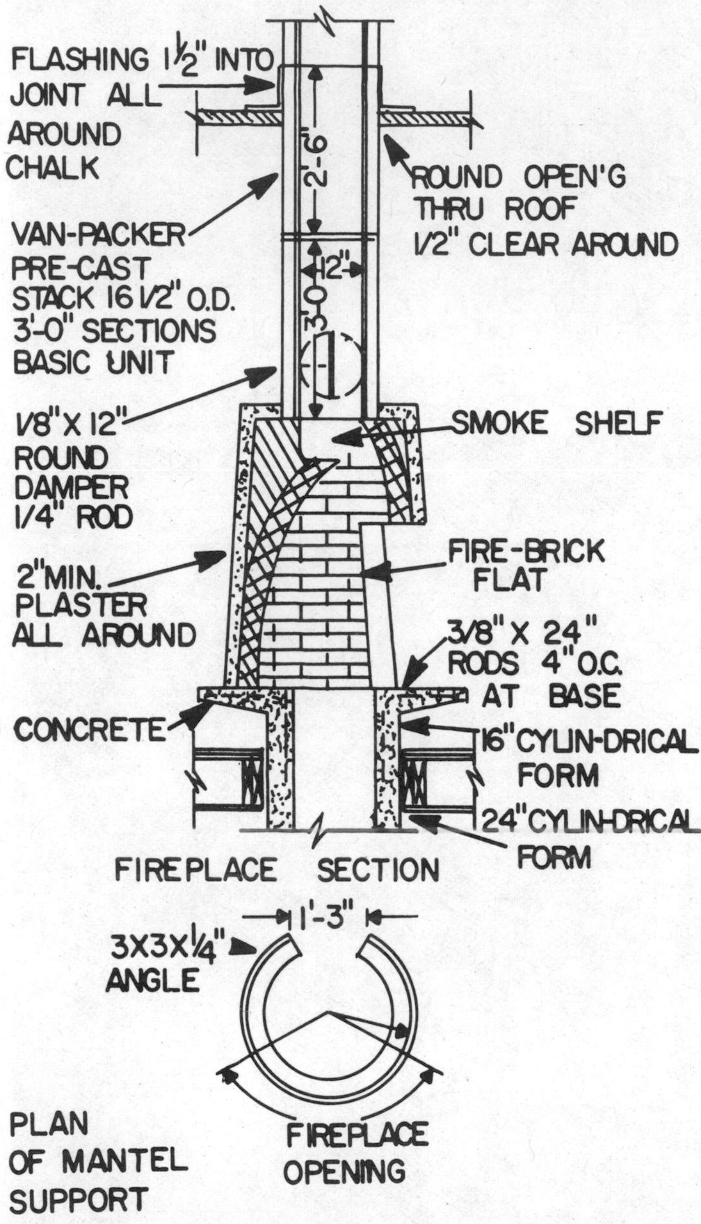

Fig. 6-7. Semicircular fireplace with cast cylindrical foundation.

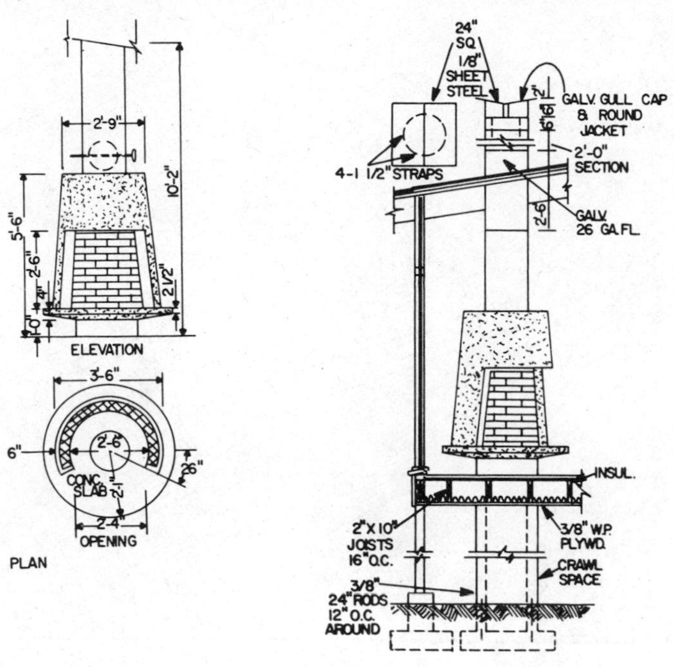

Fig. 6-7. Semicircular fireplace with cast cylindrical foundation (continued from page 210).

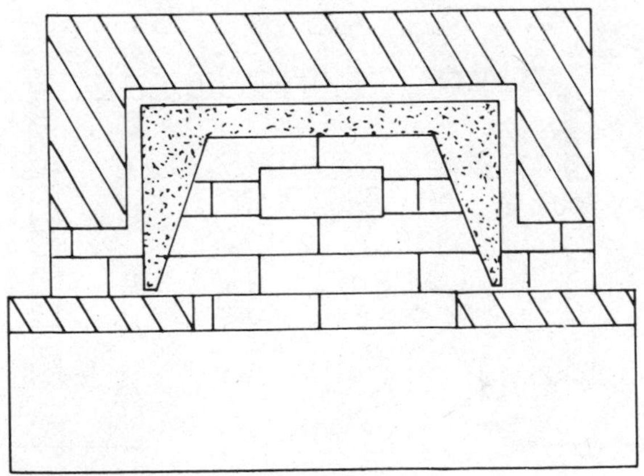

Fig. 6-8. Hearth plan at floor level.

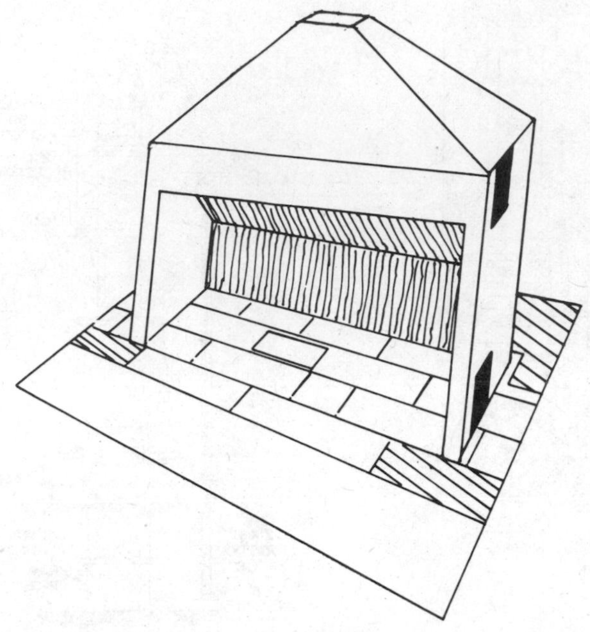

Fig. 6-9. Circular unit in position.

used in the circulator, and the power line to the fan is concealed, it may be desirable to locate the conduit and junction box in the masonry. When fans are used, two fans—one located in each cold

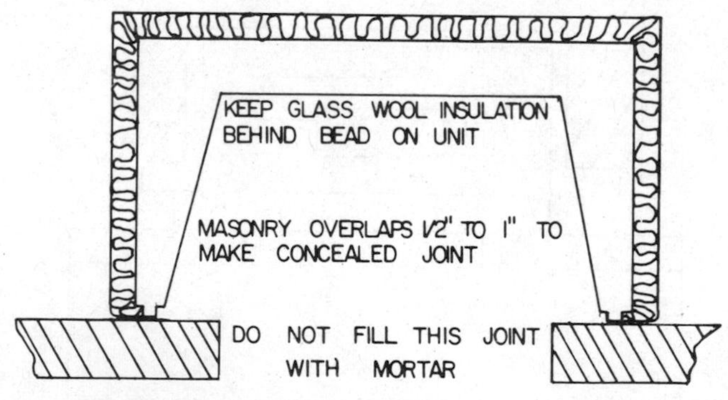
KEEP GLASS WOOL INSULATION
BEHIND BEAD ON UNIT
MASONRY OVERLAPS 1/2" TO 1" TO
MAKE CONCEALED JOINT
DO NOT FILL THIS JOINT
WITH MORTAR

Fig. 6-10. Insulation and concealed joint.

air intake—are needed. Never locate the fans in the warm air outlet. Set the cold air intake grilles in place. Do not remove the top grille face until the boxes are installed in the masonry. This assures a neat and level fit and protects the grilles.

After dimensions are checked and the location of the grille and thickness of the mortar joints are determined, the dry course of masonry can be taken up and laid permanently with mortar. See Fig. 6-11. With this start, proceed with the masonry in the regular way. Keep in mind the following:

- Glass wool insulation goes around the circular unit.
- The concealed joint is at the fireplace opening.
- The cold air intake and warm air outlets must be planned for and located in the masonry and must be separated by masonry or ducts.
- All weight of the chimney must be supported by the masonry and not the circulator unit.

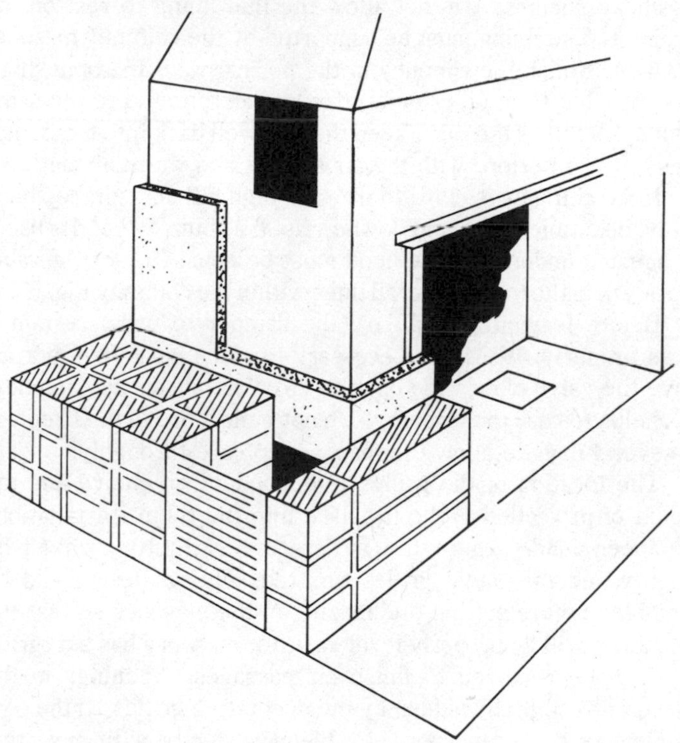

Fig. 6-11. Starting brick work and locating grilles.

- When the top of the fireplace is reached, use a steel angle (lintel) of adequate strength to support the masonry work above the unit. Set the lintel low enough to conceal the metal apron of the circulator unit. Pack loosely generous quantities of insulation behind and at the end of the lintel. See Fig. 6-12.

Plan the location of the warm air outlet grille in the same manner as the cold air intake. If the warm air outlets are extended any distance beyond the masonry, the duct work should be insulated. Air outlets and inlets may be located in so many different positions that it is beyond the scope of these instructions to cover specific details Fig. 6-13. When the face of the fireplace has been built up to the desired height, start corbeling the masonry back to meet the dome of the smoke chamber and the flue lining. Be sure the smoke chamber is covered with insulation. See that tight connections are made to the flue linings and that plenty of insulation is packed loosely around the place where the flue lining meets the smoke chamber. Do not allow the flue lining to rest on the circulator. The lining must be supported by the chimney masonry Fig. 6-14. Finish the chimney in the normal way. In some chimneys, the flue from other units may be incorporated in the same chimney. If this is the case, keep the flue well back into the corner so as not to interfere with the air intakes and warm air outlets.

If the chimney is close to trees or high hills, a chimney hood may be desirable to prevent downdrafts. If a chimney hood is used, the opening underneath the hood must be equal to, or preferably greater, than the total area of all flues within the chimney Fig. 6-15.

Before leaving the job, try the damper to make certain it works properly. It may be necessary to clean out fallen mortar. Leave the valve plate wide open to circulate air up the chimney. This helps to cure the masonry. Do not build a fire in the fireplace for several days to allow the masonry to cure throughly.

The location of the grilles is dependent on choice and the amount of projection of the fireplace into the room. Installations have been made where the outlets are skillfully masked by masonry and the metal grilles omitted. The grilles should be assembled before setting the housing in the masonry so that the grille faces will be properly leveled. After masonry has set, grille faces can be removed to finish air passages. Openings in the masonry are skillfully hidden by the decorative grilles on the cool air inlets of the fireplace. They blend perfectly with any style mantel and can be painted to match the surrounding walls or

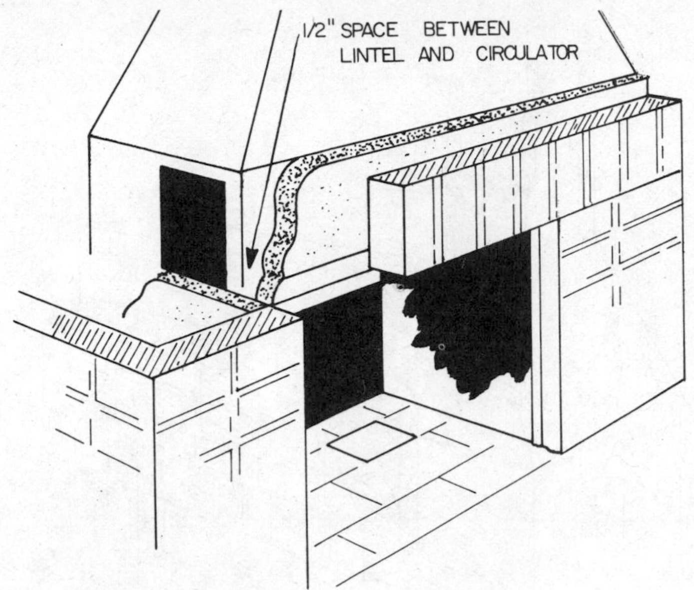

Fig. 6-12. Setting the lintel.

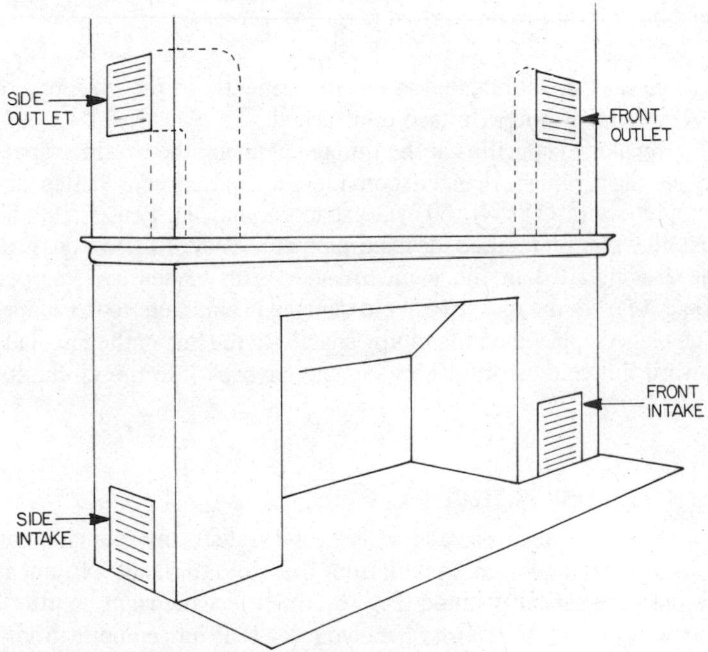

Fig. 6-13. Air outlets may be above the mantel.

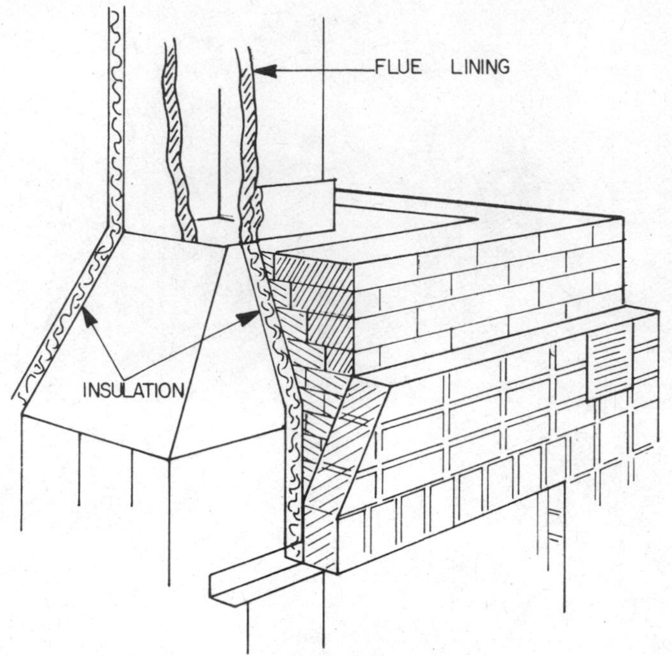

Fig. 6-14. Brick should be corbeled to support a chimney.

masonry. A metal housing is set permanently in the masonry or wall to which the grille face is attached.

By using fan grilles at the intake openings, the heating capacity of the fireplace can be considerably increased. Grilles are complete with 115 volt, 60 cycle ac motor and fan. Fans should be installed at both intakes for maximum efficiency. Electric fan grilles are installed in the same manner. Fan blades are shipped separate from the motor to avoid damage in shipment to the blade. The blade is placed on the motor shaft with the hub of the fan blade toward the cold air inlet blowing the air back into the circulator unit.

PLAN OUT YOUR PROJECT

A new fireplace can add warmth and style to any room in your home. For the average installation, it is not a difficult job, but it should be carefully planned (Fig. 6-16). Select the right position. Choose a place in the room where you won't run into complications. Make sure ceiling rafters or wall studs will not interfere at the point you plan to run the chimney. The required distance of placement of a fireplace from combustible materials varies by type.

Check the fireplace installation instructions before positioning the unit. Wherever the chimney passes through walls, ceilings or roofs, it should be an insulated steel chimney that meets local building code approvals. The selected chimney diameter size should be the same size or larger than the fireplace smoke outlet regardless of the fuel used. Even if you plan to use a gas log burner, the chimney must be the same size as the fireplace outlet to avoid invisible smoke pollution. Once the position of the unit has been decided, the chimney installation will require cutting through the ceiling, wall or and roof. Do not use a gas vent (type B)) flue with a woodburning fireplace, even if you plan to install a gas log burner.

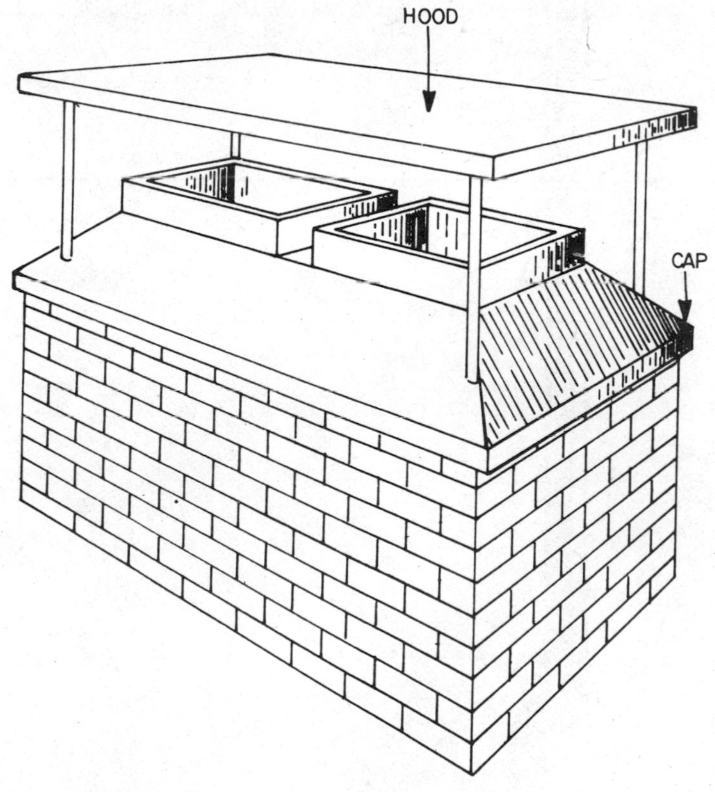

Fig. 6-15. Chimney may be hooded if desired.

FACTORY-BUILT CHIMNEYS

If there is no existing chimney that can be used for adding a unit, a pre-built or factory built chimney may be used. These units are made of metal, insulated, built in short lengths and fastened

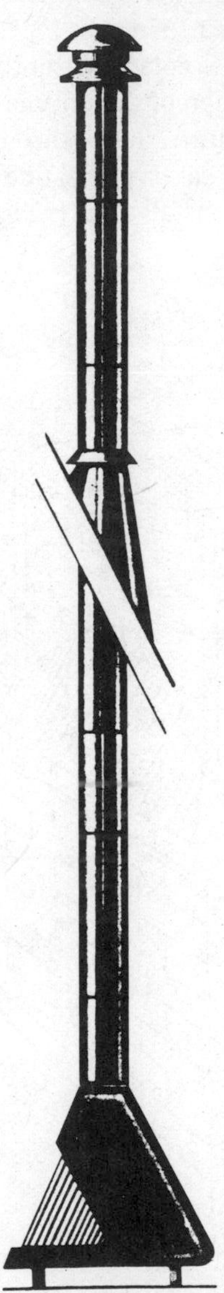

Fig. 6-16. Plan your project carefully (courtesy of Metalbestos Systems).

together. They are efficient and easy to install. Soot and creosote buildups are minimized because of rapid warming of the inner surface. This is a safety factor and reduces the possibility of danger. The minimum clearances are labeled on the units. A factory-built chimney can also be used where existing chimneys are below standard (Figs. 6-17 through 6-20).

A factory-built chimney is permitted to pass through floors if it has an approved continuous enclosure, having a fire rating of at least one hour and two hours, for four or more stories high. Most fireplace chimneys, other than masonry types, are usually supported by the building framing. This is normally done in one of the following ways.

Flat Ceiling

With a flat, joist type ceiling, simply cut and frame an opening in the ceiling and then fasten the ceiling support member (Fig. 6-21). This unit will support sections of the insulated chimney above. The wall smokepipe from the fireplace is inserted into the bottom of the support. This support also has a decorative finish plate to cover the hole in the ceiling.

Side Wall

In venting the fireplace through a side wall, an insulated tee and wall support kit can be used to support the chimney that runs up an outside wall (Fig. 6-22). Wall bands placed every 8′ will stabilize the chimney sections along the wall.

Cathedral Ceiling

With a cathedral or open beam type ceiling, the weight of the chimney can rest on the roof and be suported by a roof support assembly (Fig. 6-23). A maximum of 20′ of insulated chimney can be carried by this unit. A segmented black trim collar can be used to cover the irregular opening at the ceiling. The single wall smokepipe from the fireplace inserts into a finishing collar mounted on the bottom of the insulated pipe. The single wall smokepipe usually supplied with the fireplace must remain at least 18″ away from any combustible material in the room and cannot be enclosed. Whenever the chimney has to pass through occupied areas of a building, it must be enclosed. If it must be placed closer than 18″ to a combustible wall, use the insulated pipe. It can then be enclosed safely in wooden paneling at only 2″ of space between the wood and the chimney.

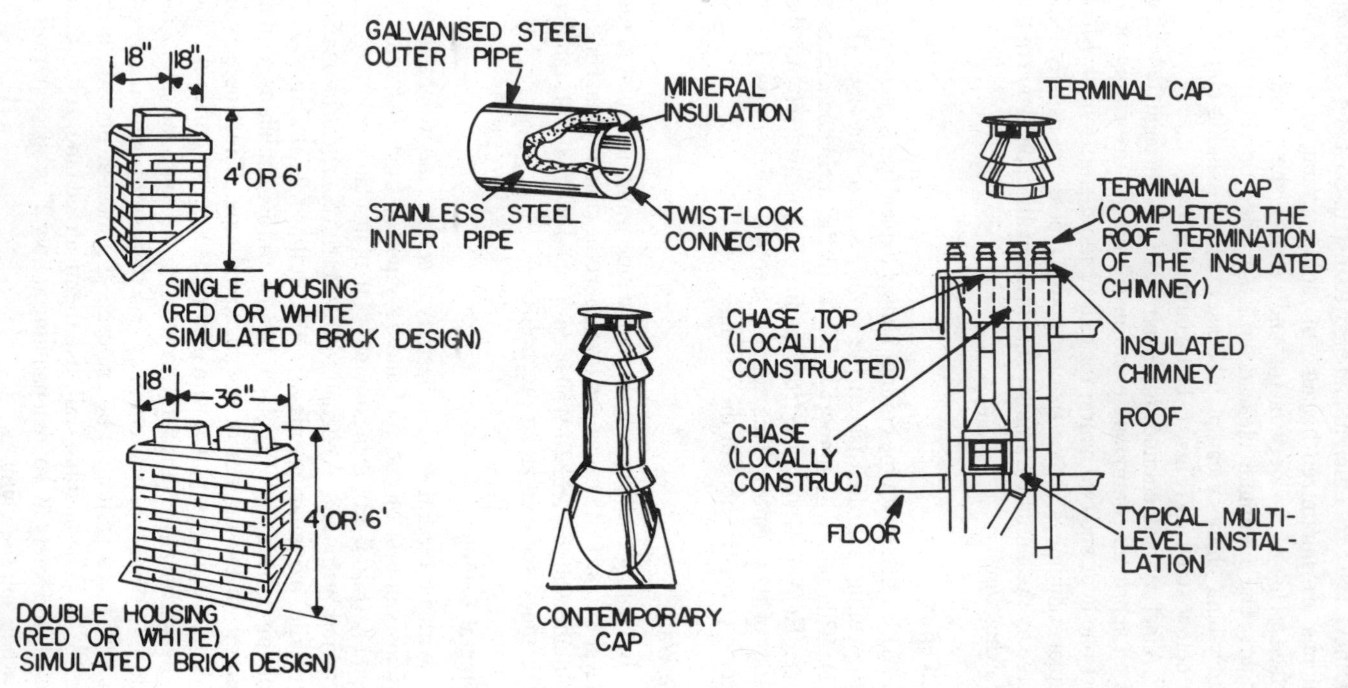
18"
18"
4' OR 6'
SINGLE HOUSING
(RED OR WHITE
SIMULATED BRICK DESIGN)
18"
36"
4' OR 6'
DOUBLE HOUSING
(RED OR WHITE)
SIMULATED BRICK DESIGN)
GALVANISED STEEL
OUTER PIPE
MINERAL
INSULATION
STAINLESS STEEL
INNER PIPE
TWIST-LOCK
CONNECTOR
CONTEMPORARY
CAP
TERMINAL CAP
TERMINAL CAP
(COMPLETES THE
ROOF TERMINATION
OF THE INSULATED
CHIMNEY)
CHASE TOP
(LOCALLY
CONSTRUCTED)
INSULATED
CHIMNEY
ROOF
CHASE
(LOCALLY
CONSTRUC.)
FLOOR
TYPICAL MULTI-
LEVEL INSTAL-
LATION

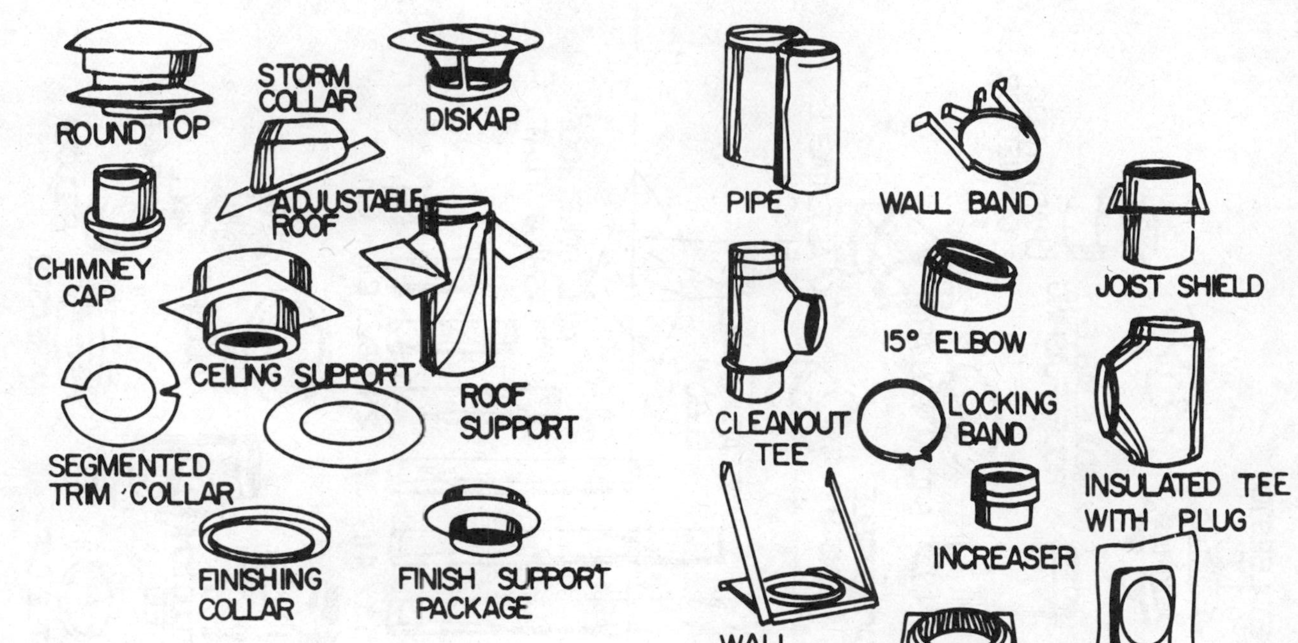

Fig. 6-17. Parts and accessories for a metal chimney.

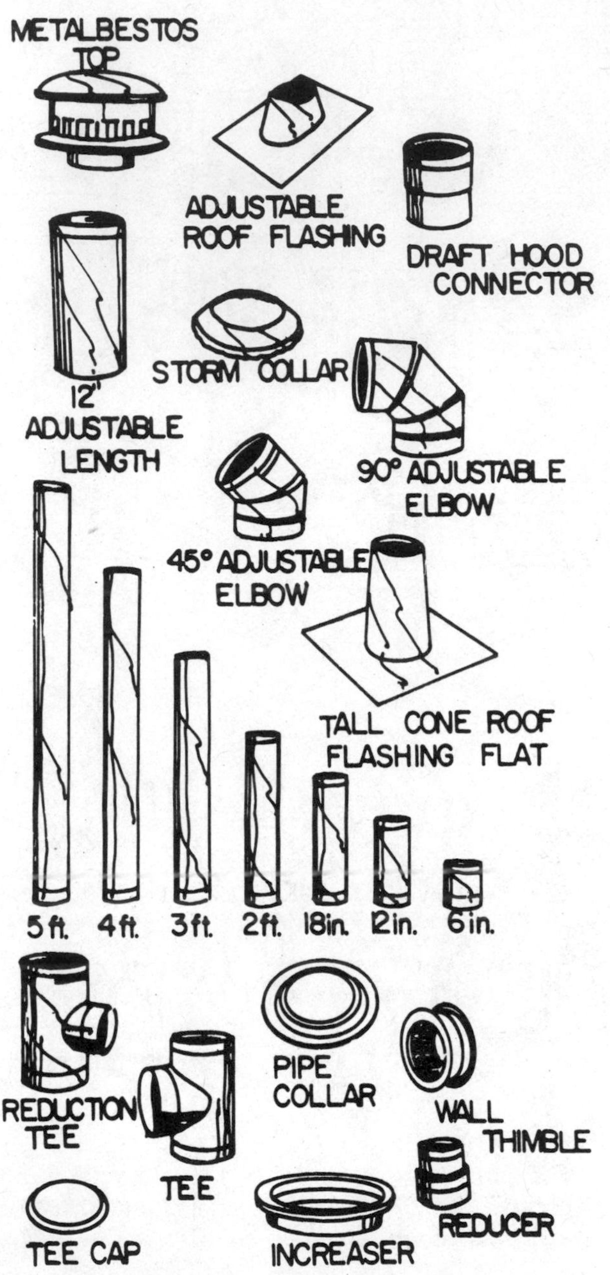

Fig. 6-18. More chimney parts and accessories.

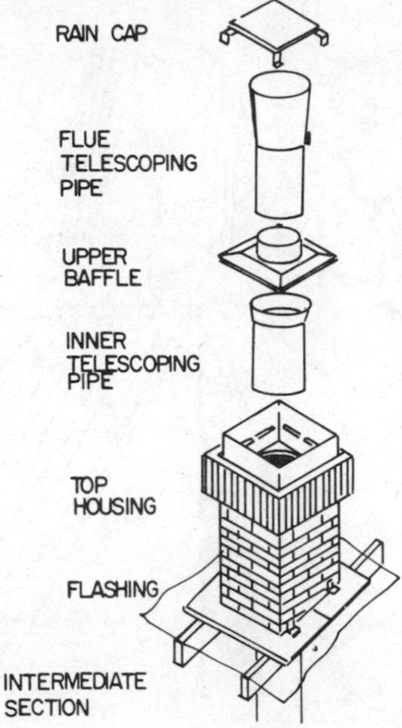

Fig. 6-19. Assemble the chimney parts carefully.

Through Floor

Framing of chimney passages through walls, ceilings above the support, and roof structures must allow at least a 2″ clear space between the insulated pipe and the combustible framing material (Fig. 6-24). The use of a joist shield or wall spacer holds the pipe in a fixed position and assures that this required clearance will be maintained.

Roof Pitch

The roof flashing must fit the pitch of the roof (Fig. 6-25). By using two rulers and a level, the roof pitch can be determined. Measure the number of inches from the end of a level ruler down to the roof. This would be the rise for 12″ of run. A rise of 3″ would be a 3/12 pitch, 4″ a 4/12 pitch, etc.

Above Roof

Once the chimney has been installed on up through the roof, the round chimney assembly with the flashing storm collar and top can be installed (Fig. 6-26). When installing the assembly, be sure the chimney is the proper height. The clearance of the chimney above the roof line is important for safety and function. Make sure

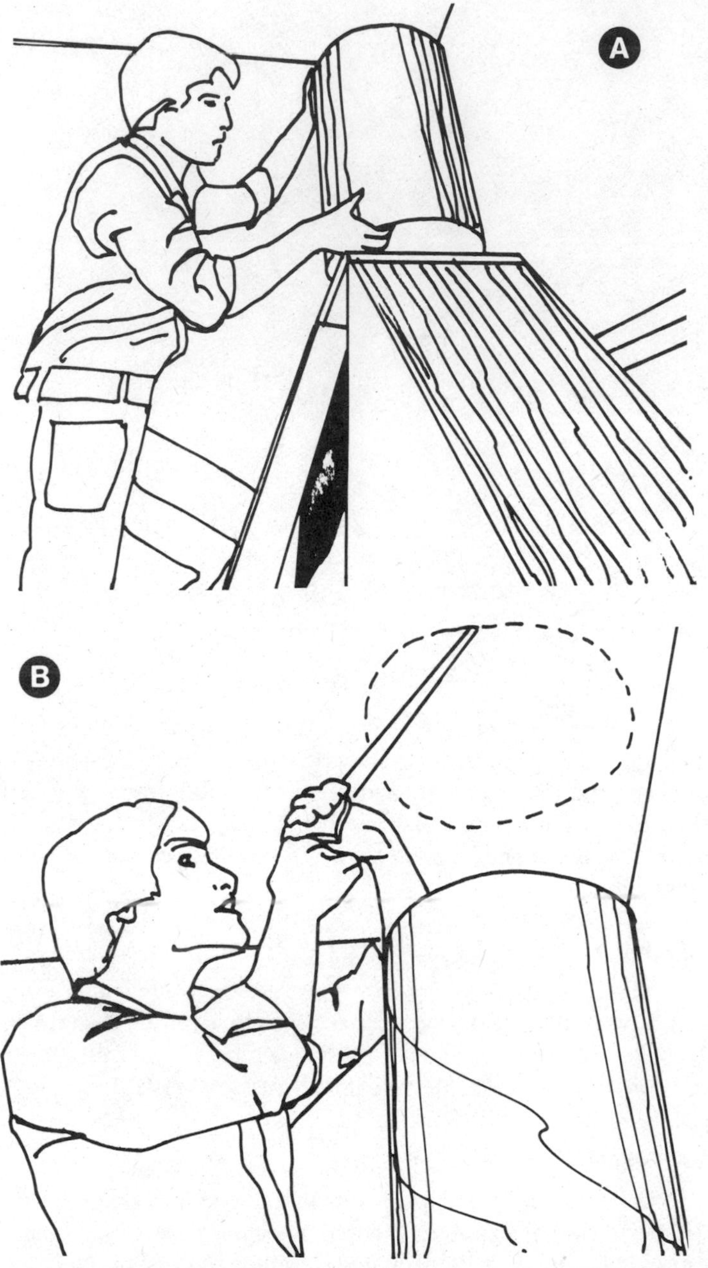

Fig. 6-20. (A). Fasten chimney starter section to fireplace. (B). Cut openings in ceiling and roof. (C). Fasten firestop to the top of the header at the ceiling. (D). Position chimney termination and cap.

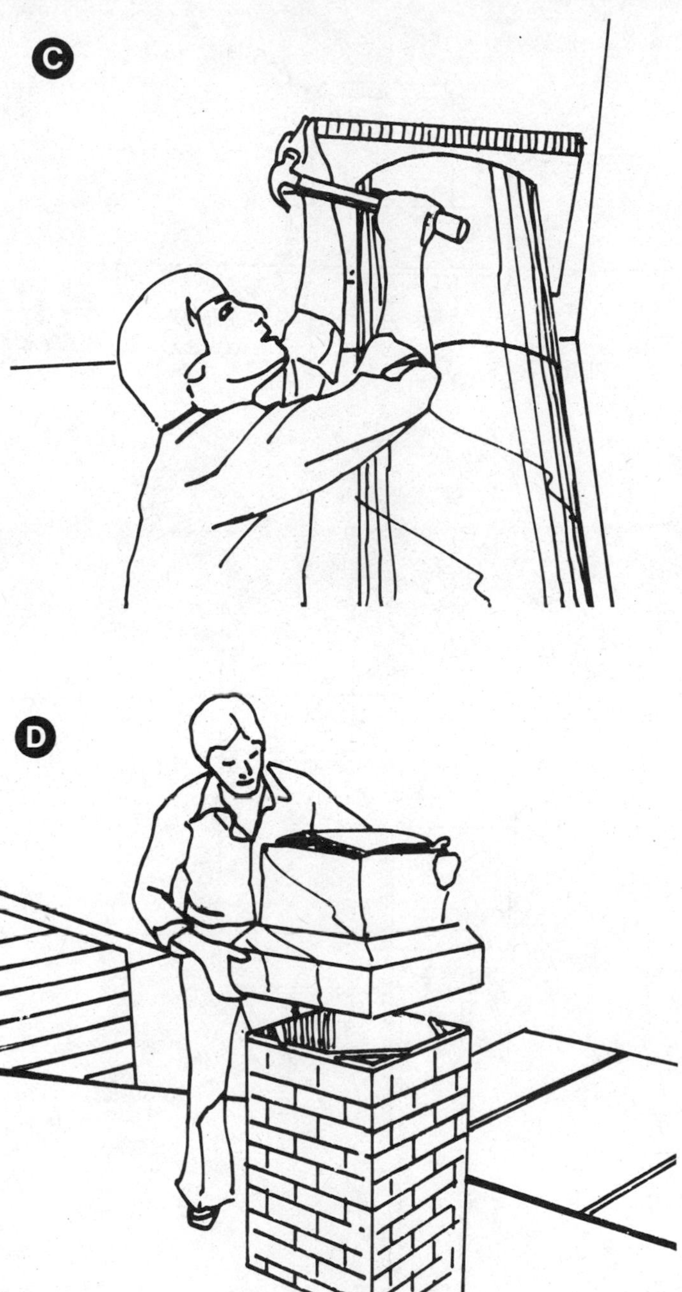
C
D

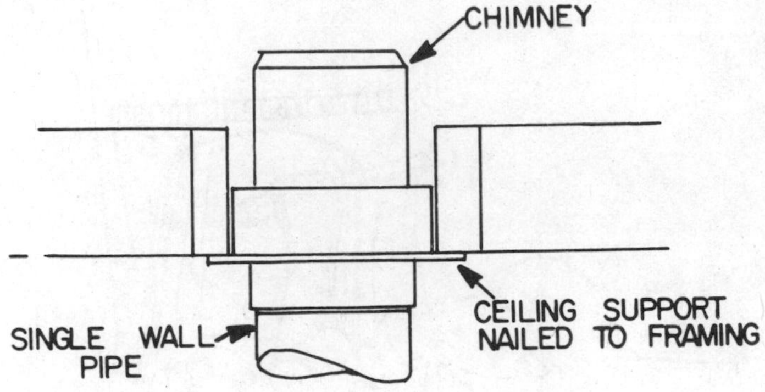

Fig. 6-21. Flat ceiling detail.

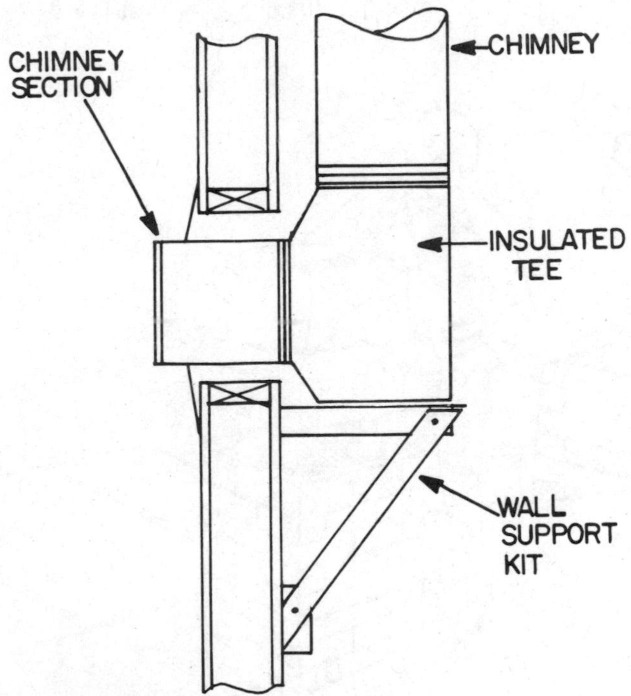

Fig. 6-22. Side wall detail.

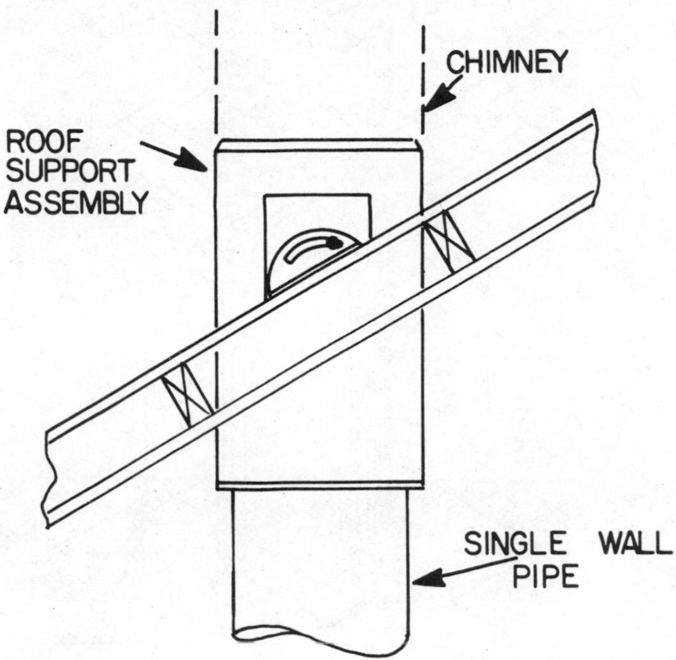

Fig. 6-23. Cathedral ceiling detail.

the insulated chimney pipe extends at least 3′ above the highest point of the roof and at least 2′ higher than any other object around within 10′. Be sure to use insulated pipe to extend the chimney above the roof. Excess heat loss from a single wall pipe can cause poor fireplace operation. Place the round flashing over the chimney pipe and nail securely to the roof through side and top flanges. Do not nail through the bottom. Finish roofing around the chimney covering the side and upper areas of the flange with roofing material. The unnailed lower portion of the flange should go over the finished roofing material. A storm collar over the top of the flashing and waterproof mastic will prevent any leaks around the chimney. A variety of chimney tops are available to give the chimney a rain cover (figs. 6-27 through 6-29).

Following are standard installation instructions for safe use of pre-built fireplaces and chimneys:

—Anchor the chimney to the building in such a manner that any settling of the building or the chimney will not cause the joints to open between chimney sections.

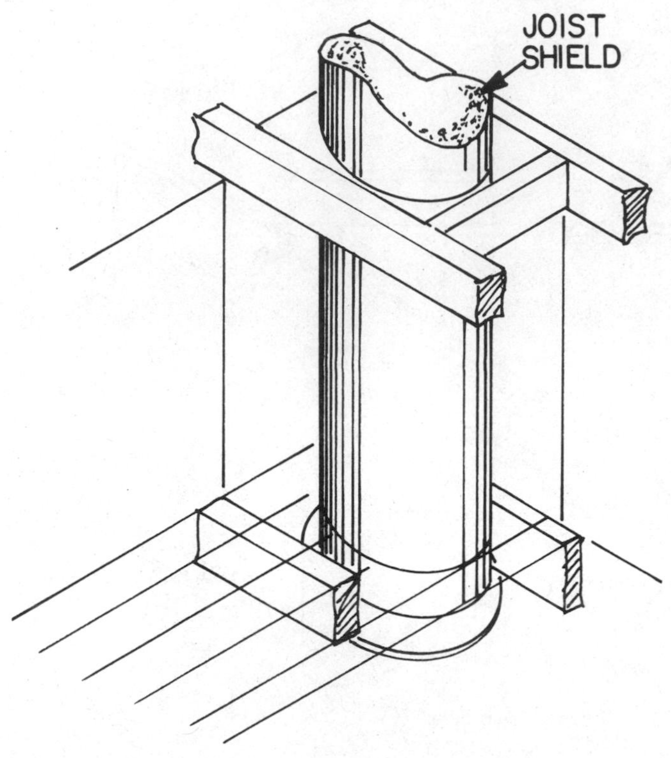

Fig. 6-24. A joist shield holds the pipe in a fixed position.

—Join chimney sections to provide an integral flue structure with joints arranged to prevent condensation from penetrating into the interior of the chimney construction. Joint cement compounds, where used, must be resistant to acids and high temperatures.

—Insulation must be impervious to high temperatures, protected from mechanical damage and should extend at least 2′ above the highest point of the opening of the roof where the chimney passes.

—The chimney flue lining should extend up to the underside of the top of the chimney roof housing in a smokeproof and sparkproof joint, or should extend through the top of the housing. When lining is of clay, it should be at least ⅝″ thick.

—Parts of the chimney located in accessible spaces should be protected from contact and mechanical damage by enclosing with rigid construction equivalent to at least ⅜″ thick wallboard.

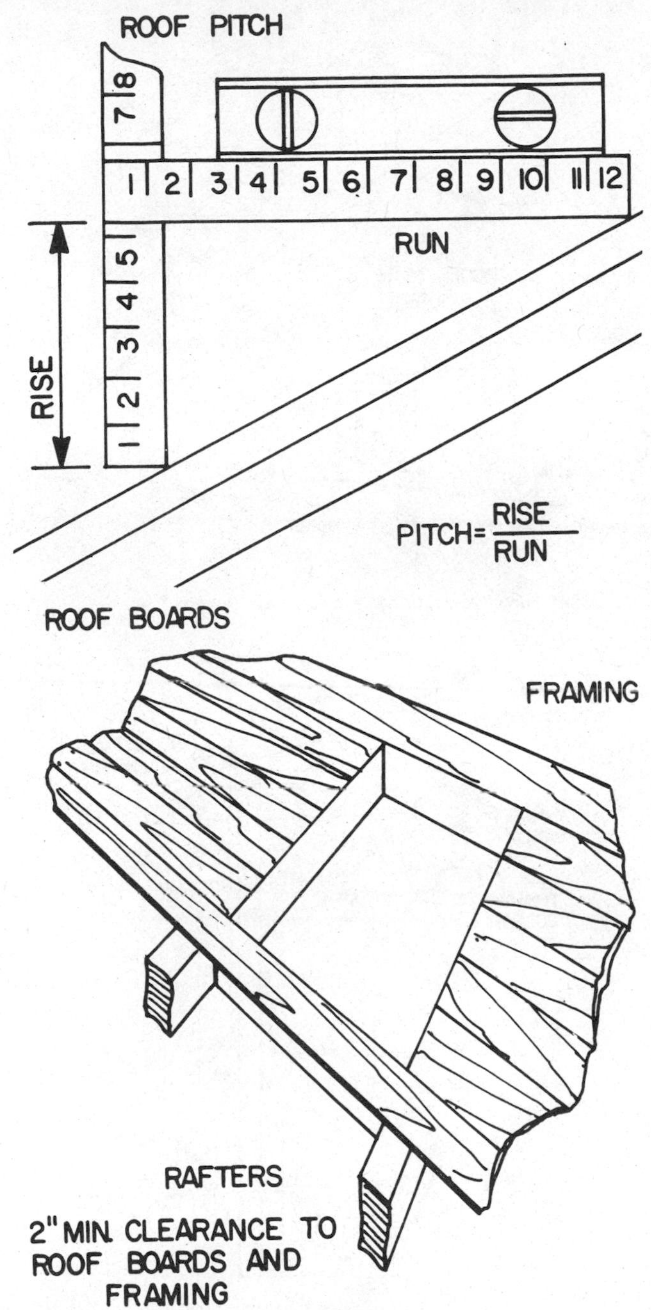

Fig. 6-25. Roof flashing must fit the pitch of the roof.

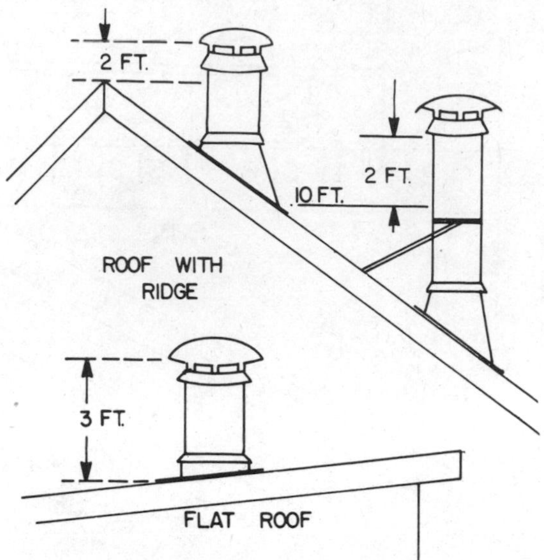

Fig. 6-26. Make sure the chimney is at the right height.

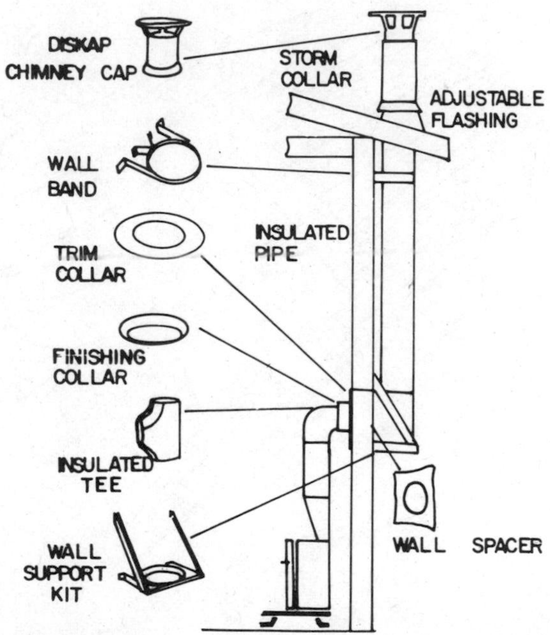

Fig. 6-27. Chimney installation through an exterior wall (courtesy of Metalbestos Systems).

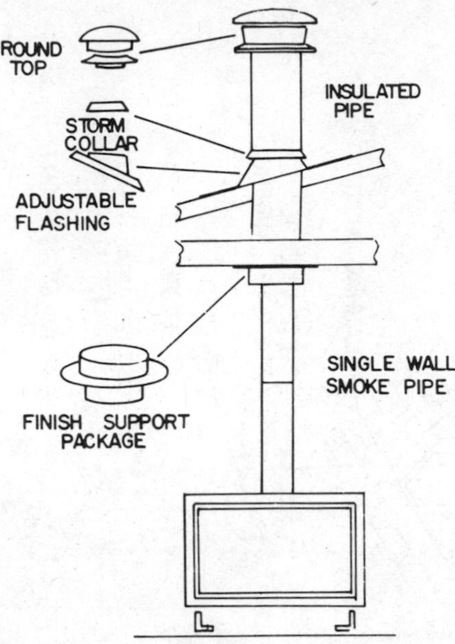

Fig. 6-28. Chimney installlation through a ceiling and normal pitch roof (courtesy of Metalbestos systems).

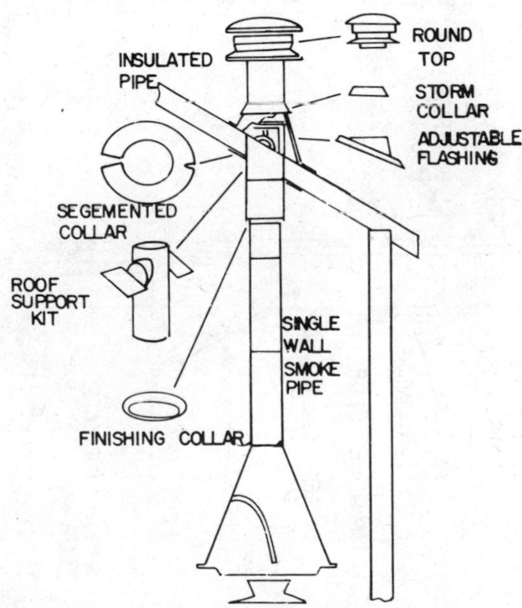

Fig. 6-29. Chimney installation through a high pitch or chalet ceiling (courtesy of Metalbestos Systems).

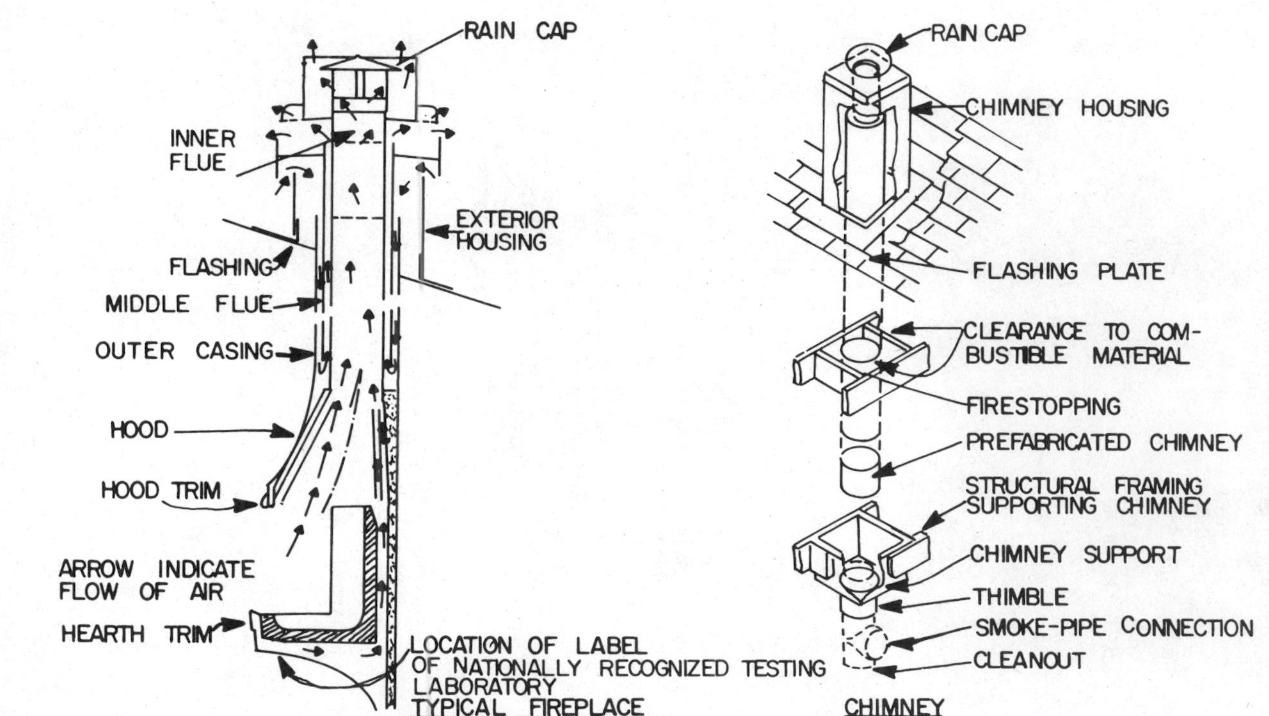

Fig. 6-30. Factory-built fireplace and chimney details.

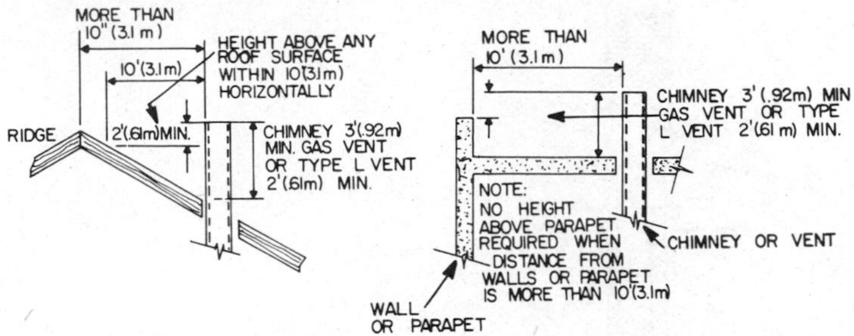

Fig. 6-31. Example of terminations more than 10′ from the ridge, wall or parapet.

—Clearances to combustibile material from the particular prefabricated chimney must be approved by a recognized testing laboratory.

—A rain cap is recommended to protect against downdrafts and to prevent rain and snow from entering the chimney.

—A cleanout below the smoke pipe connection should be installed.

—Structural framing should be doubled or otherwise designed to carry the load without settlement or cracking of the chimney (Figs. 6-30 through 6-33).

Framing

Cut and frame openings with 2″ × 4″ or 2″ × 6″ framing lumber. Install all equipment including intermediate sections, which must extend through the roof opening. Install firestops at ceiling and roof openings (Fig. 6-34). Dimensions A and B are measured horizontally and do not vary with the roof pitch. Determine minimum dimension E (Fig. 6-35). Add 24″ to dimension E to obtain minimum dimension C. Scribe the C dimension on one side

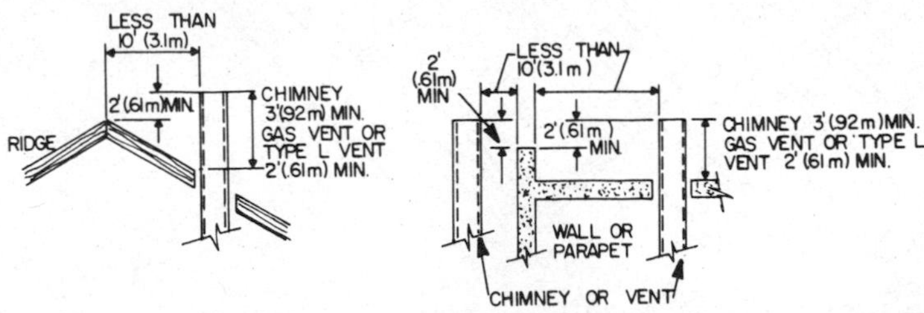

Fig. 6-32. Example of termination less than 10′ from the ridge, wall or parapet.

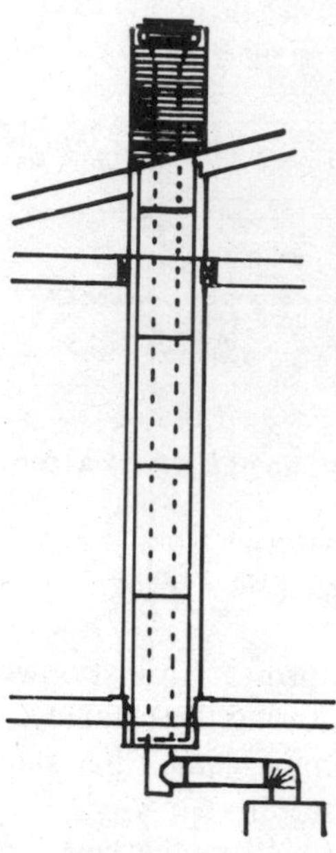

Fig. 6-33. Typical installation of a factory-built chimney in a house.

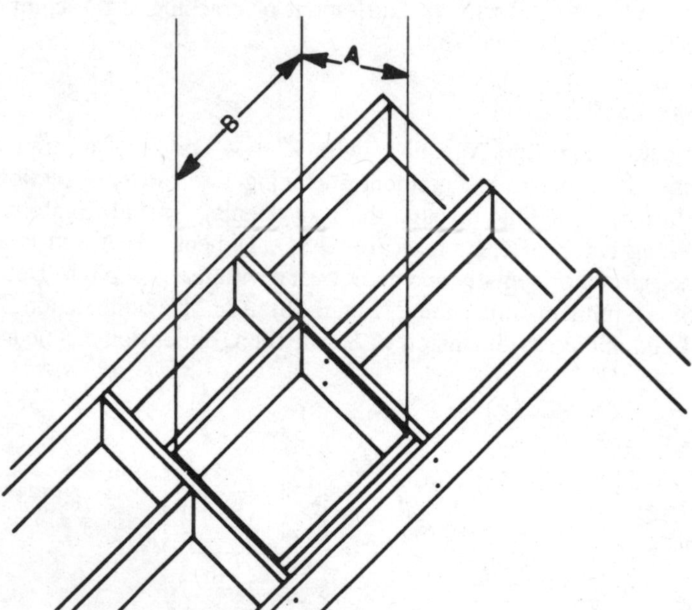

Fig. 6-34. Dimensions A and B vary horizontally and do not vary with the roof pitch.

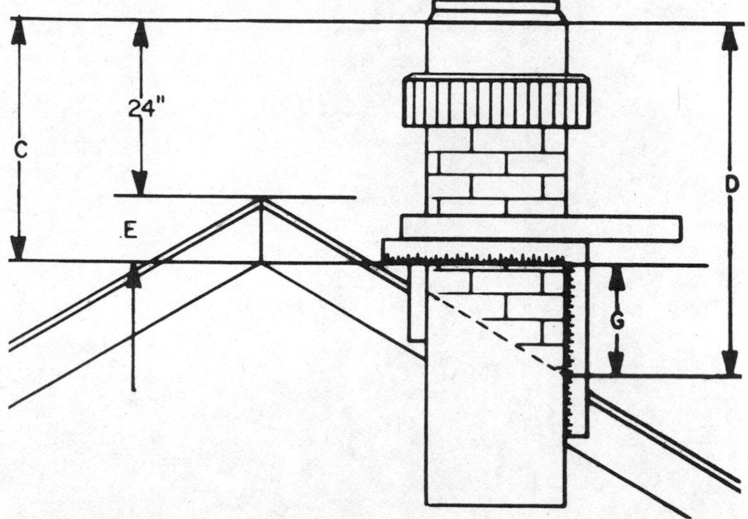

Fig. 6-35. Roof asembly. Determine minimum E dimension. Add 24" to E to obtain minimum C dimension. Scribe the C dimension on one side of the top housing. Determine the D dimension by using a level an a square. The G dimensions plus the C dimension equals D. Scribe the D dimension on the opposite side of the housing. Scribe connecting lines on adjacent sides of the housing. Cut along these lines with tin snips. A hacksaw may be needed at heavy corners.

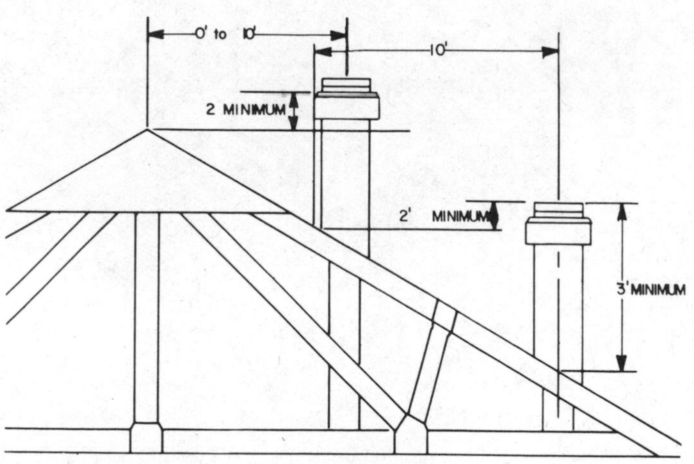

Fig. 6-36. Minimum dimensions above the roof.

Fig. 6-37. A smokeless fireplace unit (courtesy of Martin Industries).

of the top housing. Determine D dimension by using a level and square.

If the chimney is within 10′ of the roof ridge, the top should extend a minimum or 24″ above the roof top. When further than 10″ from the roof ridge, the chimney should be positioned so that it is 10′ or more from the closest point on the roof in a horizontal direction, and a minimum or 24″ above that point but never less than 36″ in height above the roof at the centerline of the chimney. Minimum distance is for most building codes. These minimum dimensions are recommended in the interest of safety and operation. (Fig. 6-36).

Smokeless Fireplaces

Smokeless fireplaces offer the easiest installation procedures. These units are fired by gas or electricity and will reduce the installation costs. Electric-fired units are ash free and require no flue lining. Fire starting is instant with the flick of a switch. Gas-fired units have push button control. If no flue is available in the house, a standard 4″ type B1 gas vent is required (Fig. 6-37).

7

Wood Burning Stoves

Your needs and requirements must be determined before purchasing a wood burning stove. What do you expect the stove to do? How much space do you want the stove to heat? This is measured by cubic feet capacity and will probably yield only about 80 percent capacity of the manufacturing label. Too large a stove will result in inefficiency. It will never burn at the rated capacity to function best. Too small a stove will not heat the area properly and you may load it beyond its rated capacity. To determine the room capacity to be heated, multiply the length by the width by the height.

How long do you want the fire to burn? Stoves are traditionally built to hold a fire only a couple of hours for every one loading. An airtight high efficiency stove will hold a fire for eight to 12 hours. They need cleaning more often and cost more. This type stove is the least expensive on a long term basis.

How important is appearance? Some efficiency stoves are not very attractive and some inefficient stoves are extremely attractive. There are a few that will give you both.

If you are planning to burn coal in addition to wood, be sure the stove can handle the heat. Some wood stoves need only a coal grate to burn coal.

Power loss may deprive you of cooking with electricity. A cook top stove can be pretty handy under those circumstances. Some units have a usable top to be used for cooking.

Stoves with a visible fire are equipped with screen or glass front. Such a stove is diminished in efficiency. If you want a stove with a visible fire, be prepared for the loss in heat.

Some stoves are equipped with a low voltage electric blower to circulate the heat. If this is your choice, be sure to get one with a ventilated motor. They will last longer than the enclosed type.

Stovepipe is important. The stove manufacturer will recommend the size to be used. The heavier the metal, the longer it will last. Twenty-four gauge is standard. The lower the number of gauge, the thicker the metal. Be sure to install a non-combustible floor under the stove. Cover at least 6″ beyond the dimensions of the stove and at least 1′ on the fuel feeding side. The manufacturer will recommend the minimum distance the stove should be from the wall.

Wood is becoming one of our favorite alternative fuels. Attracted by the prospect of saving energy and money, thousands of homeowners all across the nation are installing wood stoves. Unfortunately, many of these stoves are being improperly installed or carelessly operated so wood stove fires are becoming more and more common. Wood stoves are not inherently dangerous. Most of these fires could have been prevented by common safety measures.

STOVE MODELS

There are about 1,500 new wood stove models to choose from. Some are unattractive and some are beautiful.Some reflect the late 19th century styling (Figs. 7-1 through 7-12).

A thorough inspection is necessary to restore an old stove back into service. If the firebox and grates are in good condition, the stove is as good as new. Although cracks can be repaired, it may be a danger because the heat inside the firebox is so intense that a bad patch presents a danger, possibly causing the house to burn down.

The Franklin Fireplace. These units have doors which will permit some degree of control, and can raise the efficiency level to about 15% to 20 percent.

Pot Belly-Parlor Stove and Box Heaters. These are closed stove type heaters with manual damper control and can be as much as 40 to 50 percent efficient with proper damper setting.

Air Tight. These are thermostatically controlled units with 50 to 60 percent efficiency. Any desired temperature level can be maintained because of precise combustion control and draft intake. One fueling can last as long as 14 hours.

Fig. 7-1. Wood stoves help to save energy and money.

Fig. 7-2. You can cook on this wood stove.

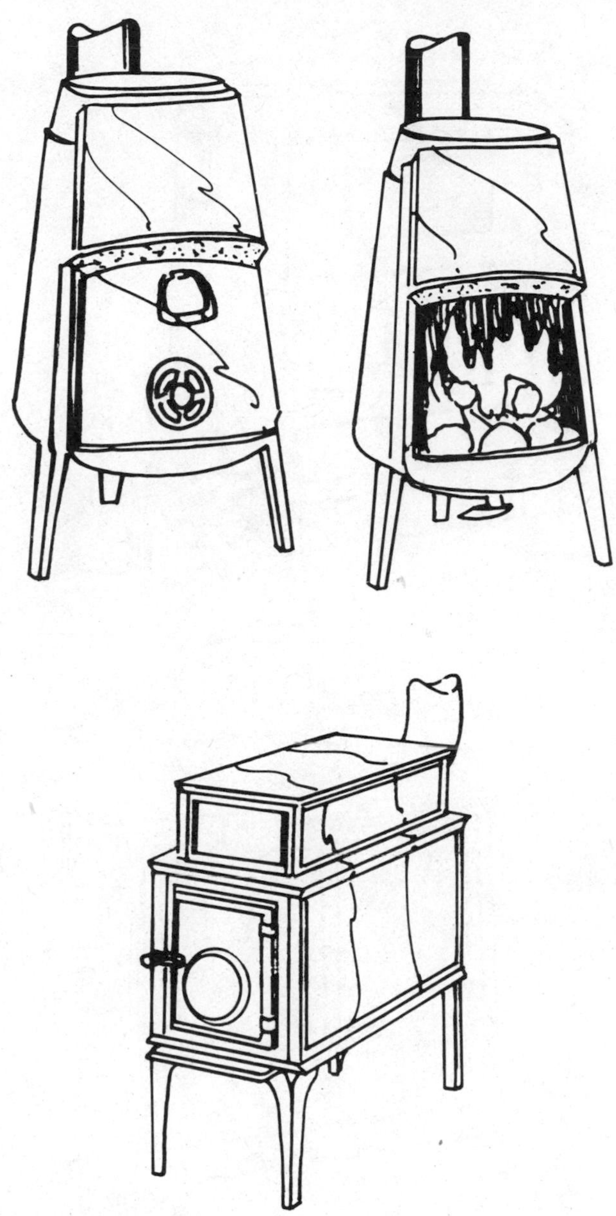

Fig. 7-3. Wood stoves come in numerous styles (courtesy of Majestic Company).

Fig. 7-4. Avoid fires by installing wood stoves properly.

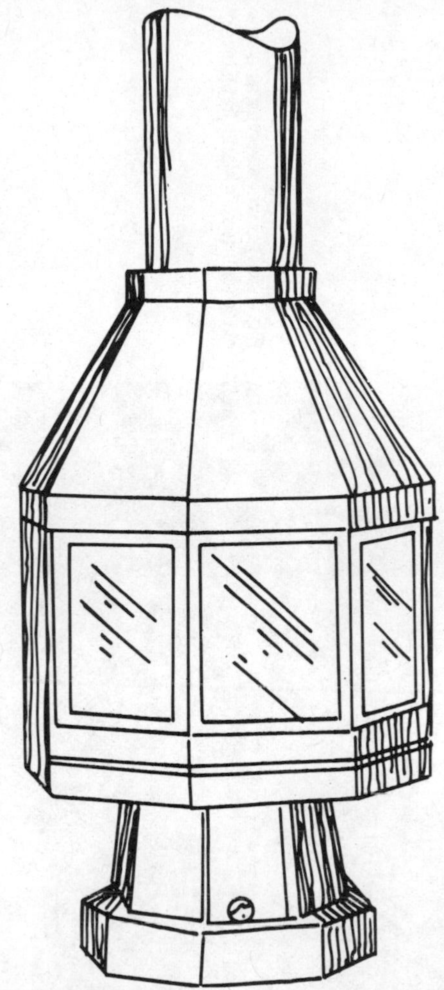

Fig. 7-4. Avoid fires by installing wood stoves properly (continued from page 242.)

CAST IRON VERSUS STEEL

Either cast iron or steel are accepted as stove building material. Cast iron's reputation of holding heat longer is a myth. It stems from the days when cast iron stove walls were thicker than steel stove walls. Given equal thickness, either metal will give identical performance. Light gauge metal without fire brick lining can be very dangerous in any unit and will have a limited life. The heating capacity of a stove is governed by the weight, mass or thickness, not the metal type.

Fig. 7-5. This stove serves as a fireplace (courtesy of Martin Industries).

Fig. 7-6. Get a wood stove which goes well with the room's decor (courtesy of Martin Industries).

Fig. 7-7. Thoroughly inspect your stove before installing it (courtesy of Martin Industries).

A used stove should be checked for cracks and repaired with stove cement. If the cracks are wide open, they should be welded. Buy a substantial good stove with good workmanship and design. The thicker the metal, the longer the stove will last. The high efficiency stoves are more expensive to buy but are less expensive to operate because they deliver more heat.

A closed wood burning stove has a different effect on heat. The stove is completely enclosed except for air entering the stove for control. Heat from the stove will heat the room with little or no loss in addition to reducing the amount of wood burned.

A fireplace stove might be the happy medium, which is nothing more than a wood burning stove inserted into the firebox using the flue as a chimney. A fan built within the system will help circulate the heat from the stove into the room. The surface temperature is about 400°F. This thin layer of hot air around the stove is called *Langmuir's film.* The fan will blow Langmuir's film into the room away from the stove. Any heat not able to radiate away from the stove will be lost through the chimney.

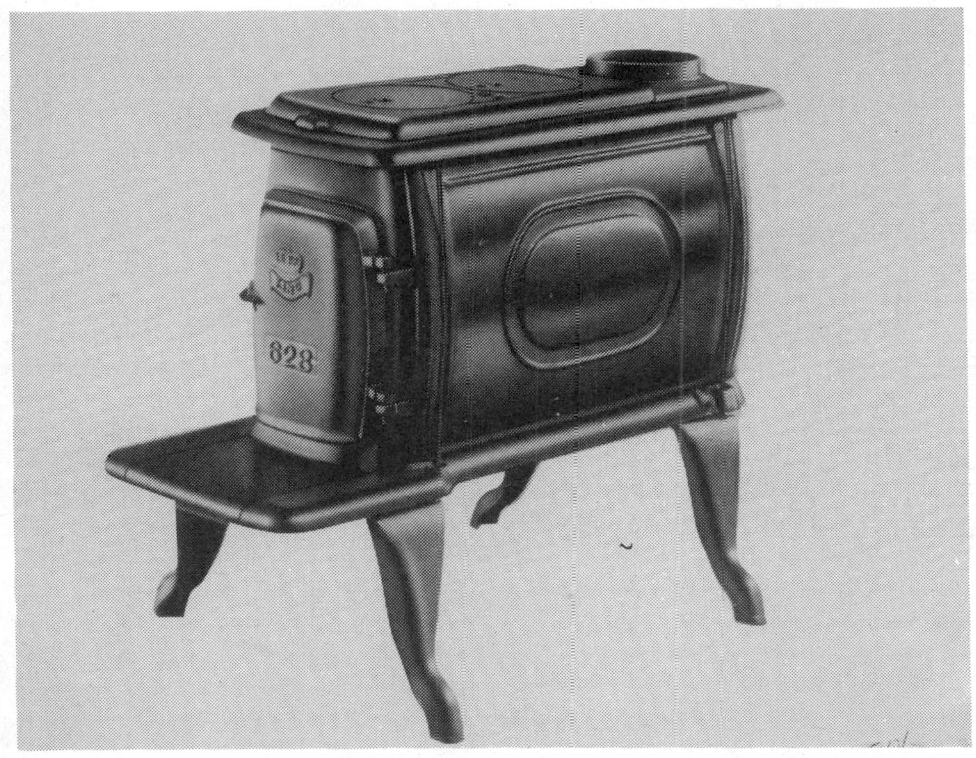

Fig. 7-8. An older wood stove design (courtesy of Martin Industries).

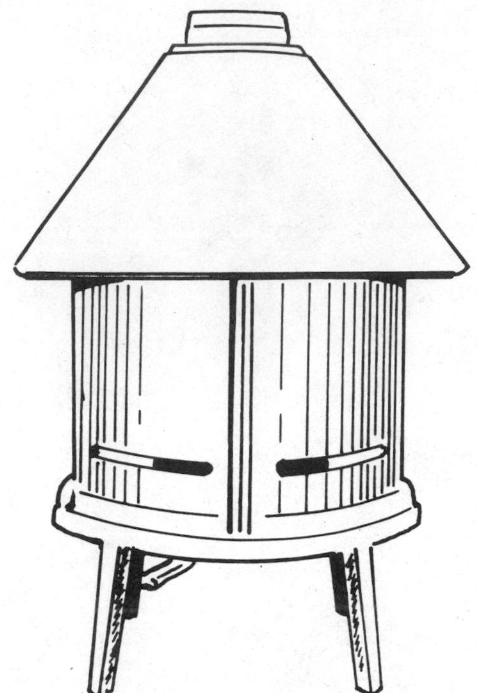

Fig. 7-9. This wood stove is uniquely designed.

Adequate wall, floor and ceiling clearances must be provided for safety. Place the stove at least 36″ from a combustible or unprotected wall. Sheet asbestos with a 1″ clearance from the wall will allow 18″ clearance. If 28 gauge sheet metal is used in lieu of asbestos, the clearance can be 12″.

Floor clearance is generally not as severe a problem because the ashes reduce radiation and act as an insulation. However, stoves with 18″ legs or more should sit on 28 gauge metal. Shorter legs will require a fireproof floor such as concrete, brick, tile or asbestos. Stovepipe installation should have a minimum of turns or bends. Plan to replace the pipe about every two years.

The connector must have an internal cross-sectional area of not less than that of the flue collar of the stove. The connector must be straight and as short as possible, preferably with not more than one or at most two sweeping 90° elbows. If you connect into an existing chimney, be sure the flue lining is clean and not cracked. The local fire department or building inspector will inspect the chimney. It should be inspected every year.

Fig. 7-10. A closed stove type heater.

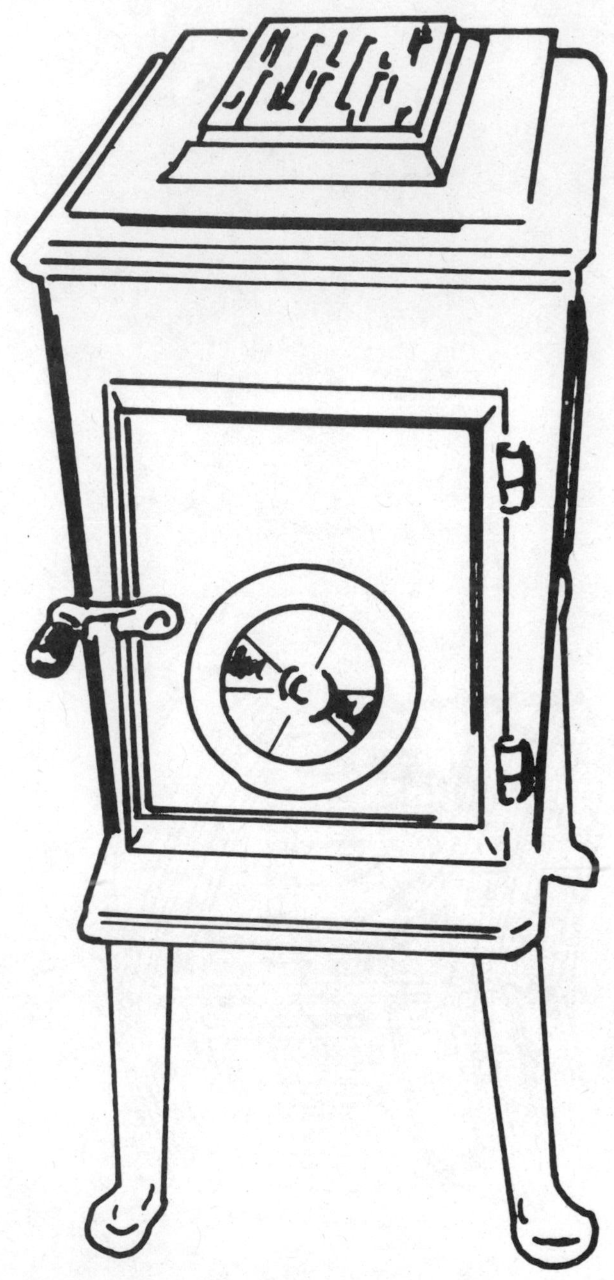

Fig. 7-11. The door permits a degree of efficiency control.

Fig. 7-12. A large Franklin fireplace unit.

Keep firewood, kindling and newspaper well away from the stove or fireplace. The sides of the stove should be at least 36″ away from any combustible material. Use only the fuel which the stove was designed to burn. If a wood burning stove does not burn coal, and if a coal burning stove does not burn wood, do not burn both unless you purchase one that will burn either. Keep a fire extinguisher handy. Install smoke and fire detectors and finally plan an escape route from your house.

SMOKEPIPE INSTALLATION

The smokepipe is connected to a thimble or flue ring built into the wall extending to the flue lining (Fig. 7-13). The rings are available with inside diameters of 6″, 7″, 8″, 10″ and 12″, and lengths of 4½″, 6″, 9″ and 12″. When installed into the wall, these rings should be airtight with a full bed of mortar around the ring. When installing a metal stovepipe, it should be installed no farther than the inner face of the flue lining with an airtight joint, along with boiler putty or asbestos cement. The top of the smokepipe should not be less than 18″ below the ceiling and no wood should be placed within 6″ of the thimble.

An improperly installed smokepipe from a wood burning stove is a dangerous fire hazard (Fig. 7-14). Do not extend the pipe too far into the flue. A metal or clay collar should be built into the wall or brickwork to receive the smoke pipe and a collar slipped over the pipe. Smokepipes should be kept at least 10″ away from the woodwork of the house.

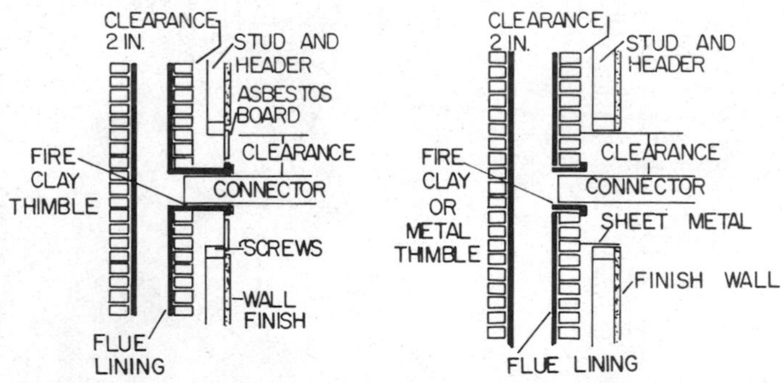

Fig. 7-13. Two methods of connecting a chimney connector to a chimney flue where the connector must pass through a combustible partitition wall.

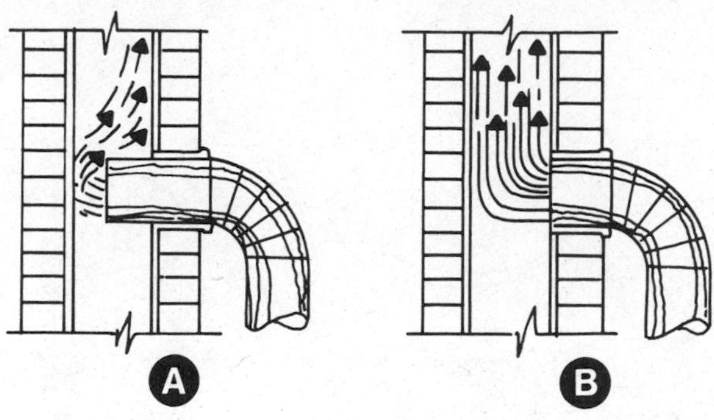

Fig. 7-14. (A). Improper stovepipe connection. (B). Proper stovepipe connection.

Some building codes will require fireproof ceilings and walls in stoved rooms. Some communities may require local building permits for installation.The building inspector will offer assistance for installation if requested.

The clearance of a chimney connector should be not less than 18″ from the nearest combustible material. Where connected to a masonry chimney, a chimney connector is required to extend through the masonry wall to the inner face of the liner but not beyond the inner surface. The connector must be mortared to the masonry wall. In lieu of this, a thimble may be connected to the masonry wall of the chimney without mortar (Fig. 7-15). If mortar is used, it must be the high temperature type. If the thimble is used, the joint must be tight to prevent back draft smoke from leaking through. A damper should be installed on the stovepipe.

A manual operated damper must be installed close to the stove. It may be horizontal or vertical. An alternative is an automatic draft regulator.

SETTING A STOVE

A wood stove must be a certain distance away from combustible materials to prevent fires from radiated heat. If your stove is listed by a national laboratory such as Underwriters' Laboratories, Inc., follow the clearances they specify. If your stove is not listed, diligently adhere to the specifications given here. Be aware that the sides, bottom and stovepipe attain quite different temperatures while the stove is in operation, so there are quite different specifications for each of them.

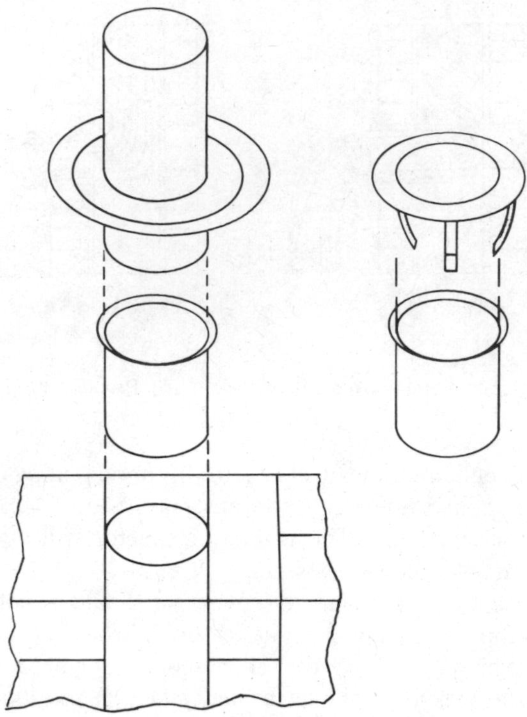

Fig. 7-15. The thimble is removed and a chimney connector is installed.

The sides of an unlisted stove should be at least 36″ from any combustible materials. A foot or two of clearance will not do. Even though very high temperatures are needed to ignite most combustible materials, over time, high temperatures can change the composition of the material by slowly darkening it so that it accepts more and more radiated heat. Finally, it may begin to smolder and burn at temperatures as low as 200 to 250°F. These temperatures are easily reached by an unprotected wall exposed to a stove without adequate clearance, so strict adherance to the clearance standards are advised.

An unlisted stove may be positioned closer to a wall than 36″ only if a noncombustible material is spaced at least 1″ away from the wall to allow air to circulate behind the material and carry heat away. But placing a noncombustible material directly on the wall has no real protective value. The material will easily conduct heat to the wall behind it creating dangerous conditions.

Asbestos millboard spaced 1″ away from a wall will allow an 18″ stovewall clearance. If 28 gauge sheet metal is installed in the same manner, the acceptable clearance is only 12″.

Remember that these clearances are for all combustible materials. This eliminates some dangerous but common practices such as stacking wood or paper next to a stove or moving a sofa temporarily closer. It may be difficult to install a stove where it is convenient, aesthetically pleasing and safe. Don't compromise. Your priority is safety.

At one time, separate standards were specified for stoves with sheet metal cabinets (also called circulating stoves), but the National Fire Protection Association now recommends that all wood stoves be treated the same (Table 7-1 and Fig. 7-16).

FLOOR PROTECTION

Safe floor clearances are substantially less than those for walls because the heat radiated from the bottom of a stove is generally less than from either the sides on the top. During a fire, ashes fall to the bottom of a stove. This has an insulating effect, resisting the flow of heat downward. This process may be started in a new stove by placing a layer of sand in the bottom.

Clearances for proper floor protection are classified according to leg length, and are listed in Table 7-2. Floor protection materials can be covered with attractive *materials* such as stone, brick or tile as long as they are noncombustible. Do not use these materials instead of an asbestos sheet or metal plate.

Falling embers and sparks present an additional safety problem that is often ignored. Avoid this potential problem by extending the floor protection 18″ from the front of the stove and 6″ around the sides and back. This affords a reasonable amount of protection, but you should still take care when loading and tending the stove. Make sure that ashes and hot coals fall only on the protected area.

Table 7-1. Minimum Clearances.

Type of protection	Stove Sides	Stovepipe
Unprotected	36″	18″
1/4″ asbestos millboard	36″	18″
1/4″ asbestos millboard spaced out 1″	18″	12″
28 ga. sheet metal on 1/4″ asbestos millboard	18″	12″
28 ga. sheet metal spaced out 1″	12″	9″
28 ga. sheet metal on 1/8″ asbestos millboard spaced out 1″	12″	9″

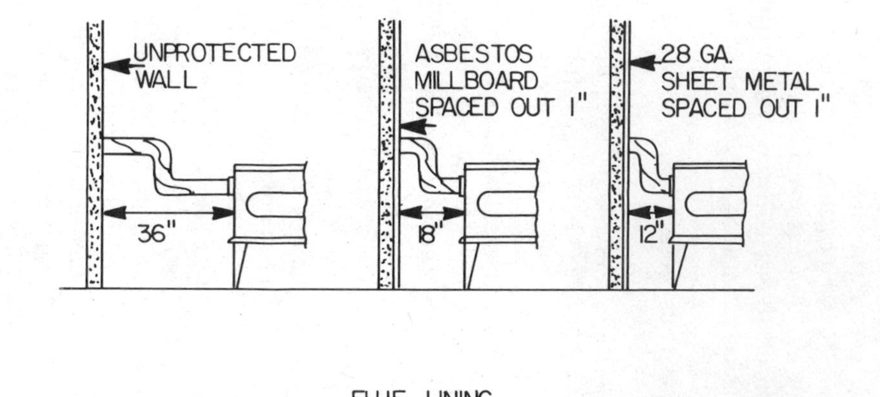

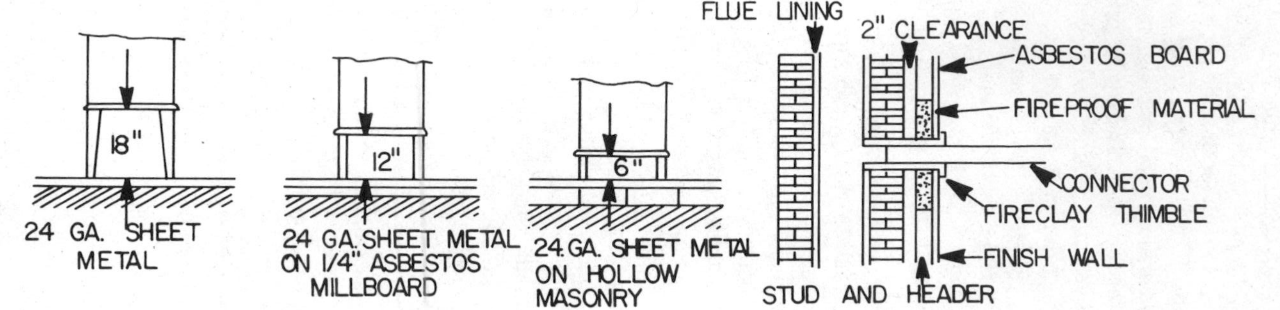

Fig. 7-16. Tips on burning wood safely (courtesy of Providence Journal).

Table 7-2. Leg Length and Floor Protection Information.

Leg Length	Protection Needed
18″ or more	24 ga. layer of sheet metal
6″ to 18″	24 ga. layer of sheet metal over 1/4″ layer of asbestos millboard
6″ or less	Use 4″ of hollow masonry laid to provide air circulation through the masonry layer covered by a sheet of 24 ga. sheet metal.

STOVEPIPE

Stovepipe and chimneys, although they are often mistakenly used interchangeably, are two completely different things. When a stovepipe is used for a chimney, dangerous conditions may occur. Creosote may build up rapidly and the wind and rain may soon corrode the pipe. Consequently, if a stovepipe fire should occur, there will be little to contain it. Chimneys, in contrast, keep the smoke and gases hotter to prevent the buildup of creosote. They are made of corrosion resistant materials so they do not need frequent replacement, and most chimneys are able to contain a fire.

A stovepipe must be installed so that there is a good draft to carry the hot gases away quickly and safely. This can be a tricky proposition unless you follow these guidelines carefully:

- Keep the stovepipe short.
- Keep turns and bends to a minimum.
- The horizontal portion of the stovepipe should be no more than 75 percent of the vertical portion.
- The stovepipe should enter the chimney well above the stove outlet. Horizontal portions of the stovepipe should rise at least ¼″ per foot.

Stovepipes come in different diameters and gauges. Measure the pipe connector on the stove and get the proper size stovepipe. Pipe gauge 24 or thicker is a good investment because it will last longer lower gauge numbers indicate thicker metal. The stovepipe pieces should be fitted together tightly, then permanently joined with two or three sheet metal acrews to prevent the stovepipe from being shaken apart during a chimney fire. Since stovepipe cannot be expected to last long, inspect it regularly and plan on replacing it every two or three years.

All stoves should have some sort of damper. Dampers are used to control the air flow to a stove, and in the event of a chimney fire, they should have the capability to shut off the air flow to the chimney completely. Generally, airtight stoves have sufficient

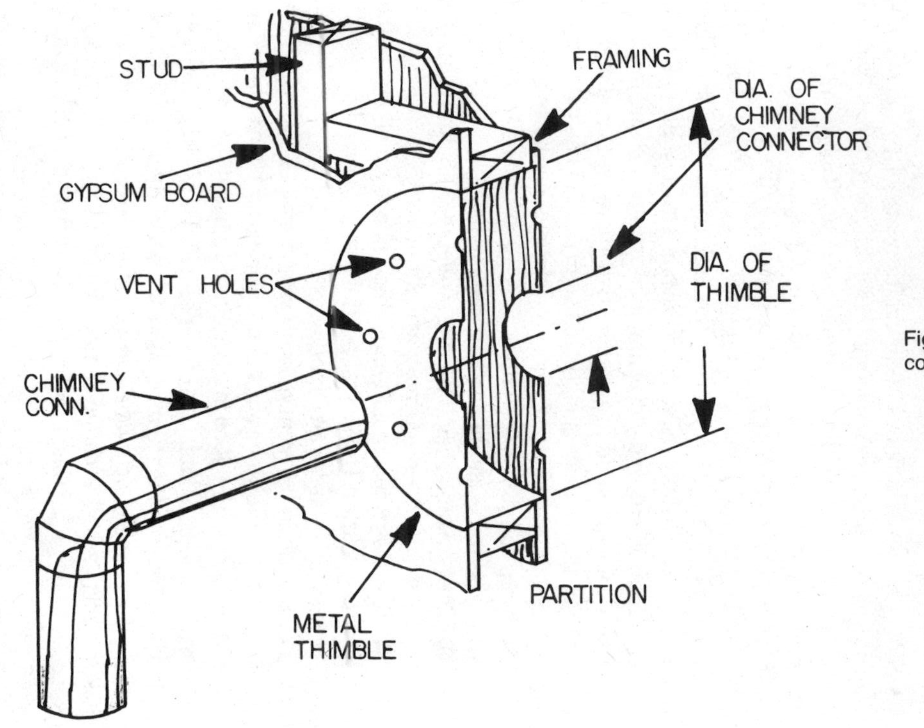

Fig. 7-17. Through wall stovepipe connection.

dampers built in, but any non-airtight stove should have a damper in the stovepipe. It is a good idea to install a second damper in the stovepipe as a safety control. Most of the dampers sold in hardware stores are not solid. Although they can be used to control air flow, they cannot shut it off completely. You may have to replace this damper with a solid piece of metal cut the same size.

Passing a stovepipe through a wall should be avoided if possible (Figs. 7-17 and 7-18). If it cannot be avoided, special precautions must be taken. An insulated wall thimble may be installed (be sure it is nationally listed for use with wood stoves) according to manufacturers' instructions, or you can use a ventilated thimble that must be specifically made for wood stoves. This thimble should be made of sheet metal or asbestos millboard and must be at least three times larger in diameter than the stovepipe. Stovepipes should never run through concealed places like closets or attics.

Care must be taken when attaching the stovepipe to a chimney, and to allow for proper cleaning of the chimney (Fig. 7-19). Stovepipe clearances must be maintained from all combustible surfaces and, in a masonry chimney, a special connector thimble must be installed. The stovepipe should fit into this thimble, and the thimble must fit into the chimney and be permanently cemented in place. Do not extend the thimble into the flue.

STOVE MANUFACTURING MATERIAL

There are three choices: cast iron, plate steel and sheet metal. Cast iron stoves are made by pouring molten pig iron into a mold forming the component parts of a stove. There pieces are machined to fit, sand blasted and acid dripped (pickled) to remove scale and corrosion, assembled and either enemeled or blackened.

Plate steel stoves are heavy sheets of steel (typically ¼"-½" thick) cut to size and then welded together. They are wire brushed or pickeld and then blackened. Sheet metal is thin steel sheet (less than ⅛" thick) that is either welded or bolted to form the stove. The material difference between plate steel and cast iron is different enough not to warrant significant concern. The thicker the metal, the longer the stove will last. Both materials retain roughly the same amount of heat per pound and both stove types cost roughly the same. One difference is taht a cast iron stove can be dressed up with designs in the casting.

A well made stove will have clean castings, smooth welds and good workmanship. Some stoves have firebrick or metal plates to prevent burnout; this may increase the lifetime of the stove and also increases the *thermal mass* (the storage medium for the heat-A

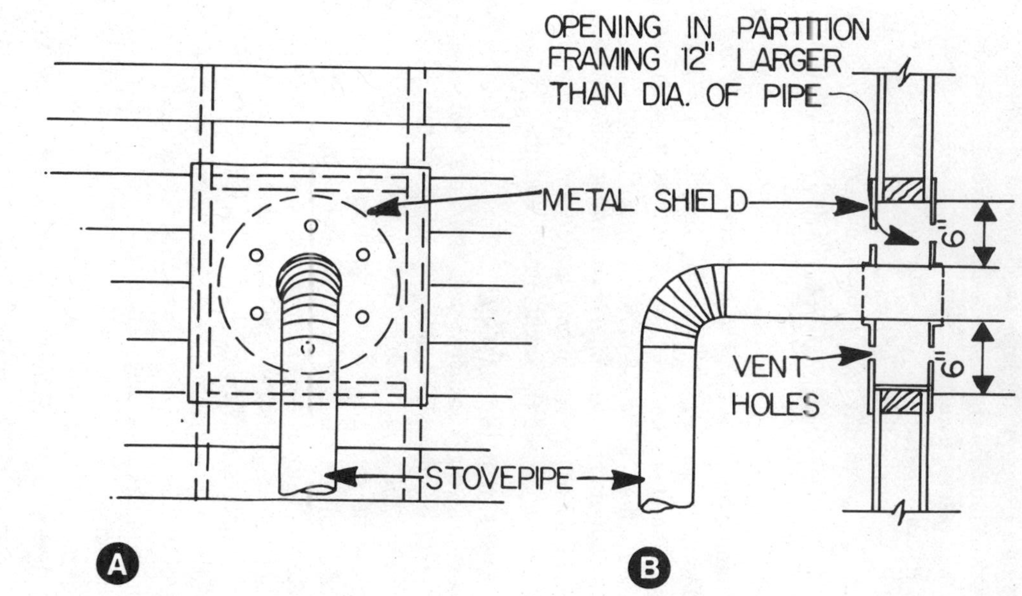

Fig. 7-18. One way of protecting a wood partition when a smoke pipe passes through it. (A). Elevation of protection around the pipe. (B). Sectional view.

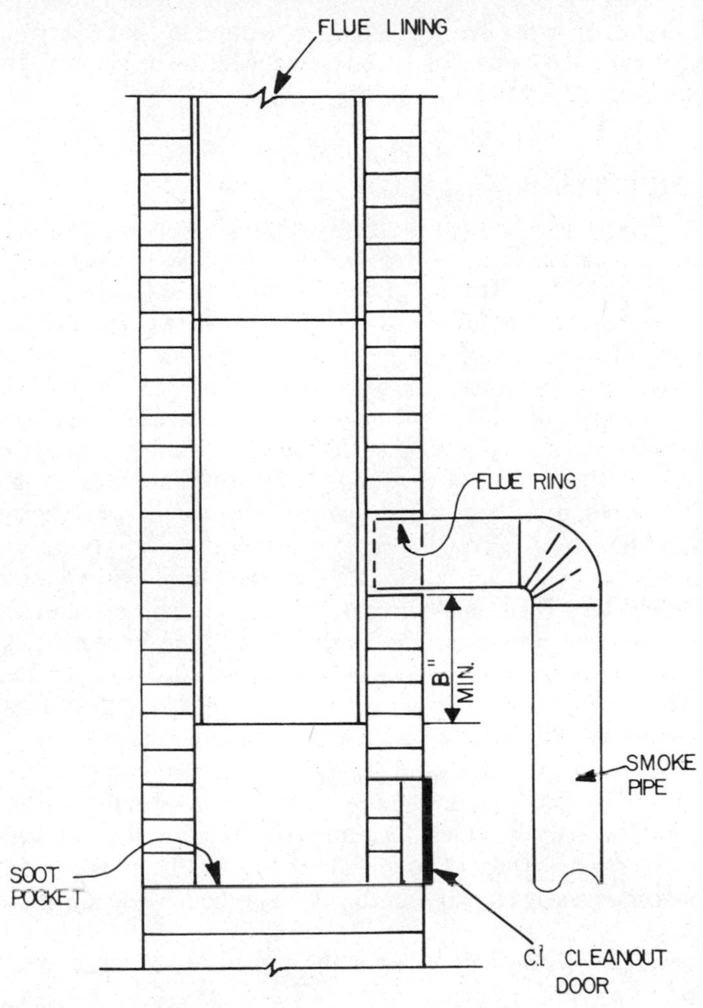

Fig. 7-18. One way of protecting a wood partition when a smoke pipe passes through it. (A). Elevation of protection around the pipe. (B). Sectional view.

500-pound stove can continue to give off usable heat four hours after the fire is out).

In general, the material a stove is made from is secondary to the workmanship and design. Sheet metal stoves are made from sheet metal (thin sheets) that burn out fast. They may be inexpensive, but they will need frequent replacement.

Plans are available for constructing a stove from a discarded oil drum. They are ideally suited for heating a garage, barn or camp, but are not recommended for extensive home heating. The sides get red hot.

STOVE DESIGNS

The design of a stove in any given category may vary significantly from stove to stove, yet the basic principle remains that of extracting heat from the fire. Low efficiency stoves (20-30 percent efficient) are technically the simplest. They have a straight air path either across or through the fire allowing sufficient air for combustion of the wood (primary air) with no accomodations for additional air to support the flame combustion (secondary air). They have excessive air leaks due to unsealed beams resulting in poor fire control. Simple box stoves, Franklin stoves, chunk stoves, pot belly stoves, parlor stoves and sheet metal stoves are representative of the category.

Medium efficiency stove (35-50 percent efficient) are more sophisticated. They have better control of the amount of primary and secondary air and are built without excessive air leaks. The common term for this category is *airtights*. Air flow to the fire is controlled to ensure maximum utilization of the burn. A thermostat is commonly utilized to insure a constant burning rate.

High efficiency stoves (50-65 percent efficient) are the most technically sophisticated. They regulate air flow as in the simpler airtights but employ baffles, long smoke paths and heat exchangers to extract as much heat as possible from the fire. These stoves are the most expensive to buy, but they deliver the most heat per unit of fuel.

When selecting a stove, the following considerations are rated in priority order:

- Decide on what your end use will be.
- Decide on location(s) of the stove(s).
- Select the correct size for your application.
- Pick a general type that best fits your use.
- Take to a stove dealer, tell him what you want to buy and why.
- Pick a stove that fits your use and taste, not just your pocketbook. Consider the purchase of a stove a major investment that will pay a handsome dividend over its lifetime.

FURNACES

Many modern homes were designed for the convenience of central heat. The layout of the house may make heating with stoves virtually impossible due to many small scattered rooms sealed off from each other by walls, closets and other heat blocking barriers. All electric homes are especially notorious for this quality. This type of layout is ideal for a wood or multi-fuel heating system. Furnaces are available that will heat any size home and are designed for use, either hot air or water transfer mediums. In most cases, the furnaces are designed to replace the existing furnace using the pipes or ducts currently in place. Maintenance of such a unit is more demanding than for a conventional oil burner. The fire must be fed, the ash box cleaned out, and the heat exchanger must be cleaned more frequently due to creosote deposite. They burn large amounts of fuel. Typical burning times are 12 plus hours. They may not be legal in some states, as code requirements have not been suitably developed to insure safe construction and maintenance. The design of a totally automatic system is still in the prototype stages. It wiil be some years before a unit will be available for general use at a reasonable price.

The one prerequisite for a wood burning furnace is a large supply of fuel. The average furnace used eight cords of wood per year. A multi-fuel heating system can use any fuel source with oil as a backup, or gas as a backup if the alternative fuel burns out. The furnaces are thermostatically controlled. When no heat is required, the damper is closed off so the fuel barely burns. When heat is required, the dampers open and the fire comes back to life.

FIREPLACES

At best, fireplaces are poor heaters. The volatile gases are drawn up the chimney before they adequately release their energy to the surrounding room. The draft created by the fire draws room air up the chimney along with the burning gases, sometimes resulting in a net loss for the whole house. Additional heat is lost if the damper is left open after the fire dies out. A typical masonry fireplace averages about 10 percent efficiency.

Modifications to a fireplace can include a metal lined heat exchanger that allows room air to be heated and be remitted out of the top of the unit. By adding tightly fitted glass doors and outside air vents, the performance of a fireplace can be more than doubled.

Hollow tube grates can be placed in the fireplace to extract additional heat from the fire. With a blower or by natural convection, a significant amount of energy can be extracted from the fire. Manufacturers claim a heat gain of 5,000 to 50,000 BTU/hours from these devices.

A conventional stove can be adapted to a fireplace in any number of ways. A tight fitting metal or asbestos sheet can be installed in place of the damper or a covering for the fireplace can be fitted over the opening. An opening can be cut into the chimney over the damper and the stovepipe installed there. In any case, the object is not to allow warm room air to escape up the chimney. If both heat and beauty are your objectives, another solution exists. Buy a Franklin stove. Although there are many high efficiency stove/fireplaces on the market today, a Franklin stove is about 25 percent efficient with the doors open and about 30 percent efficient with the doors closed. The airtight combination units are about 30 percent efficient with the doors open and about 50 percent efficient with them closed.

The atmosphere of an open fire is by far the most important reason people buy or install fireplaces. The fireplace is not an efficent heating device, even with extensive modifications..Except for supplemental or emergency usage, the fireplace is best left to being a pleasant experience.

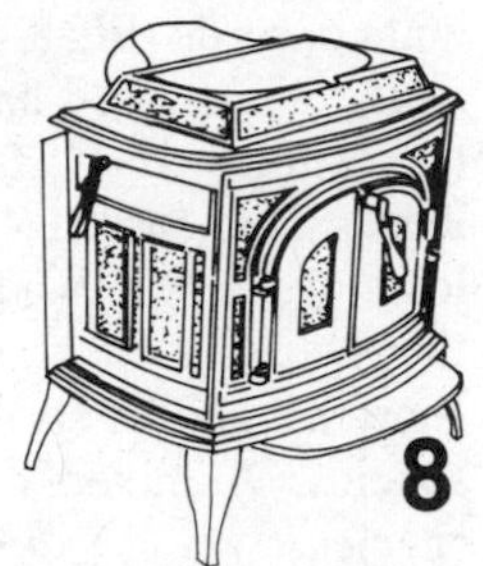

8

Wood and Coal As Fuels

The phrase "please turn up the heat" requires more than just the flick of a switch. It means going outside to get wood to restock the woodbox,removing the right amount of ashes, mixing the right seasoned wood for a long even burn, adjusting the air flow and feeding the fire for an even burning lasting heat. No chemicals should be used in a wood stove such as commercially produced sawdust logs. No garbage should be used for kindling. Wood storage requires a great deal of space. It tends to be somewhat messy with dirt, wood wastechips, sawdust and insects that are part of burning wood.

Household solid fuel combustion is a complex chemical reaction between oxygen and fuel. The result is heat and gases. Several conditions must be followed to assure maximum combustion:

- Continuous supply of fresh air.
- Proper amount of fuel in the combustion chamber not enough to overheat, but enough to avoid a cool flue liner which will result in poor draft and buildup of residues and creosote.
- Proper fuel burning to avoid waste and toxic products of combustion, such as carbon monoxide.
- Removing unwanted products of combustion.

Combustion occurs when all the fuel is oxidized by the air. Stoves and fireplaces are designed to operate with a considerable amount of excess air to prevent intermittent periods of incomplete combustion. When incomplete combustion occurs, carbon monoxide is produced.

WOOD BUYING

Wood buying is not a simple matter. In order for you not to "get burned," decide on an amount of wood, know the moisture content, the degree of preparation and the price. Wood is sold in units of cords (Fig 8-1). A full cord measures 8′ long, 4′ high and 4′ wide. A face cord has wood lengths of 12″ to 16″ to 24″, which makes it less than a full cord and the price should be less; 24″ long logs is a full cord, 16″ long logs is one-third less a full cord and 12″ long logs is ¼ less a full cord. When purchasing firewood, be sure the stacking of the logs is fairly tight so you will not be shortchanged. A straight cord is made up entirely of one grade or species. A mixed cord is made up of several different wood species.

The kind of wood is important. The best firewoods are the hardwoods because they produce more heat when burned. As a rule, hardwood trees are those that shed leaves and change seasonally. Softwoods generally are evergreens with needles.

A full cord of wood can weigh as much as 1 ton. From 3 to 10 cords of wood may be required to heat a house during one winter season. Beware of buying a truck load of wood. A standard pickup truck will hold only about one-third or one-half a full cord. The average wood burned per year is about 1 to 2 cords for fireplaces, 4 to 6 cords for stoves and 6 to 8 for woodburning furnaces. Wood heating value is the most important characteristic we should be concerned about. The more dense the wood, the more heat it will give off when burned. Woods are broken into hardwood and softwood with heating values between. Following are the groups broken down:

- The woods with the highest heat values, 28-30 million BTU per cord, are apple, birch, black locust, hickory, hop horn bean and white oak. One cord of these woods is equal to approximately 191 gallons of fuel, 228,000 cubic feet of natural gas and 5020 KWH of electricity.
- 25-26 million BTU per cord include ash, beach, red oak, sugar maple and yellow birch. These equal approximately 176 gallons of fuel oil, 211,000 cubic feet of natural gas and 4,600 KWH of electricity.
- With 21-23 million BTU per cord are black cherry, elm, grey birch, red maple, tamarack and white birch. These equal about 150 gallons of oil, 180,000 cubic feet of gas and 3971 KWH of electricity.

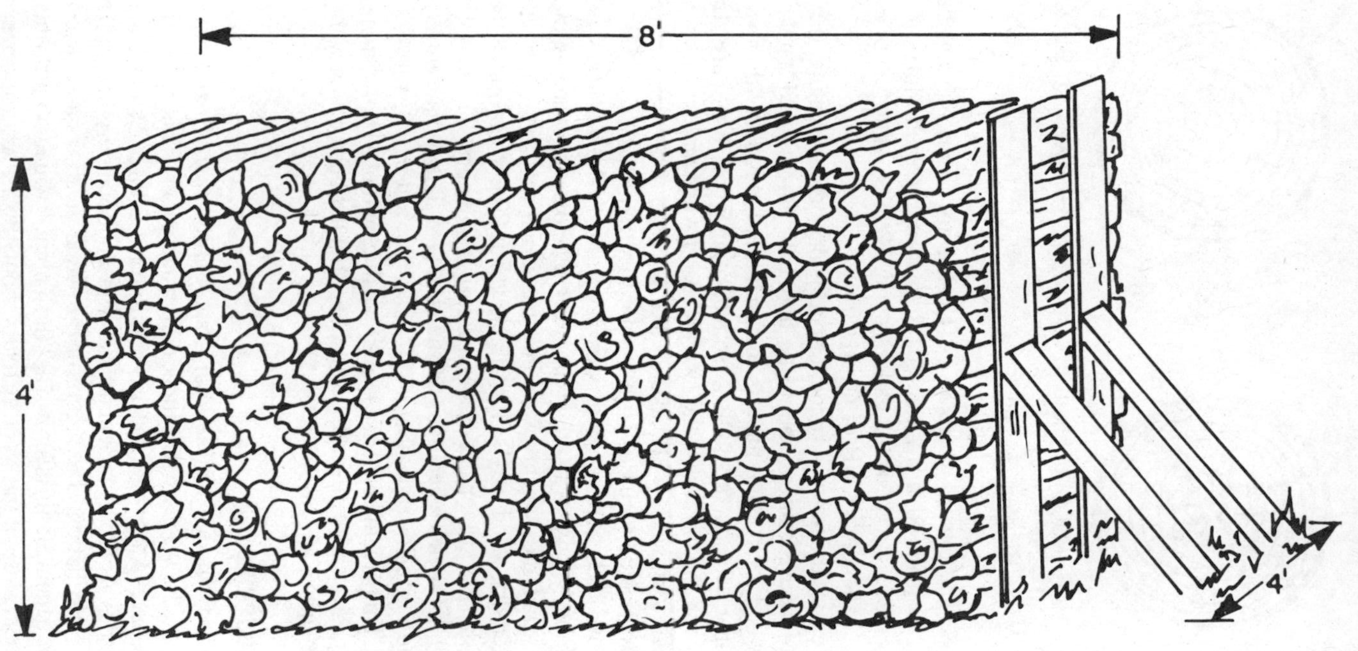

Fig. 8-1. A full cord of firewood.

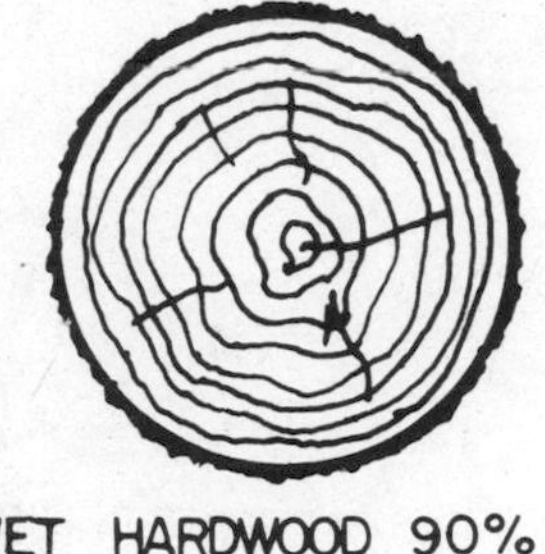

Fig. 8-2. Moisture content of wood.

- The lowest woods in heat value are alder, balsam, fir, basswood, adar, hemlock, poplar, spruce and white pine, equal to about 108 gallons of oil, 129,000 cubic feet of gas and 2800 KWH of electricity.

Be sure the firewood used, or cut, is dry before burning. (Fig. 8-2). Moisture content should be about 20 percent and it takes fresh wood about eight months to reach that level. Only then will you achieve the maximum heat from burning wood. If you are still not sure of the dryness, take two pieces of wood and knock them together. Dry wood will make a clear almost hollow sound. Wet wood will come together with a solid firm thud.

The BTU value of woods vary according to the density. One-fifth of the wood is wasted by moisture evaporation changing into steam. Half the weight of freshly cut wood may be water and so-called dry wood may still contains about 20 percent moisture. Water must be driven out of wood before it will burn. The greener the wood, the more heat loss up the chimney. The temperature of the flue normally runs about 400° and any water will turn into steam. This steam condenses on the inside wall of a cold chimney and deposits creosote on the walls. If you must burn green wood, burn it with a hot fire.

WOOD BURNING

Wood will burn in several stages (Fig. 8-3). Heat is first applied to the wood by burning kindling and paper. This raises the temperature of the wood and drives out the moisture. At this stage, the wood is absorbing heat and raises the wood temperature until it reaches distillation. The fibers of the wood give off gases which burst into flame. This is known as "flash point," which occurs when the temperature of the wood reaches about 480°F. After the gases are burned, charcoal remains which when burned gives off a high heat output. As the charcoal continues to burn, carbon is consumed leaving ashes which will not burn. When wood is burned, it releases carbon dioxide, water and ashes. If the burning process is complete and efficient, the energy is released as heat and the original components are recycled back to the earth. There is no pollution from harmful chemicals (Figs. 8-4 and 8-5).

Wood burns with a higher flame because of the high percentage of volatile matter. The combustion space above the burning wood must be greater than needed for coal. Most of the air mixture is introduced around the burning wood to assure complete combustion and prevent unburned gases from entering the chimney. If a moderate sized hot fire is maintained, any creosote or gases that enter the flue as a result of incomplete combustion will be

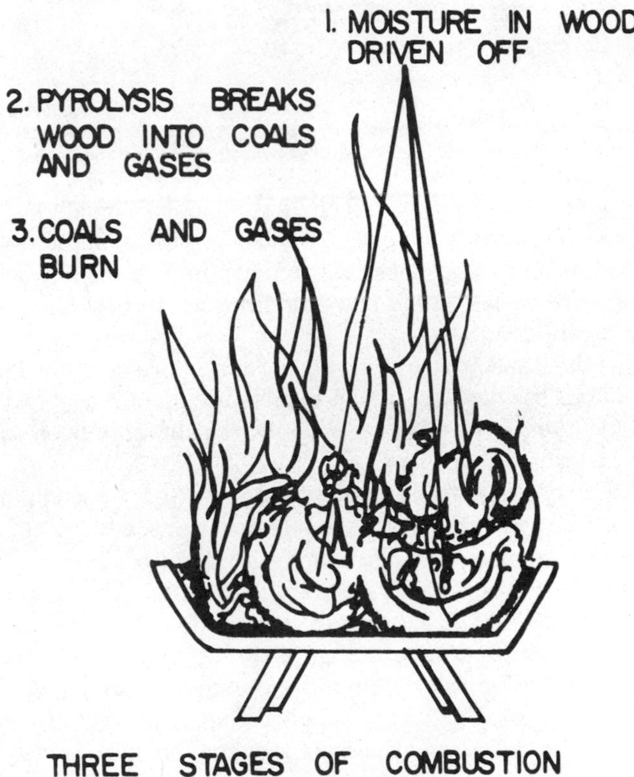

Fig. 8-3. Three stages of combustion. Three essentials are required to begin the combustion process. You need fuel, air and a high temperature to start and keep the fire going.

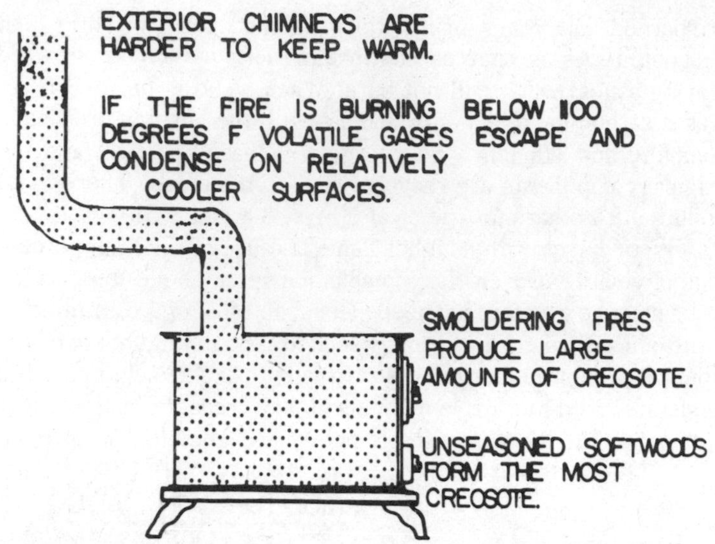
EXTERIOR CHIMNEYS ARE
HARDER TO KEEP WARM.
IF THE FIRE IS BURNING BELOW 1100
DEGREES F VOLATILE GASES ESCAPE AND
CONDENSE ON RELATIVELY
COOLER SURFACES.
SMOLDERING FIRES
PRODUCE LARGE
AMOUNTS OF CREOSOTE.
UNSEASONED SOFTWOODS
FORM THE MOST
CREOSOTE.

Fig. 8-4. Burn wood properly. If the fire is burning below 1100°F volatile gases escape and condense on relatively cooler surfaces. Smoldering fires produce large amounts of creosote. Unseasoned softwoods form the most creosote.

exhausted out through the hot chimney. A cooler smoldering fire will cause these gases to condense and accumulate on the wall of the flue lining, causing a possible chimney fire. A shallow bed of ashes should be left in the stove or fireplace to provide a heat reflecting surface.

Use the same principle for starting a coal fire as a wood fire. Once a draft has been created in the chimney, more coal may be added to the fire. The damper or draft must be fully open when starting a fire.

Wood should be stored in a dry location before use, and should be stacked so that both ends of the logs are exposed to the air. Do not burn waste paper like gift wrapping in the fireplace.

Firewood would be dried before burning. This involves loosely stacked rows to allow air to circulate for 4 to 12 months. If the logs are split, less time is required for drying. A close look at the ends of the log will determine the extent of drying. A well seasoned log will show cracks or splits running at right angles to the rings. This is caused by shrinkage as the moisture leaves the wood. If you attempt to burn green or unseasoned logs it becomes difficult to ignite the logs. If successful in igniting, it will not produce as much heat as seasoned wood. It also builds up creosote

Fig. 8-5. Stages in the cycle of wood.

in the flue lining which is one of the causes of chimney fires. Even with dry seasoned firewood, creosote can build up from a continuous slow burning overnight fire. A frequent hot fire will retard creosote buildup.

Stoves and fireplaces can be altered to burn coal or wood. A stove and chimney connection used to burn coal should be of heavy metal thickness. Either a stove ore fireplace requires grates in burning coal. Wood burning usually requires andirons.

Open fires like the sun give off radiant heat, which is the most comfortable of all types of heat. A draft free grated area requires low temperatures of radiant heat for comfort. Oxygen must be provided to keep the fire burning. Normal air leakage through the house (infiltration) is usually sufficient. If the house is extremely tight with insulation, a window may need to be opened slightly to supply the needed oxygen. Do not burn wood covered with shellac, paint or other preservatives. These are highly flammable and can produce chimney fires or toxic gases.

COAL BURNING

Most coals are highly volatile. An easy way to start a coal fire is to place a small amount of crumbled paper at the bottom of the grate and cover with a few sticks of kindling wood. Place the coal on top of the pile. The damper must be open completely before the fire is started. Ignite the paper and the heat will ignite the coal. After the coal is ignited, the damper may be adjusted slightly, but never fully closed as long as fire is burning. Coal will emit a large amount of carbon monoxide.

As the fire progresses, a bed of glowing coal is developed. These coals are overlaid with a fresh supply of coal as needed. The glowing coals ignite the volatile gases in the fresh coal before the gases accumulate. If the coal bed becomes cool, do not add more coal until the coal bed is relighted and glowing. If the gases are left to accumulate, a mild explosion may occur before being ignited. A hand fired stove or fireplace should be constantly attended while in use. Never use flammable liquids to ignite a fire.

ADVANTAGES OF WOOD

If the price of fossil fuel is making you consider wood, you are not alone. Over 50 percent of cold climate homes are already using wood either to supplement or totally supply heating needs. Historically, wood has supplied up to 90 percent of our energy needs, but as fossil fuels became cheaper our reliance on wood as a fuel declined to less than 1 percent by 1970. After the 1973 oil embargo and the increasingly high coat of "clean-modern fuels" began ruining budgets, more and more people began returning to wood as a fuel in 1976. Over that time span, the stove business suddenly became a multi-million dollar industry. In 1973 there were less than a dozen stove manufacturers left in America. Now they cannot be counted.

Wood is a form of solar energy. Sunlight, through photosynthesis, turns carbon dioxide and water into organic material. When the tree dies, bacteria converts it back to carbon dioxide and water with the nutrients returning to the soil. When a tree is burned, it releases the same ingredients: carbon dioxide, water and ashes. If the burning process is complete and efficient the energy stored is released as heat and the original components are recycled back to earth. There is no disruption of natural cycles, no pollution from harmful chemicals, just the speeding up of a natural process. Trees are renewable. As poor quality and commercially undesirable trees are removed from the forest for firewood, new growth occurs. As long as the forest is properly managed, and only the amount of wood that can be replaced is taken, little or no significant environmental damage occurs. By encourageing new growth a greater diversity of wildlife habitats are created.

Because of the environmentally soft characteristics of wood, it has become one of the favorite alternative fuels for heat. It cannot totally replace oil, coal or nuclear power in the energy future of heating, but it can complement the energy mix and make the land less dependent on imported, expensive and increasingly scarce fuels.

WOOD PREPARATION

Preparing wood is labor intensive and the price is largely dependent upon how much work you are willing to do yourself. If you want to have your firewood split into fine pieces and stacked near your doorstep, expect to pay premium prices. If you want to go the cheapest route, cut the wood yourself from standing trees. Wood can be bought in almost any stage between these extremes. It is fairly common to buy wood in 4 to 16′ lengths and do some of the cutting and splitting yourself. Wood delivered in this form usually costs about half that of wood cut and split, but involves about eight hours of hard work.

Table 8-1. Seasonal Moisture Effects, with Relative Heat Value and Moisture Content.

Time	Relative Heat Value	Moisture Content
Green in fall, winter or spring	89	80
Green in summer	93	65
Trees leaf-felled in summer after 2 weeks	96	45
Spring wood seasoned three months	97	35
Spring wood seasoned six months	98	30
Dry wood seasoned twelve months	100	25

There are no real "deals" in buying wood, just your sweat for the dealer's sweat. If you enjoy cutting and splitting wood as many people do, you can be paid handsomely for your recreation. Other sources of wood may include scavenging the local tree dump, picking broken pallets at a local mill or warehouse, purchasing ends, slabs and other waste from a local sawmill, buying cutting rights from a private landowner (many times done as shares—one cord for you and one for him), and cutting wood on state and federal lands. The possibilities are endless. The only determinant is one's ambition and resourcefulness. See Table 8-1 and 8-2.

The same type of wood will vary from place to place on price, all according to labor costs, transportation costs, and supply and demand. Shop around, try to buy when demand is low and be sure you understand exactly what you are buying.

OPERATING A STOVE

A wood stove is not like a conventional oil or gas heating system. It can't be forgotten, There is no electronic wizardry to do the thinking for you. It needs periodic attention. Still most people consider this part of the lure of heating with wood and they thoroughly enjoy the stoking, poking and tending that their stove demands. Operating a stove is not as simple as setting a thermostat, but it is a subtle blend of science and art. The science is the thing we learn from experience and the art comes only from time and practice.

Combustion is the process that rapidly turns the chemical energy stored in wood into light and heat. This process is actually quite complicated but it can be broken down into three separate stages. First, the moisture in the wood must be driven off. Then, at high temperatures, a reaction called *pyrolysis* occurs which breaks the wood into coals and gases. Finally, at still higher temperatures, the coals and gases burn. Complicating the picture is the fact that all of these steps may be occurring at the same time in different stages and parts of the fire. Generally, a fire must go through all of these stages at one time or another.

Obviously you need a match to start the fire and high temperatures to keep it going, but you also need fuel and air. Learning to operate a stove is simply learning to control these three variables: temperature, oxygen and fuel.

The air controls not only determine the rate of burning. They also determine the efficiency of the combustion process and affect the third essential for combustion, temperature.

Turning the damper down, as is often done for long burns, results in a cool fire. Because of the low temperatures, the gases produced by pyrolysis leave the fire unburned, and a potentially valuable amount or heat is lost. Contrast this with a fire burning with the damper wide open. The fire is hot enough to burn the gases, but the temperatures create a draft so strong that heat is lost up the chimney before it can be transferred to your home. It seems like there is no way to win, so a compromise is necessary. All we can tell is that the best position is somewhere in between these two. A little experimentation will help to descover that position best for your particular stove.

FACTORS AFFECTING WOOD FUEL QUALITY

A great deal of attention is usually paid to purchasing wood and rightfully so. You should be aware of the wood species, which determines the energy content, and how long it was seasoned, which gives a good indication of the moisture content.

Hardwoods are generally preferred over softwoods because they pack more energy into the same volume as softwoods. Actually all wood has the same amount of energy per pound, but hardwoods are more dense so they have more energy in a given

Table 8-2. Labor Involved in Various Methods of Buying Firewood.

Method of Sale	Labor Involved
Truck load of green logs	Eight hours/cord
Truck load four foot rough split wood	Six to eight hours/cord
Cut and Split, you pick up	One to two hours/cord
Cut split and delivered	0
Stumpage	Eight to twelve hours/cord
Slabs, ends, etc.	Varies
Pallets & scrap wood	Varies

volume. For example a cubic foot of poplar wiighs 26 pounds compared to 39 pounds for a cubic foot of sugar maple. Sugar maple has 1.5 times the energy of an equivalent volume of poplar. Since different species have different amounts of energy, you can match the amount of heat you need to a wood species. In reality, we need not be quite that precise. On cold days burn hardwoods, on warm days burn softwoods, and on moderate days a mix of hardwoods and softwoods will do. In time you will learn the different species of wood, their heating qualities, and be able to match them to your needs.

The moisture in the wood is a second important factor affecting fuel quality. Burning wet wood wastes energy because every bit of moisture in wood must be evaporated before it will burn. Evaporating this moisture takes energy. Naturally, the wetter the wood the more water to be evaporated and the more energy you lose. Burn wood that has dried for at least six months and your fire will start more easily and give off more heat.

The second essential for combusion, oxygen, is controlled by the damper or air inlet of the stove. There are many different types of dampers and air inlets, but all of these have the same function. They allow you to control the flow of air going to the fire. Shut the air controls way down and the fire will burn slowly. Open them and the fire burns quickly.

STARTING A FIRE

Nothing can be quite so frustrating to a beginner as failing to start a fire. Once you learn the basic principles, nothing could be easier. Again the three essentials, fuel, oxygen and temperature—come into play. To start a fire you need dry fuel, plenty of oxygen and high temperatures.

—Open the dampers and air inlets on the stove all the way.

—Crumble or shred newspapers and place them in the stove. Burning these will provide temperatures needed to ignite the wood.

—Stack small pieces (up to 1″ in diameter) of very dry kindling on the paper, log cabin or teepee style, to insure that plenty of oxygen will create circulation in the fire. Softwoods like pine and cedar split into thin pieces make the best kindling. Any wood will do if dry and finely split. If you use your stove intermittently, it will be wise to secure a supply of pine scraps as kindling.

—Light the paper, wait until the fire is blazing and then add larger pieces of fuel. Stack them so that air can circulate freely around them.

—After 10 minutes or so, close down the air controls to the desired location.

MAKING FIRE LAST

Most people seem to enjoy tinkering with a stove during the day or evening but when night comes, they get down to business. No one likes to wake up to a cold house. Learning to make a fire last is essential.

Set your heating system thermostat at 55° to 60°F. so that the heating system will take over when the fire goes out. Overheat your home to perhaps 80 to 85°F. Even if the house cools 15 or 20° by morning, the temperature will still be a comfortable 60°.

Glossy magazines contain a lot of filler which does not burn and leaves behind a large amount of ashes. Lay 15 or 20 sheets of such paper on the fire. It will burn, leaving a thick layer of ash on top of the wood. This reduces the amount of air that can get to the fuel and slows down the burning rate. When splitting wood, you will come across large knots that defy hammer and wedge. So be it. These will insure they burn slow. Save these and your densest woods for the coldest nights.

Close the dampers for long burns. Some of the heat loss due to unburned gases will be compensated for by better heat transfer between the fire and the stove walls. Remember that these unburned gases end up as creosote in the stove pipe or chimney. Periodically check your flue or pipe and clean as necessary. Try to begin a new burning cycle at the beginnings of long periods of inattention. Before bedtime all that should remain of the previous fire is a bed of coals. This insures that a fuel change will last for the maximum period of time. If seasoned wood is scarce, mixing green wood with dry wood will extend the wood pile and make the fire last a little longer. This technique should be approached with caution as green wood produces excessive creosote, and even more so when the stove is tightly dampered. If forced to use this method, it is good advice to start a good hot fire every morning to burn off the creosote formed the night before. Obviously the alternative to making a fire last is to get up early in the morning to stoke the stove. Then go back to sleep.

One fo the by-products of burning wood is ash. Eventually you will have to remove some or it will fill you stove. Remove ash with a shovel and place it in a heavy bucket. Assume that there are still hot coals mixed in with the ashes (there usually are) and do not place them in the garbage in or near anything combustible. You may wish to save the ashes in a metal drum. They make excellent fertilizer and can be used to give traction on icy walks and steps. They can even be used to make soap.

WOOD STORAGE

Split as much wood as possible. Remove the bark because it seals the wood and retains the moisture, preventing the logs from drying out. Small diameter pieces need not be split because they dry quickly. Whether you cut your own wood or buy it, try to get as many split logs as possible in your wood pile.

Stack the wood neatly, bark side up, in an area with plenty of sun the logs in length parallel to the prevailing winds. This will help to dry out the logs. Keep the bottom of the pile off the ground by stacking the wood on rot resistant lumber such as 2 × 3″. A sheet of plastic on the ground under the log pile will help to keep ground moisture from penetrating the logs. Cover the log pile with a protective cover such as tar paper or plastic film to guard against rain, snow and ice.

Check to see if insects or spiders are beginning to nest in the wood pile. If this happens don't use insect repellents or pesticides on the wood. When the logs are burned, this will cause dangerous fumes. Move the pile to another location where it is drier and there are stronger winds. Keep the area clean to discourage termites and carpenter ants or other wood eating pests. If you do see them, take precautinos so they will not find their way into the house or other buildings. Never place a log on the ground in contact with the house or building that might provide a home for the insects. After about three months of temperatures around 50°F., the wood will be as dry as this method will allow it to be. Store the wood where it will protected against the weather. Don't store wood inside the house. Carry in as many logs as the fire will support. Any dormant insects nesting in the logs will come alive from the heat inside the house.

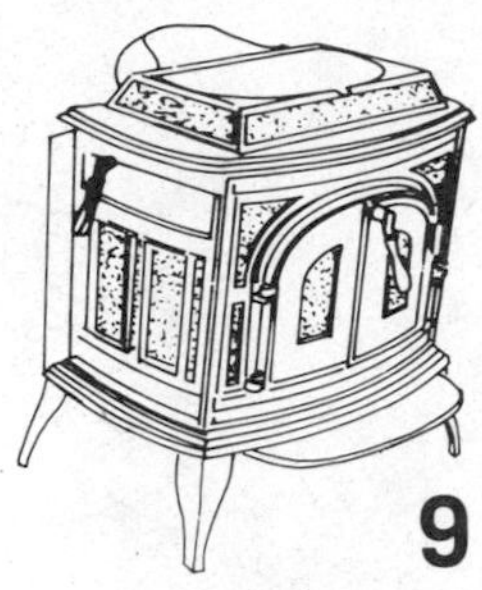

9 Safety

Of prime importance is safety, your safety. Follow instructions from manufacturers carefully. Do not follow the adage, "When all else fails read the instructions." Careful and proper use of tools, especially power tools, will develop a strong feeling toward safety. This means giving time and attention to your work. It means that you will be certain to work carefully and follow the rules. Following are examples of actual accidents which occured because proper safety measures were not followed.

REPORTED ACCIDENTS

- The back of a fireplace chimney faced an open porch; the porch was later enclosed. Wood furring strips were nailed over the brick with 2″ long case hardened nails, penetrating the chimney. Wood paneling was nailed to the furring strips and the heat from the fireplace heated the nails, igniting the furring strips, which in turn ignited the wood paneling. A woman was killed and a man was injured.
- A living room wood burning stove was overfired before the family retired for the night. While asleep, the heat from the overfired stove ignited the wall paper. The fire spread quickly, burning three children to death (Fig. 9-1).
- Seven children aged 4 to 12 were killed while unattended because one of the children overloaded the wood burning stove, setting the walls of the house on fire.

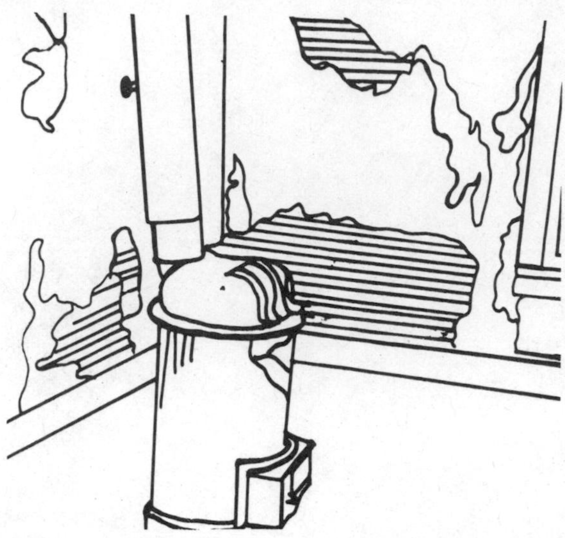

Fig. 9-1. Damage caused by an overfired wood burning stove.

- An ice storm caused a power outage. The owner lighted his fireplace, overloading, so he could not place the screen in front of the fire. He then poured charcoal lighter fluid on the wood to ignite it and left the lighter fluid container and some newspapers on the hearth and went to bed. The fireplace overheated and ignited the lighter fluid and the newspapers, completely destroying the wood frame.
- A wood burning stove was installed too close to a wall and the flue pipe connector was installed straight up through the ceiling and roof, without proper precautions. Two people were killed and the house was destroyed (Fig. 9-2).
- A wood burning stove with 6″ legs was installed on a rug covered floor within 4″ from a combustible wall. The rug and wall ignited.
- The chimney connector of a wood burning stove was installed through the side wall. The heat from the connector ignited the wall (Fig. 9-3).
- A Franklin stove was installed using an 8″ chimney flue connection, vertically from the stove. The clearance between the connector and the structural members of the house was not adequate. After several hours of continuous use, the wood was ignited.

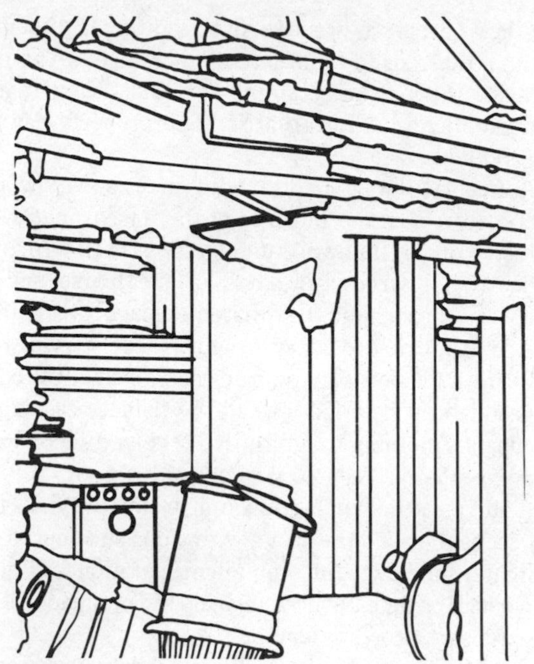

Fig. 9-2. Results of a fire where a chimney connector was used as a chimney and run through the ceiling and roof with no clearances.

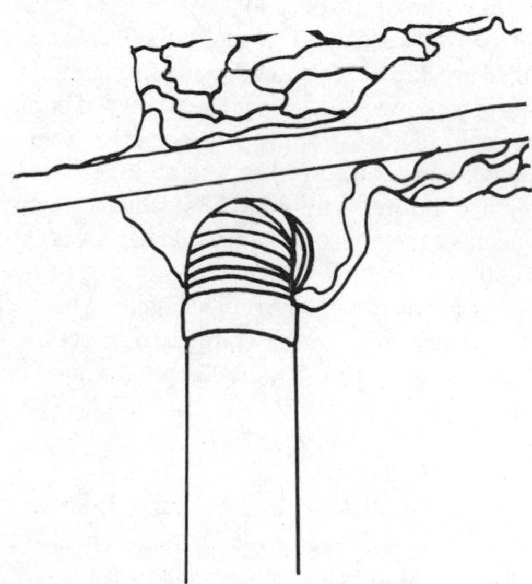

Fig. 9-3. Results of a chimney connector fire where the connector was improperly installed with inadequate clearances.

- A large fireplace was overfired igniting the floor joists in the attic, caused by a defective chimney. The occupant heard the crackling sound and dismissed it as being caused by mice in the attic. The property damage was $150,000.
- A fireplace was loaded with unseasoned wood. The creosote from the burning of the unseasoned wood collected on the flue walls and ignited. The hot fire ignited, destroyed structural parts of the house and quickly spread throughout. Estimated damage was $100,000.
- A fire appeared to be out in a fireplace. In trying to relight the fire, the occupant poured gasoline over the coals. The gasoline flashed and spread the flames, causing the occupant's clothing to ignite. He received second and third degree burns over 20 percent of his body.
- A stove had hot coals remaining from a previous fire. The occupant loaded the stove with wood and poured charcoal lighter fluid over the wood in preparation for lighting the wood. The fluid flashed, injuring the occupant and causing extensive property damage.
- Rags were used to plug holes in a defective chimney. The heat from the chimney ignited the rags and the fire spread, killing four people.
- Wood joists were used to support a fireplace. After prolonged use, the heat from the open fire ignited the joists.
- Piles of paper were stored close to a wood burning stove. The paper ignited, trapping the occupant from escaping.
- Matches had been stored on a mantel shelf. Heat from the fireplace ignited the matches which quickly spread throughout the house. Property damage was estimated at $15,000.
- A fire originated from a fireplace igniting hay, which was used for insulation in the chimney be a previous owner. Several people were hospitalized for smoke inhalation.

CLOTHING

Dress properly for the work to be done. Remove coats and jackets in warm weather. Trousers and overalls should fit properly without any loose clothing such as sleeves or pant legs. No cuffs should be worn on trousers. Button sleeves or roll them all the way up.

Shoes should be thick soled, preferably rubber, and reinforced at the toes to withstand a load of 2500 pounds. Do not wear sneakers or lightweight canvas shoes. A hard hat is a must for protection against falling objects. Be comfortable. Good visibility is important, but safety glasses are also vital. Have enough light without straining your eyes. Standard specifications state that safety glasses lens must withstand the blow of a ⅛" steel ball dropped from a height of 50" without breaking.

Keep your hands free of any grease or oil. Wear gloves of an appropriate type without restriction to the use of fingers and hands. If you are working in a dusty area, wear a face mask.

TOOLS

Select the proper size and type of hand and power tools for the job. Be sure they are sharp, clean and properly adjusted. Do not use tools with loose handles or in poor condition. Dull tools require excessive force to make them cut and become hazardous. They may slip and cause serious injury. When carrying tools, keep the edges and pointed end turned down. Do not swing or raise your arms over your head with tools in hand. Carry only what you need. Do not carry sharp tools in your pocket. When using tools, hold them correctly and all cutting should be away from you. If you use your fingers or hand as a guide, be very careful. Hitting the wrong nail can be very painful. When tools are not in use, they should be stored in a tool chest or box. Do not use your finger to test the sharpness of a tool. Use a strip of paper or block of wood.

Do not rush the job through. A good steady unhurried pace will accompolish more and better work. If you become over confident, you become careless.

Become thoroughly familiar with power tools before use. Be sure you have the correct electric wire size extension cord. More importantly, it should be of the waterproof type. The manufacturer of power tools will list the safety precautions and the proper use of the tool. All electrical tools should be grounded. Grounded plugs have three prongs; the third prong acts as a ground. If it were not there, electricity could pass through your body in the event of an electrical problem. If you do not have a three prong plug, do not cut the third prong from the power plug cord. Use an adapter for the third plug, a very inexpensive hardware store item.

Keep the construction site neat at all times. This requires good housekeeping and an organized plan. Do not pile tools one upon the other. Never allow a sharp or pointed tool to hang over a table, bench or scaffold. Manintenance is in order. This leads to efficiency and is important to prevent accidents. Place building material in a neat pile ready for use, but not in a passage or aisle. Contain waste, scrap and rubbish until ready for disposal. Do not permit brick, block, empty mortar bags or other building material to accumulate since they interfere with traffic and may constrict working, forming a tripping hazard.

To perform a safe task with hand tools or power tools, stand on a firm solid base, smooth but not slippery. Do not work or reach over rough piles of earth of stacks or building materials. Stay well away from edges such as walls, excavation or scaffolding, or install guard rails. In cold weather, remove any ice or melting snow or cover it with sand or chemicals. If materials is stored overhead, be sure it is properly placed and stacked so it will not fall off. If any liquid is spilled, wipe it up immediately.

LADDERS AND HEAVY LOADS

Check ladders frequently and at regular intervals. Limit their use to climbing from one level to another. Do not use a ladder as a horizontal working platform. Working on a ladder, even in a proper position, is hazardous and dangerous. To erect a ladder, place the lower end against a solid object, such as a wall, so it cannot slide. Raise the top end and walk toward the bottom, raising the ladder by each rung as you walk. When the ladder is vertical, place it against the structure at a proper angle so that the horizontal distance from the lower end to the wall or structure is at least one-fourth the length of the ladder. Before climbing the ladder, be sure both rails rest on solid footing and also that the extension is firmly locked into place. The ladder bottom should have safety shoes to prevent slippage. Always carry a ladder slightly elevated at the front end over your shoulder. Do not allow the ladder to drop. Place it down. Dropping could weaken the ladder. When storing, be sure the ladder is in a horizontal position to prevent distortion. Do not use metal ladders where there is a possibility of coming in contact with electric wires. Face a ladder when climbing up or down. Both hands must be used for support when climbing a ladder.

When carrying a heavy load, do not turn or twist your body. Make adjustment in position by shifting of the feet. If the load is bulky, seek help. Never underestimate the weight to be lifted or overestimate your strength.

Protect your back muscles when lifting heavy objects. Lift with your leg and arm muscles, not with your back muscles. Seek help if the object is too heavy for you.

FIRE PREVENTION

Become familiar with different classes of fire because they can occur on any building site. Class A fires are form burning wood and debris. Class B fires involve volatile materials such as gasoline, oil, paints and oil-soaked rags. Class C fires are caused by electricity and faulty electrical equipment such as extension cords and power tools.

Always check the electric cords on power tools and keep oil and grease-soaked rags contained. Fire extinguishers should be easily available on all construction sites. Be sure to use the proper extinguisher for the class fire.

FIRST AID

A knowledge of first aid is extremely important. Be sure you understand the approved procedures and be able to use good judgement. Knowing what not to do and doing nothing without professional help is sometimes as important as knowing what to do properly. An accident victim may receive further injury from treatment by an unqualified person. First aid information is available from the local Red Cross office. Keep a first aid kit handy and use it to treat even the slightest of cuts or scratches.

Nothing is more important than your safety and safety to others. Besides a physical handicap, which may result from an accident you may be deterred from your regular job for a period of time. Loss of time is loss of money, probably far more than the savings on your do-it-yourself project. Many accidents can be avoided by using common sense and not taking short cuts. The quickest way is not always the safest and best way.

Other reasons for injury on the job are due to lack of interest, inattention, tiredness, carellessness and sloppy methods. It is easy to become careless when you feel overconfident, and this attitude should be avoided. Construction work is very dangerous because one must work with sharp tools, electric power tools and on and under scaffolding.

Exceptionally long hair poses another danger in construction. Tuck the hair well under the hard hat or tie it back to prevent possible injury.

MORTAR BOARD AND SUPPLIES

Always space the mortar board about 24″ away from the wall under construction. This makes it wasy to pick up and spread the mortar by merely pivoting around from the mortar board to the wall in one motion without taking any unnecessary steps. Elevate the mortar board about 20″ using concrete blocks. This will avoid unnecessary bending. Check mortar boards or pans for cracks, breaks or splinters. Metal mortar boards sometimes split as a result of rough usage. This creates sharp dangerous edges which may cause serious injury. Do not use mortar board if it cannot be repaired.

Stack the masonry units the same distance away from the wall as the mortar board. The units should be stacked in the same position as they will go onto the wall without having to be turned over or around. Keep them about 12″ away from the mortar pan on both sides. This will prevent mortar from splashing onto the masonry units. They should be interlocked when stacked to prevent them from falling over.

LIGHTNING PROTECTION

The probability of injury to a person from lightning is remote. Nonetheless, it does happen. The principle in the protection of chimneys against lightning is to provide means by which a lighting discharge may enter or leave the earth without passing through a nonconducting part of the chimney such as building material of wood, brick, tile, stone or concrete. Damage may be caused by the heat and mechanical forces generated by the discharge.

Lightning discharges to chimneys tend to travel in metal parts which extend in the general direction of the discharge. Damage can be reduced if the parts are properly grounded. Lightning has such a wide range of characteristics that it is difficult to provide protection under all conditions. If the installation is properly made and maintained, the degree of damage is reduced considerably. The purpose of lightning protection is to protect the chimney in case a lightning bolt occurs or strikes the chimney. It is not to prevent such a strike. The protection involves placing metal air terminals on the upper part of the chimney with conductors connected with the terminals and to the ground.

When building a new chimney, lightning protection should be considered in the planning stage. If already built, installation is not a difficult job. When designing and installing a lightning protection system, the following should be considered.

- The purpose is to intercept the discharge immediately and to direct it into the ground. The air terminals, or lightning arresters must be placed high enough above the chimney to prevent danger of fire from the arc.

- The system must be installed in a direct path from the top of the chimney to the ground. There should be no sharp bends or loops.
- When lightning is about to strike, a radius of several miles carries an electrical charge. As the strike takes place, these electrical charges concentrate in the spot where the strike occurs. At that point, the current becomes high. If it flows through the house foundation, damage may result. For that reason, the grounding should be placed away from the building. A least two ground connections should be made spaced on opposite sides of the building.
- If the lightning system is installed near metal objects of considerable size, within a few feet of the system, sparks or flashes of electricity could jump from the conductor to the metal object. To prevent such damage, interconnecting conductors should be provided at all places where this is likely to occur.
- All material used in the lightning protection system should be resistant to corrosion.

Conductors

How do we determine how far we should go in the protection system, or even if we should put one in at all? The frequency of thunderstorms varies throughout the United States. A few severe thunderstorms a season may be reason enough to install the system. The lightning hazard to human beings in a house should not be overlooked. Casualities from lightning have occurred. The exposure of the building or chimney is also a factor. In closely built-up towns and cities, the hazard is not as great as in open country. In hilly or mountainous districts, a building upon high ground is usually subject to greater hazard than one in a valley or sheltered area.

The conductors used in the system shall be a grade ordinarily used for electrical wiring. Following are material used:

—Copper should be of a grade designated as being 98 percent conductivity when annealed. Wire size should be not less than No. 17 American Wire Gauge (AWG) (0.045″ diameter).

—Alloys should be substantially resistant to corrosion as copper. Wire size should not be less than No. 16 AWG (0.051″).

—Copper clad steel covering shall be permanently welded to the steel core. The proportion of copper should be such that the conductance is not less than 30 percent of the conductance of an equivalent cross section of copper. Wire size should be No. 16 AWG.

—Aluminum should not be in contact with ground because it will deteriorate rapidly. Precautions should be taken at connections with dissimilar metals. Cable conductor should be of electrical conductor grade aluminum. Wire size should not be less than No. 14 AWG (0.064″). Do not use copper, copper-covered or copper alloy fixtures. Only aluminum fittings should be ued except direct ground connections. These should be galvanized iron.

Joints shall be as few in number as possible and they should be made mechanically tight and strong. The height of the terminal should be no less than 10″ above the chimney height. No less than two conductors should be installed and a separate ground connection should be made for each conductor. Where a metallic water pipe enters the building at least one conductor should be connected to it, preferably at a point away from the building.

Making Ground Connections

Properly made ground connections are essential to the effective functioning of a lightning protection system. Every effort should be made to provide ample contact with the earth. This does not necessarily mean that the resistance of the ground connection must be low, but rather that the distribution of metal in the earth, or upon its surface in extreme cases, shall be such as to permit the dissipation of a stroke of lightning without damage.

Low resistance is, of course, desirable, but not essential, as may be shown by extreme cases on one hand of a building resting on moist clay soil, and on the other by a building resting on bare solid rock. In the first case, if the soil is of normal resistivity, the resistance of the ground connection made by extending the conductor 10′ into the ground will be greater. Under these conditions, adequate means for collecting and dissipating the energy of a flash of lightning without chance of damage is a simple and comparatively inexpensive matter.

In the second case, it would be impossible to make a ground connection in the ordinary sense of the term because most kinds of rock are insulating, or at least of high resistivity. In order to obtain effective grounding, other and more elaborate means are necessary. The most effective means would be an extensive wire network laid on the surface of the rock surrounding the building, connected to the down conductors. The resistance to earth at some distant point of such an arrangement would be high. At the same time the potential distribution about the building would be substantially the same as though it were resting on conducting soil. The resulting protective effect would also be substantially the same.

In general, the extent of the grounding arrangement will depend upon the character of the soil, ranging from simple extension of the conductor into the ground where the soil is deep and of high conductivity to an elaborate buried network where the soil is very dry or of very poor conductivity. Where a network is required, it should be buried if there is soil enough to permit it. This adds to its effectiveness.

Some essential features of good practice in grounding for protection against lightning are as follows:

- Where practical each artificial ground connection should extend or have a branch which extends below and at least 2″ away from the foundation walls of the building. Otherwise, there is a chance of the wall being damaged.
- The metal composing the ground connection should make contact with the soil from the surface downwards. If contact is made below the surface, there may be flashing at the surface with the danger of burning the building.
- During a stroke of lightning on a system of conductors, the grounding electrodes are to be thought of as the points through which the heavy current flows between the air terminals and the surface of the earth about the building. They should, therefore, be distributed with the view of carrying this flow of current in the most advantageous manner. This will be generally realized by placing the electrodes at the outer extremities, such as the corners, and avoiding as far as possible current flow under the building.

A LAST WORD

Well, you've followed these guidelines, so you're safe, right? Wrong. Safety demands vigilance. Maintain and inspect your equipment regularly. Don't let a dangerous situation begin. Prepare your family for a fire. Plan escape routes from every room in your home and make your family aware of fire survival techniques. Have a practice drill so that everyone understands exactly what to do in the event of a fire. Only when you have done all you can should you be confident of safety.

Glossary

abutment—the skewback of an arch.

anchors—metal ties which have a bend on each end; used for tying stone and backing masonry together by building in with mortar.

arch—a section of masonry work that spans an opening and supports both its own weight and the weight of the masonry work above it.

arch axis—the median line of the arch ring.

ash dump—flat, metal door with a flange built flush with the fireplace's inner hearth; used for dumping ashes into the ash pit.

ashlar stonemasonry—stone that is cut to the dimensions shown on shop drawings. It is cut, dressed, and finished to precise job requirements at the mill, and shipped to the job as a completed product. Ashlar stone is set in a constant mortar joint thickness, and is laid in a definite repeated pattern or in a varied bond known as random ashlar.

ash pit—area directly below a fireplace's inner hearth where ashes from the fire are collected via the ash dump.

backfilling—the process of packing earth in around a foundation.

barbecue—a raised masonry structure for the drying, smoking, or preparing of food; a small outdoor fireplace without a chimney.

basket weave bond—bricks are alternated in a vertical and horizontal position every 8″. A brick masonry pattern bond.

batter—the upward and backward slope of a masonry wall (such as a retaining wall) from the face side. It is built to fight off the pressure of the earth fill behind the wall.

batter boards—right-angle corner posts and boards, built on the job to hold and maintain the actual wall lines of the building during the period of excavation and construction of the foundation.

bearing wall—a masonry wall that supports a load, such as joists, concrete floors, or roofs other than its own.

belt course—a course of stone or brick that completely surrounds a structure at one level for decorative purposes.

bench mark—a definite mark put on some object on the work site, to be used as a reference point in deciding on heights for a building. This mark is based on height of the ground above or below sea level.

bituminous—term used to designate materials that are derived from petroleum, coal tar, and so forth.

bond beam—course of masonry units inserted with steel reinforcing rods and filled solidly with mortar.

bonded arch—an arch that is comprised of alternating bricks that are bonded together, like a jack arch that is 1 ½ bricks high.

bonded jack arch—the strongest type of jack arch. It is higher than one brick and is bonded by alternating the mortar joints so they are staggered in appearance.

brick buggy—a cart that can be driven by a mounted gasoline engine, with or without hydraulic controls. It is used to transport masonry units to the mason.

brick veneer—the brick facing laid around an existing frame building. It is not considered a load-bearing wall and supports only its own weight.

building code—regulations governing the building construction; established by local, state, and federal agencies.

building line—the main line used to lay out a building; ususally the front wall of the structure.

building paper—paper applied to floors or walls as a cushion and dampproofer in the construction of a building. Thirty-pound felt paper is the best type to apply to framing walls before laying the brick veneer.

bush hammer—a heavy, steel forged hammer with a toothed head either on one end or both ends. It is used for dressing soft stone. The toothed head grinds the stone to a fine edge without cracking or splitting the stone.

calcium chloride—chemical that is combined with water for the mixing of mortar. It should not exceed more than 2 percent of the portland cement by weight. Do not use in mortar that contains metal wall ties because it can cause corrosion.

camber— a jack arch's relatively small rise.

casting—manner of fabrication of masonry panels involving the combining of masonry units and grout in a form. This can be done either vertically or horizontally.

caulking—the process of filling in cracks or cavities around expansion joints, doors or windows by using an elastic material usually from a caulking gun.

caustic soda—a chemical that removes old paint from masonry work. It is also known as sodium hydroxide or lye.

ceramic glazed brick—brick is made from shale and clay, fire-clay or a mixture of both,and glazed on the face before firing in a kiln. Glazed bricks are needed where a brick with a very dense, water-repellent finish is specified.

chill factor (or windchill)—wind speed plus temperature. The windchill makes the air seem much colder than the thermometer indicates.

chimney pad—a chimney's footing.

cleanout door—metal door placed in the masonry work below a flue at the chimney bottom. It is used for cleaning out soot from the chimney.

closure—the last masonry unit (such as the last brick) laid in a wall or step. A closure unit is usually placed in the middle of a wall.

cmu—abbreviation for concrete masonry unit.

colonial ring-around fireplace—fireplace with only the facing of bricks stacked up the jambs with an exposed soldier course over the top.

common jack arch—a jack arch which is only one soldier brick in height.

constant cross-section arch—an arch whose span has a constant depth and thickness throughout.

correlated—mutually related to each other or to work together efficiently. The laying of six standard courses of brick together, backed up with 2 courses of concrete block, would be level with each other, or correlated.

cove—the angled, thickened coat of portland cement mortar troweled on at the bottom of the outside of the foundation wall.

cove base—specially made glazed tile with projected curved lip at the bottom made for the finished floor to fit against.

creepers—bricks next to the arch which are cut to fit the curvatures of the outer edges of the arch ring.

crown—the apex (center) of the arch ring. The crown is at midspan in symmetrical arches.

cube—A pallet of concrete blocks or a banded stack of bricks.

damper—metal device installed over the fireplace's firebox to control the draft from the firebox into the chimney flue.

dead load—the weight of the superstructure such as floors, roofs, and walls. Dead load is steady, constant, and unmoving.

density—an object's hardness.

depth (of an arch)—the dimension perpendicular to the tangent of the axis. The depth of a jack arch is its greatest vertical dimension.

diamond bond—bricks are arranged to form a series of diamond designs; a brick masonry pattern.

dowel pin—a metal pin, usually made of brass or galvanized metal, used in stonework. The dowel pin is inserted in the top of a masonry wall with the end projected to fit into the coping stone's dowel hole.

draft—the current of air created by the variation in pressure resulting from differences in weight between the cooler air outside the chimney and hot gases in the flue.

drain tile—terra-cotta or concrete pipe laid on a bed of crushed stone to drain water away from a masonry building.

dry bonding—laying out masonry units without mortar to establish a wall's bond.

dummy flue—flue lining installed at the top of the chimney that is not hooked up to any source of heat. It is used only to appear as a flue and balance out a chimney with only two flues but a large empty space between them. Dummy flues should be filled with mortar on the side to keep birds or insects from building in them.

efflorescence—the whitish deposit found on the exposed face of a wall's masonry units. It is caused by the leaching of soluble salts from within the wall.

end construction—the vertical coring of a structural clay tile's cells.

engineered brick masonry—load-bearing brick masonry walls that are constructed following a careful analysis of the structure and based on generally accepted analysis methods. The brick walls are built to the story height and the floor is installed bearing on the wall. The next story is then built and the process is repeated until the structure is finished. No steel or concrete frame is needed.

epoxy mortar—mortar used for pointing up head and bed joints in glazed tile work; consists of a hardener, resin and powder. The finish of epoxy mortar is very hard and durable, and recommended for a joint finish where a sanitary condition exists.

expansion joint—elastic joint of rubber or fiber used in masonry to allow masonry movement to prevent cracking from expansion and contraction.

extrados—the convex curve which bounds the arch's upper limits.

face hammer—a heavy hammer weighing 4 to 6 pounds used for breaking and dressing stone for masonry work. It has a tapered edge on one end and is also sometimes called a stone axe or stone hammer.

fill—a coarser grade of earth used to fill in and around walls or foundations.

firebox—fireplace area built of firebricks or bricks where the fire is built.

fixed arch—an arch that has a skewback which has set position and inclination. Plain masonry arches are fixed arches.

flagstone—a hard flat-faced stone usually no more than 1½″ thick. It is laid either in mortar or sand for walks, patios, and floors. Flagstone can be laid in a squared section bond or a random pattern with irregular pieces.

flash set—the rapid setting of portland cement caused by adding water that is too hot (usually in excess of 160°F.).

floor joists—wood or metal supports that span from wall to wall, usually 2″ × 10″ or 2″ × 12″; used in the construction of a building to support the floor.

flue lining—fireclay or fireproof terra-cotta, used to line the flue of a chimney. It may be rectangular or round in shape, and is usually 2′ long.

footboard—a wood board that is laid on concrete blocks or bricks and is used by the mason to stand on when setting stone or laying brick. Sometimes called a hopping board, a footboard is the simplest type of scaffolding.

footing—the enlarged concrete base, usually, that the foundation rests on. Its function is to support the building and distribute the weight over a greater area.

formed footing—concrete footings that are set into a form on the job.

foundation—walls of a building that are built below grade (or below the first floor joists) and support the structure that will set on it.

Franklin stove—cast iron stove resembling a fireplace; created by Benjamin Franklin.

frost line—the depth of the earth where it is probable that frost will occur. The frost line varies in different places according to the temperatures in each area.

fullback—concrete block that has all of the cell webs cut out except the last one that holds the block together.

gauge rod (or sill stick)—shortened version of the story pole usually about 4 feet high. It is used for building the corner to the sill height.

gin pole—a wood metal pole that is held in place by guy wires and cable. The end of the pole has a block and tackle hook attached on a cable for the lifting of stones with a winch.

glass wool—insulation comprised of glass fibers.

Gothic arch (or pointed arch)—an arch with a rather high rise, with sides consisting of arcs of circles, the middles of which are at the level of the springing line. The Gothic arch is often referred to as a crop, equilateral, or lancet arch, depending upon whether the spacings of the centers are less than, equal to, or more than the clear span.

grade—the ground level around a building in relation to the building. When the earth is on a slope, it is said to have falling or rising grade.

grade beam—concrete reinforced beam placed just below the finish grade line for the purpose of supporting a masonry wall.

grading—the process of filling around a building with soil so the grade slopes away and downward from the building to carry the water away.

grout—very thin, proportioned mortar which is placed between two walls for reinforcement or liquid concrete that is set in the center of a reinforced masonry wall; consists of aggregates, lime and portland cement.

hacking—the process of unloading bricks from a truck by manual labor using brick tongs.

half-high block—a rip block that is cut in half lengthwise.

halfback—concrete block that has the inside of two cells cut out.

hawk—a square platform made of metal or wood, hand-held using a vertical handle in the center. It is used to carry plaster or mortar.

header brick—brick laid lengthwide in the wall with its tiniest end facing out; used for corbeling in the smoke chamber.

herringbone bond—pattern bond used in brickwork in which bricks in alternate courses are placed on an angle in opposite directions. It presents a zigzag, diagonal pattern.

high-bond mortar—portland cement mortar with a special additive for extra strength. High-bond mortar makes it possible to build masonry panels in 4-inch wythe thicknesses in a factory.

inner hearth—the flat bottom part of the firebox that the fire is built on.

intrados—the concave curve which bounds an arch's lower limits. The difference between the soffit and the intrados is that the intrados is linear, while the soffit is a surface.

island fireplace—fireplace built in a room's center that is open on more than one side.

jack arch—a flat arch capable of carrying a load, but should be supported on steel angle irons if the openings are over 2 feet long. It is the weakest of all arches.

keystone—the wedge-shaped piece (stone or brick) at the top center of an arch. It locks together the other pieces that form the arch ring.

lewis pins—steel pins that are placed in a predrilled hole in a stone, on an angle of approximately 60°, in an opposite direction to each other. The pair of pins are connected by a chain to a large center ring to which a rope or cable is attached, for lifting a stone to the wall.

live load—load applied to a structure other than the structure's weight itself; examples are snow on the roof, furniture, people and any moving load.

making the count—the adding together of the number of masonry units laid by the mason in one day. This count is necessary to determine if enough work is being laid by the mason to keep the work on schedule.

mantelpiece—the projection of wood or masonry materials that forms a shelf on the front of a fireplace.

membrane—thin sheets or layers of cloth or tar paper used with tar against the foundation wall to waterproof the wall.

metal heat-circulating fireplace—prebuilt metal fabricated form fireplace unit. It has hollow walls and vented openings to allow the passage of heat.

modular—masonry work laid out on a 4″ grid called the module.

modular bricks—bricks made to fit the 4″ grid system of measurement.

modular coordination—based on the 4″ grid, this method applies the techniques of mass production to lower the cost of construction work. Different types of construction materials can be built together with no alternation. The plans are drawn on a modular scale. Building materials are also manufactured on a 4″ grid.

module—the unit of measure used as a standard for modular construction; a module is 4″.

multicentered arch—an arch whose curve consists of several arcs of circles which are usually tangent at their intersections.

multiple-opening damper—type of damper used in a multiple-opening fireplace.

multiwythe construction—masonry wall made of at least three thicknesses of masonry units in width.

nominal—a dimension greater than a specified masonry dimension because of an amount allowed for the thickness of a mortar joint not exceeding ½″.

nonmodular bricks—bricks which do not fit into the 4″ modular grid system of measurement.

outer hearth—the part of the hearth that is built out in front of the firecplace; can be flush or raised.

pallet—a portable platform for moving, storing or handling materials.

parging—the application of portland cement mortar to the outside of the foundation wall to keep water from entering.

perch—unit of measure for stonework. A perch of stone is 16′6″ long, 1′ high, and 1′6″ thick. This equals 24¾ cubic feet of stone. In some localities 16½ cubic feet or 22 cubic feet are used as a perch.

pinch bar—a small crowbar that is made with a hooked end. Pinch bars are used for pulling nails out of wood or prying objects.

pitching chisel—a heavy-duty chisel with a beveled edge, available in different widths. It is used for cutting and dressing the face of building stone.

plain chisel—chisel built to withstand rugged use in stonecutting. It has a beveled blade, 1¼″ to 2¾″ wide. This chisel is used for cutting and trimming of building stone.

point chisel—chisel used for removing small stone knobs, that project off a stone face. The point chisel is drawn to a point on the end.

prefabricated masonry—masonry wall panels built in a factory-type environment using high-bond portland cement mortar with special additives. The design is based on engineering standards used by the mason.

prefaced concrete masonry units—lightweight concrete blocks with a thermoplastic resin finish applied to the face. They have been fired in a kiln to make the finish and block inseparable.

prehydration—the process of premixing water with pointing mortar. Use only enough water so that the mortar will form into a damp ball when squeezed with the hand. After the mortar has set for one hour, more water is added to bring the mortar to the consistency needed for pointing in mortar joints with a tool.

quarterback—concrete block with the inside of two cells cut out.

radial center joint—the point where the radius line begins.

raised flat joint—a method of tooling the mortar joints by forming a smooth, raised flat joint.

raised hearth—masonry hearth built above the finished floor level.

rise (or an arch)—the rise of a minor arch is the maximum height of arch soffit above the level of its springing line. The rise of a major parabolic arch is the maximum height of the arch axis above its springing line.

rock cut face—term used to describe building stone cut with the pitching chisel, leaving the face in a roughly squared shape.

rolling bead joint—a method of tooling mortar joints with a concave striking tool that forms a rolled projected mortar joint.

Roman arch—the name given a semicircular arch because Romans use it in buildings and bridges.

roof buck—scaffold frames made of lumber, built to fit the slope of a roof.

rubblework—stonemasonry in which the stone is laid either as it comes from the quarry or roughly squared with a chisel and hammer by the mason at work.

runway—a wood (or metal) platform that extends from the outside of a structure to the inside at floor level.

salamander—type of metal stack heater that burns fuel oil in the bottom and radiates heat from the chimney stack pipe. It is used for heating areas where masonry or construction work is being done.

scratch coat—roughening the first coat of cement mortar parging with a wire lath or stiff brush to permit a better bond between the coats.

sedimentary stone—stone formed over a long time by the sediments of minerals and other natural resources.

segmental arch—an arch that has a circular curve less than a full semicricle.

semicircular arch—an arch that has a full semicircular curve; a Roman arch.

serpentine wall—masonry unit wall (usually bricks) built on an alternating curve from an established centerline. The unique feature of a serpentine wall is that it is usually only 4 inches thick and resists movement due to its curving design.

setting derrick—a wood-framed derrick used in stone setting. It is mounted on wheels and can be moved from place to place.

shooting points—establishing level marks around a foundation with the aid of a builder's level or transit.

shop drawings—the drawings showing construction details and identification of the stone by numbers.

shove joint—method of forming a solid mortar joint by spreading the mortar on the brick and flattening out the mortar with a trowel instead of furrowing with the trowel point. The brick is then shoved into the mortar, forming a solid joint.

side construction—the horizontal coring of the cells in a structural clay tile.

silicones—chemical liquid dampproofer for either brushing or spraying on masonry walls to make them water-repellent. They are effective in preventing absorption of water because they change the contact angles between the water and the walls of the capillary pores in the wall.

skewback—inclined (sloping) masonry units built into the wall, with the beginning arch bricks resting against the units at each end of an opening, such as over a window or door.

slicker—metal tool used to strike a flat joint.

slings—heavy canvas, fiber, or leather straps used for lifting stones to the wall. The sling is attached to a cable and lifted by a crane or derrick.

smoke chamber—the area of a fireplace extending from the level of the damper up to the first flue lining. Slopes of all sides should be equal.

smoke shelf—brick ledge or shelf, laid level with the bottom edge of the damper and back of the firebox. It serves to deflect the air currents that come down the chimney back up the flue's opposite side.

smoke test—test conducted by the mason after the fireplace is completed, consisting of building a fire at the bottom of the flue and then covering the flue's top tightly.

soffit—an arch's bottom or underside.

soft joints—the joints between panels of prefabricated masonry in curtain wall construction. Panels are supported by the structural frame. Joints are either pointed with mortar or filled with an elastic sealant.

span—the horizontal distance between abutments. For minor arches, the clear span of the opening is used. For a major parabolic arch, the span is the distance between the ends of the arch axis.

splay—an inclined surface or angle such as the angled sides of a fireplace's firebox.

springing line—for minor arches, the line where the skewback cuts or intersects the soffit. For major parabolic arches, the intersection of the skewback with the arch axis.

starter piece—a masonry unit or glazed tile cut specially for use at the corner to establish the proper bond lap.

stepped footing—concrete footings built in the shape of a set of steps. They are used because of a sharp drop in the grade or the presence of soft ground.

stocking or materials—placing masonry materials in the work are so masons have ready access to them.

stone masonry—the art of cutting and building stone walls either with or without mortar.

stone setter—term applied to a mason who specializes in setting large, precut stone. This type of stonework concentrates on the skills of handling and settign large stone.

story high—the height of the masonry story from the floor line to where the wood plates will be set for the ceiling joists.

story pole—wood pole approximately ¾″ × 2″ × 10′ on which all of the various heights and individual courses of masonry units are laod off.

stretcher stack bond—stack bond in which all masonry units are laid in a soldier position.

striking hammer—a heavy steel hammer used in settling stone into place or driving stakes. The striking hammer weighs from 2 to 4 pounds. Also called a mash hammer.

structural clay tile—a fired masonry unit consisting of light burning, de-aired fireclay used in masonry wall construction.

thermal movement—expansion and contraction of masonry caused by changes in temperature.

thimble—a round terra-cotta or fireclay insert which fits into a chimney to take in the furnace pipe and form a fireproof connection into the masonry wall.

throat—the part of the fireplace that narrows at the firebox's top. The gas smoke passes through this part. If a damper is set, it becomes the throat.

tile shapes—various shapes of structural tile that adapt to special needs in the construction of structural clay tile walls.

tooth chisel—a steel chisel in which the blade forms a series of teeth; used for dressing stone.

topping out—the process of laying the last section of the masonry wall to the finished height of the building.

trench footing—concrete footings that are placed in an earthen trench.

trimmer arch—masonry arch used in fireplace construction to support the rough hearth or the rough opening over the firebox.

tuck-pointing—the process of refilling mortar in mortar joints using a slicker.

washing down—process of cleaning masonry work with water and acid.

water table—a masonry unit or stone that forms a ledge usually at the top of a story of a building or ground level.

weep holes—small holes left in the mortar bed joints just above the grade line to allow water to rush out.

working to one's hand—working a left or right-handed mason to the best use off of the center. A right-handed mason is more at ease working from the left end of a wall toward the center, and a left-handed person is more comfortable working from the right end of the wall to the center.

working overhand—the process of building a masonry wall by workign only from one side, although the wall may be tooled on both sides.

wythe—wall comprising only one masonry unit in thickness.

Appendix

Table A-1. Brick and Block Courses.

Block No. of Courses	Brick No. of Courses	Height of Course	Block No. of Courses	Brick No. of Courses	Height of Course
	1	0′ 2-5/8″		37	8′ 2-5/8″
	2	0′ 5-3/8″		38	8′ 5-3/8″
1	3	0′ 8″	13	39	8′ 8″
	4	0′ 10-5/8″		40	8′ 10-5/8″
	5	1′ 1-3/8″		41	9′ 1-3/8″
2	6	1′ 4″	14	42	9′ 4″
	7	1′ 6-5/8″		43	9′ 6-5/8″
	8	1′ 9-3/8″		44	9′ 9-3/8″
3	9	2′ 0″	15	45	10′ 0″
	10	2′ 2-5/8″		46	10′ 2-5/8″
	11	2′ 5-3/8″		47	10′ 5-3/8″
4	12	2′ 8″	16	48	10′ 8″
	13	2′ 10-5/8″		49	10′ 10-3/8″
	14	3′ 1-3/8″		50	11′ 1-3/8″
5	15	3′ 4″	17	51	11′ 4″
	16	3′ 6-5/8″		52	11′ 6-5/8″
	17	3′ 9-3/8″		53	11′ 9-3/8″
6	18	4′ 0″	18	54	12′ 0″
	19	4′ 2-5/8″		55	12′ 2-5/8″
	20	4′ 5-3/8″		56	12′ 5-3/8″
7	21	4′ 8″	19	57	12′ 8″
	22	4′ 10-5/8″		58	12′ 10-5/8″
	23	5′ 1-3/8″		59	13′ 1-3/8″
8	24	5′ 4″	20	60	13′ 4″
	25	5′ 6-5/8″		61	13′ 6-5/8″
	26	5′ 9-3/8″		62	13′ 9-3/8″
9	27	6′ 0″	21	63	14′ 0″
	28	6′ 2-5/8″		64	14′ 2-5/8″
	29	6′ 5-3/8″		65	14′ 5-3/8″
10	30	6′ 8″	22	66	14′ 8″
	31	6′ 10-5/8″		67	14′ 10-5/8″
	32	7′ 1-3/8″		68	15′ 1-3/8″
11	33	7′ 4″	23	69	15′ 4″
	34	7′ 6-5/8″		70	15′ 6-5/8″
	35	7′ 9-3/8″		71	15′ 9-3/8″
12	36	8′ 0″	24	72	16′ 0″

Mortar Joint is 3/8″

Table A-2. Safe Loads in Pounds per Square Foot on Different Types of Soil.

Material	Safe Load Lbs. Sq. Ft.
Soft, wet clay or soft clay and wet sand mixed	2,000
Sand and clay—Firm clay or wet sand	4,000
Dry solid clay or firm dry sand	5,000
Hard clay—Firm coarse sand—Gravel	8,000
Firm coarse sand and gravel mixed	12,000
Hard Pan	20,000

Table A-3. Decimal Equivalents.

Decimal Equivalents							
Decimal of a Foot						Decimal of an Inch	
Fraction	Decimal	Fraction	Decimal	Fraction	Decimal	Fraction	Decimal
1/16	0.0052	4-1/16	0.3385	8-1/16	0.6719	1/64	0.015625
1/8	0.0104	4-1/8	0.3438	8-1/8	0.6771	1/32	0.03125
3/16	0.0156	4-3/16	0.3490	8-3/16	0.6823	3/64	0.046875
1/4	0.0208	4-1/4	0.3542	8-1/4	0.6875	1/16	0.0625
5/16	0.0260	4-5/16	0.3594	8-5/16	0.6927	5/64	0.078125
3/8	0.0313	4-3/8	0.3646	8-3/8	0.6979	3/32	0.09375
7/16	0.0365	4-7/16	0.3698	8-7/16	0.7031	7/64	0.109375
1/2	0.0417	4-1/2	0.3750	8-1/2	0.7083	1/8	0.125
9/16	0.0459	4-9/16	0.3802	8-9/16	0.7135	9/64	0.140625
5/8	0.0521	4-5/8	0.3854	8-5/8	0.7188	5/32	0.15625
11/16	0.0573	4-11/16	0.3906	8-11/16	0.7240	11/64	0.171875
3/4	0.0625	4-3/4	0.3958	8-3/4	0.7292	3/16	0.1875
13/16	0.0677	4-13/16	0.4010	8-13/16	0.7344	13/64	0.203125
7/8	0.0729	4-7/8	0.4063	8-7/8	0.7396	7/32	0.21875
15/16	0.0781	4-15/16	0.4115	8-15/16	0.7448	15/64	0.234375
1-	0.0833	5-	0.4167	9-	0.7500	1/4	0.250
1-1/16	0.0885	5-1/16	0.4219	9-1/16	0.7552	17/64	0.265625
1-1/8	0.0938	5-1/8	0.4271	9-1/8	0.7604	9/32	0.28125
1-3/16	0.0990	5-3/16	0.4323	9-3/16	0.7656	19/64	0.296875
1-1/4	0.1042	5-1/4	0.4375	9-1/4	0.7708	5/16	0.3125
1-5/16	0.1094	5-5/16	0.4427	9-5/16	0.7760	21/64	0.328125
1-3/8	0.1146	5-3/8	0.4479	9-3/8	0.7813	11/32	0.34375
1-7/16	0.1198	5-7/16	0.4531	9-7/16	0.7865	23/64	0.359375
1-1/2	0.1250	5-1/2	0.4583	9-1/2	0.7917	3/8	0.375
1-9/16	0.1302	5-9/16	0.4635	9-9/16	0.7969	25/64	0.390625
1-5/8	0.1354	5-5/8	0.4688	9-5/8	0.8021	13/32	0.40625
1-11/16	0.1406	5-11/16	0.4740	9-11/16	0.8073	27/64	0.421875
1-3/4	0.1458	5-3/4	0.4792	9-3/4	0.8125	7/16	0.4375

1-13/16	0.1510	5-13/16	0.4844	9-13/16	0.8177	29/64	0.453125
1-7/8	0.1563	5-7/8	0.4896	9-7/8	0.8229	15/32	0.46875
1-15/16	0.1615	5-15/16	0.4948	9-15/16	0.8281	31/64	0.484375
2-	0.1667	6-	0.5000	10-	0.8333	1/2	0.500
2-1/16	0.1719	6-1/16	0.5052	10-1/16	0.8385	33/64	0.515625
2-1/8	0.1771	6-1/8	0.5104	10-1/8	0.8438	17/32	0.53125
2-3/16	0.1823	6-3/16	0.5156	10-3/16	0.8490	35/64	0.546875
2-1/4	0.1875	6-1/4	0.5208	10-1/4	0.8542	9/16	0.5625
2-5/16	0.1927	6-5/16	0.5260	10-5/16	0.8594	37/64	0.578125
2-3/8	0.1979	6-3/8	0.5313	10-3/8	0.8646	19/32	0.59375
2-7/16	0.2031	6-7/16	0.5365	10-7/16	0.8698	39/64	0.609375
2-1/2	0.2083	6-1/2	0.5417	10-1/2	0.8750	5/8	0.625
2-9/16	0.2135	6-9/16	0.5469	10-9/16	0.8802	41/64	0.640625
2-5/8	0.2188	6-5/8	0.5521	10-5/8	0.8854	21/32	0.65625
2-11/16	0.2240	6-11/16	0.5573	10-11/16	0.8906	43/64	0.671875
2-3/4	0.2292	6-3/4	0.5625	10-3/4	0.8958	11/16	0.6875
2-13/16	0.2344	6-13/16	0.5677	10-13/16	0.9010	45/64	0.703125
2-7/8	0.2396	6-7/8	0.5729	10-7/8	0.9063	23/32	0.71875
2-15/16	0.2448	6-15/16	0.5781	10-15/16	0.9115	47/64	0.734375
3-	0.2500	7-	0.5833	11-	0.9167	3/4	0.750
3-1/16	0.2552	7-1/16	0.5885	11-1/16	0.9219	49/64	0.765625
3-1/8	0.2604	7-1/8	0.5938	11-1/8	0.9271	25/32	0.78125
3-3/16	0.2656	7-3/16	0.5980	11-3/16	0.9323	51/64	0.796875
3-1/4	0.2708	7-1/4	0.6047	11-1/4	0.9375	13/16	0.8125
3-5/16	0.2760	7-5/16	0.6094	11-5/16	0.9427	51/64	0.828125
3-3/8	0.2813	7-3/8	0.6146	11-3/8	0.9479	27/32	0.84375
3-7/16	0.2865	7-7/16	0.6198	11-7/16	0.9531	55/64	0.859375
3-1/2	0.2917	7-1/2	0.6250	11-1/2	0.9583	7/8	0.875
3-9/16	0.2969	7-9/16	0.6302	11-9/16	0.9635	29/64	0.890625
3-5/8	0.3021	7-5/8	0.6354	11-5/8	0.9688	29/32	0.90625
3-11/16	0.3073	7-11/16	0.6406	11-11/16	0.9740	59/64	0.921875
3-3/4	0.3125	7-3/4	0.6458	11-3/4	0.9792	15/16	0.9375
3-13/16	0.3177	7-13/16	0.6510	11-13/16	0.9844	61/64	0.953125
3-7/8	0.3229	7-7/8	0.6563	11-7/8	0.9896	31/32	0.96875
3-15/16	0.3281	7-15/16	0.6615	11-15/16	0.9948	63/64	0.984375
4-	0.3333	8-	0.6667	12-	1.0000	1-	1.000

Table A-4. Various Measures and Conversion Factors.

Unit	Current U.S. term (multiply factor)	Conversion Factor*	SI term (divide factor)	SI Symbol
Length	inch	25.400	millimeter	mm
	foot	0.305	meter	m
	yard	0.914	meter	m
	mile	1.609	kilometer	km
Area	square inch	645.2	square millimeter	mm^2
	square foot	0.093	square meter	m^2
	square yard	0.836	square meter	m^2
	square mile	2.590	square kilometer	km^2
	acre	0.405	hectafe	ha
Mass	ounce	28.350	gram	g
weight)**	pound	0.454	kilogram	kg
	ton (2000 pounds)	0.907	metric ton	t
Volume	fluid ounce	29.574	milliliter	ml
	pint	0.473	liter	L
	quart	0.946	liter	L
	gallon	3.785	liter	L
	cubic foot	0.028	cubic meter	m^3
	cubic yard	0.765	cubic meter	m^3
	barrel (petroleum)	0.159	cubic meter	m^3
Force	pound force	4.448	newton	N
Pressure and Stress	psi (pounds per square inch)	6.895	kilopascal	kPa

	psf (pounds per square foot)	.048	kilopascal	kPa
	ton per square foot	95.760	kilopascal	kPa
Electric Current†	ampere	no conversion	ampere	A
Light	lumen	no conversion	lumen	lm
	candela	no conversion	candela	cd
	foot candle	10.76	lux	lx
Heat, work or energy	Foot pound	1.356	joule	J
	kilowatt hour	3.600	megajoule	MJ
	BTU	1.055	kilojoule	kJ
Power	foot pound per second	1.355	watt	W
	BTU/hour	0.293	watt	W
	horse power	0.746	kilowatt	kW
	tons (refrigeration)	3.517	kilowatt	kW
Heat factors	U value	5.679	metric U value	undecided
	K value	1.730	metric K value	undecided
Temperature	degree Fahrenheit	††	degree Celcius	C
	degree Fahrenheit	††	Kelvin	K

* conversion factors have been rounded to the third decimal place

** mass and weight are not synonymous.

† electric terms already in common use.

††to convert °F to °C subtract 32 and multiply by 1.8; to convert °F to K add 459.67 and multiply by 1.8

Table A-5. Metric Measures and Equivalents.

LINEAR MEASURE

10 millimeters	=	1 centimeter
10 centimeters	=	1 decimeter
10 decimeters	=	1 meter
10 meters	=	1 decameter
10 decameters	=	1 hectometer
10 hectometers	=	1 kilometer

SQUARE MEASURE

100 sq. millimeters	=	1 sq. centimeter
100 sq. centimeters	=	1 sq. decimeter
100 sq. decimeters	=	1 sq. meter
100 sq. meters	=	1 sq. decameter
100 sq. decameters	=	1 sq. hectometer
100 sq. hectometers	=	1 sq. kilometer

CUBIC MEASURE

1000 cu. millimeters	=	1 cu. centimeter
1000 cu. centimeters	=	1 cu. decimeter
100 cu. decimeters	=	1 cu. meter

LIQUID MEASURE

10 milliliters	=	1 centiliter
10 centiliters	=	1 deciliter
10 deciliters	=	1 liter
10 liters	=	1 decaliter
10 decaliters	=	1 hectoliter
10 hectoliters	=	1 kiloliter

WEIGHTS

10 milligrams	=	1 centigram
10 centigrams	=	1 decigram
10 decigrams	=	1 gram
10 grams	=	1 decagram
10 decagrams	=	1 hectogram
10 hectograms	=	1 kilogram
100 kilograms	=	1 quintal
10 quintals	=	1 ton

LINEAR MEASURE

1 inch	=		=	2.54 centimeters
1 foot	=	12 inches	=	0.3048 meter
1 yard	=	3 feet	=	0.9144 meter
1 rod	=	5 1/2 yds. or 16 1/2 ft.	=	5.029 meters
1 furlong	=	40 rods	=	201.17 meters
1 mile (statute)	=	5280 ft. or 1760 yds.	=	1609.3 meters
1 league (land)	=	3 miles	=	4.83 kilometers

SQUARE MEASURE

1 sq. inch	=		=	6.452 sq. centimeters
1 sq. foot	=	144 sq. inches	=	292 sq. centimeters
1 sq. yard	=	9 sq. feet	=	0.8361 sq. meter
1 sq. fod	=	30 1/4 sq. yards	=	25.29 sq. meters
1 acre	=	43,560 sq. feet or 160 sq. yds.	=	0.4047 hectare
1 sq. mile	=	640 acres	=	259 hectares or 2.59 sq. kilometers

CUBIC MEASURE

1 cu. inch	=		=	16.387 cu. centimeters
1 cu. foot	=	1728 cu. inches	=	0.0283 cu. meter
1 cu. yard	=	27 cu. feet	=	0.7646 cu. meter

ANGULAR AND CIRCULAR MEASURE

1 minute	=	60 seconds
1 degree	=	60 minutes
1 right angle	=	90 degrees
1 straight angle	=	180 degrees
1 circle	=	360 degrees

Table A-6. Weights of Building Materials.

Material	Weight	Material	Weight
CONCRETE		WOOD CONSTRUCTION (CONTINUED)	
With stone reinforced	150 pcf	Ceiling, joist and plaster	10 psf
With stone plain	144 pcf	Ceiling, joist and 1/2" gypsum board	7 psf
With cinders, reinforced	110 pcf	Ceiling, joist and acoustic tile	5 psf
Light concrete (Aerocrete)	65 pcf	Wood shingles	3 psf
(Perlite)	45 pcf	Spanish tile	15 psf
(Vermiculite)	40 pcf	Copper sheet	2 psf
		Tar and gravel	6 psf
METAL AND PLASTER			
Masonry mortar	116 pcf	STONE	
Gypsum and sand plaster	112 pcf	Sandstone	147 pcf
		Slate	175 pcf
BRICK AND BLOCK MASONRY (INCLUDING MORTAR)		Limestone	165 pcf
4" brick wall	35 psf	Granite	175 pcf
8" brick wall	74 psf	Marble	165 pcf
8" concrete block wall	100 psf		
12" concrete block wall	150 psf	GLASS	
4" brick veneer over 4" concrete block	65 psf	1/4" plate glass	3.28 psf
		1/8" double strength	1.63 psf
WOOD CONSTRUCTION		1/8" insulating glass with air space	3.25 psf
Frame wall, lath and plaster	20 psf	4" block glass	20.00 psf
Frame wall, 1/2" gypsum board	12 psf		
Floor, 1/2" subfloor · 3/4" finished	6 psf	INSULATION	
Floor, 1/2" subfloor and ceramic tile	16 psf	Cork board 1" thick	.58 psf
Roof, joist and 1/2" sheathing	3 psf	Rigid foam insulation 2" thick	.3 psf
Roof, 2" plank and beam	5 psf	Blanket or bat 2" thick	.1 psf
Roof, built-up	7 psf		

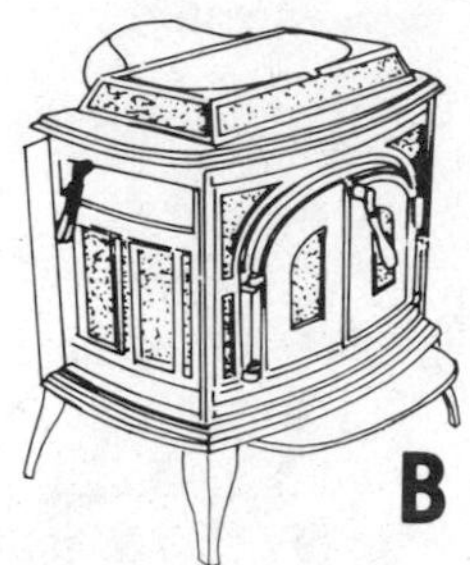

B

Sample Of A Building Code

ARTICLE 10: CHIMNEYS, FLUES AND VENT PIPES

Section 1000.0 General

1000.1 Scope. The provisions of this article shall control the design, installation, maintenance, repair and approval of all chimneys, vents and connectors hereafter erected or altered in all building and structures.

1000.2 Other Standards. Unless otherwise specifically provided herein, conformity to the applicable requirements for chimney construction and vents contained in the mechanical code shall be deemed to meet the requirements of this code.

1000.3 Minor Repairs. Minor repairs for the purpose of maintenance and upkeep which do not increase the capacity of the heating apparatus or appliances, or which do not involve structural changes in the permanent chimney and vents of a building, may be made without a permit.

Section 1001.0 Plans and Specification

1001.1 General. The structural plans and specifications shall describe in sufficient detail, the location, size and construction of all chimneys, vents and ducts and their connections to boilers, furnaces, appliances and fireplaces. The thickness and character of all insulation materials, clearances from walls, partitions and ceilings and proximity of heating devices and equipment to wall openings and exitways shall be clearly shown and described.

1001.2 Appliances. All appliances required to be vented shall be connected to a vent or chimney, except as provided in Section 1006.3 and as provided in the standards for special venting arrangements.

Section 1002.0 Performance Test And Acceptance Criteria

1002.1 Tests. The building official may require a test or tests of any chimney or vent to insure fire safety and the removal of smoke and products of combustion.

1002.2 Acceptance Criteria. The system shall be accepted if the following conditions are fulfilled.

- There shall not be spillage at the draft hood when any one or combination of appliances connected to the system is in operation.
- Temperature on adjacent combustible surfaces shall not be raised more than limits acceptable to nationally recognized testing or inspection agencies.
- Condensation shall not be developed in a way that would cause deterioration of the vent or chimney drip from joints or bottom end of the vent or chimney.
- The draft reading taken at the place recommended in the installation instructions shall be within the range specified by the appliance manufacturer.

1002.2.1 Approved Installations. Factory-built chimneys and gas-vents which have been tested and listed by a nationaly recognized testing or inspection agency shall be accepted as complying with the requirements of item 2 of Section 1002.2 when installed in accordance with the clearance specified in their listing.

Section 1003.0 Chimneys

Chimneys as used in this article shall be classified as:

- Factory-built chimneys.
- Masonry chimneys.
- Metal chimneys (smokestacks).

Section 1004.0 Appliances Requiring Chimneys

1004.1 General. All heating appliances except those appliances specifically exempted by the provisions of Section 1006.3 shall be connected to chimneys as specified in the chimney selection chart contained in the mechanical code.

Section 1005.0 Existing Buildings

1005.1 Raising Existing Chimneys. Whenever a building is hereafter erected, enlarged or increased in height so that a wall along an interior lot line, or within 3′ thereof, extends above the top of an existing chimney or vent of an adjoining existing building, the owner of the building so erected, enlarged or increased in height shall carry up at his own expense, with the consent of the adjoining property owner, either independently, or in his own building, all chimneys connected to fuel burning appliances. Vents within 6′ of any portion of the wall of such adjoining building shall be extended 2′ above the roof or parapet of the adjoining building.

1005.2 Size Of Extended Chimneys. The construction of an extended chimney shall conform to the requirements of this article for new chimneys, but the internal area of such extension shall not be less than that of the existing chimney.

1005.3 Notice To Adjoining Owner. It shall be the duty of the owner of the building which is erected, enlarged or increased in height to notify in writing, and to secure the consent of, the owner of existing chimneys affected at least 10 days before starting such work.

1005.4 Existing Chimneys. An existing chimney, except one which does not endanger the fire safety of a building or structure and is acceptable to the building official, shall not be continued in use unless it conforms to all requirements of this article for new chimneys.

1005.5 Cleanouts And Maintenance. Whenever a new chimney is completed or an existing chimney is altered, it shall be cleaned and left smooth on the inside. If the chimney is constructed of masonry or tile, the interior mortar joints must be left smooth and flush. Cleanouts or other approved devices shall be provided at the base of all chimneys to enable the passageways to be maintained and cleaned.

Section 1006.0 Vent Systems

1006.1 Listed Appliances. For the purpose of determining vent requirements, gas-fired and oil-fired appliances shall be classified as "listed" or "unlisted." A listed appliance is one that is shown in a list published by an accredited authoritative testing agency, qualified and equipped for experimental testing of such appliances, and maintaining an adequate periodic inspection of current production of listed models and whose listing states either that the appliance or accessory complies with nationally recognized safety requirements or has been tested and found safe for use in a specific manner. Compliance may be determined by the presence on the appliance or accessory of a label of the testing agency stating that the appliance or accessory complies with nationally recognized safety requirements. An unlisted appliance or accessory is one that is not shown on such a list or does not bear such a label. In cases where an applicable standard has not been developed for a given class of appliance or accessory, approval of the authority having jurisdiction should be obtained before the appliance or accessory is installed.

1006.2 Appliances Required To Be Vented. Appliances shall be connected to a listed venting system or provided with other means for exhausting the flue gases to the outside atmosphere in accordance with the Venting system selection chart.

1006.3 Exemption. Connections to vent systems shall not be required for appliances of such size or character that the absence of such connection does not constitute a hazard to the fire safety of the building or its occupants. The following appliances are not required to be vented unless so required to their listing:

- Listed gas ranges.
- Built-in domestic cooking units listed and marked as unvented units.
- Listed hot plates and listed laundry stoves.
- Listed domestic clothes dryers.
- Listed gas refrigerators.
- Counter appliances.
- Space (room) heaters listed for unvented use, only upon prior approval by the building official.
- Specialized equipment of limited input such as laboratory burners or gas lights.
- Electric appliances.

When any or all of the appliances listed in items 5, 6 and 7 above are installed so that the aggregate input rating exceeds 30 British thermal units (BTUs) per hour per cubic foot of room or space in which they are installed, one or more of them shall be vent connected or provided with approved means for exhausting the vent gases to the outside atmosphere so that the aggregate input rating of the remaining unvented appliance does not exceed 30 BTU per hour per cubic foot of room or space in which they are installed. Where the room or space in which they are installed is directly connected to another room or space by a doorway, arch, or other opening of comparable size, which cannot be closed, the volume of such adjacent room or space may be included in the calculations.

1006.4 Types Of Vents. Vents of common type include: Type B vents, Type B-W vents, and Type L low temperature vents.

Section 1007.0 Fireplaces

1007.1 General. Fireplaces, barbecues, smoke chambers and fireplace chimneys shall be of solid masonry or reinforced concrete or other approved materials, and shall conform to requirements of this section.

1007.2 Construction. Structural walls of fireplaces shall be at least eight (8)″ thick. Where a lining of low duty refractory brick (ASTM C64) or the equivalent at least 2″ thick laid in fire clay mortar (ASTM C105, medium duty), or the equivalent, or other approved lining is provided, the total thickness of back and sides, including the lining, shall be not less than 8″. Where such lining is not provided, the thickness of back and sides shall be not less than 12″. The firebox shall be 20″ in depth and will be permited to be open on all sides, provided all fireplace openings are located entirely within one room.

1007.3 Lining. The lining shall extend from the throat of the fireplace to a point at least 4″ above the top of the enclosing masonry walls.

1007.4 Clearance.

1007.4.1 Distance. The distance between fireplace and combustibles shall be at least 4″ and such combustibles shall not be placed within 6″ of the fireplace opening. Wood facings or trim normally placed around the fireplace opening may be permitted when conforming to the requirements of this section; however, such facing or trim shall be furred out from the fireplace wall at least 4″ and attached to noncombustible furring strips. The edges of such facings or trim shall be covered with a noncombustible material. Where the walls of the fireplace are 12″ thick, the facings or trim may be directly attached to the fireplace.

1007.4.2 Metal Hoods. Metal hoods used as part of a fireplace or barbecue shall be at least 18″ from combustible material unless approved for reduced clearances.

1007.5 Metal. Metal hoods used as a part of a fireplace or barbecue shall be at least No. 18 B&S(0.0403″) Gage sheet copper, No. 18 Galvanized Steel Gage (0.052″) galvanized steel or other equivalent corrosion-resistant ferrous metal with all seams and connections of smokeproof unsoldered construction. The hoods shall be sloped at an angle of 45° or less from the vertical and shall extend horizontally at least 6″ beyond the limits of the firebox.

1007.6 Metal Heat Circulators. Approved metal heat circulators may be installed in fireplaces, provided the thickness of the fireplace walls is not reduced.

1007.7 Smoke Chamber. All walls, including back walls, shall be at least 8″ in thickness.

1007.8 Areas of Flues, Throats And Dampers. The net cross-sectional area of the flue and of the throat between the firebox and the smoke chamber of a fireplace shall be at least that required in Article 7. When dampers are used, damper openings shall be at least, when fully opened, equal to the required flue area and shall be of No. 12 Galvanized Steel Gage (0.018″) metal.

1007.9 Lintel. Masonry over the fireplace opening shall be supported by a noncombustible lintel.

1007.10 Hearth. Every fireplace shall be constructed with a hearth of brick, stone, tile or other noncombustible material. For fireplaces with an opening of less than 6 square feet, the hearth shall extend not less than 16″ in front and not lessthan 8″ on each side of the fireplace opening. For fireplaces with an opening of 6 square feet or more, the hearth shall extend no less than 20″ in front and not less than 12″ on each side of the fireplace opening. Such hearths shall be supported on trimmer arches of brick, stone, tile or concrete not less than 4″ thick or other equally strong and fireresistance rated materials. All combustible forms or centering shall be removed after completion of the supporting construction.

1007.11 Firestopping. Firestopping between chimneys and wooden construction shall meet the requirements specified in Section 919.0 and the mechanical code.

1007.12 Support. Fireplaces shall be supported on foundations designed in conformity with Section 726.0.

1007.13 Screens. Screens or other acceptable protection devices shall be provided for all fireplace openings.

1007.14 Other Type Fireplaces. Other fireplaces not conforming to the requirements of this section shall be subject to approval by the department prior to installation. Imitation fireplaces shall not be used for the burning of gas, solid or liquid fuel. Approved factory-built fireplaces may be installed and shall conform to the applicable portions of this code. Factory-built fireplaces shall bear the seal of a nationally recognized testing or inspection agency.

1007.15 Solid Wastes. Solid waste shall not be burned in a fireplace.

Section 1008.0 Incinetators

1008.1 Mechanical Code. Incinerators of all types shall be installed in accordance with the applicable provisions of the mechanical code.

Section 1009.0 Construction Of Metal Ducts And Vents

1009.1 Mechanical Code. All metal vents, ducts and duct systems required under the provisions of Articles 10 and 11 for heating systems and equipment, and under the provisions of Articles 5 and 18 for ventilating and air-cinditioning systems shall be constructed and installed in accordance with the requirements of the mechanical code.

1009.2 Construction Of Ducts. Ducts and plenums may be constructed of approved material constructed in accordance with the requirements of the mechanical code. Non-metallic ducts shall be constructed and installed in accordance with their approval and the applicable standards. Aluminum ducts shall not be used in equipment rooms with fuel-fired equipment, encased in or under concrete slabs on grade, for kitchen or fume exhausts or in systems where air entering the duct is over 250°F.

Section 1010.0 Spark Arrestors

1010.1 Mechanical Code. All chimneys, stacks and flues, including incinerator stacks, which emit sparks shall be provided with a spark arrestor conforming to the requirements of the mechanical code.

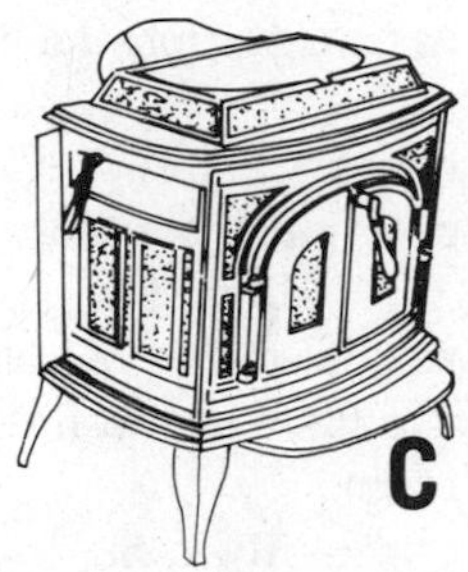

C

Safety With Heating Devices

The U.S. Consumer Product Safety Commission estimates that each year over 6,000 people receive hospital emergency room treatment for injuries associated with fireplaces. Most of these injuries are cuts and bruises caused by handling wood, andirons and other equipment. But the most serious injuries are burns, and most of the victims are children.

- Five-year-old Steve was standing too close to the fireplace and his clothing ignited. He received serious burns over 80 percent of his body.
- A spark from an unguarded fireplace ignited a small carpet. The fire spread to a nearby sofa and soon engulfed the entire room. Two people died in the fire.
- Mr. Allen used gasoline to "stoke" a smoldering fire in the fireplace. The flammable vapors exploded, and he was burned severely.
- After starting a fire in a poorly ventilated fireplace, Lois threw in some wrapping and polystyrene which had been used as packaging. The polystyrene produced so much carbon monoxide that Lois fell unconscious and died from the poisonous gas.

The typical accident patterns associated with fireplaces include:

- *Clothing ignition* from the open flames.
- *Sparks from the fire landing on nearby flammable material.*
- *Using flammable liquids to kindle or rekindle the fire*. It is hazardous to use flammable liquids anywhere near the

fire because the vapors can travel to the flames and be ignited.

- *Carbon monoxide poisoning* caused in inadequate ventilation.

The U.S. Consumer Product Safety Commission offers the following suggestions for the safer use of fireplaces:

—Check to make sure the fireplace was constructed to be used as a fireplace, not just for decoration. Have it inspected to determine whether it has all necessary linings and clearances.

—Don't use gasoline or other flammable liquids to kindle or rekindle a fire because the flammable vapors can explode. Never use fuels near a fire; explosive vapors can travel the length of a room.

—Always keep the damper open while the fuel is burning to provide for efficient burning and to prevent the accumulation of poisonous or explosive gases.

—Don't use coal, charcoal, or polystyrene packaging in a fireplace unless the fireplace is well-ventilated.

—Don't treat artificial logs (made from sawdust and wax) the same way you treat real wood logs. Use only one at a time. If you use more, they can produce too much heat for some fireplaces to withstand.

—Always use a screen that completely covers the opening around a fireplace to keep sparks from flying out. Don't put combustible materials, such as carpets or furniture, near a fireplace.

—Keep children away from the fire because their clothing can easily ignite. Warn the entire family about this hazard.

—Check fireplaces regularly (at least once each year) to determine that all vents and chimneys are operating properly.

—Be sure that all ashes have thoroughly cooled before you dispose of them.

—Make sure the fire is out completely before retiring for the evening.

—Use chimney guards. Squirrel and bird nests can stop up chimneys.

FURNACES

The U.S. Consumer Product Safety Commission estimates that last year 6,500 consumers received hospital emergency room treatment for injuries associated with central furnaces, and 1,600 received treatment for floor furnace accidents. These are some of the accident patterns:

- A two-year-old boy crawled onto the hot grate of a floor furnace. He received second and third degree burns to his hands and legs.
- A woman stuffed a towel into the intake vent for her furnace because the air was making her utility room cold. The deprived the furnace of oxygen which it need to burn the fuel, and large quantities of carbon monoxide were produced. The woman was found dead from carbon monoxide poisoning.
- In trying to light the pilot light in his furnace, a man ignited the gas which had accumulated in the combustion chamber. His shirt caught fire, and he received burns over 50 percent of his body.

These illustrations represent the following accident patterns associated with furnaces:

- *Contact with hot metal grates and other hot surfaces*—Children can crawl onto or push each other against hot floor furnace grates. Adults also can fall and get burned by hot surfaces.
- *Carbon monoxide poisoning*—All fuel-burning appliances need air in order to burn the fuel properly. If an oil, gas coal, or wood furnace is "starved" of its necessary intake air, it will operate inefficiently and produce large quantities of carbon monoxide. In addition, if the exhaust pipes are clogged or cracked, carbon monoxide can leak into your home.
- *Ignition of accumulated fuel vapors*—Trying to light a pilot light or to perform maintenance procedures can be hazardous if you're not familiar with the furnace. The accumulated vapors can ignite and cause a fire or burns.

In an effort to save energy, many consumers are insulating their homes and closing off all drafts and air leaks. This can be hazardous if necessary air intake vents are blocked. In some older homes, furnaces actually need a drafty door or window in order to get enough air to burn the fuel properly. Have your furnace checked regularly by a service company to make sure it is getting enough air to burn the fuel safely.

The U.S. Consumer Product Safety Commission has the following suggestions for selection, use, and maintenance of furnaces:

Selection. Be sure that the furnace has a "safety pilot" that automatically stops the flow of fuel when the pilot light goes out.

Have the furnaces installed according to all local codes. These usually specify the air-intake and exhaust requirements for safe operation of the furnace.

Use. Cover the metal grates of furnaces with a metal screen which will prevent children—and adults—from touching the hot surface.

If you are insulating your house or trying to block air drafts around doors and windows, be sure that you don't cut off air necessary for the furnace to burn its fuel properly. Have a service company check for this. (Generally, you need 1 square inch of intake air piping for every 5000 BTUs/hour of heat produced by the furnace. If the furnace doesn't get adequate air to burn fuel efficiently, it will produce large quantities of carbon monoxide which could leak out and kill you.)

Keep flammable liquids (such as gasoline) away from furnaces because the flammable vapors could be ignited by the pilot light in the furnace. Keep flammable liquids in tightly-capped safety cans in a shed outside, away from any flame or heat sources.

Don't attempt to light a pilot light unless you are familiar with the furnace and the proper techniques. If the pilot light goes out or if the furnace needs adjustment, call an experienced service company or the gas company.

Maintenance. Have your furnace checked at least once every year, before the heating season begins, to be sure that there is adequate intake air and that the exhaust system is working properly. Have flue checked to be sure they are not blocked by debris, which could permit fumes to enter the house.

SPACE HEATERS AND WOOD AND COAL BURNING HEATING STOVES

The U.S. Consumer Product Safety Commission estimates that each year over 5,000 people receive hospital emegency room treatment for injuries associated with oil, gas, kerosene, and electric space heaters and with wood and coal burning heating stoves. Here are some accident patterns:

- Four-year-old Jenny was standing close to the gas space heater to keep warm. Her dress was ignited by the open flame and she suffered severe burns over 70 percent of her body.
- Mr. Bloom turned on the gas for his space heater and lit a match to light the heater. The accumulated gas exploded and Mr. Bloom died from resulting burns.

- An unvented space heater was left on all night and produced enough carbon monoxide to asphyxiate a family of three. They were found dead in their small house.
- Karen was running in the living room when she tripped and fell against the electric space heater in the center of the room. She was seriously burned on both hands and on her right arm.
- Richard received a serious electrical shock when, just after taking a shower, he turned on the electric space heater in his bathroom.
- Mr. Johnson tried to build up a smoldering wood fire in his heating stove by squirting gasoline on it. The flammable vapors from the gasoline ignited and traveled up the gasoline stream to the can, which exploded. Mr. Johnson was seriously burned.

These illustrations represent some accident patterns associated with space heaters and heating stoves:

- *Contact with the flame, heating element, or hot surface area*. Your clothing can ignite and cause severe burns. Falling against or touching exterior surface can also cause severe burn injuries.
- *Explosion of accumulated gas* while attempting to light the burner.
- *Carbon monoxide poisoning*. An unvented space heater or one which is poorly adjusted and dirty can produce deadly quantities of carbon monoxide. Incomplete combustion of solid fuel in a heating stove can also produce carbon monoxide. In addition, combustion consumes oxygen in the air. Therefore, you need adequate fresh air when you use an unvented heater.
- *Electrical shock*, often because the victim was wet and touched the control.
- *Using flammable liquids to "stoke" a fire*. The flammable vapors can ignite and cause an explosion. Using flammable liquids (such as gasoline) in the same room with a heater or stove can create the same hazard.

Most space heaters involved in accidents are gas space heaters, but electric heaters also can cause burns and electrical shocks. The use of improper fuel, such as charcoal in a heating stove, poses special hazards of carbon monoxide and overheating, especially if the stove is not vented properly.

The U.S. Consumer Product Safety Commission offers the following suggestions for the selection, safe use, and maintenance of space heaters and heating stoves:

Selection. Buy a heater or stove that can be vented to the outside. Old-fashioned or second-hand heaters and stoves may be cracked, improperly adjusted, or improperly vented, producing deadly quantities of carbon monoxide.

Be aware that unvented heaters are more likely to produce deadly amounts of carbon monoxide than are vented heaters. Unvented heaters are prohibited in some communities because of the carbon monoxide hazard.

Buy a space heater or stove with an adequate guard around hot surfaces or the heating coil. Keep children, pets and clothing away from the heat source.

If you buy an electric space heater, be sure that it has an automatic switch which cuts off electric power if the heater is tipped over. Be aware that you must keep at least 3′ safety clearance on all sides of the space heater. This distance requirement should influence your purchase.

Use. Keep a window partially open if you must use an unvented space heater. Plenty of oxygen is required for proper combustion, and the fresh air will help prevent the accumulation of carbon monoxide.

Use the proper fuel for each heating device:

- Don't use coal in a wood burning stove because it can overheat.
- Don't use flammable liquid on a wood or coal fire because it can cause an explosion.
- Don't use charcoal or polystyrene in a heating stove which is not properly vented because these fuels can produce deadly amounts of carbon monoxide.
- Don't use oil in a kerosene heater, or kerosene in an oil heater; do not convert any heater to use another fuel without expert advice.

Keep children away from space heaters and stoves because they can be burned simply by touching the hot surface. Keep at least 3′ clearance in all directions around space heaters or stoves. Don't put a space heater near drapes, furniture, or other flammable materials or near traffic lanes.

Pay attention to the fire to maintain proper ventilation and rate of burning. Try to keep a fire at a moderate heat, neither too cool nor too hot. If the fire is too cool, it may permit the accumulation of flammable gases and residues which can explode when reheated by adding more coal or wood.

Always use a screen around a stove or space heater which has open flames.

Keep the damper open while the fuel is burning. This will provide for efficient burning and will prevent the accumulation of explosive gases and the leaking of carbon monoxide into the room.

Learn how to light a gas space heater properly. If you smell gas, turn off all controls and open a window or door. Don't turn on the gas until you have a match ready and lit. Don't give gas time to accumulate, and if you fail to light the heater on the first try, allow sufficient time for the gas to dissipate before trying again.

Never use flammable liquids (such as gasoline) around a space heater or heating stove. The flammable vapors can flow from one part of the room to another and be ignited by the open flame. Never leave an unvented space heater or stove on overnight because deadly quantities of carbon monoxide gas may accumulate and kill you while you are sleeping.

Do not use an extension cord for an electric heater unless it is a heavy duty cord (which usually is available only in electrical supply shops) rated for at least 15 amps. Have an eelectrician check the wiring in the room if you plan to use a heater with higher than usual wattage.

Never place an electric heater near a bathtub, shower, or sink; avoid use of a portable electric heater anywhere in a bathroom. Never touch an electric heater if you are wet.

Place a metal sheet under a coal or wood burning stove to protect the floor from live coals or burning wood and from overheating. Never fill a heater with cold oil because as the oil warms, it expands and could spill and flare.

Be aware that mobile homes are smaller than most houses and may have less adequate ventilation, more closely installed electrical and fuel-burning appliances, and more combustible construction. Consequently, the use of a space heater or heating stove can be more hazardous.

Maintenance. Have gas, kerosene, and oil space heaters inspected annually to insure that they are properly adjusted and clean. Also, have heating stove inspected once a year to insure that all linings and chimneys are intact, that the stove is properly adjusted, and that it is clean. Check stoves for cracks or faulty legs and hinges. Replace loose or missing guards on electric, gas, oil, and kerosene heaters and on heating stoves. Keep all electrical wiring in electric space heaters in good working condtion. Be sure that all ashes have thoroughly cooled before you dispose of them.

If your clothing *does* catch fire, don't run! Drop down immediately and roll to smother the flames. Teach your children how to react to fire. **Caution:** Never use a cooking stove as a heater. Never leave the oven door open more than a few minutes at a time because an oven can overheat and cause a fire.

D

List Of Manufacturers

American Standard Company—Majestic *pre-built fireplaces*
245 Erie St.
Huntington, IN 46750

Castle Rock Enterprises, Ltd. *simulated brick and stone*
Box 2564 Centre Station
Framingham, MA 01701

Eldorado Stone *sumulated brick and stone*
P.O. Box 125
Kirkland, WA 98033

Franklin Cast Products *wood burning stoves*
1800 Post Road
17 Airport Paaza
Warwick, RI 02886

Frontier—J & J Enterprises *wood burning stoves*
4065 W. 11th Ave.
Eugene, OR 97402

Martin Industries *pre-built fireplaces*
P.O. Box 1527
Huntsville, AL 35807

Stucco Stone Products, Inc. *simulated brick and stone*
P.O. Box 237
Napa Valley, CA 94558

Suscon Stacks *pre-built chimneys*
42 Fort Road
Magnolia, MD 21101

Tekton Corporation *wood burning furnaces*
Conway, MA 01341

Universal Stone Corporation *simulated brick and stone*
1525 N. Herdelback Ave.
P.O. Box 4312
Evansvill, IN 47711

Vega Industries, Inc.—Heatilator *pre-built fireplaces*
19409 W. Saunders St.
Mt. Pleasant, IA 52241

VMC Corporation—Z Brick *simulated brick and stone*
Woodville, WA 98702

Wallace Murray Corporation *pre-built chimneys*
Metalbestos Systems
1820 E. Fargo
P.O. Box 372
Nampa, ID 83651

Concrete and Cement Information

E

Table E-1. Recommended Maximum Permissible Water-Cement Ratios for Different Types of Structures and Degrees of Exposure.

Type of structures	Exposure conditions**					
	Severe wide range in temperature or frequent alternations of freezing and thawing (air-entrained concrete only) (gallons/sack)			Mild temperature rarely below freezing, or rainy, or arid (gallons/sack)		
	In air	At water line or within range of fluctuating water level or spray		In air	At water line or within range of fluctuating water level or spray	
		In fresh water	In sea water or in contact with sulfates†		In fresh water	In sea water or in contact with sulfates†
A. Thin sections such as reinforced piles and pipe	5.5	5	4.5	6	5.5	4.5
B. Bridge decks	5	5	4.5	5.5	5.5	5
C. Thin sections such as railings, curbs, sills, ledges, ornamental or architectural concrete, and all sections with less than 1-in. concrete cover over reinforcement	5.5			6	5.5	
D. Moderate sections, such as retaining walls, abutments, piers, girders, beams	6	5.5	5	††	6	5
E. Exterior portions of heavy (mass) sections	6.5	5.5	5	††	6	5
F. Concrete deposited by tremie under water		5	5		5	5
G. Concrete slabs laid on the ground	6			††		
H. Pavements	5.5			6		
I. Concrete protected from the weather, interiors of buildings, concrete below ground	††			††		
J. Concrete which will later be protected by enclosure or backfill but which may be exposed to freezing and thawing for several years before such protection is offered	6			††		

*Adapted from Recommended Practice for Selecting Proportions for Concrete (ACI 613-54).

**Air-entrained concrete should be used under all conditions involving severe exposure and may be used under mild exposure conditions to improve workability of the mixture.

†Soil or groundwater containing sulfate concentrations of more than 0.2 per cent. For moderate sulfate resistance, the tricalcium aluminate content of the cement should be limited to 8 per cent, and for high-sulfate resistance to 5 per cent. At equal cement contents, air-entrained concrete is significantly more resistant to sulfate attack than non-air-entrained concrete.

††Water-cement ratio should be selected on basis of strength and workability requirements, but minimum cement content should not be less than 470 lb. per cubic yard.

Table E-2. Age-Compressive Strength Relationship for Types I and III Air-Entrained Portland Cement.

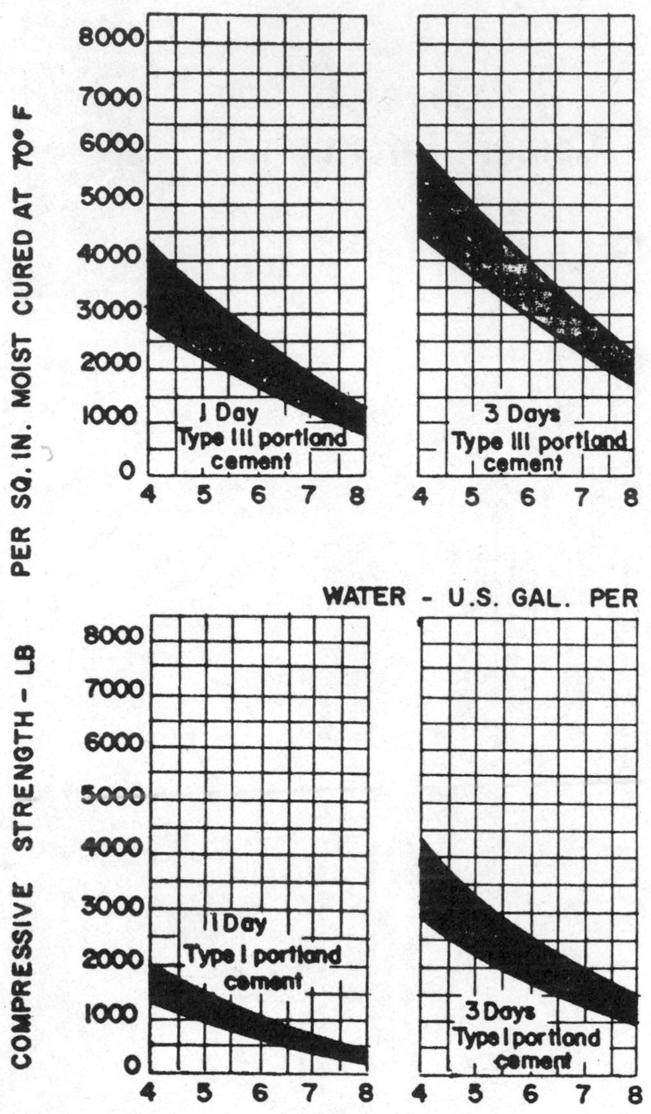

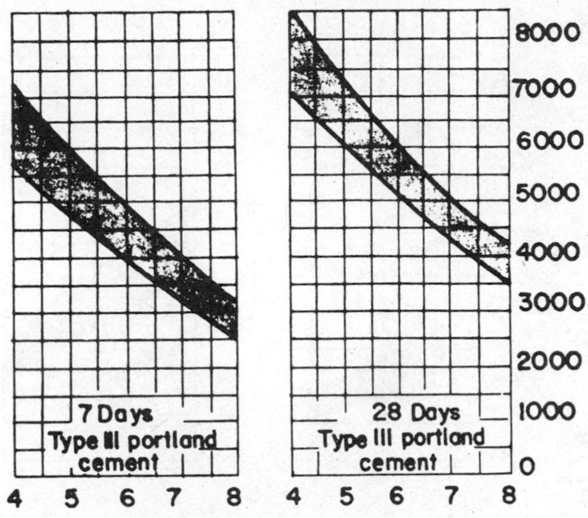

SACK OF CEMENT

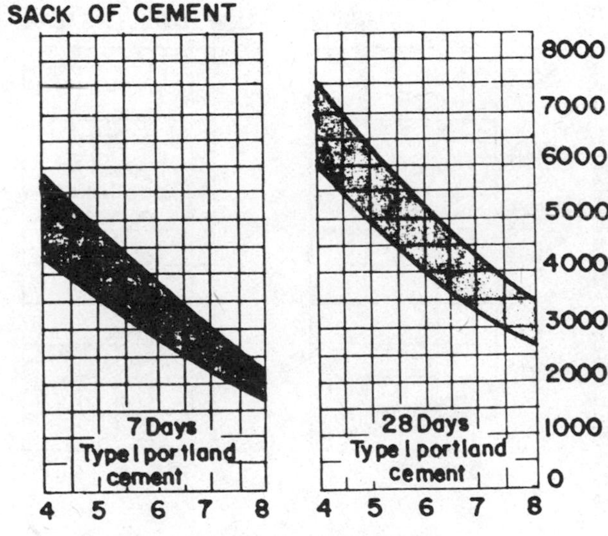

(Cont on next page.)

Table E-2. Age-Compressive Strength Relationship for Types I and III Air-Entrained Portland Cement.

(Cont. from previous page.)

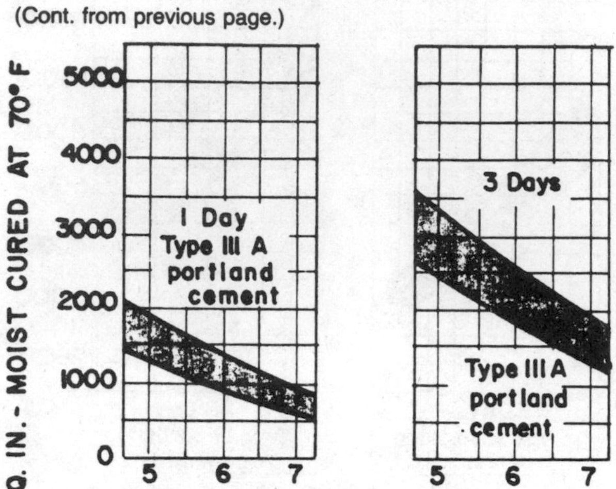

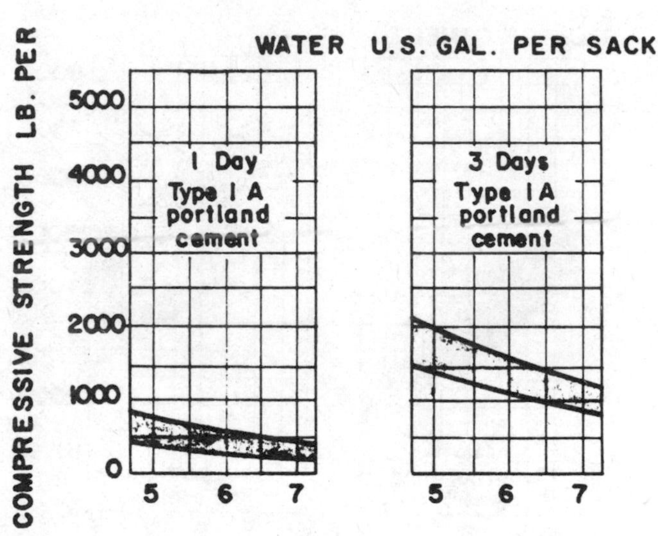

OF CEMENT

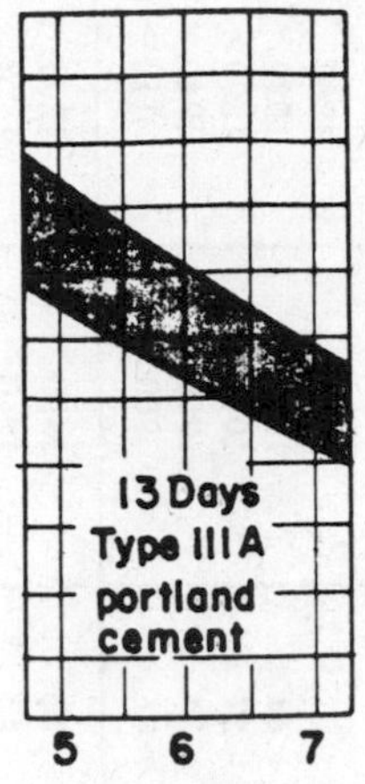

13 Days
Type III A
portland
cement
5
6
7

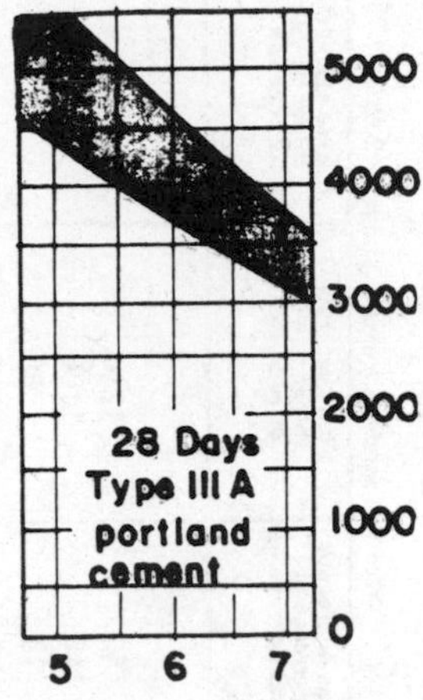

28 Days
Type III A
portland
cement
5000
4000
3000
2000
1000
0
5
6
7

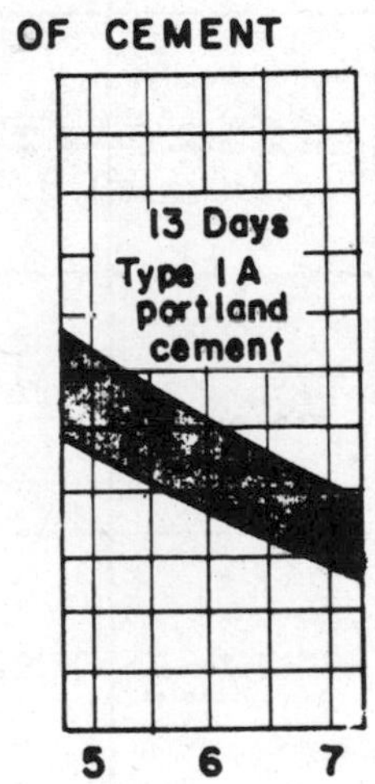

13 Days
Type I A
portland
cement
5
6
7

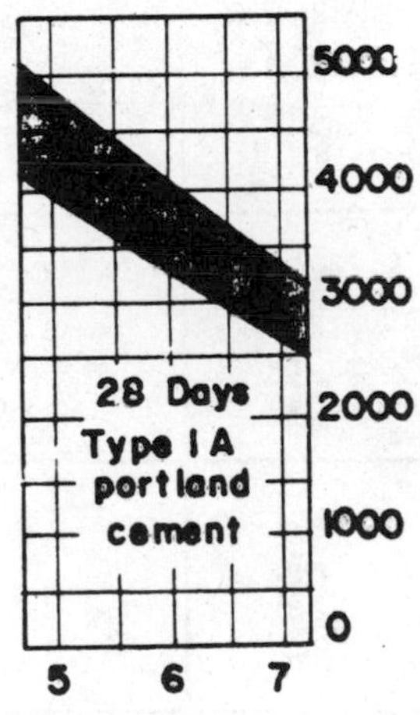

28 Days
Type I A
portland
cement
5000
4000
3000
2000
1000
0
5
6
7

Table E-3. Suggested Trial Mixes for Non-Air-Entrained Concrete of Medium Consistency with 3 to 4" Slump.

Water-cement ratio Gal per sack	Maximum size of aggregate inches	Air content (entrapped air) per cent	Water gal per cu yd of concrete	Cement sacks per cu yd of concrete	With fine sand—fineness modulus = 2.50		
					Fine aggregate per cent of total aggregate	Fine aggregate lb per cu yd of concrete	Coarse aggregate lb per cu yd of concrete
4.5	3/8	3	46	10.3	50	1240	1260
	1/2	2.5	44	9.8	42	1100	1520
	3/4	2	41	9.1	35	960	1800
	1	1.5	39	8.7	32	910	1940
	1 1/2	1	36	8.0	29	880	2110
5.0	3/8	3	46	9.2	51	1330	1260
	1/2	2.5	44	8.8	44	1180	1520
	3/4	2	41	8.2	37	1040	1800
	1	1.5	39	7.8	34	990	1940
	1 1/2	1	36	7.2	31	960	2110
5.5	3/8	3	46	8.4	52	1390	1260
	1/2	2.5	44	8.0	45	1240	1520
	3/4	2	41	7.5	38	1090	1800
	1	1.5	39	7.1	35	1040	1940
	1 1/2	1	36	6.5	32	1000	2110

6.5	3/8	3	46	7.1	54	1480	1260
	1/2	2.5	44	6.8	46	1320	1520
	3/4	2	41	6.3	39	1190	1800
	1	1.5	39	6.0	37	1120	1940
	1 1/2	1	36	5.5	34	1070	2110
6.0	3/8	3	46	7.7	53	1440	1260
	1/2	2.5	44	7.3	46	1290	1520
	3/4	2	41	6.8	39	1130	1800
	1	1.5	39	6.5	36	1080	1940
	1 1/2	1	36	6.0	33	1040	2110
7.0	3/8	3	46	6.6	55	1520	1260
	1/2	2.5	44	6.3	47	1360	1520
	3/4	2	41	5.9	40	1200	1800
	1	1.5	39	5.6	37	1150	1940
	1 1/2	1	36	5.1	34	1100	2110
7.5	3/8	3	46	6.1	55	1560	1260
	1/2	2.5	44	5.9	48	1400	1520
	3/4	2	41	5.5	41	1240	1800
	1	1.5	39	5.2	38	1190	1940
	1 1/2	1	36	4.8	35	1130	2110
8.0	3/8	3	46	5.7	56	1600	1260
	1/2	2.5	44	5.5	48	1440	1520
	3/4	2	41	5.1	42	1280	1800
	1	1.5	39	4.9	39	1220	1940
	1 1/2	1	36	4.5	35	1160	2110

*See footnote at end of table.

(Cont. on next page.)

Table E-3. Suggested Trial Mixes for Non-Air-Entrained Concrete of Medium Consistency with 3 to 4″ Slump.

(Cont. from previous page).

Water-cement ratio Gal per sack	With average sand—fineness modulus = 2.75			With coarse sand—fineness modulus = 2.90		
	Fine aggregate percent of total aggregate	Fine aggregate lb per cu yd of concrete	Coarse aggregate lb per cu yd of concrete	Fine aggregate percent of total aggregate	Fine aggregate lb per cu yd of concrete	Coarse aggregate lb per cu yd of concrete
4.5	52	1310	1190	54	1350	1150
	45	1170	1450	47	1220	1400
	37	1030	1730	39	1080	1680
	34	980	1870	36	1020	1830
	32	960	2030	33	1000	1990
5.0	54	1400	1190	56	1440	1150
	46	1250	1450	48	1300	1400
	39	1110	1730	41	1160	1680
	36	1060	1870	38	1100	1830
	34	1040	2030	35	1080	1990
5.5	55	1460	1190	57	1500	1150
	47	1310	1450	49	1360	1400
	40	1160	1730	42	1210	1680
	37	1110	1870	39	1150	1830
	35	1080	2030	36	1120	1990
6.0	56	1510	1190	57	1550	1150
	48	1360	1450	50	1410	1400
	41	1200	1730	43	1250	1600
	38	1150	1870	39	1190	1830
	36	1120	2030	37	1160	1990

6.5	57	1550	1190	58	1590	1150
	49	1390	1450	51	1440	1400
	42	1240	1730	43	1290	1680
	39	1190	1870	40	1230	1830
	36	1150	2030	37	1190	1990
7.0	57	1590	1190	59	1630	1150
	50	1430	1450	51	1480	1400
	42	1270	1730	44	1320	1680
	39	1220	1870	41	1260	1830
	37	1180	2030	38	1220	1990
7.5	58	1630	1190	59	1670	1150
	50	1470	1450	52	1520	1400
	43	1310	1730	45	1370	1600
	40	1260	1870	42	1300	1830
	37	1210	2030	39	1250	1990
8.0	58	1670	1190	60	1710	1150
	51	1520	1450	53	1560	1400
	44	1350	1730	45	1400	1680
	41	1290	1870	42	1330	1830
	38	1250	2030	39	1280	1990

*Increase or decrease water per cubic yard by 3 per cent for each increase or decrease of 1 in. in slump, then calculate quantities by absolute volume method. For manufactured fine aggregate, increase percentage of fine aggregate by 3 and water by 17 lb. per cubic yard of concrete. For less workable concrete, as in pavements, decrease percentage of fine aggregate by 3 and water by 8 lb. per cubic yard of concrete.

Table E-4. Suggested Trial Mixes for Air-Entrained Concrete of Medium Consistency with 3 to 4" Slump.

Water-cement ratio Gal per sack	Maximum size of aggregate inches	Air Content (entrapped air) per cent	Water gal per cu yd of concrete	Cement sacks per cu yd of concrete	With fine sand—fineness modulus = 2.50		
					Fine aggregate per cent of total aggregate	Fine aggregate lb per cu yd of concrete	Coarse aggregate lb per cu yd of concrete
4.5	3/8	7.5	41	9.1	50	1250	1260
	1/2	7.5	39	8.7	41	1060	1520
	3/4	6	36	8.0	35	970	1800
	1	6	34	7.8	32	900	1940
	1 1/2	5	32	7.1	29	870	2110
5.0	3/8	7.5	41	8.2	51	1330	1260
	1/2	7.5	39	7.8	43	1140	1520
	3/4	6	36	7.2	37	1040	1800
	1	6	34	6.8	33	970	1940
	1 1/2	5	32	6.4	31	930	2110
5.5	3/8	7.5	41	7.5	52	1390	1260
	1/2	7.5	39	7.1	44	1190	1520
	3/4	6	36	6.5	38	1090	1800
	1	6	34	6.2	34	1010	1940
	1 1/2	5	32	5.8	32	970	2110
6.0	3/8	7.5	41	6.8	53	1430	1260
	1/2	7.5	39	6.5	45	1230	1520
	3/4	6	36	6.0	38	1120	1800
	1	6	34	5.7	35	1040	1940
	1 1/2	5	32	5.3	32	1010	2110

6.5	3/8	7.5	41	6.3	54	1460	1260
	1/2	7.5	39	6.0	45	1260	1520
	3/4	6	36	5.5	39	1150	1800
	1	6	34	5.2	36	1080	1940
	1 1/2	5	32	4.9	33	1040	2110
7.0	3/8	7.5	41	5.9	54	1500	1260
	1/2	7.5	39	5 6	46	1300	1520
	3/4	6	36	5.1	40	1180	1800
	1	6	34	4.9	36	1100	1940
	1 1/2	5	32	4.6	33	1060	2110
7.5	3/8	7.5	41	5.5	55	1530	1260
	1/2	7.5	39	5.2	47	1330	1520
	3/4	6	36	4.8	40	1210	1800
	1	6	34	4.5	37	1140	1940
	1 1/2	5	32	4.3	34	1090	2110
8.0	3/8	7.5	41	5.1	55	1560	1260
	1/2	7.5	39	4.9	47	1360	1520
	3/4	6	36	4.5	41	1240	1800
	1	6	34	4.3	37	1160	1940
	1 1/2	5	32	4.0	34	1110	2110

*See footnote at end of table.

(Cont. on next page).

Table E-4. Suggested Trial Mixes for Air-Entrained Concrete of Medium Consistency with 3 to 4″ Slump.

(Cont. from previous page).

Water-cement ratio Gal per sack	With average sand—fineness modulus = 2.75			With coarse sand—fineness modulus = 2.90		
	Fine aggregate percent of total aggregate	Fine aggregate lb per cu yd of concrete	Coarse aggregate lb per cu yd of concrete	Fine aggregate percent of total aggregate	Fine aggregate lb per cu yd of concrete	Coarse aggregate lb per cu yd of concrete
4.5	53	1320	1190	54	1360	1150
	44	1130	1450	46	1180	1400
	38	1040	1730	39	1090	1680
	34	970	1870	36	1010	1830
	32	950	2030	33	990	1990
5.0	54	1400	1190	56	1440	1150
	46	1210	1450	47	1260	14000
	39	1110	1730	41	1160	1630
	36	1040	1870	37	1080	1830
	33	1010	2030	35	1050	1990
5.5	55	1460	1190	57	1500	1150
	46	1260	1450	48	1310	1400
	40	1160	1730	42	1210	1680
	37	1080	1870	38	1120	1830
	34	1050	2030	35	1090	1990
6.0	56	1500	1190	57	1540	1150
	47	1300	1450	49	1350	1400
	41	1190	1730	42	1240	1680
	37	1110	1870	39	1150	1830
	35	1090	2030	36	1130	1990

6.5	56	1530	1190	58	1570	1150
	48	1330	1450	50	1380	1400
	41	1220	1730	43	1270	1680
	38	1150	1870	39	1190	1830
	36	1120	2030	37	1160	1990
7.0	57	1570	1190	58	1610	1150
	49	1370	1450	50	1420	1400
	42	1250	1730	44	1300	1680
	38	1170	1870	40	1210	1830
	36	1140	2030	37	1180	1990
7.5	57	1600	1190	59	1640	1150
	49	1400	1450	51	1450	1400
	43	1280	1730	44	1330	1680
	39	1210	1870	41	1250	1830
	37	1170	2030	38	1210	1990
8.0	58	1630	1190	59	1670	1150
	50	1430	1450	51	1480	1400
	43	1310	1730	44	1360	1680
	40	1230	1870	41	1270	1830
	37	1190	2030	38	1230	1990

*Increase or decrease water per cubic yard by 3 per cent for each increase or decrease of 1 in. in slump, then calculate quantities by absolute volume method For manufactured fine aggregate, increase percentage of fine aggregate by 3 and water by 17 lb. per cubic yard of concrete. For less workable concrete, as in pavements decrease percentage of fine aggregate by 3 and water by 8 lb. per cubic yard of concrete.

Table E-5. Approximate Mixing Water Requirements for Different Slumps and Maximum Sizes of Aggregates.*

Maximum size of aggregate, in.	Air-entrained concrete				Non-air-entrained concrete			
	Recommended average total air content, per cent†	Slump, in.			Approximate amount of entrapped air, per cent	Slump, in.		
		1 to 2	3 to 4	5 to 6		1 to 2	3 to 4	5 to 6
		Water, gal. per cu.yd. of concrete**				Water, gal. per cu.yd. of concrete**		
3/8	7.5	37	41	43	3.0	42	46	49
½	7.5	36	39	41	2.5	40	44	46
¾	6.0	33	36	38	2.0	37	41	43
1	6.0	31	34	36	1.5	36	39	41
1½	5.0	29	32	34	1.0	33	36	38
2	5.0	27	30	32	0.5	31	34	36
3	4.0	25	28	30	0.3	29	32	34
6	3.0	22	24	26	0.2	25	28	30

*Adapted from Recommended Practice for Selecting Proportions for Concrete (ACI 613–54).

**These quantities of mixing water are for use in computing cement factors for trial batches. They are maximums for reasonably well-shaped angular coarse aggregates graded within limits of accepted specifications.

†Plus or minus 1 per cent.

Index

Index

Homeowner's Guide to Saving Energy

Revised Edition

Other TAB Books by the authors:

No. 820 *Central Heating & Air Conditioning Repair Guide*
No. 1176 *Master Handbook of ALL Home Heating Systems—Tuneup, Repair, Installation & Maintenance*

Homeowner's Guide to Saving Energy

Revised Edition

by Billy L. Price & James T. Price

TAB BOOKS Inc.
BLUE RIDGE SUMMIT, PA. 17214

FIRST EDITION

FIRST PRINTING

Printed in the United States of America

Library of Congress Cataloging in Publication Data
Price, Billy L.
Homeowner's guide to saving energy.

Includes index.
1. Energy conservation—Handbooks, manuals, etc.
I. Price, James Tucker, 1955- joint author.
II. Title.
TJ163.3.P74 1980 644 80-19968
ISBN 0-8306-9923-6
ISBN 0-8306-9691-1 (pbk.)

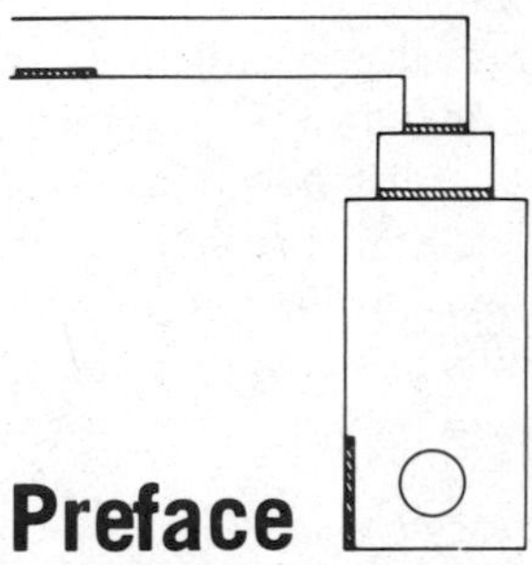

Preface

No aspect of home improvement and maintenance is changing more rapidly than energy conservation. New recommendations and new energy saving products are being developed with amazing, even alarming frequency. As energy costs have continued rising with no end in sight, the claims and counterclaims of manufacturers and sellers of "energy conservation" products have reached a frenzied pitch. Fast-buck artists and hucksters have sold shoddy products at inflated prices in an attempt to cash in on America's sudden energy consciousness.

This revised edition has been written out of our desire to keep the homeowner, renter and home builder abreast of this ever changing field. Energy conservation products and recommendations have changed dramatically. In revising this book we have included much more detailed information to help you easily and economically reduce the energy consumption of your household. We have also pointed out some areas of product manufacturing where shoddy "energy conserving" products have become a serious problem. In this edition you will find considerably more material on how to wisely select energy saving products for your home—from insulation to appliances, from fireplaces to heat pumps.

This edition includes new chapters on heat pumps, buying the right amount of insulation, and wood heating—some of the most controversial and rapidly changing areas of energy conservation and use. In these chapters we have included information to help you decide whether these products will save you money, which is the bottom line consideration in energy conservation.

This edition also includes many more simple recommendations for everyday energy saving. There are suggestions on how you can use your appliances more efficiently every day and on how you can purchase efficient appliances to cut your energy bills significantly.

Simplicity is still the key to this book. Most of the new material added for the second edition requires no more mechanical knowledge than how to use a screwdriver. You don't have to be a mechanical whiz to conserve energy in your home. By utilizing the suggestions outlined in this book, hundreds of dollars a year in utility bills are yours for the saving!

Billy L. Price
James T. Price

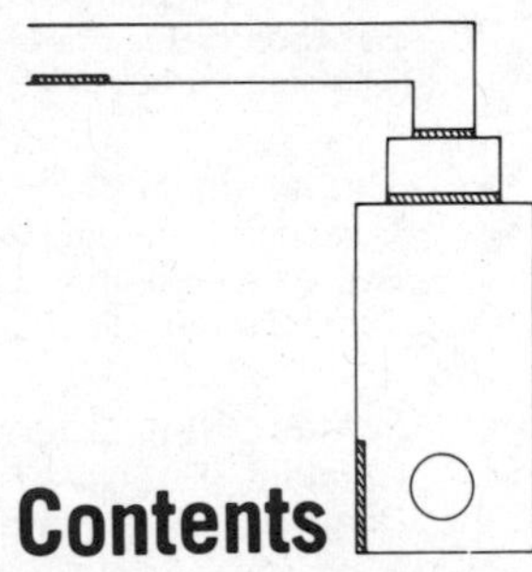

Contents

1 Fundamentals of Heating and Cooling

The first step in reducing energy consumption and fuel bills is to understand some the basic principles of heating and cooling. Most energy is consumed in the home through the operation of furnaces, air conditioners, ovens and refrigerators. By understanding how heating and cooling take place, you can gain a real insight into the factors that make these units work efficiently. You can then readily see what adjustments are needed to improve their efficiency and reduce their workload.

To start with, you must always remember that your total heating or cooling bill depends upon *two* factors, not just one. It is not enough to consider only the *efficiency* of a furnace, air conditioner, or other appliance; you must also consider the amount of *work* you are asking it to do. Today there is far too much emphasis on efficiency, probably because it is a banner that manufacturers can wave at you in their advertisements. Simply speaking, *efficiency* is just a measure of how much energy is wasted in doing a particular job; 100% efficiency means no wasted energy, while 50% means half is wasted. A fact too often ignored is the actual amount of work required to do the job. A poorly insulated house requires far more energy to heat and cool than a well insulated house. Sealing up air leaks, adding more insulation, and doing other simple jobs can do far more to reduce your fuel bills than buying the most sophisticated, expensive, high efficiency furnace or air conditioner on the market.

HEATING AND COOLING YOUR HOME

Most homes today have fully controlled temperatures all year round. In the winter the home is heated by a furnace; in the summer it is cooled by an air conditioner. The inside temperature is regulated by a thermostat. Although there are many different types, brands, and models of heating and cooling equipment, the basic purpose is the same—to keep the occupants comfortable, neither too hot nor too cold.

Of course, you don't get something for nothing. Heating and cooling a home cost money. Electricity is consumed, gas and oil are burned, and you pay for what you use. The object, then, is to use as little energy as possible to heat and cool your home. Using efficient equipment is one way to cut down energy consumption, and adding insulation is another. Efficient equipment makes it possible to use energy in the least wasteful manner, while insulation slows down the escape of heat energy in the winter and the entrance of heat in the summer.

People are concerned about energy conservation today, mostly because of its effect on their utility bills. But the total impact of energy costs invade practically every aspect of housing. With energy prices rising significantly, contractors are forced to install thicker insulation, add better weather stripping, and include double-pane windows in new homes. Even the fireplace—recently considered a mere luxury—is fast becoming an essential part of every new home because it provides supplemental heat in addition to beauty and comfort (Fig. 1-1). In rural areas especially, the plentiful supply of relatively inexpensive firewood makes a fireplace almost mandatory. The increased cost of electricity and fuel is therefore rapidly pushing up the cost of new homes because energy-conscious buyers are demanding better construction methods to reduce fuel bills.

Older homes are affected by the energy crunch too. Fifty years ago there was little concern over fuel, so the majority of homes were built without insulation. As fuel prices went up over the decades, homeowners were forced to install insulation, particularly in walls and attic spaces (Fig. 1-2). Recent homes have had insulation installed when they were built, but not the amount recommended as a result of today's energy prices. Consequently, most homes can still benefit by the addition of more insulation and better weather seals.

Apartment renters are also conscious of heating and cooling costs. They may not be able to do much about the insulation, but

Fig. 1-1. This concrete pad indicates that the home is being built with a fireplace that will provide added heat as well as beauty. By the same token, a poorly sealed damper in a fireplace chimney can allow heat to escape when the fireplace is not being used.

when it comes time to pick out an apartment, the electric and fuel bills are high on their list of questions. They are also more conscious about the direction their prospective apartment faces in relation to the sun and whether or not it has a large amount of window area. If you have a basic knowledge of what factors affect energy consumption, you can save yourself a lot of money by renting the right apartment and using the right techniques to lower your energy bills.

ENERGY IS MEASURED IN UNITS

Energy is something you buy in measured amounts. Different kinds of energy come in different forms and so are measured using different units. For example, you buy natural gas by the cubic foot, gasoline and fuel oil by the gallon, and coal by the ton. But energy consumption doesn't take place instantly—it takes time to use up the fuel. (When you fill up the tank of your car with gasoline, you pay for the fuel in advance, but it will last for many hours of driving.) When thinking about energy, keep in mind that a time factor is involved in its use.

Electrical energy is sometimes confusing because it is not measured in a unit of quantity that you can see. Your electrical appliances are rated in *watts*, which is an indication of the *power* they consume. Power and energy are not the same thing, though. Your electric meter records your energy consumption in *watt-hours* or *kilowatt-hours*. (The prefix *kilo* means 1000, so a kilowatt is 1000 watts.) In other words, energy is equal to the product of power and time. If you burn a 100-watt light bulb for one hour, you will have consumed 100 watt-hours of electrical energy. If you burned the same bulb for two hours, you would have consumed 200 watt-hours, or 0.2 kilowatt-hours. If your electric power company charged you 5 cents per kilowatt-hour, then 0.2 kWh would cost you $0.2 \times 5 = 1$ cent.

The *British thermal unit* (BTU) is the basic unit used in measuring heat energy. The energy capacity of both heating and cooling equipment is measured with this unit. For example, a moderate-sized home in one of the northern states might have a furnace rated at 100,000 BTU and a central air conditioner rated at 36,000 BTU. The furnace is rated on the basis of how much heat it can deliver to the house, while the air conditioner is rated by how much heat it can remove from the house. As these figures indicate, one BTU represents a fairly small amount of heat energy. Technically speaking, a BTU is the amount of heat required to raise the temperature of one pound of water by one degree Fahrenheit. However, it is easier to visualize if you just think of a BTU as being about equal to the heat delivered in one hour by the flame of one candle on a birthday cake. The *one hour* comes into the picture because the heat output of the candle is actually one BTU *per hour*, so it takes one hour to deliver one BTU of heat energy. (The one hour is often implied in the ratings; for example, a 100,000 BTU furnace takes one hour to deliver 100,000 BTU, so the actual furnace capacity is 100,000 BTU per hour.)

Home heating requirements are also figured in BTU. The *heat load* is the amount of heat that escapes from the structure—through walls, windows, doors, ceilings, floors, etc. If a house has a 100,000 BTU heat load (figured on the coldest expected temperature), it will require a furnace with at least 100,000 BTU capacity to heat the home (Fig. 1-3).

When air-conditioning a home, the terms *heat gain* or *cooling load* are used to specify the amount of heat that must be removed from the home. A home having a summer heat gain of 36,000 BTU (figured on the hottest typical day) would require an air conditioner rated at 36,000 BTU. This cooling capacity is easily accomplished with a moderate-sized central air conditioning unit, though you

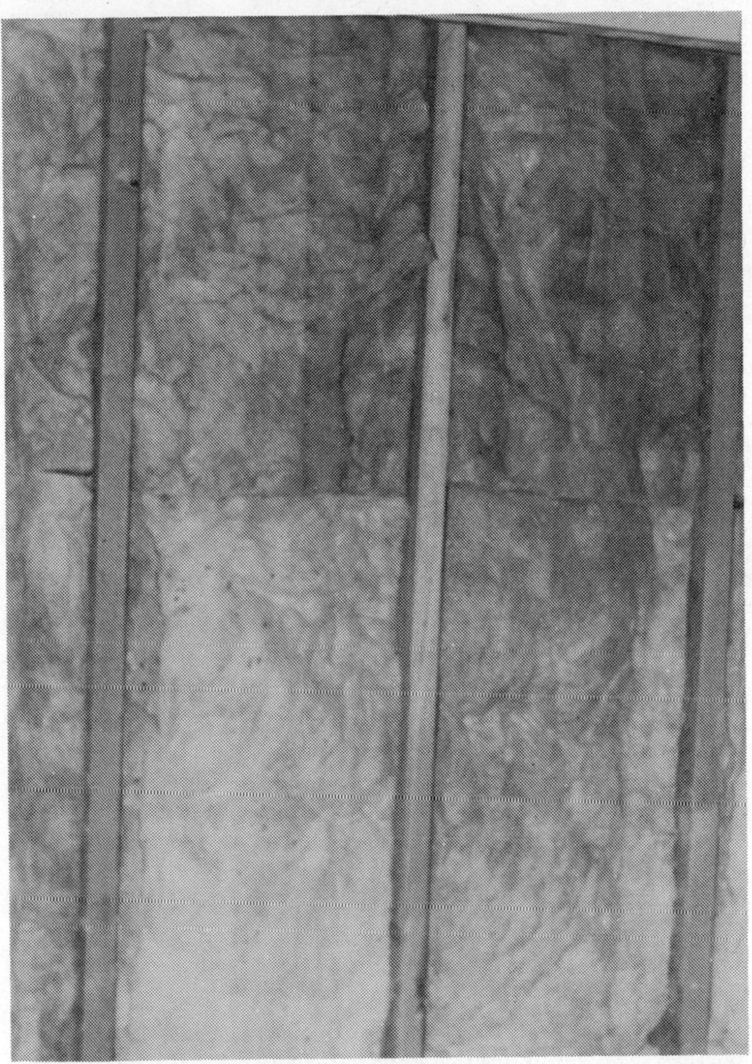

Fig. 1-2. Insulating walls, ceilings and floors is one of the best ways to cut energy consumption. With higher energy prices, it can pay the homeowner to add insulation. The insulation shown here is fiberglass batting, available in precut lengths of 4 and 8 feet—perfect for insulating the space between wall studs. Rolls of fiberglass insulation are also available.

could also use several smaller window-mounted units totaling 36,000 BTU.

Large air conditioners are normally measured in *tons of refrigeration*, which has nothing to do with the air conditioner's actual

Fig. 1-3. Furnaces must be sized to the heat load of your home. The furnace capacity is given in BTU and is generally stated on the identification plate inside the furnace. The furnace rating must exceed the heat load of your home if the furnace is to be able to heat your home properly on cold days. Note that fuel furnaces have two BTU figures: gross and net. The gross BTU figure indicates how much fuel is consumed, while the net BTU figure tells you how much heat energy is delivered to your home. The net BTU value is the one you are interested in. The difference between the two BTU figures is the heat lost up your chimney.

weight. In this system, one tone of cooling capacity corresponds to 12,000 BTU. Thus our 36,000 BTU air conditioner could also be rated as a 3-ton air conditioner. This interesting unit came about in the early "icebox" days of refrigeration because it represented the amount of heat energy required to melt one tone of ice in 24 hours. But all you need to remember is that one ton equals 12,000 BTU.

Since the BTU and the watt-hour are both units of heat energy, there is a simple conversion factor that can be used to relate them. One watt-hour is roughly 3.4 BTU. Similarly, one kilowatt-hour is about 3400 BTU. To convert watts to BTU, jsut multiply the number of watts by 3.4. Alternatively, to convert BTU to watts, divide the BTU rating by 3.4. Electrical heating equipment is sometimes sized in watts instead of BTU. This is particularly the case with baseboard heaters and space heaters.

The energy efficiency ratio (EER) is a handy way of comparing the efficiencies of various air conditioners. The EER is equal to the BTU rating divided by the input watts. Your might, at first, think that this would simply equal 1/3.4, or about 0.3, but it doesn't. Air conditioners do not produce heat directly, instead they merely transfer or pump heat energy from one place to another. In a refrigerator, for instance, the motor pumps Freon gas through coils located on the inside and outside of the refrigerator. One coil absorbs and removes heat energy from the inside, making it cold, while the second coil dissipates the heat into the outside air circulating over its fins. The advantage here is that it takes less energy to pump heat around than it does to generate it, as in a heater. This is proven by the fact that typical air conditioners have an EER between 5 and 10, which is much larger than 0.3. What these figures prove is simply that a typical air conditioner is capable of removing about 25 times as much heat energy from your home as the unit itself consumes in electrical energy.

Of course, the EER for an air conditioner is determined under prescribed test conditions of temperature and humidity, and this is done so that you can easily compare the performance of all air conditioners. But it must be pointed out that temperatures will vary in actual operation and so will the efficiency with which your air conditioner can pump heat out of your house. The official EER rating reflects a typical summer-operating condition; however, you can expect that your air conditioner will use more electrical energy on really hot days and less on cool days.

TEMPERATURES DETERMINE ENERGY CONSUMPTION

Temperatures are generally measured in degrees *Fahrenheit* in the U.S., although the metric *Celsius* (or centigrade) scale—used almost everywhere else in the world—is catching up with us. On the Celsius scale, 0°C (32°F) represents the freezing point of water and 100°C (212°F) represents the boiling point of water. In terms of room temperature, 20°C (68°F) is just a bit on the chilly side, while 25°C (77°F) is just a bit on the warm side. Throughout this book, temperatures will be given in Fahrenheit unless otherwise noted.

The *temperature difference* is the difference between the inside and outside temperatures of a building. As the temperature difference increases, the heat load or cooling load also increases. Consequently, it will take more fuel to heat a house when the difference between the inside and outside temperatures is 70 degrees than when the temperature difference is only 30 degrees.

Design temperatures vary according to your location in the nation. The winter design temperature tells you how cold it will get in your area. It will determine the heat load of your home and, therefore, the size of the required heating unit. For example, the winter design temperature in Milwaukee, Wisconsin is—17°F. The temperature difference for a home in Milwaukee with its thermostat set at 68°F would then be 85 degrees. Similarly, the winter design temperature in Jacksonville, Florida is 33°F, so for the same thermostat setting, the temperature difference would be 35 degrees. Obviously, the Milwaukee home would require a much larger heating unit than an identical home in Jacksonville.

Summer deisgn temperatures also vary according to your location. The summer design temperature tells you how hot it is expected to get in the summer. In Milwaukee the summer design temperature is 95°F, while in Jacksonville it is 104°F. The air conditioners used in these areas must be sized according to the summer design temperatures.

Design temperature information is available from weather stations and from stores in yoru area that specialize in heating and air conditioning equipment. These design temperatures are used when determining the heating or cooling load of your home. The stores in your area can often provide heating and cooling load estimates based on typical homes in your area, but adjusted for such factors as the amount of insulation you have.

The *inside temperature* in your home is regulated by using heating and cooling equipment. But the inside temperature also affects the temperature difference between the inside and outside of the house. Thus the setting of the thermostat changes the heating and cooling load of the home. Lowering the thermostat in the winter lowers the heat load of the home, meaning that less energy is consumed by the furnace in maintaining the home at the desired temperature. Raising the inside temperature of the home during the summer means that the cooling load is reduced and the air conditioner doesn't have to work as hard.

A point to remember is that the heating and cooling loads for a home will not be the same because different temperatures are involved. A house with a heat load of 80,000 BTU will not have a cooling load of 80,000 BTU except possibly in some southern state. In a typical northern state, the house might have an 80,000 BTU heat load and a 36,000 BTU cooling load. The difference in heating and cooling loads results because the loads are figured using different design temperatures and inside temperatures, and also because they include solar heating effects due to sunlight. The heating and cooling loads in your area can be found for almost any structure by using charts and tables designed for that very purpose. Most stores will readily cooperate in helping you find your specific requirements if it means a possible sale.

The heating and cooling loads, and hence your fuel bills, are also affected by what is inside the building. Appliances such as stoves, toasters, irons, ovens, washers, and driers produce heat. Lamps, in addition to giving light, also contribute heat. People, whether sitting or actively moving about, also generate varying amounts of body heat. In the winter this extra heat is welcomed because it lowers the heating load, but in the summer this extra heat places an added burden on the air-conditioning system that must remove it.

HUMIDITY AFFECTS YOUR COMFORT

Humidity refers to the amount of water vapor or mositure in the air. Warm air can hold more water vapor than cool air, so warm air speeds up evaporation. *Relative humidity* is a way of expressing the percentage of moisture contained in the air at a specific temperature. For example, 50% relative humidity means that the air is holding only half as much moisture as it is capable of holding at that temperature. Raising or lowering the temperature will change the relative humidity. In a sealed house, as the temperature rises, the relative humidity decreases; and as the temperature falls, the relative humidity reaches 100% and water begins to condense out of the air, forming drops of water on the glass.

High humidty and condensation can be very bad in a home, making the air feel clammy, rotting window moldings, and rusting

Fig. 1-4. A humidifier attaches to the duct system of a furnace to allow the furnace air to absorb additional moisture. Water is held in the plastic basin and brought into the air flow on the plastic bristles. Humidifiers are discussed at length in a later chapter.

tools and equipment. On the other hand, too little humidity makes the air feel dry, increases static electricity, and causes wood to dry and shrink. Consequently, both *humidifiers* and *dehumidifiers* are often used in homes to control the relative humidity to within comfortable limits (Fig. 1-4). Since air conditioners also dehumidify the air by condensing and removing water vapor, it is desirable to select a unit with the right cooling capacity so that it will properly control both the humidity and temperature of your home.

Humidity can be measured in several ways. Today there are weather instruments, called *hygrometers*, that show you at a glance what the relative humidity is. But most humidity information is given in tables and graphs using the temperatures recorded on two different thermometers—a *drybulb* thermometer and a *wet-bulb* thermometer (Fig. 1-5). The dry-bulb thermometer is just a conventional thermometer like the ones you have around your home. The wet-bulb thermometer, however, is a thermometer with a wet cloth or wick wrapped around its bulb. As water evaporates from this cloth, the bulb of the thermometer is cooled. The wet-bulb thermometer thus indicates the effect of moisture in the air, since the rate of evaporation is affected by the air's humidity as well as temperature. If the air is very dry, evaporation is rapid and the wet-bulb thermometer will indicate a much lower temperature than the dry-bulb thermometer. But if the relative humidity is 100%, the wet-bulb and dry-bulb thermometers will indicate the same temperature because no evaporation takes place.

The wet-bulb temperature is important for another reason—it indicates the approximate ***dew-point*** temperature, which is the temperature at which water vapor will begin to condense out of the air. The wet-bulb thermometer is cooled by the evaporation of water into the air, but the temperature cannot drop below the dew-point temperature; otherwise, evaporation would stop and moisture in the air would begin to condense back onto the wick around the bulb. In your home, the dew point tells you at what

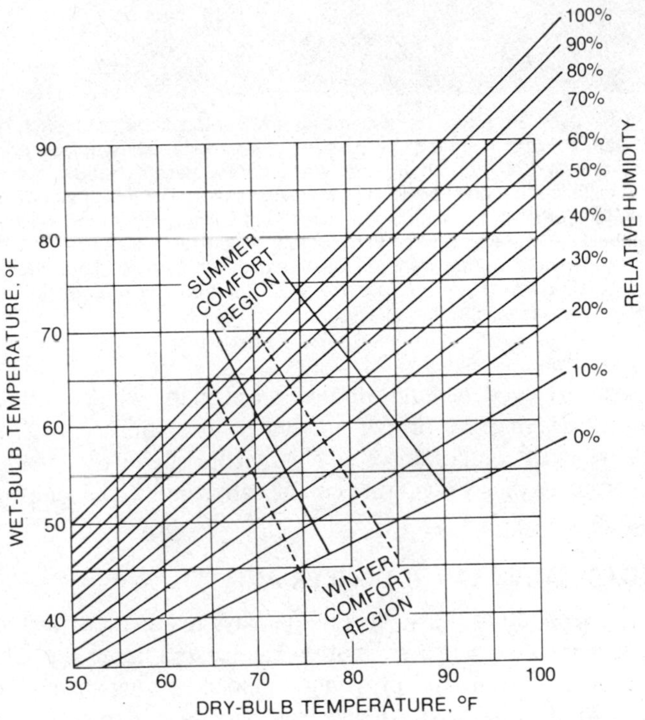

Fig. 1-5. A graph has long been used to determine the relative humidity by using the temperature obtained from dry-bulb and wet-bulb thermometers. The relative humidity effects the apparent warmth of the air. This effect is indicated on the graph by the two comfort regions for summer and winter. Of course, the apparent temperature of the air is only one comfort factor. Most people also prefer the relative humidity to be between 30 and 70% for maximum comfort.

Fig. 1-6. Attic vents may be installed in several locations, and each has its advantages. When installed in the eaves of the roof as shown, they are sheltered from wind-driven rain and snow and do not mar the beauty of a home. Vents installed in higher positions, however, do a better job of removing heat during the summer, but will also let more heat escape during the winter. Thermostatically controlled attic fans mounted on the roof can provide additional ventilation in hot summer weather. Be careful that you do not cover these vents with insulation when you insulate the attic—the vents are needed to remove moisture that collects in the attic space.

temperature condensation will take place on the windows and wall surfaces. Having the proper amount of insulation will normally keep the wall temperatures in your home above the dew-point temperature, thus preventing condensation and its accompanying problems.

AIR CIRCULATION CAN BE GOOD OR BAD

The motion of the air in a home plays many important roles. For example, too much air motion can make a home feel drafty, while too little air motion prevents a uniform heating and cooling of the air. Air coming into the house from outside, and the subsequent loss of air from inside, is also a major source of heat loss and heat gain. Sometimes this outside air is desirable, sometimes it is not. Fresh air can supply oxygen and remove stale odors, but most homes ordinarily have enough air entering through the opening and closing of doors that no additional air is needed. In general, the air movement into and out of a home can occur in two different ways: *ventilation* and *infiltration*. An understanding of what these two terms mean is quite helpful.

Ventilation occurs when air is intentionally brought into the home and made to mix with the air in the building. Ventilation air can be brought into the home with a separate fan, or it can be introduced using a special vent connected in the duct system. In either case, it is necessary to control the *amount* of outside air brought in as well as its temperature. The outside air is generally not at the same temperature as the inside of the building, making it necessary for the heating or cooling system to work harder.

Many buildings are required by law or local building codes to have a certain amount of outside ventilation air. The usual buildings having this requirement are nursing homes, hospitals, factories, and office buildings. The purpose of this ventilation air is to mix fresh air with the circulating air in order to reduce the amount of odors, bacteria, and noxious gases. The ventilation air also insures that an acceptable level of oxygen is present in the air.

The average home, though, does not need to have outside air brought into it. More than enough outside air usually manages to come into the building unintentionally! And this air runs up the heating and cooling bill. But while ventilation air should not be brought into the living areas of the home, other areas can benefit by circulating fresh outside air.

Fig. 1-7. The crawl space under a home needs two or more vents so that air can circulate to dry out the crawl space if it gets damp. The best kind of vent is to install is the closable type that permits the air circulation to be shut off from the outside of the house during the winter months. All vents should be screened to keep out termintes and other insects.

The attic and crawl space, for example, do need ventilation. The attic space usually needs ventilation all year round to remove heat buildup in the summer and moisture in the winter (Fig. 1-6). The crawl space needs venting in the summer to remove moisture that would rot beams and produce musty odors, but such ventilation is not usually desirable in the winter because it increases the heat load of the home and results in cold floors (Fig. 1-7).

Ventilation in the furnace room is sometimes required by insurance and loan companies. This requirement is intended to prevent the furnace from burning up all the oxygen in the house. The furnace room is thus equipped with an outside vent to provide fresh air to the furnace burners, and the combustion gases are then exhausted safely up the chimney. In many European countries, the vent is opened and closed automatically to increase furnace efficiency, but at present this scheme is not approved in the U.S.

Infiltration air enters the home through cracks around windows and through tiny openings in the walls, ceilings, and floors. When you hear whistling noises around doors and windows while the wind is blowing hard, you are listening to infiltration air. The same is true when you see window shades and blinds move as the wind blows outside. This infiltration air is not intentional—a perfectly sealed home would not have any. Since infiltration air must be heated and cooled, it contributes to the heating and cooling load of your home. Even the best homes have some infiltration air, which is another reason why no extra ventilation is needed. You can cut down the amount of infiltration air that enters your home by caulking and weather-stripping your windows and doors to seal up cracks and places that air can get through (Fig. 1-8).

METHODS OF TRANSFERRING HEAT

Heat energy is moved or transferred from one place to another by three chief methods: *conduction, convection* and *radiation*. All homes are heated or cooled using at least one of these methods. The reason it is important to know something about them is that they greatly affect the efficiency of your heating and cooling equipment. When the transfer of heat becomes inefficient, it costs you more to heat and cool your home, and that is a plenty good reason for knowing what's going on!

Conduction is a fancy word that just means heat is transferred by direct contact. When you place a pot on the burner of your stove, the heat energy is transferred from the burner to your pot. If the stove is electric, the pot rests directly on top of the heating coil. If

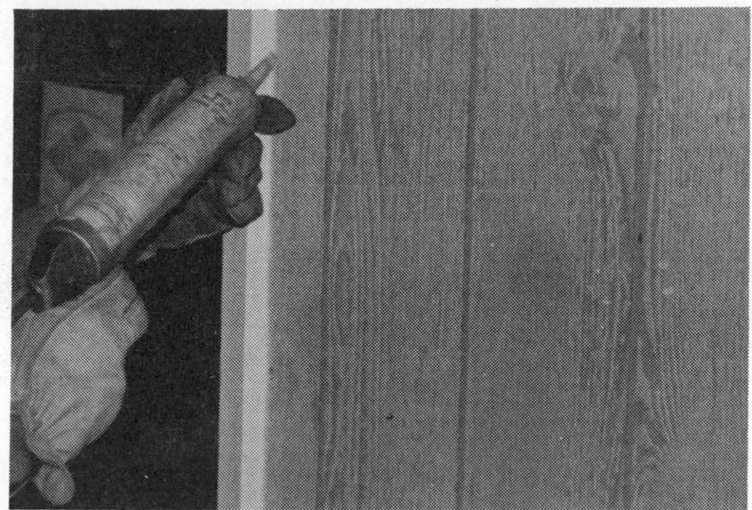

Fig. 1-8. Caulking around doors, windows and any other seams reduces the amount of infiltration air that enters the house. Caulking is a good investment of time and money because it reduces the heat load of the house and lowers the fuel bill.

the stove is gas, the flame touches the pot. In either case, the important thing to remember is that conduction requires a good contact between the *source* of the heat and the *object* to be heated. Dirt and soot between the source and object can destroy the efficiency of heat conduction in a furnace by acting as an insulator to slow down the transfer of heat. On the other hand, good insulation in your home can reduce the heat load and heat gain (Fig. 1-9).

Convection simply refers the heating or cooling of liquids and gases. When heating a gas such as air, the air molecules are free to move about and mix together. Warm air rises and cool air sinks, but the air currents that are created in this way tend to churn and mix the air so that its temperature becomes nearly uniform. Some conduction heating does take place, but the mixing or convection process dominates. The cool air drawn into a gas furnace is heated by convection in the burner box. Similarly, a baseboard electric heater draws cool air in at the bottom, where it is heated by convection as it passes over the hot fins inside, and then the entire room is heated by convection as the hot air rises and circulates throughout the room. Steam and hot-water furnaces also use the principle of convection heating. Air conditioners use a more complex process involving Freon on the inside, but the heating and cooling of the air on the outside works by simple convection. The efficiency of convection heating and cooling is reduced by dust and dirt, and by restrictions that slow the circulation of the air.

Radiation is the third method of heat transfer, and it differs quite a bit from either conduction or convection. The best example of radiation is sunlight or solar heat. When you stand out in the sun, rays of heat energy from the sun warm your body. But only that part of your body exposed to the sun is actually warmed by radiation; the shaded part is not warmed at all. Radiation is also at work when you stand in front of a fireplace or any other very hot source of heat. Heat lamps and even ordinary light bulbs give off heat radiation. Anything that is hot enough will emit infrared (heat) radiation, though it doesn't have to be hot enough to glow or give off light. The important characteristic to remember about radiation is that it always travels in a straight line; it cannot go around corners. However, heat radiation can be reflected just as light can, so shiny and light-colored surfaces can be used to reduce the heating effect of radiation. Radiation heat can be very effective in some applications, and it is the main principle behind the operation of electric and gas-fired space heaters.

Another method of heat transfer deserves mentioning, although it is really a combination of conduction and convection. *Evaporation* is an important form of heat transfer that enters into most heating and cooling operations. Evaporation was mentioned earlier when discussing relative humidity, and it was pointed out that evaporating water draws heat from objects that are in contact with the water, reducing their temperature. Both water and water vapor may feel just as warm to you when they are at the same temperature, but the fact is that water vapor contains more heat energy. Thus, as water evaporates, the vapor draws heat energy out of the remaining water, making it cooler. Furnace humidifiers use heat energy in himidifying the air, but the air feels warmer and much more comfortable, making it possible to turn the thermostat down a couple of degrees.

Evaporation works both ways, however. For in order to condense the water vapor from the air, the extra heat energy must be removed from the water vapor to turn it back into water. In fact, an air conditioner has to work almost as hard to reduce the humidity of the air by one percent as it does to reduce the temperature of the air by one degree. That is why it is so important in summer weather to use an exhaust fan to remove steam from cooking and showers, rather than to make the air conditioner work extra hard to remove it. The exhaust fan is a much cheaper way to cope with water vapor.

Fig. 1-9. Insulation reduces the conduction of heat through the walls of a house. There are several different kinds of insulation. These walls and cracks are being filled with fiberglass batting insulation.

QUICK WAYS TO CUT COSTS

Just looking at some of the fundamental principles of heating and cooling we have discussed should give you all sorts of ideas as to how you can reduce your electric and fuel bills. One quick way is to simply reduce the temperature difference between the inside and outside of your home. The less the temperature difference, the less it will cost to heat or cool your home. This was the basic idea behind the recent campaign to *dial down to 68°* in the winter to save heating fuel. The same idea can be used in the summer by setting your thermostat higher, say 78° instead of 74°.

Increasing the relative humidity of a home in the winter will make the occupants *feel* warmer because of a slowdown in the evaporation of perspiration, even though the air temperature remains the same. This makes it possible to set the thermostat at a lower temperature in the winter without sacrificing comfort. Similarly, decreasing the relative himidity of your home in the summer will speed up evaporation, and this will make you feel cooler with the same air temperature. So humidifiers and dehumidifiers can both be used to advantage in your home. It is wise, however, to keep a dehumidifier located in the basement or some low part of your home, since that is where the cool damp air collects and can be treated most easily and economically.

Air circulation can also be used to heat and cool your home more economically. Furnace registers and ducts should be adjusted to furnish heat to the room you spend most of your time in during the day. Bedrooms do not require heating during the daytime, and you can always use an extra blanket at night. Fans can be used to circulate air during the summer, especially if you are not using an air conditioner. Fans are very effective when used to draw hot air out of the house while windows are opened in occupied rooms, allowing cool air to come in. And if you have your air conditioner on, fans can also be used to increase air motion in the room, making the air feel cooler. Often, fans do a good enough job of circulating the air in a home that they can reduce or eliminate your dependence on air conditioning.

Ventilation air is responsible for much heat gain and heat loss in your home. Attic vents and exhaust fans can cool the upper levels of your home and reduce your cooling costs. Closeable vents in the foundation and crawl spaces of your home should be shut in the winter to prevent heat from escaping. Cold floors increase the temptation to raise the thermostat setting, which is a problem that can be partly solved with closed vents, although insulation, carpeting, and good air circulation help greatly.

Infilitration air is not desirable during either the summer or the winter. This cause of fuel waste can be solved by weather-stripping and caulking doors and windows to seal off gaps and cracks. Insulation can also reduce air leaks through floors, walls, and ceilings.

Insulation lowers both heat gain and heat loss. While adding insulation may not be a particularly quick way to cut costs, it is quite effective in the long run. The best thing about insulation is that it works in both the summer and winter to reduce heating and cooling costs. Detailed chapters are included in this book on how to insulate your home, as well as how to add weather stripping.

Solar radiation can significantly increase the costs of air-conditioning your home. Awnings, blinds, shades, and draperies can all be used to prevent this source of heat energy from entering your home.

Efficient heating and cooling rely greatly on obtaining the best possible heat transfer. This means that furnaces and air conditioners must be periodically inspected and cleaned. Replacing or cleaning a dirty, clogged air cleaner doesn't take long, but it can sure have a big effect on your fuel costs.

While the simple jobs described here can have an immediate effect in cutting your monthly bills, there are many other things you can do with not much more effort. The remaining chapters in this book describe many of the energy-saving techniques you can use to reduce your bills year after year. And a little energy-wise common sense can also pay off when using your household appliances, both large and small.

2 It Pays To Know Your Insulation

Every material used in building a home has insulation properties. Some materials insulate better than others. The trouble is that appearances are sometimes misleading. For example, suppose you had a 1-foot-thick concrete wall and a 1-inch-thick piece of fiberglass. Which would you say was the better insulator? If you guessed that the fiberglass was the better insulator, you were right. But would you have guessed that that flimsy thin sheet of fiberglass was almost *twice* as good an insulator as that sturdy, thick concrete wall? As you can see, you need hard facts and figures to tell you which insulating materials are better than others.

INSULATION AND HEAT TRANSFER

The heat load and heat gain of a building are affected by many factors, but insulation is by far the most important. We have already discussed heating and cooling loads briefly. However, their relationship with insulation, temperature, and fuel consumption merits further discussion. For the moment, we will concentrate on heat loads, realizing that the same principles apply to cooling loads. In general, whatever you do to reduce the heat load of your home will also reduce the cooling load.

There are four factors that have an effect on the heat load of a building: the exposed area of the walls, ceiling, and floor; the type of insulation used; the thickness of insulation used; and the temperature difference between the indoor and outdoor temperatures.

The exposed area of a building has an effect because heat loss is proportional to the exposed surface area. You would expect that a larger home would have a greater heat load than a smaller home, and this will be true if they are built the same way and located in the same part of the country. The larger home, of course, will have a larger outside surface area, so more heat energy will be conducted through the walls to the outside air. It also stands to reason that compact cubical homes provide less exposed surface area than sprawling ranch-style homes having an equivalent amount of living area.

The type of insulation and building materials used in the construction of a house determines how easily heat will pass through the building to the outside air. Some materials conduct heat better than others. Obviously, materials that are good conductors of heat must *not* be good insulators and therefore would not be desirable for building a home. What you really want for building materials are good insulators, and a good insulator will not let much heat pass through to the outside air. The insulating properties of many materials can be improved by the way in which they are processed or put together, so the final product—rather than the material itself—is of major concern. And there is also the question of cost, since, in general, the better the material or construction is for insulation purposes, the more costly it will be.

It is also reasonable that the more insulation you use, the more heat energy you will prevent from passing outside the building. Putting more insulation in the walls, ceiling, and floor of a home will reduce the heat load. There is, however, a point of diminishing returns, a point where the extra cost of more insulation outweighs the benefits received. You would certainly question the idea of adding so much insulation that it would take 20 years or more to repay your investment with the money saved in your fuel bills. Yet there are some contractors who would suggest that you do just that!

The temperatue difference has a direct effect on the heat load of a building. The heat load varies with the temperature difference, so the colder it gets outside, the greater the heat load and the more it costs to heat your home. As mentioned earlier, it is possible to reduce the temperature difference by lowering the inside temperature of your home. However, the whole idea behind having a thermostat is to make yourself comfortable, so there is a limit to how low you will set your thermostat. This means that you are at the mercy of the outside temperature, and your heating requirements will vary accordingly. The winter design temperature represents the coldest expected outside temperature and therefore determines the largest temperature difference. In turn, the largest temperature difference determines your maximum heat load, which determines the size of the furnace or heating system that you will need.

These four factors are used to find the heat loss or heat gain through the walls, ceilings, and floors of a building. This is the heat energy that is transferred through your home by conduction. Heat is also lost by infiltration air as warm air escapes from the house through openings and cracks in the building, or as cold air enters through similar openings. Therefore, the total heat loss or gain in your home is due primarily to the combined effects of conduction and infiltration. Heat loss by conduction is reduced with insulation. Heat loss by infiltration is reduced by caulking around cracks and weather-stripping door and window openings. It is often the case, though, that the addition of insulation also reduces infiltration air by closing off openings inside the walls, ceilings, and floors. There are a wide variety to tiny openings around baseboards, ceiling fixtures, electrical receptacles, and switchplates that permit infiltration air to pass, but the amount of this air is reduced by the presence of insulation that fills up the wall cavities.

HEAT TRANSFER FACTORS

The conducting or insulating properties of different materials are rated using three factors. Actually, all three factors give you essentially the same information, but they are used in slightly different ways. The proper understanding and use of these factors can help you in selecting everything from basic building materials to complete walls, ceilings, and floors. The heat transfer factors are represented by the letters K, U and R. You will see at least one of these letters appearing in a variety of tables and charts that list the insulating properties of either basic building materials or standard structures already containing various types of insulation.

For convenience in comparing and working with these factors, they are all based on a one-square-foot section of the material and on a one-degree temperature difference between surfaces. The thickness of the material may vary, but it is always listed in the table with the heat transfer value.

The K Factor

The K factor is a *conduction* factor that tells you how much heat energy will pass through a piece of insulating material. The K factor is given in BTU per hour for 1 square foot of surface area and

Table 2-1. K Factors for Common Building Materials.

MATERIAL	THICKNESS	K FACTOR
cork board	1″	0.27
fiberglass	1″	0.27
glass foam	1″	0.40
polystyrene foam	1″	0.15
rock wool	1″	0.29
fir	1″	0.67
pine, soft	1″	0.86
particle board	1″	0.50
sawdust	1″	0.41
brick, face	1″	10.00
brick, common	1″	5.00
gypsum wall board	1″	0.70
stone	8″	0.70
stone	12″	0.50
cinder block	8″	0.50
	12″	0.35
concrete, block	8″	0.55
	12″	0.45
concrete poured	8″	0.70
	12″	0.50

a temperature difference between surfaces of one degree. All heating and cooling loads, furnaces, and air conditioners are rated in BTU per hour, so the K factor gives you information that is immediately usable.

Tablc 2-1 gives some K factors for common materials. For example, the K factor for a 1-inch-thick piece of cork board is 0.27. This means that a piece of cork mesuring 1 foot by 1 foot will allow BTU per hour to pass through if the temperature difference is one degree. Doubling either the temperature difference or the surface area will double the heat conduction, but doubling the thickness of the material will cut the heat conduction in half. In other words, you can use K factors for any thickness material covering any size area and for any temperature difference. All you have to do is multiply the K factor by the actual temperature difference and by the surface area, while you divide the K factor by the proportionate increase in thickness. For example, if you are tiling and 8 by 12 foot wall with cork board that is 2 inches thick, and the temperature difference is 10 degrees, the heat conduction would be:

$$\frac{(\text{K factor}) \times (\text{width}) \times (\text{length}) \times (\text{temperature}) \text{ difference})}{(\text{increase in thickness})}$$

$$= \frac{0.27 \times 12 \times 8 \times 10}{2} = 129.6 \text{ BTU per hour}$$

Be careful when using any of these heat transfer factors that you carefully note the thickness of the material given in the table. Often the thickness is given for standard product sizes, as for concrete blocks. But in other cases the thickness is for just one inch. If you use, say, 6 inches of fiberglass and the K factor was for 1 inch, you would divide by 6 since you were using 6 times as much insulation. But if you use 6 inches of poured concrete when the K factor given is for, say, 8 inches, then you would have to divide by 6/8, or ¾, since your were using only ¾ as much materials.

All building materials—fir, pine, brick, concrete, foam insulation, etc.—have their own K factors. Materials that conduct heat more rapidly have higher K factors than materials that insulate well. So when comparing K factors, the lower the K factor the better.

The U Factor

The U factor is sort of a *universal* factor because it applies to wall construction rather than to specific materials. If you knew how the wall in a home was constructed, you could use the various K factors for each material to find out what the heat conduction would be through the wall. But this approach would be rather tedious, and it might not be very accurate either. If available, the U factor is the one to use because it often takes into account the effect of wind speed and surface finishes on each side of the wall. For our purposes, we will ignore such details as finishes, air films, and wind speeds, since they have only a minor effect on the final heat conduction value.

Like the K factor, the U factor is also expressed in BTU per hour for a 1-square-foot area of wall and a one-degree temperature difference. Knowing the U factor of a wall allow you to figure out what amount of heat is escaping. You can then compare the U factors of different wall constructions to determine what type of construction has the lowest heat conduction and, therefore, the best insulation properties. Knowing the U factor also helps in quickly determining the heat load of a home, since the same BTU energy units are used in calculating heat loads.

Heating contractors and utility companies use charts and tables for estimating heat loads that are based on typical constructions and home designs in their location. These charts already include the winter design temperatures in your area, so it is only necessary to know the general size and home style (ranch, bungalow, etc.) in order to estimate your heating requirements to a fair degree of accuracy. But if such detailed charts are not readily available, or if your home differs greatly from the typical homes listed, then the heat load can be determined by multiplying the U factor of each wall by the area of the wall and by the temperature difference.

To find the U factor of a wall from the K factors of each material in the wall, use the following formula:

$$U = \frac{1}{\frac{\text{thickness of A}}{\text{K factor of A}} + \frac{\text{thickness of B}}{\text{K factor of B}} + \frac{\text{thickness of C}}{\text{K factor of C}}}$$

where A, B, and C are the materials in the wall. To illustrate how this formula is used, let's find the U factor of the wall shown in Fig. 2-1. This wall is constructed using ¼-inch fir lap siding, ¾ inch pine boxing, and ¼ inch wood paneling inside.

From Table 2-1, the K factor for the fir lap siding is 0.67 per inch, the K of pine is 0.86 per inch, and we will assume that the K for the wood paneling is the same as for the pine, 0.86 per inch. Putting these numbers into the formula, we get:

$$U = \frac{1}{\frac{0.25}{0.67} + \frac{0.75}{0.86} + \frac{0.25}{0.86}}$$

$$= \frac{1}{0.373 + 0.872 + 0.291}$$

$$= \frac{1}{1.536} = 0.65$$

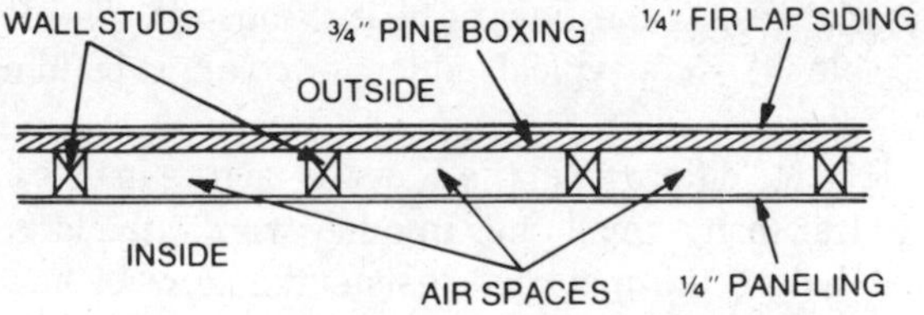

Fig. 2-1. The U factor for a wall is a composite of the K factors of each material in the wall. The K factors for the materials in this wall are 0.67 for the siding and 0.86 for the boxing and paneling. The U factor for the entire wall is 0.65, as described in the text. Note that this wall does not have its air spaces filled with insulation. Note also that the studs in the wall do not contribute any insulating effect in this calculation because the large air spaces allow heat to pass around the studs from the inside wall to the outside wall.

Table 2-2. R Factors for Common Building Materials.

MATERIAL	THICKNESS	R FACTOR
insulation, spun rock or fiberglass	2″	7
	3–4″	11–14
	5–8″	19–22
plywood	⅜″	0.47
	½″	0.62
	⅝″	0.78
	¾″	0.94
brick, common	1″	0.20
brick, face	1″	0.11
gypsum wall board	1″	0.90
pine, soft	1″	1.20
shingles, asphalt		0.44
shingles, wood		0.94

It is easy to see that this would be a fairly cumbersome method of figuring the heat loss through a wall. For this reason, the charts and tables for complete walls are much more desirable to work with. Such charts can tell you at a glance what effect added insulation can have on your home, whether it is already built or still in blueprint form. You will also be able to see what effects different sidings and insulation materials have, as when adding aluminum siding over an existing lap or shingle siding. (Aluminum siding, by the way, also comes with insulation on the underside.) The U and K factors can be of great help when designing a new home, permitting you to select materials that can prevent a lot of heat loss.

The R Factor

The R factor is a *resistance* factor that tells you how much a given material resists the flow of heat through it. The R factors given in Table 2-2 show typical values for common building materials.

The R factor differs from the K and U factors in that a large R factor is better than a small one. In other words, the larger the R factor, the better the material resists the flow of heat. Most insulation materials have R factors printed on them. If you look closely at a roll of fiberglass insulation, you'll see an R number printed on it. For example, a roll of 3½-inch-thick fiberglass might have the number R-11 printed on it, which indicates that its R factor is 11. Building specifications will often list an R number for the insulation and leave it up to the contractor to meet the requirements with the most economical materials available. For example, in the northern states, it is presently recommended that you use at least R-33 ceiling insulation and R-19 insulation in floors.

The R factor is just the reciprocal of the U factor; that is, $R = 1/U$ and $U = 1/R$. The wall in the previous example had a U factor of 0.65, which is equivalent to an R factor of 1/0.65, or 1.54. So the R factor of the wall was 1.54. Reversing the calculations, if you knew the R factor of the wall, you could find the U factor, since $U = 1/R$.

The R factor is the principal factor used to rate the effectiveness of insulation, and most materials have an R factor printed on them. But most building materials such as wood, brick, siding, etc. are usually rated in K and U factors, although it is simple to convert them to R factors. Heating contractors and most fuel companies normally use U factors to figure the heat load of a house, while electric power companies seem to favor using R factors (probably because of the similarity to electrical resistance). Both U and R factors, however, give you the same sort of information, though the R factors are much easier to work with since you just add them up directly. Figure 2-2 shows how the U factor of a wall is found using the R factors of the various materials. Note that the total R factor of the wall (14.35) is just the sum of the individual R factors.

The most important use of the R factor is as an aid to the homeowner in determining the resistance of the various types of

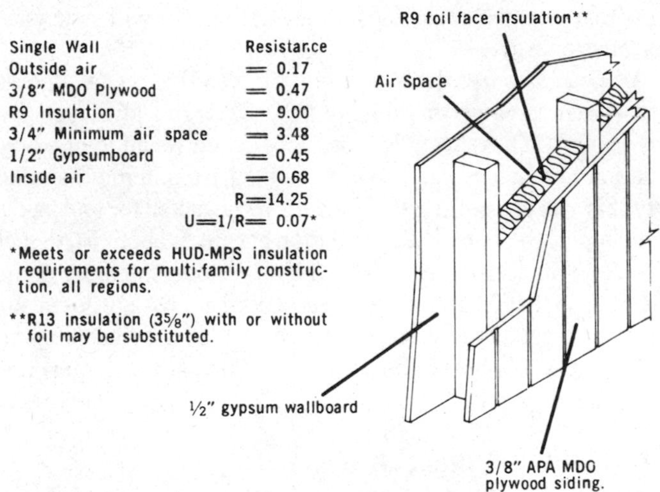

Single Wall
Resistance
Outside air = 0.17
3/8" MDO Plywood = 0.47
R9 Insulation = 9.00
3/4" Minimum air space = 3.48
1/2" Gypsumboard = 0.45
Inside air = 0.68
R=14.25
U=1/R= 0.07*
*Meets or exceeds HUD-MPS insulation requirements for multi-family construction, all regions.
**R13 insulation (3⅝") with or without foil may be substituted.
R9 foil face insulation**
Air Space
½" gypsum wallboard
3/8" APA MDO plywood siding.

Fig. 2-2. R factors are used here to find the U factor of a residential wall (courtesy American Plywood Association).

Fig. 2-3. While very attractive, face bricks actually add very little insulating ability to a wall, since the R value for face brick is only 0.10 per inch. Adding insulation between the bricks and the outer boxing will greatly increase the insulating qualities of the wall.

insulation. With the *R* values, you can compare the insulating qualities and costs to decide which type is best for your particular use. This is especially true when planning to remodel a home or add on to an existing home (Fig. 2-3). At that time, it is a fairly simple matter to select and install insulation that will save you the most heat energy.

You can also use the *R* factor as an effective means of quality control when having a custom home built, or an addition such as a family room. The advantage of the printed *R* numbers on the insulation is that you can inspect the insulation being installed to verify that you are getting the insulation you asked for and paid for. For example, R-19 and R-22 insulation batting is about 5 to 8 inches thick; R-11 and R-13 is usually 3 to 4 inches thick. A point to remember is that insulation requirements for FHA approved housing are measured in *R* values, so if you anticipate financing under this plan, it would be a good idea to check what the requirements are in your area.

HEAT CONDUCTION THROUGH WALLS

Adding insulation to a wall will increase its *R* value or decrease its *U* value. In either case, the amount of heat escaping through the wall will be reduced (Fig. 2-4). Adding 1 inch of insulation to an uninsulated wall will reduce the heat loss through the wall by 40—50%. Adding 2 inches of insulation will reduce the heat loss by 60—65%. Adding 3 inches will cut heat loss by 70—75%, and adding 4 inches will cut heat loss by 75—80%. All of these quoted percentages depend on the particular type of insulation used and on the construction of the wall before insulation is installed, but they represent typical figures.

The temperature difference between the inside and outside of your home is the main factor in determining how much insulation

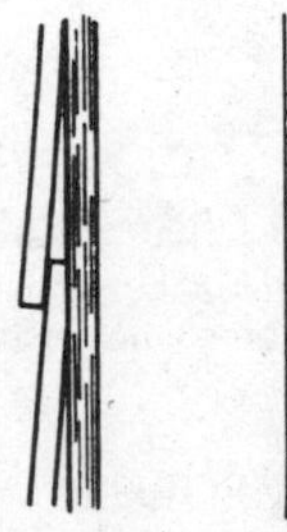

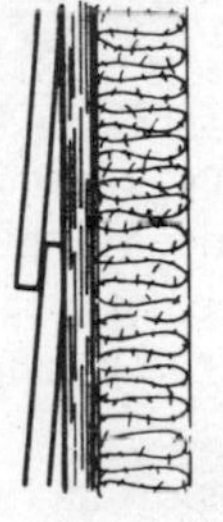

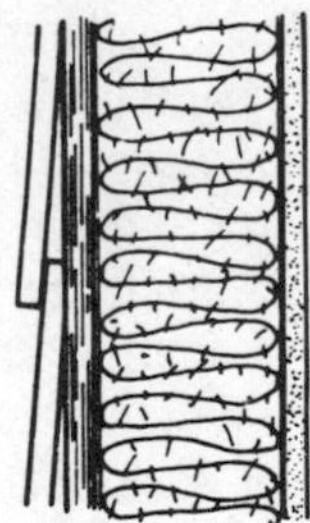

Fig. 2-4. This demonstrates the difference insulation can make in a typical wall. The effects of adding insulation are magnified a little, since we ignored the insulating effects of the air film on each side of the wall. But in most cases, 4 inches of insulation will reduce the heat loss by 75 to 80%.

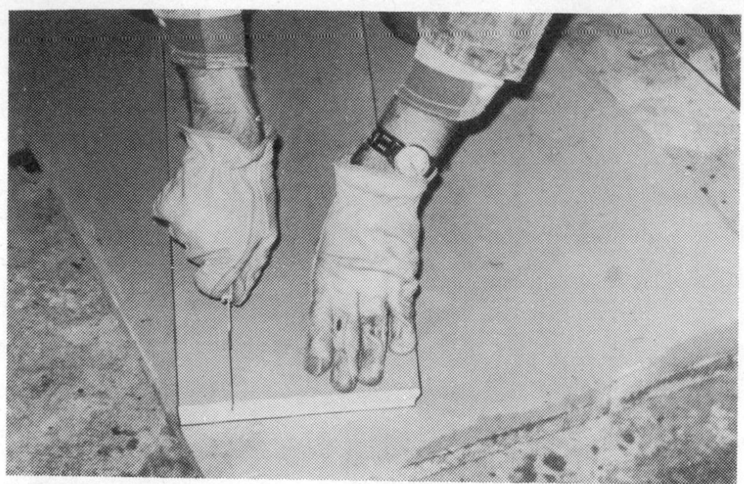

Fig. 2-5. Plastic foam insulation is made with millions of dead-air spaces fused together. This is called closed cell insulation. The R value for some types of this insulation is 6 per inch.

should be used in the walls, ceilings, and floors. If you live in the northern part of the U.S., where cold winters are the rule, you will spend more money in obtaining more and better insulation than if you lived in the south. In some regions of the country, the cost of fuel is especially high, and this too dictates the use of more insulation. Aside from the heating aspect of your home, there is also the cooling side, which would also benefit from added insulation. So in the southern states, insulation can reduce the cost of air conditioning your home more than it would reduce the cost of heating it.

In the northern states, heating costs are most important, so insulation is always installed on the basis of the lowest expected winter temperature, which is known as the winter design temperature. To find out how much insulation you need and what types you should use, contact you local builders, building material suppliers, and central heating and air conditioning shops. Beware, though, of biased information from people who are interested primarily in selling insulation, for they may try to sell you more insulation than would justify the cost. Often, the most reliable source of information can be obtained from the service departments of electric and fuel companies, which can often provide year-round estimates of how much it would cost to heat a home based on just the blueprints.

The addition of insulation to the walls, ceilings, and floors of a home reduces heat transfer—convection, conduction, and radiation. Air is actually a very poor conductor of heat, even though it is able to transfer large amounts by convection. The trick is to prevent the air from moving or circulating, and this is the way most foam, spun, or batting insulation materials work. Some insulation, such as plastic foam and closed-cell insulation, actually creates dead air pockets by holding the air in sealed bubbles (Fig. 2-5). Other insulation, such as batting and spun fibers, merely prevents the air from circulating freely (Fig. 2-6). In either case, the motion of the air is drastically reduced and only a small amount of heat is transferred by conduction through the air.

The dead air space between the studs in an uninsulated wall is much too large to provide any insulating effect. The air is able to freely circulate, transferring large amounts of heat energy by convection. Filling the wall with insulation prevents convection and therefore increases the insulating capabilities of the wall (Fig. 2-70. It may seem truly amazing that the light, fluffy materials used to fill these wall cavities could have such a tremendous effect on stopping heat transfer, but that is the way it works. These insulation materials simply divide the air space between the studs into thousands of tiny dead air spaces that have almost no air motion and therefore have very little convection heat loss.

Good insulation has a high R factor and a high resistance to the conduction of heat through the wall. Even though convection may

Fig. 2-6. Insulation fills the space between the walls with material that stops convection currents in the wall. This fiberglass insulation batting has an R factor of about 4 per inch, compared to soft pin wood, which has an R factor of about 1.2 per inch.

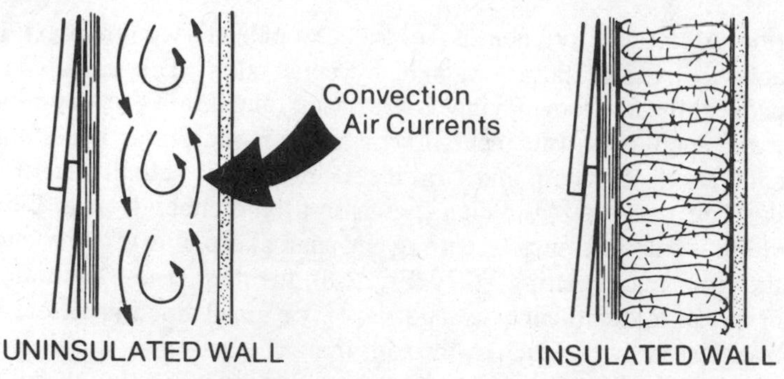

Fig. 2-7. The uninsulated wall has a large amount of heat transfer as the convection currents inside the wall freely transfer heat and create heat loss. The insulated wall reduces heat loss, since the insulating material almost completely eliminates convection currents.

be a significant factor of heat transfer within the wall cavity, the insulation properties of the wall itself are treated as a conduction effect (Fig. 2-8). Therefore, the addition of insulation within the wall acts to lower the conduction of heat through the wall. The more insulation that is added to the wall, the higher the *R* value and the resistance to heat flow.

Moist air has a higher conduction factor than dry air, so many types of insulation have a vapor barrier that is intended to keep moist air on the outside of the home. The vapor or moisture barrier is formed by a layer of plastic, foil, tar paper, or a combination of these. When installing insulation having a vapor barrier, the barrier side faces toward the living area. An advantage of plastic foam insulation is that the individual air cells are completely sealed and pass very little air or moisture at all.

Even some of the best insulating materials can become rather poor insulators if they are allowed to get wet. The problem with moist air is that it can condense and saturate some insulations, permitting the water, which has a very high heat conductivity, to transfer heat energy through the wall. Even worse, though, the presence of water or high amounts of moist air can rot and warp wooden beams and paneling. In particularly moist locations such as basements or other masonry walls, the best vapor barrier is obtained by using large sheets of plastic installed directly against the masonry wall. Large rolls of heavy gauge plastic are available from most building material suppliers for just this purpose, and the rolls are wide enought to extend from floor to ceiling and from wall to wall. Since concrete and cement-block walls are fairly poor insulators, it is a good idea to use at least some insulation behind the paneling in basements.

How much heat energy does adding four inches of insulation save? Let's consider our earlier example in which we calculated the U factor of a wall with ¼-inch fir lap siding, ¾-inch pine boxing, and ¼-inch wood paneling. The K factors of the materials were 0.67, 0.86, and 0.86, respectively. We had calculated that the U factor for the uninsulated wall was 0.65. If this wall were 60 feet long and 8 feet high, there would be 480 square feet of wall area. Multiplying the U factor by the wall area yields a heat loss through the wall of $0.65 \times 480 = 312$ BTU per hour for each degree of temperature difference. With a 70 degree temperature difference, the heat loss would be $312 \times 70 = 21{,}840$ BTU per hour. This, remember, is the heat loss through a wall with no insulation.

Now let's see what happens when we add 4 inches of fiberglass insulation (K factor, 0.27). The U factor of the wall then becomes:

$$1U = \frac{1}{\frac{0.25}{0.67} + \frac{0.75}{0.86} + \frac{0.25}{0.86} + \frac{4}{0.27}}$$

$$= \frac{1}{0.373 + 0.872 + 0.291 + 14.8}$$

$$= \frac{1}{16.63} = 0.06$$

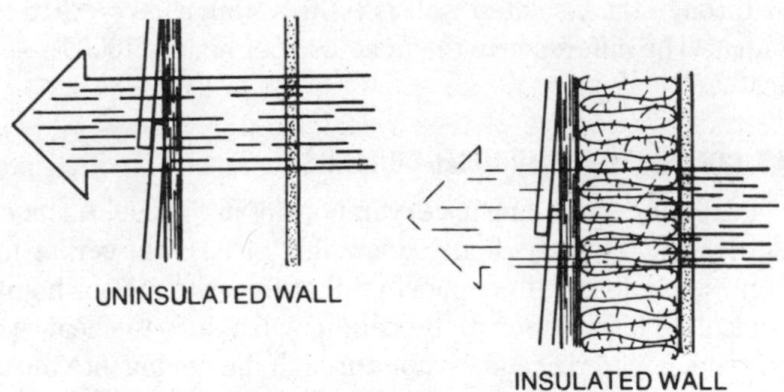

Fig. 2-8. The air between the inside and outside walls transfers heat readily, allowing a large heat loss by conduction through the wall. The insulation has a higher resistance to heat flow and does not conduct heat as easily. Adding insulation increases the R value of the wall and reduces the wall's ability to conduct heat.

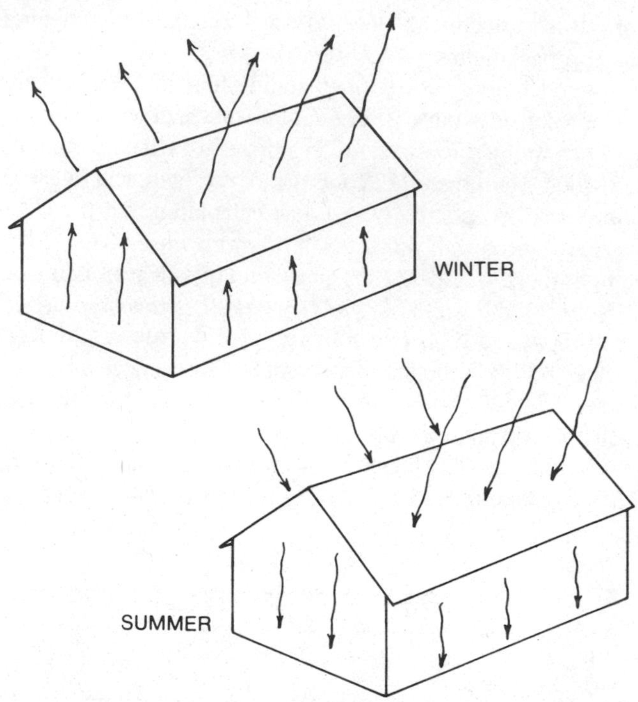

Fig. 2-9. This shows the importance of insulating the ceiling. In the winter, the heat in the house rises to the ceiling and escapes to the outside. In the summer when attic temperatures reach 125°, heat comes into the living area from above.

The *U* factor of the insulated wall is 0.06, and the heat loss per hour through the insulated wall is 0.06 × 480 × 70 = 2016 BTU per hour. The difference in the heat loss per hour is 1000%—or 10 times!

HEAT CONDUCTION THROUGH CEILINGS

Insulating the ceiling is very important in a house. As much as 75% of the heat loss in a house goes right through the ceiling in the winter, so obviously it is important that this part of your home be well insulated. Insulation in the ceiling will hold in the heat, which has a tendency to rise and escape through the ceiling into the attic space. In the summer, the heat flow reverses and extremely hot temperatures in the attic warm the rooms in the living area below (Fig. 2-9).

For most applications, 6 to 10 inches of fiberglass batting insulation in the ceiling is needed to prevent excessive heat gain or loss through the ceiling. Again, this will depend on your area, the winter and summer design temperatures, and other factors. You should contact a local builder or insulation company to get recommendations. More than 10 inches of insulation (R-33) may cost more than the extra insulation is worth, but this varies. Twelve inches of insulation (R-38) is justified in some northern states where fuel costs are especially high. There are several different ways that the ceiling can be insulated, including blown-in insulation, fiberglass batting insulation, or a combination of insulation types.

There are other ways to reduce the energy loss through the ceiling besides insulation, although this is the most important. One way to reduce heat gain in the summer is to lower the temperature of the attic above the living area of the house. When the attic is cooler, less heat will be transferred into the rooms below, and the air conditioner will have less of a load. The temperatures in attics can often exceed 125°F, and this adds a considerable amount of heat to the living space.

You can lower the temperature of the attic by installing an automatic attic fan and vents. Just installing vents at each end of the attic will often allow enough air circulation to lower the temperature of the attic quite a bit. Forcing the ventilation with a fan can lower the attic temperature even more. A section discussing attic fans and giving installation tips appears in Chapter 4.

Fig. 2-10. This house is being built with white asphalt shingles covering the roof. A dark-colored roof will increase the heat gain through the ceiling by as much as 20% and can add significantly to the summer cooling load. Even though a dark roof will absorb some heat in the winter to reduce the heat load, this contribution is normally considered to be insignificant.

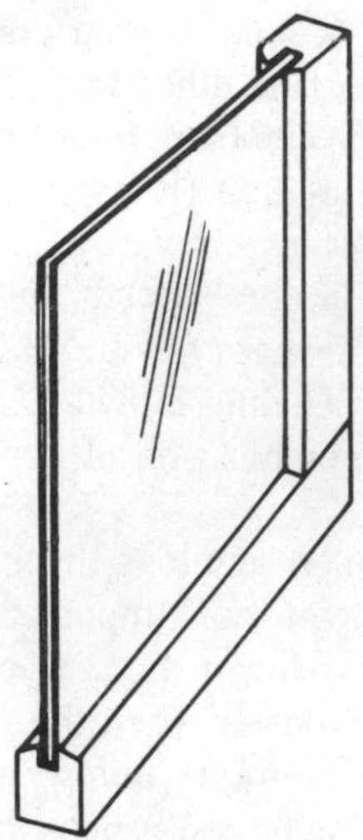
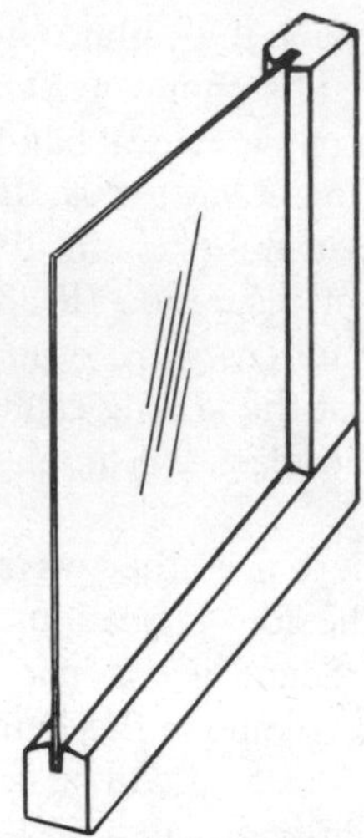

Fig. 2-11. A window with a single glass pane has a U factor of about 1.13, whereas a double-pane window has a U factor of about 0.5. Adding a second pane of glass in the window lowers the heat conduction by 60%, which is more than half, because the captive air between the panes contributes added insulation.

The color of the roof has an effect on the amount of heat gain in the house. An important thing to remember here is that heat gain is undesirable in the summer, but it is desirable in the winter. This presents somewhat of a dilemma for the homeowner. While a dark-colored roof will absorb sunlight and add some desirable heat to the attic in the winter, this same dark roof will add heat to the attic in the summer when it is undesirable. A light-colored roof will help relfect the sun's rays and leave the attic somewhat cooler than a dark roof in the summer. From the standpoint of energy conservation, we would recommend a light-colored roof (Fig. 2-10) because most homes stand to benefit more from a light roof in the summer than they would from a dark roof in the winter. This is purely a energy saving suggestion, however, since design or style will probably have more to do with the color and type of roof selected for a home than matters of energy conservation.

HEAT CONDUCTION THROUGH WINDOWS AND DOORS

Figue 2-11 compares the U factors and construction of two windows. It points out the large amount of heat loss that is possible through the windows of a home. A single-pane window, with a typical U factor of 1.13, has a heat loss more than 10 times greater than a residential wall or ceiling having a typical U factor of 0.10. Double-pane windows (also called insulating glass and double-glazed windows) have a U factor of about 0.50, which is less than half as much as a single-pane window.

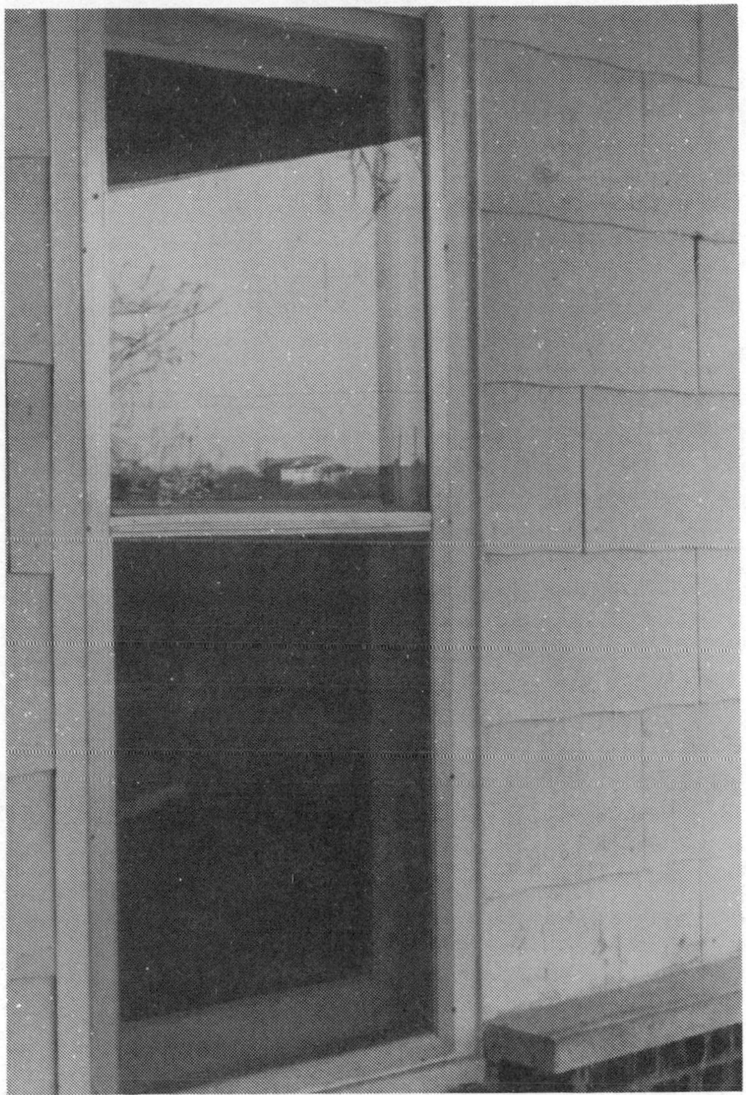

Fig. 2-12. A storm window attaches to the window frame and adds a second pane of glass to reduce heat flow through the window area. Special insulating-glass models are also available that are constructed with two sealed panes of glass in each sash.

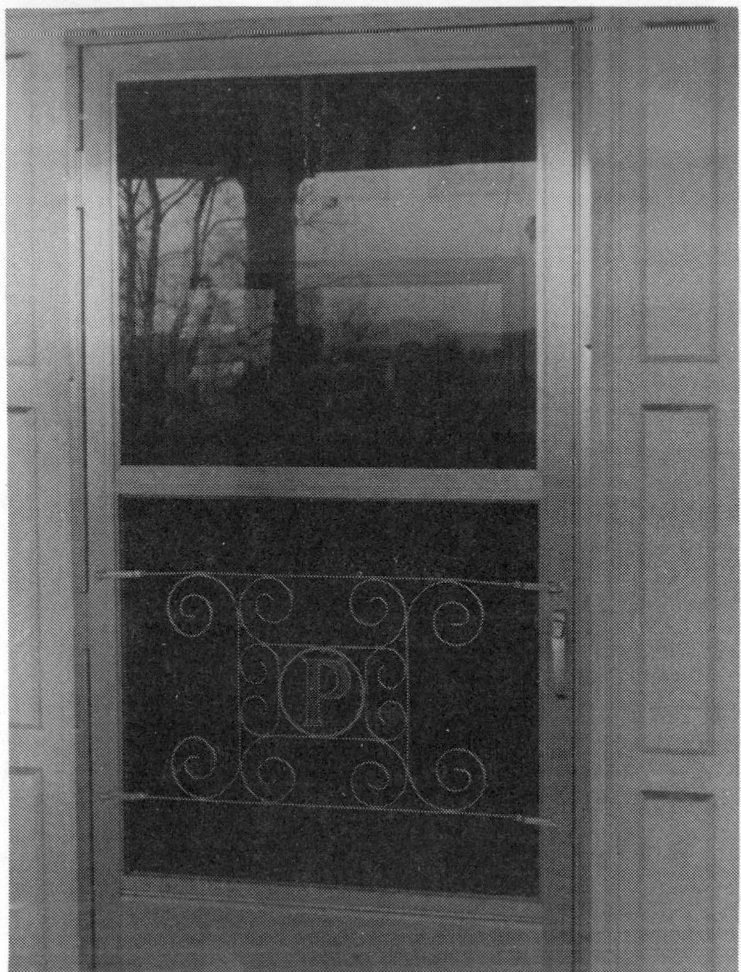

Fig. 2-13. A storm door is easy to install to the existing door frame, and it reduces the flow of heat through the door area. Storm doors are available in many different materials, styles and constructions. Aluminum storm doors are the most popular, but wooden units are also available.

Adding storm windows over the single-pane windows of your home will accomplish much the same task as double-pane windows (Fig. 2-12). Storm windows and double-pane windows, which will reduce the heat loss through the windows by 40 to 60%, should be installed on any house in the northern two-thirds of the United States. Some areas in the northern third of the country will benefit from triple-glazed windows or double-glazed windows with storm windows.

Storm doors will similarly reduce the heat loss through the door (Fig. 2-13). Such a door may not be necessary, however, if your doors are solid wooden ones with small window areas. Foam core doors are also available to provide additional insulating qualities.

Window awnings may be used during the summer to reduce radiated heat passing through the window by about 15%. Storm doors, storm windows, and window awnings are discussed in Chapter 6.

TYPES OF INSULATION

Materials used to insulate buildings have a low conductivity for heat. That is, they have a low K factor and a high R factor. Some common materials used for insulating purposes are spun/fiberglass (K factor, 0.27 per inch), rock wool (K factor, 0.29 per inch) and foamed plastic (K factor, 0.15 per inch). Wood and particle board also exhibit some insulating qualities, but their K factors are much higher (around 0.70 to 0.80 per inch). Insulating properties for some common materials are compared in Tables 2-3, 2-4 and 2-5.

As you can see, there is a wide variety of insulation types. Some of these types have properties that make them particularly well suited for specific insulation uses. The best way to select the right insulation for your use is to contact a local builder or insulation dealer.

Most types of insulation are interchangeable with other types for many uses. For instance, all types of insulation listed in Table 2-3 are suitable for insulating walls. This is an advantage for the homeowner who is planning to insulate his walls but cannot obtain the type of insulation he perfers, due to short supply.

Table 2-3. Facts On Common Insulating Materials (courtesy of Department of Housing and Urban Development).

	BATTS OR BLANKETS		LOOSE FILL (POURED-IN)			
	glass fiber	rock wool	glass fiber	rock wool	cellulosic fiber	
R-11	3½"-4"	3"	5"	4"	3"	R-11
R-19	6"-6½"	5¼"	8"-9"	6"-7"	5"	R-19
R-22	6½"	6"	10"	7"-8"	6"	R-22
R-30	9½"-10½"*	9"*	13"-14"	10"-11"	8"	R-30
R-38	12"-13"*	10½"	17"-18"	13"-14"	10"-11"	R-38

*two batts or blankets required.

*two batts or blankets required.

Table 2-4. Approximate R Values Per Inch.

Material	R value
Fiberglass blankets	3
Fiberglass loose fill	2.2
Rock wool blankets	3.2
Rock wool loose fill	2.5
Cellulosic fiber	3.2-3.7
Urea-formaldehyde	4
Polystyrene	4-6
Polyurethane	6
Perlite, expanded	2.7
Vermiculite, expanded	2.1

When the supply of one type of insulation is low in your area, you can easily substitute another type of insulation. Since R values provide a universal system of comparing the insulating qualities of different materials, you can be reasonably sure of the insulating value per dollar for your insulation, no matter what type it is. The R factor also makes comparison shopping simple by allowing the purchaser to compare the R value per dollar for the different types of insulation and brands available in his area.

As a general rule, you should pay more money only for a higher R value. Of course, different types of insulation have different properties (such as fire resistance, longevity, and freedom from settling) that make them worth a bit more money. And you certainly should not hesitate to pay slightly higher prices for good quality insulation from a reputable dealer.

But the common denominator in all insulation is the R factor, and that is the figure you should use in all your comparisons. You need not concern yourself with pounds per dollar or inches per dollar—it's the R value per dollar that tells you how much insulating quality you are getting for your money. The R factor lets you instantly compare fiberglass insulation with plastic foam and cellulosic fiber insulation.

In the following sections we have summarized the major properties of some of the best known insulation materials. We have also included some general information about prices of the various insulation types, but this is one point regarding insulation that you will have to determine for yourself. Insulation prices have risen rapidly in the past few years, and they are almost certain to continue rising. Any cost figures may be quickly out of date. Also, prices vary widely from area to area, depending on demand and the available supply of insulation. The only way you can compare the cost of using the various types of insulation for your home is to go out and ask for yourself.

Table 2-5. Good and Bad Points Concerning Structural and Insulating Materials.

PLYWOOD	+ good nailing surface, good durability, great strenght – would not be used for insulation because of its expense
FIBERBOARD	+ inexpensive sheathing material, decent insulating value – not a good nailing surface, not waterproof
SOFTWOOD T&G DECKING	+ provides roof structure over beams 8′ on center, attractive celing material, nominal insulating value, great nailing surface – would not be used solely for insulation because of its expense
URETHANE	+ provides walls with flat surface, easily installed directly over studs, light-weight, good insulator, can be used below-grade – expensive, extremely flammable, when it burns it emits toxic fumes
CELLULOSE	+ inexpensive, needs less cavity for same insulating value as fiberglass, fireproof – may settle in walls, may collect moisture
FIBERGLASS	+ inexpensive, easily installed, can be bought with vapor barrier, foil-faced stops reflective heat loss, may be used in walls and ceilings, batts won't settle in walls – needs more space to match other insulations "R" value
UREA-FORMAL-DEHYDE FOAM	+ can be installed in uninsulated homes, highest "R" value per inch of all the fill insulations – must be properly formulated by the installer, cannot be used in ceilings, inferior products may deteriorate.

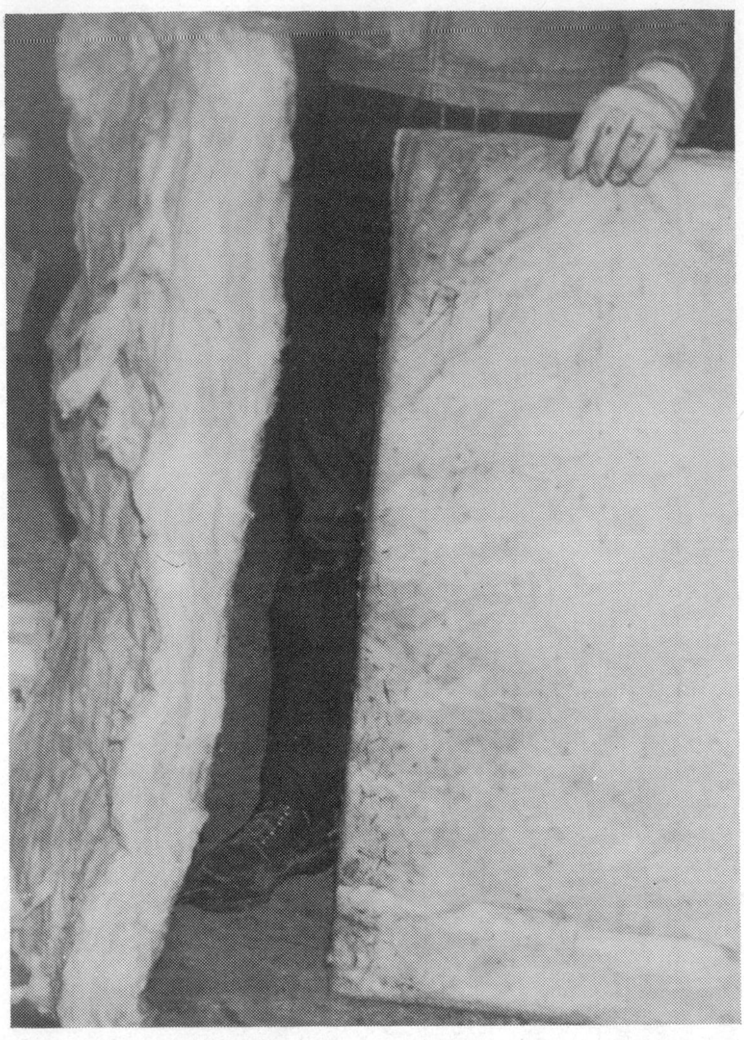

Fig. 2-14. Fiberglass insulation batting is available in a variety of thicknesses to give varying insulating qualities. The R factor of the insulation should be marked plainly on the package.

FIBERGLASS AND ROCK WOOL

These materials are the standbys of modern insulation materials. Both have been used with great success for decades, and many builders claim they would not insulate a home with anything else. In general, fiberglass and rock wool (also known as mineral fiber) are among the least expensive insulation materials, both in terms of absolute cost and cost per R value. In many areas, however, mineral fiber insulation is in short supply, which has forced homeowners and contractors to use other materials.

Both fiberglass and rock wool are formed from rock-like substances, which gives them their fireproof qualities. Rock wool, also called mineral wool, is made by blowing air through molten limestone or slag to obtain wooly fibers (hence the name *rock wool*). Fiberglass is made by spinning molten sand (glass) into long fibers. The rock wool or fiberglass fibers are then stuck together to trap air between the fibers and create the insulating material that comes in either bolt or pellet form.

Insulation Batts and Blankets

Mineral fiber insulation can be purchased in several different forms. One very popular form is the insulation *batt*, shown in Fig. 2-14. These batts are precut to fit between the studs or joists on 16-inch or 24-inch centers. They are available in 4-foot and 8-foot lengths and can be purchased with or without a vapor barrier backing. Their popularity comes from the ease in handling the short lengths of insulation.

The insulation is also available in large rolls or blankets. Unlike the batts, which are cut in relatively short lengths, the

Fig. 2-15. Rock wool insulation has much the same insulating qualities as fiberglass insulation. Loose rock wool insulation also comes in pellet form. In some ways this type of insulation is more versatile than insulation batting, especially in the ceiling and in sealed walls. The homeowner can spread the insulation to any desired thickness to get the R value he wants. The insulation container has a chart showing how thick you must spread the insulation to obtain the desired insulating factor. This type of insulation is prone to settling over time, however.

installer cuts the blankets to the length he desires from a large roll of insulation.

Loose Fill Insulation

The third form of mineral fiber insulation is the pellet, or loose, insulation shown in Fig. 2-15. This insulation comes in large bags, and the installer can pour the insulation and spread it over the area he wants to insulate. Many people like to use loose fill insulation in attics because the insulation covers ceiling joists and fills around braces more easily than blanket insulation. This can be an advantage when the homeowner installs 8 to 10 inches of insulation in his attic.

Loose fill insulation is seldom used to insulate newly constructed walls because the inside wall surface must be completed to form a cavity that will hold the pellets. It is very popular, however, for insulating walls in older uninsulated homes. When used this way, the insulation pellets are blown into the walls by a contractor using an air pressure apparatus. The contractor removes siding from the outside of the house along the top of the walls. He then drills holes into the wall cavities—one hole between each pair of studs—attaches a hose, and fills the cavities with insulation.

You will notice from the figures in Table 2-3 that it takes somewhat more loose fill fiberglass and rock wool insulation to achieve the same R value as the blanket forms. This is of little concern if you are insulating your ceiling, where space is no problem. Remember the R value is the important figure, not the number of inches. In insulating your walls, however, space may be at a premium. Most wall studs leave only a 3-⅝-inch wide cavity for insulation, which may not be enough space to fit the recommended R values of loose fill insulation.

Backing Material

Blankets and batts are often backed with kraft paper or foil which serve as a *vapor barrier* (See the discussion of vapor barriers in Chapter 4.) Insulation with no backing is called *friction-fit* insulation, because the insulation will support itself by fitting tightly between the studs. Insulation with a backing should be used to hang from roof or floor areas, since the backing can be stapled to the joists to support the insulation (Fig. 2-16).

You must be certain not to leave the insulation backing exposed, because most of these backings are flammable even though the insulation itself is not. Some manufacturers sell insulation with

Fig. 2-16. This fiberglass insulation has a backing that serves as a vapor barrier and allows the insulation to be stapled between the roof joists. Notice the R-11 markings on the backing.

a nonflammable backing for use when the insulation backing material is to be exposed.

The insulation is installed with the backing material facing the living area of the home to reduce the circulation of air and to prevent mositure from condensing and saturating the insulation. The insualtion is stapled in place through the backing material as it is held against the studs or joists. The insulation should be pressed firmly against the back wall but should not be overly compressed, since its insulating abilities will be reduced. Insulation with a reflective backing should be installed so there is an air space of about ¾ inch between the backing and the wallboard. A reflective backing acts as an additional insulator, but it gains insulating properties only if it is facing a dead-air space.

Problems With Fiberglass and Rock Wool Insulation

Although the batting and blanket forms of this insulation are not prone to settling or packing down over the years, the pellet and loose fill forms are. As the insulation settles, it compresses and the insulation qualities are reduced. For this reason, good insulation contractors always add an extra inch or so of insulation when insulating areas such as ceilings to account for the expected settling.

Fiberglass and rock wool can create itching and irritation on the arms, hands, eyes and throat because of the sharp particles in the fibers. This problem can be reduced by wearing gloves and enough clothing to protect the skin from contact with the insulation. You should also wear goggles to protect your eyes and a respirator, if necessary, to protect your throat.

Advantages of Fiberglass and Rock Wool Insulation

These are some advantages of fiberglass and rock wool insulation. It is fireproof and will melt only at extremely high temperatures. It is also not prone to decay. Even if used in damp locations, the insulation will not deteriorate, although its insulating qualities will be reduced when it is wet. Since there is no food value in this insulation, it is insect and rodent proof.

The manufacturers' quality control seems to be excellent, so there is little chance of purchasing an inferior product. Most of this insulation is produced by a relatively few manufacturers who carefully monitor the quality of their products. Fiberglass and rock wool insulation have not been the brunt of consumer and government complaints about poor quality.

Disadvantages of Mineral Fiber Insulation

There are some disadvantages of mineral fiber insulation. The materials require more space to provide R values than some other materials. This can be an important consideration if you live in an area where the recommended wall insulation is R-19. Standard 2 × 4 studs do not provide a large enough wall cavity to fit the 6 inches of fiberglass blanket insulation required to produce this R value.

Mineral fiber insulation is in very short supply in many areas. The exploding demand for insulation has far outstripped the ability of manufacturers to produce mineral fiber insulation, and the insulation is being allocated at a fixed rate to most building suppliers.

CELLULOSIC FIBER INSULATION

A relative newcomer to the insulation scene, this material is now one of the largest selling types of insulation. Its rise in popularity is due primarily to the shortages of fiberglass and rock wool insulation.

Cellulosic fiber insulation is made from any ground wood pulp product such as recycled newspapers. It is available only as loose fill insulation that can be poured from bags or blown into the attic and walls by a contractor.

You will notice from Tables 2-3 and 2-4 that cellulosic fiber insulation *generally* has a higher R value per inch than loose fill mineral fiber insulation. This may be an advantage if you wish to put R-16 insulation inside the wall cavities created by 2 × 4 studs. Cellulosic fiber insulation is about the same price per R value as fiberglass or rock wool insulation, but this may vary according to the availability and the quality of insulation in your area.

Because it is a loose fill insulation, cellulosic fiber insulation is used almost exclusively to insulate ceilings and finished frame walls in uninsulated houses. It easily fills spaces between irregular spaced ceiling joists and around obstructions above the joists.

There are many properties of this insulation that cause some building experts to feel it is not as good an insulator as rock wool or fiberglass. Cellulose is inherently flammable and prone to attracting insects and rodents, so the chopped fibers must be chemically treated to prevent these problems. In fact, untreated cellulosic fiber insulation is capable of *spontaneous combustion* in proper conditions—that is, heat generated within the insulating material itself, can create a fire without any external source of flames.

The two primary flame retardant chemicals now used to treat cellulosic fiber insulation are *boric acid* and *aluminum sulfate*. Boric acid, however, has been in short supply due to large demands of insulation manufacturers. Aluminum sulfate has been reported to cause wiring and plumbing corrosion.

Insulation Fraud

The shortage of fiberglass and rock wool insulation, coupled with similar shortages of flame retardant chemicals to treat cellulosic fiber insulation, has opened the door to insulation fraud. Governmental and private consumer protection groups estimate that fraudulent insulation sales number in the millions. The bulk of those center on the sale of cellulosic fiber insulation.

Because cellulosic fiber insulation, unlike mineral fiber insulation, is manufactured by a countless number of producers, it can be very difficult for the consumer to know exactly what he is getting. Many unscrupulous manufacturers and dealers have sprouted like weeds in recent years, peddling untreated and highly flammable cellulosic fiber insulation onto unsuspecting customers. By the time the customer realizes he has purchased an inferior product, the dealer is long gone. The lucky ones discover that their "20-year guaranteed insulation job" has deteriorated in five years to walls full of damp, rodent-eaten newspaper shreddings. The unlucky ones are those whose houses ignite like tinderboxes when the untreated insulation begins burning.

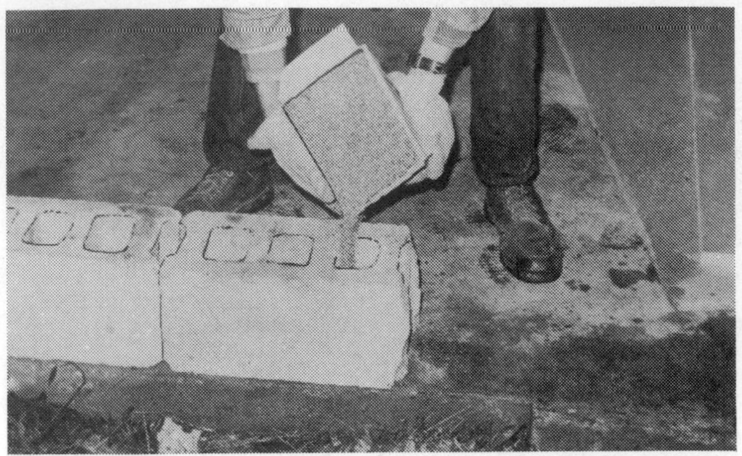

Fig. 2-17. Fill insulation is in granual form, and it is used to pour block walls to increase their insulating qualities.

It is much easier to begin producing and selling cellulosic fiber insulation than it is to produce mineral fiber insulation. While mineral fiber insulation requires large investments in plant and equipment to increase production, anyone with an empty garage and a massive stack of old newspaper can go into the business of producing cellulosic fiber insulation. And some people have done just that!

Checking For Untreated Insulation

There are a number of things you can do to protect yourself from untreated insulation. Check the insulation bags for information on flame retardant treatment. If the insulation has been treated, it will say so clearly. This alone is no assurance that the treatment meets minimum standards, so check to make sure the insulation meets the Federal General Services Administration specification (HH-I-515D), a voluntary specification for flammability (ASTM C-739-77), and the trade group specification (N-101-73).

You also should take a handful of the insulation, place it in a wind-free area, and attempt to set it afire. If the insulation has been properly treated, it will smoke when the match is applied to it but will go out when the flame is removed.

You should perform these checks whether you are purchasing the insulation from a supplier for your own use or if you are having the insulation installed by a contractor. Do not deal with any contractor who does not use bagged insulation but instead manufactures or shreds the material with a portable machine at the site.

EXPANDED MINERALS FILL INSULATION

This type of insulation comes in loose fill granular form that may be blown or poured into place (Fig. 2-17). Two of the more popular fill minerals are *vermiculite* and *perilite*, which are commonly used to pot plants.

Because expanded mineral fill insulation pours easily, it is commonly used to fill the cavities of concrete blocks. Cement and concrete are relatively poor insulators, but their insulation properties can be increased significantly by filling the center air pockets with fill insulation. A similar use is filling the space between face bricks and wall boxing on a brick wall. See Fig. 2-18.

Expanded mineral insulation can also be used in the walls and attic spaces, but all holes must be sealed because this insulation will flow easily. Holes and cracks permit substantial amounts of insulation to run out, not only reducing the insulation but creating a mess as well. Expanded mineral insulation have R values of 2.1 to 2.7 and are generally more expensive than mineral fiber or cellulosic fiber insulation.

PLASTIC FOAM INSULATION

Foamed plastic insulation is available in two forms: rigid boards and a liquid that is pumped into wall cavities where it foams

Fig. 2-18. The insulating qualities of a wall faced with brick are increased considerably with the addition of fill insulation. Pour the insulation in the ½ inch to 1 inch crack between the bricks and the boxing on the wall of the house.

up and hardens. This insulation material is often used in refrigerators, ice chests and frezers, where insulation space is at a premium. One of the prime features of plastic foam insulations is its high R value (R-4 to R-6 per inch), which is almost double that of fiberglass and rock wool.

Rigid Boards

Rigid board foam insulation is available in different thicknesses, and the boards can easily be cut with a knife (Fig. 2-19). This material is considerably more expensive per R value than mineral fiber insulation, but it is difficult to beat for some applications. It is especially useful in insulating basement walls or crawl spaces (see chapter 4).

Two popular materials used for rigid board insulation are *polystyrene* (R factor, 4 per inch) and *polyurethane* (R factor, 6 per inch). These materials have an added advantage in that they also serve as a vapor barrier, so a separate vapor barrier is not needed. Some other materials also used as rigid board insulation, such as fiberglass, are not vapor barriers.

Many foamed plastics are flammable and emit toxic fumes when they burn. Consequently, this insulation should *never* be used on an exposed wall because of the toxic fumes it would produce in a fire. It must always be covered with at least ½-inch gypsum wallboard to assure fire and smoke safety.

Plastic foam board insulation can be glued in place with a special adhesive, it can even be glued to cement walls. Because of its rigid nature, this material can be covered with cement when pouring a slab floor to provide added insulation, but it must be securely anchored to prevent it from floating. Because of its high R value per inch, it is more often used in narrow wall cavitites and places where space is limited. Plastic foam is affected by some petroleum-based liquids, such as paint, paint solvents and gasoline, which can soften and dissolve the insulation.

Foam-In Insulation

This type of insulation is the newest and most expensive form of home insulation. But it can also be the most effective, since plastic foam insulation has a high R value per inch.

This insulation is installed by a contractor, who drills holes into the wall cavities and fills the spaces with foam under slight pressure. This foam then "cures," or hardens, to form plastic foam insulation similar to the rigid board foam insulation described earlier.

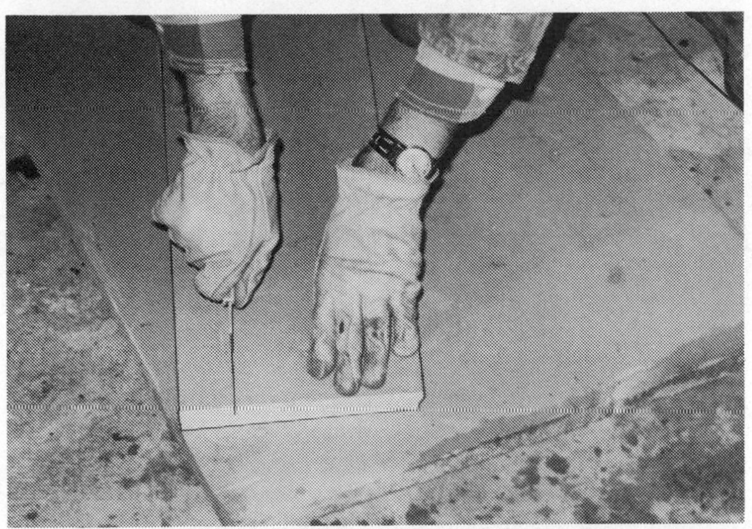

Fig. 2-19. Foamed plastic insulation has one of the lowest conductivity factors per inch available in insulation. It comes in ridig boards that can easily be cut with a pocket knife.

Urea-formaldehyde is the most widely used foam-in insulation material, but other types are also available. Besides the advantage of a high R value per inch, foam-in insulation is also moisture resistant. Some plastic foam materials act as a vapor barrier, which solves the problem of installing a vapor barrier in finished walls to protect the home from moisture condensation.

One of the largest drawbacks to foam-in insulation is its cost. Urea-formaldehyde does have a higher R value than mineral fiber insulation (R value 4 per inch compared to R value 3 per inch), but it may cost 50% more than other forms of insulation installed by contractors. The cost may be about twice as much as other insulations installed by the homeowner. And foam-in insulation cannot be installed by the homeowner.

Since some foam-in materials emit highly toxic fumes when they burn, they can present a danger if a fire should ever begin in the home. This presents problems not only for the occupants if they do not escape a burning home quickly, but there may also be delays and problems in fighting fires.

A possible hazard linked with urea-formaldehyde insulation is the emission of fumes after the product has been installed. This problem is said to be preventable with proper mixing and installation, however.

The necessity of proper mixing and installation underscores the requirement that you hire a reputable contractor to install foam-in insulation in your home. If the foam is not mixed and installed properly, it will present a danger to the occupants and a poor insulation.

Because foam-in insulation is so new, it is largely untested by use in the field. Some tests have shown there are possible problems due to shrinkage and varying quality of application, but it would appear there are probably no more drawbacks to this type of insulation than most others.

Certainly there are some large potential advantages to foam-in insulation. In northern areas where R-19 insulation is recommended in walls, foam-in insulation can fill the R value recommendations within the space created by 2 × 4 studs instead of the 2 × 6 studs that may be required for other types of insulation. Also, the foam insulation will fill all cracks and crevices of a wall with insulation. It is not as prone to leaving uninsulated gaps in the walls as are some forms of blown-in insulation.

Foam Sheathing

Another application of plastic foam insulation is in exterior sheathing panels. As shown in Fig. 2-20, these panels may be used in place of normal plywood or pine boxing to seal the exterior of the home. These sheathing panels have an R value of about R-6 per inch, so they can provide a good deal of extra insulation to the wall. These insulating sheathing panels might be especially attractive to homeowners wishing to achieve R-19 wall insulation in a northern part of the country. See Chapter 4 for recommended amounts of insulation. You will notice from Table 2-3 that you must have a 6-6½ inch wide wall cavity to fit enough fiberglass insulation to achieve R-19. This is, of course, a much larger wall cavity than provided by standard 2 × 4 studs. Therefore, using foam sheathing, you can achieve R-19 insulation and still use 2 × 4 studs, R-13 fiberglass insulation blankets and R-6 sheathing.

If you are remodeling your home, some types of this sheathing can be added on top of your old siding, which means you will not have to remove your old siding to install the sheathing material. Some of these materials will also act as a vapor barrier, which will protect the insulation inside the walls. You should check with your building materials supplier or with your insulation dealer to determine the exact properties of the sheathing/insulation material you intend to purchase.

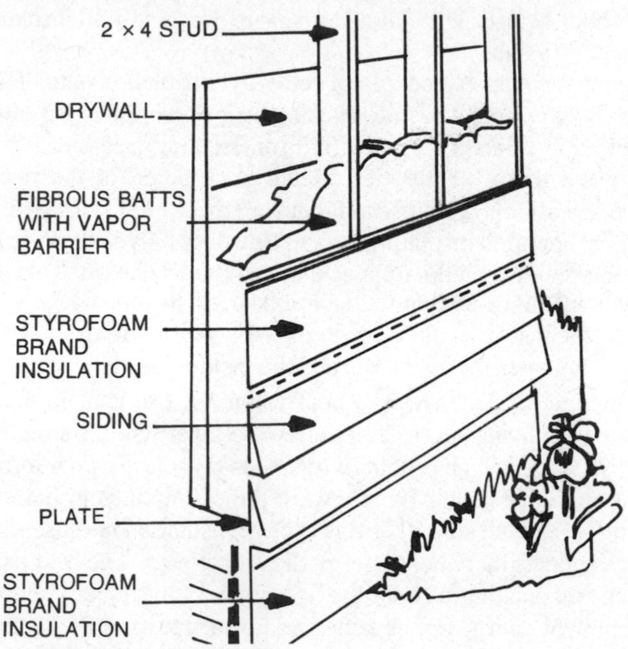

Fig. 2-20. STYROFOAM® Brand Sheathing Insulation from the Dow Chemical Company is made of polystyrene and is said to save about 24% in heating costs over a conventionally insulated home. The foam sheathing is nailed to the outside surface of the wall studs, replacing the standard plywood or fiberboard sheathing. An additional benefit of adding tongue and groove foam sheathing of this type is that the tongue and groove reduces air infiltration, thereby keeping the home warmer in winter and cooler in summer.

Another recent use for foam insulation is in insualted aluminum siding. A small layer of foam material lines the underneath side of the siding, increasing its insulation properties. Again, you should check with your supplier before purchasing to determine the material's properties, especially the R value. You may discover that you can increase the R value of your wall in less expensive ways.

REFLECTIVE INSULATION

Polished metal sheets are normally used to make reflective insulation, which is used to insulate against radiant heat energy. This type of insulation works on the principle that a polished surface reflects heat. You can use it either to keep outside heat energy from entering a room or inside energy from leaving. However, reflective insulation works only when it faces a dead-air space of about ¾ inch. Without an air space, practically all insulating properties vanish.

The most common example of reflective insulation is the foil layer that is often applied to the backing strips on bolts of mineral fiber insulation. Since this reflective foil backing faces into the living areas when installed, it reflects back some of the heat energy, preventing it from escaping during the winter. However, as noted earlier, this insulating property works *only* if there is a dead-air space between the foil backing and the wallboard. Therefore, if you install insulation with a foil backing in your walls, you must push the insulation far enough into the wall cavity to leave a ¾-inch gap between the insulation and the inside face of the studs.

Reflective insulation works best when used to contain heat energy within a living space. The reflective layer itself is a metal foil, so it was a very high conductivity and is therefore a poor form of insulation. Since hot air rises toward the ceiling in your home, the ceiling is not well suited for this type of insulation because the foil layer conducts more heat energy than it reflects. The best use for reflective insulation is under the floor joists of the house, where the radiant heat energy can be reflected upward toward the room. The shiny surface will reflect heat, which warms the air in the space beneath the floor, making the floor warmer. This type of insulation also has uses behind paneling or other wallboard material, where it can serve both as insulation and as a vapor barrier.

INSULATING PROPERTIES OF BUILDING MATERIALS

When you figure the R-value of your wall, you will want to account for the R factors of the wall's building materials, as well as the insulation inside the wall. Figure 2-2 is a good example of how the total R-value of a wall is figured.

As shown in the diagram, the main additional R factors are in the outside sheathing and the inside wallboard. Notice, however,

Table 2-6. K and R Factors of Wood Products.

MATERIAL	K FACTOR PER INCH	R FACTOR PER INCH
fir	0.67	1.3
oak	1.16	0.9
particle board	0.50	2.0
pine, soft	0.86	1.2
pine, hard	1.10	0.9
plywood	0.80	1.2

that there is also a bit of insulating quality attributed to the inside and outside air films.

There are several different types of wood and lumber you can use for building, and each one has a different conductivity, or K factor, that depends on the hardness of the wood. In general, the harder the wood, the higher the heat conductivity and the lower the R value. Most lumber used for framing, subflooring and sheathing has a K factor of about 0.80 per inch, or an R factor of about 1.2 per inch. Tables 2-2 and 2-6 compare the K and R factors of various building materials. Notice that most of the K and R factors are based on *1 inch* thickness. Thus, to determine the R factor of a given building material, you must determine its thickness and multiply that thickness by the R factor per inch. Another material sometimes used for exterior sheathing is insulating foam sheathing, discussed in the previous section on plastic foam insulation.

3 Buying The Right Amount Of Insulation

One of the most important aspects of energy conservation is weighing the costs of energy saving improvements against the benefits of those improvements against the benefits of those improvements. The question is not, "How much energy will such-and-such an improvement save me?". Rather, the question you should ask is, "How much money will the improvement save?" Once you know the answer to that question, you then compare the dollar savings to the cost. If the cost is greater than the savings, the improvement should not be made.

Nowhere is this cost-benefit approach to energy conservation more helpful than in deciding how much insulation you should install in your home. It is quite true that you could save a little bit more energy and a little bit more money on heating costs by installing R-25 wall insulation and R-100 ceiling insulation. But you would not really save any money at all, because the additional cost of installing these amounts of insulation would far outweight any savings you could achieve over a more sensible insulation plan.

It is especially important to keep these points in mind in the current state of energy conservation frenzy. Hucksters selling insulation will tell you to fill your entire attic with insulation in order to make another sale to a homeowner who may already have a sensible amount of insulation. These fast-buck artisits will oversell their shoddy products, dupe some customers into purchasing twice as much insulation as they need, and then move along to other quick money schemes where you will never be able to find them again.

The simple fact is that you can't save any money if you install so much insulation that it would take 30 or more years to repay the purchase cost in energy savings. Yet, some insulation salesmen would have you do just that!

Determining the right amount of insulation for your home is not an easy chore, however. It is difficult to make broad generalizations because weather conditions and fuel costs—the two largest factors in determining the most profitable amount of insulation—can very widely even within the same geographic region. For this reason, only a person familiar with these factors in your area can give you a firm figure as to the exact amount of insulation that is just right for your home. Some sources for such information are discussed later in this chapter. See Appendix A.

FUTURE FUEL COSTS

Added to the general fluctuations in weather patterns and fuel costs from area to area is the problem of determining future fuel costs. The cost of fuel 10 years from now will determine whether it is economical to add an extra R-6 insulating value to the walls of the home you are constructing this year. Future fuel costs are very uncertain. Witness the four-fold jump in prices of some fuels in just the last few years! Such an increase could never have been predicted a decade ago.

Even though future fuel costs are uncertain, some expected increase must be taken into account in determining the best amount of insulation. Most experts in the field are using a fuel cost increase factor of about 7 to 10% per year. Given the current state of fuel availability and recent experience, this seems to be an accurate estimate. When the future fuel cost factor is considered in the insulation calculation, the result will be a recommendation to install a bit more insulation. If you plan to keep your home 10 to 20 years, the expected future cost of fuel is a factor you centainly must take into account in determining how much insulation will be the most economical over the life of the home.

There are a lot of uncertainties in figuring the best amount of insulation for any given home, but there are some general recommendations that can be made. In this chapter we discuss some of the leading recommendations, as well as sources where you can get more exact information on your particular locality, if you want it. If you consider the generalized recommendations that follow in this chapter and then modify those recommendations a bit, according to the recommendations of building and insulation experts in

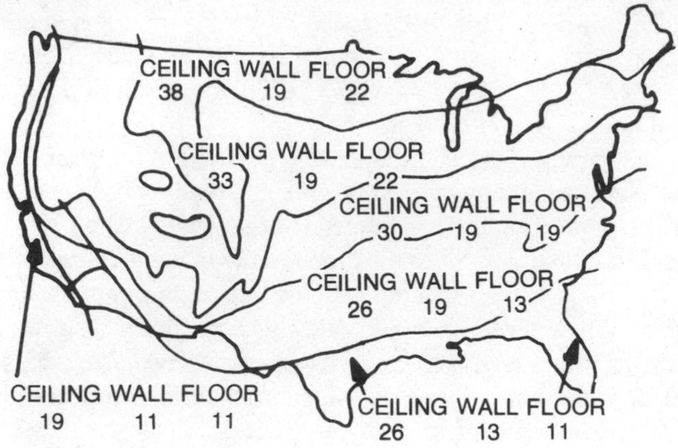

Fig. 3-1. The recommended insulation standards for ceilings, walls and floors shown on the map were developed by Owens-Corning from a computer analysis of 71 American cities. These recommendations provide a general guide to the correct amount of insulation to install in your area, but the exact recommendations for your home may vary according to utility costs and the type of fuel you heat with.

your locality, you should have an accurate estimate of the amount of insulation you can economically install in your home.

THE INSULATION ZONE MAP

One widely circulated set of insulation recommendations was developed by Owens-Corning, the largest manufacturer of fiberglass insulation. Owens-Corning has developed a map, shown in Fig. 3-1, that divides the country into zones and establishes recommendations for insulation amounts according to zone.

The insulation map is simple to use. All you need to do is find your location on the map, and the figures show you the recommended amounts of insulation. Table 3-1 shows the thicknesses of Owens-Corning Fiberglas brand blanket insulation necessary to achieve the R-values listed in the map.

Owens-Corning developed its insulation recommendations from a computer model using 71 American cities. The computer analysis considered insulation costs, weather data, heating and cooling costs, and a 7% projected annual utility rate increase factor. The analysis also based the calculations on a 20-year term, with savings discounted 10% each year. Thus, even if you have to borrow the money to finance the insulation recommendations, you will still save the largest amounts of money at these insulation levels, according Owens-Corning.

Table 3-1. Thickness Needed for R-Value Fiberglas Blanket Type Insulations (courtesy Owens-Corning).

R-Value	Thickness	R-Value	Thickness
R-38	12″ (two layers 6″)	R-22	6½″
R-33	10″ (3½″ plus 6½″)	R-19	6″
R-30*	9½″ (6″ plus 3½″)	R-13	3⅝″
R-26°	7¼″ (two laqers 3⅝″)	R-11	3½″

It is our understanding that the Owens-Corning map was developed to determine the most economical levels of insulation for homes with air conditioning and electric resistance heat, which is becoming a leading heating fuel as natural gas shortages get worse. Therefore, these recommendations may be a bit high for your home if you have natural gas heat or oil heat, with no air conditioner. You can convert the map's ceiling/insulation recommendations for electrically heated homes to recommendations for a gas heat home by using Table 3-2.

The Owens-Corning insulation map gives you a general gauge of how much insulation is economical to install in your home. Since the map gives recommendations according to zones, however, it cannot take into accound varying fuel costs between nearby communities. Therefore, if your locality has fuel costs significantly higher or lower than the average community in your zone, you should compensate accordingly.

If your fuel costs are higher, use a bit more insulation than in recommended for your zone. If your fuel costs are lower, use a bit less.

This map and chart give you a somewhat more exact measure of the correct insulation for your locality, because they allow you to take into account varying fuel costs between communities. If you

Table 3-2. Attic Insulation Recommendation Conversion Chart. Substitute R-Values in the Right Column for R-Values in the Left Column When They Appear on the Map.

ELECTRIC RESISTANCE HEAT RECOMMENDATIONS	RECOMMENDATIONS FOR GAS OR OIL HEAT WITHOUT AIR CONDITIONER
R-38	R-30
R-30	R-22
R-22	R-19
R-19	R-11

compare this map's recommendations to those obtained from the Owens-Corning "insulation zone" map, you should be able to get a general range of the proper insulation amount for your home.

LOCAL SOURCES OF INFORMATION

It would be a mistake to assume that any generalized system of determining insulation recommendations can tell you exactly how much insulation is best for your home. There are simply too many variables. As we have mentioned, fuel costs vary widely from community to community. The cost of insulation can also vary, and this is obviously an improtant factor in determining whether an additional 2 inches of insulation are worth the expense. The availability of the insulation material you prefer and the availability of financing are also considerations that you must account for. Your home's construction and the insulating value of the building materials used are other factors the insulation maps cannot account for.

There are severla local sources of good information as to the right amount of insulation for you to install. Local builders may be of some help, but only if they have kept up with recent trends in insulation practices. You will probably find many who are still insulating the homes the same way they did 10 years ago. Your insulation dealer or building materials supplier may also be a great deal of help, especailly if he is conscientious and takes the time to figure your insulation needs. Comprehensive charts and tables allow him to calculate insulation recommendations according to local climate, utility costs and the amount of insulation you already have in your home.

Utility Company

Another excellent source of information is your utility company. Many companies have developed comprehensive programs for insulating their customers' homes. The utility company may be able to provide you with insulation recommendations, names of approved contractors and insulation suppliers, and financing information. The recommended levels of some utility companies run significantly below those developed by Owens-Corning.

There are several possible reasons for this. One is that the Owens-Corning recommendations were developed for new homes, and many of the recommended insulation levels might cost more than they would be worth in older homes because of the additional costs of installation—especially in walls. Another is that some utility company recommendations apparently have been developed with a more critical eye toward the diminishing benefits of adding insulation above a certain point. Thus, even though there may be some overall savings to adding more insulation than the utility comapnies' recommendations, the extra insulation is not included in the recommended levels because the payback period is considered too long or the savings are considered too small.

Estimates

As you can see, recommended levels of insulation can vary quite a bit according to the factors considered. Your best bet is to get two or three local estimates, if possible, and compare those to the national charts and maps in the previous sections. These figures will give you an acceptable range of recommended levels that you can tailor to your own needs. If you intend to live in your home for more than 10 years, you should select from the figures on the higher side of the range. If insulation shortages or financing are problems, you may want to select figures from the lower end. You can always add more insulation later—especially in the ceiling.

Building Codes

State and local building codes sometimes prescribe minimum levels of insulation acceptable in new buildings. You certainly should check these codes before building or insulating a new home. Homes whose purchase is financed by the FHA also must meet certain minimum insulation standards. Although these various government standards for insulation are changing rapidly to reflect higher energy costs, they generally are well below the optimum insulation levels. Generally, you should rely on them only as an absolute minimum standard, not as an optimum insulation recommendation.

USING 2 × 6-INCH WALL STUDS

Most homes in the United States have been constructed with 2 × 4-inch wall studs. Steadily increasing energy costs have caused many building experts to reconsider this custom. Many new homes are being constructed using 2 × 6-inch wall studs to allow space for 5½ inches of mineral fiber insulation. This change increases the R factor of the insulation inside the wall from R-13 to R-19. But old customs die hard, and 2 × 6-inch wall studs are far from gaining widespread acceptance. In fact, their use is essentially prohibited by building codes in some areas.

The standard 2 × 4-inch wall studs are placed on 16-inch centers and create a cavity in the wall 3-⅝ inches wide. This is enough space to fit mineral fiber blanket insulation of about R-13. Escalating energy costs have led many energy experts to recommend R-19 wall insulation, especially in new homes. This R value cannot be achieved with standard mineral fiber insulation inside a 3-⅝ inch cavity. There are a number of ways this higher R factor can be achieved. One is to use some type of foam insulation inside the walls to achieve the higher R value. Another is to add exterior wall insulation, such as foam sheathing. See Chapter 2 for a discussion of various types of foam insulation.

Using 2 × 6-inch wall studs in place of the normal 2 × 4-inch studs is another alternative. These studs are placed on 24-inch centers and provide a wall cavity of about 5½ inches. This is roughly enough space in which to fit R-17 to R-19 mineral fiber blanket insulation (Fig. 3-2).

Using 2 × 6-inch studs on 24-inch centers is really very little more expensive than using 2 × 4-inch studs on 16-inch centers. In some localities, however, building codes set the maximum distance between studs at 16 inches, which would make 2 × 6-inch studs considerably more expensive. These codes are likely to be changed, however, as 2 × 6-inch studs on 24-inch centers come into more common usage.

If you are building or remodeling a home and live in the northern half of the country, you should consider using 2 × 6-inch studs. This is especially true if you plan to live in your home more than 10 years.

COPING WITH INSULATION SHORTAGES

You may find that you are unable to get the right amount of the type of insulation you prefer. Insulation sales have surged since 1973, with the demand far outstripping supply in most areas. As described in Chapter 2, insulation shortages have hit the mineral fiber insulation supply the hardest, while cellulosic fiber insulation and other insulation types remain generally available. Cellulosic fiber insulation is much easier to manufacture than mineral fiber insulation, which means supply can be kept in step with demand.

If you prefer a type of insulation that is in short supply in your area, such as fiberglass blanket insulation, for example, there are a number of alternatives. One is to use a different form of the same general type of insulation. Thus, you might be able to get rock wool blankets or loose fill mineral fiber insulation. If you can get only

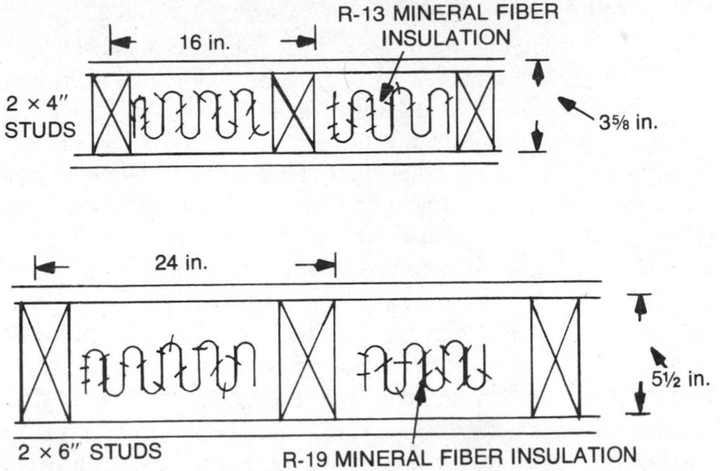

Fig. 3-2. You can achieve an extra 50% insulating value in your home's walls if 2×6″ studs are used instead of the more common 2×4″ studs. The cost for the studs is comparable, although the insulation cost itself is higher.

part of your needs in the blanket form, plan to use what you can get to insulate your floor and walls. You can use the loose fill insulation to insulate your ceiling.

Another solution is to switch to another insulating material. This is relatively easy because all insulation materials are rated in the common R values, so you can easily switch to another type of insulation if you know the R value of the insulation you need. The drawback to this solution is that some insulating materials may have significantly different properties than your insulation preference, and some may be significantly more expensive. And there have been widespread problems of poor quality alternative insulation materials manufactured by fast-buck insulation dealers who have taken advantage of the insulation shortages. See the discussion in Chapter 2 on insulation types and materials.

A final alternative is to delay your insulation project until you can get the material you want. This will only work, however, if you already live in a home that has some insulation already installed. If you are building a new home or live in an older uninsulated home, you probably cannot afford to wait until the insulation arrives. You may be able to do your insulation in steps as the material becomes available. Then install more later. Remember that R-11 insulation in the ceiling should be your first priority—then the walls, the remainder of the ceiling—and the floor.

FINANCING AND TAX PLANS

There are several sources of information on loans and financing plans that are available for your home improvement insulation projects. Your utility company or insulation dealer should have information of this type. Some utility companies are experimenting with plans where the homeowner can arrange through his utility company to have his house insulated. The homeowner is then billed by the utility company in monthly installments.

Your commercial bank, savings and load association, or credit union can give you information on home improvement loans. The terms of these loans will vary with the type of loan and the interest rate in your area. When you inquire about loans, be sure to tell the person you talk with that you want the loan to finance insulation improvements. Some state and federal loan programs have been established to finance these improvements, and terms can be quite favorable.

Since 1973, there has been much talk in Congress of providing a federal tax credit plan that would reduce federal income taxes for homeowners who insulate their homes. As of this writing, such a plan is still being discussed and no federal insulation tax credit has been enacted. Your state government may provide tax incentives for insulation purchasers, however, so you should inquire about this if you have made any recent insulation purchases.

Because of pending legislation on insulation tax credits, you should save all receipts and tickets for insulation purchases. If such plans are later enacted, you will have the documents necessary to prove your purchases. Even if the tax plans are not enacted for a couple of years to come, some of them may apply retroactively to give you credit for insulation purchases you make now.

Whether insulation tax plans are enacted or not, you should save your insulation purchase receipts. They can become valuable documents when you later decide to sell your home. You will be able to show a prospective buyer that he is indeed buying a well-insulated home.

4

Insulating Your Home

The first step in successfully insulating your home is to decide what and what not to insulate. The rule is: Insulate any wall or surface that has a cold space on one side and a heated space on the other. Following this rule, you should be able to divide your home into heated and unheated areas as shown in Fig. 4-1. No insulation is required in walls that divide two heated areas, nor is any insulation required in the floor between the living area and the basement.

If you were to follow the same rule, you would not ordinarily need insulation in walls separating two unheated areas, as in the outside wall of an unheated garage. But often there are advantages to insulating unheated areas, such as garages, entrance ways, and attached buildings, that are normally not heated during the winter. These areas would definitely be warmer when insulated, since they would capture heat energy escaping through the main walls of your home. As a result, there is no fixed rule that can be applied to insulating unheated areas because the choice is often made on the basis of comfort or convenience rather than cost. For example, you might want to add insulation to an attached workshop or toolshed to protect stored goods from freezing or rusting, though you would not be interested in heating the area all or even part of the time. Or you might want to insulate your unheated garage because your car would start easier on cold days, or because it would be more comfortable for you to work in a garage that was just cold rather than freezing in the winter.

If you wonder whether or not your home has enough insulation, here is a simple test that is often used. On a cool day with the outdoor temperature at least 20 degrees less than the indoor temperature, take a thermometer that has been hanging on an indoor wall of your home and move it to an outdoor wall in the same room. If the temperature indicated on the thermometer drops more than 1.5 degrees for each 10 degree indoor/outdoor temperature difference, your wall is not providing the recommended amount of insulation. For example, if the outdoor temperature is 30°F and the thermometer read 70° when hanging on the inside wall of the room, the temperature difference is 40 degrees. Moving the thermometer to an outside wall, the temperature should be no less than 64°F if the insulation in the wall is adequate. When making this simple test, avoid wall areas that are close to radiators, baseboard heaters, windows, doors, and lamps, since these can all affect your temperature readings.

In the following topics, you will see how to insulate your home from the ground up, starting with the foundation areas and working upwards to the attic. Here we are concerned only with installing insulation in your home; insulating your garage and weatherstripping doors and windows are subjects covered in later chapters.

STOPPING MOISTURE PROBLEMS

Although basements and crawl spaces are most prone to moisture problems, all the walls in your home need moisture protection. High humidity and condensation are to be avoided in the home because they encourage fungus, mildew, and deterioration in most building materials. The additional moisture from exposed ground areas also adds to the humidity of the air already present in the home, increasing the load on air conditioning equipment and possibly causing personal discomfort. Adding insulation without considering the moisture problem is just asking for trouble, and this is particularly true of basements and crawl spaces.

Sources of Moisture

There are three primary sources of moisture—exterior leaks, ground moisture, and vapor-laden air within the home. All air contains varying amounts of water vapor, but the warm air within the home is capable of holding more moisture than the colder outside air. Thus, when warm moist air comes in contact with a cold wall surface, some of the moisture condenses into water. Our modern homes today are very tightly sealed compared to older homes, so there is noway to remove this condensation from inside

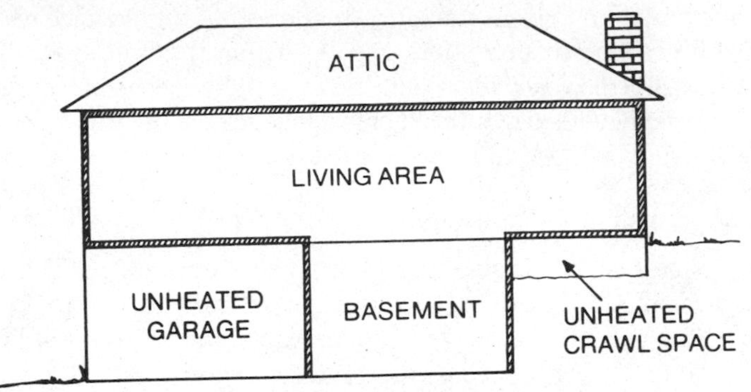

Fig. 4-1. Insulation should be installed between a warm area and any unheated area. Insulation is normally installed between the living area and an unheated garage or crawl space, though in some houses the garage and crawl space are also heated. To decide whether you should insulate the floor above your home's crawl space or insulate the walls of the crawl space instead, see the section on floor and crawl space insulation later in this chapter.

wall spaces. The only avenue of escape we have is to prevent this condensation from occurring in the first place.

When a wall is insulated, a vapor barrier is put up with the insulation to stop the passage of moisture through the wall. The vapor barrier keeps the insulation in the walls dry and prevents the condensation of water on the wall surface and in the insulation material itself. Some types of insulation are manufactured with a waterproof backing material that serves as a vapor barrier. Fiberglass batting is available with this type of backing. Plastic foam insualtion is a vapor barrier as well as an insulation material. Rolls pf plastic film are also available for making large vapor barriers.

There is moisture present in the air, both inside and outside your home. In most cases it is the moisture inside your home that presents the biggest problem. Outside moisture from rain and snow are of little concern and account for very little damage. Basements and crawl spaces occasionally present special moisture problems when the moisture is the result of seepage through the walls from the outside rather than simple condensation from the air inside. But in general, most moisture problems result from warm inside air condensing water onto colder outside wall surfaces. (This is the major cause of cracking, peeling, and blistering paint.) Since insulation reduces the temperature of the wall surface, it also reduces the chance of water condensing from the air. However, a vapor barrier is needed to prevent warm moist air from passing completely through the insulation to the colder wall surface where it will produce condensation, usually within the wall space. For best results the vapor seal should be as airtight as possible, and it is even recommended that the seams and cracks in the vapor barrier be caulked or taped to prevent air leakage.

External Sources of Moisture

Water vapor can also enter your home from outside. This can be prevented by providing proper drainage and weatherproof construction of roofs, eaves, and outside walls. In most homes, however, it is the walls that pass moist air, and this is particularly true of homes that have central air conditioning. A single vapor barrier on the inside wall of these homes is not adequate, since the hot and cold surfaces of the walls reverse during the winter and summer months. A vapor barrier is needed on the inside walls during the winter, while a second vapor barrier is needed on the outside walls during the summer. Most new homes are sheathed in exterior plywood or tar paper before the siding is installed, so these homes already have an outside vapor barrier.

Unless the homesite is on well drained ground, water vapor from the ground may be added to moisture from other sources in the house. Basement walls may tend to bleed water after rains, and crawl spaces may become especially damp during summer months. The moisture problem occurring in crawl spaces is prevented by insuring adequate clearance between the ground and the floor joists (at least 18 inches), providing proper drainage, installing vapor barriers over the ground, and making sure that the crawl space is adequately ventilated during the summer. Basement walls may seep water due to poor drainage, as when the drain tiles become clogged or when the house is built in an area having a high water table. Many types of masonry sealers are available in paint and plaster-like forms, and if you have this type of moisture problem, these should be used to seal the walls before installing any insulation. Sometimes a second plastic film barrier can be installed directly against the masonry wall, but this method is not advisable if there is a chance that water may collect behind the barrier and drain out the bottom.

Installing Vapor Barriers

Vapor barriers are usually made from combinations of plastic, film, metal foil, tar paper, and kraft paper, and these may be included as part of the backing on insulation batting. Plastic foam is

Table 4-1. This chart shows that exterior plywood exhibits sufficient resistance to moisture penetration to qualify as a vapor barrier. When plywood sheathing is used on the outside walls, no other vapor barrier will be needed between the outside walls and the insulation. The seams where the sheets of plywood join should be caulked. An inside vapor barrier will still be required.

Vapor Permeance*:

Values tabulated below represent the average water vapor transmitted through plywood in grains per sq. ft. per hour, per inch of mercury pressure (perms). Materials with vapor permeance of one perm or less are considered effective vapor barriers.

PRODUCT	SURFACE FINISH	PERMS
Exterior Type Plywood 3/8"	None	0.8
Exterior Type Plywood 3/8"	One coat exterior primer plus two coats exterior house paint (solvent thinned system)	0.2
Exterior Medium Density Overlaid Plywood one-side 3/8"	None	0.3

*Values shown are based on the physical properties of Douglas Fir.

a vapor barrier as well as an insulation. However, exterior plywood is also a vapor barrier (Table 4-1) and can be used in a wide variety of home remodeling projects. The essential characteristic of all vapor barriers is that they are airtight and waterproof, being unaffected by water vapor and condensation.

Place the vapor barrier on the warm side of the wall so that moist air cannot pass through to the cold side. In most homes, the vapor barrier will be installed on the inside wall surface, as illustrated by the plastic film over the studs in Fig. 4-2. For a really good job, a plastic sheet is best, since you can seal an entire wall with one single piece. If necessary, any seams can be taped over, or the two ends can be overlapped with a bead of caulk between. Film barriers of this type are especially recommended in basements or other naturally moist locations.

Vapor barriers are installed next to the insulation material, usually just beneath the wall board or paneling. This encloses the insulation and protects it from harmful moisture, provided that the vapor seal is tight. Puncture holes resulting from the nails used to hold the wall boards and paneling in place permit very little air to pass through because the wall board or paneling is pressed tightly against the film and stud. Care should be taken when installing electrical outlets and switches that the vapor barrier not be punctured or ripped needlessly.

Fig. 4-2. A vapor barrier must be installed between the insulation and the wall covering to prevent moisture condensation on the walls. Polyethylene film is frequently used as a vapor barrier.

Vapor barriers also contribute to the insulating value of a wall and are extremely effective at reducing infiltration air currents. The insulating value of the vapor barrier depends on the material used, but it is usually quite small. Vapor barriers made as part of the backing material on insulation batting do not provide as good an air seal, and the insulation value of the barrier is included in the rating of the insulation material as a whole.

FLOOR VERSUS CRAWL SPACE INSULATION

The homeowner has two options open to him for reducing heat loss under his house: insulate the floor or insulate the crawl space. Both approaches are quite effective in cutting down heat loss, but the costs can be surprisingly different.

When the crawl space is insulated, we say that the house has a heated crawl space. This doesn't mean that you actually open a heating duct into the crawl space; however, the crawl space will stay quite warm just from the heat escaping from the rooms above.

A crawl space should be maintained at a temperature of at least 50°F if the uninsulated floors above the crawl space are to be at a comfortable temperature. Figures given by the American Plywood Association show that a typical house in Minneapolis, Minnesota will maintain a crawl space temperature of 50°F even when the heating ducts passing through the crawl space are insulated. Normally, if the heating plant and ducts are located in the insulated crawl space, the crawl-space temperature can exceed 70°F.

The area of the crawl space under a house is fairly small compared to the total living area, and the heat loss through the floor or crawl space normally accounts for only about 10% of the total heat load. If you are concerned about the additional heat loss from a 70°F crawl space, you can easily insulate the duct system to reduce the loss. This will still provide you with a 50°F crawl space, enough to qualify as a heated crawl space.

Table 4-2 was prepared by the American Plywood Association to illustrate the money savings obtained by insulating the crawl-space foundation instead of the floor above. The figures are based on a typical house measuring 30 feet by 50 feet (You could make a similar table based on your home's dimensions and insulation costs.) The APA table shows a cost difference of more than $400, making it far less expensive to insulate the foundation walls than to insulate the floor. The major cost of insulating the floor goes into the 1500 square feet of insulation that gets stuffed between the

Table 4-2. Comparative Cost Summary of Installing Foundation Wall Insulation Versus Installing Floor Insulation.

Item	Quantity	Installed Unit Cost	Foundation Wall Insulation	Floor Insulation
Floor Insulation – R11 Reverse Flange[1]	1500 SF	$0.17/SF		$255.00
Foundation Wall Insulation – R11 Blanket[2]	400 SF	$0.14/SF	$ 56.00	
Vapor Barrier – 4 mil Polyethylene	1500 SF	$32.00/MSF	$ 48.00	
Foundation Vents – 12"x24" Screen	8	$6.50/Ea		$ 52.00
8"x16" Operable Louvres	2	$8.75/Ea	$ 17.50	
Heating Duct Insulation – 2" Flexible Wrap	264 SF	$0.55/SF		$145.20
Water Pipe Insulation – 1" Thick	50 LF	$1.75/LF		$ 87.50
			$121.50	$539.70
				−121.50
			COST DIFFERENCE	$418.20

Fig. 4-3. A vapor barrier can be put on the ground under a house after the house is constructed, but it is much easier to put the vapor barrier down before the floor joists are put in place.

floor joists and the 264 square feet of duct insulation for the heating system. On the other hand, the foundation can be insulated with only 400 square feet of insulation, since the perimeter of the foundation wall is just 160 feet and the wall is insulated only to a height of 2½ feet. But to properly insulate the crawl-space foundation, you must install a vapor barrier over the ground and closable vents in the foundation. The vents for the insulated crawl space cost less than with floor insulation because a smaller number is needed with a vapor barrier installed over the ground. Water pipes and heating ducts do not need to be insulated if the crawl-space is heated, though some builders elect to insulate them anyway, especially in colder climates.

Calculations show that by insulating the foundation, it is possible to maintain crawl-space temperatures at 75°F in many areas of the country. The benefit from such a high crawl-space temperature is that the floors feel warm in the house, so the homeowner can often reduce the thermostat setting by several degrees with no change in comfort. In homes without warm floors, the homeowner must often increase the thermostat setting to raise the temperature of the air near the floor, particularly in rooms where children spend much time playing on the floor and adults spend much time sitting.

Traditionally, floors have been insulated, so the idea of having a heated crawl space is new to most people. Unfortunately, many people are likely to reject the idea of a heated crawl space just because it is new, despite the proven fact that it can be a much cheaper way to effectively insulate a home. We suggest that you talk with some local building contractors or insulation suppliers for pricing information, and with several people who have recent experience with heated crawl spaces for their opinions.

INSULATING THE FOUNDATION

When the foundation is insulated, a vapor barrier must be installed on the ground to keep the crawl space dry. If a vapor barrier is not used, moisture will enter the crawl space from the ground and it will condense on the insulation. Heavy plastic is most often used as a vapor barrier under houses. It is easiest to install this plastic before the floor joists of the house are put up (Fig. 4-3). Frequently this is not possible, so the plastic must be layed over the ground after the house has already been built.

Figure 4-4 shows the crawl space with an insulated foundation and a vapor barrier. The plastic material is held down by a three-inch layer of crushed limestone, small gravel, or sand. Some provision must be made to hold the plastic to the ground or it will get torn loose as people crawl under the house. The plastic must be lapped several inches at the seams and at the foundation to provide a good seal.

Sealing the Foundation

Whether you insulate the foundation or not, several steps can be taken to reduce heat loss by sealing the foundation against air

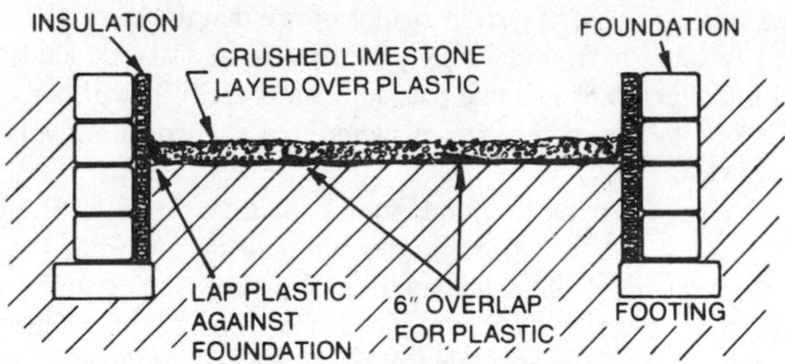

Fig. 4-4. A typical foundation is insulated with either R-11 insulation batting or about 1 inch of rigid insulation. A vapor barrier has been installed here using plastic sheets with their seams overlapped. The plastic is then covered with about 3 inches of crushed limestone, sand, dirt, gravel or cement depending primarily on local building codes.

leaks that would pass infiltration air. Should you decide to insulate the foundation, these sealing steps will have to be taken before you begin installing insulation. Here is a checklist of things to do:

- Check the mortar between all foundation blocks and repair all openings with fresh mortar.
- Check for cracks in the foundation blocks and where the house rests on top of the foundation. Fill these with mortar or a suitable caulking compound.
- Locate where power lines, water lines, and sewer lines enter and leave the foundation. Fill large holes with mortar and caulk small holes and cracks.
- Check basement doors for possible air leaks. Use weather-stripping and caulking as required to seal all openings.
- Check the access door to the crawl space for air leaks. Seal all openings with weather-stripping and caulk. If the crawl space does not have a door, you can make one using a wood frame and plywood. Insulate the inside of the door and frame to cut down heat loss.
- Make sure that all crawl-space vents can be sealed off during the winter months to conserve heat. Vents that can be closed easily from the outside are desirable, but a plywood or metal sheet tacked over the opening will do just as well.

Installing the Vapor Barrier and Insulation

In a house that has already been built, a rigid insulation material like plastic foam is probably the easiest type to install. The advantages to using rigid insulation are that the insulation also acts as a vapor barrier and can be easily attached to the foundation wall in several ways. Since plastic foam is rigid, it will not compress or soak up water, which would make it lose its insulating properties.

A trench around the foundation should be dug 6 to 8 inches deep to allow the insulation to extend into the ground when the dirt is replaced (Fig. 4-5). The insulation is glued or nailed to the wall using concrete nails and a 1- by 2-inch board strip. Some of the dirt from around the foundation shoudl be saved to cover the ends of the plastic vapor barrier.

Put the plastic down last to avoid tearing and pulling it while you are working under the house. A little dirt on top of the plastic should be enough to hold it down, since there shouldn't be much

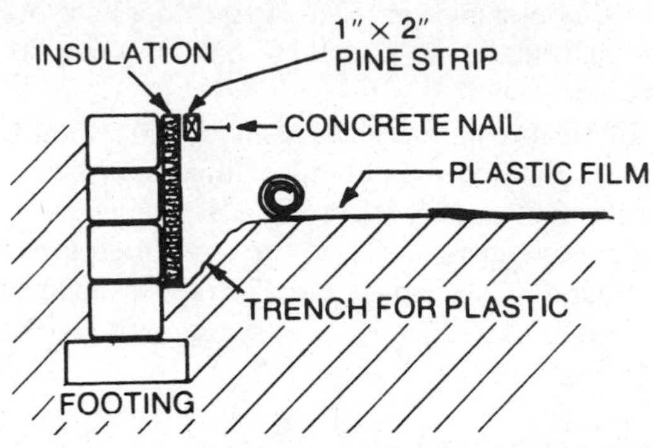

Fig. 4-5. The insulation material extends into the ground, with the ends recovered with dirt. Rigid insulation is probably best and can be glued to the foundation or held in place with pine strips and concrete or masonry nails. If fiberglass batting is used as the insulation material, the vapor barrier backing should face into the crawl space.

more work in the crawl space. On a new home, though, the vapor barrier should be installed before the floor joists are installed, and a 3-inch cover of dirt should be put on top of the plastic.

A good material to use for the vapor barrier is four- or six-mil-thick polyethylene. The lap joints between sheets should be 3 to 6 inches. With rigid insulation on the foundation, the plastic film should extend up the face of the insulation for about three inches, but it should not extend to the top of the insulation. If fiberglass insulation is used, the plastic should extend completely to the top of the insulation.

How deep the insulation should extend into the ground depends on the climate in your area. Houses in areas with lower winter temperatures should have the insulation extending deeper into the ground than in warmer areas. If practical, the insulation should extend 14 to 18 inches below ground level. A good guide is to extend the insulation to the footing of the foundation. Putting the insulation this deep will probably not be practical on a house already built, due to the limited work space under the house.

Sealing the Floor Joists

A lot of heat energy is lost through the lumber and cracks where the house sits on the foundation. Figure 4-6 shows the construction of the joist header and sill plate, indicating where to install vapor seals and insulation. The insulation with the vapor barrier should be installed with the barrier facing the crawl space.

The vapor barrier is stapled or tacked to the floor joist on each side. The subfloor and outside wall should be finished before this insulation is installed.

A full four inches of fiberglass insulation is recommended for this application. Fiberglass insulation with a vapor-barrier backing is most suitable for this purpose, and it will save you the trouble of having to install a separate vapor barrier. Fiberglass insulation with an aluminum foil backing is popular, since the aluminum foil serves both as a vapor barrier and a reflector of radiant heat energy.

Water Standing Under the House

Wet basements and crawl spaces are a serious problem, not only from the standpoint of water damage to the home, but from the point of energy conservation. Water under your home can encourage insects such as termites, rot the joists and subfloor, and rust your furnace, ductwork, and any other steel parts lying around. Wet insulation is of little value in preventing heat loss, and the evaporating water draws heat energy from the air, stealing more energy from your home.

This problem is not one that can be solved by merely adding a vapor barrier over the ground. A vapor barrier can only prevent vapor from coming up through the ground beneath your house—it can't hold back the water. If water is actually standing on the surface of the ground, you have a serious problem that must be corrected. Perhaps your drain tiles are clogged with leaves or tree roots; if so, there are drain-cleaning services that can be called to the rescue. In other cases, the problem may be caused by improperly graded land that permits water to run off from surrounding ground to fill your crawl space; this calls for regrading the ground to make it slope away from your home rather than toward it.

When water stands in the crawl space, the ground outside should be filled, trenched, and sloped away from the foundation. Guttering should be installed so that water from the roof will run away from the house. A drain tile should be installed around the foundation to carry off water, and another installed through the foundation so that any water that does enter can be drained out. If water enters the crawl space, the foundation vents and the crawl space door will have to be opened to allow air circulation to dry the dirt in the crawl space. Any work necessary to prevent water from running into the crawl space should be completed before any insulation or vapor barrier is installed under the house.

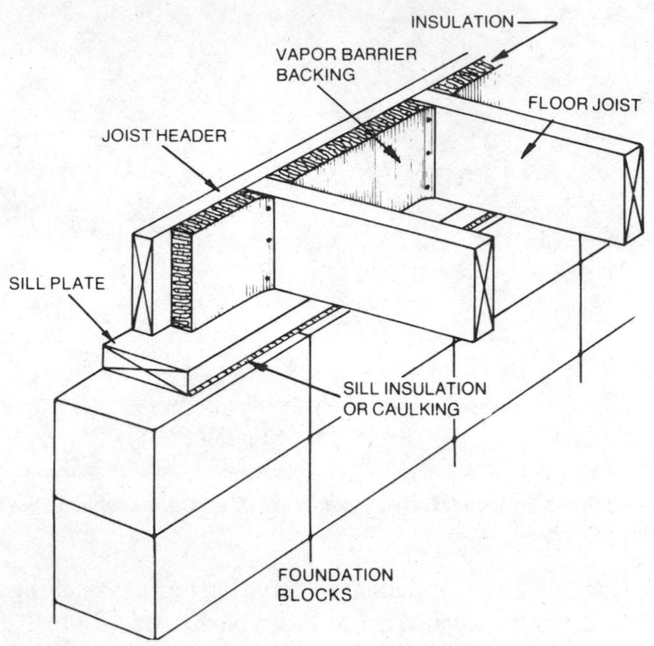

Fig. 4-6. Four inches of fiberglass insulation should be placed between the floor joists and the joist header. This insulation should have some type of vapor barrier backing, and it is installed with the backing facing toward the crawl space and tacked to the floor joists.

Sill Insulation and Termite Shield

If you are building a new house or adding a room onto an older home, you will want to install insulation between the foundation and sill plate to eliminate air leaks. This insulation has to be a least as wide as the sill plate, so if a 6-inch-wide sill plate is used, the insulation should be at least 6 inches wide. Normally, 1 inch of fiberglass insulation is adequate, and there are rolls of insulation fiber available for this purpose. Figure 4-7 illustrates a foundation wall with insulation squeezing out from under the sill plate. The insulation must be reasonably thick so, when the sill plate is installed, the insulation will fill all gaps caused by low places in the foundation.

In most areas of the country, termites and other insects present a problem. A termite shield is therefore installed on top of the foundation to prevent insects from crawling up the foundation and into the wooden portion of the house. The termite shield should be installed between the foundation and the sill insulation

Fig. 4-7. This is the foundation wall after the plate and termite shield have been installed.

strip (Fig. 4-8). The insulation will force the termite shield against the foundation and seal off any air leaks on that side. Note that the lip of the termite shield extends into the crawl space, not outside, since termites prefer to enter the house from the moist, protected side of the foundation.

VENTING THE FOUNDATION

The foundation must be vented, whether it is insulated or not. Vents are necessary to provide the air circulation necessary to remove moisture from the crawl space. Closable vents, like that shown in Fig. 4-9, are best because they can be opened when needed to remove moisture, and they can be closed at other times to prevent cold air from blowing under the house to increase the heat load.

When the crawl space is insulated, the vents should be closed during the winter. A vapor barrier should be installed on the ground when using closable vents so that excess moisture will not build up when the vents are closed. The foundation vents can be opened during warmer weather to keep the crawl space dry, and they can be closed again during the hot summer cooling season. Leave the vents open in new homes to let the lumber dry out.

Different building codes have different requirements for foundation vents. Be sure to check the local building codes in your location because they will often affect the cost tradeoffs in building

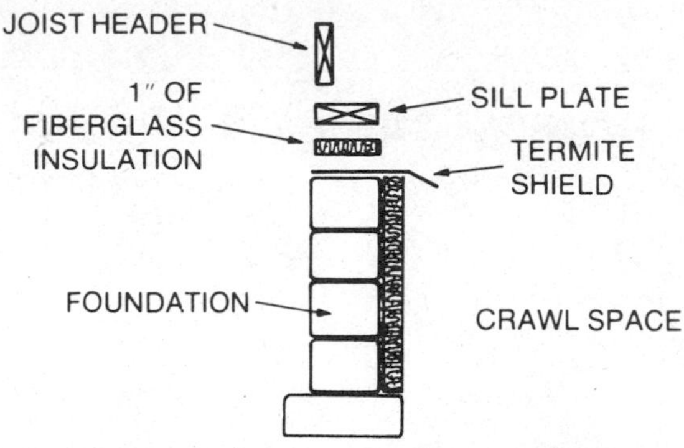

Fig. 4-8. Place 1 inch of fiberglass insulation between the termite shield and the sill plate to seal any lower places between the foundation and the plate. This insulation is sometimes called sill sealer, and it is sold in rolls, ready-cut by the factory in the widths needed.

and remodeling your home. Some codes allow the vent area in the crawl space to be reduced by 90% if a vapor barrier ground cover is used in the crawl space. Others allow reduction in vent area for a vapor barrier on the ground. At least two vents are needed to provide cross-circulation of air. In many areas only two vents are required if a vapor barrier is used, but this is another item that is regulated by building codes.

INSULATING THE FLOOR

If the crawl space foundation is not insulated, the floor of the house must certainly be insulated to prevent heat loss through the

Fig. 4-9. If the foundation is insulated, vents closable from the outside are a must. Even if the foundation is not insulated, closable vents are better than nonclosable vents because you can shut off most of the air circulation under the floor during cold weather. Stopping this air flow reduces the heat load.

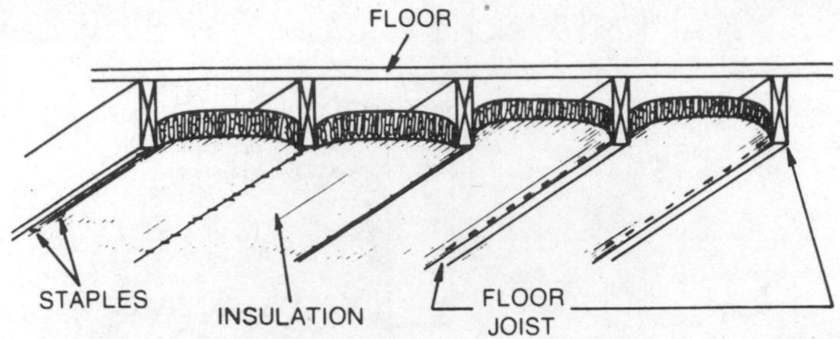

Fig. 4-10. If the insulation has a backing material, it can be stapled to the floor joists using either of the methods shown above. At the left, the backing is pulled over the bottom of the joist and stapled, while at the right the backing is stapled to the sides of the joists. In either case, the vapor barrier must face toward the heated side of the floor. This may make it necessary to use a separate vapor barrier or insulation having two layers, a vapor barrier and a paper backing with the insulation in between.

floor. Stuff fiberglass or rock wool batting between the floor joists, holding them in place with wire, wood lathe, or staples, Sometimes the backing of the insulation can be stapled to the floor joists as shown in Fig. 4-10.

A vapor barrier should face the floor above, no matter what method of fastening is used. If the insulation has an aluminum foil vapor barrier, there must be an air space of at least ¾ inch between the foil backing and the floor; otherwise, the reflective value of the insulation will be lost.

Wire or wood lathe can also be used to support the insulation, as shown in Figs. 4-11 and 4-12. The wire can be stapled to the floor joists, but sometimes the weight of the insulation may cause the staples to pull out. An alternative method of supporting the insulation is to lace wire across the joists in a crisscross fashion, nailing the wire in place. Heavy-gauge wire supports are also available that fit in between the floor joists (Fig. 4-12). Another alternative is to nail chicken wire under the floor joists to support the insulation. The insulation may have a tendency to sag, but if you do a good job of supporting it, you shouldn't have any problems.

To protect the insulation, it is a good idea to have a vapor barrier covering the ground (described in the section on insulating the foundation). Such a vapor barrier is definitely required when the crawl space is to be insulated and heated; but if the floor is to be insulated, the ground vapor barrier is not required, since the floor insulation has a vapor barrier. Nevertheless, it is still a good idea to install a ground barrier, since it will prevent ground moisture

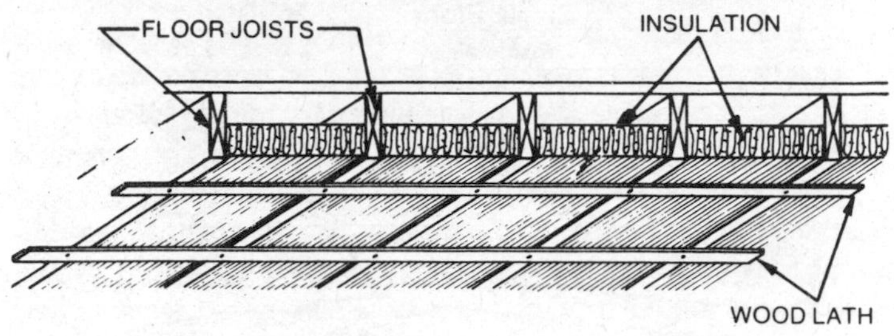

Fig. 4-11. Small wood lath strips can be nailed to the bottom of the floor joists to support the insulation. The strips are ¾ inches by 1½ inches and they are spaced 24 to 36 inches apart.

from entering and condensing in the crawl-space to damage the insulation. Having a ground vapor barrier reduces the need to have crawl space vents open during the heating season, and if you can close the vents, you will reduce your heat load.

If the crawl space under your house is open or you are having extreme problems with water under the house, you should provide some method to protect the floor insulation. You might consider nailing inexpensive plywood to the bottom of the floor joists, or you might staple a polyethylene vapor barrier over the bottom of the insulation if the insulation does not have a vapor barrier on both sides.

Building experts recommend using R-11 insulation under the floor of a house for most parts of the United States. Colder climates need R-19 insulation, and expecially cold areas may need insulation with even high *R* values. The amount of insulation you need will

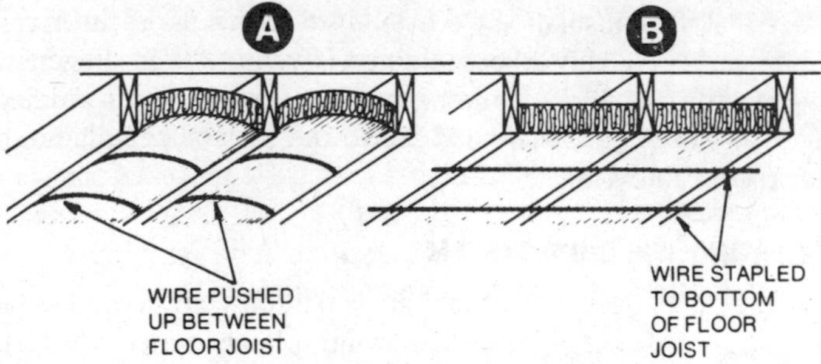

Fig. 4-12. (A) Heavy gage steel wire is used here to support the insulation. This wire is cut long enough that it bows upward, and the ends of the wire grip the sides of the joists. (B) Light wire is held to the floor joists with stables to support the insulation. An alternative is to lace the wire in a criss-cross fashion, using nails to hold the wire.

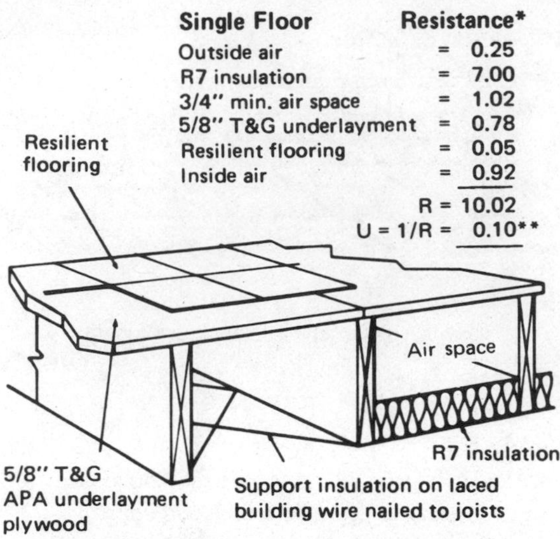

Single Floor
Resistance*
Outside air = 0.25
R7 insulation = 7.00
3/4" min. air space = 1.02
5/8" T&G underlayment = 0.78
Resilient flooring = 0.05
Inside air = 0.92
R = 10.02
U = 1/R = 0.10**
Resilient flooring
Air space
R7 insulation
5/8" T&G APA underlayment plywood
Support insulation on laced building wire nailed to joists

***R values from ASHRAE Guide. Actual thickness and species groups affect plywood insulation values.**

Fig. 4-13. The addition of R-7 insulation to this typical floor over an unheated crawl space increases the resistance, or R value, of the floor by almost five times, from R = 2.25 to R = 10.02. Most climates in the United States need R-11 or R-19 insulation under the floors (courtesy of American Plywood Association).

depend largely on the price of heating energy in your area; when prices are higher, it pays to use more insulation.

Figure 4-13 shows a floor that has been insulated using R-7 insulation. While R-7 would not be enough insulation for most parts of the U.S., it would be sufficient in areas that have mild winters. Notice that if the insulation were not used on this floor, the *R* value of the floor would only 2.25, yielding a *U* value of 0.44. In general, the *U* factor of a floor should never be more than 0.10. Adding a carpet and fiber pad would add 2.0 to the resistance value of the floor (see Table 4-3).

INSULATING THE DUCT SYSTEM

The ducts used to heat and air-condition your home can be a major source of energy loss. In the winter, heat energy is lost from the ducts into cooler unheated spaces; in the summer, heat energy is absorbed by the air conditioning ducts passing through spaces. Cool air conditioning ducts are also susceptible to water condensing on them, and this can rust out a duct system in just a few years.

Table 4-3. R Factors of Floor Coverings.

MATERIAL	R FACTOR
carpet with fiber pad	2.00
carpet with foam pad	1.25
hardwood flooring (per inch)	0.85
tile or linoleum	0.05

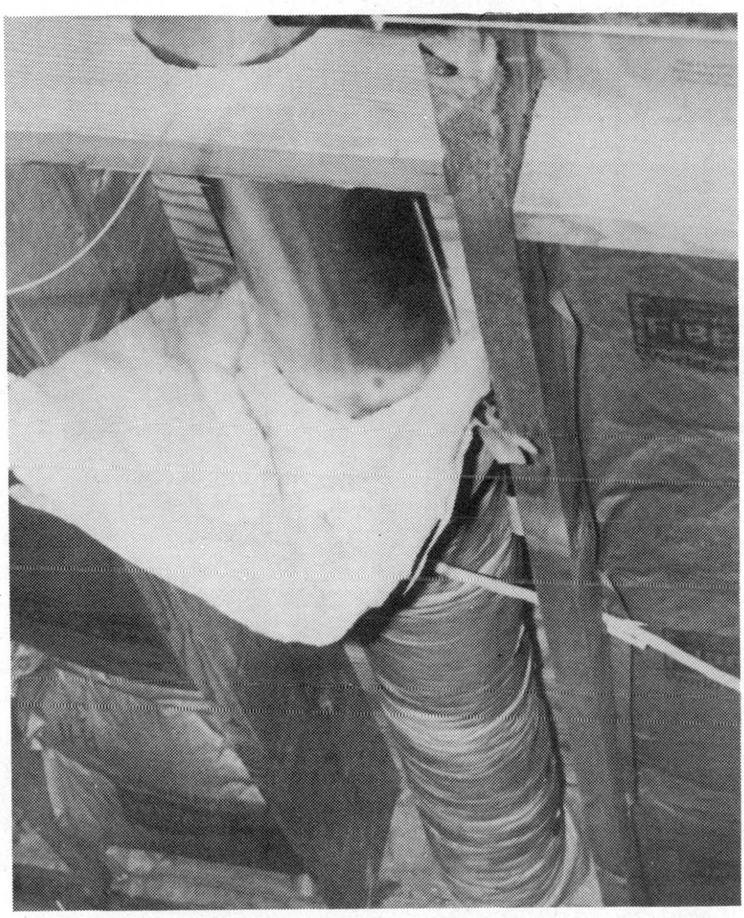

Fig. 4-14. This 6-inch round pipe has been wrapped with insulation batting from a 2-foot wide roll, which provides a good fit. Insulation having a vapor barrier backing is desirable to prevent rusting. Pieces of furnace tape hold the insulation to the duct, but you could also lengths of light wire, looped around the insulation and twisted together. Always insulate a duct that carries cool air when it passes through an area that is not cooled, since a cool duct will cause condensation and its accompanying moisture problems. Insulation is optional for ducts passing through an insulated crawl space, although it can save heat energy.

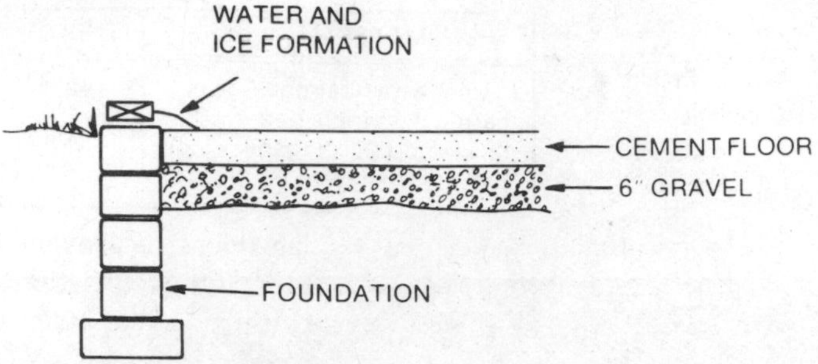

WATER AND
ICE FORMATION

CEMENT FLOOR

6" GRAVEL

FOUNDATION

Fig. 4-15. When the weather gets cold, the concrete foundation and slab floor will cool and may even drop below 32° Fahrenheit if the foundation and floor are not insulated. The cold temperature of the floor and foundation will cause water and ice to form on the floor, which is very bad for carpets.

In heating system, a duct running through any unheated area, such as an attic, garage, or unheated crawl space, should be insulated to reduce heat loss. While special duct-wrapping insulations are available for this purpose, you might find it more economical to use regular batting insulation. Figure 4-14 shows a duct being insulated with batting. Normally, two inches or more of insulation are needed to adequately insulate heating ducts. The insulation should have a protective covering or backing, although a vapor barrier is usually not required over the outside of the insulation *if the duct is used only for heating*. If the heating ducts run through an insulated crawl space, the ducts will not usually require insulation. In the winter, the crawl space will be sealed off, so the temperature in the area will be high enough to prevent much heat loss through the exposed ducts. Your money is better spent on insulating the foundation walls than on insulating the ductwork.

When air conditioning ducts run through any area that is not temperature controlled, the ducts must be insulated and covered with a vapor barrier. Exposed air conditioning ducts not only increase your cooling load, they also cause the warm surrounding air to condense water vapor on the ducts, and this encourages rusting and other moisture problems. During the cooling season, the insulated crawl space is generally cool enough that no moisture will condense on the ducts. If you do have a condensation problem, a simple solution is to cut an outlet in the duct system to blow some cool air into the crawl space. This method normally results in an insignificant increase in your cooling load because the crawl space is sealed, insulated, and fairly cool to begin with. Just install a vent in the duct outlet so that you can regulate the amount of cool air that enters the crawl space, and be sure to close the vent during the winter heating season.

INSULATING SLAB FLOORS

It is very important to insulate slab floors to prevent the formation of water and ice during the winter. If the foundation and floor are not adequately insulated, moist air inside your house can condense and even freeze when it comes in contact with the cold floor (Fig. 4-15). Ice formation is very possible in cases where carpeting is installed over the floor, for then the carpet acts to insulate the condensed water from the warm room air above, permitting it to freeze to the floor surface This condensing and freezing action is damaging to most carpets and can promote the growth mold and mildew at the carpet edges.

Installing insulation between the floor and the foundation as shown in Fig. 4-16 actually serves two purposes. First, it will insulate the floor from the cold outside air. Secondly, it will allow for the normal expansion and contraction of the floor. At least 6 inches of gravel should be placed on top of the fill dirt beneath the slab floor. Then a heavy plastic vapor barrier is placed on top of the gravel, and the concrete floor is poured on top. The vapor barrier is necessary to prevent moisture from seeping upward through the concrete and collecting on the top of the floor. Figure 4-17 shows how the insulation is covered with trim strips where it appears

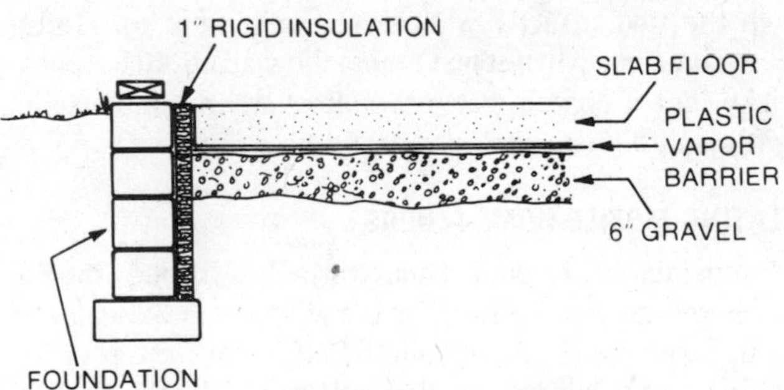

Fig. 4-16. One inch of rigid insulation should be used between the foundation and the slab floor. This insulates the floor from the outside cold and allows for floor expansion at the same time. Six inches of gravel or crushed limestone should be placed over the fill dirt, with a vapor barrier placed between the gravel and the floor. One inch of rigid insulation may be used under the slab floor for better insulation.

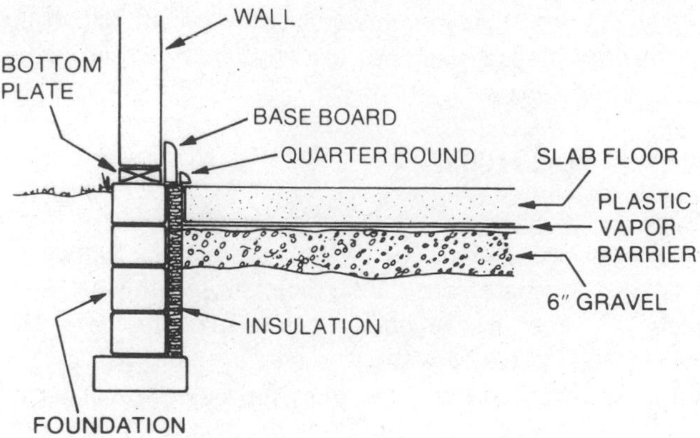

Fig. 4-17. Plan the foundation and wall placement so that the wall trim will cover the insulation.

above the top of the concrete surface. Here a baseboard and quarter-round molding are used to hide the top of the insulation.

The duct system used to carry the air for a central heating/air-conditioning system has to be installed before the slab floor is poured. Figure 4-18 shows how the duct system is installed. The fill dirt is trenched out enough to allow the ducts to come just to the top of the fill gravel. Concrete is then poured in the trenches to encase the ducts and hold them down when the floor is poured. Fill gravel is added until it comes to the top of the ducts, and the vapor barrier is layed over the top of the fill gravel and ducts. An important thing to remember when installing the duct system in a slab floor is that the duct must be positioned so that they will come through the floor exactly where you want them to. Getting the outlet to come up so that it just meets the wall at the baseboard can be tricky, but it is well worth the effort when you consider how unsightly and difficult an error would be to correct.

INSULATING MOBILE HOME FLOORS

A considerable amount of heat can be lost through the floor of a mobile home unless the floor or crawl space is adequately insulated. In some cases, the mobile home is set on top of a closed foundation, and this in itself will greatly reduce heat loss. But many mobile homes are set on pillars, leaving the under side exposed to cold winds that rob the home of much heat energy. Mobile-home owners are not usually interested in doing much work on the foundation, particularly if they are merely renting a site in a mobile

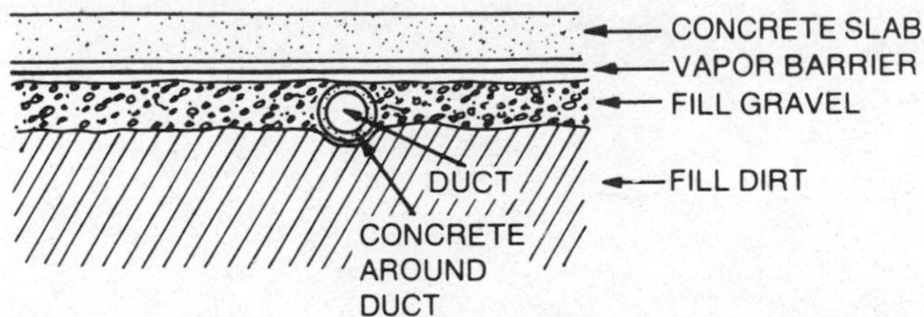

Fig. 4-18. A cross-section of the concrete floor shows that the duct lies in a trench. One inch of concrete is poured and let dry around the duct before the floor is poured. The top of the duct is at the top of the fill gravel, and the vapor barrier goes over the fill gravel and the duct.

park. Instead, they are interested in insulation improvements that will upgrade the value of the mobile home itself.

A mobile home can be insulated in much the same way as a conventional home, by installing floor insulation and skirts around the home. There is only one way to reduce heat loss through the floor of a mobile home, and this is to insulate and enclose the floor area above the unheated space.

The floor of a mobile home should have insulation placed between the floor joists, with a vapor barrier on top of the insulation. Sometimes a half inch of Celotex or some similar rigid material is placed across the bottom of joists to create a dead air space under the floor. The Celotex can be used in addition to 4 inches of fiberglass batting insulation between the floor joists. The advantage to using Celotex or some other rigid insulation material is that it acts to support the fiberglass batting, making it unnecessary to use wire, staples, or lathing to hold the batting in place (Fig. 4-19).

The heat loss through the floor of a mobile home can be greatly reduced if a skirt is placed around the bottom edge to close the area

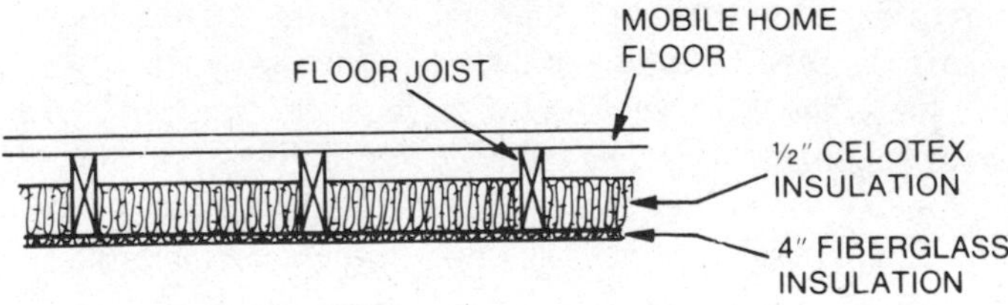

Fig. 4-19. Since the area under the mobile home is frequently exposed to wind, rain and snow, the insulation must be protected from the weather. While inexpensive exterior plywood or waterproof particle board would also support and protect the insulation, the use of a rigid insulation material is preferred because it significantly increases the insulation value of the floor. The space between the floor joists is insulated using about 4 inches of batting insulation with the vapor barrier backing positioned upward toward the floor.

Fig. 4-20. This mobile home has an attractive skirt that seals and insulates the crawl space beneath the home, greatly reducing heat loss through the floors.

under the trailer. The skirt becomes an attractive part of the mobile home and should be insulated with one inch of rigid plastic-foam insulation to further reduce the heat loss (Fig. 4-20). The skirt can be constructed in several different ways, using aluminum sheets, aluminum siding, Masonite, particle board, plywood, or almost any type of building material.

Figure 4-21 shows the construction details of a skirt made from aluminum or Masonite siding that covers 1 inch of rigid insulation. The foundation and footing around the perimeter of the mobile home insulate the space under the structure and provide a base to build the skirt on. This foundation can also be used to help anchor the home if some type of anchoring mechanism is put into the concrete when it is poured. When a good, tight, well insulated skirt is built around a mobile home, the heat loss through the floor can be reduced by 10—20%, depending on the materials used.

Just as there should be air vents in the crawl space under a home, there should be vents in the skirt under a trailer. These air vents are opened and closed as needed to allow air circulation when work is being done under the mobile home and when it is necessary to dry up any moisture that has entered the crawl space.

INSULATING WALLS

The best time to insulate the walls of a home is before the interior wallboards are put up. At this time, you have free access to all wall cavities around windows and doors, so the insulating job goes quickly. After the wall has been constructed, the insulation task is somewhat more difficult, and you have to rely on loose or granular insulation materials that can be poured or blown into the walls.

New Homes

When installing insulation in a new home, the walls should be filled with at least 3 to 4 inches of fiberglass insulation, grades R-11 to R16. See Chapter 3. The insulation batting is placed between the wall studs and pushed firmly against the back side of the wall. If the insulation has a backing material, the backing can be stapled to the studs to support the weight of the insulation and help form a good air seal. Begin stapling the insulation at the top, fitting it tightly against the top plate over the stud. Then work toward the bottom of the wall, placing staples about every 8 to 10 inches along the sides of the studs. If the insulation has a reflective foil backing, be sure to allow at least ¾ inche of air space between the foil and the inside

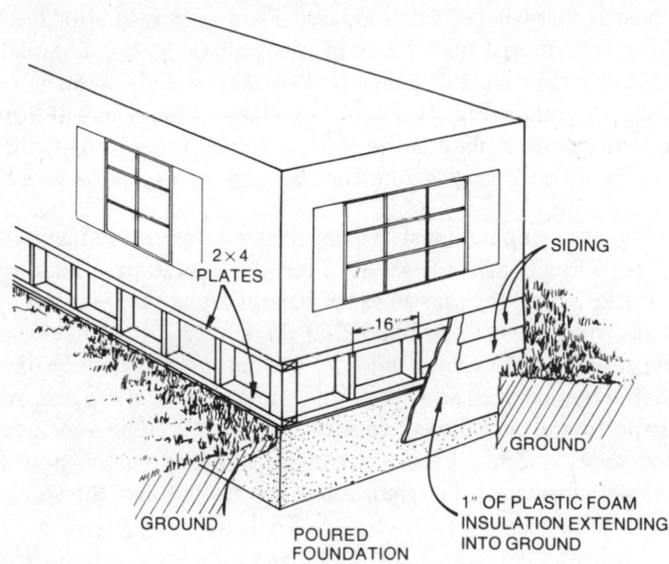

Fig. 4-21. This inexpensive but effective mobile home foundation has skirts to insulate and seal the crawl space. The poured foundation is low to permit easy installation and removal of the mobile home. A two by four-inch base plate or sill goes on top of the foundation. Supporting studs are then erected on 16-inch centers around the mobile home between the bottom and top plates. Rigid insulation covers the insulation and protects it from damage. The siding should be flush with the side of the trailer, so you should recess the foundation and framework.

Fig. 4-22. This fiberglass batting is a friction-fit insulation available in 4 or 8-foot lengths for studs placed on 16 or 24-inch centers.

wallboards that will be installed later. Fricton-fit insulation has no backing, but it will hold itself in the wall (Fig. 4-22). Smaller lengths of batting should be installed so that the ends of the batting fit snugly together (Fig. 4-23). The insulation should also fit firmly against the bottom plate of the wall. If you do the job right, there should be no air spaces at the top, bottom, sides, or back of the insulated wall.

The next step is to install a vapor barrier over tthe insulation (Fig. 4-2). For this, use a sheet of polyethylene film at least two mils thick. Unroll the plastic vapor barrier along the length of the wall and cut off what you need. Lift up an edge of the sheet and staple it across the top of the wall so that it hangs freely like a curtain. Then go back and staple the sheet securely in place from top to bottom. Cover the entire wall with polyethylene—including all doors and windows. Later you can cut out the openings, stuff any cracks with insulation, and then staple the insulation to the window and door frames.

An alternative to a plastic vapor barrier is special foil-backed gypsum board available from many building supply stores. The cost is comparable to using polyethylene sheets, but check with your supplier to see if there are any local restrictions to its use. The foil backing forms an airtight seal as the wall board is nailed against the studs, so a large sheet of vapor barrier is not really required.

It is easy to forget to insulate the many cracks and openings around doors and windows, but this must be done before installing

Fig. 4-23. Four-foot lengths of batting are often easier to handle and install. Be sure to press the ends of the batting firmly together where they meet at the center of the wall, however, to cut down on heat loss through convection air currents.

any wallboard. These cracks and openings are major sources of infiltration air in your home and contribute to a great deal of heat loss. Stuff pieces of insulation batting in all cracks and holes, sealing off every air leak you can find. Windows are installed between the rough-in studs; there are cracks around the window between the frame and the rough opening (Fig. 4-24). Doors have

Fig. 4-24. A window has cracks to fill with insulation on all four sides. Use scraps of batting insulation to stuff in these spaces. This will stop heat flow and infiltration air around the windows. Doors have similar spaces that should be filled with insulation.

Fig. 4-25. Fill all holes in the walls with insulation or caulk. A hole such as this can permit a lot of air flow.

similar openings. Don't forget to cover this insulation with the vapor barriers!

Other openings and cracks abound in the wall cavities, and these are just as easy to miss. Plumbing and electrical wiring requires access holes to be cut into studs, walls, top plates, and base plates (Figs. 4-25 and 4-26). Large openings can be easily filled with pieces of insulation batting; small cracks and openings may be easier to fill with caulk. Stuff insulation behind and around pipes. Seal all holes drilled through studs and plates where electrical wires are run up into the attic space.

Normally, a wall constructed with exterior sheathing or, plywood siding, R-13 insulation, an inside vapor barrier, and gypsum wallboard will provide good enough insulation for most regions of the country. If you feel that more insulation is required, a layer of ½-inch fiberboard sheathing (*R* value, 1 to 1.5) can be added between the outside sheathing and studs. You could also use rigid plastic-foam insulation between the studs, since this has a higher *R* value per inch than fiberglass batting, though you will find it a bit more difficult to install.

Old Homes

After a wall has been constructed and sealed, it is much more difficult to install insulation. Loose rock wool or mineral wood is good for filling sealed walls, but you will have to find some way to get the wood into the wall. Your best bet is to pour this material into the walls from the attic, provided that your house is constructed so you can do this. Another solution is to contact an insulation contractor who can blow the insulation into the walls with special equipment.

Insulating Masonry Walls

Basement and other masonry walls can be insulated by first nailing 2-inch by 2-inch wood strips to the walls and then stapling the insulation to the strips (Fig. 4-27). Nail the wood strips into the wall with concrete nails. The insulation normally used is R-7, which will just about fill the 1¾ inch space that the wood strips leave. This insulation can be purchased in batting and rolls for convenient use on 24-inch centers, so place the strips on 24-inch centers unless you want to use narrower insulation on 16-inch centers. If you want more insulation, you will have to attach wider studs to the wall to give more space. Paneling or wallboard can be nailed to the studs if a finished wall is desired.

Another way to insulate a masonry wall is to glue rigid foam insulation to the walls. Use a strong waterproof glue to attach the insulation to the walls. Gypsum wallboard can be glued over the insulation. One inch of rigid insulation also serves as a vapor barrier and will give you an R-6 to R-8 thermal resistance.

INSULATING THE CEILING

Probably the most important part of your house to insulate is the ceiling. The amount of heat lost through the ceilings account for

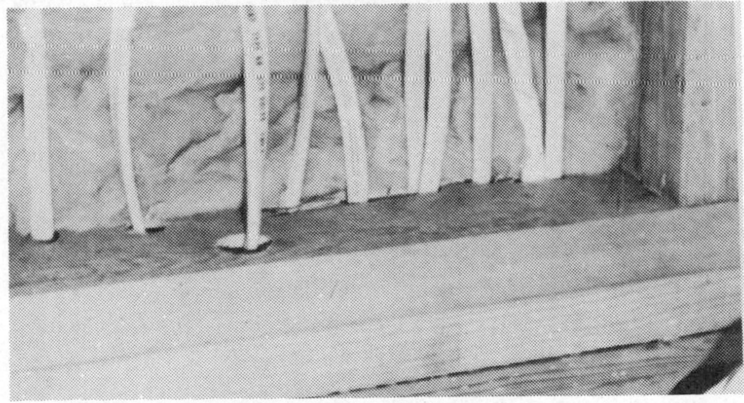

Fig. 4-26. Insulation has been stuffed behind the electrical wires here to prevent drafts. Insulation batting will also be placed over the front of these wires, so there should be no problems with air leakage. Caulking could also be used, but here it is easier to use batting.

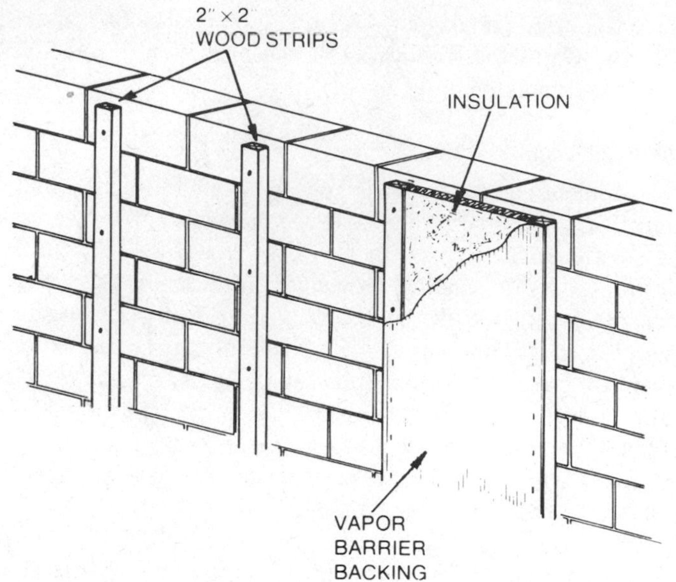

Fig. 4-27. To insulate a masonry wall, first attach wood strips to the wall using concrete nails. Staple the backing of R-7 insulation batting to the lath and then cover the wall with wallboard. Use insulation with a vapor barrier backing and be sure the backing faces toward the heated living area.

a big percentage of your total heating bill. By installing adequate insulation in the ceiling or attic floor, you can save 25/50% on your heating bills, depending on the style of your home. Ranch-style homes have very large ceiling areas that lose a lot of heat energy during the winter and gain a lot of heat energy during the summer.

Ceilings are insulated in most houses, especially those in colder climates. With higher fuel costs, however, homes in all parts of the country probably do not have enough insulation. Houses in cold winter climates should have insulation with a rating of R-30 or more (about 10 inches of fiberglass batting). Houses in warmer climates should have at least (6 inches of fiberglass batting).

The recommended amount of insulation for cilings has steadily increased in recent years as heating and cooling costs have soared. When heating costs were lower, it didn't pay to install a lot of insulation in your home. But as experts keep revising their insulation estimates, it becomes clear that cheap sources of energy are a thing of the past. Even the amount of insulation that is presently recommended may not be enough based on the heating costs of tomorrow, so the investment you make today in insulation may pay surprising dividends in the future.

Whether you are building a new home or adding insulation to an older home, be sure to find out what the most recent estimates of insulation are in your area of the country. Talk with several builders, building suppliers, and insulation suppliers; try to find people in your area who have kept up with recent developments in energy cost increases and who know about the insulation needs in your location. These people should be able to tell you how insula-these people what amounts of insulation they were recommending these peopel what amounts of insulation they were recommending and installing several years ago when energy was inexpensive; if they were recommending the same amounts then as they are now, their advice may not be very good.

Adding More Insulation

Check the insulation you now have in your ceiling (Table 4-4). If you have less than 6 inches, you should add more. If you have less than three inches, add 6 inches of insulation batting or 8 of loose fill (R-19). If you have 3 to 6 inches of insulation, add at least 4 inches of insulation batting or 5 inches of loose fill (Fig. 4-28). A total insulation value of about R-19 is considered near the minimum for most climates in the United States, and you will need more if you live in a cold winter climate, or if your heating costs are higher than average. See Chapter 3. You should also remember that energy costs are increasing, so if you plan to live in your house for several more years, you can afford to insulate more heavily. Over an extended period, the extra insulation will pay for itself.

Adding more insulation to your attic is fairly simple. You can install insulation batting or pour in loose wood yourself, or you can hire an insulation contractor to blow loose wool insulation into your attic.

If you decide to add insulation batting, it is best to use insulation that does not have a backing or vapor barrier. Just lay the

Table 4-4. Approximate Insulation Value and Thickness.

R FACTOR	BATTING	LOOSE FILL
7	2–3″	3–4″
11–13	3–4″	4–7″
19–22	6–8″	8–10″
30–33	10–12″	12–18″

Fig. 4-28. Fiberglass batting insulation (bottom) is easy to handle and install in attics. To install batting, work from the outside wall toward the center, laying the batting between the joists. You will have to take up any floor boards covering the joists in the attic to lay the insulation. Pouring loose rock wool insulation (top) is also very popular in attics. Simply dump the insulation in the area and level it out with a board, shovel or rake. Watch that you don't have any thin spots in the insulation. Over time, this loose insulation tends to settle a bit, but it is still one of the easiest types to install.

insulation between the joists over the old insulation. If the batts do have a backing, use a knife to slash the backing so moisture can pass through freely. If the old insulation comes to the top of the joists, lay the new insulation over the joists, as well as the old insulation (Fig. 4-29).

Loose mineral wool insulation is often used in attics. Simply dump it out of the bag and level it off. The bag has a chart showing how thickly the insulation should be spread to give the desired *R* value. Loose insulation will eventually pack down and settle, so it usualy takes a greater intial thickness of this insulation to obtain a given *R* value for batting. Do nto allow any thin places in the insulation or there will be heat leakage, and do not put a vapor barrier between the new insulation and the old insulation.

Insulating a New or Uninsulated Ceiling

A vapor barrier is not needed over the ceiling if there is adequate ventilation in the attic area. Federal Housing Administration (FHA) requirements state that a house does not require a vapor barrier in the ceiling if there is at least one square foot of ventilation area for each 300 square feet of attic space. To meet these requirements, half of the ventilation area must be at the top of the attic and the rest must be in the eaves.

Place insulation batting face down on the ceiling with the vapor barrier (if one is required) on the warm side of the ceiling. Use at least R-19 insulation, more if you live in a cold area or have high energy costs. Cover the top plate over the wall stud, but do not let the insulation touch the roof, otherwise the eave vents will be cut off.

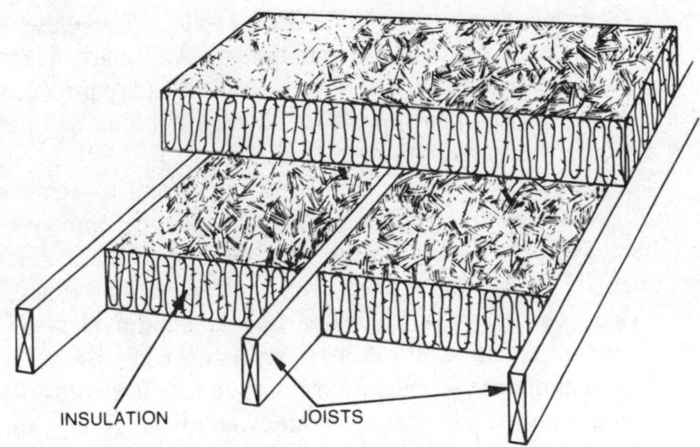

Fig. 4-29. Use two layers of insulation to cover the tops of the joists as well as the rest of the ceiling. The first layer should be installed between the joists with the vapor barrier (if there is one) facing the room below. The second should be installed crosswise over the first layer and should not have a vapor barrier.

If more than R-19 insulation is to be installed, put down two separate layers of insulation. The first layer should be thick enough to bring the insulation level to the top of the joists. The second layer should cover the entire attic area—joints and all, as shown in Fig. 4-29. Fit the batting snugly together to stop air circulation between them.

Loose fill insulation can also be poured over the ceiling to insulate the area. Be sure to spread it to the correct thickness to get the insulating value you want. An insulation contractor can blow loose wool insulation into the uninsulated attic through a hose.

Do not cover eave vents with loose insulation; construct a retainer to keep the wool away from the vents. A simple retainer is made from pieces of insulation batting placed next to the vents. Recessed light fixtures coming through the ceiling must not be covered with insulation because they will overheat.

Fill all holes in the attic. Stuff insulation in holes drilled in the top plate of the wall for electrical wires. Be sure to insulate the plates too. Do not forget to insulate the back of the attic doorway. And if your house has an attic stairway, be sure to insulate the walls and beneath the steps.

TIPS ON HIRING AN INSULATION CONTRACTOR

Insulation contractors, generally blow mineral fiber or cellulosic fiber insulation in the walls or ceiling of a house. Contractors are often called upon to insulate sealed walls because they can install the insulation without having to take the wall apart. At most, they may have to drill a hole in the wall between each pair of studs, but if you remove the baseboards for them, the holes will never show and you will have nothing to patch.

The thickness of blown insulation necessary to achieve a given *R* value varies according to the manufacturer and type of insulation. Typical ranges are given in Table 4-4. Federal regulations require that each bag of blowing-wool insulation be marked with a chart showing the thickness and maximum square-foot coverage of the insulation necessary to achieve the given *R* values.

When dealing with an insulation contractor, you should always specify ther thermal resistance value you want, giving him a specific *R* value. If you specify only the thickness of insulation, you may not get the *R* value you need, since different insulations require different thicknesses to achieve the same *R* value.

From the maximum coverage specified on the insulation bags, calculate how many bags the contractor will need for your house to achieve the *R* value you want. Be home the day the contractors show up and *count the bags* they use to insulate your home so you can be sure you are getting the insulation you want and are paying for.

ATTIC VENTILATION

The final step to insulating your home is insuring that there is adequate ventilation in the attic to remove moisture and to help your air conditioner do its job more efficiently. Installing several vents will permit air to circulate by natural air convection. Installing an attic fan will provide more air circulation through the vents by forcing more air to flow.

Ventilation will lower the temperature of your attic during the summer cooling season. If ventilation is not provided, the heat from the sun can warm the attic to temperatues of 125°F or more, Without vents, the attic air is trapped, so the heat just keeps building up. This hot air is conducted through the ceiling insulation and into the living space below.

For natural air circulation using only vents, you should install vents under the eaves and at the top of the gable at each end of the attic (Fig. 4-30). The size of these vents depends upon the ceiling area and whether or not you have a vapor barrier in the ceiling. When no vapor barrier is used, you need about one square foot of

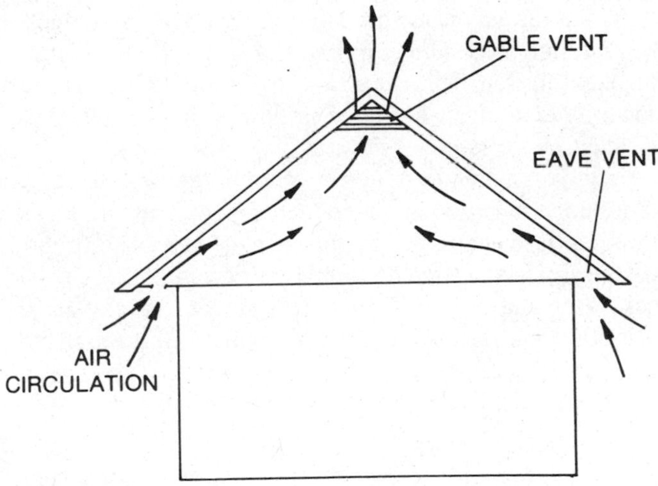

Fig. 4-30. Best air circulation is obtained with two eave vents and one gable vent at each end of the attic. Adequate ventilation will protect your home from moisture during the winter and will keep your home cooler during the summer.

gable vents, since the air that flows in through one vent must flow out through the other. If a ceiling vapor barrier is used, you can reduce the vent area by half.

If the vents are covered with louvers, screens, or panels, the effective area of the vents will be reduced. This means you will have to increase the vent area to allow for more air flow. Some louvers and grilles actually leave less than 50% of the vent area exposed for free air flow, so you would need a vent area twice as large to achieve the required air flow.

Using fans to circulate the attic air gives more effective ventilation and can save money on air conditioning bills. An attic fan may be placed in one of the gable vents or attached to the roof of the house. The fan forces the circulation of cooler air through the attic, which lowers the temperature of the attic and reduces the load on the air conditioner. The best type of attic fan has a thermostat that turns the fan on automatically when the attic temperature reaches about 90°F or so.

Attic fans can also be used to provide air circulation in the living area of the house, cutting down on air conditioner usage. A two-speed attic fan with a remote switch can be installed in the gables or on the roof near the ridge. At night when outside air is cool, you can turn this fan on high speed and open the windows and doors. An opening for air flow is needed in the ceiling between the living area and the attic, such as the crawl way or attic stairway. With the fan turned on and the attic access open, cool night air is sucked through the windows into the house, while the warm air is blown out at the fan. This can eliminate the need for you to run the air conditioner at night. For good air flow, however, all other attic vents must be closed.

A similar cooling system has vents in the roof and a special ventilation fan mounted in the ceiling. The ceiling fan draws cool air through the windows in the house and blows it into the attic where the air is exhausted through the attic vents, thereby cooling both the attic and the living area. This system has the advantage that the attic vents are always open to circulate air through the attic space. The fan opening in the ceiling should have closable louvers to seal it off during cold weather.

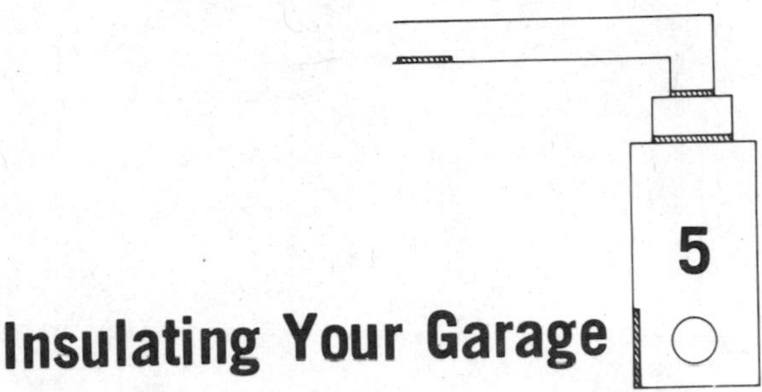

Insulating Your Garage

Garages and other structures attached to your house require special consideration when it comes to insulation. These structures may or may not be heated during the winter. If they are to be heated, you would than go about insulating them in much the same way you would the rest of your house. But if they are not to be heated, you may still decide whether to insulate and weather-strip them to capture some of the free heat escaping through the wall of your house. This would raise the inside temperature of the garage during the winter months, making it more comfortable to work there and easier to start your car. Other attached structures such as workshops, toolsheds and storage areas might benefit from insulation too. With the increase in home gardening, for example, you could store canned goods in such areas—provided they had sufficient insulation to prevent the goods from freezing.

INSULATING AN UNHEATED GARAGE

The wall separating an unheated garage and the living area of the house is easy to forget. If the garage is to be unheated, you will want to insulate this wall thoroughly to cut down on heat loss. Ordinarily, this would be done while you were insulating the rest of your house, but an attached garage is often neglected, even though it is one of the easiest structures to insulate.

If you are not going to heat your garage, you must insulate the wall connecting to your house. In many homes, a room is situated over the garage, so you must also insulate the ceiling of the garage, which is the floor of the room above. The connecting wall partition

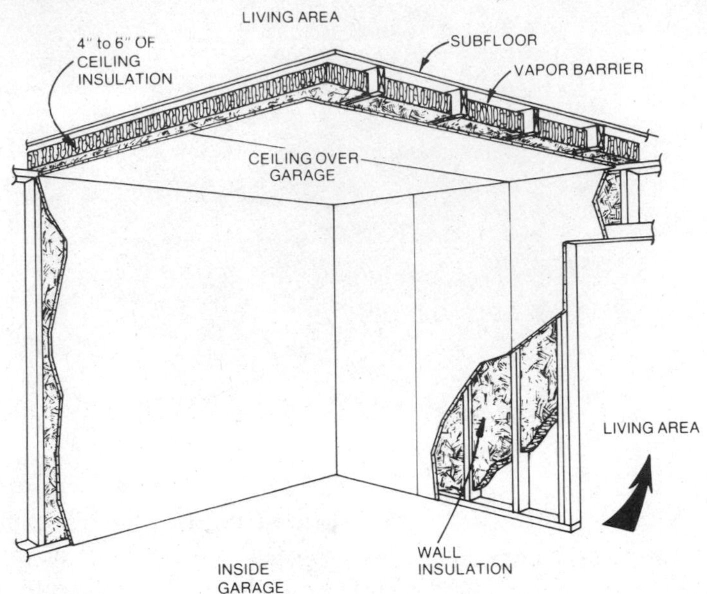

Fig. 5-1. If a garage is unheated, insulate the walls and ceiling adjoining living areas just as you would any other outside partitions in your house. The vapor barrier must face toward the heated living area of the house.

is insulated like any other outside wal in your house (see Chapter 4). The ceiling of the garage, however, is treated as a floor over a crawl space (Fig. 5-1).

The walls can be insulated using 3 to 4 inches of fiberglass batting (R-11 to R-13). Often, you can install even more insulation because the inside wall of the garage is not usually sided. A vapor barrier should be installed against the heated surface of the dividing wall, with the insulation covering the barrier. A layer of plywood or particle board will provide added insulation and protect the insulation from damage.

If there is a room over the garage area, the ceiling of the garage should be insulated, using 4 to 6 inches of fiberglass batting. You can use more insulation here because the floor joists are larger than wall studs. Use R-11 to R-19 insulation in the ceiling as illustrated in Fig. 5-1. A vapor barrier should be installed against the floor boards of the room above. In this case, the vapor barrier will not only protect the house from moisture condensation, it will keep dangerous automobile exhaust fumes from traveling into the rooms above, which are often bedrooms.

If heating or cooling ducts run through the unheated garage, be sure to insulate these too. Normally these ducts are encountered in homes having rooms located above the garage. Wrap the ducts with at least R-11 insulation to reduce heat loss and moisture condensation (Fig. 5-2). If the ducts are part of your air conditioning system, be sure to use a vapor barrier over the insulation to keep them from rusting out.

When the garage door is open, the inside temperature of the garage will quickly become as cold as the outdoors. With the door closed, however, the air space in the garage becomes sealed off, behaving as an unheated crawl space of sorts. The heat energy escaping from the house then warms the air in the garage, and this lowers the temperature difference between the living area and the garage, which in turn reduces the heat loss through the walls. It is therefore desirable to keep the garage door closed as much as possible in cold weather to conserve heat energy.

If the unheated garage is sealed off so that there are few air leaks, the temperature in the garage will always be warmer than the cold outdoors. The actual temperature depends in part upon how thoroughly you insulated the wall and ceiling partitions separating the garage from the living area. With only one attached wall, the heat energy captured by the garage will be relatively small. Many homes, though, have other rooms both above the

Fig. 5-2. R-11 insulation has already been installed in the ceiling of this garage; the duct system is now being insulated. The ceiling of this garage is located beneath a living area in a split-level house. A square feed duct supplies warm air to the round ceiling duct. In a heated garage, this square duct might also be used to supply warm air to the garage area, although this generally proves to be a very inefficient way to heat the garage.

garage and behind it. With this larger wall area to contribute heat to the garage, the garage will stay much warmer in the winter.

Adding some insulation or sheathing to the remaining walls of the garage will also help to increase the temperature in the unheated garage. This step will rarely reduce your heating bill enough to justify the added cost, though personal comfort and convenience often overrule the economics of the matter. For example, you may occasionally work in the garage area and heat it with an electric or gas space heater while you are working. Additional insulation can save some money on your heating bill, but you would probably save much more money by being able to purchase a less powerful space heater.

INSULATING A HEATED GARAGE

Sometimes a heating duct is run into the garage so that it can be heated. This is often a great convenience when you use the garage as a work or storage area. The energy crisis has also raised the cost of gasoline and auto maintenance, so many homeowners have been using their garages for more than just a place to park their car. The problem with heating a garage is that it can add a lot to the heating bill. A garage occupies a rather large area, and it can cost quite a bit to heat. Since the garage is rarely used much of the time, the benefits from heating it full time are small.

To compound the heating problem, the garage is the most poorly insulated and sealed part of the house. The garage door doesn't fit well, is filled with cracks, and has practically no insulation properties. The garage walls are usually not insulated, so the garage has little ability to retain heat energy. And the concrete floor is cold and damp most of the time because cold air sinks to the floor. All in all, the typical garage is not a very comfortable place to work in during the winter months.

The garage has a huge doorway that lets all the heat in the garage escape when it is opened for even a moment. When the garage door is then closed, you have to heat all the air in the garage again. The garage door is usually made of thin fiberglass or metal these days, but even heavy wooden garage doors provide little insulation. To be of any value in keeping the heat inside the garage, the garage door must be sealed and insulated.

Most new houses provide insulation in all the walls of an attached garage. If the garage does not have such insulation, you should install R-11 insulation batting in the walls, always placing the vapor barrier on the *heated side* of the wall. If the wall is between the garage and the living area, place the vapor barrier on the living-area side; otherwise, put the vapor barrier facing toward the inside of the garage. In general, just insulate the walls of the heated garage as you would any other wall of the house.

Insulate the ceiling of the garage even when heated rooms are above the garage, since the garage is often left unheated. Place the vapor barrier against the floor above the garage ceiling if the area above the garage is heated; otherwise, place the vapor barrier facing into the garage area.

The slab floor of the garage should also be insulated just as you would inside the house. Place a sheet of rigid foam insulation between the slab floor and the outside wall of the garage.

Because the garage door is frequently opened and closed, the garage is somewhat of a challenge to heat efficiently. Large amounts of heated air escape every time the garage door is opened. If you plan to heat the garage, be sure to install a small door to the outside so the large door need only be opened to move the car. And when you do open any outside door of the garage, close it again as quickly as possible. An automatic-garage door opener is especially good for cutting down on this kind of heat loss.

While it is possible to use the heating duct from your furnace to heat the garage, this usually proves to be a very expensive method. Most often, the cheapeast way to heat the garage is to use supplementary heaters that can be turned on and off as you need them. Electric space heaters and baseboard heaters permit you to heat the garage as much as you want to without affecting the House's heating system. If you do not want the garage to be heated all of the time, you can turn the heat completely off when the garage is not being used. You can also use the thermostat on the heaters to lower the temperature when you are not using the garage, but not so far that the garage cannot be quickly heated again. The thermostat can be set to prevent to prevent the temperature in the garage from dropping below the freezing point, thus protecting bottled goods and perishable foods stored in the garage area.

Another way to heat a garage cheaply is to run the flue pipe of your furnace through the garage area. The heat energy that goes up the flue is normally wasted energy, but since you've already paid for this heat, you might as well use it to help heat your garage. Just by itself, the flue will give off quite a bit of heat into the garage area. You can increase the heat from the flue by installing a small fan to blow air over the flue pipe and to circulate the warm air throughout the garage. Other exposed heating ducts could be left exposed for added heat, but this often interferes with the temperature regulation of the rooms fed by these ducts. Ducts used for air conditioning should never be used in this way because condensation during warm weather would soon rust them.

GARAGE DOORS

There are several different materials used to construct garage doors: most have very little insulating value. Since the garage door occupies such a large area, a great deal of heat energy is conducted through the door. For homes that have insulation between the unheated garage and the living area of the house, this factor may not be important. But homes with little or no insulation between the garage and house let a large amount of heat escape through the wall of the house and into the garage, and from the garage through the garage door. So whether or not you plan to heat your garage, the garage door should have good insulating qualities, and the door should be caulked and weather stripped to stop air leaks.

A wooden garage door generally has the best insulating value, but its main drawback is its weight. Lightweight fiberglass, plastic, and aluminum doors have gained popularity over the years, but they offer considerably less insulating value.

Fig. 5-3. Caulk the trim around the garage door to reduce air flow through these cracks.

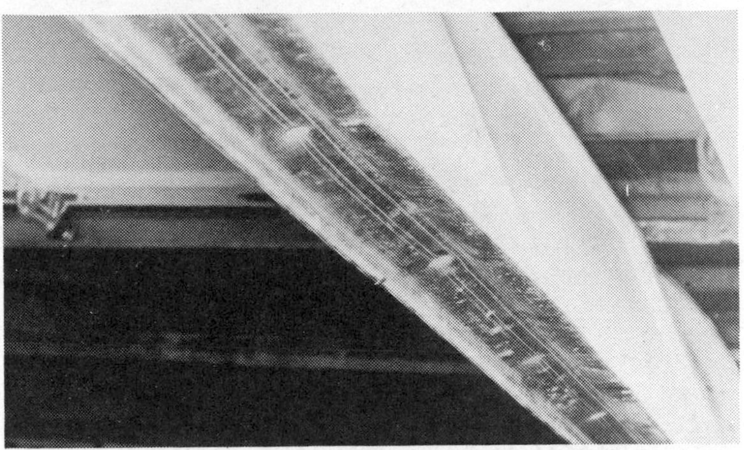

Fig. 5-4. To prevent heat loss under the garage door, attach a metal and rubber weather strip to the bottom of the garage door. When the door closes, this strip will form a seal against the floor and stop air flow under the door. Flexible weather stripping can also be added at the side and top of the garage door openng to seal those areas.

Garage doors have many cracks and openings that should be sealed. You can start by caulking the door casing (Fig. 5-3). Cracks between the hinged door panels can be taped over on the inside of the garage with a flexible tape that will not crack when the door is opened and closed; furnace duct tape does a fairly good job. You should also apply weather stripping to the bottom of the door to provide a snug seal when closed; this is usually made of a flexible rubber or vinyl material (Fig. 5-4).

A difficult part of the door to seal is the track along the sides of the door. To prevent air from entering around the door when it is closed, this track must be set close to the door facing. Of course, if the track is set too close to the facing, the door will not open and close properly. To weather-strip this track, you must use a very flexible type of stripping that will not make the door bind or stick, yet that will completely seal the opening when the door is closed. There are many types of soft vinyl strips and tubes that can be used for this purpose, and they are generally installed on the outside door facing so they press against the sides and top of the garage door when it is closed. Be careful that you do not install this weather stripping too snugly against the door, or the door may pull and tear the strip as it moves up and down. The weather stripping will also hold up better if the garage door has a smooth surface where it meets the strip.

6 Weather-Stripping Doors and Windows

A considerable amount of heat energy is lost through doors and windows. Some of this heat is lost through conduction as heat energy passes through the solid parts of the doors and windows, but a lot of heat is lost through air leaks around the edges. Weather stripping is used to reduce infiltration air that brings cold air into the house or carries warm air outside. Most new windows have built-in weather stripping, so heat loss of this nature is not much of a problem. Unfortunately, though, most older homes have large unfilled cracks where the parts of the windows come together. Doors—both old and new—have similar cracks where the door edge meets the jambs and threshold. All these air leaks must be eliminated by adding weather stripping and caulking.

Figure 6-1 shows a diagram of a window not having weather stripping. In order for this window to slide up and down, there must be spaces between the sash and jamb. But these spaces permit air to flow into the house. When these windows were new, the sash and jamb fit closely together and worked easily. But as they age and weather, the spaces between the sash and jamb grown increasingly larger, permitting more air to flow freely into the thouse.

SIMPLE WEATHER SEALS

There are several different types of weather stripping and sealing materials available at hardware stores and building suppliers. One of the easiest materials to install is a caulk com-

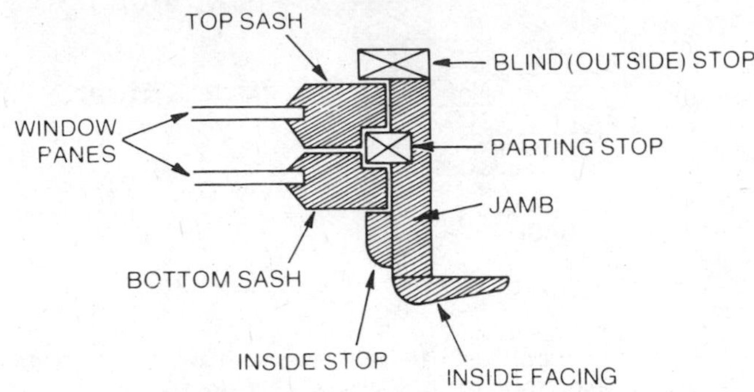

Fig. 6-1. Top view of window showing cross section of right-hand side. The sash is the part of the window that holds the pane, and the jamb is the side of the window frame that holds the sash in place. An older window will probably not have weather stripping. Outside air will then move through the cracks between the sash and jamb. The infiltration air flow will be especially bad during windy winter weather.

pound that can be applied around the inside sash and window stop. This material will stop the air flow around the window sash, but the window cannot be raised or lowered while the stripping material is in place. This means you must remove the caulking material in the spring if you want to raise and lower the windows again. Consequently, this type of caulking material is removable and never hardens completely.

Felt weather stripping is a material that can be tacked to the inside window stop. It presses against the window sash, stopping the air flow around the window assembly. To install the felt weather stripping, push the lower sash against the parting stop to obtain a snug fit; then tack the weather stripping to the inside stop. The top sash is pushed against the blind (outside) stop and the felt is tacked to the parting stop. With this weather stripping added, the air flow will be reduced, yet the windows can be raised and lowered.

During the winter when the windows will be closed all the time, it is a good idea to seal the crack between the two windows where the lower sash and the upper sash come together. This can be done either with caulking matterial or by wedging some felt material in the crack. This seal must be removed before the windows are raised and lowered in the spring.

Another simple method of weather-stripping windows is to tack up a sheet of plastic over the window frame. Several types of clear plastic are available for this use; some are very clear, while

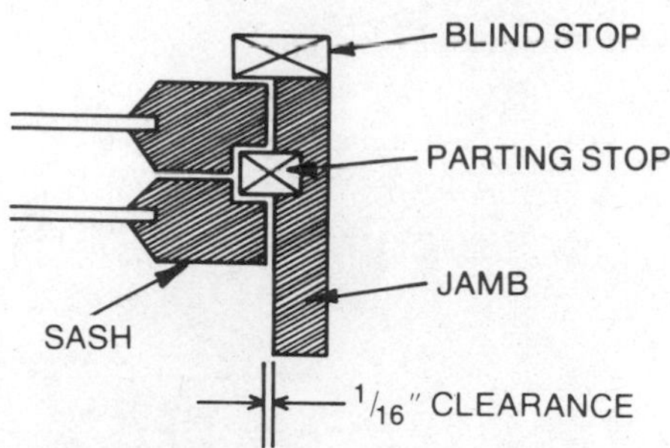

Fig. 6-2. There should be at least 1/16-inch clearance between the window sash and the window jamb to give room for two weather strips to fit in the channel; more clearance is needed with plastic strips. Plane the sides of the sash to obtain the proper clearance and a smooth sliding edge.

others are a bit cloudy. The plastic is tacked or taped to the window casing or screen, using heavy cardhboard strips or small wooden strips. This method not only stops the air flow through the cracks in the window assembly, but it acts like a storm window and provides another dead air space to give more insulation to the window. Some manufacturers supply storm-window kits for standard size windows, using attractive adhesive-backed strips that do not have to be tacked down.

WEATHER STRIP INSERTS

If the windows are to be raised and lowered with the weather stripping in place, you will have to use a weather strip that fits inside the window between the sash and jamb. Weather stripping of this type requires that you dismantle the window to install it. A thin metal or plastic weather strip can be installed as shown in Figs. 6-2 and 6-3. This strip acts as a spring to press against the sash, thereby cutting off any air flow.

To install this kind of weather stripping, you will have to remove the stops at the sides of the window that hold the sashes in place. Many homeowners are only interested in raising and lowering the bottom window sash because that is the only one they use. If you decide to do this, you should caulk and seal the top sash. The advantage to using both windows, however, is that you can ventilate your home easier in the summer by lowering the top sash and raising the bottom sash equal amounts. Since hot air rises toward the ceiling, the top sash will allow the hot air to leave the house while the bottom sash allows cooler air to enter through the same window. This is one instance in which you can make natural convection air currents work *for* you instead of *against* you.

The weather stripping takes up extra room in the window channel, so you will probably have to plane the edges of the sash to obtain the necessary clearance. Be careful, however, not to plane off too much wood, or the windows will not fit snugly enough to make the weather stripping effective. If you have to do any planing, do just enough to allow the windows to slide smoothly up and down in the channels. Sometimes applying a little soap film in the channel will help if the window is just a little on the tight side. On the other hand, if the sash has too much clearance, a thin piece of shimming wood can be glued to the sash to make a good fit; if you anticipate this problem, you will find it easier to shim out the channel before tacking in the weather strip.

Before buying the stripping, you will have to decide how much you will need for each window. You can buy the stripping in rolls and in precut lengths at most hardware and building supply stores. If you want to weather-strip both the top and bottom sashes, you will need enough weather stripping to go up both sides and across the top and bottom jambs, plus about 2 feet extra for channel extensions. If you decide to weather-strip only the lower sash, measure across the bottom and up the two sides of the sash, and then allow 1 foot more. The extra lengths in each case are needed so that the shases can be completely raised or lowered without sliding off the strip and possibly jamming the window open.

To dismantle the window, remove the inside stop and take out the bottom sash. To remove the top sash, the parting stop must be removed, and this can be done by carefully prying it out of its

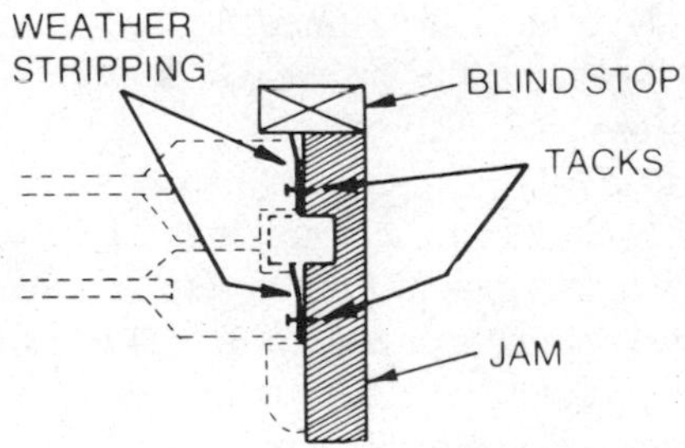

Fig. 6-3. With the sashes and stops removed, the weather stripping is tacked into the channel. The outer edge of each strip must spring toward the outside to keep out rain and snow, as well as air. Cut the stripping about 6 inches longer than the window sashes so that the sashes will not slide off the stripping as the windows are raised and lowered. Be careful with metal stripping that you do not bend or deform it, preventing it from making a good seal. Plastic stripping is sometimes considered to be better because it can take more abuse and remains quite flexible.

groove in the jamb. If the windows have window weights, these will have to be removed before the weather stripping can be installed. (If the cords on the weights are broken or worn, now is a good time to replace them.)

The weather strips are tacked along all four sides of the window assembly, but they must be installed in the proper channels. If you take the top sash out, start by tacking the strip in the top channel occupied by the upper sash. This strip is needed to seal the upper sash when it is pushed against the top jamb. Cut this top strip to exactly the length of the channel. Note that the flexible or springy side of the strip faces toward the outside of the house so that the stiff winds will force it tightly against the sash rather than blowing it open. Next, cut two lengths of weather stripping for the side channels of the upper sash, allowing about 6 inches extra on each side so the sash won't slide off the strip when the sash is lowered all the way. Tack these two strips in place.

After the stripping has been installed in the upper channels, put the top sash back into the window and check for clearance. The sash should fit snugly, but not so tightly that the window can't be raised and lowered with moderate effort. The top of the window sash should also fit firmly against the top jamp. If the window jambs are not exactly perpendicular, the window may gap a little at the top, so you may have to plane the top edge of the sash to make the clearances the same. When you've got the sash to fit right, lower it to the bottom of the window to make it easier to put the parting stop back.

With the upper sash and the parting stop in place, install stripping in the bottom sash cahnnel. Again, cut the side strips about 6 inches longer than the sash and tack them in place. Install another strip across the bottom channel to seal the bottom sash when it is fully closed. After all the stripping has been installed, put the bottom sash back in and check its fit at the sides and bottom. Also check the window lock at this time to see that it forces the sashes firmly against the upper and lower weather strips when it is closed. When you've got the right clearances, replace the inside stops and any trim you might have removed.

COMBINATION WEATHER STRIP AND PARTING STOP

Figures 6-4 and 6-5 illustrate a unique type of weather strip that is often seen in new windows. This type is ideal for renovating older windows because it does away with the old parting stop between the two sashes, which is often the cuase of many problems. When the weather stripping is in place, the sashes slide up and down in the window, following the tracks molded into the strip. Because of the many contact surfaces, this type of stripping produces an excellent weather seal while allowing the sash to move with less effort.

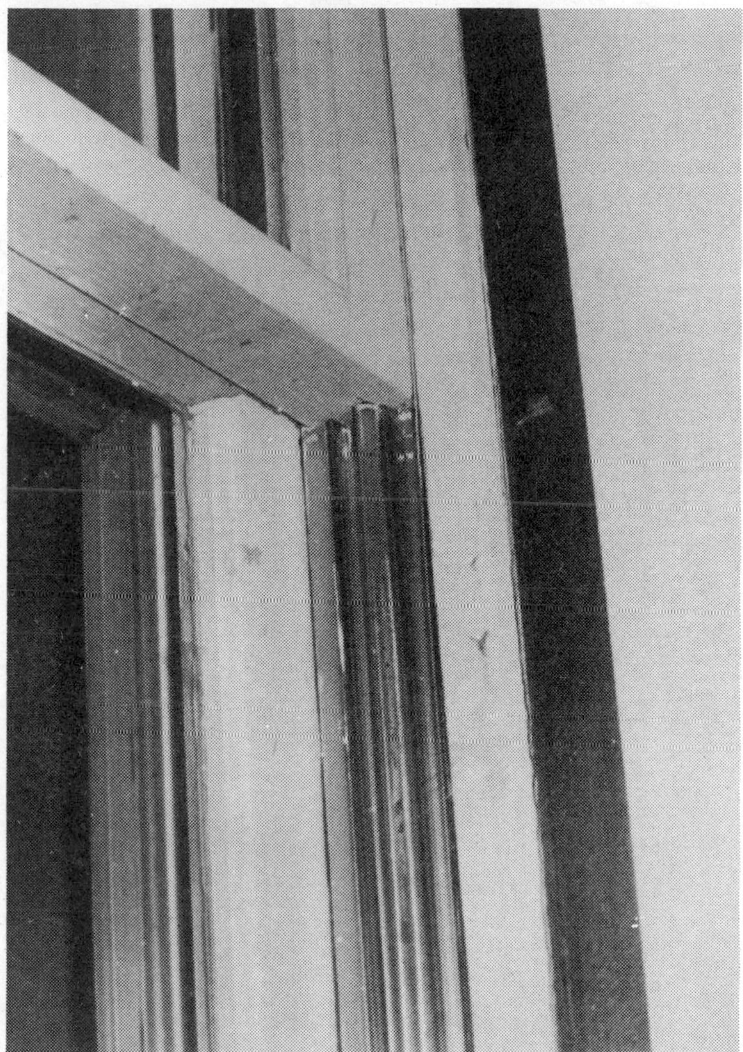

Fig. 6-4. This type of weather stripping serves both as a barrier to air flow and as a parting stop to guide the window up and down. To install this weather stripping, a groove must be cut in the side of the window sash, which is easily done with a power saw.

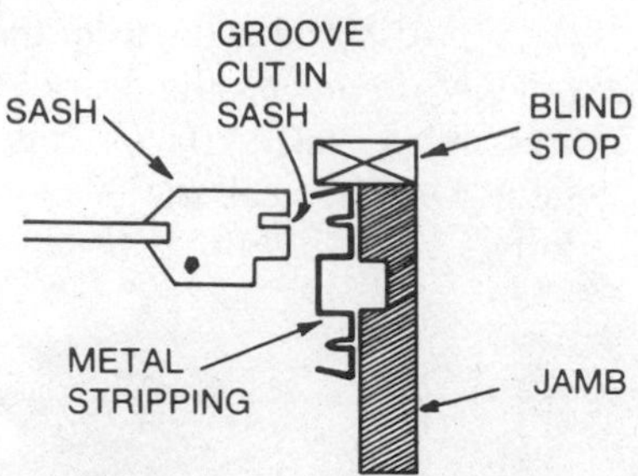

Fig. 6-5. To install this type of weather stripping, first remove the inside stop and lower sash. Then pry the parting stop and remove the sash. Be sure to check the clearance between the sashes and window jamb. Cut the metal stripping to the proper length on each side. A groove will have to be cut on each side of the window sash, large enough for the ridge to fit in.

The window is taken apart as before, by removing the inside and parting stops that hold the sashes in place. A groove is then cut in the sides of the sashes with a power saw. This must be done carefully so that the groove matches the ridge in the weather strip. The groove must be cut straightly and deeply enough that the sash will slide up and down without binding. This type of weather stripping usually comes in a kit with complete directions on how to cut the grooves. The whole operation is really quite simple and goes quickly.

Before cutting the grooves, though, check the overlap area of the sashes in the center. These two frames are supposed to meet in the middle to cut off any air flow between the sashes (Fig. 6-6). Normally, you can cut the grooves to make the two check rails seal correctly, but this is not always the case. You may have to plane the check rails to clean off old paint, or if they are too far apart, you may have to add felt weather stripping or caulking along the crack to form a good seal.

After cutting the grooves in the sashes, insert the stripping into the grooves and place the sashes and stripping into the window jamb. The sashes and stripping have to be installed together because of the raised ridges that hold the sash in place. Note also that the weather stripping extends the full length of the window, from top to bottom, and must be installed in one piece. So with the back edge of the stripping pressed against the blind (outside) stops of the window, nail the exposed portions of the stripping in place. Then slide the sashes to the other end of their channels and nail down the remaining half of each weather strip. The sashes should now slide easily up and down.

To complete the window, install weather strip inserts (discussed in the preceding section) to seal the top and bottom of the window. After these have been installed, you can replace the inside stops, which now serve only as trim since the new channel strips actually hold the windows in place.

INSTALLING NEW WINDOWS

Most new windows have weather stripping installed. Some of these windows, however, may not fit well. You may have to add shimming to reduce the air flow around the factory-installed weather stripping, or add weather stripping to the bottom of the sashes, or fix the sashes so they seal tightly in the middle. Buying a new window doesn't automatically guarantee a good weather seal, especially in these days of mass production, so you can expect to make a few adjustments to make them airtight.

When you install a new window in a house or remodel the window area of an older house, be sure you stuff insulation in the cracks around the window itself (Fig. 6-7). Batting insulation can be cut into strips and shoved into the cracks between the window jamb and the rough opening. Prehung windows and doors are shimmed and braced so they can be installed plumb and true in the rough-in opening, but this is no guarantee that they will be installed properly. If the window is not kept square when installing it, gaps

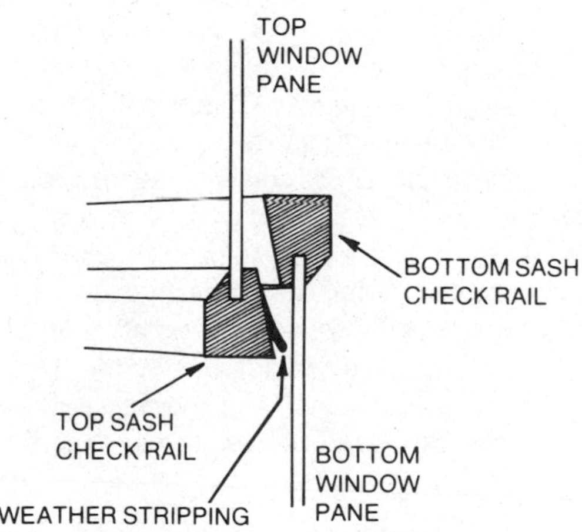

Fig. 6-6. The top and bottom sashes should fit together in the middle of the window to prevent air flow through the joint. Since the check rails are cut with a slope, a good fit can usually be obtained by planing a little off the bottom of the lower sash. If this approach won't work, weather stripping material can be installed in the crack to stop air flow.

Fig. 6-7. This new window is being installed in an unfinished wall. Before the wall and trim are put up, be sure that insulation is added to fill the cracks around the window casing. This is important to prevent air flow and heat loss. Such cracks are typical in home construction, since the rough-in studs and horizontal braces are made slightly oversized so that the window can be easily inserted and shimed squarely in place at a later time.

will occur around the edges that may be too wide to permit the weather stripping to work effectively. Always check to see that the window opens and closes easily since this is a good clue as to how well the window has been installed.

New windows and replacement windows are usually made of wood or aluminum, and they may have a vinyl coating on the outside so that you do not have to paint the outside trim. A vinyl coating over aluminum windows is a very good idea, since it adds to the insulation value of the window and reduces the amount of water condensation on the inside during the winter. Double-pane windows and windows with self-storing storms are especially desirable because they decrease heat loss through the window areas of your home.

INSTALLING STORM WINDOWS

Adding a second pane of glass to a window can reduce the heat loss through the window by 50—75%, as was shown in Fig. 2-11. The dead air space between the two panes raises the insulation value of the window making the insulation value greater than that of just two panes. Recent cost figures show that a storm window will pay for itself in only two or three years, so a storm window is definitely a good investment. When adding a storm window over an existing window in your home, be sure to caulk around the storm window to form an airtight seal. Do not, however, seal off the tiny drain or *weep* holes at the bottom of the storm window, since these prevent water from collecting and rotting the window frame and also keep the windows from steaming up.

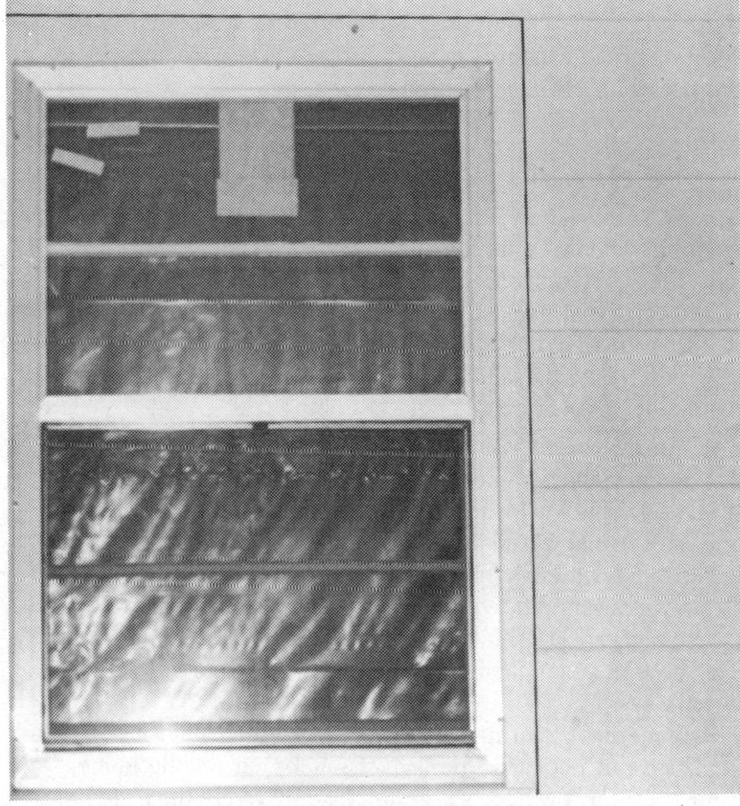

Fig. 6-8. Storm windows are easy to install—a screwdriver and screws will attach most of them to the window casing or blind stop. Storm windows add significant insulating qualities to the window area. They are available in different styles and sizes, and they can be purchased in single-pane or double-pane models. (The reflections on this storm window are caused by its protective plastic wrapping). The weep hole, shown enlarged, should never be caulked shut because it is needed to prevent the windown from fogging up and to let condensation drain out.

Two materials are commonly used for storm window assemblies: wood and aluminum. Aluminum is the most popular, since wooden storm windows do not ordinarily allow the window to be raised and lowered. Wooden storms are installed on the window frame in the fall and removed in the spring. When a wooden storm is removed, a screen is usually put in its place. Most wooden storm windows are found on older houses.

Aluminum storm windows can be mounted to the blind stop or window casting on the outside of the window (Fig. 6-8). Aluminum storm windows are permanent installations, and they can be raised and lowered easily. They usually consist of three movable sections: two with clear panes and one with a screen. All three sections of the window can be quickly removed from the inside of the house for cleaning or repair.

Aluminum storm windows cna be purchased at most building supply stores. You should make sure that the parts of the window work smoothly and fit snugly when you purchase them. Storm windows are easy to install, since they attach with screws to the existing window casing or blind stop. If a supply store does not have the size you need, the windows can be custom made to fit the windows in your house. When taking measurements, be sure you measure the right dimensions. These storm windows are designed to fit either over the outside window casing or recessed against the blind stop; measure your windows both ways.

Storm windows should be caulked at all seams where the aluminum window frame contacts the window casing or blind stop (Fig. 6-9). This will insure a tight seal and a dead air space between the inner window and the storm window. Usually there will be a wider aluminum strip at the bottom of the window to make the storm window fit different length casings; when the storm window is fastened in place, move this strip so it will firmly contact the sill. The bottom seam should be caulked everywhere except at the drain holes.

Sometimes storm windows are installed on windows that crank or roll out. This is fairly common on mobile homes and campers. Storm windows are then installed from the inside of the home and are held in place with clips or some other type of holder (Fig. 6-10).

When a storm window is added to a house that is to have an outside brick facing, the brick facing will have to be installed so that it comes to the edge of the storm window (Fig. 6-11). First install the wall boxing. Then when the bricks are added, caulk the seam where the bricks touch the window assembly.

Some window assemblies are now available with both the inner windows and storm windows made together as one unit. These are becoming more popular in the construction of new homes. They are installed by putting the entire window assembly, inner window and storm window, in the window frame of the

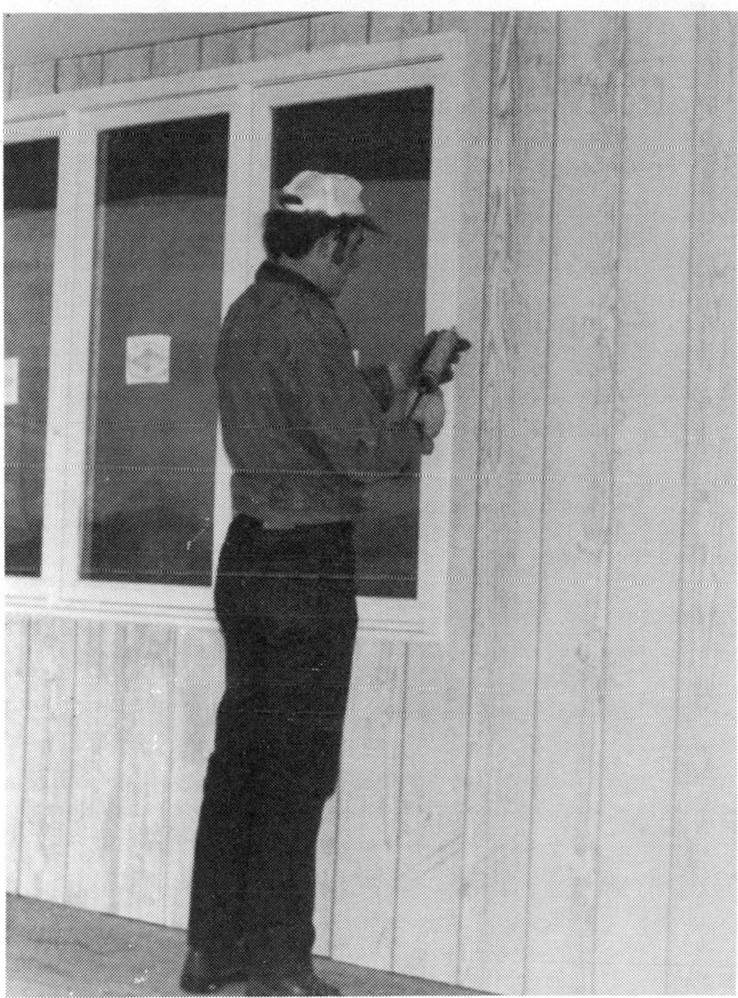

Fig. 6-9. These storms windows are being caulked along the outside trim. The caulking prevents cold air from blowing around the cracks in the trim and going into the house. When caulking, be sure to fill the seam with a smooth bead of caulking compound, since thin layers tend to crack as they age. Use a good grade of exterior caulking that will remain flexible during hot and cold weather.

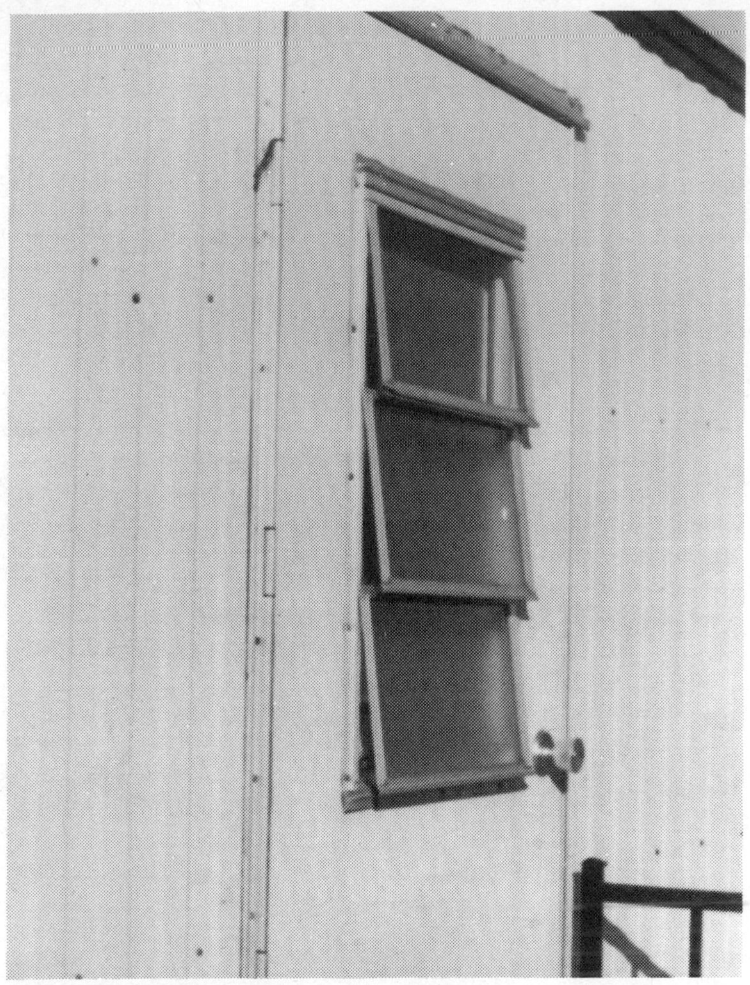

Fig. 6-10. Since the window on this mobile home cranks out, the storm window is installed on the inside with clips holding it in place. During warm weather, the storm window has to be removed to provide air circulation.

unfinished house. These units normally have a considerable amount of weather stripping and insulation built into the assembly to reduce heat flow to the outside.

OTHER WINDOW TRICKS

Weather stripping and storm windows can provide a big return on your investment of time and money, but there are other tricks you can use too. For example, a double-pane window can cut your heating load quit a bit in the winter, but its effect on the summer cooling load is much less because of solar heat radiation through the glass. To combat the summer heat, you can take other steps to cut energy costs.

Special heat reflecting glass is available at many building supply stores that will reduce the solar load through your windows

Fig. 6-11. Storm windows can also be added to brick homes or homes with brick facing. The job is usually much easier, however, if the storm windows are already in place when the brick is laid. If you are considerng having brick facing installed on your home, try to have the storm windows installed first. If you already have storm windows, they should be caulked before laying the brick.

Fig. 6-12. Window awnings can be very effective in reducing the summer heat gain, especially for windows facing the east and west. Awnings on windows can reduce the heat gain through the windows by as much as 75%.

by about 25%. Heat-absorbing double-pane windows can thus reduce the solar load through a window by as much as 50%. Some commercially applied coatings work in much the same way by tinting the glass—similar to the tinted glass on cars having factory-installed conditioning.

Window awnings are one of the simplest and least expensive additions that you can make to cut down on solar heat (Fig. 6-12). Awnings are even better than tinted glass in reducing heat gain through your window by about 75%. They are especially effective on windows facing the east and west, where direct sunlight is worst. Ventilated awnings that have slats or holes for air circulation are best. If you wanted to get the most benefit from the sun's heat, you could put up window awnings in the summer to cut out direct sunlight and take the awnings down in the winter to allow sunlight to enter the house. Not many people would go to this effort, but the winter sunlight would add to the heat in the house and reduce the winter heat load.

Roller shades, draperies, and venetian blinds are effective and very versatile for reducing the solar gain of a window. Draperies and venetian blinds can reduce the solar gain by 40-50%. Roller shades will reduce the solar gain by 25-30%.

Drapes shouls be open during the day in the winter and closed during the night. This allows the sun's rays to warm the house during the day, and when the drapes are closed at night, they insulate the window area from the cooler outside air. The closed drapes also stop radiation of the inside heat to the outside. Insulated draperies are particularly effective at reducing heat loss and heat gain in your home.

INSULATING AND WEATHER-STRIPPING DOORS

Some doors have weather stripping installed on them when they are purchased; others are constructed so that installing weather stripping is an easy job. Many older doors, however, either never had weather stripping or the original weather stripping has worn out with years of use. Weather-stripping doors, like weather-stripping windows, can greatly reduce the infilitration air that enters the house.

When a new door is being installed in a house, insulation should·be placed between the door frame and the rough opening (Fig. 6-13). The door frame is the wooden frame that the door fits into. The rough opening is the opening left in the wall for the door when the house is built. Insulating the space between the door frame and the rought opening helps prevent outside air from enter-

Fig. 6-13. When the door facing on the inside door is installed, the spaces between the door jamb and the rough opening should be filled with insulation. Strips of fiberglass batting can be cut and shoved in the cracks to do the job. The inside trim is nailed in after the insulation is added and the inside wall is put up.

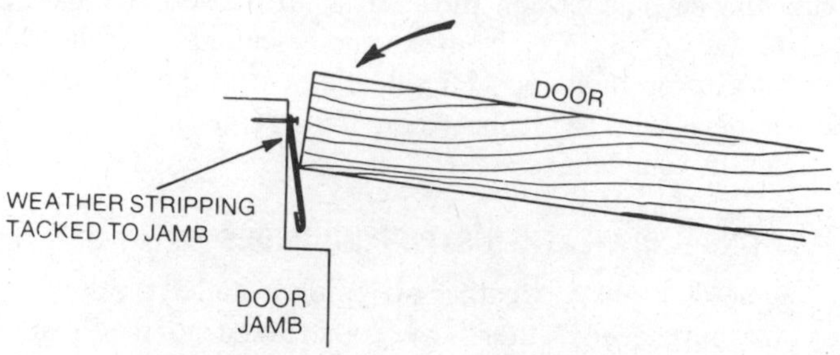

Fig. 6-14. The metal strip is tacked to the door jamb. As the door closes, it applies pressure to the strip and help seals out the air.

ing around the door, and it provides extra insulation to stop the loss of heat around the door. After the insulation has been installed, the inside door trim is added.

Many door frames have grooves for installing weather stripping on the door jambs. But if grooves are not provided on your door frame or door jamb, you can easily add weather stripping to the door jamb as shown in Fig. 6-14. This weather stripping is the same as used for windows, and the same techniques are used for installation. A metal strip, purchased at hardware stores or building suppliers in rolls or precut lengths, is tacked to the door jamb. The spring action of the weather stripping seals the door to cut off wind. When this weather stripping is installed, the open side of the strip should face the outside to permit the door to close. The door must fit tightly to seal the opening and shut out the wind, but the addition of the weather stripping may not allow the door to close properly. In this case, the edge of the door can be planed to give enough clearance.

A small groove is cut in the door frame (as shown in Fig. 6-15) to install another type of metal weather stripping. The weather stripping is simply pushed into the groove where it holds itself in place. The spring tension of the strip seals the crack when the door closes.

Another type of weather stripping comes mounted on strips of wood or aluminum that are attached to the outside of the door jamb (Fig. 6-16). A felt or vinyl weather stripping is attached to these mounting strips so that the door presses and seals against the weather stripping as it closes. Some care is required in installing these strips. If the weather strip is installed too tightly, the door may not close. If the strip is too loose, the door will not seal. On the

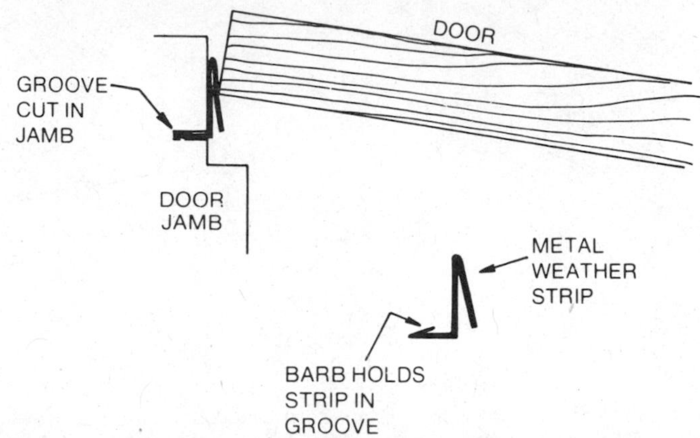

Fig. 6-15. Some door frames are made with a groove cut in them for easy installation of weather stripping material. The weather stripping is pushed into the groove to seal out the air when the door closes.

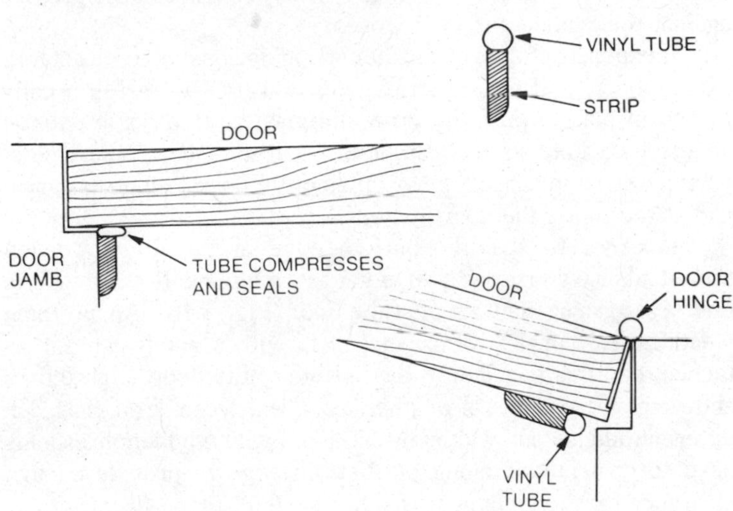

Fig. 6-16. This type of weather seal attaches to the outside part of the jamb, facing toward the door as it closes. An alternate way to install the stripping on the hinge-side of the door is also illustrated. The vinyl tubing compresses and seals against the door as the door is closed. The tubing comes attached to wood or metal strips that are screwed or nailed in place The best way to install this type of weather stripping is to close the door completely; set the weather strip in place against the jamb; push the strip forward until the tubing compresses about half way; then nail or screw in place. Weather strips of this type also come with felt stripping attached, and the are installed in the same way.

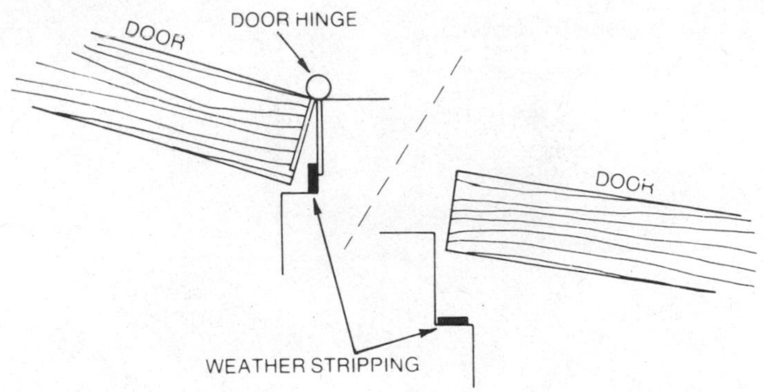

Fig. 6-17. Rolls of felt, foam or plastic strips can be tacked or stuck in place along the door stops of the jamb. As the door closes, the weather stripping is squeezed between the door and the stops, sealing off air flow.

hinge side of the door, in particular, the door may scrape and tear the weather stripping as it closes. A cure for this last problem is to install the hinge-side strip on the door itself so that it presses against the jamb as the door closes.

Inexpensive forms of weather stripping consist of rolls of felt, foam rubber, and plastic strips (Fig. 6-17). The felt is usually tacked in place, while the foam and plastic often come with an adhesive backing so they can be pressed in place. Some type of weather stripping should be installed on all doors, along each side and at the top of the door frame.

In order to seal the bottom edge of the door, wooden thresholds have given way to metal assemblies with vinyl inserts that seal against the bottom of the door (Fig. 6-18). An alternate weather seal consists of a metal strip with a vinyl material attached, and this is added to the bottom of the door. Figure 6-19 shows these two types of weather seals, which can be purchased in different heights and widths. Most doors with wooden thresholds have to be trimmed along the bottom edge to provide enough clearance for the aluminum weather seals to fit.

STORM DOORS

Both wooden doors and aluminum doors can be used as storm doors, though aluminum doors are much more popular on new homes because they are light and easy to install. Aluminum storm doors can be bought in many different designs and colors for any installation (Figs. 6-20 and 6-21). Storm doors, both wooden and

Fig. 6-18. This metal and vinyl threshold replaces older wooden thresholds. Proper installation requires that the vinyl insert press against the bottom of the door when it is closed. When installing this type of threshold, stuff fiberglass batting underneath it to prevent air currents from entering the house from under the threshold. Some thresholds include rubber sealing strips on the bottom side to make a weather seal, but not all thresholds have this feature.

aluminum, can be custom made to fit any opening. Some aluminum storm doors have two panes of glass and a section of screen in the door, the same as in a storm window; the lower glass section may be raised and lowered to allow more or less air to enter through the screen.

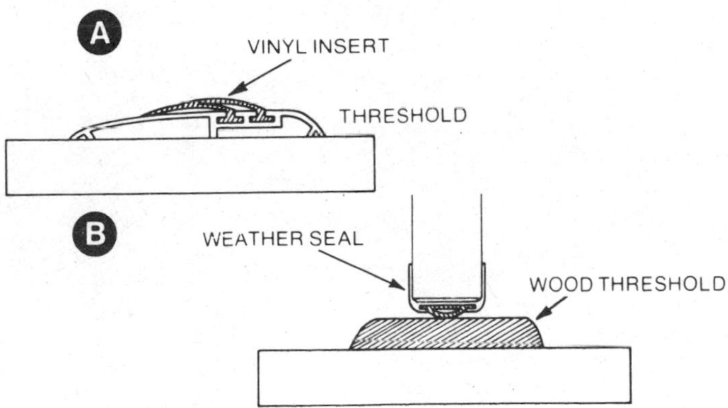

Fig. 6-19. The bottom of the door can be sealed using two different methods. In (A) an aluminum threshold with vinyl insert is used to replace the older wooden threshold; if necessary, a shim can be used to raise the aluminum threshold so that it firmly contacts the bottom edge of the door. In (B) a similar aluminum and vinyl seal is added to the bottom edge of the door where it seals against the usual type of threshold.

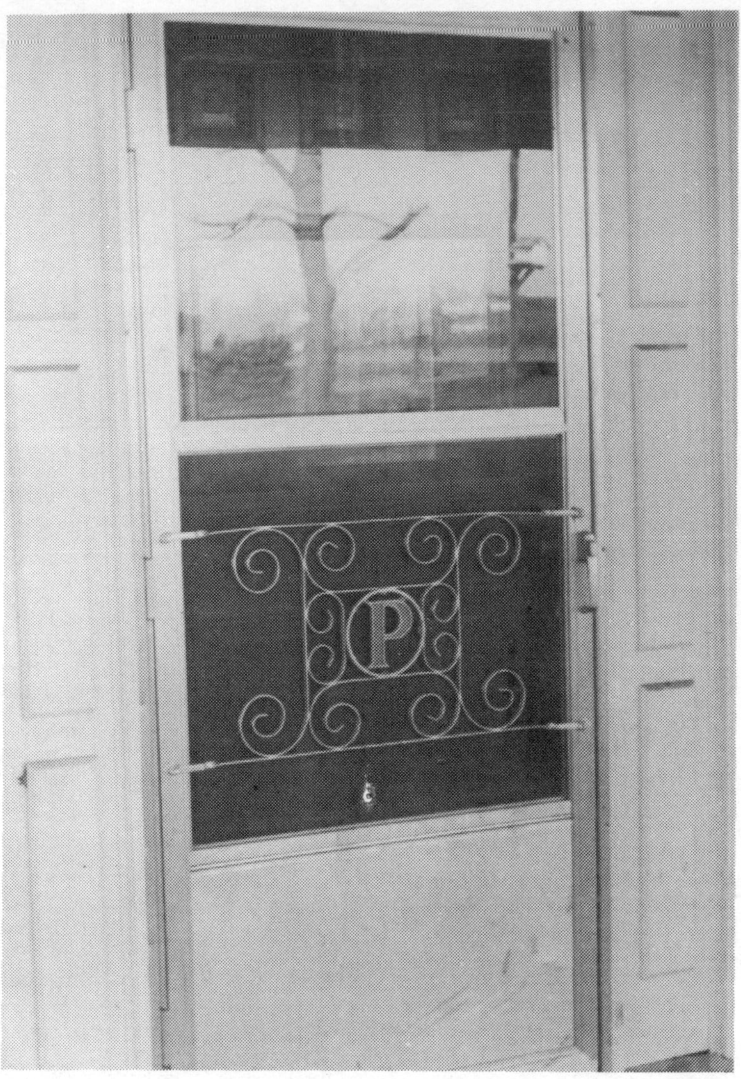

Fig. 6-20. Aluminum storm doors having a natural metal finish are not very expensive. Standard sizes are available to fit most door widths, and there are left-hand and right-hand versions. A special bottom panel can be removed to permit the storm door to be shortened if necessary; the panel is then replaced to cover the cutting marks. The storm windows can be replaced with screens during the summer.

An aluminum door is purchased with a frame that fits either to the door casing or to the door jamb. The aluminum door frame is screwed into the casing or jamb. Care must be taken to get the door frame perfectly square and plumb; if it is not, the door wil not close into the frame.

When installing the door, temporarily put two or three nails through the screw holes at the top of the aluminum frame to hold the storm door in position until it can be plumbed. Start by driving a small nail in the top of the frame on one side; then adjust the other side until the door is square and plumb. When you have lined up the frame, drive another nail in the other top corner to hold the door in the proper position. Finally, put screws along the remaining holes in the door frame and remove the nails.

The cahin, spring, and closer are installed to complete the door, as shown in Fig. 6-22. The strip at the bottom of the door can be adjusted to fit to the door sill and help shut out infiltration air. Some storm doors have an additional vinyl strip on the bottom of the door to help keep the air out. Caulk any seams around the door frame to reduce air flow.

Wooden storm doors (Fig. 6-23) are not used much any more on new houses, although they can still be purchased at hardware stores and building suppliers. Their main disadvantage is that they do not have self-storing screens like many aluminum doors have. Instead, wooden storm doors have removable screen and glass sections that must be changed with the seasons (Fig. 6-24). They are not as versatile for modern homes because if the screen is put in the door in the summer, any insulating value the storm door has is lost, adding to the summer cooling load. But if the glass is left in the

Fig. 6-21. Decorative storm doors are available in many colors and styles to add a touch of elegance to your home.

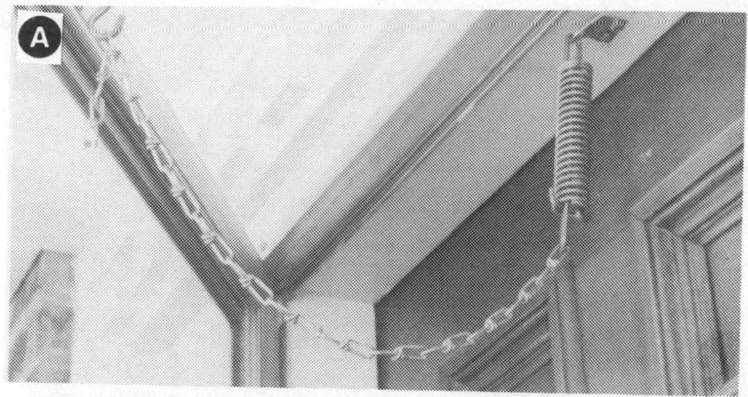

Fig. 6-22. The last steps to installing a storm door. (A) Attaching the chain and spring at the top. (B) Attaching the door closer. (C) Adjusting the weather strip to seal the bottom edge of the door.

door in moderate summer weather, the homeowner cannot get a breeze through the door to help cool his house without air conditioning.

Fig. 6-23. The wooden storm door is found mostly on older houses today, although it can still be purchased at most building suppliers. It has separate screen and glass panel inserts that are changed with the seasons.

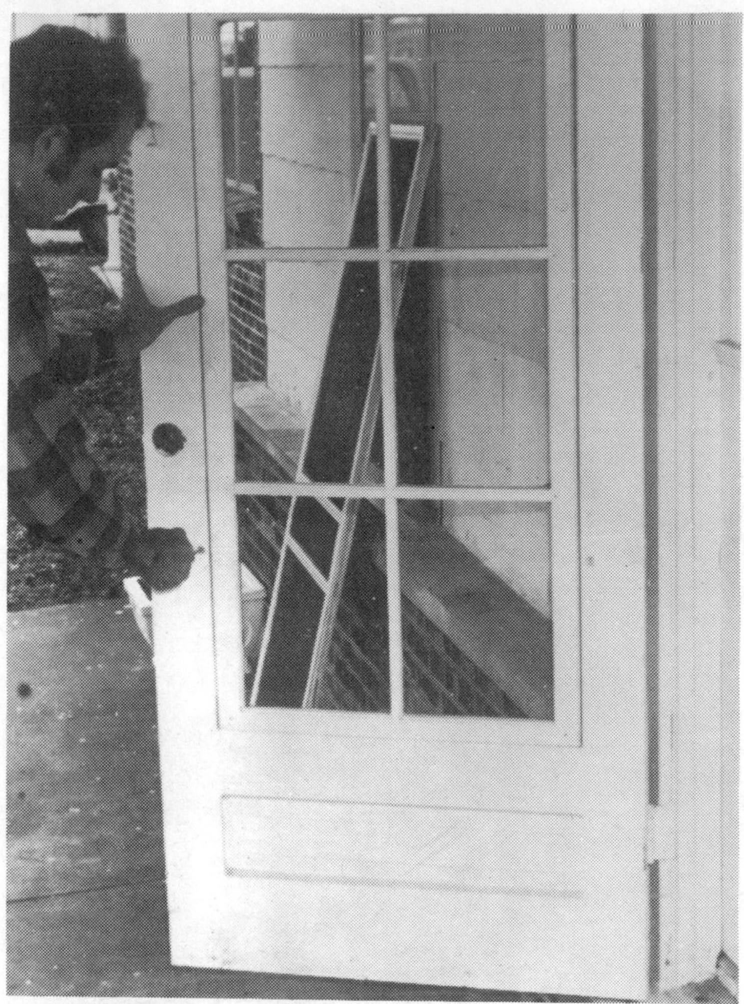

Fig. 6-24. The wooden storm door has two separate panels, a screen panel and a window panel. Here the homeowner is removing the window panel in the spring. The screen panel that will replace it is leaning against the house in the background.

Wooden storm doors are more difficult to install than the aluminum doors because they have hinges and latches that must be installed and the stops for the door must be attached to the door casing. An aluminum door frame has its own stops, latches, and weather stripping built into the frame. Hence, the wooden door must be installed to fit snugly and it must be weather stripped.

CAULKING MATERIALS

Several different types of caulking compounds are sold in hardware and building supply stores. Some compounds will last for years; others will last only a year or two before they will have to be replaced. Some of the better compounds have a synthetic rubber base. These caulking compounds are soft, can be applied with a caulking gun, can be painted over, and will last five or more years.

Silicone caulking compounds are generally used for caulking around showers and bathtubs; they are too expensive for exterior applications on doors and windows. This is a superior compound that is thoroughly waterproof and will remain flexible for many, many years. It is now available in colors that match bathtub and tile colors. However, its flexibility and ability to repel water make it nearly impossible to paint over.

Butyl rubber and latex caulking compounds are good for exterior applications, since they are made to stand up to extreme temperatures. Some latex compounds, however, are better suited for interior use, so read the instructions carefully. These exterior caulking compounds are usually white and dry to provide a moderately hard surface, but they remain somewhat pliable to resist cracking and peeling. They are easily painted over, which is a

Fig. 6-25. Caulking comes in tubes that are inserted in a caulking gun. Squeezing the handle on the gun forces the caulking compound from the tube, making it easy to apply the caulking around windows and doors. A wide variety of caulking, sealers, adhesives, masonry cements, spackling and other patching compounds are available in tube form for use with these guns.

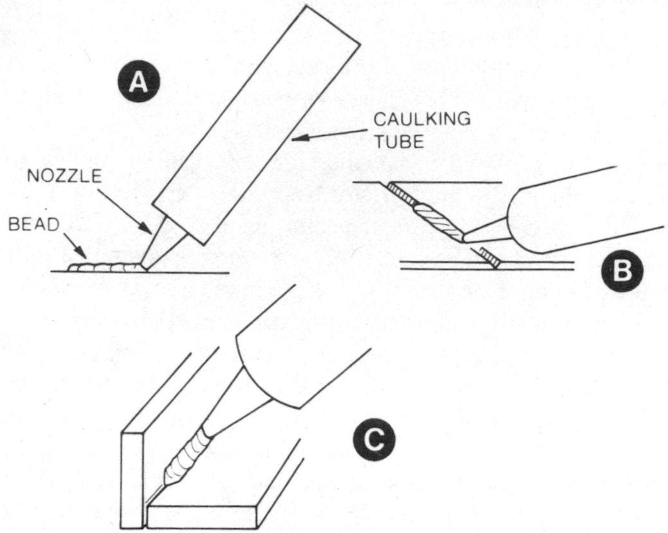

Fig. 6-26. Controlling the flow of caulk is the secret to doing a good caulking job. (A) A rounded bead is not very useful when caulking. (B) A flat bead is good for filling notches and grooves so the surface remains flat. (C) A slightly rounded bead is best for caulking corners around windows and doors.

desirable feature. Some varieties of these caulking compounds are specially colored to match aluminum siding, though you may have to purchase them through an aluminum siding contractor or supplier.

Cheaper caulking compounds are also available, and these fill a variety of needs in interior caulking applications where cracks and small holes must be filled. In most cases, these are putty-like substances for use with wallboard and woodwork. When used in more severe locations outdoors, they have a tendency to dry out and flake off after a couple of years.

Most caulking compounds are available in tubes for use with a caulking gun (Fig. 6-25). This makes the caulking easy to apply and smooth out. When applying the caulking in cracks and seams, it is essential that the caulking compound not be spread too thinly, since this encourages it to crack and pull loose. The tip of the caulking tube can be cut to let the caulk squeeze out in a round bead, a flattened bead, or anything in between (Fig. 6-26).

There are also string-like caulking materials that come in rolls. These are made to be pressed into cracks by hand. The caulk contains fibers that help it to maintain its shape and also permit it to be quickly removed by pulling it loose. You can use this type of caulking material around the seams of windows removed during the summer, treating it as a temporary sealer.

Masking tape and furnace tape can also be used to seal cracks temporarily. The adhesives on these tapes are not always easy to remove, however, and they have a tendency to pull the paint loose. Furnace tape is the most durable tape for sealing jobs, since it is made with a fabric material and an adhesive that withstands wide variations in temperature. Masking tape and most other tapes usually dry out in hot weather, making them harder to remove. Some tapes are also affected by moisture and soon work loose from surfaces that collect water.

7 Heating Systems and Routine Maintenance

Unless your heating system is operating at maximum efficiency, you are losing money. Any time a furnace is out of adjustment or the air circulation is restricted, the heating efficiency is reduced and the operating cost is increased. Once you understand how a heating system works, you will be able to correct and even anticipate common problems that affect its efficiency. Most of the time, all it takes is a little routine maintenance to keep your system operating near peak efficiency. But even if the job becomes more complicated, you can still follow the guidelines presented in the next chapter to tune up your furnace the way most repairmen would. In any event, if you can at least recognize when something is wrong with your heating system, you will know when to call in a repairman to fix it, and that is bound to save you money in the long run.

FURNACE EFFICIENCY

There are several different types of fuel used in heating systems. Table 7-1 shows the efficiencies of several of the most popular heat sources. The efficiency of a heating system is based on the amount of heat energy that actually goes into the living area, which is compared to the total amount of heat generated inside the furnace. Clearnly, not all the heat generated goes into the living area—some of it goes up the flue and some of it is lost in the ductwork as the heat passes through unheated parts of the house. The advantage to electric heating, of course, is that no flue is

Table 7-1. Heating System Efficiency.

HEAT SOURCE	EFFICIENCY
wood furnace or stove	30–50%
coal furnace	30–60%
natural gas furnace	75–80%
propane furnace	75–80%
butane furnace	75–80%
oil furnace	75–80%
electric furnace	90–100%
electric baseboard	95–100%

needed, since there are not exhaust gases due to combustion. Electric baseboard heaters, for example, have an efficiency approaching 100% because practically all of the heat generated inside them is delivered to the area being heated.

FUEL FURNACES

Fuel furnaces must have flues to expel the combustion fumes. Since these exhaust gases are hot, they carry away considerable amounts of heat energy. Wood-burning units, such as wood furnaces and wood stoves, have the lowest efficiency rating—as much as 70% of the heat produced from the burning wood is wasted as it goes up the flue (Fig. 7-1). Coal furnaces are almost as bad.

Since a large percentage of heat energy is lost up the flue, it makes sense that the damper that controls the flue has a lot to do with the efficiency of the heating system. Ideally, a fuel-burning furnace needs only enough air to assure that all of the fuel is cleanly burnt. Not enough air will prevent the fuel from burning completely, producing soot and dangerous carbon-monoxide fumes. Too much air, on the other hand, only serves to cool the combustion temperatures and carry away more heat up the flue. Hand-fed heating systems are therefore very inefficient because the damper setting must also be controlled by hand; so there is a lot of room for error in managing the fire. A hand-fed and hand-operated wood stove or coal furnace has an efficiency of about 30%. But if an automatic feeder and automatic damper are added, the efficiency of these units can be increased to about 50%.

Natural gas, propane, butane, and oil furnaces have much higher efficiency ratings, hovering around 70%. When the gross input BTU and net output BTU ratings are computed for these furnaces, manufacturers sometimes use a figure of 80%, though this is meant to be a ballpark figure rather than an actual rating. For example, if the gross input BTU to a furnace is listed as 100,000 BTU, you would expect to see the net figure given as 80,000 BTU.

But in practice, you could achieve a slightly higher net heating capacity with a finely tuned furnace—and a lot lower output with a poorly tuned one! So the figures given on the nameplate of the furnace are not entirely trustworthy.

The higher efficiencies of gas and oil furnaces are due primarily to their construction. In the first place, the amount of fuel fed into the furnace is carefully and automatically controlled, and when properly adjusted there is little room for human error. The heat exchanger in such furnaces is also constructed to extract the maximum amount of heat energy from the hot gases produced as the fuel burns. And finally, the air flow through the combustion of the fuel. However, if the furnace is not properly adjusted and cleaned for maximum heat transfer, you cannot expect to obtain good heating efficiency.

If the air flow to the burner of a gas or oil furnace is not correct, the efficiency of these furnaces can drop to less than 50%. The flame of a gas furnace should have a bright blue color next to the burner where it comes out. Check the flame at the burner—if it is yellowish in color, the air flow could be adjusted too low or it may be that the gas pressure is too high; if the flame is erratic or jumps off the burner, the air flow may be adjusted too high or the gas pressure may be incorrect. When the adjustments are not correct on an oil-burning furnace, the flame smokes, causing problems with smut build-up in the flue or chimney. Step-by-step instructions for making these adjustments are given in the next chapter.

Air flow through the heat exchanger in a furnace is also quite important. In general, you cannot expect your furnace to deliver its rated heat energy to your house unless the ductowrk and furnace fan are able to provide the correct air flow. If the heating ducts or cold air returns are too small, the furnace will never be able to deliver its rated heat capacity. A safety thermostat on the heat duct leaving the furnace prevents the air temperature from exceeding safe levels. If the temperature rises too high, the high-temperature-limit thermostat turns off the burners until the air temperature drops to a safe level again. If the burners on your furnace turn on and off even though the room thermostat in your house is demanding more heat, that means the limit thermostat is operating, and this in turn indicates that there is probably not enough air flow through the ductwork. It is always best to have a reputable company or dealer install your furnace and ductwork or you may be wasting money later on your heating bills. It might also be a good idea for you to learn to size your own duct systems and

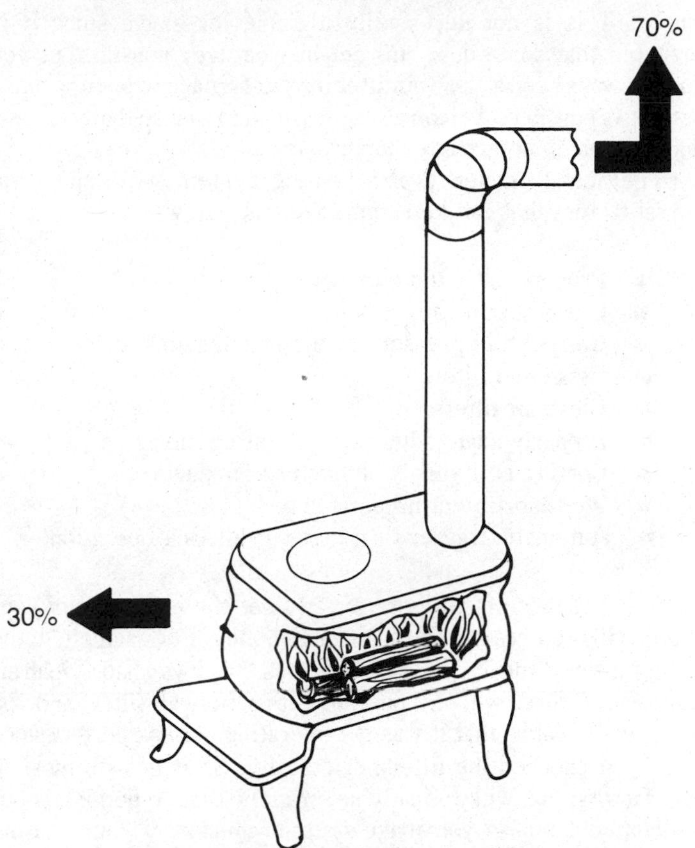

Fig. 7-1. A hand-fed wood stove is one of the most inefficient of all heating systems. As much as 70% of the heat produced in the stove leaves the house through the flue and is wasted. Home fireplaces normally have even worse efficiencies, but they can be constructed to retain more heat energy and deliver it into the living space of the home. Gas and fuel furnaces are rated at 80% efficiency, at least if you look at the BTU capacities given on their nameplates, but you can get more or less efficiency. Electric baseboard heaters approach 100% efficiency because they do not have a flue to let heat energy escape.

furnaces, particularly if you plan to save money by installing part of the system yourself.

Every forced-air furnace has air filters in the cold air intake to prevent dust particles from collecting in the furnace and ductwork. If dust collects in the burner box, it not only decreases heat conduction to the air, it also poses a fire hazard because it might ignite and burn. If you smell scorched air from the heat registers, it is likely that some dust has gotten into the burner box of your furnace. This is not necessarily a cause for alarm since it is inevitable that some dust will get in whatever you do, but you should always keep a clean air filter in your furnace to keep as much dust out as possible. A clean air filter will also assure that you have maximum air flow through your furnace.

The actual efficiency of a heating system will depend on several factors that can be summarized as follows:

- Properly adjusted burners
- Clean nozzles and jets
- Correct fuel pressure at the nozzles and jets
- Clean fuel filters
- Clean air filters
- Properly adjusted nozzle and jet openings
- Correct size supply and return air ducts
- Well lubricated furnace blower
- Automatic (rather than manual) furnace operation

If any of these factors are out of line, the efficiency of your system will drop, wasting both fuel and money. For example, if the air filter is dirty, the efficiency will be less than if you had a clean air filter. Your furnace will still operate with a dirty air filter, and you might never realize that it was not operating at peak performance unless you checked the filter periodically. So it is with most of these factors; you will probably never know that something is out of adjustment unless you make routine checks on your heating system. Of course, if you let things go too long, your furnace might stop working altotether! Just think of your heating system as you would your car—routine maintenance is essential to keeping everything working efficiently.

The heat energy escaping through the flue in a fuel furnace has fascinated people for a long time. Perhaps the thought of wasting all that energy has encouraged them to devise schemes for recovering at least part of the escaping heat energy. Although most of the schemes are impractical for most homewoners (if indeed they work at all), here is one suggestion that is fairly easy to use: The flue pipe is hot because of the exhaust gases, so it can be used to give off heat into the surrounding air. If local ordinances permit, you can route the flue pipe through nearby unheated spaces such as garages, attics, attached sheds, and even greenhouses (Fig. 7-2). This idea will not work in every home, of course, but it is well worth mentioning because it will work in many.

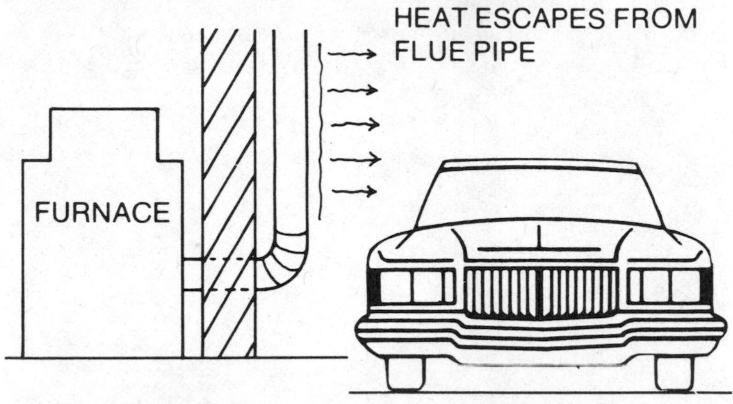

Fig. 7-2. If you are heating your garage, you might save some heat if the flue pipe were run through the garage. In a gas, butane or oil furnace, about 20% of the heat produced in the heat chamber is lost, mostly up the flue. But if the flue pipe is run through a garage or work area before it goes to the outside of the house, some of the heat in the flue can be used to warm the surrounding air. You might get enough heat from the flue that you would be able to close off the furnace duct to the garage area. There are limits to how far you can reroute the flue pipe, however, and most building codes restrict you from ever running a flue pipe downwards; since hot exhaust fumes naturally move upwards, you would not want the fumes to go back into your house.

ELECTRIC FURNACES

Electric furnaces resemble fuel furnaces but differ in that no combustion takes place. As a result, there are no burner adjustments to make and no flue pipe to waste heat. An electric furnace, therefore, requires little maintenance to keep the unit operating at maximum efficiency, which is around 90—100%.

Electric furnaces still have much in common with fuel furnaces when it comes to the ductwork and blower that circulates the heated air through out the house. For this reason, most of what has been said about the size of the ducts, clean air filters, and routine maintenance also applies to electric furnaces.

Because of the relatively high cost of electricity as compared to other fuels, the efficiency of your electric furnace system is of paramount concern. Heat losses cannot be tolerated, and every step must be taken to thoroughly insulate and seal your home. Most of the heat loss occurs in the duct system, so it is important to properly insulate and seal ducts passing through garage areas and open crawl spaces (Fig. 7-3). Most all-electric homes are built with

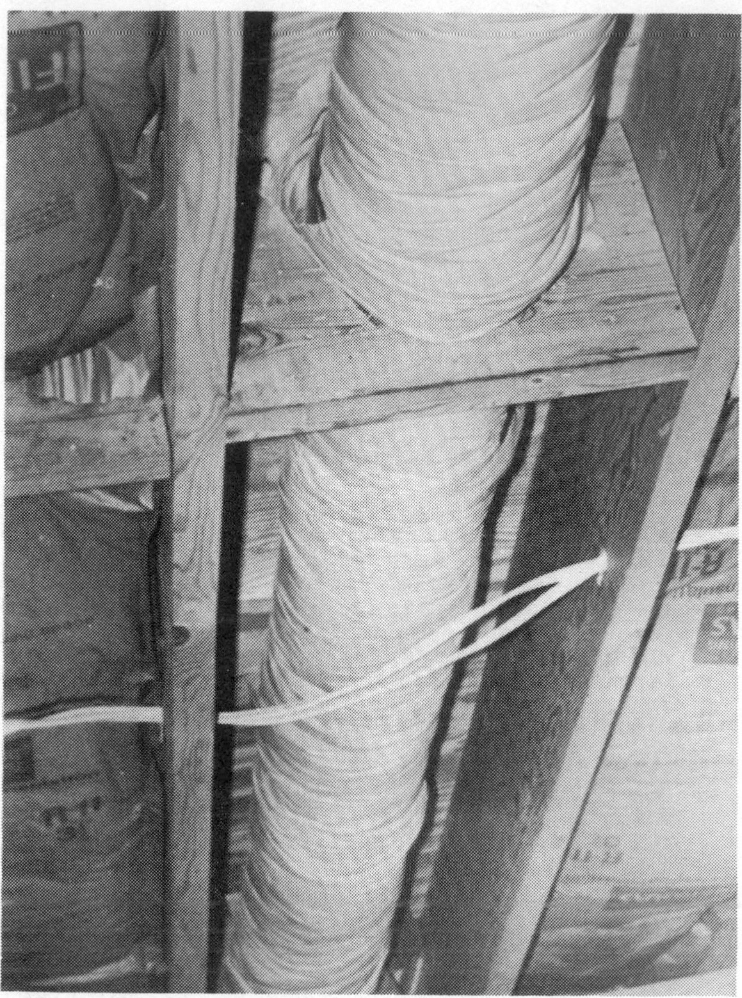

Fig. 7-3. Insulating the duct system will keep some of the heat in the ducts from being lost into the attic or crawl space air. Insulating a duct system can make the efficiency of an electric furnace approach 100%.

considerably more insulation than other homes to offset the higher cost of electricity, so adding more insulation to your house is usually a good idea.

ELECTRIC BASEBOARD HEATERS

An electric baseboard heater may operate at nearly 100% efficiency, since there are no fans and no duct system to waste heat. This assumes, however, that the unit is wired properly and is perfectly clean. The efficiency of a baseboard heater will be reduced if the heating element gets dirty. Dirt, dust, and lint collecting on the heater can reduce the transfer of heat that should go into the room. Baseboard heaters should be cleaned with a vacuum cleaner at least once a year to avoid this problem (Fig. 7-4).

If the heater does not get the right amount of electric current, as when there is a voltage drop in the lines or if it is wired on a 120V circuit when it requires a 240V circuit, the heating capacity of a baseboard heater will be greatly reduced. In fact, if a 240V heater is wired on a 120V circuit, you will get less than 35% of the rated heat from the unit—it may get warm, but not warm enough to heat a room properly.

HEAT PUMPS

A heat pump is the most efficient type of mechanical heating system. A heat pump does not have to burn fuel to produce heat, and it does not have to waste electrical energy by running it

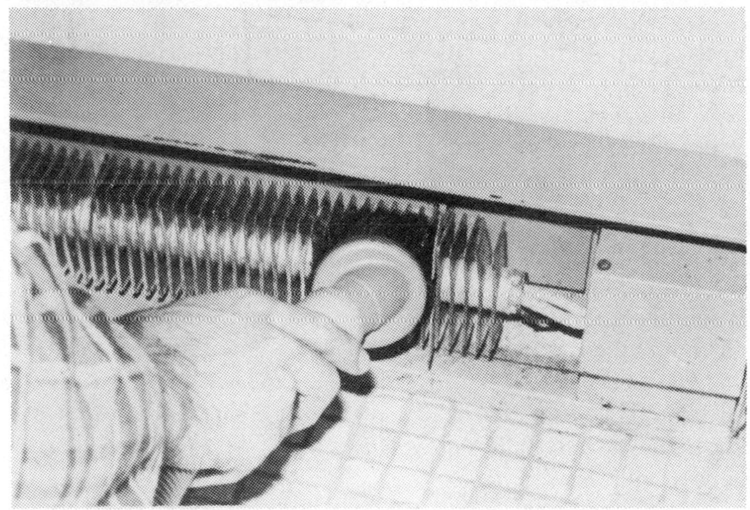

Fig. 7-4. Vacuum the heating element of a baseboard heater at least once a year to remove dirt and lint. This will keep the baseboard heater operating as it should, circulating an adequate amount of heated air through the room. An internal thermostat limits the maximum temperature of the heating element to a safe value that will not ignite dust particles, so restricting the air flow over the heating element causes it to heat up more and eventually turn itself off. In addition, if the heating element operates at higher than normal temperatures, more heat energy is lost through the wall it is attached to, thus lowering its heating efficiency.

through a resistive wire element to produce heat. The heat pump only requires enough electricity to run a compressor motor, which takes the heat out of the air on the outside of the house and deposits this heat inside the house.

The heat pump is actually a kind of refrigeration or air-conditioning system that can work in reverse, In the summer, the heat pump cools your house in the usual manner, removing heat from within the house and depositing it outside. In the winter, the heat pump works in reverse, removing heat from the outside and depositing it inside.

The efficiency of a heat pump is measured in terms of how much easier it is to *pump* heat energy than to *generate* it by conventional means, as in electric baseboard heaters. When used to heat your house, the efficiency of a heat pump depends primarily on how cold it is outside. As the temperature drops, the efficiency also drops. If it gets too cold outside, the heat pump automatically switches on an electric heating element, when it becomes easier and more economical to generate heat energy that way. Normally, though, as long as the outside temperature is above about 20°F, the heat pump can heat your house more cheaply than an electric furnace can. And as the outside temperature approaches the inside room temperature, the efficiency continues to climb dramatically.

Taken on a year-round basis, a heat pump can usually heat your house for only a third to half the cost of conventional electric heat. Heat pumps are discussed in detail in Chapter 12.

FUEL COSTS

We all know that there are different costs involved for each type of heat. When planning a house, you will want to know how much it will cost you to heat your house with each type of fuel. If you can find out that information, you can then make a rational decision about what type of furnace to install—or even if it will save you money to get a different type of furnace when your present one needs replacing.

All energy sources are bought in units, such as the gallon or the kilowatt-hour. But the cost per unit doesn't tell you what it actually costs to heat your house. To figure this out, you also need to know how much heat energy you can get from one unit of each energy source. That is, how many BTU are produced from each unit that you buy. This important information is given in Table 7-2.

By checking with your local fuel suppliers, you can find out the price of one unit of each type of fuel. A problem often encountered

Table 7-2. Common Fuels and Their Heat Energy Per Unit.

FUEL	UNIT	BTU PER UNIT
natural gas	cubic foot therm (100 cu ft)	1,000 100,000
propane butane	gallon gallon	90,000 130,000
No. 1 fuel oil No. 2 fuel oil	gallon gallon	136,000 140,000
electricity	killowatt-hour	3,413

Note: Propane and butane are gases that become liquids when they are pressurized, so they are sold by the gallon. Liquid petroleum gas (LPG) is a name commonly applied to both propane and butane, or even a blend of the two. In general, propane is used in the north while butane is used in the south.

here, though, is that many fuel suppliers use *graduated rates*—a system in which the cost varies with how much fuel you buy each month. In most cases, the companies give you quantity discounts, reducing the cost per unit as you buy more and more fuel. An exception to this general rule is the practice lately of many electric companies that penalize you for excessively high fuel consumption during the summer air-conditioning season. The best approach is to estimate your approximate fuel consumption for a typical winter heating month; then ask the fuel supplier what the cost would be so you can figure the average cost per unit.

Your fuel costs can then be found by using the following formula:

$$C = \frac{F \times E}{P}$$

where C = cost per BTU of heat energy, in BTU per dollar
F = BTU value of fuel
E = efficiency of your heating system, in percent
P = price of fuel, in cents per unit

To illustrate how this formula is used, let's consider a house with an electric furnace having an efficiency of 90%, and located in a city where the utility company charges 2.5 cents per kilowatt-hour. Putting these numbers into the formula, we get:

$$C = \frac{3413 \times 90}{2.5} = 122{,}868 \text{ BTU per dollar}$$

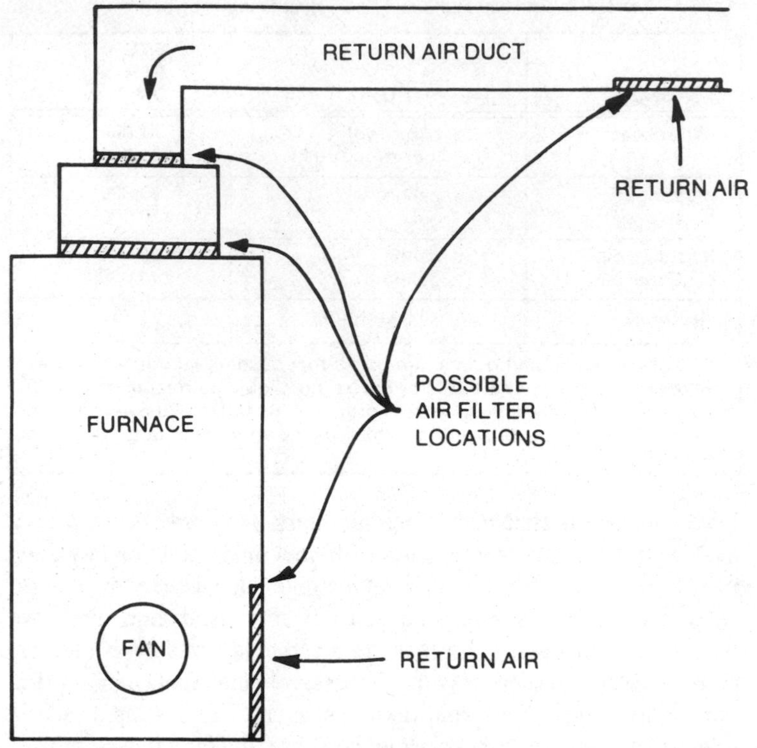

Fig. 7-5. The air filter may be found at any of several possible locations in a furnace. Usually it will be near where the cool return air enters the furnace. The filter is normally laid or slid edgewise into position. Some furnaces have a door or grill that must be removed to expose the filter.

As another example, let's consider a house with an oil furnace having an 80% efficiency and located in an area where No. 2 fuel oil costs 40 cents per gallon. In this case, the formula tells us that the cost is:

$$C = \frac{140{,}000 \times 80}{40}$$

$$= 280{,}000 \text{ BTU per dollar}$$

Of course, the fuel costs in these two examples do not tell you the whole story. You would also have to weigh the cost of installing the particular heating system and any additional insulation you might add to your house. Then too, there is the question as to what fuels are available in your area. So you can see there are actually many factors to consider.

CHANGING AND CLEANING FURNACE FILTERS

All central heating systems have filters. These filters all get dirty—that's their job! They take the dust and lint particles out of the circulating air so dirt does not clog up the working parts of the furnace. The air filter is usually located in the return air duct where the cool air enters the furnace to be heated. As the filter removes the dirt from the air, the filter itself becomes clogged and restricts the air flow, which cuts down on both the efficiency and capacity of the furnace. The efficiency is cut down because the slower moving air is not able to pick up all of the heat energy produced by the furnace, and what is not picked up is wasted as it goes up the flue. The heating capacity of the furnace is also reduced as the filter becomes clogged, since a full, unrestricted air flow through the furnace is needed to obtain the maximum rated output.

Air filters and cleaners fall into three general categories: disposable, washable, and electronic. The location of these filters in and around the furnace varies with the installation, but you will usually find some kind of filter compartment near the fan intake or some place around the return or cold air ducts leading to the furnace (Fig. 7-5).

Disposable Filters

Disposable filters (Fig. 7-6) come in a variety of sizes and can be located in a variety of places. Most often, though, these will be located in the fan compartment just before the return air goes into the fan. If the furnace does not have a separate return duct, there will be an opening in the furnace where such a duct could have been attached, and that will be where the air filter is located. In some furnace systems, the air filter has been moved to the other end of the return duct, where the cool air first enters, and this is often done for convenience when the furnace is located in a crawl space that is difficult to get into.

Disposable filters are ordinarily thrown away when they get dirty, but their life can be increased if you will dust or vacuum them periodically. When they are really dirty, they should never be washed with water or blown out with compessed air—just throw them away and buy new ones. The disposable filter is usually constructed with fiberglass material between two metal grills and housed in a cardboard frame.

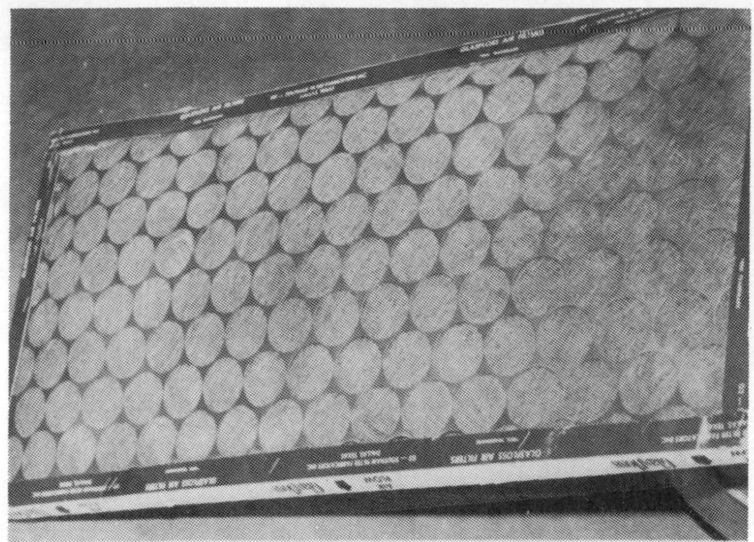

Fig. 7-6. Disposable air filters are made to be thrown away when they are dirty, but periodic dusting and cleaning can prolong their life. When you replace an air filter be sure to use the proper size, which is clearly marked on the sides of each filter. The filter should also be installed according to the indicated direction of air flow, since the rigidity of the filter and its filtering action depend on how it is installed. The fiberglass threads in the filter are often coated with a sticky substance to help trap dust particles.

After a filter has been in use for about a month or two, it will probably not be too dirty, but the furnace will still get more air flow if the filter is dusted out. This can be done every month or so, but some dirt will remain in the filter. After about four months of heavy use, the filter usually will accumulate enough permanent dirt that it should be replaced.

When cleaning the filter, be careful not to bend the filter or damage the cardboard. Take the filter out of the furnace and tap it upside down on a hard surface so the lint on the incoming side of the filter can fall out. Alternatively, you can gently clean it with your vacuum cleaner.

Replace the filter if it is torn or broken. The size should be easy to locate on the sides of the filter. Be sure to get a replacement filter that is the *same size* as the one removed. A one-inch-thick fiberglass filter must not be replaced with a two-inch filter—even if it will fit—because the thicker filter will restrict air flow into the furnace. This can cause the furnace to overheat, and it will reduce the efficiency of the furnace. Using the wrong size replacement just defeats what you are trying to accomplish—increasing the efficiency of the furnace. Normally, a filter should be replaced about three to four times a year under heavy use. You can go for as long as six months without replacing a disposable filter if you are conscientious about dusting the filter, and the air circulating in the house is reasonably clean.

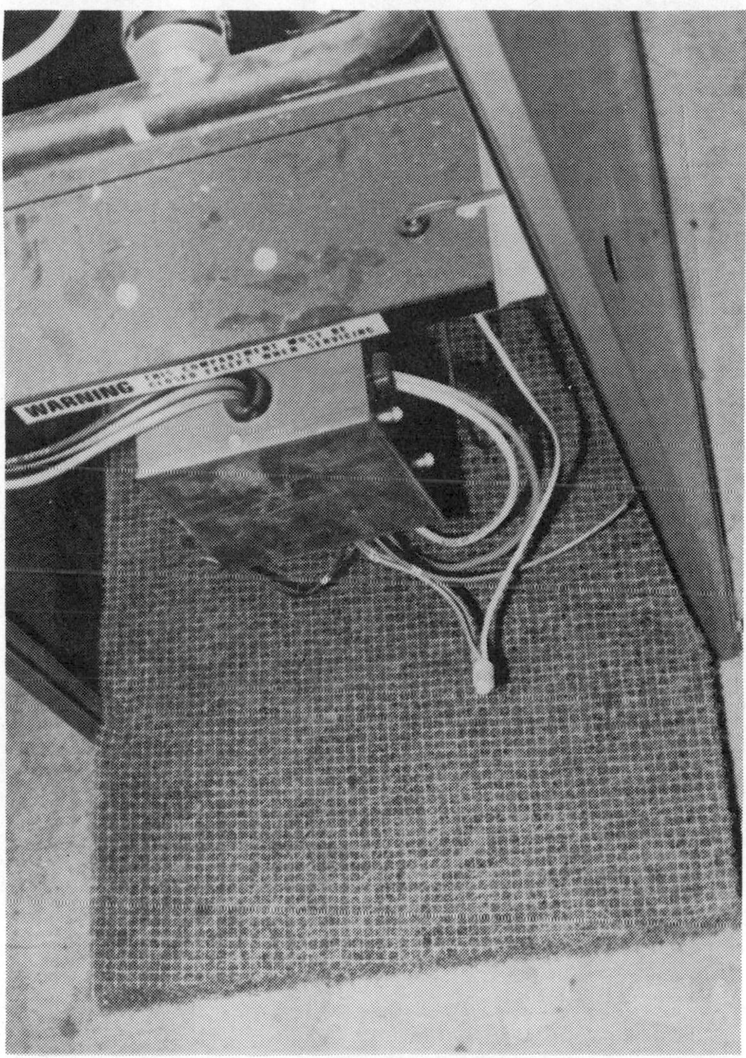

Fig. 7-7. This gas furnace has a washable air filter at the bottom of the furnace. Filters can be located in several different places; you should check your furnace over carefully to find yours. Sometimes there may be more than one air filter.

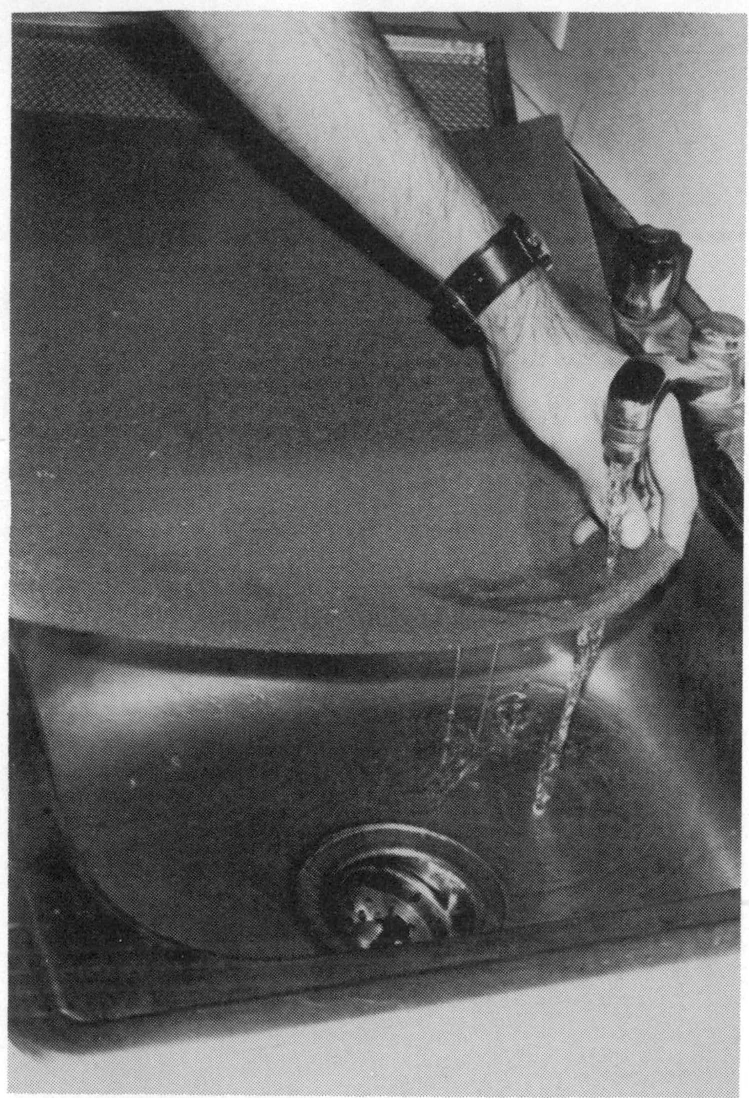

Fig. 7-8. Clean the washable filter material by running water through the element in a direction opposite to normal air flow.

Washable Filters

Washable filters are usually made with a plastic foam of aluminum mesh. Many of these filters are thin and fairly fragile, so you have to treat them carefully. They are prone to tearing, and if they are torn you will have to replace them (Fig. 7-7). Wash them gently with warm soap and water or with plain water. Run the water through the filter in the *opposite* direction to the air flow so the flow of the water will flush out the dirt (Fig. 7-8).

You can usually purchase a washable filter element from a furnace dealer in precut sizes or in large sheets that you can cut yourself. Be sure to get a filter element that will fill the entire filter frame (Fig. 7-9). If the filter is too small, unfiltered air will enter the furance around the edges of the filter element. Any filter replacement should be made with an element as identical as possible to the size and material of the original. If you have to replace a washable filter, don't take any chances—take the original to a reputable furnace dealer so he can recommend a good replacement.

A washable filter should be cleaned about once every three months. It will usually not need to be replaced unless it is torn or allowed to go for a long period without cleaning.

Electronic Air Filters

An electronic air filter is a fairly delicate instrument, but it is not a difficult thing to clean if the cleaning is done right. The electronic air filter operates by generating a large elecrical voltage that attracts dust, pollen, and lint particles from the air onto charged plates, much like electricity does. Before the air

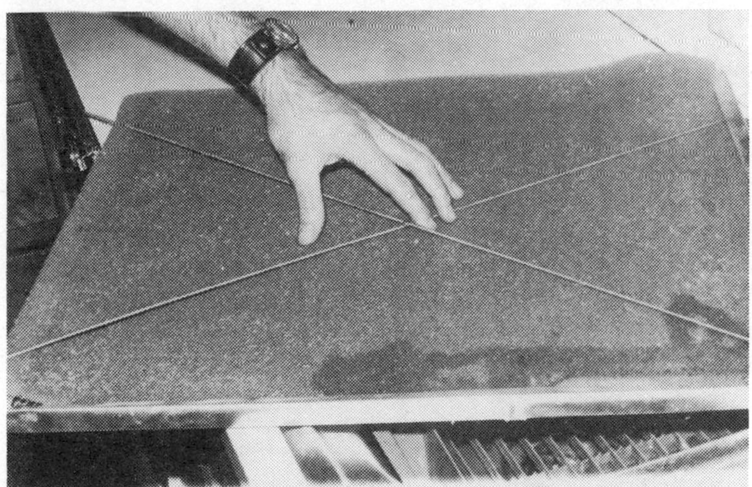

Fig. 7-9. When installing a new filter element or merely replacing one that you have just washed, be sure it fills the entire frame. Also be sure you do not tear the element as you fit it into its frame—a torn filter element will allow large dust particles to pass through.

reaches the charged plates, however, it is first filtered through a disposable or washable filter. This first filter element should be cleaned like any other filter of its type.

After the air passes through the first filter, any remaining particles are attracted to the charged plates of the electronic element. For best operation, these plates must be cleaned periodically according to factory recommendations. A factory service manual will tell you how often the plates should be cleaned by wiping or immersing them in a special cleaning fluid. The electronic air filter usually has an indicator to tell you when these plates need to be cleaned.

Be careful when you check an electronic filter—the filter elements are charged with 12,000 or more volts. If the filter is not disconnected from the powre supply, it can give quite a shock to an unsuspecting homeowner. Most filters have a safety switch that shuts off the power when the service door is opened, but disconnect the power to be sure because the switch may stick.

Tuning Up Your Heating System 8

If you own a car, you know that for trouble-free operation and good gas mileage you have to give it a tuneup about once a year or every 12,000 miles. Surprisingly, though, most homeowners seem to expect their furnace to operate without any maintenance at all for 15 to 20 years! Most furnaces can indeed operate that long, but it is only because manufacturers have designed their furnaces to take such abuse and neglect. No furnace was meant to be ignored for that long, and you have only to look at the owner's manual (if it hasn't been lost) to see that some kind of regular maintenance is required.

A car will go for a long time without any sort of maintenance, but when it does break down, watch out! All too often, a little routine maintenance will prevent more serious problems from happening. Your furnace is much like a car in that respect—it needs regular maintenance too. Perhaps its only a matter of checking the air filter a couple times a year, but that's important if you want to keep your furnace operating at peak efficiency. A lot can happen over a year's time—filters get clogged up, fans get dirty, parts need oiling, adjustments get out of adjustment. You might not see any obvious changes in your furnace's operation, but your fuel bills will creep higher. Of course, with the rapidly increasing prices of energy these days, it's hard to see what part of your fuel bill is due to rising energy costs and what part is due to inefficient operation. Like so many other people, you may be tempted to attribute the entire rise in cost to inflation, setting aside the possibility that your furnace might also be to blame.

Fig. 8-1. A squirrel cage fan consists of a motor, a fan cage with many blades, and a housing (not shown) which fits over the cage. The motor should be removed once every two years for cleaning, but the external fan blades and motor parts should be cleaned every year.

Most routing maintenance can be done with a minimum of tools and equipment. A couple of screwdrivers and wrenches, together with a free afternoon, will enable you to make the minor adjustments and clean the few parts that can have such a big effect on your fuel bill. Generally speaking, a furnace should be adjusted and checked once a year—just before the heating season begins is the best time. Air filters should be inspected more often and cleaned more often during the heating season—two to four times a year is about right.

CLEANING YOUR FURNACE FAN

The fan most used in heating systems is the *squirrel cage* fan (Fig. 8-1). This fan circulates the air through the furnace and duct system. Over a period of time—even with regular filter replacements—the blades and motor of the fan will become covered with dirt, reducing air flow in the furnace. Figure 8-2 shows a dirty squirrel cage blade assembly that came from a furnace. With good filtering and periodic cleaning, the fan blades should never get this dirty. Although large amounts of dirt on the fan blades will obviously reduce the air flow, even a much smaller amount of dirt and lint has a measurable effect.

Cleaning the Fan and Motor Housing

Clean the fan blades with a brush and soapy water. Be careful not to move any of the balance weights from the fan blades. The blades can be cleaned without removing the fan if there is enough room. But never use water to clean the blades unless they are taken off the motor shaft, since the water might spill or drip into the motor or some electrical connection, causing a short circuit. If you are going to clean the inside of the motor, the entire assembly will have to be removed; the blades can then be cleaned after you remove them from the motor shaft.

Figure 8-3 shows a squirrel cage fan as it appears inside. Usually, the complete fan assembly can be removed by loosening a couple of screws or wing nuts on the sides of the fan housing. The fan and motor assembly should come out as one unit. In some cases, the flue pipe gets in the way and has to be removed before the fan can be taken out. When the motor is taken out of the furnace, be sure to mark the connecting wires so you can put them back on the correct terminals when you reinstall the motor.

The fan on your furnace may not have the fan blades connected directly to the end of the motor shaft. If not, they are then attached to the motor by a belt and pulley (Fig. 8-3). This type of fan is basically the same as the direct-drive fan and the motor is cleaned

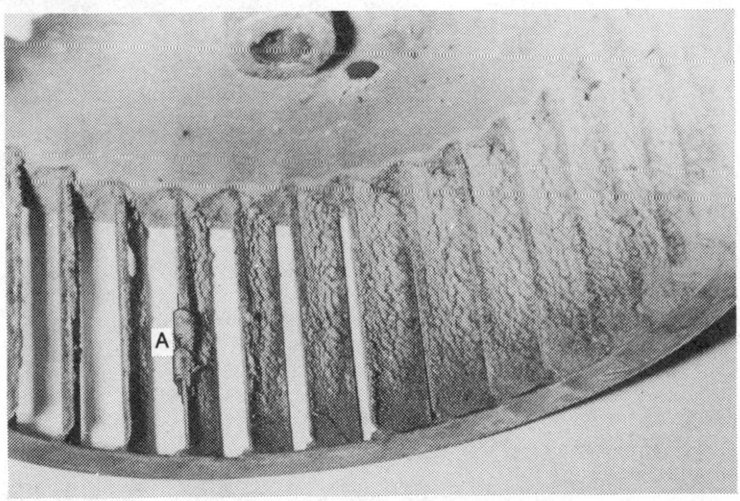

Fig. 8-2. Dirt, grease and lint are caked onto these squirrel cage fan blades so badly that the air flow from this fan is greatly reduced. These blades can be cleaned with a rag, brush or cleaning solvent. Be careful not to bend the blades or move the balance weight, which is clipped to the blade at (A).

Fig. 8-3. To remove the squirrel cage fan from the furnace, loosen the nuts on each side of the fan housing at (A). Remove the motor, fan and housing as one unit. This unit has a belt-driven fan, so the motor can be removed by itself without taking out the entire fan assembly. (B) is the fan housing. (C) is the terminal box for the fan relay, transformer and other connections. (D) is the pulley and fan belt. Be sure to mark or tag the connecting wires on the motor when they are removed so you can attach them to the same terminals when the motor is put back in place.

in the same way. In this case, though, it is possible to remove the motor without removing the entire fan assembly.

With a belt-driven fan, you should check the belt periodically to see that it is good repair and in proper adjustment. The belt should have about an inch of play as you push down on it. If the belt is too loose, it will slip; if it's too tight, it could burn out a bearing.

The fan on a furnace should be brushed and cleaned about once a year. The fan motor does not need cleaning quite as often; about once every two years or so should keep it in good shape, unless you are having problems with it. When you clean the fan each fall, it would be a good idea to give the motor housing a good brushing to remove dirt. Dirt on the housing can cause overheating. Do not use water to clean the motor housing.

Disassembling the Motor

Figure 8-1 shows the motor and blade assembly after it has been removed from the fan housing. The blade assembly will pull off the motor shaft when the allen screw in the blade hub is loosened. If you have a long allen wrench, it can be inserted through the special hole in the fan blade (as shown in Fig. 8-4) to loosen this screw. Remove the fan blades and clean them.

After cleaning the fan blades, clean the motor. Dirt and lint buildup on the outside housing of a motor can cause it to overheat, which can lead to more trouble. A common problem occurs when

Fig. 8-4. To loosen the fan blades and remove them from the shaft, you will have to loosen the allen set screw on the bottom side of the fan hub. A long allen wrench can be inserted through the hole in the fan blades to loosen the screw; a short wrench will reach from inside the blades. Pull the fan blade completely off the motor shaft for cleaning.

Fig. 8-5. To disassemble the motor, remove the blades from the motor shaft. Clean the shaft with sand paper or cleaning solvent. The nuts on the through bolts are removed at (A) so the motor can be separated. Mark a line across the side of the two bellhousings (B) and the stator (C) so the parts can be lined up after assembly.

the bearings overheat and bind, causing the motor to pull more current, which heats the motor still more. If the bearing is dirty and does not turn freely, the motor may fail to start or run, opening the circuit breaker. In Fig. 8-5, the motor is ready to be dismantled for a thorough inside cleaning. Using a sharp tool, nail, or pen with ink that will not rub off, mark a line across the outside housing of the motor so the parts can be reassembled in the correct position. There are three or four bolts that go through the housing of the motor from one end to the other; these should now be removed. The motor shaft should always be clean before you attempt to pull the motor apart. If it is not clean the bearing in the bellhousing may be damaged when the motor is pulled apart. Clean the shaft with sandpaper or a cleaning solvent (Fig. 8-6).

The bellhousings are removed by inserting a screwdriver or cold chisel in the crack between the bellhousing and stator. By gently tapping on the screwdriver, you should be able to loosen the bellhousing enough to remove it (Fig. 8-7). Be careful not to dent or bend the bellhousing.

Fig. 8-6. The rotor (A) and front bellhousing (B) are being separated in the upper picture from the stator (C) and rear bellhousing (D). The lower picture shows the parts pulled completely apart.

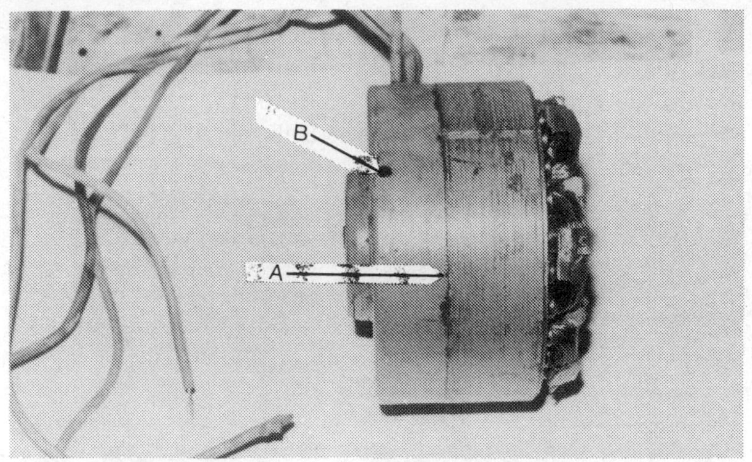

Fig. 8-7. This is the rear bellhousing and stator after the rotor has been removed. If you wanted to separate the remaining bellhousing from the stator (there is really no need for cleaning), you could insert a screwdriver or cold chisel in crack (A) and tap gently. Do this all around the bellhousing until the unit has separated and loosened. Be careful not to bend or dent the bellhousing. The motor is oiled through the oil hole (B).

Cleaning the Stator and Rotor

The stator windings are now ready for cleaning (Fig. 8-8). Clean the motor windings initially with a dry cloth or paper towel to remove the worst part of the dirt. Never scrape or scratch the electric motor windings or try to clean them with solvents—this might remove the enamel coating on the wires and cause a short circuit. Loose particles of dust and lint can be blown out with air. You can finish wiping the windings with a clean cloth to remove the remaining dirt.

Carefully pull the rotor out of the front bellhousing (Fig. 8-9). The rotor contains no wires that can be damaged by petroleum solvents, so you can thoroughly wipe the rotor clean with a rag and cleaning fluid. Do not, however use water when cleaning any motor parts, since this might cause rusting. Do not sand the rotor shaft where it touches the bearings—this surface must remain polished to prevent bearing wear.

Cleaning and Lubricating the Bearings

The bearings located in each bellhousing should be thoroughly cleaned with a solvent to remove as much dirt and grime as possible (Figs. 8-8 and 8-9). After cleaning the bearing surface, lubricate it generously with SAE 10 motor oil. If there is a cloth wick or packing around the bearing, saturate it thoroughly with oil.

Insert the rotor into each bearing, testing one at a time to see if it moves freely. Turn the rotor shaft in the bearing; if it grates as you turn it, replace the bearing. Parts of this nature are available from furnace repair shops and factory distributors.

Some of the newer fan motors have a sealed or life-time lubricated bearing that can go for years without additional lubrication or cleaning. Such motors have a shaft cut with tiny grooves that force oil to circulate through the bearing. An extra-large reservoir around the bearing holds sufficient oil to last for five or more years. While such motors would not require a major cleaning and lubricating job every year, they should be given an external cleaning each year to limit the buildup of dust and dirt. Certainly, though, if the motor shows signs of turning stiffly or tends to slow down after it has been running a while, the motor probably needs a good cleaning—inside and out.

Reassembling the Motor

After cleaning the windings and oilings the bearings, begin reassembling the motor. First, place the rotor in the front bellhousing as shown in Fig. 8-9. Now place the rotor and bellhousing assembly into the stator rear bellhousing (Fig. 8-6). Line up the marks you made earlier on the outside of the housing (Fig. 8-5). If

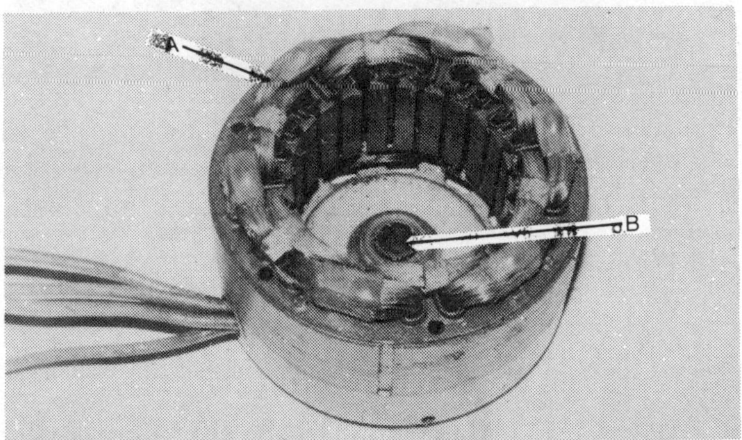

Fig. 8-8. The stator and rear bellhousing should be cleaned with a cloth and compressed air. Do not scrape or damage the windings (A). Clean and oil the bearing (B).

Fig. 8-9. Carefully remove the rotor (A) from the front bellhousing (B) and clean it with a cloth and petroleum solvent. Never sand the surfaces (C) of the rotor shaft that turn in the bearings of each bellhousing because this will ruin the rotor shaft and cause the softer bearing material to quickly wear out. Clean and oil the bearing (D).

they are not lined up evenly, the bearings and shafts may bind and burn out the motor.

After the motor is reassembled turn the shaft to see that the rotor turns freely. Install the fan (Fig. 8-4) and be sure you put it on the proper end of the shaft if you have a double-shaft motor. The motor and fan assembly are now ready to go back into the fan housing.

ADJUSTING THE FAN CONTROL AND LIMIT SWITCH

The limit switch is just a thermostat that keeps the furnace from getting to hot. The limit switch is usually located near the heat exchanger or burner box. When too much heat is generated in the heat exchanger, the limit switch cuts off the burner. An electric furnace usually has a bimetal limit switch located near the heating elements.

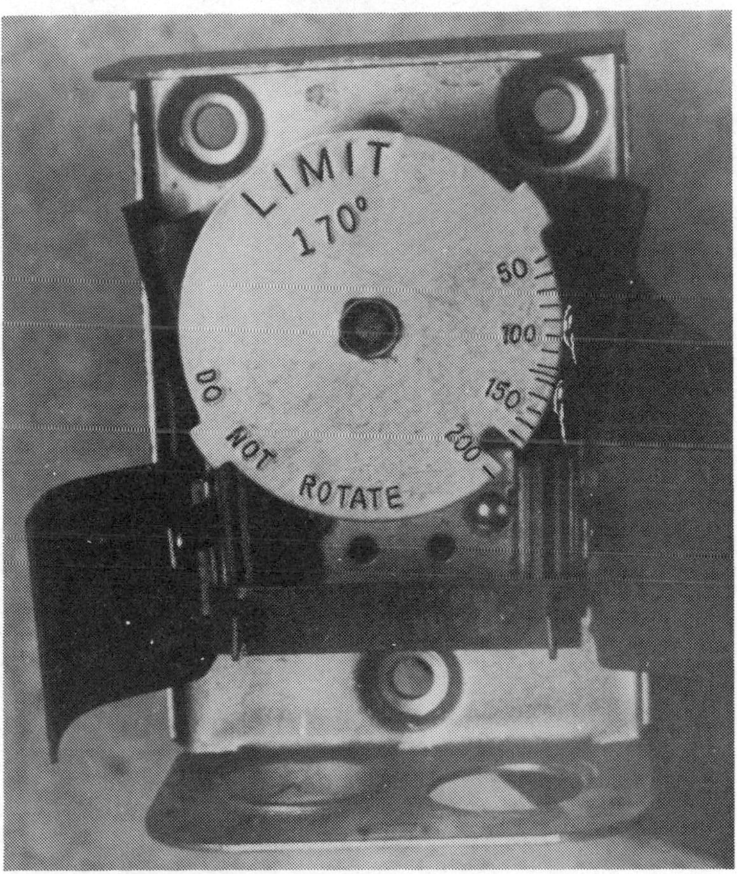

Fig. 8-10. This limit switch has a fan cntrol built into the unit levers beside the temperature dial that can be set to control the on and off temperatures for the fan. The slot cut in the dial permanently sets the 170° Fahrenheit furnace limit; it should not be adjusted. To change the temperature settings for the fan, simply slide the levers to match the proper temperature settings on the dial.

The limit switch is essential to protect both you and the furnace. For example, if the burners or heating elements are on and for some reason the fan does not come on, too much heat would quickly build up in the heat chamber. Without a limit switch, this heat would keep building and eventually damage the furnace or start a fire. But the limit switch keeps this from happening.

The limit switch is set by the factory to a temperature that is less than 225°F. This limit switch should not be adjusted. Raising the limit temperature is unsafe, while lowering it reduces furnace efficiency.

The limit switch on a fuel-burning furnace usually has a fan control built into the switch, as in the control shown in Fig. 8-10. But an electric furnace often has a separate switch for the fan control. There are normally two levers or tabs on the switch that you can adjust to control the temperatures at which the fan turns on and off. (IF there are three levers, the one set at the highest setting is the limit control, which should not be adjusted.) For instance, the fan control may be set so that the fan comes on when the temperature in the heat exchanger reaches 150°F and will stop when the temperature drops to 125°F. In general, though, the on and off temperatures will vary with different furnaces.

You can adjust the fan control temperatures to suit your individual needs. The adjustment itself is matter of moving levers or tabs, but you should first consider what the adjustment does before you attempt making any changes. While the two levers work independently, it is best that you do not set the on and off temperatures too close together, otherwise the furnace may begin to *short-cycle*. When a furnace short-cycles, the fan clicks on and off at short intervals, which is hard on the fan motor and often leads to similar on/off behavior in the furnace burners as well. Short cycling should be avoided because it producers inefficient furnace operation and soon wears out many expensive furnace parts.

To illustrate how short cycling can happen, let's say that you left the fan *turnon* temperature at 130°F and raised the *turnoff* temperature to 125°F. Now when the furnace is turned on by your room thermostat, the temperature of the air held in the heat exchanger will rise, turning on the fan when it reaches 130°F. But when the fan turns on, it draws cool air into the furnace from the return air duct to be warmed in the heat exchanger. If the furnace can't warm this cool air to at least 125°F by the time it leaves the heat exchanger, the furnace fan will quickly turn off. Of course, with the fan now off, the heat exchanger will once again be able to heat up the air to 130°F, the fan will turn on, and the process repeats. Short cycling is most likely to occur when the turnoff temperature is too high or when the temperature of the air in the return air duct is cooler than normal, such as when you turn the room thermostat down for the night.

You can usually make your furnace operate more efficiently by lowering the on and off temperatures of the fan. For example, if you lower the turnon temperature of the fan, the fan will start blowing air over the heat exchanger sooner, drawing off more heat energy from the heat exchanger before it is lost up the flue. Similarly, by lowering the turnoff temperature of the fan, you can draw more heat out of the heat exchanger after the burners turn off. A disadvantage of using lower on/off fan settings is that the initial air coming out of the register will feel cooler when the fan first turns on , though it quickly warms up. If the turnoff temperature is set too low, the fan may run for a long time after the burners turn off, increasing your electric bill and making your house feel drafty.

Clearly, some compromise is called for when it comes to setting the temperatures in the fan control. Ordinarily, a turnon setting of about 115—125°F will cause the fan to come on very soon after the burners turn on, while a turnoff setting of about 100°F will draw out most of the heat energy in the heat exchanger so that it will not be lost up the flue. These on/off temperatures are low enough and far enough apart that short cycling will not occur when the furnace turns on. The fan may turn on and off a few times after the furnace turns off, but this can be stopped by raising the turnon temperature just a little.

The high temperature limit switch has no actual effect on the efficiency of the furnace. As mentioned before, this limit switch is primarily a safety device that prevents demage to the furnace and your home. If the limitt switch on your furnace happens to be adjustable, do not tamper with it. Raising the limit temperature may permit the air in the heat exchanger to become so hot that it will ignite dust and wood particles, whereas lowering the limit temperature may cause short cycling of the burners and reduce the heating capacity of your furnace.

Some fan controls cannot be adjusted. The only way to change the on/off temperature settings on these controls is to replace the control with another unit having different temperature settings. But if the fan control and limit switch are separate units, it is sometimes possible to replace the fan control with a control having adjustable settings.

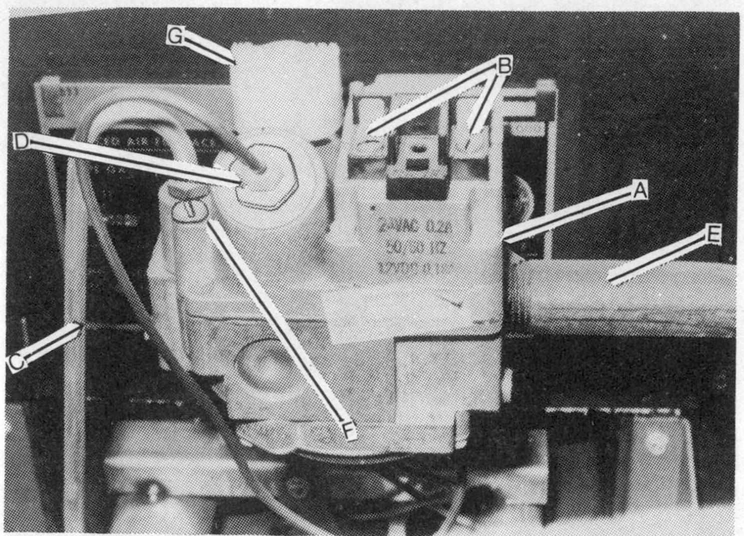

Fig. 8-11. The gas valve (A) is connected to the manifold (E). The terminal connections at (B) are used to connect the thermostat wires to the gas valve. (C) is the pilot light tube and (D) is the thermocouple tube that shuts off the gas valve when the pilot light goes out. Remove cap screw (F) and insert a screwdriver to adjust the pilot light flame. Knob (G) is used to turn the gas on and off and to light the pilot.

ADJUSTING LPG AND NATURAL GAS FURNACES

A gas furnace may burn natural gas (methane), propane gas, or butane gas. Natural gas is delivered to the house through underground gas lines, while liquid petroleum gas (LPG) is stored near the house in supply tanks with direct feed lines to the furnace. The gas flow to the furnace is regulated by a gas valve in the line, which meters the amount of gas entering the burners within the heat exchanger. Air is mixed with the gas there and is ignited to produce heat.

To get the highest amount of heat energy from the furnace, the gas and air mixture must be just right. To accomplish this feat, a series of regulators control the flow of gas to each burner, and each burner has an adjustment mechanism to control the air flow. If you can set these regulators and adjustments properly, you will be that much closer to having a furnace that operates at peak efficiency.

Gas Valves

The manifold is a pipe that connects between the gas valve and the burners. Gas flows from the valve into the manifold, which distributes the gas to the burners. The purpose of the gas valve is to control the flow of gas into the manifold. When the furnace is not heating and the thermostat is not calling for heat, an electrical solenoid in the gas valve opens, permitting gas to flow through the valve into the manifold. The gas valve and inlet manifold pipe are shown in Fig. 8-11.

If the pilot light goes out, the gas valve is shut off to safely prevent gas from escaping into the furnace room and house. The gas valve closes when the pilot light goes out because the thermocouple, a temperature-sensing device, is no longer heated by the pilot light. Figure 8-12 shows the burner assembly with burners, manifold, pilot light, and thermocouple.

Lighting the Pilot

If the pilot light goes out in your furnace, it must be lighted by hand. To do this, first turn down the room thermostat so that furnace will not come on as you are working. Then turn the large knob on the top of the gas valve (Fig. 8-11G) to the position marked

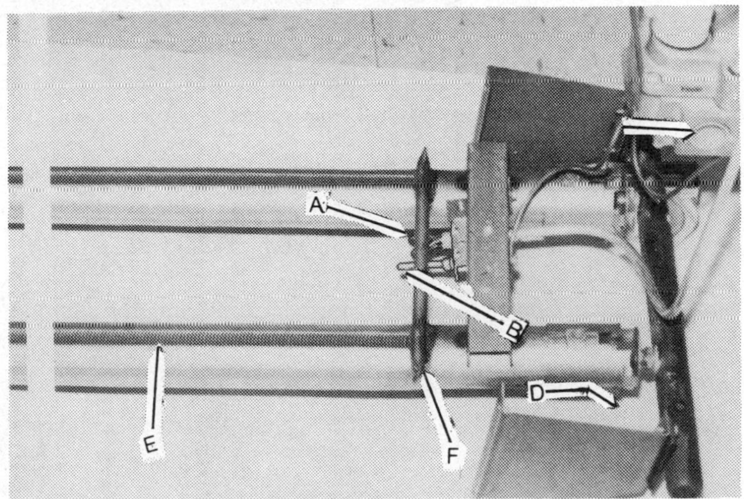

Fig. 8-12. The pilot light (A) and thermocouple (B) are attached to the burner assembly. The thermocouple should extend into the pilot light flame. When the thermocouple is hot, it will allow the main gas valve (C) to open when the room thermostat calls for heat. When the furnace turns on, gas flows through the jet on the manifold and into the burner (D) where it mixes with air. The gas and air mixture then passes through the openings (E) in the burner, where it is ignited. The openings are too small to permit the flame to pass back into the burner chamber, so the flame remains over the burner openings. The burners are lighted by the gas flowing toward the pilot light through the pilot tube (F).

PILOT. Press down on this knob and hold it down to permit gas to flow to the pilot. The pilot can now be lighted with a match.

Continue to hold the knob down until the pilot has a chance to heat up the thermocouple. If you release the knob before the thermocouple is hot, the pilot light will go out. Once the thermocouple is hot, though, a mechanism in the gas valve will keep gas flowing to the pilot light after you release the knob. The knob can now be turned to the ON position, which will allow gas to flow to the burners when you turn the room thermostat back up. When the burners light, the pilot light should remain lit; if it goes out, turn to the section titled *Adjusting the Pilot Light*.

If the termocouple is not working, the pilot light will go out every time you release the knob on the gas valve. If this happens, it may be that the thermocouple is not working, the pilot light will go out every time you release the knob on the gas valve. If this happens, it may be that the thermocouple is out of position. It should be set so the flame of the pilot touches the thermocouple. If you have not held the gas valve knob down long enough for the thermocouple to warm up, this will also cause the pilot light to go off again, but it shouldn't take more than a minute to heat up the thermocouple. If you are reasonably sure that the thermocouple is set in the right position and that the thermocouple has had a chance to get warm, your furnace may have a bad thermocouple, which will have to be replaced.

If everything is working properly, the gas valve will open and gas will flow into the manifold (Fig. 8-13). The gas jets are located on the manifold and extend into the burners (Figs. 8-12 and 8-13). The jets direct a stream of gas into each burner where it picks up air. The gas and air mix in the burner before passing through the holes of the burner. The gas-air mixture is lighted by the pilot tube (Fig. 8-12).

Leaking Gas Valve

If the gas valve leaks, gas can enter the furnace and room even when the pilot light is off. This not only wastes gas and money. it can also be very dangerous, leading to fire or explosion.

To check for a leaky gas valve, a pressure gauge must be attached to the valve. This gauge is an instrument that measures the amount of gas pressure by the amount the level of a water column rises in a glass tube. The pressure gauge usually has a ¼-inch pipe fitting, so an adapter is needed to join the gauge to the manifold port in the valve housing.

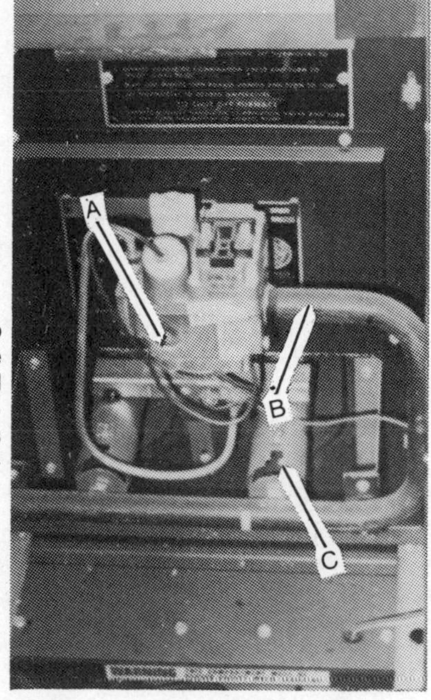

Fig. 8-13. Gas valve (A) connects to the manifold (B). The gas jets are located on the manifold and extend into the burners. (C) is the air adjustment for the burners. As the jets direct a stream of gas into the openings, the gas mixes with air.

The pressure gauge is connected to the gas valve after removing the manifold. Most often this is an easy job, but sometimes you must first remove the pilot-light tube and thermocouple, disconnect the thermostat wires, unscrew the main gas feedline, remove the manifold, and then reconnect the gas line back to the valve. Be sure to turn off the gas to the furnace if you have to remove the gas line from the valve.

With the pressure gauge installed and the gas line connected, turn the gas valve to the ON position. If the pressure gauge shows a pressure reading, the valve is leaking and should be replaced.

Adjusting the Air Mixture

The flame should be a bright blue color down close to the burner. If the flame is not burning correctly, the first place to check is the air adjustment. When there is not enough air, the flame will usually have a yellowish color. This means the flame is not burning hotly, so it will take more gas than it should to heat an area. Too much air causes the flame to burn with a pale blue or white color.

Figure 8-14 shows the air adjustment on the burners of a gas furnace. To adjust the air flow into the burner, loosen the screw on the collar and slide the collar back and forth until the flame burns with a bright blue color. Each burner has to be adjusted separately. Some burners have a dial to adjust, but the procedure is basically the same—open or close the air hole to control the mixture.

Cleaning the Burners

If the air flow is out of adjustment on the burners for a long time, soot may collect around the burners. The flame may even burn inside the burner body or at the gas jet opening and build up quite a bit of carbon and soot inside the burner. Sometimes dust and lint in the air will also collect in the throat of the burner and partially block the air flow. In damp locations, the burner can become spotted with rust.

To clean the burners, they must be removed from the heat chamber. But before you got to a lot of unnecessary work, check to see if the burners can be removed without having to disassemble the gas valve and gas lines. On many furnaces it is possible to remove the burners by simply taking out the mounting screws that hold the burner's bracket in place (Fig. 8-14A). By sliding the burners away from the manifold gas jets, the burners may then drop down far enough to slip right out. Of course, you will still have to disconnect the thermocouple and pilot light tube that are attached to the burners, but this can usually be done without having to disconnect them from the gas valve as well. Be careful not to bend or kink the tubes.

If the burners cannot be removed the easy way, you will probably have to move the manifold and gas valve before you can slide the burners out. Begin by shutting off the gas supply at the supply line, the gas tank, or the nearest shutoff valve. Then disconnect the supply line that connects to the gas valve. Remove the thermostat wires and screws, making sure they are identified so you can reattach them in the right places. Finally, remove the screws on each side of the burner housing supports, so the gas valve, manifold, and burners can be pulled out.

Clean the burners with compressed air to remove dirt, lint, and loose soot. If the burners are oily, you may want to wipe them carefully with a cloth, but be careful not to bend or break the burners. As a last resort, if there are some really tough buildups of soot, you can use some type of cleaning solvent to dissolve the dirt.

Adjusting the Gas Pressure

The gas pressure also affects the mixture of the gas and air going to the burners. If you have tried adjusting the air flow to the burners, have cleaned the burners, are sure that all gas connections are tight, and still have a flame that does not burn properly at the burners, you are probably justified in suspecting that the gas pressure may not be correct. A sure indication of pressure problems is a flame that is too large or too small.

Pressure regulators are located in two possible places. A supply-line regulator is sometimes located at the beginning of the gas line, either at the main natural gas meter or at the LPG supply tank. A second pressure regulator is often located in or near the gas valve of your furnace. Supply-line regulators are usually adjusted by the gas supplier, who generally resents anyone but authorized company servicemen adjusting these pressure regulators. If you have reason to suspect that the pressure may be wrong, though, the gas company will ordinarily check it at no charge. Gas-valve regulators, on the other hand, are set by the factory; you can adjust these regulators if you can get a set of gauges to do the job.

The instruction manual for your furnace ordinarily gives complete information on what the gas pressure should be. If the gas valve or furnace includes a pressure regulator, the instruction manual usually indicates where and how to make pressure adjustments. It is not advisable for you to attempt making any pressure adjustments without having the proper gauges or knowing what the

Fig. 8-14. To remove the burners, first shut the gas off at the tank or at the regulator valve. Loosen the gas line at the gas valve. Remove screws (A) so the gas valve, manifold and burners can be slipped out. The air adjustment collars (B) on the burners are vaired to control the amount of air mixing with the gas. Inlet gas pressure can be measured by removing the plug (C) in the gas valve and connecting a pressure gage.

pressure should be. A flame too large may quickly fatigue and crack the heat exchanger in the furnace, while one too small will be inefficient and waste gas. An experienced serviceman might be able to adjust the pressure by eye, but the typical homeowner would be foolish to risk it.

You can, however, check the gas pressure without any risk to see if it is correct. This is done by connecting a pressure gauge to the gas valve or manifold to measure the gas pressure inside the manifold, which controls the amount of gas flowing through the jets to the burners. To check the gas pressure, first turn the gas valve to the OFF position. Then remove the ¼-inch plug located on the gas valve, as in Fig. 8-14C, or on the manifold pipe. If you can't find a plug in either place, you will have to remove one of the gas jets, connecting the other end of the hose to the pressure gauge. The rubber hose will permit you to measure the gas pressure within the manifold, but the burners for that jet will not work while the hose is in place. Be sure that the hose fits tightly over the jet so that it will not pop off when the pressure builds up.

To measure gas pressure, a special gauge is used that measures the pressure in *inches of water*, indicated by the height of the water column in a glass tube. You may be able to borrow or rent such a gauge; gas companies and repair services have them. Do not attempt to adjust the gas pressure without using the proper set of gauges.

Relight the pilot light and turn the gas valve to ON. Set the thermostat so the burners will light. Be sure all the pipe fittings are tight, and be sure the rubber hose does not come off. The gauge should give the proper pressure reading. The instruction manual for the furnace should have a chart showing how the pressure is to be set. If the pressure is not correct, the regulator will have to be adjusted.

If there is only a supply-line regulator, it will be located near the source of the gas supply: at the gas meter if you are in a city with natural gas lines, or at the supply tank if you have liquid petroleum gas. Figure 8-15 illustrates a typical supply-line regulator.

Most—but not all—furnaces have pressure regulators built into the gas valve. If this is the case, you will have to follow the furnace manufacturer's instructions on how to locate and adjust this regulator. Some furnaces have a separate pressure regulator such as that shown in Fig. 8-16. This small regulator is generally located inside or near the furnace, on the gas supply line going to the gas

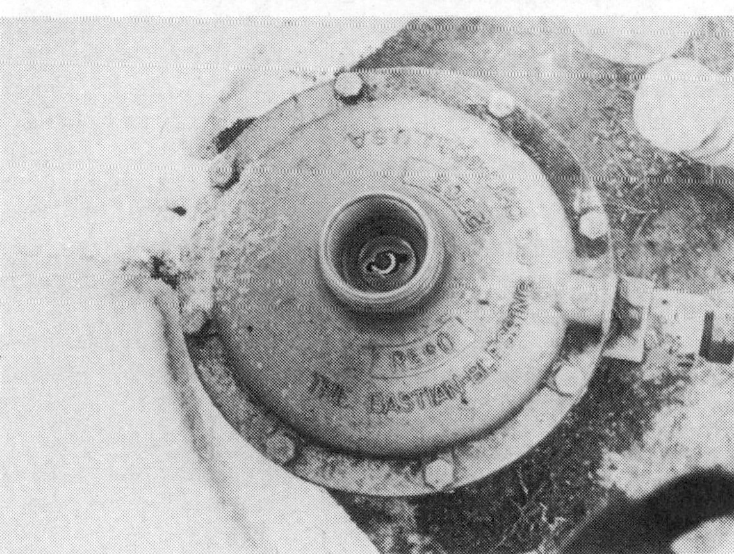

Fig. 8-15. The gas pressure can be regulated at the furnace or at the supply source. This regulator is used on an LPG tank and controls the gas pressure coming out of the tank. Remove the cap to adjust the gas pressure. The lower picture shows the internal adjustment after the cap has been removed. The gas company should be contacted before attempting any adjustments, since their policies may prohibit unauthorized people from tampering with their equipment. The gas company will probably make the adjustment for you.

valve. The pressure adjustment on most regulators is protected by a cover that must be removed to gain access to the adjustment screw. This cover is included to prevent you from accidentally turnign the adjustment as well as to protect the inside of the regulator from dust and dirt.

After the pressure has been set, turn the gas valve knob to the OFF position and replace the plug or remove the hose from the burner. Relight the furnace and set the air adjustment for the best flame. If both the gas pressure and air flow are not adjusted correctly, the furance will waste fuel.

Adjusting the Pilot Light

The pilot light in most gas furnaces is on all the time, though some new furnaces use a form of electric ignition. Before adjusting the pilot light, it's a good idea to inspect it to insure that everything is reasonably clean. A dirty or clogged pilot is often resonsible for the pilot light going out, and a pilot light that is too small often causes noisy ignition of the burners.

To clean the pilot light, you have to remove it from the burner assembly. Some pilot lights can be removed without removing the burners, since they are usually clipped or bolted to a bracket near the burners. To remove the pilot light, you should first disconnect the small gas tube of the pilot light where it connects to the gas valve. Be sure not to twist any fittings or kink the tube. Remove the pilot light from the burner, take it apart, and clean it with compressed air or some lightweight solvent. The small orifice inside the pilot light should be cleaned to clear any blockages. The diameter of the orifice is not critical, so you can safely clean it with a pin, wire, or toothpick.

If the burner assembly has to be removed, be sure to disconnect both the gas tube and the thermocouple tube to prevent damaging them. The pilot tube and thermocouple (Fig. 8-12) should also be cleaned at this time. Sometimes the pilot light has a deflector to focus the pilot flame toward the pilot tube or thermocouple; be careful that this deflector is aimed in the proper direction when you reassemble the pilot light and burner.

The size of the pilot light is adjusted by a tiny screw in the gas valve. This adjustment is covered with a protective cap that has to be unscrewed to gain access to the adjustment. The pilot adjustment is usually located near the pilot tube, as it is in Fig. 8-11F. Adjust the size of the pilot flame so that it touches the tip of the thermocouple and is sufficiently large to insure quick ignition of the

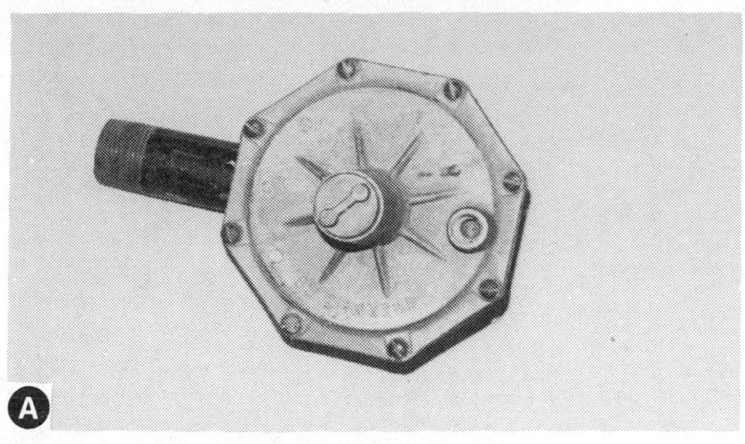

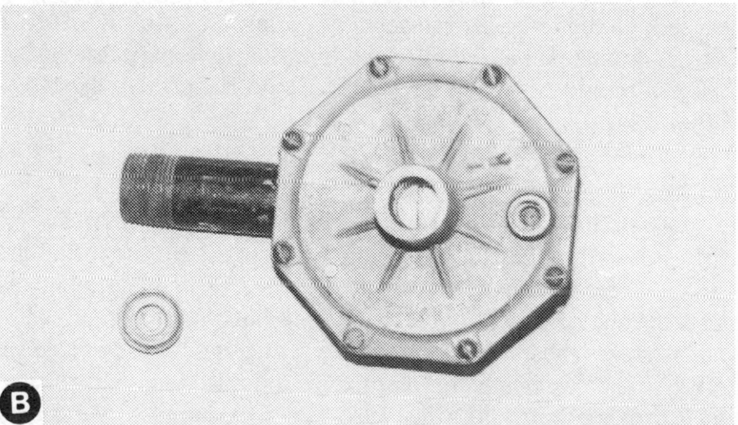

Fig. 8-16. (A) Not all gas furnaces have a furnace pressure regulator located in the gas valve—some depend on correct gas pressure from the supply line. This pressure regulator is a separate unit located near the gas valve. (B) To adjust the gas pressure, the cap of the regualtor is removed to expose the adjustment screw. Always use a pressure gauge when adjusting the gas pressure.

burners when they turn on. If the burners do not ignite quickly, too much gas will fill the combustion chamber and a small explosion will occur when the burners finally do light. In some cases, the explosion snuffs out the pilot light, turning off the furnace.

Some forms of electric ignition use a hot wire to ignite the pilot, which then heats the thermocouple, which in turn allows the burners to turn on. Oil furnaces generally use arc igniters to light the fuel. Electric ignition systems can save fuel, but they have their

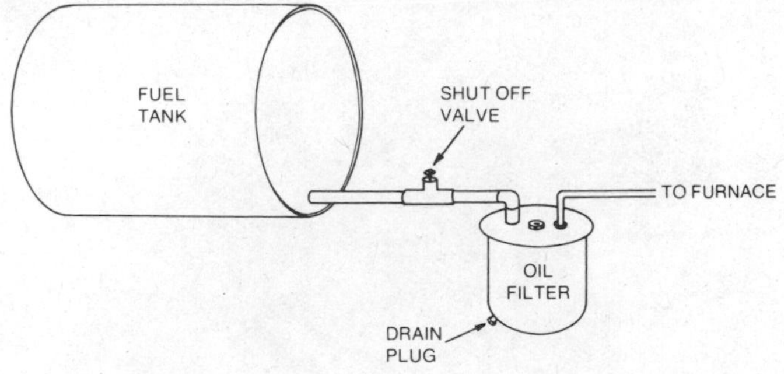

Fig. 8-17. Drain and clean the filter at the supply tank. If this filter is not kept clean, the flow of fuel to the furnace will be restricted and dirt may pass into the furnace.

problems too. In hot-wire systems, for example, the wire element can fail, but this is easily replaced with a new unit. An advantage of such systems is that the pilot and thermocouple parts are not on most of the time, so they do not have to be cleaned or adjusted as often.

OIL FURNACES

An oil furnace draws fuel from a nearby supply tank. The oil first passes through a furnace pump, which pressurizes the fuel and sprays it through the nozzles in the furnace. The oil spray mixes with air and passes through an arc-ignition system comprised of electrodes. These electrodes (also called igniters) produce an electric arc through the oil-air mixture to ignite the mixture. The mixture then burns in a fire box, which is similar to the heat exchanger in a gas furnace. The house is heated by air passing through a heat chamber above the fire box, and this air is forced through the furnace and ductwork by a fan. A stack control thermostat senses when the burners are lit, accomplishing much the same job as the thermocouple in a gas furnace—if the stack control thermostat does not heat up shortly after the fuel begins spraying into the furnace, the furnace turns off automatically. A limit switch and fan control completes the furnace equipment by regulating the burners and turning the fan on and off.

Cleaning the Tank Filter

A filter is located at the supply tank (Fig. 8-17) and removes moisture and dirt from the oil as it flows to the furnace. This filter

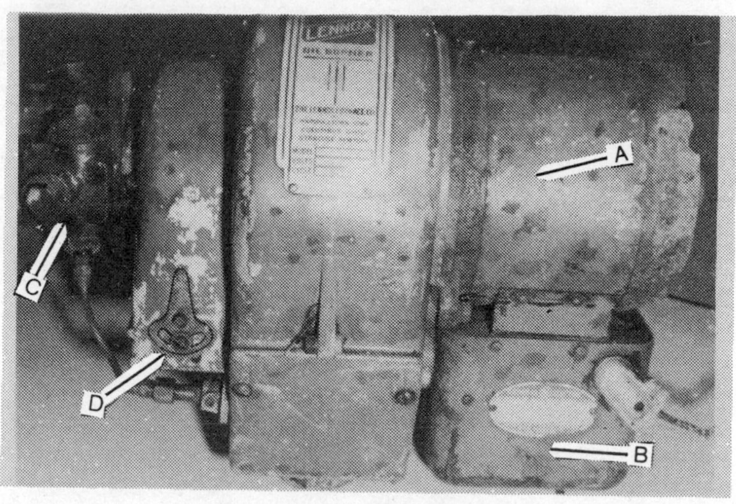

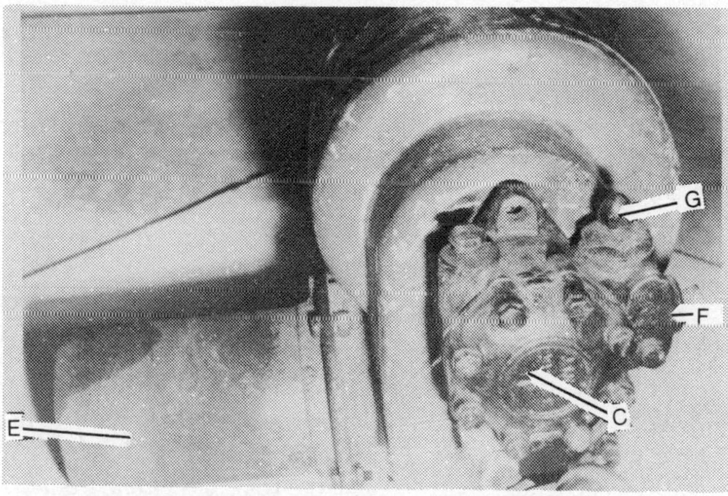

Fig. 8-18. The oil burner is made up of several different parts combined into one unit. (A) is the motor. (B) is the power transformer that produces about 15,000 volts for the igniter electrodes. (C) is the pump that draws fuel from the supply tank and pressurizes it to spray through the nozzles. (D) is the air-adjustment mechanism for obtaining the proper air-fuel mixture. A side view of the oil burner assembly shows the barrel (E) that houses the igniters and the nozzle. The fuel-air mixture burns at the end of the barrel. Pipe plug (F) is removed to install the oil pressure gauge, and cap (G) is removed to gain access to the pressure adjustment screw.

Fig. 8-19. This is a view of an oil burner looking into the nozzle end of the barrel. The center nozzle sprays the fuel-air mixture, which is ignited by the igniter electrodes (arrow).

has a drain plug to remove water and dirt from the filter bowl; the bottom of the filter can also be removed for cleaning.

To drain this filter, first close the main valve between the filter and the tank. Some filters contain disposable paper filtering elements that should be replaced periodically. Other filters simply use a sediment bowl that must be drained and cleaned.

Cleaning the Burners

Most burner assemblies have a motor on one side that is connected to a blower fan and pump on the other (Fig. 8-18). A high-voltage transformer steps the 120V from the power line up to about 15,000V. this high voltage is then sent to the igniters, which provide an arc to light the fuel-air mixture as it passes through the burner (Fig. 8-19).

Disconnect the supply line and the transformer line from the igniters and nozzle so they can be removed for cleaning (Fig. 8-20). Scrape the electrodes (Fig. 8-21) and smooth them with sandpaper. Unscrew the end of the nozzle and clean the nozzle with compressed air or a cleaning solvent. The screen and jet behind the nozzle end should also be cleaned. If the electrodes are burned off too short you will have to replace them. Check the porcelain base of the electrodes for cracks that might cause shorts to the metal case.

Fig. 8-20. The cover has been removed to reveal the igniter and nozzle assembly (A). To clean the assembly, disconnect the power supply, the fuel line (B) and the transformer terminal (C).

Fig. 8-21. The nozzle and igniter assembly has been removed for cleaning. Scrape the carbon and soot deposits from the assembly and reset the gap distance between the tips of the electrodes.

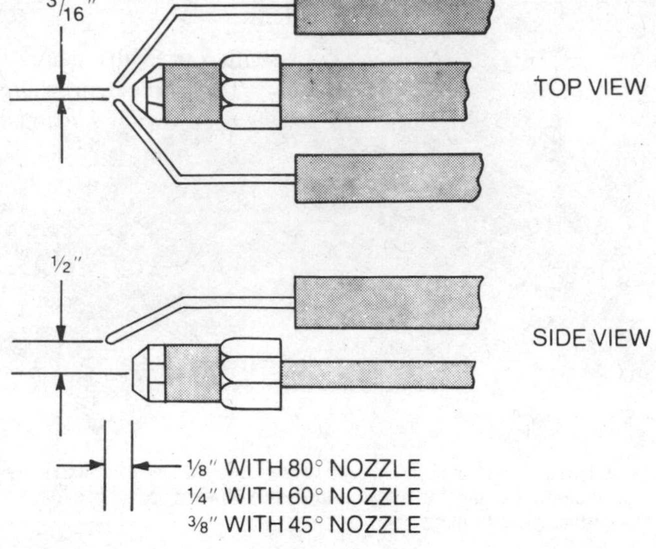

Fig. 8-22. If the two electrodes are not in adjustment, the proper arc will not be obtained for igniting the fuel. If the electrodes are burned off or damaged, replace them.

After the electrodes and nozzle are clean, reassemble the unit and adjust the setting of the electrode gap as shown in Fig. 8-22. Adjust the electrodes by loosening the set screw holding them in the porcelain base, turning the electrodes to move them in or out as required. The electrodes must be adjusted correctly so they will form the proper arc to ignite the fuel. After cleaning and adjusting the igniters and nozzle, replace the parts of the assembly and tighten all connections.

Adjusting Air Flow and Pump Pressure

After the igniters have been cleaned and replaced, the air flow must be adjusted to produce an efficient flame. The flame should make just a little smoke as combustion takes place. Loosen the screw or nut shown in Fig. 8-18D and open or close the air supply vent as needed. Some units may have a flange that must be moved back and forth over the air intake to adjust the air flow. Increase the air supply until no smoke is produced and then close the vent slowly until you begin to see the onset of smoking. You can usually see the flame as it burns by looking through a peep hole or removing a flap on the burner for this purpose. Tighten the screw or nut to lcok the adjustment in place.

The pump pressure is measured with a pressure gauge that reads in pounds per square inch (psi). The correct pressure is usually about 180 psi, but check the furnace owner's manual or service manual to be sure. Remove the pipe plug, Fig. 8-18F, to install the pressure gauge. Remove the cap (G) and use a screwdriver to adjust the pressure when the unit is in operation. If you must adjust the pump pressure, the air flow will have to be readjusted.

Cleaning the Pump Filter

Figure 8-23 shows a pump filter that is so filled with sludge that it severely restricts the flow of fuel through the pump. You can gain access to the filter by removing the bolts and housing of the pump. Clean the filter by placing it in clean fuel oil and gently brushing it with a paint brush. As in cleaning all filters, be careful not to tear or damage the screen. If you plan to clean the pump filter, you should do this before adjusting the pump pressure and air flow.

Cleaning the Flue and Fan

For normal operation, the oil furnace should produce a small amount of smoke. While a little smoke is no problem, a lot of smoke will soon produce carbon deposits in the flue. You should check the flue pipe to be sure that there are no buildups of carbon that would restrict air flow, since this can make the furnace smoke, and the smoke will likely end up in the house rather than outside. Carbon deposits usually collect in horizontal sections of the flue pipe, particularly where these sections connect to vertical pipes.

The fan in an oil furnace is the same as that in a gas furnace. Follow the same procedures discussed earlier for cleaning the squirrel cage fan motor and fan blades, also checking to see that the fan is mounted tightly on the motor shaft and that the fan belts have the proper tension.

ELECTRIC FURNACES

An electric furnace will usually operate properly and at maximum efficiency for many years without adjustment. Since there is no fuel combustion taking place, you will not have problems with carbon and soot buildup as in other furnaces. So any dirt that could decrease efficiency in an electric furnace must come from the air circulated inside the house. Keeping the air filters clean is therefore an important part of maintaining an electric furnace. Since there is no combustion, the electric furnace also has no flue to waste heat energy. As a result, almost all of the heat produced by the furnace elements ends up in the house.

Heat is generated in an electric furnace by passing electric current through resistance wires. When these heating elements raise the temperature of the air enough in the heat chamber, the fan starts up and circulates the warm air throughout the house. These electric heating elements draw a lot of electrical power, so it is essential that adequate sized wires are run to the furnace to supply all the current it needs. Normally, the local building codes insure that the proper size wiring is used, since the current passing through these wires also produces heat, which is wasted.

Maintaining the Fan

The fan controls on an electric furnace are usually preset and cannot be adjusted. The switches that turn the fan on and off, for example, are sealed units mounted in the heat chamber. The limit switch is usually a metal fuse (rather than a circuit breaker), and this fuse melts when the furnace elements get too hot. Consequently, if the fan does not come on for some reason, the fuse will open, requiring that it be replaced after the fan is fixed. If you want to save yourself the expense and nuisance of replacing the limit fuse, always make certain that you reconnect the fan wiring exactly where it belongs when you work on the fan.

About all you can do in an electric furnace is to keep the fan blades, fan motor, and filters clean. If you follow a regular maintenance schedule, you should have few problems with your furnace, and it will always be working near peak efficiency. You should clean all filters two to four times each year. And once a year you should remove the fan assembly and clean the blades, motor, and housing. The fans used in an electric furnace are the same as discussed earlier in the chapter.

Checking the Thermostat

An electric furnace usually has a special two-stage thermostat that prevents waste of energy. For example, consider an electric furnace with four heating elements. When the thermostat calls for heat, the first two elements come on immediately. The second two elements will not turn on unless the thermostat senses a big drop in

Fig. 8-23. (A) Remove the eight end bolts from the pump housing. (B) Remove the housing to get access to the pump filter, which here is shown removed. A filter filled with sludge will restrict the fuel flow to the burner sand reduce the efficiency of the furnace. Remove the filter screen and clean it with a brush and cleaning solvent.

temperature or unless the first two elements do not heat the house fast enough. This technique gives some energy savings to the homeowner because the second two elements are not used until they are needed.

Sometimes an outside thermostat is also attached to the two-stage thermostat inside the house. In this system, if the temperature outside remains above a preset temperature (usually about 35°F), the second stage of the thermostat can't come on. So the second stage is not used unless the temperature outside is really cold, requiring the extra heating elements. This is a very good feature to have if you frequently change the thermostat settings, as when you lower the setting for the night. When you turn the thermostat back up in the morning, the furnace is not likely to overheat the house on days that it is not especially cold outside.

HOT WATER BOILERS

Boilers heat water with gas, oil, electricity, and other types of energy. If the heating unit has burners, they should be cleaned and adjusted for maximum efficiency, jsut like the burners on gas and oil furnaces.

Since water contains minerals, lime and other residues will collect inside the boiler, and this must be cleaned out. To do this, you can buy boiler cleaners, which are specially prepared to remove the lime and scales from inside the boiler and water lines.

The water-pressure regulator valve and the automatic water inlet valve must be kept in good repair. These regulator valves are usually located near the water supply line. If these valves start sticking, they can cause major problems inside the boiler. Also check the air-bleed valves on the radiators to see that they are not frozen or sticking.

The surge tanks should have some water in it, but it should not be full. If the tank is full, drain it until it is less than half full.

Many hot water heating systems have water pumps to aid in circulating the water, particularly in new homes that use smaller diameter pipes. Since electrical energy is consumed in circulating the water, it is important to clean and lubricate the motors and pump sections so they will continue to operate efficiently. Clean the electric motor just as you would a fan motor. The pump section usually does not need more than a periodic oiling unless the pump shaft becomes hard to turn or the seals begin to leak water.

Furnace Humidifiers

9

The relative humidity of the air in a house is an important comfort factor. Sadly, humidity has varying effects on people. Some people seem unaffected by dry air, while others complain of irritated noses and throats. Many authorities feel that dry air is unhealthy, contributing to colds and sore throats. Whatever the arguments may be, it is certain that people feel more comfortable in a home when the humidity is between about 30% and 70%. Some experts claim that most people experience maximum comfort during the winter when the relative humidity is between 40% and 50%.

HUMIDITY EFFECTS

Relative humidity is the percentage of moisture in the air relative to the amount of moisture that the air could hold at that temperature. (See Chapter 1 for a discussion on humidity.) People generally feel uncomfortable when there is too much or too little moisture in the air. During the summer, for example, a relative humidity of more than 70% makes the air feel damp, close, and sultry. During the winter, a relative humidity of less than 30% makes the air feel dry, irritates the nose and throat, and encourages the buildup of static electricity in rugs, upholstery and clothing. Dry air also makes the air feel cooler because it speeds up the evaporation of moisture from the body.

During the heating season, it is difficult to maintain a suitable level of humidity because the air outside the home contains very little moisture. For example, if the temperature is 50°F outside with 100% relative humidity, the humidity will drop to less than 20% by the time the air has been heated to 70°F. For outside temperatures below freezing, the air contains practically no moisture to speak of. For this reason, the relative humidity in your home will go way down during the coldest winter months.

Some moisture is added to the home through the preparation of food, taking showers and baths, and normal body perspiration. A tightly sealed house can hold much of this moisture inside, helping to keep the relative humidity at a higher level. But the relative humidity can be lowered if moisutre condenses on cold wall and window surfaces. Without adequate insulation in the walls, moisture may condense on wall surfaces; and without insulated or double-pane windows, moisture will condense on the panes, running down and saturating the window frames to speed rotting. In slab-floor homes, moisture may condense at the wall edge near the floor, producing mold and mildew. Thus, even if plenty of moisture is added to the air, a home with inadequate insulation and poor weather stripping will not be able to keep the moisture from being condensed back out of the air, reducing the relative humidity.

In most homes, however, infiltration air leakage accounts for the major loss of moisture from the air. There will always be some air leaks around doors and windows, and you must open doors to go in and out of the house. In a typical home, up to one gallon of water in the air may be lost each day as it escapes from the house. So to maintain the relative humidity at an acceptable level, you must replace this moisutre as fast as it is lost.

Many schemes have been tried for increasing the humidity level in a home during the winter. You can boil pans of water on the stove, hang up wet cloths in the basement to dry, drape wet towels over radiators, set water-filled pans on the floor, etc. But if not inefficient, these methods are messy to say the least. Most modern furnace humidifiers require a minimum of maintenance, and a selection of models is available in a wide price range.

TYPES OF HUMIDIFIERS

There are basically two different types of furnace humidifiers, but they work in essentially the same way—they introduce water vapor into the air stream passing through the furnace ducts. Most humidifiers are purchased as separate add-on units that are installed in the duct system. You can buy these units at hardware stores, building supply stores, furnace suppliers, and many department stores. They are fairly easy to install, which is an extra benefit to the do-it-yourselfer.

All humidifiers need a supply of water, and this is usually obtained by clamping a special attachment onto a nearby water pipe. The attachment punctures the water line while forming a water-tight seal at the same time. A valve on attachment permits you to turn the water on and off as you desire. Some humidifiers also require an electrical connection, since they contain a motor.

Evaporator Types

The simplest and cheapest furnace humidifiers merely provide a wet surface for the warm furnace air to blow against, which then evaporates some of the water, carrying it throughout the house. These units rely solely upon evaporation to introduce moisture—there is no forced spray of water. The construction of these units varies widely, but they all contain a reservoir or basin of water that is kept filled to the required level by a float and valve system, much like that used in the water tank of a toilet.

The wet surface exposed to the furnace air flow may be obtained in different ways. In one system, a set of evaporator fins sits in the basin of water, soaking up the water that is evaporated by the portion of the fins extending into the furnace duct. Other systems use a motor to dunk the ends of bristles or a foam belt into the reservoir and then move the wet portion up into the stream of warm air. If the humidifier has a motor, it is usually wired together with the furnace with the furnace fan so that the motor only operates when the furnace fan does.

Figure 9-1 illustrates a motorized humidifier using a set of bristles. The water is held in the basin, where the nylon bristles pick it up. A motor turns the bristles and brings them into the flow of air through the furnace duct. Water that is not evaporated simply returns to the water basin. The water is piped to the water basin, and a float controls the water level. The water supply tube should have a shutoff valve near the humidifier so the water supply can be turned off if necessary. The humidifier is attached to the duct system where the main hot-air duct leaves the furnace.

Evaporator-type humidifiers do not usually need to have a humidity control—called a *humidistat*—to regulate the amount of moisture in the air. The humidity is controlled in part by the moisture already in the air, but mostly by how often the furnace turns on. Since these units are installed on the air duct leaving the furnace, the relative humidity of this warm air is quite low, so variations in the humidity in your house will have little effect on the amount of water being evaporated. However, your furnace will

Fig. 9-1. This humidifier is installed in the bottom of the main duct. The nylon bristles extend into the air flow, where the furnace air evaporates the moisture. A 24-volt electric motor and gearbox turn the bristles to pick up the water from the lower part of the humidifier. The motor is connected in the circuit with the furnace fan so that the humidifier will come on only when the furnace is on.

turn on more often during cold weather when the air is normally drier, so more moisture will be introduced into the air as it is needed. It is therefore important when buying an evaporator-type humidifier that you get a unit for the size furnace you have, since this is the only method you have of controlling the amount of moisture being added to the air.

Figure 9-2 shows a belt-type humidifier. In this evaporative system, some warm air is pulled out of the main duct system and

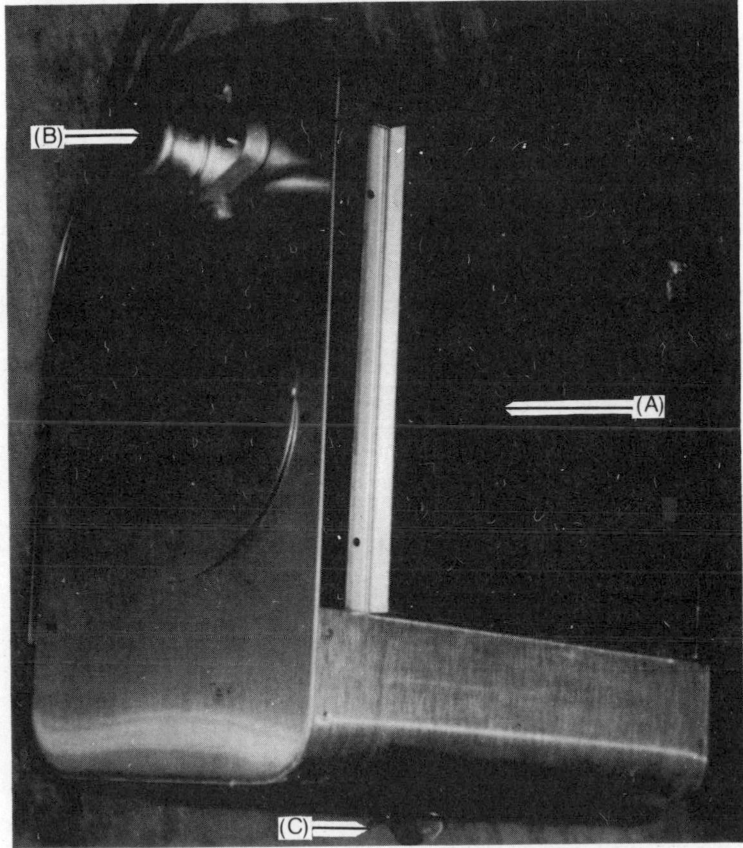

Fig. 9-2. This type of humidifier is sometimes called a semi-forced air humidifier because some air is taken from the furnace and forced through the wet belt. Cutouts are provided at the left and right sides for connecting the feed duct, while the main square area (A) exposing the belt is connected into the regular duct system. This type of humidifier does a good job of humidifying the air, so some method is needed to regulate the amount of moisture added to the air. The 24-volt motor (B) connects to the furnace fan-control system so that the belt turns only while the furnace is operating. This unit can also be installed on the air intake of the furnace, with the feed duct coming back from the hot air side of the furnace.

forced through the wet belt, which then passes humidified air back into the duct system. The motor drives the belt so that it picks up water from the basin at the bottom, keeping the belt continually saturated with water. While this unit relies only on the furnace to circulate air through the belt, this technique tends to be much more efficient than other types of evaporator-type humidifiers. It is advisable to use a humidistat with this unit, though a vent can also be installed on the feed duct to regulate the amount of air passing through the unit and, therefore, the amount of moisture added to the air.

Sprayer Types

The best type of furnace humidifier uses a pump or revolving disc to produce a fine spray or mist of water that is quickly evaporated in the furnace air. The warm air easily absorbs the additional moisture and carriers it through the air ducts to the various rooms in the house. This type of humidifier *must* have a humidity control, called a humidistat, to shut the pump or sprayer off when the relative humidity in the home reaches a satisfactory level. Without the humidistat, this type of forced-mositure humidifier will continue spraying water into the furnace air. Eventually there will be so much humidity in the air that moisture will begin condensing on walls and windows, causing the problems outlined before. Even after the humidity reaches 100%, the pump will continue to spray the water mist, and this can destroy the furnace ducts. With a humidistat, the control can be set for 40-50% or so, and the humidifier will automatically keep that much moisture in the air.

Because of their construction, sprayer-type humidifiers are among the most expensive of furnace humidifiers. However, by spraying the water directly into the air, they eliminate the need for replacing evaporator bristles, plates, and belts, which eventually become clogged with deposits left behind when the water evaporates. And since the moisture is forcibly introduced into the air stream, much higher levels of humidity can be obtained.

The reliability of sprayer-type humidifiers has proven to be much better than simpler evaporator types, which means that there is generally less maintenance to perform. But while there is less accumulation of deposits from the evaporating water within the humidifier itself, some people note that the deposits are passed into the house, slightly increasing the amount of dust in the house. While this dust might not concern the average homeowner, it might be of interest to people with allergies or with water containing a lot of minerals.

CLEANING YOUR HUMIDIFIER

All humidifiers should be inspected once a year before the heating season begins. Evaporator-type humidifiers should also be inspected a couple of times during the winter to be sure that accumulations of lime and minerals from the evaporating water do not clog the water-inlet valve or the fins, belts, and bristles.

The float, needle valve, and valve seat of a humidifier are shown in Fig. 9-3. As water is evaporated from the humidifier, lime and mineral deposits are left behind. These collect on the valve seat, so they must be removed periodically. If they are not, the valve may not turn off, causing the water basin to overflow.

To clean the humidifier, first remove it from the bottom of the duct. Take out the bristles of fins as shown in Fig. 9-4. You can drain the water from the basin of the humidifier through the drain

Fig. 9-3. Float (A) maintains the water level in the basin. This float can be adjusted to raise or lower the water level. The water line connects to the humidifier at valve (B). Overflow outlet (C) keeps the water level from getting too high in the basin, enabling the water to flow out onto the floor rather than into the furnace.

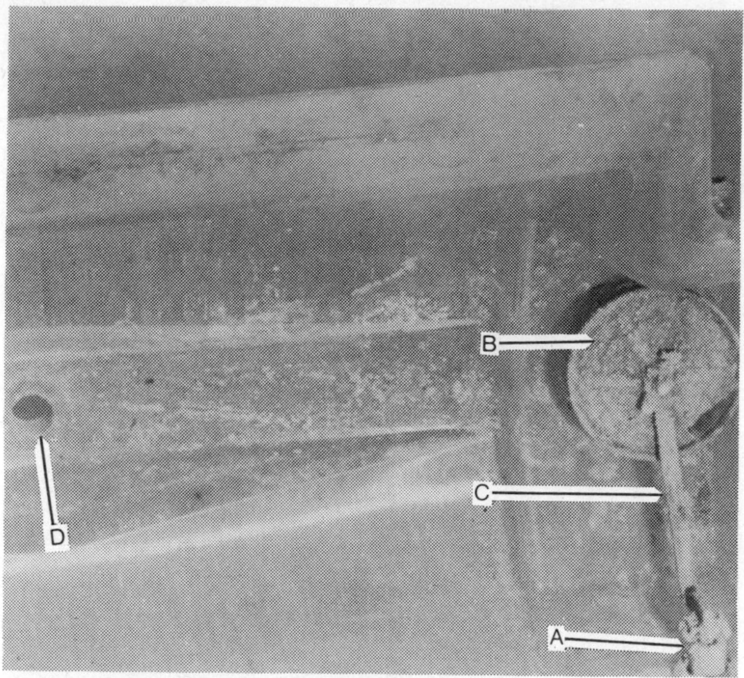

Fig. 9-4. The bristles of this humidifier have been removed so that the needle valve and valve seat (A) and the float (B) can be scraped clean. These parts are covered with mineral deposits on this humidifier. The stem (C) on the float can be bent to adjust the water level. A drain (D) in the bottom of the basin lets the water drain out.

hole in the bottom. Scrape all the mineral deposits from the float, the valve, and the valve seat. Remove the mineral deposits from any other part of the humidifier and water lines.

Figure 9-5 shows the back of a belt unit removed so that the humidifier can be cleaned. The belt goes around two rollers, one at the top and one at the bottom. These rollers can be removed easily to clean the humidifier. The belt will have to be replaced if it is worn or ripped. Scrape the water valve and float to remove any mineral deposits that could affect the performance of the unit.

FUEL SAVINGS

For years it has been common knowledge that people feel warmer when the humidity in a room is higher. Generally, you can figure that each 10% increase in relative humidity enables you to turn down the room thermostat by about one degree. This would seem to indicate that you can obtain a substantial fuel savings by using a humidifier in your home. But you have to be careful about such claims because the savings is not as great as some manufacturers would have you belive.

You will remember that when water evaporates it absorbs heat energy. Your furnace has to supply this heat energy when you use a humidifier—and it takes over 8000 BTU to evaporate just one gallon of water. Fortunately, however, the average size home needs less than one gallon of water evaporated into the air to bring the relative humidity from 0% up to 50%. Since there are many other sources or water vapor in your home, your furnace humidifier does not have to supply very much water each day to maintain the humidity at a comfortable level. Of course, this depends upon how much infiltration air enters your home, pushing out the moist air. The more tightly sealed your home is, the more moisture it will be able to retian, and the less water vapor your humidifier will have to add to the air to replace what was lost.

As an example of cost, let's use the home in Chapter 7 that had an average heat load of 25,000 BTU per hour over a six-month

Fig. 9-5. The cover of this belt type humidifier has been removed for cleaning. The sponge rubber belt (A) is held in position by two rollers (B), which must be removed to clean the float (C) and valve assembly (D). The overflow opening (E) prevents water from entering the furnace.

heating season. During the average 24-hour day, this furnace would consume 600,000 BTU of heat energy, and assuming that the humidifier used up a whole gallon of water in that time, 8000 BTU of heat energy would be needed to evaporate the water. Now, if having a 50% relative humidity inside the house would permit you to turn down the thermostat just two degrees, the furnace woudl consume 30,000 BTU less energy on a day that the outside temperature was 40 degrees less than the inside. Clearly, the 8000 BTU expended in evaporating the gallon of water saved quite a bit of fuel energy. In general, the energy savings will pay for the furnace humidifier in about two to five years, depending on how much moisture you have to add to the air in your home and how expensive the unit was.

Air Conditioners and Common Sense 10

There are several types of air conditioning systems for cooling your home during the hot summer months. You can pick from a wide range of air conditioners, central air conditioners, or heat pumps. All of these systems work in essentially the same way—some are just bigger than others. And all of these systems require similar maintennance to keep them working at top efficiency.

Most homes built today have capability of easy conversion to central air conditioning, if they do not already have it. Homes built with heat pumps to provide heat during the winter also use the same unit to provide air conditioning during the summer. Most room air conditioners are used today where only one or two rooms are to be cooled, or where central air conditioning is impractical or unnecessary. So the type of air conditioning you have or want depends on your cooling needs and the cost of installing a particular system.

ROOM AIR CONDITIONERS

A room air conditioner can be installed either in a window or wall, depending on where you want the unit to be and how much effort you want to expend on installing it. There are many different models, designs and styles of room air conditioners available today. They range in size from small units that are able to cool just one room, to large units that are able to cool three or four rooms. Large units are often mounted through the wall and become permanent installations.

The big selection of air conditioners introduces a lot of problems. Some of these problems involve minor things like style and appearance, but many of the problems are quite a bit more serious. Air conditioners are powered by electricity, for example, so you have to check the power consumption, outlets, and voltages required by the various air conditioners. You also have to be concerned about the cooling capacity of the air conditioner to be sure that it meets your needs.

There are many reasons why people complain about the performance of their room air conditioner. Some people are just hard to please, but many people have legitimate complaints. Their air conditioner just doesn't perform the way their friends' do—or the way the salesman promised them it would. Usually, a little forethought and planning before purchasing a room air conditioner will prevent most of the problems these people have.

One of the biggest reasons an air conditioner does not perform to expectations is that the unit is simply too small for the area being cooled. In a rush to make a sale, the salesman may have convinced the buyer that the smaller model—which is $50 cheaper—would probably cool the house, so the homeowner doesn't really need that big, expensive air conditioner. Sometimes the salesman is right; sometimes he isn't. Later in this chapter we discuss how to size an air conditioner.

The opposite problem of course, occurs when a person who buys an extra-large air conditioner, one that has much more cooling capacity than is needed. Perhaps they are convinced that they are getting more for their money, or maybe they think that a large unit will do a better job of cooling. Whatever their reason for buying the air conditioner, they are likely to complain that the unit makes too much noise, produces drafts, cools the room too quickly, or doesn't seem to be able to lower the humidity of the air. All of these are common problems with over-sized air conditioners, proving once again that bigger is not always betters.

A large number of people buy a room air conditioner with the idea of cooling more than one room. So they buy a large unit, install it, and often find that it doesn't do the job it was supposed to do. The problem here may be improper air circulation. Cold air is heavy and difficult to move; it has a tendency to sink down next to the walls and lie on the floor. The room air conditioner can provide only limited air circulation. It has a fan to blow the air out into the room, but it has no way to really circulate the air through the house. Cool air will not circulate by itself as readily as warm air, so you have to

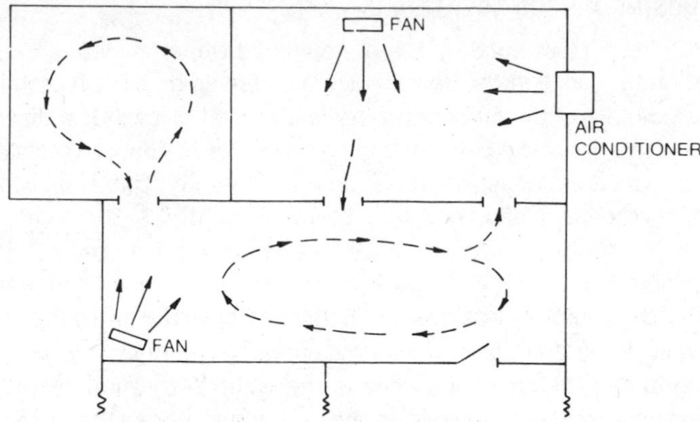

Fig. 10-1. Household fans will help distribute the cool air of a room air conditioner and improve its performance. Set the fans so they direct the air flow into the rooms to be cooled. Fans located near the floor are best because cool air sinks to the floor. If the cool air is blown through the lower half of a doorway, warm air will flow out of the room through the upper half. A room can be kept at a more even temperature by making the fan blow cool air upward toward the ceiling where the hot air tends to collect, thereby mixing and circulating the air better.

be sure that either the air conditioner's fan is able to blow the cool air into all rooms or provide an extra fan to assist the air conditioner.

If the air conditioner is installed in a room that has limited circulation to the other rooms in the house, like a bedroom, the room with the air conditioner will be much cooler than the other rooms. Using fans to help circulate the cool air can bring the air conditioners' performance up to what it should be. Set the fans up as in Fig. 10-1 to blow the cool air into the rooms you want cooled. Fans are beneficial in another way, for the air circulating from the fans will speed up evaporation from the body and make you feel cooler. You will probably find that you can turn the thermostat on the air conditioner to a warmer setting and save some electricity.

Room air conditioners are not inherently troublesome; they just require a little forethought and common sense. You have to remember that while a lot of professional planning goes into installing a large, central air conditioning system, you also have to plan ahead when installing even a small room air conditioner. And if you don't trust your own judgment, you can always go to a reputable dealer who can help you get a quality unit of the right size and give you tips on how to achieve the best possible performance.

CHOOSING A GOOD LOCATION

The performance of a room air conditioner depends a good deal on the place in the home you have chosen to have it installed. For example, if the air conditioner is installed in a window directly opposite a door, the fan on the air conditioner is going to blow cool air out the door each time it is opened. Certainly, this is no way to conserve energy and cool your room efficiently.

Of course, if you want to cool two or more rooms, it is desirable to locate the air conditioner opposite an open doorway to one of the rooms, since this will help distribute the air to the other rooms. If you don't have a window opposite the doorway, you can often install the air conditioner in the wall. You can also use the directional vents or louvers on the air conditioner to throw the air toward the open doorway. Not all air conditioners have movable louvers and not all movable louvers work very well, so you have to be careful when buying an air conditioner.

The condensers (the part of the room air conditioner that extends outside the house) must have good air circulation around it. The condenser is the part of the air conditioner that releases the absorbed inside heat into the surrounding outside air. If there is not good air circulation around the condenser, the heat cannot be carried away and the efficiency of the air conditioner is reduced. The condenser should not be placed in direct sunlight, either , since the sunlight warms the condenser and makes it more difficult to disperse the heat.

Sometimes an air conditioner is installed in a wall with the condenser extending into the garage. This is not recommended, since it can create problems with both heat and air circulation. If the garage door is left closed, circulation over the condenser is reduced, and the heat from the condenser is dispersed into the garage, raising the temperature inside the garage. Unless the garage door is left open when the air conditioner is operating, the efficiency of the air conditioner will be reduced considerably. There are times, however, when you have no alternative but to install the air conditioner in the garage wall because that turns out to be the most convenient location. In such cases, you just have to be sure to provide adequate ventilation through the garage when it is operating.

When the condenser extends outside the house, try to avoid locations that shelter the condenser from natural wind currents. While the air conditioner does have an external fan to circulate air through the condenser, it definitely helps to have fresh air available

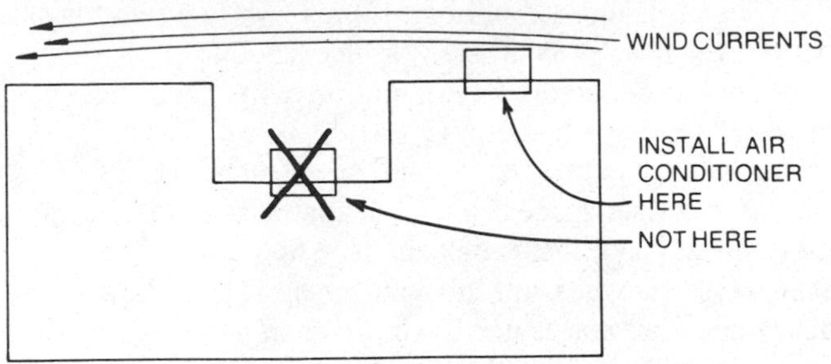

Fig. 10-2. Do not install a room air conditioner where the condenser will not receive good air circulation. Do not put it in a place where it will be surrounded on three sides by walls. Note, however, that shelter from direct sunlight is beneficial in keeping the condenser as cool as possible.

for good cooling. A sheltered location, like that shown in Fig. 10-2, cuts down on the amount of fresh air, forcing the air conditioner to recirculate warmed air over the condenser coils. In general, the cooler the air around the condenser, the more efficiently your air conditioner will perform.

SELECTING THE RIGHT SIZE AIR CONDITIONER

Size is very important. If your air conditioner is too small, the air conditioner will run all the time on hot days and still not be able to cool the room. On the other hand, if your air conditioner is too large, the unit will start up and cool the area so quickly that it will only be on a short time. And because it only runs a short time, it will have to turn on and off more often to control the temperature of the room. Given the large amount of electricity needed to start an electric motor and bring the air conditioner up to normal operation, the more often the compressor motor has to start, the more electricity will be wasted. This type of operation is also harder on the air conditioner and more likely to bring about an early failure. Another result of short operation times is that the humidity in the room will not be lowered as much, and this means the thermostat has to be set to a lower temperature for comfort, wasting more electricity.

Window air conditioners are sized in three ratings: horsepower, BTU and tons of refrigeration (12,000 BTU is equal to one ton of refrigeration). A one-horsepower unit provides about 8000 BTU, depending on the efficiency of the unit.

An average size room with good insulatin will usually require a unit rated at 8000 BTU, or ¾ ton. A one-ton air conditioner is usually large enough to cool two rooms, while a two-ton air conditioner will usually cool four or five rooms. These estimates depend, of course, on the air circulation in the house, its construction, insulation, and location.

As a rough estimate, you will need from 2.5 to 3 BTU of each square foot of floor space in a well insulated room. Before purchasing a room air conditioner, measure the floor area of the rooms you want to cool. Also measure the window area and make a note of how much window area faces north, south, east, and west, and whether or not the windows are shaded. Make a note of the number of appliances operating in the room and their wattages. Armed with these figures, you can then go to a reputable dealer, who should be able to closely estimate the right size unit for your needs.

If you wish to figure your own requirements, you can often obtain printed guides from various manufacturers, showing you how to estimate the cooling load based on the factors just mentioned. There are several magazines, such as *Consumer Reports*, that provide such information and include many helpful hints on which air conditioners are most economical and possess the most desirable features.

CHECK YOUR WIRING BEFORE BUYING

Before you go out to buy a room air conditioner, you would be very wise to check your wiring. More than one person has planned an installation and purchased an air conditioner, only to find that the receptacles are wrong, the house wiring is not adequate, or the main electrical service to the home cannot handle the extra power required. While very small room air conditioners (4000 to 5000 BTU capacity) are not likely require special wiring, even these come with three-pronged plugs that may not fit the receptacles in older homes. Air conditioners rated at 6000 BTU or more are most likely to cause problems. These units draw a considerable amount of electric current while they are starting up and operating, so you have to be sure that the wiring in your home can handle the load.

Older homes often have circuits that can handle no more than 10 amperes, while most homes today have circuits rated for 10 or 20 amperes. Each circuit usually has about six receptacles on it, and each circuit has its own fuse or circuit breaker. Under normal circumstances, each circuit will provide enough current to operate an assortment of lamps and small appliances. But the circuit may not have enough reserve capacity to handle an air conditioner *in addition to everything else*. A 6000 BTU air conditioner, for example, will typically require between 6 and 8 amperes, so even this relatively small unit will use a large percentage of the current capacity in one circuit of your home.

Large room air conditioners normally require 240V instead of the usual 120V found in most home outlets. The reason for this is that 240-volt operation needs only half as much current to produce the same amount of power. Air conditioners are primarily 120-volt units until their current demands approach about 12 amperes; above this they normally use 240V. In terms of cooling capacity, this transition occurs somewhere between 8000 and 12,000 BTU, depending on the efficiency of the unit and on whether or not 240V is available. When air conditioners come in either 120V or 240V, the 240-volt unit is generally more efficient because the lower amount of current also wastes less energy in the motor wiring. Since this is a very popular range of cooling capacities, there is a wide variety of room air conditioners that can be purchased for either 120V or 240V. If you plan on 240-volt operation, you will have to install a special outlet unless there is already one available.

Another important consideration is the service capacity that you have from the electric company. Older homes may not have 240-volt (three wire) service. Even with 240-volt service, if you Have a lot of electrical appliances, you still may not have adequate service to run a large air conditioner. So before you buy an air conditioner, contact your utility company to see if the service lines into your home are sufficient. Utility companies usually do not charge extra for upgrading your service—after all, you're going to be buying more electricity from them—but there may be a substantial delay before they can get around to doing it. In addition, your home may need new junction boxes and circuit breakers to handle the increased service, so there may be more expenses and delays before you can plug in your air conditioner.

Chances are, if you're planning to install a new air conditioner, you'll want to put in a separate circuit and receptacle just for the air conditioner, and you will probably want 240V if you're planning to install a new air conditioner, you'll want to put in a separate circuit and receptacle just for the air conditioner, and you will probably want 240V if you're planning to install a single, large air conditioner. This means you should check your present breaker. If there is no room, you have to install either a larger box or a separate smaller box. You may have to install another breaker box anyway if your home does not have enough service.

ELECTRICAL OUTLETS

Figure 10-3 show s the most common receptacles for use with room air conditioners. Outlets D and E you have seen many times before. However, outlets A, B, and C are used only for 240-volt circuits, such as on an electric range or drier. The main difference between the various 240-volt outlets is in the amount of current they can deliver to an appliance. For maximum safety, appliance cords are made to fit only those outlets that are able to handle the required amount of current. (It is assumed that the receptacle is connected back to the junction box with the correct size wire and that the correct size circuit breaker is used.)

Since a 240-volt outlet has three wires going to it, you must be extremely careful to connect the right wires to the right pins on the outlet. A wrong connection here can seriously damage any appliance plugged into the outlet. In a 240-volt outlet there are two "hot" wires that carry 120V each and a neutral wire with zero volts. In Fig. 10-3 the lower two pins of each outlet are hot and the top pin is neutral. Neutral wires are always colored white. Hot wires may be any color except white or green. The green color is reserved for the ground wire connected to the third pin of a 120-volt outlet or to the metal frame of other junction boxes and appliances.

The voltate measured between the two hot pins of a 240-volt outlet should always be approximately 240V. The voltage between any hot pin and the neutral pin should be about 120V. The two hot wires should be connected to the two hot wires entering the main service box from the utility lines. If you plan on doing the wiring yourself, determine what type of receptacle is required for the air conditioner you plan to buy, then check with a local supply store to be sure that you use the right size wires and circuit breaker.

On 120-volt outlets, such as that shown in D of Fig. 10-3, 12-gauge wire having three conductors is normally used. Sometimes this is referred to as *two conductors with ground* or as 12/2 *with ground*. Although 14-gauge wire, with its lower current capacity, can often be used with 120-volt air conditioners, it is best to use 12-gauge wire, since it can handle 20 amperes in most circuits. Referring to Fig. 10-3, the green*ground* wire goes to the round pin at the top, the white *neutral* wire goes to the wider right-hand pin, and the colored (usually black) *hot* wire goes to the smaller left-hand pin.

HOW AIR CONDITIONERS WORK

An air conditioner has two coils, one on the inside of the house and the other on the outside. In a rom air conditioner, both coils are

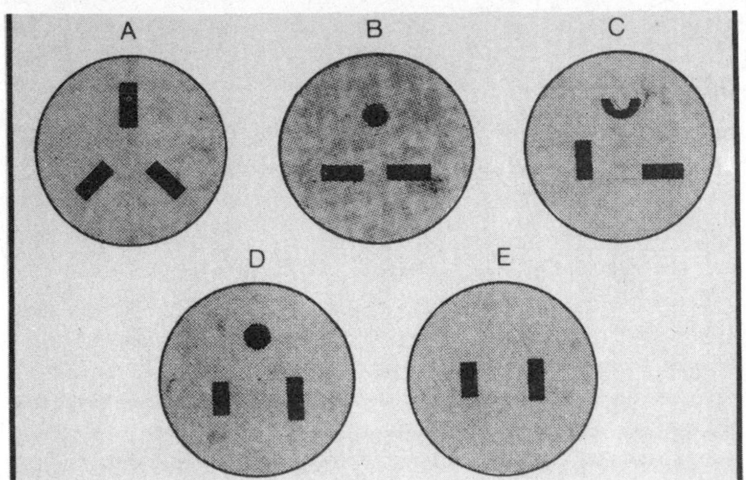

Fig. 10-3. Receptacles (A), (B) and (C) are plugs used to connect air conditioners on 240-volt circuits of different amperages. Receptacles (D) and (E) are used with 240-volt air conditioners. Although most 120-volt air conditioners need a receptacle like (D) with a ground pin, adapter plugs with ground wires may also be used for use with receptacle (E)

contained in the same box, but they are separated from each other, with one facing into the room and the other facing outside. Central air conditioners and heat pumps also have two coils, though they are separated foom each other by a much greater distance.

The purpsoe of the two coils is to absorb and release heat energy. To aid in this process, they are covered with fins or wire bristles to give them more surface area. A large surface area is important because it makes it easier for the coils to transfer heat to the surrounding air. Fans are used to circulate air through these coils when the air conditioner is running.

The two coils are connected to a compressor, which pumps the refrigerant (usually Freon) through the system, as shown in Fig. 10-4. The refrigerant is a liquid that has a very low boiling point—generally around—20°F to—50°F. So at room temperatures, the refrigerant would evaporate very quickly if it was not sealed tightly in the system. When the air conditioner is operating, the refrigerant changes from liquid to vapor and back to liquid again as it circulates through the two coils. When the refrigerant evaporates, it absorbs heat energy from the surrounding air; when it condenses, it gives of fheat.

The refrigerant enters the outside coil, or condenser, as a gas under high pressure, due to the pumping action of the compressor.

When the refrigerant gas is compressed, its temperature increases. Consequently, the condenser coils become much warmer than the surrounding air outside. By circulating the outside air over the condenser coil, the air cools the coil and removes heat energy, causing the refrigerant to condense and become liquid. The liquid drains to the bottom of the condenser coil and flows back to the inside of the house.

The returning liquid refrigerant then passes through an expansion valve, where the pressure is permitted to drop. The opposite action now takes place as the drop in pressure produces a drop in temperature. The refrigerant now becomes much cooler than the air inside the house. The refrigerant passes through the inside coil, or evaporator, and circulating air from insided the house warms the coil. The liquid refrigerant now absorbs the heat energy and becomes a vapor once again. The vapor is returned to the compressor and the cycle repeats itself.

As you can see, the real secret to the operation of an air conditioner lies in the repeated condensing and evaporating action of the refrigerant. The compressor and expansion valve make the system work by increasing and decreasing the pressure exerted on the refrigerant, which raises and lowers the temperature of the refrigerant. For really efficient operation, the temperature of the refrigerant in the condenser coil must be much hotter than the outside air, and the temperature of the refrigerant in the evaporator coil must be much colder than the temperature of the air inside the house. The efficiency of an air conditioner, therefore, depends on the temperature of the inside and outside air. If the outside temperature is less than the inside temperature, the air conditioner can transfer heat energy to the outside very efficiently. But on hot summer days, the temperature difference between the coils and the surrounding air is not as great, making it necessary for the air conditioner to work much harder to transfer heat energy.

Air conditioners use basically the same refrigeration process as that used in refrigerators, freezers, and heat pumps. Because of the pressures involved, the refrigeration system must be a sealed system in which the refrigerant is not permitted to escape. If a leak develops in a coil or one of the refrigerant lines, the refrigerant will be lost and the system will cease to function. You will never see a drop of refrigerant outside the air conditioner because it evaporates at such a low temperature—your only clue will be the poor operation of your air conditioner.

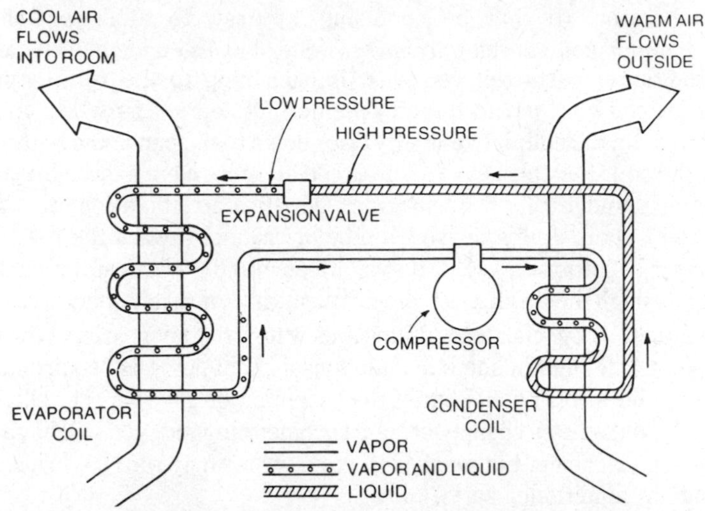

Fig. 10-4. Simplified diagram of air conditioner showing flow of refrigerant liquid and vapor. The refrigerant removes heat energy from the air as it evaporates in the evaporator coil, and it gives off heat energy as it condenses in the condenser coil. The compressor pumps the refrigerant vapor from the evaporator into the condenser. The expansion valve controls the flow of refrigerant liquid into the evaporator coil. The condenser coil operates at a much higher pressure than the evaporator coil. A motor with a fan blade on one end of the rotor shaft circulates air over the outside condenser coil. A separate fan motor is used for the evaporator coil inside the house to circulate air.

With a central air conditioning system, the two coils are widely separated. The evaporator coil is located in the furnace in a compartment known as the coil case, which is the box on the furnace with all the heat ducts coming out. In the summer cooling season, the furnace fan is used to circulate air through the evaporator coil and then through the rest of the house. The condenser coil and compressor are located in a separate unit some distance from the living areas. As Fig. 10-4 illustrates, only two lines are required to carry the refrigerant between the evaporator and condenser coils, so the two parts of the central air conditioner may be located up to about 50 feet apart. Heat pumps operate in much the same way, except with a heat pump it is possible to interchange the roles of the two coils so that heat energy can be pumped into the house as well as out of it.

Air conditioners also serve to dehumidify by condensing excess moisture from the air. Since the evaporator coil of the air conditioner is much cooler than the air inside the house, water vapor will condense on the coil as the air passes through the evaporator. (It may be confusing, at first, to think that the *evaporator* coil serves to *condense* water but the names of the air conditioner parts tell you what is happening to the refrigerant inside the coil, not to the air outside.) Of course, as water condenses on the coil, it eventually drips down to the pan at the bottom of the coil. For this reason, all air conditioners have a drain line to safely remove this condensation. On room air conditioners, the water simply drains through a tube or channel toward the rear of the air conditioner, where it evaporates into the warm air circulating through the condenser compartment. In central air conditioning systems, a special tube drains the water to the nearest sewer opening, though in some installations a sump pump is required to carry the water up and out of the basement or crawl space. Obviously, if the drain channel or tube becomes clogged, you will have a mess to clean up, but much worse, the water may rust the furnace and air conditioner parts.

TIPS ON USING YOUR AIR CONDITIONER

The efficiency with which an air conditioner can dehumidify the air depends primarily upon how cold the evaporator coil gets. If the fan of the air conditioner is set at a low speed, the coil will get colder and more moisture will be removed from the air; however, the air conditioner may not be able to cool the house on especially hot days. At high fans speeds, the air conditioner will be able to cool better, but it will not be able to dehumidify as well. For best comfort, it is usually recommended that you use a low fan setting on warm, humid days and a high fan setting on hot days.

Constantly adjusting the thermostat up and down does no good. An air conditioner will not cool a room any faster if the thermostat is set to a much cooler setting when it is first turned on, despite what many people believe. An air conditioner turns on when the thermostat senses that the room is too warm, and it does not turn off until the room is cool enough. The fastest way to cool a room is to set the fan speed on *high*; this will make the air conditioner work at maximum capacity. Set the thermostat at a comfortable temperature, then leave it alone, except for minor changes to take care of cool or hot days. In general, an air conditioner with several fan speeds will permit you to keep the room at a more uniform temperature without having to adjust the thermostat as much.

Should you open up the house during the day when you are not at home? This is not a good idea if you live in a climate with humid summers. You have to remember than n air conditioner works almost as hard to reduce the humidity of the air by 1% as it does to reduce the temperature by one degree. If you close up the house during the day, the temperature inside may increase, but the himidity will not—it will decrease. The temperature inside a sealed home will not become much hotter than it gets outside, so when you come home and turn on your air conditioner, it will only have to lower the temperature of the air. This will permit your air conditioner to cool your home faster, and it will save electricity as well. As a general rule, if the himidity of the outside air will be more than 30% on any day that you plan to use your air conditioner it will be more economical to close up your house when you leave in the morning. This is not a new trick—many people without air conditioners open up their house at night and close them up during the day; the temperature inside their house may get as hot as the outdoors, but the lower humidity inside makes the home feel much cooler.

11 Maintaining Your Air Conditioner

Whether you have a small room air conditioner or a much larger central air conditioner, there are many things you can do to keep it operating at peak efficiency. For example, an air conditioner has filters that get clogged with dust, finned coils that become dirty, and motors that need lubricating. These simple tasks are not difficult to do and require only a wrench and a couple of screwdrivers.

All air conditioners should be lubricated and cleaned each year. The best time for doing this is a month or so before the summer cooling season begins. A big advantage to making an early inspection is that you will always be ready if the first warm weather should strike early. Another advantage is that you will not have as much trouble finding parts or getting professional help if you should happen to find something seriously wrong with your air conditioner.

ROOM AIR CONDITIONERS

Figure 11-1 shows the collection of dust and dirt that quickly builds up inside an air conditioner. The outside case (Fig. 11-2) serves primarily to protect the inside parts from large dirt particles and to protect you from the moving parts, but the case does little to prevent smaller particles of dirt from entering.

Cleaning the Air Filter

As room air is drawn into the air conditioner, it first passes through a foam or aluminum-mesh filter, much like the air filters in

Fig. 11-1. The inside of an air conditioner rapidly collect dust particles on the coils,m fans and other motor parts. For optimum efficiency of operation, this dirt should be cleaned out once a year. (A) is the condenser coil that sticks out the window, (B) is the evaporator coil inside the house, and (C) is the air duct that blows cool air into the room.

many furnaces. The air filters are cleanable, and they should be cleaned several times a year. The openings in the filter are fairly large in order to pass the largest amount of air. But the relatively large openings also permit a certain amount of small dust particles and dirt to pass through to the evaporator coil. Fortunately, the evaporator coil is able to continually clean itself with the water condensing and running off, so only large dust particles pose any threat to the operation of the air conditioner.

The filter is normally located immediately behind the plastic grille or front panel of the air conditioner. The panel is most often held in place by several spring clips on one side that permit the panel to be "popped" off, usually from the top or bottom. Be careful, however, since one edge of the panel generally has a lip that holds it in place until the opposite side of the panel is swung out. Other air conditioners have plastic or metal tabs that must be pushed sideways to release the panel. Carefully inspect the front panel of your air conditioner before you attempt to force the panel loose, or you may easily break the panel.

The filter may be held in place over the evaporator coil or against the back side of the panel. Sometimes clips, springs or elastic bands are used to hold the filter in place. The foam tears very easily, so be careful when removing it for cleaning. If the filter

Fig. 11-2. The case of the air conditioner serves to protect the air conditioner parts from rough handling. The case may be mounted in a window opening or through a hole cut in the wall. The air conditioner chassis (Fig. 11-1) is completely rigid and slides easily into and out of the case. This feature makes working on an air conditioner much easier than most other electrical appliances.

is torn or especially dirty, you can buy a replacement kit in most hardware or department stores; just cut the foam to fit your air conditioner. Do not replace a filter with one that is thicker than the original because this can restrict the air flow.

Clean the air filter in warm water, possibly with a little detergent to help dissolve the dirt. Again, handle the filter carefully. (Refer to the section on furnace filters.) The filter is replaced just as it was removed, though you should check to see that there are no gaps around the filter where dust might pass through. The air filter should be cleaned at least once a year, more often if you have carpeting or some other source of lint and dust. The filter is relatively small, so it can get clogged up pretty quickly.

Evaporator Coil

The evaporator coil at the front of the air conditioner (Fig. 11-3) rarely needs attention; the cleansing action of water condensing on it usually does a good job of keeping it free of dirt. However, you should routinely inspect this coil whenever you clean the air filter. If the air filter has moved or allowed much dirt to pass through, sections of the evaporator coil may require some cleaning. After several years of use, some sections of the coil are bound to accumulate dirt.

If the evaporator coil needs cleaning, you can blow it out with compressed air or a light spray of water. Soapy water also works well. Wipe off any dirt around the condenser coil and air ducts in the front. Do not get any water on any of the controls or motor parts, and be careful not to bend or dent the fins of the evaporator, since this will restrict air flow and encourage icing.

The thermostat element is usually located on or near the evaporator coil Fig. 11-3) so that the air conditioner can sense the temperature of the room air being drawn into the evaporator. This sensing element is connected to the actuating switch by thin metal tube, which you should avoid bending or otherwise damaging.

Evaporator Icing Problems

If the thermostat on an air conditioner is set at a very low temperature, the evaporator coil may begin to ice up. What happens is that the temperature of the evaporator drops below the freezing point and ice begins to form on the evaporator. Ice usually

Fig. 11-3. The evaporator coil is under the front panel of a room air conditioner. Part of your regular servicing should include inspecting and cleaning the coil with compressed air or water. Do not get the controls or motor wet. Part of the squirrel cage fan can be seen at the back of the air duct. The tube and bulb affixed to the front of the evaporator are part of the thermostat, and they are easily damaged. Always unplug the air conditioner when cleaning it to avoid physical and electrical hazards.

starts to form along the refrigerant inlet at the top of the coil, and it gradually progresses downward until the whole coil is blocked with ice. Since the formation of ice restricts the flow of air through the evaporator coil, the more ice that forms, the colder the coil will get, and this cause even more ice to form. Some air conditioners are designed so that this icing problem cannot occur, but the majority of air conditioners can ice over under certain circumstances.

The common reason for the evaporator icing up is setting the thermostat at too low a temperature. When the thermostat is set properly, the room will stay at a fairly comfortable and uniform temperature. You should not have to touch the thermostat once it is set properly, especially if the air conditioner has several fan speeds. Of course, some air conditioners are able to control the room temperature better than others, so some minor adjustment may be required between cool days and hot days.

For some reason, many people think that you can cool a room faster when the air conditioner is first turned on by setting the thermostat at a much lower temperature. This is not ture! And it is one of the biggest causes of air conditioners icing up. When you turn the air conditioner on, the compressor will continue to operate until the room temperature drops to the setting indicated on the thermostat. As long as the thermostat "says" the room is too warm, the air conditioner is going to operate at maximum capacity, and no amount of juggling the thermostat is going to make it cool the room any faster. The best advice for adjusting the thermostat on a room air conditioner is to adjust it only after the temperature in the room has had a chance to stabilize. When you first turn the air conditioner on, turn the fan to its highest speed setting; this will cool the room the fastest.

Condenser

The moisture that collects on the evaporator drains back to a pan under the condenser coil. There, a ring on the fan blade often picks up the water and slings it onto the condenser. This technique increases the efficiency of the air conditioner because the evaporating water helps cool the condenser coil. In effect, the air conditioner is able to use the evaporating water to make up for some of the energy lost when condensing the water vapor inside the house. Another benefit of this technique is that the condensation is evaporated and does not dribble or run down the outside of the house. On especially humid days, the air conditioner may drip a little because more moisture must be removed from the air inside the house, and it is much more difficult to evaporate the condensation outside.

The condenser gets much dirtier than the evaporator (Fig. 11-4). At most, a wire screen is used to keep out leaves and other large objects, but this still lets plenty of dirt and trash through to the condenser. To do a good cleaning job, the case should be removed from the air conditioner so that you can get at all the parts inside. As with the evaporator, special care is required to prevent damage to the condenser coil and fins. Compresses air or a spray of cold water will normally clean out dirt, lint, and insects. Avoid getting water on any controls or motor parts. Larger objects may be carefully removed with a wooden stick or some soft tool. Never try to pry objects loose with a pick or sharp metal tool, or you may puncture the coil and allow the refrigerant to escape.

The condenser illustrated in Fig. 11-4 is made of aluminum fins surrounding the condenser coils. Aluminum does an excellent job of carrying heat energy away from the coils, but the metal is soft and easily crushed. When removing the case and handling the air conditioner, be very careful not to smash these fins. Bent fins restrict the air flow between the fins and cut down the cooling capacity and efficiency of your air conditioner. If the fins do become

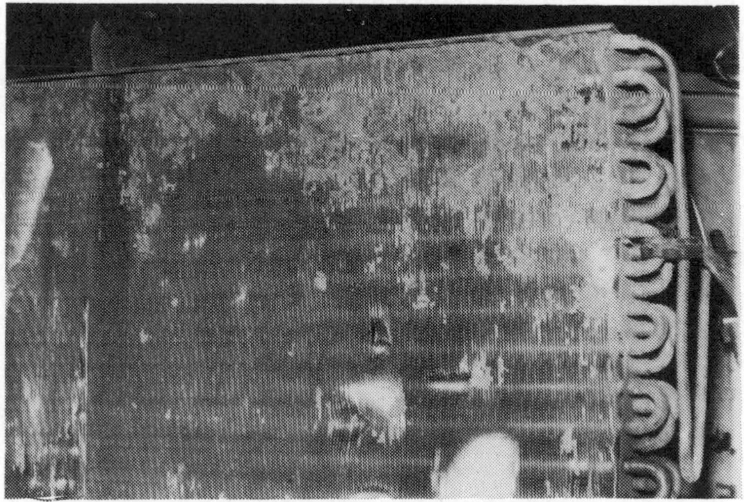

Fig. 11-4. Dirt will clog the fins of the condenser, restricting the air flow. Clean the condenser coil using compressed air or a cool spray of water. The fins surrounding the coil carry away heat energy, and they are easily bent, as shown by the shiny spots in the condenser above. Once bent, you will have only limited success in trying to straighten them, so always be careful when working around the fins.

Fig. 11-5. This double-shafter motor drives two fan blades. The fan for the condenser (A) is usually quite large. The squirrel cage fan (not visible) connects to the shaft at the other end of the motor (B), which extends through the dividing panel that separates the inside and outside portions of the air conditioner. When oiling the motor, locate the oil holes (C) at each end of the motor housing and put in a few drops of SAE 10 oil.

bent over, it is possible to straighten them a little, but you must be extremely careful not to damage the condenser coil. The metal stretches as it bends, and this prevents the fins from ever being bent perfectly back in place. The best approach is to never damage the fins in the first place.

The design of the condenser varies. While some models use aluminum fins, many use wire or toothed bristles wrapped spirally around the condenser coil. (This spiral wrap is also found in the evaporator coil of many air conditioners.) Whatever construction is used, you should always treat the fins with respect when cleaning them, for the materials are all very thin and bend easily.

Cleaning the Fan Motor

Air conditioners normally have two motors, one for the fan and the other for the compressor. In this way, the fan motor can be running all the time to circulate air in the room, while the compressor motor need only run when the thermostat calls for more cooling. The fan motor may be single-shafted or double-shafted, depending on how the fan blades are connected to the motor. The most usual arrangement is the double-shafted motor, in which the shaft extends from each end of the motor, as in Fig. 11-6. A large fan blade is connected to one shaft of the motor to circulate air over the outside condenser coil. The other end of the shaft extends through a panel to a squirrel cage fan (Fig. 11-3) that circulates air over the evaporator coil and into the room. The advantage to using a squirrel cage fan on the inside is that is much quieter in operation.

During your yearly tuneup, you should clean the fan motor and fan blades (particularly the condenser fan blades). The fan motor should be oiled too, though some of the newer fans have sealed bearings that do not require oiling every year. Most fan motors, however, have some provision for adding oil. These motors may have oil holes, tubes, caps, or small rubber plugs at each end of the motor housing. Remove the plugs or caps and add a few drops of SAE 10 motor into the hole (Fig. 11-5). Replace the plugs or caps after oiling to keep out dirt.

If the fan turns sluggishly or perhaps not at all, you have to remove it for service. There will be several bolts holding the motor in place and possibly a motor brace across the top of the motor. Loosen the squirrel cage fan blade and the condenser fan blade. These fans are usually held to the motor shaft with a set screw or bolt that you must loosen. The squirrel cage fan must be loosened from the front of the air conditioner unless there is a special coupler on the shaft near the motor. When you remove the condenser fan blade, gently push it against the condenser fins (Fig. 11-6) to

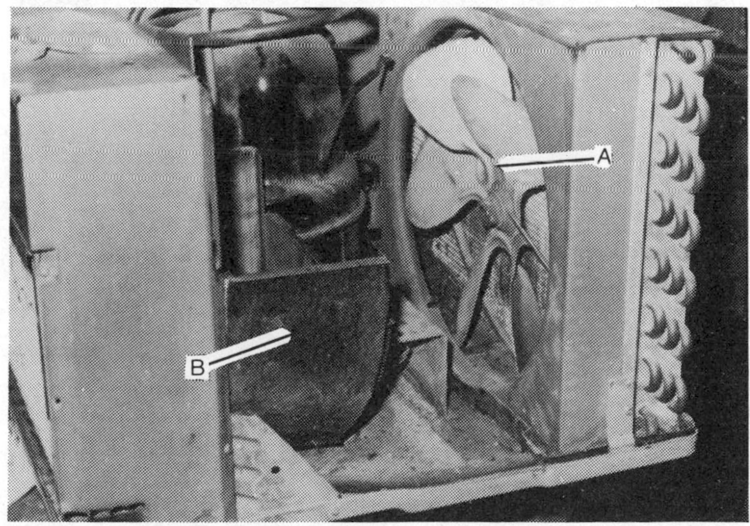

Fig. 11-6. The two-shafted fan motor has been removed from this window air conditioner. (A) is the fan for the condenser. (B) is the housing for the evaporator's squirrel cage fan.

Fig. 11-7. Dirt and leaves can collect in the bottom of an air conditioner. If they collect on the condenser or plug up the water drains, they will reduce the efficiency of the unit.

remove the motor—but do not mash the fins on the condenser. With the motor removed, take advantage of the opportunity to clean out the debris that has collected in the bottom of the air conditioner (Fig. 11-7).

The fan motor (Fig. 11-8) should be dismantled for a complete internal cleaning about once every two years or so. (Refer to the selection on cleaning furnace fan motors.) Whether the fan motor is a split-phase or shaded-pole motor, the dismantling and cleaning process is the same. Check the motor bearings and replace them if they do not rotate smoothly. Clean the outside motor housing to remove dirt and grime. Lubricate the bearings generously before reassembling the motor.

A split-phase fan motor has a starter switch located in one end of the bellhousing (Fig. 11-9). If this switch should become defective, the motor will not be able to start. When cleaning the motor parts, use a brush to dislodge any dirt on the starter switch. If the switch contacts are rough and pitted, they may be lightly sanded with fine sandpaper or emery cloth. Avoid bending the switch contacts and never allow oil deposits to form on the contact surfaces. If the starter switch is broken or obviously worn beyond repair, replace it with an equivalent switch obtained from a local service shop.

Fig. 11-8. The fan motor has been removed from the air conditioner, and it is now ready for cleaning. Before disassembling the motor, make a mark across the housing so that the parts can be lined up for reassembly.

In Case of Trouble

If your air conditioner either doesn't work at all or not as well as you think it should, there are several checks you can make to find out what may be wrong.

Fig. 11-9. A split-phase motor has a starter switch in one bellhousing. This switch can prevent the motor from starting, so you must replace it if it is defective. Before you disconnect the switch, tag the wires so you can replace them on the correct terminals during reassembly.

If the unit doesn't work at all, first check to see that it is plugged in. Locate the circuit breaker or fuse for the air conditioner circuit to see if the breaker or fuse has opened. If these two checks fail, use a voltmeter, lamp, or neon indicator to determine if power is getting to the unit. The receptacle contacts may be defective, or the breaker or fuse may be loose and not making contact.

If the unit is running but doesn't seem to be cooling properly, check the fan to see if it is running at its various speeds. Listen for the compressor turning on and off as you adjust the thermostat. The compressor will usually turn off immediately, but it may not start up immediately because of a protective thermal sensing element built into the compressor. Ordinarily, the compressor will start after resting a few minutes; if it does not, then you may have trouble with either the thermostat or the compressor.

If the unit doesn't seem to cool enough, place a thermometer in the air flow coming from the air conditioner. If the temperature of the air coming out is more than 10 degrees below the room temperature, the air conditioner is probably working right, although the unit may be too small for the area you are trying to cool. If this is the case, about all you can do to help is to buy another air conditioner or replace the one you have with a larger capacity unit.

If your temperature check showed that the air wasn't being cooled enough, you should remove the air conditioner from its case and make some internal checks. With the cover off, plug the air conditioner in and turn it on. First check to see that the compressor is running. If it isn't, warm the thermostat bulb or short the thermostat leads to make the compressor turn on. If the compressor comes on when you short the leads of the thermostat but not when you warm the bulb, the thermostat may be defective. Before replacing it, though, first check to see that the wires are not corroded or loose.

If the compressor still does not turn on when you short the thermostat leads, follow the electrical wires going to the various terminals to see that the compressor is getting eleectrical power. Another simple check is to touch the compressor carefully with your hand to see if it is hot (Fig. 11-10). If it is hot, then it's getting electricity and trying to start. Unplug the air conditioner to allow the compressor to cool off. A compressor will not start if it is too hot because of an internal protective element. It may be that your thermostat is calling for the compressor to start, but the compressor is unable to start immediately due to a lower-than-normal line voltage; the thermal breaker inside warms up quickly and shuts off the compressor.

Fig. 11-10. The compressor (A) is a sealed unit containing a motor and pump. The compressor circulates the refrigerant through the system and makes it possible for the air conditioner to cool your home. The refrigerant enters the compressor through the low pressure line (B) coming from the evaporator. The compressor then forces refrigerant through the high pressure line (C) into the condenser. The wires entering the compressor supply power to the motor; the tubular objects to either side of the junction box are starting capacitors. If the compressor fails to start, the high flow of electrical current quickly heats up the compressor motor, but a thermal breaker located inside the compressor senses this buildup of heat and interrupts the current until the compressor cools down again.

If the compressor runs, but still not cooling the air much, it may be that there is a leak in the refrigerant lines that has allowed the gas to escape. Insufficient refrigerant in the air conditioner will greatly reduce the cooling capacity. If this seems to be the case, you should take the air conditioner to a repair shop to have it recharged with refrigerant. It is not recommended that you attempt to recharge the unit yourself because so much equipment is required to do the job properly. A professional repair shop can also check the unit to determine where the refrigerant has been escaping and repair any leaks.

CENTRAL AIR CONDITIONING

A central air conditioning system operates the same way as the room air conditioner. The parts are the same and the operation is the same. The central air conditioner merely has larger parts and is designed to cool an entire house instead of just a few rooms.

The case that houses the evaporator coil is usually located in the furnace. The condenser is outside the house, connected to the evaporator by copper tubing carrying the refrigerant back and forth. An alternate type of central air conditioner is made as one unit, located outside the house and connected to the furnace duct system through a separate duct line.

Once a year, clena out the parts of the central air conditioner, the same as you would for a room air conditioner. The air filter should be cleaned or replaced about four times a year. When the evaporator coil is located in the coil case of your furnace, the central air conditioner uses your furnace fan, so this fan will require more frequent inspection and cleaning. With the alternate, single-unit system, the central air conditioner contains a separate fan to force cool air into your furnace duct system. Electricially heated homes may use this alternate system with duct work just for air conditioning.

Grass, leaves, and dirt may collect in the condensing unit located outside the house. Clean out the unit to remove any restrictions that could reduce the efficiency of the unit or impair its operation.

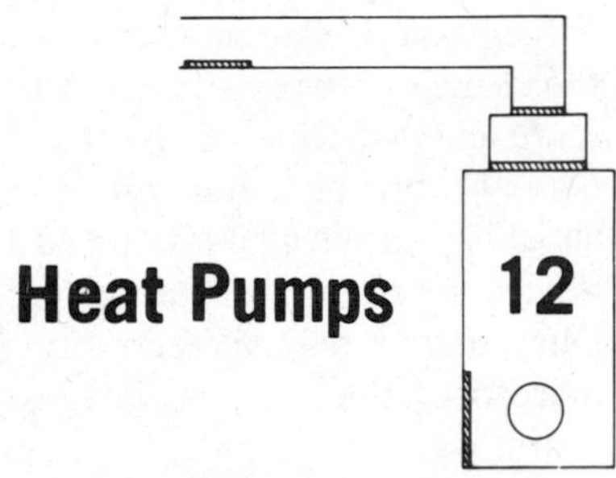

Heat Pumps 12

Without question, heat pumps have become the "in" heating and cooling system in recent years. There are a number of reasons for this. First, they are efficient—often twice as efficient as electric furnaces. The low cost of operation makes the heat pump an attractive alternative to electric heat in most parts of the United States. This can be an especially important factor in selecting a heating system in areas where natural gas shortages have precluded the extension of natural gas lines to new homes. Also, the high efficiency of the heat pump makes it cost competitive with natural gas as a heating fuel in some localties.

DESIGN IMPROVEMENTS

A second major reason for the surge in heat pump popularity is design improvement. Although heat pumps have been around for several decades, early designs were unreliable. They were very inefficient at temperatures below freezing. Special components designed to withstand the rigors of heat pump operation had not been perfected. Compressor malfunctions were one of the largest sources of breakdowns in heat pumps. The result was that early heat pumps were not economical in most areas in the northern half of the United States, and compressor problems abounded.

But these design problems have been eliminated in recent years. The heat pump no longer takes a back seat to conventional gas, electric and oil furnaces in the heating scene. The heat pump is now designed to perform efficiently in most northern climates as well as in mild weather locales. Special heat pump compressor designs have replaced the old compressors that essentially were adapted from refrigeration and air conditioning units. Now, many heat pumps are designed to operate efficiently at sub-zero temperatures without risking breakdown.

Probably one of the largest reasons for heat pump popularity (which experts claim will grow even faster in the coming years) is the changing energy scene. With natural gas availability becoming more and more limited, electricity is increasingly being used as a home heating fuel. As we have mentioned, heat pumps use only about half as much electricity as an electric furnace in many areas. Since experts predict future prices of gas and oil will climb at a much faster rate than electricity prices, heat pumps will gain even more operating cost advantages over fossil fuels in the coming years.

In this chapter we explain the basics of heat pump operation and somee things you will want to consider before buying a heat pump. Also, we have included in this chapter some simple heat pump maintenance tips that can help the heat pump owner keep his heating/cooling unit operating at top efficiency.

THINGS TO CONSIDER BEFORE YOU BUY

Probably no major climate control system sold today is more misunderstood than the heat pump. Many people do not have the foggiest notion of how a heat pump operates, except that it "pumps heat" and runs off electricity.

First of all, even though the device is called a "heat pump," it is actually a combination heating and cooling system. It heats during the winter and air conditions during the summer. Thus, if you are not interested in installing air conditioning in your home, you will not save any money by installing a heat pump. You'll save a lot more money by simply purchasing a heating-only furnace, which will cost a fraction of the initial cost of a heat pump.

Secondly, even though the heat pump runs by electricity, it is not the same as an electric furnace. This is evident to those who have any knowledge at all about heat pump operation. We wanted to make this point, though, because we have heard of cases where unwary buyers have purchased electric furnace and air conditioning systems, thinking they were getting heat pumps. We don't know if this was due to unscrupulous dealers who deliberately misled customers or to an honest mistake of communication between buyers and sellers. Before you purchase a heat pump, learn how it operates and understand the difference between the heat pump and a traditional furnace system so you don't make this mistake. Heat pump operation is discussed later in this chapter.

Heat pumps generally cost considerably more to purchase than conventional heating and cooling systems. You must consider this additional initial cost as an offset against any future savings in operating costs. As a guideline, you can expect to pay 25 to 30% more for a heat pump than for a central furnace and air conditioner. This will depend, however, on the particular models you are considering.

The heat pump is a central climate control unit, which means you must have insulated ductwork to carry the warm and cool air to the rooms. If you are considering installing a heat pump in an existing house that has individual room heaters but no ductwork, you must consider the additional cost of installing the necessary ducts.

The simple fact is that heat pumps, popular though they may be, are not for everyone. In some very cold climates, you may not save much money on heat pump operating costs because some models are not designed to operate efficiently at sub-zero temperatures. If natural gas is available, it is probably less expensive to operate a natural gas furnace than a heat pump (at least at current energy prices). If you are not planning to install central air conditioning, you should not install a heat pump. The large difference in the initial cost of a heat pump compared to a heating-only furnace would wipe out any future savings in operating costs. These factors all must be considered before you make an investment in a heat pump.

HEAT PUMP OPERATION

While the traditional furnace systems use electricity or fossil fuels to generate heat, the heat pump works on an entirely different principle. In an electric furnace, for instance, electricity is passed through resistance heating elements. These elements become hot and warm the passing air.

The heat pump, on the other hand, uses principles of refrigeration to remove heat from the air outside the house and deposit it inside the house. This is when the heat pump is on the heating cycle, of course. On the cooling cycle, the opposite occurs. See Fig. 12-1. It may seem strange that on a cold winter day a mechanical device can actually remove heat from outdoor air, but that's what a heat pump does. As long as the temperature of the outside air is above the temperature of the evaporator coil outdoors, heat can be removed.

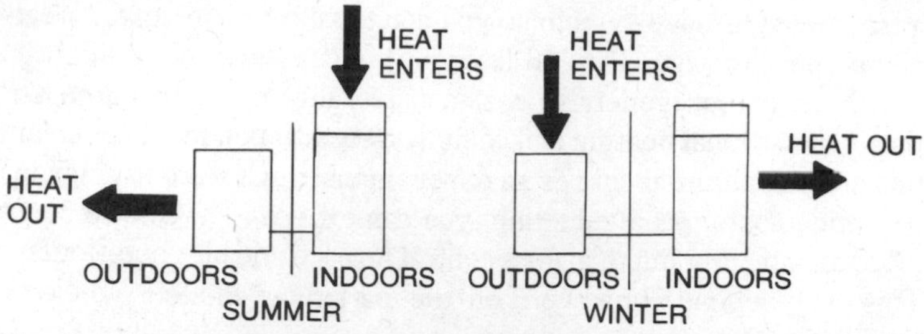

Fig. 12-1. The heat pump is a year-round climate control device. During the winter it extracts heat from the outside air and deposits that heat inside the house. During the summer the heat pump works as an air conditioner, extracting heat from the indoor air and depositing it outdoors.

Essentially, heat pump operation can be most easily explained by comparing it to an air conditioner. On the cooling cycle, the heat pump is an air conditioner. It removes heat from the air inside the house and deposits it outside the house. The operating principles are the same as those described for air conditioners in Chapter 10.

Cooling Cycle

With the cooling cycle operation, the *evaporator coil* (the coil inside the house) absorbs the heat to be carried away. This is accomplished because the refrigerant picks up heat from air passing over the evaporator and boils, forming a vapor. The refrigerant vapor travels to the compressor, and the compressor pumps this vapor into the *condenser* (the outside coil). At the condenser, the heat absorbed at the evaporator is given off into the surrounding air. As the compressor pumps the vapor into the condenser coil, a restricting device in the refrigerant line just beyond the condenser restricts the flow of refrigerant.

In a heat pump, this purpose is accomplished by a metering device. This rerstrictor slows the flow of refrigerant at the same time that the compressor pumps more refrigerant into the condenser. The pressure causes the refrigerant vapor to compress back into a liquid inside the condenser. This condensation process gives off heat contained in the refrigerant—heat that was absorbed in the evaporator—and this heat goes into the outside air. This cooling cycle is shown in Chapter 10 in Fig. 10-4.

Heating Cycle

In the heat pump heating cycle, the system reverses the direction of flow of refrigerant and, in essence, switches the functions of the indoor and outdoor coils. Now, the indoor coil is the condenser (it was the evaporator on the cooling cycle) and it gives up heat inside the house. The outdoor coil becomes the evaporator (it was the condenser on the cooling cycle) and it now absorbs heat.

An easy way to visualize this change is to imagine a room air conditioner that is cooling during the summer. The indoor coil (the evaporator) is cold, and cool air comes out the indoor side of the air conditioner. Outside, however, the air blowing over the outdoor coil (the condenser) is warm, and this warm air is dissipated outdoors. If you were to turn this room air conditioner around so that the front was outside, the warm air would now be blowing inside the house. You would be using the air conditioner condenser to warm the indoors. This is the principle of a heat pump. By the way, this idea of turning the air conditioner around is offered only as a way of illustrating heat pump operation. You *cannot* turn your air conditioner around in the window to heat your house.

Parts of a Heat Pump

Beyond the normal refrigeration components, such as evaporator, condenser and compressor, the heat pump has several additional components designed for the requirements peculiar to heat pumps. See Fig. 12-2.

To change the heat pump system from the cooling cycle to the heating cycle, there must be some way to change the direction of

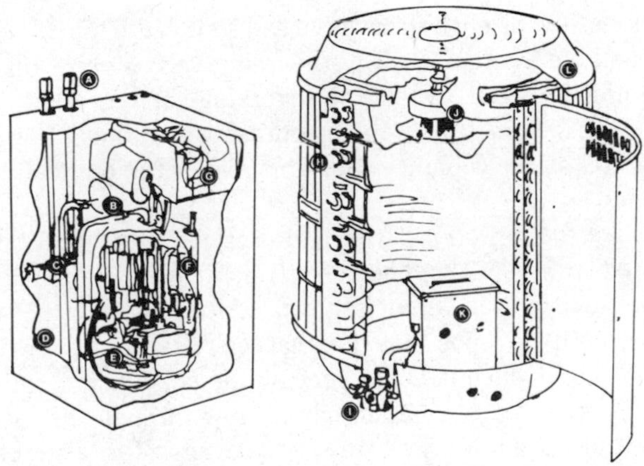

Fig. 12-2. The internal parts of a heat pump. The compressor unit, outdoor coil and indoor coil are all separated and conencted with refrigeration lines. (A) Refrigeration line fittings. (B) Internal muffler. (C) Reversing valve. (D) Insulated cabinet. (E) Heating device to keep compressor oil warm. (F) Compressor. (G) Compressor malfunction indicator. (H) The outdoor coil. (I) Service valves. (J) Fan. (K) Wiring terminal box. (L) Metal housing.

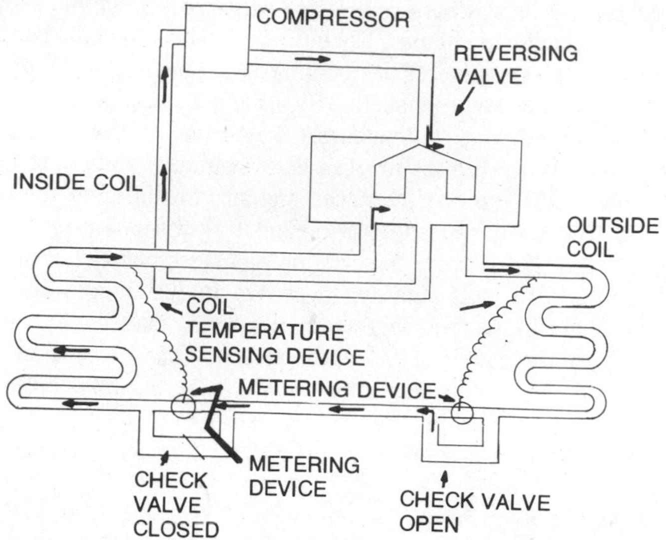

Fig. 12-3. This diagram shows the operation of the heat pump in the cooling cycle. The reversing valve is in the cooling position and directs the refrigerant flow first to the outdoor coil. The check valve on the outside coil is open, letting the refrigerant pass through unrestricted. The check valve on the inside coil is closed, forcing the refrigerant to pass through the metering device. The metering device, or expansion valve, is a restriction in the line that holds the pressure in the line between the compressor and the evaporator. After refrigerant passes through this valve, it goes into the evaporator where it expands, boils and absorbs heat.

refrigerant flow through the system and switch the functions of the indoor and outdoor coils. The reversing valve serves this function. Notice in Fig. 12-3 that the reversing valve is positioned so that the refrigerant leaves the compressor and flows toward the outdoor coil on the cooling cycle. This makes the outdoor coil the condenser.

Notice the direction of refrigerant flow in the heating cycle illustrated in Fig. 12-4. The refrigerant leaves the compressor from the same side and in the same direction. But now the reversing valve has been repositioned so that the refrigerant flows first to the *inside* coil, which now has become the condenser. The check valve closes so the refrigerant has to flow through the metering devices, causing a lower pressure in the evaporator. The refrigerant now boils at a lower temperature in the evaporator.

The metering device serves two functions. First, it restricts the flow of refrigerant so the refrigerant backs up in the condenser coil behind the metering device. Teh compressor pressurizes this refrigerant, forcing it to change from a vapor into a liquid. Secondly, the metering device serves as an expansion valve, allowing a small amount of refrigerant to enter the evaporator. This liquid refrigerant, once inside the evaporator, expands and forms a vapor when it absorbs heat.

Notice in Fig. 12-3 that on the cooling cycle the check valve at the outside coil is open to allow free flow of the refrigerant past the metering device. When the heat pumps switches to the heating cycle, the check valve at the inside coil opens and the check valve at the outside coil closes to force the refrigerant through the metering device. The reversing valve changes the direction of the refrigerant flow between the coils, and the outside coil is now the evaporator.

Supplementary Heat

As the outdoor temperature drops, so does the amount of heat the heat pump can remove from the outside air. As the air temperature approaches the temperature of the evaporator coil, less heat can be absorbed. At some point, the heat pump's refrigeration system will no longer be able to supply the necessary heat to warm the house.

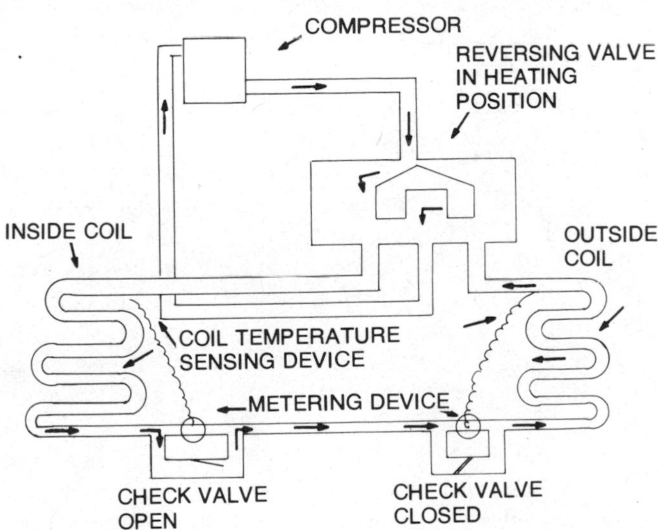

Fig. 12-4. This diagram illustrates how the heat pump operates on the heating cycle. The reversing valve has changed positions so it reverses the flow of refrigerant between the coils. The reversing valve directs the flow of refrigerant first to the inside coil, which is the condenser on the heating cycle. Notice also that the check valve at the outdoor coil is now closed to create pressure in the condenser. The check valve at the inside coil is open to allow the free flow of refrigerant past the metering device.

When the evaporator can no longer absorb enough heat to warm the house, electric resistance heating elements turn on to make up the difference. On most heat pumps, the electric heating elements begin turning on when the temperature is around 15°, but on some models it may be much higher. The exact temperature will vary with the heat pump's size, design and the heat load of the house.

As the outdoor temperature continues to drop, the unit relies more on the resistance heating elements and less on the refrigeration system. On some units the pump may be shut off completely at some temperature and only the resistance elements will supply heat. When this happens, the heat pump is operating exactly the same as an electric furnace. On other units the pump may keep running as the electric elements are used.

The use of the electric strip heaters drasitcally reduces the efficiency of the heat pump and increases the operating costs. One of the important design improvements in recent years has been in developing systems that operate at lower temperatures without turning on the electric strip heaters. Although electric resistance heat is the most common type of supplemental heat for heat pumps, some models use gas or oil supplemental heating systems.

The Defrost Cycle

When the outdoor temperature during the heating season is below 40°F, ice and frost will build up on the outdoor evaporator coil. If unchecked, this buildup will eventually stop the air flow through the coil. To prevent this problem heat pumps are equipped with an automatic defrosting system.

One way this defrosting occurs is to divert hot gas from the compressor to the outdoor evaporator long enough to melt the ice. The heat pump switches back to the cooling cycle to defrost. During this time the outdoor fan will shut off. If heat is needed inside the home, the electric strip heaters will come on. The defrosting process takes only a few minutes.

During the defrosting cycle, the homeowner may observe some steam coming from the outdoor coil. This is due to the ice and frost melting from the coil and vaporizing in the cold air. The steam ceases shortly after the defrost cycle ends.

Cool Air Problems

One frequent comment from new heat pump owners is that the air coming from the heating register is not warm enough. These people, who are accustomed to the warm air temperatures of furnaces, often think their heat pumps are malfunctioning.

The fact is, however, that the supply air from a heat pump is usually about 100°-125°, several degrees cooler than the 125° temperatures of supply air from furnaces. Don't be alarmed if the supply air coming from your heating registers is a bit cooler, with a heat pump than the temperatures you are accustomed to from a furnace.

EFFICIENCY AND COST OF OPERATION

The heat pump is the most efficient type of mechanical heating system. A heat pump does not have to burn fuel to produce heat, and it does not have to waste electrical energy by running the energy through a resistive wire element to produce heat. The heat pump only requires enough electricity to run a compressor motor, which takes the heat out of the air outside the house and deposits this heat inside the house.

On the cooling cycle, the heat pump essentially has the same efficiency as any air conditioner. Of course, some air conditioners and heat pumps are more efficient on the cooling cycle than others due to energy-efficient designs. When people talk of saving money on operating costs with a heat pump, they are referring to savings on the heating cycle.

The efficiency of a heat pump is measured in terms of how much easier it is to *pump* heat energy than to *generate* it by conventional means, as in electric baseboard heaters or electric furnaces. In fact, the efficiency of the heat pump drops quickly when the refrigeration system is unable to supply all of a home's heating requirements and the conventional electric strip heaters are turned on. Normally, though, as long as the outside temperature is above about 20° Fahrenheit or the design temperature of the pump, the heat pump can heat your house more cheaply than an electric furnace can. Plus, the electric strip heaters will not be turned on. On some models, even if the outdoor temperature is below 10°Fahrenheit, the refrigeration system will supply all the heat necessary to heat an average home. These temperatures can vary widely with the design of the heat pump, the heat pump's size, and the heat load of the house. As the outside temperature approaches the inside room temperature, the heat pump efficiency continues to climb dramatically.

Over an entire heating season, a heat pump will have an *average* heating efficiency of about 120 to 200% depending on the heat pump design, its size and the average outdoor winter temperature. This means the heat pump will yield 1.2 to 2 times the amount of heat a fully efficient electric strip heater would yield while using the same amount of electricity.

In some areas in the southern United States, seasonal efficiency averages may be even higher than 200% due to warm winter temperatures, which increase heat pump efficiency. In terms of cost, those efficiency factors translate into heating savings of about a third to half the cost of conventional electric heat. For a northern city like Columbus, Ohio, the annual heating cost for a heat pump is about 50% of that for an ordinary electric furnace, making the heat pump cost-competitive with natural gas in that area. Similar results have been reported in Washiongton, D.C., as shown in Table 12-1.

CONSIDER YOUR NEEDS

A heat pump can be a good investment that yields dividends for many years to come. But we should offer a warning. In selecting a heat pump, as in selecting any other climate control system, carefully consider your needs—present and future—along with the costs and features of all systems available. You should talk with several persons in your locale who know about the operation and success of heat pump installations in your area. Local building contractors, heat pump dealers and owners of homes with heat pumps should be able to answer your questions.

Talk with several heat pump dealers and have them figure the operating costs of a heat pump in your home. Beware of exorbitant efficiency claims. It is possible to show an efficiency of 300% for a unit that actually on a seasonal average is only twice as efficient as an electric furnace. Such figures can be derived by statistical manipulation and by laboratory conditions you could never duplicate in actual operation in your home.

Talk with reputable dealers, and talk with *more than one*. If you don't know of any heat pump owners from whom you can seek recommendations for a satisfactory dealer, ask the dealers to supply you with some references of people to whom they have sold heat pumps.

In short, do whatever you can to protect yourself from the example mentioned earlier in the chapter. Don't get stuck with an electric furnace when you wanted a heat pump!

COMPARING THE NUMBERS

There are three different figures that are commonly used to compare the efficiencies of heat pumps. By using these figures, you can

Table 12-1. Possible Annual Savings of a Heat Pump Over Othe Heating Furnaces (courtesy of Carrier Corporation)).

City	Annual cost with heat pump at 2.5c per KWH	Annual cost with electric heat at 2.5c per KWH	Annual cost with oil at 45c per gal.*	HEAT PUMP SAVINGS —over oil heat	—over electric heat
Atlanta, Ga.	167.95	417.09	281.49	249.14	113.54
Charlotte, N.C.	202.57	490.29	330.90	287.72	128.33
Chicago, Ill.	385.06	789.00	532.51	403.94	147.45
Columbus, O.	264.97	610.46	412.00	345.49	147.03
Dallas, Tex.	122.71	312.63	211.00	189.92	88.29
Denver, Colo.	365.55	756.79	510.76	391.24	145.21
Detroit, Mich.	402.29	815.32	550.25	413.03	147.96
Hartford, Conn.	388.33	798.63	539.00	410.30	150.67
Indianapolis, Ind.	311.35	673.00	454.20	361.65	142.85
Jackson, Miss.	116.10	302.04	203.84	185.94	87.74
Jacksonville, Fla.	63.99	174.34	117.65	110.35	53.66
Kansas City, Mo.	269.57	583.34	393.70	313.77	124.13
Los Angeles, Calif.	71.50	205.74	138.85	134.24	67.35
Louisville, Ky.	236.29	548.38	370.10	312.09	133.81
Memphis, Tenn.	168.14	413.47	279.04	245.33	110.90
Miami, Fla.	12.91	37.03	24.99	24.12	12.08
Minneapolis, Minn.	526.04	925.52	624.55	399.48	98.51
New Orleans, La.	65.23	179.26	120.98	114.03	55.75
Omaha, Neb.	406.50	764.46	515.94	357.96	109.44
Philadelphia, Pa.	260.20	604.15	407.75	343.95	147.55
Pittsburgh, Pa.	355.17	739.68	499.21	384.51	144.04
San Francisco, Calif.	158.98	439.78	296.81	280.80	137.83
St. Louis, Mo.	286.89	615.14	415.16	328.25	128.27
Seattle, Wash.	286.89	615.14	436.63	328.25	149.74
Syracuse, N.Y.	400.03	805.78	543.83	405.75	143.80
Washington, D.C.	243.85	573.11	386.79	329.26	142.94

*Oil furnace rated at 65% efficiency.

compare the efficiencies of different heat pumps to determine which models deliver the most performance for the amount of energy consumed.

Coefficient of Performance

The *coefficient of performance* is a comparision of the heat pump's ability to heat the home. It is the ratio of the amount of heat absorbed by the system to the amount of energy required to produce the amount of heat absorbed:

$$\frac{\text{Heat absorbed}}{\text{Electrical energy requirements}}$$

The ratio shows how much heat is produced by the system compared to the amount of heat that would be produced by electric resistance heaters using the same amount of electricity. Thus, the coefficient of performance (COP) of an electric resistance heater is 1. A 3.00 coefficient of performance represents a 3:1 ratio and means the unit is absorbing three times as much heat as would be produced by an electric resistance heater using the same amount of electricity.

The COP for any given heat pump at any given time will vary according to the outside temperature, because the heat pump efficiency varies with the outside temperature. At warmer outdoor temperatures, the COP can go well over 3.00. When the temperature is cold, however, the COP will approach 1. Heat pump models are rated according to an average COP that makes instant comparison quite easy. Average COPs for most heat pumps are usually between 2.0 and 2.8.

Seasonal Performance Factor

The *seasonal performance factor* (SPF) is the ratio of the heat pump's heat energy output to its electric energy input over an entire heating season. This figure is also a measure of the unit's heating efficiency. However, the SPF averages the heat output ratio over an entire heating season, and the same heat pump model will have a different SPF in different cities, according to the cities' climate patterns. The SPF, therefore, is the most meaningful figure for comparing the overall heating performances of heat pumps and for comparing the potential savings by using a heat pump instead of another type of heating system. An SPF of 2.2 means that particular heat pump will deliver 2.2 times the heat that would be produced by electric resistance heaters using the same amount of electricity over the entire heating season in the city. In colder climates, the same heat pump will have a lower SPF.

Energy Efficiency Ratio

The *energy efficiency ratio* (EER) is a figure used to rate the heat pump's cooling efficiency. The EER figure tells you how many BTUs the unit will cool for the amount of electricity it uses. The EER equation is:

$$\frac{\text{BTU rating}}{\text{Size of unit in watts}} = \text{EER}$$

The EER is a single figure, usually carried to one decimal place. Average EERs for heat pumps usually run from about 6.0 to 8.0. The EER for a heat pump is basically the same as the EER for refrigerators or air conditioners. See Chapter 15 for a further discussion of the EER.

MAINTENANCE

Because heat pumps are refrigeration systems, the routine maintenance that the homeowner can perform is almost the same as routine maintenance for air conditioners. You should insure a good air flow through the heat pump and the duct system by cleaning or replacing the air filter about three or four times a year.

Once a year, examine the coils and remove any dirt or debris that would block the air flow. Check belts for proper tightness and for wear. During the winter, periodically examine the outdoor coil on cold days to see that the evaporator is not blocked with ice. If it is, there may be a defective defrosting control that will have to be replaced.

Have your heat pump examined at least once a year by a competent serviceman. Because of the peculiar demands on the heat pump refrigeration system, the refrigerant pressure must be set correctly. If it is not, it may cause a compressor to burn out—an expensive item to replace.

Service is another reason you should purchase a heat pump only from a reputable dealer. In many instances it is difficult, if not impossible, to obtain service from anyone but the dealer who sold you the unit, especially if the unit is under warranty.

Sometimes it is possible to purchase a service contract from a serviceman or dealer. For a fixed yearly fee, the contractor will repair and maintain the heat pump.

SINGLE ROOM HEAT PUMPS

Some room air conditioners are used as a type of heat pump, although they operate quite differently than the full-sized central heat pump. These units have no reversing valves or defrosting relays because the direction of refrigerant flow does not reverse.

These units operate as typical room air conditioners when on the cooling cycle. When switched to the heating cycle, a solenoid

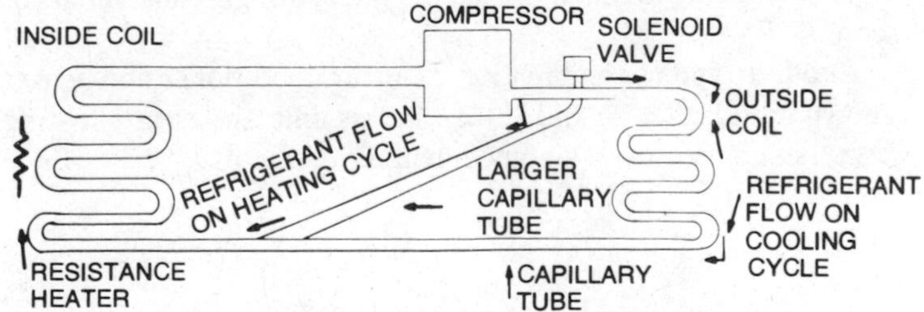

Fig. 12-5. On a room-size combination heating/cooling system, a solenoid valve controls the flow of refrigerant through the unit. On the heating cycle the refrigerant is directed into the larger capillary tube, bypassing the outside coil and the small capillary tube. This system of heating delivers some compressed heat into the living area, but most of the heat from a unit like this comes from the resistance heating element at the front of the unit.

Fig. 12-6. (A) This room heating/air conditioning system uses electric resistance heaters to provide heating in the winter. (B) The indoor evaporator is connected to the outdoor condenser by refrigeration lines (courtesy of Heat Controller, Inc.).

valve opens and the refrigerant flows through a large-diameter capillary tube and bypasses the outdoor coil, as shown in Fig. 12-5. The refrigerant now is allowed to move through the system relatively freely, since the small capillary tube that normally restricts its flow is bypassed. In traveling through the system, the refrigerant will heat up because it is compressed by the compressor. This heat is deposited inside the room when the refrigerant leaves the larger capillary tube and has room to expand inside the indoor coil.

These units are not nearly as efficient as a central heat pump. The only heat they are "pumping" is the heat produced by compressing the refrigerant. These units rely very heavily on electric resistance heating elements to supply the heating requirements of a room.

Another type of combination room air conditioner and heater is shown in Figs. 12-6A and 12-6B. In this unit, the entire heating energy is supplied by resistance heating elements.

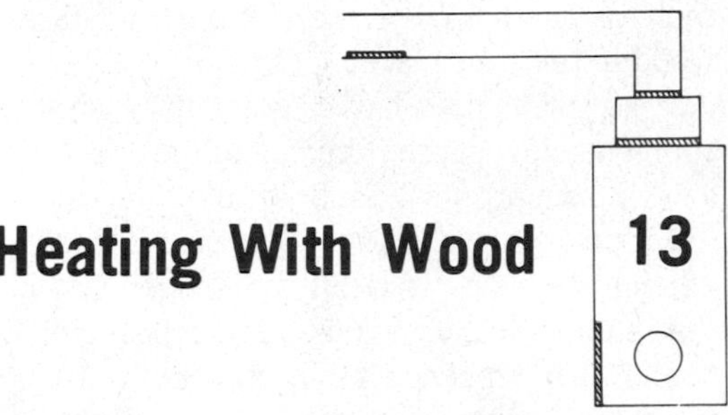

Heating With Wood 13

As our modern heating systems have become more efficient, complex and more reliant on fossil fuels, we have forgotten the heating systems our ancestors used for ages. For our forefathers, the wood stove and the fireplace were necessities of survival. To most of us today, they are more decorative than useful.

With recent increases in the prices of the once cheap fossil fuels and the difficulty in obtaining those fuels when they are most needed, the wood stove and the fireplace have become conservation pieces instead of conversation pieces. America's consumption of wood as a heating fuel has been declining in the twentieth century, but this trend may be reversing itself as families begin to rely more on wood to deliver part of the heat for their homes.

Wood is not only generally less expensive to burn than the fossil fuels (an innovative person can locate several sources of a free wood supply), but you can rest assured that when the temperature drops no foreign countries will shut off America's wood supply. During years of extremely cold winters when natural gas supply shut-offs have been looming in areas of sub-zero temperatures, thousands of families undoubtedly looked longingly at the smoke wisping from their neighbor's fireplaces.

A family with a fireplace is assured of having at least some source of heat, even if the gas company does stop delivering gas to the furnace.

DISADVANTAGES AND ADVANTAGES OF WOOD

Wood, of course, is not without its disadvantages. It takes a considerable amount of room to store, and it can be difficult and messy to handle. If you live in a city, you know that wood is not easy to come by—and it can be expensive. Added to that is the fact that many wood-burning heaters are notorious for sending more heat up the flue than they put into the room. These are just some of the reasons that our fathers and grandfathers gave up heating by wood in the first place.

But wood does have a good many advantages, especially as a supplemental source of heat. Almost every home has room to store a week's supply of wood. If you use your imagination and keep your eyes open, you will find sources of free or inexpensive wood. As for efficiency, thermostatically controlled wood heaters are available that automatically regulate the amount of heat put out. These heaters have a respectable efficiency. Also, there are many devices today that dramatically increase the efficiency of even the wasteful fireplace. A standard fireplace,—with no efficiency modifications has an efficiency of about 10%.

TYPES OF WOOD

Firewood types are classified basically in two general groups: *hardwoods* and *softwoods*. Hardwoods are generally used in home wood heating and include such popular fuel woods as oak, hickory, maple and walnut. Softwoods include most woods commonly used for commercial lumber production. Pine, fir and cedar are softwoods.

Hardwood is usually recommended for burning in home heating systems because hardwood logs give off more heat. Oak gives off almost twice as much heat per cord as aspen or pine. All wood produces about the same heat per pound, but wood is commonly sold by the cord, a volume measurement (4 feet × 4 feet × 8 feet.) Since softwoods weigh less per cord, a cord of softwood produces much less heat than a cord of hardwood.

Even if the price of softwood is discounted enough to compensate for its lower heating value (it seldom is), there are other good reasons for choosing hardwood. Hardwoods burn longer, so the fire doesn't have to be tended as often. One of the most important points in wood selection, however, is that hardwoods contain no resin that causes creosote to cake up in the chimney. Softwoods typically contain about 15% resin, a highly flammable material that forms creosote soot to collect on the chimney walls.

This creosote itself is highly flammable and can cause a chimney fire if ignited. With hardwoods creosote is not formed, so the fire burns cleaner and maintenance of the chimney is easier.

This is not to say, however, that softwoods have no use for home heating. Softwoods provide fires that are quick starting and supply a large amount of heat for a short time. They are often used in firebuilding as starter logs that will ignite easily and, in turn, will ignite the hardwood logs.

AMOUNT OF HEAT IN A LOG

Before you can know the savings (if any) you would gain from using wood heat, you must know how much heat you get from your present fuel and the logs you burn. The heat value per pound is about the same for all types of wood, hardwood or softwood—8,500 BTUs per pound. Part of that heat energy is used to evaporate the moisture present in virtually all wood. Even seasoned wood contains about 15 to 20% moisture. That leaves about 7,000 to 7,200 BTUs of heat, after moisture evaporation, that will be released when seasoned dry wood is burned.

Unseasoned (also known as "green" wood), wood, however, robs even more of the wood's heat energy. As much as 50% of the log's heat energy can go to evaporate the moisture within the log. And that is heat energy which is lost forever—heat energy that goes for nothing more than to boil the water out of the log.

As a rule of thumb, you can figure that one cord of hardwood holds about the same BTU heat potential as one ton of coal. For softwood, it will take almost two cords of wood to get the same heat potential found in one ton of coal. Table 13-1 shows how wood compares to other common fuels in heat potential.

The other important point, of course, is how much of the log's heat actually goes into the house. You can figure that a thermostatically controlled wood stove will be about half as efficient as a gas or oil furnace and about 40% as efficient as an electric furnace. Therefore, for wood heating to save you any money at all on your heating bill, it must cost less than half as much for the amount of heat produced as gas or oil, if you have a wood stove. If you have a heat circulating fireplace, your wood must cost about one-third as much for the amount of heat produced in order to save you money.

Table 13-1. Conversion Table for Heat Value of Some Woods (Per Cord).

	GAS. CU FT.	OIL, GAL.	COAL, TONS	ELECTRICITY, KWH
Hardwood (Maple)	20,000	135	1	5500
Hardwood (Oak)	24,000	165	1.25	6700
Softwood	14,500	95	.65	3900

Fig. 13-1. This wood burning stove costs about $200 and is large enough to heat a single room such as a den, game room or workshop. It also can be used to provide supplementary heat to as many as three or four rooms if your house has good air circulation (courtesy of Shenandoah Manufacturing Company).

BUYING A WOOD STOVE

Wood stoves are available in many styles and designs from the traditional cast iron potbelly stoves to the modern attractive porcelain-finished stoves. If you take the time to shop around at several hardware stores, you will likely find a new stove that is just right for your tastes in use and design.

Although the traditional potbelly stoves are still available, those have given way to the modern square wood stoves that can be purchased in a large array of imitation wood grain finishes and colors. The modern porcelain finish is practically maintenance free. Two wood stove of quite different designs are shown in Figs. 13-1 and 13-2.

The wood stoves of yesterday had to be tended often. The wood was fed into the stove by hand, and the draft regulator had to be frequently adjusted to be sure the right amount of air reached the burning wood. You can still buy a stove that requires this much attention, but you don't have to. Wood stoves have become increasingly convenient over the years to the point that some stoves can now go unattended for more than half a day.

You don't have to add wood as often because some stoves can store as much as 100 pounds of logs—about a 12-hour supply. You don't have to adjust the damper, either, to keep the wood burning at

Fig. 13-2. This modern wood stove is equipped with a blower to distribute heat to as many as six rooms. It has a black porcelain finish; a thermostat and weighs about 260 pounds. It costs about $400. Notice that if a wood stove is place on a carpet, it must be insulated from the carpets with a fireproof asbestos pad (courtesy of Shenandoah Manufacturing Company).

just the right level. Today you can buy a number of wood stoves that have thermostatic controls to adjust the air draft for maximum heating efficiency (Fig. 13-3). Just put a large supply of logs in the stove's woodbox, and the thermostat will take care of the rest. You don't have to tend the fire again for 12 hours. Now, that is convenience our forefathers never dreamed of!

Other features are also available on many wood stoves today. Some stoves are accompanied with a blower system that allows the stove to heat four or five rooms. Removable glass windows are available on some models so you can watch the fire. Some stoves have intricately designed flues to decrease the amount of heat that escapes up the flue. Most stoves will burn coal as well as wood.

Although the traditional stove designs have a nostalgic appeal, their inefficiency is their most serious drawback. Since traditional wood stoves are hand-fed, they have an efficiency of about 25%, depending on the stove model and how skillfully the fire is maintained. This means that for every 10,000 BTU of heat the burning wood produces, 2,500 BTU are sent into the room and 7,500 BTU are sent up the flue. The more inefficient your stove is, the less money you'll save by using wood.

A thermostat controls the fire much better than a person manually feeding the fire and adjusting the air draft by hand. Thermostatically controlled wood stoves have an efficiency of about 50%, which is a significant difference. This means that for the same money and effort in obtaining wood fuel, the thermostatically controlled stove will give you twice as much heat.

STOVE CONSTRUCTION

Stoves must be well constructed to withstand the temperatures reached in burning wood. Unfortunately, many models sold today are not well constructed but are manufactured by firms anxious to cash in on growing wood heater sales. Many manufacturers guarantee their stoves for a year, and you should ask about a warranty before you invest money in a stove. If there in no warranty, you'd better consider another dealer or another brand.

Cast iron stoves are the sentimental favorite, but steel stoves are also popular today. You will find that steel stoves are lighter and easier to move about, and they are also less expensive than cast iron stoves. Steel heats up faster, but cast iron holds heat longer after the fire dies. Since steel heats faster, steel stoves are more prone to warpage and cracked seams. This effect can be minimized, however, by using care in tending the fire to prevent

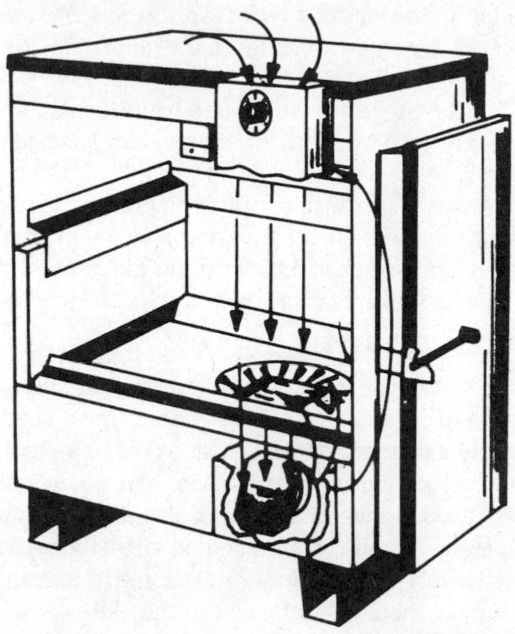

Fig. 13-3. The arrows show how air moves through one model of a modern wood stove to achieve an efficient burning process. The air passes through the preheated channel to the thermostat damper. From the thermostat damper at the bottom of this channel, most of the air enters the fire box as primary air through the cast iron grate. As the fire calls for secondary air, it passes between the grate and door into the upper part of the burning chamber. This stove will hold a 12-hour supply of wood.

excessively hot fires. A very hot fire will also crack a cast iron stove, especially when the stove is new. The first few fires in a cast iron stove must be relatively small to season the iron.

Black painted stoves are another sentimental favorite over the more modern porcelain-covered stoves. The enameled porcelain has the advantage of being easier to care for, since the finish doesn't fade or rust. The black stove may lose a good deal of its sentimental value about the time you have to polish it. Some porcelain finishes have an attractive wood-like look that helps the stoves blend in with the furniture.

Examine the stove with an eye toward what you will think of it after a year's use. Are the ashes easy to move? Is the firebox accessible? What size logs will it accept? That quaint wood stove with the daintily small opening may not seem nearly so quaint a year from now after you purchase a load of wood and discover that half of the logs will not go through the door.

It's a lot more work to saw and split wood into small chunks. That means either more work for you or more money that you'll have to pay for smaller wood.

Look at the stove's features and handles. Are they easy to reach and easy to use? Will you burn your hand just trying to operate the stove?

The stove's craftmanship is very important. Since the stove has to withstand intense heat, any weak welds will break. Look for cracks around the seams and be sure the metal parts join tightly. Use a flashlight to inspect the firebox for cracks or weak joints.

INSTALLING A WOOD STOVE

Before you buy a wood stove, you should check your local building code to determine what restrictions are placed on its use, location and installation. You should also give some thought to how and where you will install the stove in your home.

Since a wood stove is light enough that it does not require special floor support, it can be installed virtually anywhere in the home. The largest consideration, therefore, in locating the stove becomes how it should be attached to the chimney or where the chimney should be placed.

Chimney

No two combustible heating units should share the same flue. You will not be able to use the existing flue from your operating fireplace or the flue from your furnace for an additional wood stove. You may, however, vent the stove to a chimney that is not in use, as long as you inspect the chimney first to insure it is safe for a wood-burning appliance. A building inspector should inspect the chimney before it is used. The chimeny must be lined with a flue liner, because mortar in brick chimneys breaks down with time and use, creating chinks between the bricks that can allow a spark to ignite the surrounding wood. Needless to say, a house can burn down because of a wood stove vented to an unlined chimney.

If you do not trust an existing chimney or you must build a chimney for your stove, there are two possible solutions. You can build a masonry chimney with a flue liner, or you can install a chimney using asbestos-lining chimney pipe. The chimney must extend above the roofline at least 2 feet above any ridge or wall closer than 10 feet. You must be careful to leave a 2-inch clearance between the chimney pipe and any combustible materials. The chimney can be angled and offset if necessary to take it around obstructions in the upper rooms, attic or roof of the house.

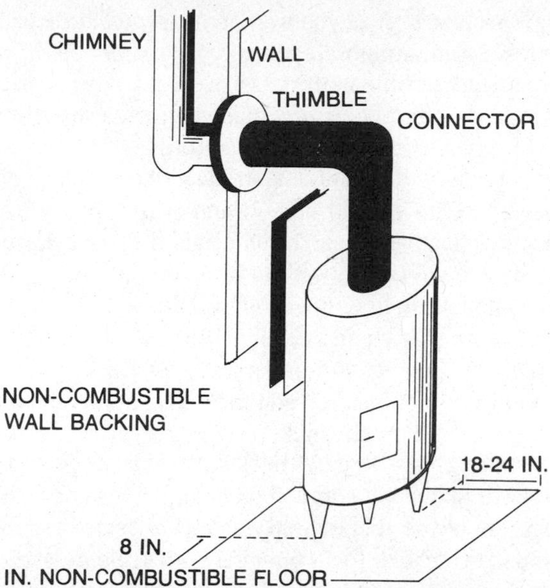

Fig. 13-4. The connecting pipe must be run through a thimble to protect a combustible wall from heat if the pipe goes through a wall before connecting to the chimney. Non-combustible materials should be placed on the wall if the stove is closer than 3 feet to the wall. Non-combustible materials must be placed on the floor.

Connector

The connector, or stove pipe, attaches the stove to the chimney, as in Fig. 13-4. The connector may be a double-wall asbestos-lined pipe, or it may be single wall stovepipe. If an asbestos-lined pipe goes through a wall or ceiling before connecting with the chimney, you must allow at least 2 inches clearance between the pipe and any combustible materials. However, you should check the pipe and stove manufacturers' recommendations in case they recommend a larger amount of clearance.

If single-wall connecting pipe is used, allow an area three times larger than that of the pipe as clearance for combustible materials. In other words, if you run a 6-inch single-wall stovepipe through a wall, allow an 18-inch diameter thimble to run the pipe through.

Floor and Wall

The floor and walls surrounding the stove should be covered with non-combustible materials. Generally, you can figure that a stove should be placed at least 3 feet from a wall constructed of combustible materials. If the wall is non-combustible, you can place the stove as close to it as you wish, unless your state or local building codes set a minimum clearance.

A good non-combustible material to protect walls is asbestos millboard. It is more effective if it is placed 1 inch away from the wall to allow air circulation behind the material.

A number of non-combustible materials will protect the floor. The stove may be set in a small box of sand or pebbles. Masonry blocks, bricks and fireplace hearth materials may also be used. Asbestos boards are another possibility.

The non-combustible floor covering should extend 8 inches to each side of the stove. It should extend 18 inches in front of the stove to protect the floor from sparks and embers that may fall when the stove door is opened to add fuel. The non-combustible floor material must be ⅜-inch thick.

Before installing your stove, check with your stove and fireplace supplier. He may have some good suggestions and installation tips, and he should be able to help you devise a safe installation plan. Also be sure to check local building codes. Some are quite explicit about requirements for wood stove installation.

WOOD FURNACES

The most effecient way to take advantage of wood for heating your home (assuming wood is less expensive than other heating fuels in your area) is to install a wood furnace. A wood furnace can be connected to a duct system to provide a central heating system and to distribute heat evenly throughout the house.

The wood furnace has many of the same components as any combustible fuel furnace, such as a gas furnace. It is larger, however, because of the larger size required to handle wood fuel. But the basic components are the same. A wood furnace has a combustion chamber, a heat exchanger, a plenum chamber, a duct system and a fan to push the heating air through the system.

If you think a wood furnace might save you money on your heating bill and you are considering installing one, you should think about installing one of the combination furnaces that burns wood or coal—but also switches to burn gas or oil if needed. This adds extra flexibility to your heating system and prevents catastrophes if you are unable to cut a load of wood when you need it to burn.

You must also carefully plan the wood furnace's location, since it will probably be heavy enough to require special floor supports or foundation support. Talk with your furnace dealer to get help in planning modifications to your house before you buy a wood furnace.

THE USE OF FIREPLACES

The use of fireplaces in American homes has almost come a full circle from the colonial days when fireplaces were the main sources of heat for homes. Fireplaces lost their place of necessity in the American home as furnaces were developed and became more sophisticated. The reasoning went: why bother with starting and tending a messy wood fire when we can sit back and let the furnace do the same thing automatically? As gas and electric furnaces replaced the older oil and coal home furnaces, the fireplace was almost forgotten for many families. In those homes where fireplaces were installed, they were luxury items—an attractive addition to a living room. In many homes, building a fire in the fireplace was a special event—a time for a family to gather around a beautiful wood flame.

Rapidly escalating home heating costs have dramatically changed Americans' views toward their fireplaces. The fireplace is now being seen as it was before the twentieth century—a source of heat for the home.

Americans are realizing that they can cut down their gas and electric heating bills by burning wood in their fireplaces. That, of course, is true as far as it goes. But the simple fact is that many fireplaces in homes today are not energy efficient. Depending on the cost of wood in your area, it may cost you more on your total heating bill (wood plus gas or electricity) to use your fireplace as a supplementary heat source. Many of the fireplaces built in homes in the last few decades were installed for their beauty—not to be energy efficient. When many of these fireplaces were installed, the amount of heat they gave out was scarcely considered. If the fire in some fireplaces is not tended very carefully, the end result of using a fireplace is a higher, gas or electric heating bill.

Fig. 13-5. The heat circulator fireplace draws air from the living area and passes it through a double-wall fire chamber lining. The air is warmed by the walls at the back and side of the fire, and the warm air is forced into the living area. A large amount of the heat that would normally escape up the chimney is recaptured and returned to the living area. The warm air exits at the top of the assembly. Electric fans usually are included in these assemblies to increase the warm air flow.

Many of these energy wasting problems with fireplaces are being overcome today as fireplaces once again take their place as important heat sources for our homes. Most of these energy saving design improvements mean that a fireplace costs a bit more money, but the extra expense is well worth it. In fact, the additional $200 or so you would spend on energy saving devices for your fireplace would probably meant the difference between cutting your total heat bill and sending a lot of wasted heat up the flue.

If you are interested in the fireplace only for its attractiveness and visual appeal, you can have a conventional fireplace installed in your home. If you want attractive visual appeal and lower heat bills, modern fireplaces can provide both.

Designs

The basic fireplace designs are pretty much the same today as they have been for decades, but there are a number of additions to most modern fireplaces that increase their energy efficiency tremendously. These devices are discussed at length later in this chapter, but briefly here are some of the main features in modern energy saving fireplaces.

Heat circulating fireplaces go far beyond the conventional fireplaces in heat production by providing a second way to get heat from the burning wood into the living area. The circulator fireplace uses a double-wall steel lining surrounding the fire chamber (Fig. 13-5). Cold air from the living area is drawn into the air chamber between the two steel walls that surround the burning wood. Once inside the air chamber, the air is warmed and returned to the living area with the help of a circulator fan (Fig. 13-6). Whereas a conventional masonry fireplace provides heat only from the radiation of the fire, the circulator provides the same radiated heat plus the additional heat from air currents around the back of the fire. The circulator greatly increases the fireplace's heat output by capturing much of the heat that otherwise would escape up the flue.

Glass doors are another energy saving feature of modern fireplaces. Wire screens in front of burning fires have long been a necessity to stop burning sparks from popping out of the fireplace and into the living area. Glass doors provide this safety plus another important feature. They block the fireplace opening so warm air inside the house cannot be sucked up the chimney. Because an open fireplace draws warm air inside through the fireplace opening and sends it outside through the chimney, an open fireplace can actually add to the furnace heating bill instead of

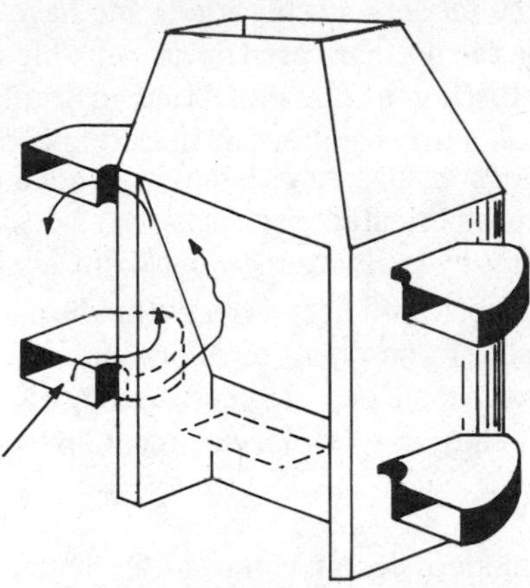

Fig. 13-6. The heat circulating fireplace draws air into the air chamber through vents at the bottom of the unit. The air circulates through the air space between the walls of the fire chamber lining. Here the air is warmed from the heat on the sides and back of the fire, and the warm air flows out vents at the top of the unit into the living area. Most heat circulators have small fans in the air inlet ducts to push more air through the system.

lowering it. Glass doors prevent this and also allow you to leave the fireplace a damper open at night while the fire burns down. You can just close the doors and go to bed while the fire continues burning.

When the fire goes out, the closed doors will prevent warm house air from being drawn up the flue. The doors allow radiated heat to warm the living area, but they work best with circulator fireplaces.

Another energy saving addition to a fireplace is a hollow tube grate that draws air from the living area, passes through the grate tubes and around the burning logs, and expels it back into the room. These grates operate with both natural convection air currents and circulator fans. Some designs have the hollow tube grates built as part of a glass door assembly. This design allows you to use the grates with closed glass doors.

Masonry and Prefabricated Fireplaces

The traditional fireplace design is the masonry fireplace. It is this fireplace that is largely giving way today to the newer heat-saving designs. The masonry fireplace uses a brick lining around the fire chamber and relies on radiation from the fire to heat the living area. The masonry fireplace with no heat saving additions is a very inefficient heating device.

Some very modern fireplace designs have become popular. One of these is the prefabricated fireplace, which is designed to be added quickly to a home. The prefabricated fireplace is a metal unit that comes with a firechamber and flue. It is installed without the concrete footings or masonry chimneys needed for a built-in fireplace. Some prefabricated fireplaces can be placed in a typical fireplace setting by building them into a masonry wall.

Other prefabricated fireplaces are modern freestanding metal designs available in an array of colors and styles. Prefabricated fireplaces have become popular because they are easy to install and are versatile. They can be placed almost anywhere in a home.

Gas Fireplaces

Another modern design is the gas or electric fireplace. These fireplaces are popular with persons who are primarlily interested in the attractive appeal of a fireplace, but who do not want or cannot have burning wood. Gas and electric fireplaces may be attractive, but they have almost no value as energy-saving devices. In fact, some designs may be energy wasting devices because of inefficient heat transfer. Since the fireplaces burn a conventional fuel, they won't cut your fuel bill.

One way the fireplaces might save money is by providing heat in the main living area and allowing you to lower the furnace setting for the rest of the house. This would maintain a comfortable temperature in the room that is used most, and the rest of the house could be cooler. The same result can be obtained at a lower cost, however, by installing individual room heaters or electric baseboard heaters, which are discussed in another chapter. About the only thing you'll get from an electric or gas fireplace is its appearance and some heat.

Wall Fireplaces

Fireplaces may be built in several different styles, but the most popular is the wall fireplace. These fireplaces are set into a wall along one side of a room.

A two-way fireplace has openings on two sides of the fire and, in effect, has no back. Usually a two-way fireplace will be in a wall divider between two rooms so the heat warms both rooms. Some fireplaces may have three open sides.

Hooded and Freestanding Fireplaces

In the hooded fireplace design, the fire is moved out into the room a bit so it will be under a large hood that projects from the wall. The hood usually extends out from the wall a foot or two. A hooded fireplace can be more efficient than a wall fireplace because the hood (usually made of metal) radiates heat into the living area.

A *freestanding* fireplace refers to any fireplace that is located away from walls in the living area of a room so there is space between the fireplace and the walls on all four sides. Usually freestanding fireplaces are the prefabricated metal type, but they may also be masonry fireplaces.

The easiest place in a house to locate a fireplace is along an outside wall. You will have to use a masonry footing for most built-in fireplaces, and you won't have to add so much extra footing along an outside wall since the foundation is already in place. Metal prefabricated fireplaces, however, do not require this footing, so they can easily be installed almost anywhere in a house.

Fireplace Size

One of the most commmon complaints about fireplaces is from owners who wish they had installed a larger one. That does not mean you should install the largest fireplace the brick masons will install, but it does mean you should take a long look at fireplace sizes and your intentions before you have one put in.

If wood in your area is inexpensive or if you have located a source of free wood, the larger the fire you build in your fireplace means the more money you'll save on your furnace heating bill. One of the biggest considerations in selecting a fireplace size is the size of the fires you intend to build. This point is crucial for masonry fireplaces, which rely on fire chamber walls to radiate heat into the living area. If a tiny fire is built in a large fireplace, the distance from the flames to the walls will be so great that little heat will be radiated.

On the other hand, you have to take into account the size of the wood you'll be burning. You won't be able to burn a very large log in a 2-foot wide fireplace. If you can get small wood and you're putting the fireplace in a small room a 2-foot fireplace may be just right. Small wood will likely cost more to buy and, at the very least, it's more work to cut.

If your main reason for installing a fireplace is to save on your heating bill, you will probably want to install a 36-inch (measured across the front opening) or larger fireplace. The larger sizes allow you to use larger wood, and you can stack larger quantities on the fire so it can be tended less often. This also gives you a larger fire that will produce more heat.

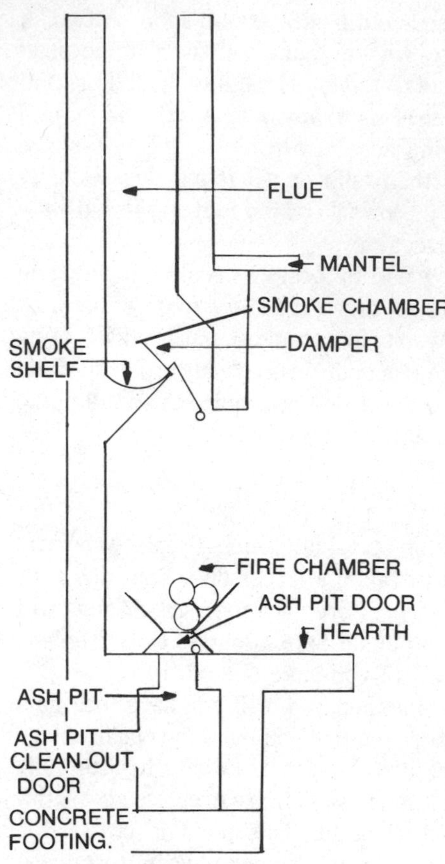

Fig. 13-7. The parts of a fireplace.

FIREPLACE PARTS

Figure 13-7 is a diagram of a fireplace showing its basic parts. The heart of the fireplace is the *fire chamber* where the wood burns. In traditional fireplace designs the fire chamber was lined with fire bricks, but much better heating is obtained when a double-wall steel liner of a heat circulating fireplace system is used. Circulator fireplaces are discussed later in the chapter.

The fire chamber cannot be shoddily constructed or your fireplace will have an abundance of problems. It must be proportioned correctly or the fire will not burn properly and smoke will enter the living area. This is another advantage of using a circulator fireplace—the fire chamber is already correctly shaped and ready to install.

Since the fire chamber walls radiate heat into the living area, these walls must be built correctly or a lot of heat will be wasted.

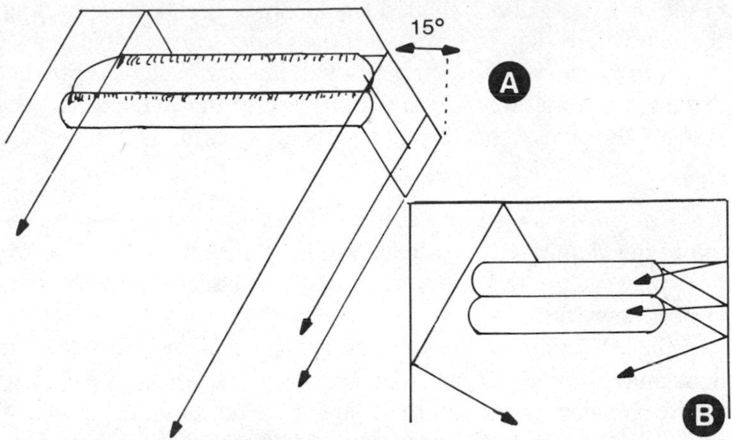

Fig. 13-8. (A) The best heat radiation into the living area will be obtained if the fireplace walls slope toward the back wall at a 15° angle. At this angle the rays from the fire are reflected into the living area. (B) When the fireplace's side walls are perpendicular to the back wall, many of the fire's rays are reflected back into the fire chamber where they are of no value in heating the living area.

The greatest amount of heat will be radiated if the sides slope inward toward the back wall of the fire chamber at about 15°. If the sides go straight back to the wall, very little heat will be radiated. (Figs. 13-8A dna 13-8B).

The top of the fire chamber slopes inward toward the living area, and this also reflects radiated heat into the room. At the top of the slope is the fireplace's *throat*, where the *damper* is found. The damper controls the opening to the flue, and it is closed when there is no fire. Closing the damper prevents cold drafts coming down the flue from entering the living area, and it keeps warm inside air from escaping up the flue.

Improper use of the damper is one of the biggest sources of fireplace inefficiency. If the damper is left open when there is no fire in the fire chamber, you will waste more heat than you will save by burning wood in the first place. One of the big advantages of installing glass doors on a fireplace is these doors can serve to close off the flue from the living area while a fire is burning low. The damper does not have to be tended nearly as closely when glass doors are used because the closed doors will prevent most of the problems caused by an open damper.

The *smoke shelf*, at the throat of the fireplace and behind the damper, serves the very important function of deflecting cold downdrafts. Downdrafts are present especially in the early stages of the fire. The curved-shaped smoke shelf directs them back up the flue where they can mix with the rising warm air currents.

The *smoke chamber* combines with the smoke shelf to prevent downdrafts from directing smoke back into the living area. The sides of the smoke chamber slope evenly inward toward the flue.

Flue

The *flue* is lined with a masonry flue lining that extends to the top of the chimney. If you have two fireplaces in your home, the flues may run through the same chimney. But each fireplace must have its own flue.

Since the flue is a source of downdrafts and the size of the flue determines how much inside air (and fireplace heat) will be drawn up the chimney, the smaller the flue is the better up to a point, of course. If the chimney is more than 15 feet high (as measured from the fireplace throat to the top of the chimney), the flue area must be one-tenth the area of the fireplace opening (height × width of the front opening). If the chimeny is less than 15 feet high, the flue area must be one-eighth the area of the fireplace openings. At altitudes over 2,000 feet, the flue area and chimney height must be increased by 5% for each 1,000 feet of elevation.

The flue runs through the *chimney* to the top of the chimney, at least 2 feet above any part of the roof or house walls closer than 10 feet. The flue will project a few inches above the top of the chimney.

Possible obstructions near the chimney may influence the location of the fireplace within the home. Nearby obstructions such as walls, trees or buildings can creat downdrafts in the flue that will force smoke into the house. The chimney must be at least 2 feet taller than the highest part of the roof. It must extend 2 feet above any wall closer than 10 feet from the chimeny.

Hearth

The *hearth* is the floor of the firechamber. It is built of firebrick or other heat resistant materials and extends in front of the fire-placeopening to project the floor from the heat in the firechamber. The hearth may be flush with the floor, or it may be raised above the floor. Some hearths are high enough above the floor to allow a person to sit on them.

The hearth should extend about 1 foot to the side of the fireplace opening and about 1½ feet int front of it. Local building codes may vary on these requirements, however, and you should check to be sure.

Some fireplaces have a metal door in the hearth that opens to let the homewoner push the ashes into an ashpit under the fire chamber. The ashpit occupies the space between the fireplace foundation walls. Another small metal door allows you to clean this pit periodically.

SAFETY PRECAUTIONS

Because of the amount of heat generated in a fireplace, especially one designed to be an important part of the home heating plan, there are a number of safety precautions in fireplace construction you should know. Any combustible material, such as wood trim, paneling or the fireplace mantel, must be at least 4 inches from the fireplace opening. If the mantel extends more than 2 inches out from the wall, it must be no closer than 12 inches above the fireplace opening.

The fireplace chimney must have a flue lining to prevent the chimney from becoming too hot and igniting nearby combustible framing boards. There should be a 2-inch air space between the fireplace and all combustible framing boards.

Metal parts, such as the damper or a combination damper-smoke chamber, should be well constructed. The damper should be relatively easy to open and close, but it must not move so easily that it might move by itself. The damper must seal tightly.

AIR SUPPLY

Burning wood requires oxygen—a lot of it! The problem homeowners face in burning wood and trying to conserve energy is that one of the easiest places for the fireplace to pull this oxygen from is the living area. The overall effect, then, is the fireplace draws in air from the living area. This air is replaced by colder outside air that can enter the house through any of hundreds of tiny air leaks in a house. This infiltration air must be heated, and that adds to the heat load of the house.

If the house is sealed tightly so that little air can enter by infiltration, other problems crop up. The fire will not burn properly because of a small air supply, and it may deplete the supply of oxygen in the living area. That can be a danger for inhabitants. If the fire cannot draw enough air from the house to create an updraft in the chimney, it will begin drawing it down the chimney instead.

There are a number of possible solutions to this problem. Certainly for energy saving you want to have a tightly sealed

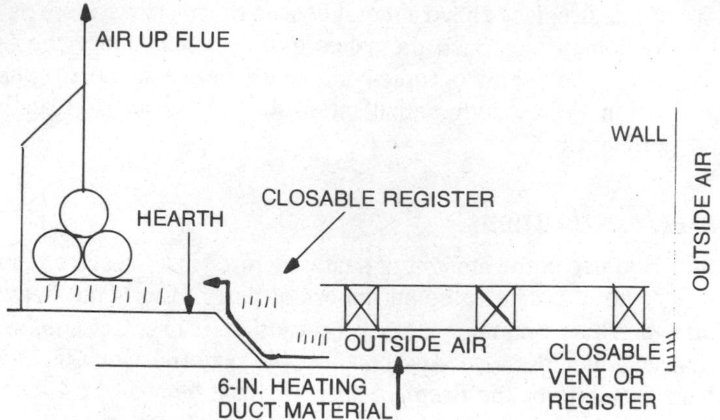

Fig. 13-9. To prevent the fireplace from drawing heated air from the house to burn the wood, you should provide an independent air supply. This can be done by running a duct from the front of the hearth to the outside so that outside air, and not heated inside air, is drawn into the fireplace for combustion. This duct must have closable vents to prevent the cold outside air from entering the house when the fire is not burning.

house, so that rules out opening windows to provide a draft for the fire. If your fireplace has an ashpit, a simple way to provide needed air for the fire is to open the ashpit door in the hearth and slightly open the ashpit's outside foundation door. This will allow the fireplace to pull a draft from the outside instead of through the house. You should be careful, however, to close off the draft through the ashpit when there is no fire. Otherwise, the cold outside air will come into the house. This is especially true if your fireplace does not have glass doors.

If your fireplace does not have an ashpit, another solution is to run an air duct from the outside, under the house, to the hearth in front of the fireplace. The same result is achieved—the fireplace is drawing its draft from outdoors instead of sending warm inside air up the chimney and replacing it with cold air. The outside air duct should be installed with an adjustable register that can be regulated as needed and closed when there is no fire (Fig. 13-9).

MORE ON PREFABRICATED AND FREESTANDING FIREPLACES

If you want to add a fireplace to your home but cannot find a good location for a masonry fireplace, or you have found the cost of a masonry fireplace to be prohibitive, a prefabricated fireplace may be just what you need. These fireplaces are built of metal instead of bricks and mortar as masonry fireplaces are, and they are purchased as an entire unit. Many hardware stores and home decorating centers will sell you an entire kit that includes all the parts of the fireplace: a metal fire chamber, flue, damper, chimney, hearth and even the fireplace trim. They come in many styles and designs to complement any room, but there are two basic types.

The freestanding fireplace is usually a contemporary design that uses the fireplace's metal construction in its overall design (Figs. 13-10 and 13-11). The freestanding fireplace is built away from the room walls so there is space on all sides of the fireplace. Some of these fireplaces have a 360° fire opening and are designed to dominate the center of a room.

The second type of prefabricated fireplace is designed to look like a masonry fireplace. These fireplaces are installed in a wall or a corner of a room and are trimmed with the traditional brick or wood surroundings of a masonry fireplace. In fact, it is very difficult to distinguish these built-in prefabricated metal fireplaces from the masonry fireplaces.

Fig. 13-10. An attractive freestanding prefabricated fireplace (courtesy of Martin Industries).

There are a number of advantages to both freestanding and traditional looking prefabricated fireplaces. One of the biggest advantages is almost any homeowner can install these fireplaces himself. This saves costly labor expenses for masonry work. Most of these fireplaces can be bought with all necessary parts included, and the directions should be complete and easy to follow. Be sure to check this out before you buy if you plan to install one of these fireplaces yourself. If the directions are cryptic notations that can be understood only by persons completely familiar with installing the fireplace, they won't do you much good. You'll have a lot of problems putting your fireplace in.

Prefabricated fireplaces require no foundation and no footing. They can be installed right on the subfloor and against a wood wall. These fireplaces usually are well-insulated or are built with double-wall construction to protect against fires. You should check these features before you buy.

Because they require no foundation and generally require no special support, prefabricated fireplaces can be installed virtually anywhere in a home—along an inside wall, in an upstairs room and even in the center of a room. These fireplaces usually come with their own flues and chimneys, but they may be connected to masonry chimneys by using special chimney connecting pipes.

Traditional Looking Prefabricated Fireplaces

When the traditional looking prefabricated fireplace is built into a wall or into a corner of a room, few people will be able to tell it is not a masonry fireplace. These fireplaces may usually be installed against a wall without any air space. The metal flue may be run through a false wall behind the fireplace, or you can build a box-like frame around the flue. When the frame is covered with wood paneling or imitation bricks, it won't even look like a metal fireplace.

You should follow the manufacturer's directions for your fireplace, but these units are usually installed on a hearth constructed of fire-resistant material. The hearth must extend outward from the fireplace about 18 inches in front and about 12 inches to the side of the fire opening, just as in a traditional fireplace.

The materials around the fireplace should complement the room—imitation brick or wood paneling are two possibilities. As with a masonry fireplace, you must not install any combustible materials within 4 inches of the fireplace opening.

Fig. 13-11. Another beautiful prefabricated fireplace (courtesy of Martin Industries).

Purchasing Freestanding Fireplaces

The flexibility of freestanding prefabricated fireplaces has given designers a free hand to make these fireplaces in a wide variety of styles, shapes and colors. You can buy one of these fireplaces with a 360° fire opening, or you can purchase one designed more like a wood stove. You can place these fireplaces almost anywhere in a room—in the center or against a wall. About the only requirement is that you place them on a hearth of a fire-resistant material and extend the chimney at least 2 feet above the ridge of the roof. Outside of these constraints you're limited only by your imagination.

In purchasing a freestanding fireplace you should be sure to check the manufacturer's recommended minimum clearance between the fireplace and the wall. Not all freestanding fireplaces are insulated well enough to be installed next to a wall. Most of these fireplaces use double wall construction or insulation to keep the outside surfaces safely cool and to prevent accidental burns. You should check this before buying. Especially if you have small children, you won't want a stove that will cause burns.

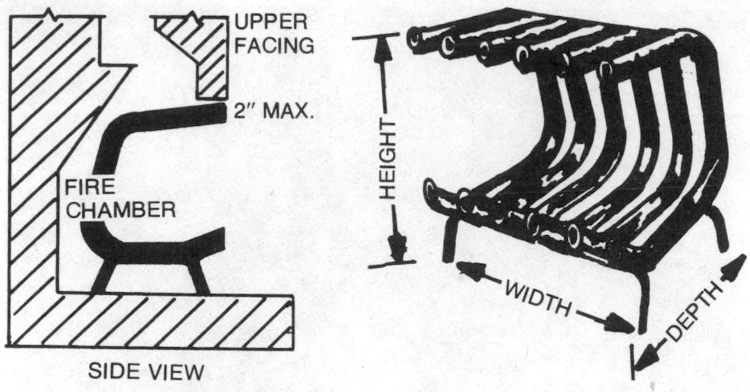

Fig. 13-12. (A) Side view of a hollow tube fireplace grate. (B) The hollow tube fireplace grate increases a fireplace's efficiency by drawing in room air, routing it around the fire and expeling the hot air back into the room.

As in purchasing a wood stove, look at a metal fireplace for solid construction, strong welds and convenience in use. When lighting a fire, give the metal fireplace some time to warm up by adding fuel slowly. This will prevent warping the fireplace.

MORE HEAT FROM YOUR FIREPLACE

Fireplaces are notoriously inefficient heating units. A plain, ordinary fireplace with no efficiency increasing modifications will send about 90% of the heat it produces up the flue. A few years ago that waste was all right because heat from wood and fossil fuels was cheap and fireplaces were used largely for decoration anyway. Today that is not the case. Families are using their fireplaces more and more to help heat their homes.

Obviously, for the family trying to stretch its heating dollars, 90% heat energy up the chimney is no longer acceptable. In fact, unless you get your firewood free, you probably won't save money on your heating bill if your fireplace is only 10% efficient because the heat per dollar supplied by firewood will be more expensive than the heat from your regular heating system.

Fortunately, there are a number of devices available that dramatically increase the heat produced from a fireplace. These devices will make the initial cost of your fireplace more expensive, but they are well worth the money in the long run. They are almost essential if you have to pay for your firewood. Even if you have a free supply of wood, it makes sense to get as much heat from it as you can.

Hollow tube grates, glass doors and circulator fireplaces are among the most popular heat increasing additions. These can be used alone or in combinations.

HOLLOW TUBE GRATES

Figures 13-12A and 13-12B show a hollow tube fireplace grate and a side view of it. These grates are available in many different sizes to fit virtaully any fireplace. The grates are constructed of six to ten 14-gauge steel tubes that use the natural convection air current to move air around the fire and return the air into the room.

Figure 13-13 shows how the cool air is drawn into the bottom of the grate and the warmer air moves out. The cool air passes under the burning wood and is warmed. Since warmer air is lighter than cool air, the air rises through the tubes as it is warmed by the fire. The air, now hot after passing through the grate's hollow tubes, leaves the tubes at the top of the grate and goes into the room.

Cool air entering the grate tubes prevents the tubes from getting as hot as a conventional fireplace grate. This prolongs the grate's life. Before buying one of these grates, however, you should be sure it is constructed of heavy-gauge steel that will withstand high temperatures one would expect in a fireplace. Check the manufacturer's warranty. Better models carry a two-year warranty against failure.

The hollow tube fireplace grates are also available with a blower system to further increase the heat output. A 110-volt fan blows air through the grate faster than natural convection currents, which increases the volume of air heated by the unit. See Fig. 13-14.

One disadvantage to the standard hollow tube grate system is that it will work only with unrestricted air flow into the fireplace.

Fig. 13-13. This cutaway side view shows how the cool air is drawn into the hollow grate at the bottom and is expelled back into the room at the top.

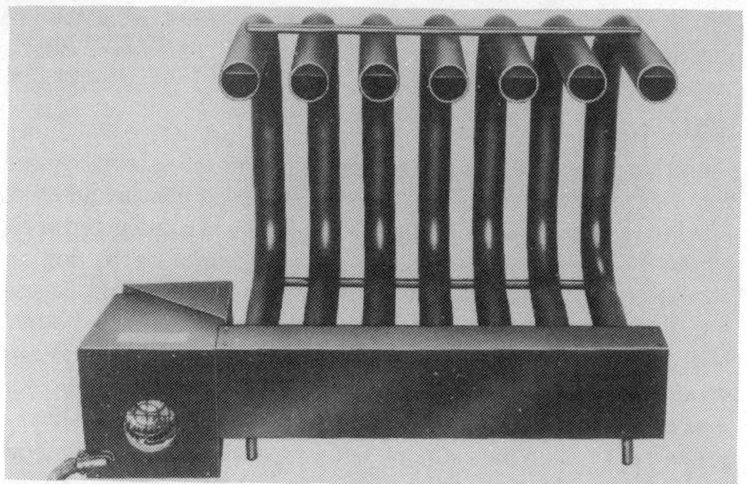

Fig. 13-14. Hollow tube fireplace grates are available with a blower system that increases the heat output of the grate (courtesy of Shenandoah Manufacturing Company).

Conventional glass fireplace doors, which reduce the flow of air from the living area into the fireplace, cannot be closed with hollow tube grates because that would shut off the air flow through the tubes. However, a combination of hollow tube grates with glass doors and a blower is also available.

HEAT CIRCULATING FIREPLACES

One of the ways to increase the heat output of a fireplace is to install a heat circulating fireplace (Fig. 13-15). These units are designed with steel double-wall construction that allows air to enter through vents near the floor circulate around the sides and back of the fire chamber, and exit at the top of the fire chamber. The heat circulating fireplace is essentially a unit that repalces the traditional firebrick lining in the fire chamber. It usually includes the throat, damper and smoke chamber along with the fire chamber as a single unit.

The heat circulating fireplace is still basically a masonry fireplace. It has a masonry flue, and a masonry surround still encircles the fire chamber. The prefabricated metal fire chamber lining is really nothing more than a mold for the masonry—it is not a self-contained fireplace.

The traditional masonry fireplace provides only one way to get heat from the fire chamber to the living area—radiation from the fire and from the sides of the fire chamber. The heat circulating fireplace, however, provides a second way to transfer the fireplace heat. Air from the living area is drawn into vents at the floor level, usually with the help of small fans. This air then passes between the steel walls of the fire chamber lining. The warm walls at the back and side of the fire chamber warm the moving air. The warm air leaves the fire chamber lining at a vent at the top of the fireplace.

There are several advantages to installing a heat circulating fireplace. Since the factory has done all the work in the complicated shaping and forming operations for the fire chamber, throat and smoke chamber, heat circulating fireplaces are easy to install. Even if you aren't skilled with bricks, mortar and trowels, you can probably do much of the installation work yourself and save large labor expenses. The steel lining provides a form for the masonry, so the bricks are laid around it (Fig. 13-16). The sloping and measuring required to build a traditional fireplace are eliminated.

Because the shape of the fire chamber and the throat are determined by experts at the factory, you are virtually assured that your fireplace will have a correctly shaped interior and that fires

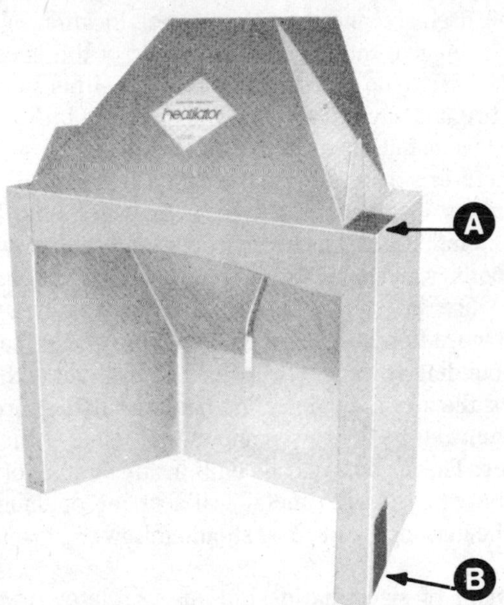

Fig. 13-15. The heat circulating fireplace is a double-wall steel fireplace form that incorporates many of the parts of the fireplace in the prebuilt unit. The circulating system draws in air in the lower vents (A) and circulates it around the sides and backs of the unit. Warm air leaves the unit at the top vents (B) and may be sent into the living area through ducts (courtesy of Heatilator Fireplaces).

Fig. 13-16. Because the heat circulating fireplace is prefabricated to the correct dimensions, the difficult measuring and shaping of a masonry fireplace is eliminated. The masonry work is placed around the steel fireplace form. (A) is the lower vent installed in the masonry work.

will burn properly. You also can be sure the damper is the correct size for the fireplace and is in the proper location. With a heat circulating fireplace, the factory takes care of the guesswork for you! All you have to do once the fireplace is built is sit back, enjoy your cozy fire and save money on your heating bills.

When you install a heat circulating fireplace, be sure to follow the manufacturer's instructions. Basically, however, the heat circulating unit is installed on a typical fireplace hearth made of fire-resistant materials. The heat circulating fireplace will require the same footings and foundation supports as a traditional masonry fireplace. Once in place, the steel lining is surrounded with masonry. One difference between installing the circulator fireplaces and building a masonry fireplace is the air vents that must be provided for the air circulation. The heat circulating fireplace has air intake vents at the floor level and output vents at the top of the fire chamber. These vents may be built in any number of ways, and they may be covered with metal grills or air openings may be formed in the masonry work. You should follow the manufacturer's directions.

A number of sizes and designs of circulator fireplaces are available. You may install a circulator fireplace anywhere you might install a conventional masonry fireplace. Circulator units also may be purchased for corner fireplaces and for two-way fireplaces.

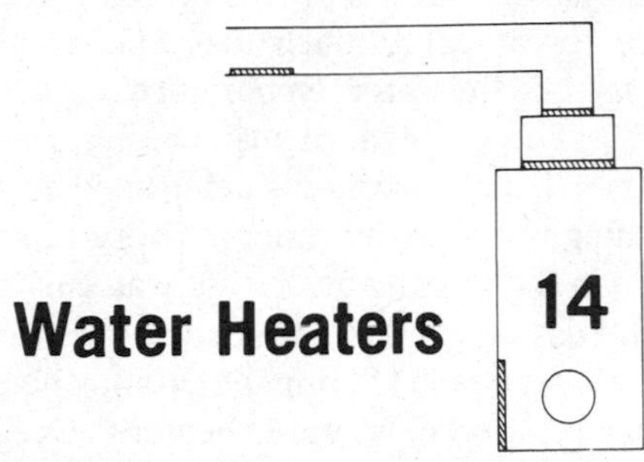

14 Water Heaters

Water heaters are virtually forgotten in the home until something goes wrong with them. But if you stop to consider that your water heater is one of your largest energy consuming devices (only the furnace and air conditioner use more energy), and that the water heater accounts for about 15 to 20% of your energy bill, you immediately realize its importance in an energy conservation program.

A family of four or five with a dishwasher and a clothes washer in the home will roughly 30,000 gallons of hot water in a year. There are a large number of variables that determine the total cost of heating that much water. If the water is heated to 165°, it may cost more than $250 annually to heat the water with electricity. Lowering the water temperature to 140° will reduce the cost of hot water by 20%, and lowering the temperature to 120° will reduce hot water costs by 40%.

LOWER TEMPERATURES SAVE MONEY

The important thing to realize about water heaters is that they spend an incredible amount of time and energy just maintaining the temperature of the water inside the tank. The result is that the water heater is using energy throughout the day, even though the entire family may be away from home and will not need much hot water for 10-12 hours after leaving the house in the morning. Likewise, the water heater continues warming the water to maintain its temperature at night when everyone is asleep and will not need hot water until the morning.

This is why setting the water heater at a high temperature is so wasteful and so costly. If you set the water heater at 165°, it will have to use enough energy to keep the water at about 165° throughout the day and night, even though the water will not be needed for several hours. On the other hand, if you set your water heater at 120°, much less energy and money are required to maintain the water temperature when no one is going to be using it.

The problem of maintaining a constant water temperature even though no water is being used may be alleviated somewhat by using water heater timers. These timers turn the heater elements on in the mornng before hot water is needed, turn them off during the day when it is not needed, and turn them back on before hot water is needed during the evening hours. But these timers are not available on most water heaters. Even where timers are used, it still makes sense to set the water temperature as low as convenient for washing and showering.

You may argue that lowering the water temperature will cause problems. There may not be enough hot water available for washing clothes and showering. With modern detergents and fabrics, however, the water temperature in the laundry appliances is not nearly as important as it once was. Studies show that most clothes will come just as clean when washed in warm or cool water as they will when washed in hot water. And the life of the fabric is longer if cooler temperatures are used. Warm water rinses have been shown to be unnecessary. The result is that laundry can be done with much less hot water than you may think.

The problem of having enough hot water for baths and showers can be a more diffcult problem when the temperature of the water heater is lowered. This can be overcome, however, by making sure baths and showers are taken before laundry or dishes are washed and by scheduling bathing for some family members for mornings and some for evenings. Hot water consumption during showers can also be reduced by using shower heads that reduce the water flow. These are discussed later in the chapter.

THE RIGHT WATER TEMPERATURE FOR YOUR HOME

If you lower the temperature setting on your water heater and later discover you are continually running out of hot water during showers or baths, you may want to raise the thermostat setting a bit. Many water heates are adjusted at the factory to a setting of 160°, but is usually relatively easy for the homeowner to readjust this setting. It is inefficient and costly to set your water heater over

140°. As mentioned earlier, your energy bill will increase by about 3% for each additional 10°.

The simple fact is that 140° is more than adequate for most modern hot water applications. If you have a dishwasher without a water heating element, you will likely need to maintain a 140° temperature setting in order to get proper cleaning. On the other hand, if you do not have a dishwasher or if experience with your dishwasher has shown a lower water temperature setting will bring acceptable results, you should lower the setting to 120°. From the 120° setting you may have to do some experimenting to get the hot water results you want—especially with hot water for showers and baths. But the result will be well worth your time, because you may be able to save $50-75 a year!

ADJUSTING YOUR WATER TEMPERATURE SETTING

An electric water heater usually has two heating elements: one at the top and one at the bottom of the water heater. Each heating element has its own thermostat. When you adjust the temperature setting, you must adjust the thermostat for each element.

The thermostat of a water heater works the same as a thermostat of a furnace or air conditioner. When the thermostat senses that more heat is needed to maintain the proper water temperature, it turns on the heating element. On an electric water heater, the thermostat and heating element terminal are located behind a removable front panel (Fig. 14-1).

To adjust the thermostat setting, remove the front panels to reveal the thermostats. With a screwdriver, you should be able to adjust the thermostats to the temperature setting you want. If your water heater has "high," "medium" and "low" settings instead of temperature degree settings, you should try to find out from your owner's manual or from your dealer exactly what those designations mean. If you cannot, you'll just have to experiment with different settings until you get one that works best. You can begin by expecting that the "low" setting will probably be about 110-125°, the "medium" setting will probably be about 140-150°, and the "high" setting will probably be somewhere around 165-180°.

If you have a gas water heater, you have only one thermostat to adjust. The thermostat is located near the bottom of the water heater on the gas valve assembly on the outside of the case.

If you will be gone from home for several days, there is no reason to leave your hot water on. It only will use energy need-

Fig. 14-1. The front panel has been removed from this electric water heater to reveal the terminals of the top heating element (A) and the thermostat (B). This water heater also has its own circuit breaker (C), which would trip is the heating element shortened. This circuit breaker appears only under the top removable panel. It is not normally found in the lower lement assembly.

lessly. An electric hot water heater can be shut down by turning off the unit's circuit breaker at the electrical breaker box. A gas water heater can be turned off by switching the control on the gas valve to the "pilot" position, which keep the burner from going on but allows the pilot light to continue burning. An alternative with either the gas or electric water heaters is to turn the thermostats to the lowest setting available. This will cut energy consumption, but it does not save as much as turning off the unit completely.

GAS WATER HEATERS

Gas water heaters have many of the same parts as a gas furnace, and they require much the same type of maintenance. The gas water heater usually has one burner at the bottom of the unit with a flue going up the center of the unit (Fig. 14-2). The flue is vented to the outside with stove pipe.

The thermostat and gas valve are usually combined in one assembly that is located on the outside of the heater case near the bottom of the unit. This thermostat is adjusted when you want to raise or lower the temperature of your hot water. When you leave the house for several days, you should turn the gas valve to the *pilot* position. This keeps the burner from turning on, but it allows the pilot light to stay lit.

The gas water heater burner is much like the furnace burner, but it is usually round rather than long. The burner works on the same principles as the furnace burner. The water heater, like the

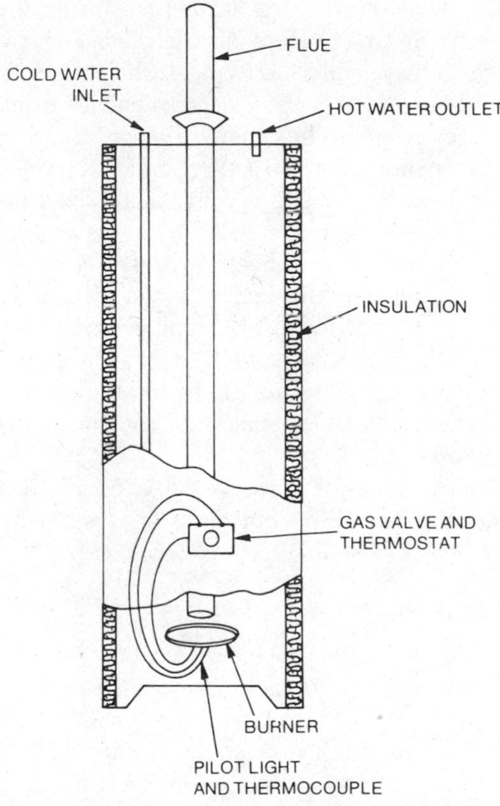

Fig. 14-2. The gas water heater has a circular burner at the bottom of the unit and flue that goes up the center. The operation of the parts of the gas water heater are very similar to those in a gas furnace.

gas furnace, has a *thermocouple* to shut off the gas valve if the pilot light should go out. Like gas furnaces, gas water heaters can be purchased to operated on either natural gas or propane.

Routine maintenance is needed to keep the gas water heater in top working condition. Check the burners about once a year. Clean them off, look for cracks or breaks, and keep them in good working order. Follow the procedure outlined in Chapter 8 for a gas furnace. The procedures for adjusting the burner, air vent, pilot light, thermocouple, etc., are almost identical to those for a gas furnace.

ELECTRIC WATER HEATERS

The construction of electric water heaters varies, depending on the type and placement of the heating elements. Unlike gas water heaters, the heating elements of an electric water heater can be wrapped around the tank or submerged inside the tank. In addition, electric water heaters may have one or two heating elements, which may require 120V or 240V for operation.

The size of an electric water heater depends primarily upon how much water it holds. In general, though, the most popular sizes for home use hold about 50 gallons, which is more water than for gas water heaters serving a comparably sized family. The electric water heater requires a larger water capacity to compensate for the fact that it can't heat the water quite as fast as a gas-fired unit. But the electric heater has the advantage that it can be completely surrounded with insulating materials, so less heat energy is lost to the surrounding air. The absence of a fire pipe also means the electric water heater can be located anywhere in the home. The closer it is to the sinks and appliances that use hot water, the better.

Most electric water heaters use 240V. Small electric water heaters frequently use 120V, but most large water heaters and dual-element heaters use 240V.

Heating Elements

Dual heating elements provide an economy feature similar to the dual element electric furnace. The main heating element is located near the bottom of the water heater, where the cold water enters. As hot water is drawn from the storage tank, cold water enters the bottom of the tank, causing the lower heating elment to turn on. For normal usage, this is the only heating element that turns on. But if hot water is much in demand, a lot of cold water will enter the water heater. This will cause a second heating element

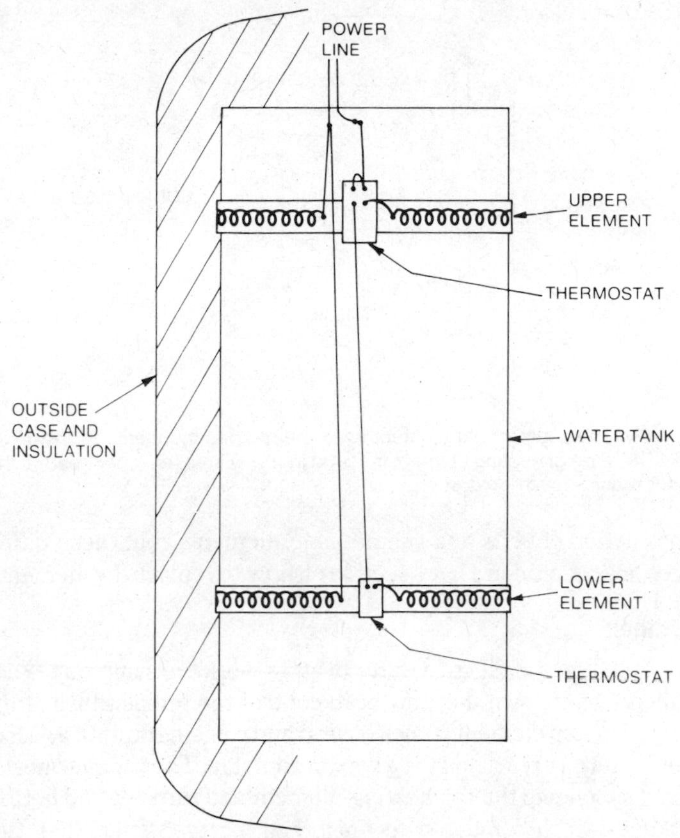

Fig. 14-3. Fig. 14-3. The belted-element electric water heater has two resistive heating elements surrounding the water tank. These heating elements work like other electric heaters. The top element of the water heater is used only when a lot of hot water is in demand. The lower heating element is an economical low-power heater that does most of the work in holding the water in the tank at the desired temperature.

near the top of the storage tank to turn on. This top element insures that the water leaving the tank is hot, even though the water in the bottom of the tank is not.

The heating elements themselves may be either belted or submersible. The belted-element water heaters have their heating elements wrapped around the outside of the tank, as in Fig. 14-3. The insulation and outside casing of the water heater cover the heating belts so they cannot be seen. The submersible-element water heaters have heating elements that extend inside the storage tank as shown in Fig. 14-4. There are some variations in the

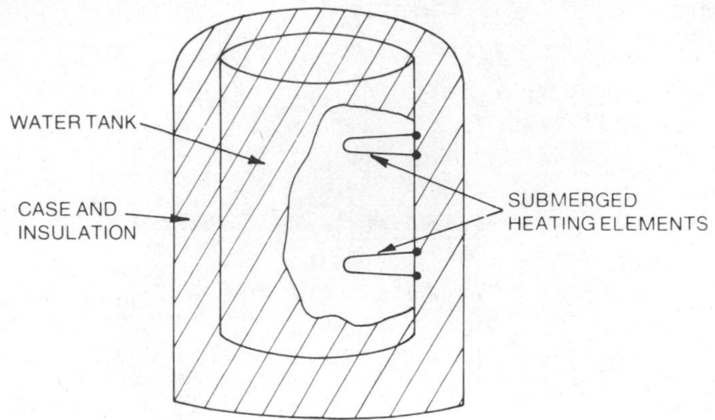

Fig. 14-4. The submersible-element water heater has the elements inside the tank. This type of heating element is found in many smaller water heaters that do not require much heat energy.

construction of belts and submersible elements, but these differences are covered in a later section on how to replace the elements.

Operation

Both types of electric water heaters work the same way. Each element has its own thermostat to control the temperature of the water. The top element comes on first and remains on until a preset temperature is reached at the top thermostat. The top thermostat then disconnects the top heating element and turns on the bottom element, which comes on to finish heating the water. The two elements may have the same wattage rating or different wattage ratings. For example, the top element might be 4500 watts, while the bottom element is only 2500 watts. Quick-recovery water heaters have higher wattage ratings than regular models, since they have additional heating capacity to heat the water quicker if much hot water is being used. A quick-recovery water heater should have 10-gauge wire going to the higher wattage heating element to supply the extra electrical current it requires Be sure to ground the water heater to prevent shock.

The outer case on a belt-type heater may crack andallow water to get into the heating element. When this happens the element will still usually operate, although it will draw more current since the water provides a path for electricity to flow to ground. If this happens on a 240V unit, even if the thermostat is off, some current will follow the water path to ground, wasting electricity and running up your electric bill.

INSULATING THE WATER HEATER

Because so much energy is used in a water heater just to maintain the temperature of the water inside the unit, you will save on your utility bill if you can slow down the flow of heat from the water into the air surrounding the water heater. An easy way to do this is to wrap a blanket of R-11 or R-14 fiberglass insulation with a foil backing that can be exposed to the living area. Be sure this back is inflammable.

You should cut the insulation blankets to the size needed to wrap arround your water heater. Tape them in place with heavy cloth tape (furnace duct tape works well). Tape all seams to prevent heat leakage.

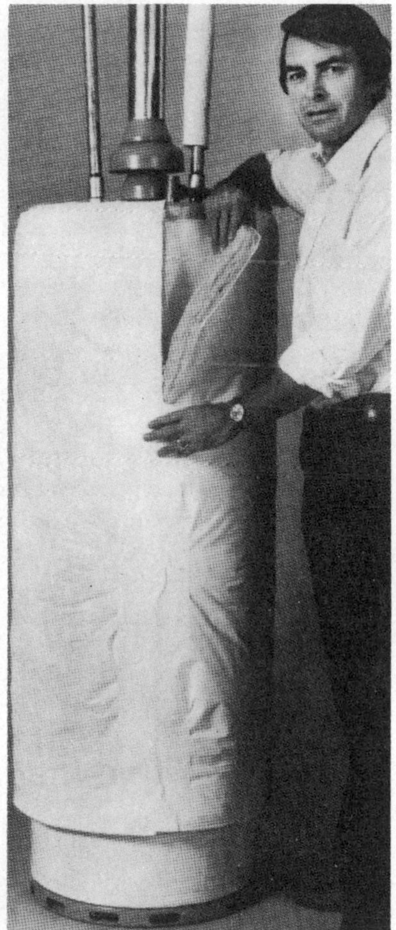

Fig. 14-5. Water heater insulation kits help prevent heat loss from the hot water to the outside air (courtesy of Johns-Manville).

If you have a gas water heater, this insulation should cover only the sides of the water heater. Insulation should not cover the top of the water heater because it may block air vents and create a fire hazard. Be careful in insulating a gas waterheater that you do not restrict air flow through any vents. Never cover the top of a gas water heater.

With an electric water heater, you should cut a piece of insulation the size of the top and then cover the top of the water heater. It will be easier to adjust the thermostat control if you remember to place the seam of the insulation blanket over the removable panels.

This wrap-around insulation can be added very easily and cheaply. If you have recently added insulation to your home, you probably have some extra batts or pieces of insulation that can be used for this purpose. If you can use extra insulation pieces, the cost of insulating your water heater is practically nothing. This addition can save about 5-10% a year on your hot water costs.

An alternative is to purchase a water heater insulation kit from your building supplier. These kits include everything you need to attractively insulate your water heater: insulation with a protective backing, tape and instructions (Fig. 14-5). Many of these kits also come with a warranty.

INSULATING WATER PIPES

The hot water lines between the water tank and the hot-water supply faucets in bathrooms, kitchens and laundry rooms should be insulated to prevent the loss of heat as water travels through the pipes. This is especially important if the water lines run through an unheated crawl space or through some other cold area. Insulating the water lines will help keep the water warm in the lines. You will find you do not have to waste water by running it into the sink while waiting for hot water to arrive at the faucet.

Local building supply outlets can furnish you with insulation specially prepared for insulating water lines. You simply fit the insulation around the pipes and seal it in place. All joints should be closed and sealed with tape.

SELECTING AN EFFICIENT WATER HEATER

If you are building a new houuse or will be replacing your water heater soon, you should give some serious thought to selecting a water heater that will be energy efficient. If you are planning on purchasing a new water heater, you may want to also consider relocating the water heater so it will be nearer the main hot water outlets: laundry room, bathroom and kitchen. The closer you can place the water heater to these outlets, the shorter the hot water lines can be and the less heat you'll waste through the pipes. These considerations are discussed later in more detail.

With recent concern over energy efficiency, many manufacturers are adding energy saving features to their water heaters. The better models are constructed with about 2 inches of fiberglass insulation to prevent heat from the water from escaping into the outside air. These well-insulated water heaters do cost somewhat more than conventional models, but the extra insulation will probably pay for itself in about two years. Even with the extra insulation on these more efficient hot water heaters, more savings will be realized if you also add a blanket of insulation around the outer shell as described earlier.

Another feature you should look for when you purchase a new water heater is a "clean-out" opening. The "clean-out" is a 6-inch plate near the bottom of the heater that can be removed with the tank is drained. Through this hole, you can scrape, chisel and flush much of the lime deposits from inside the water tank. Removing these deposits will increase the efficiency of your heater because the heater will no longer have to spend so much money and energy heating up the deposits of lime and minerals.

Many water heaters do not come with these "clean-outs" because of the public's disinterest in doing this chore. The concern over energy, however, will likely make " clean-outs" more generally available on water heaters.

While you want a water heater large enough to provide the amount of hot water your family will need, if your water heater is too large you will waste precious energy dollars maintaining the temperature of that extra water inside the tank. As a general guide, you can figure that a 40-gallon water heater will be large enough for a family of four. But a 50-gallon heater may be required if you have a clothes washer and a dishwasher. For a family of five, a 50-gallon heater should be adequate. If you select a gas water heater, you may be able to get by with slightly smaller sizes because the gas heaters have somewhat quicker recoveries.

You should talk with a reliable plumbing and building supplier before selecting your water heater to determine what size will be best for your uses. The dealer should also be able to help you determine if you would save a significant amount of money in operating costs by using a gas heater instead of an electric heater.

You will likely find that a natural gas heater is cheaper than an electric water heater to operate, but this depends on the costs of those fuels in your area. Propane, on the other hand, likely will cost about the same as electricity.

You have to be careful in selecting a propane or natural gas water heater. Be sure to check the *availability* of these fuels before you buy an appliance such as a water heater that uses them. In many localities, natural gas is simply not available to new customers. Check this out for yourself by calling your local gas supply company. Do not rely on the assurances of a salesman eager to make a quick sale of a water heater.

WATER HEATER MAINTENANCE

Lime and mineral deposits form inside the water heater, especially in hard-water localities. They are energy robbers. If there is a large amount of lime and mineral deposits inside the water tank, as much as 50% of the water heater's energy may go to warm those deposits before the heater can ever begin warming the water. It is as though you had insulated the heating element from the water tank!

As little as one-eighth of an inch of lime and mineral buildup can noticeably affect the water heater's performance. This can especially be a problem with gas water heaters and belt-type electric heaters where the burner is outside the water tank. Water heater salesmen tell horror stories of customers insisting they need larger water heaters, when the fact is that their old heaters are half-filled with mineral deposits that make the heaters so heavy it takes three men to carry them always.

This problem can be avoided and money can be saved by taking some routine steps each year. The best way to rid your water tank of energy robbing mineral deposits is to completely drain your tank. If your water heater has a "clean-out" opening near the bottom, you can open that, reach inside and scrape and flush most of the deposits away. The "clean-out" is a plate about 6 inches in diameter that gives you access to the inside of the tank so you can remove unwanted mineral deposits. Many water heaters, however, do not have these openings because of the public's disinterest in cleaning out water heaters.

The next best alternative is to drain about a gallon of water out of the bottom of the tank to remove the mineral deposits. If your water heater has a drain plug at the bottom, this can be removed for drainage. If there is no drain plug, you may be able to drain some water from a water inlet near the bottom or by removing the lower heating element in a submersible type electric water heater.

CHANGING ELECTRIC HEATING ELEMENTS

If your electric water heater suddenly stops working or begins to quickly run out of hot water, there is a good chance that one of the heating elements is defective. To test the heating element, turn the heater off, remove the cover plate, disconnect one wire from the terminals of the element, and use an ohmmeter to check for continuity through the element as indicated in Fig. 14-6.

The ohmmeter is used by touching one probe to each terminal of the element. If the element is good, you should get a fairly low resistance reading (usually between 10 and 50 ohms); if it is bad, the resistance will be quite different. For example, if the meter needle swings all the way across the scale and goes to zero, the element could be shorted. If the needle barely moves, the element could be burned out, a condition that we often call "*open*." If the reading ranges from several hundred ohms up to several thousand ohms, the element could be flooded with water as well as be burned out.

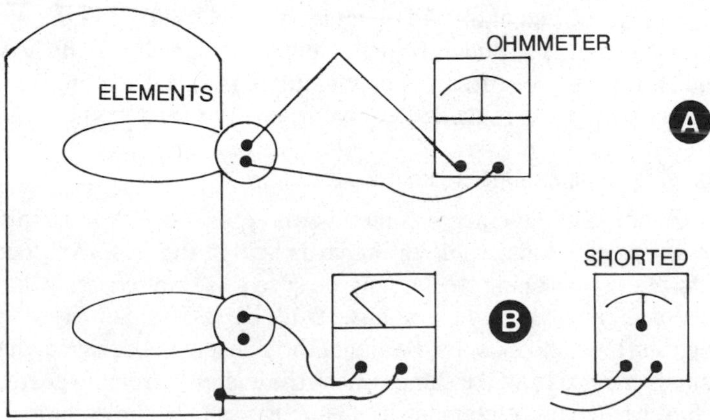

Fig. 14-6. To check the belt type element or the submersible type electric element for continuity, disconnect the wires from the element terminals and attach theleads of the ohmmeter. If the element is good, the ohmmeter will show a low resistance reading of about 10 to 50 ohs. (A). If the water heater's circuit breaker or fuse has been tripped, the element may be shorted to the case. Place one ohmmeter lead on an element terminal, and place the second lead on the water heater case (B). iF the needle stays on the left side of the scale, there is no short. But if the meter's hand moves across the scale, indicating there is continuity between the element and the water heater case, the element is shorted to the case.

If you found that the water heater's circuit breaker or fuse was open, the heating element might be shorted to the case of the water heater (Fig. 14-6). In this instance, you should remove both wires from the element terminals and measure the resistance between the terminal of the element and the metal case of the water heater. If you get a low resistance reading, the element is shorted to the case.

If for any of the preceding reasons the heating element is found to be bad, it will have to be replaced. Follow the procedure outlined here for the type of heating element you have. Inspect your water heater carefully and determine the type of heating element it uses. If the replacement type is not listed on the heater's nameplate, copy down the make and model number of your heater and take it to a heating supply store. They will assist you in finding the correct repair part. You should have the new part in your hand before you attempt to remove the old one.

Changing Belt Elements

To change a belt type element, disconnect the wires at the thermostat and at the element. Loosen the clamp on each end of the element, but do not remove the element yet. First attach the new element to one end of the old element. Then carefully pull the old element out. As you pull the old element out, you will pull the new element into place. After the new element is tightened in place, connect the wires, replace the cover plate and turn the unit on.

Changing Submersible Elements

Submersible elements come in two types—one type simply screws into the tank, while the other is held in the tank with four bolts. Before changing an element, be sure you know exactly what kind of element your heater has. While it is obvious that the mounting brackets must be the same, the size and the design of the element must also be the same. Check the nameplate on the heater to find what type of element it uses. Figure 14-7 shows how to measure the bolt-mounted element to get the correct replacement size.

Before removing the old element, you must first drain enough water from your tank to bring the water level inside below the level of the element. The easiest way to do this is to turn off the water supply line going to the water tank, connect a hose to the drain fitting at the bottom of the tank, and then open a hot-water faucet to allow the water to drain out through the hose. A by-product of this procedure is that it also drains out the mineral deposits from the bottom of the tank as it lowers the water level.

To remove a bolt-mounted element, remove the wires, loosen the mounting bolts and pry the element loose. It may be necessary to use a hammer and cold chisel. Replace both the element and gasket with new parts. Tighten the bolts evenly to assure a water-tight seal.

To remove a screw type element, remove the wires on the element and turn the element counterclockwise with a large wrench—preferably a socket wrench. A hammer and cold chisel may be required to loosen the element so it will turn. Remove the element and gaskets and replace them. Reattach the wires and turn the power back on.

A defective heating element can be changed without first draining the water from the tank. To do this, you must be fast. Prepare to get some water on you and the floor around the water heater. This method is most often used to replace the lower element.

Shut the water supply off on the tank; then open and close a faucet to bleed off the pressure in the water lines. If the tank has a

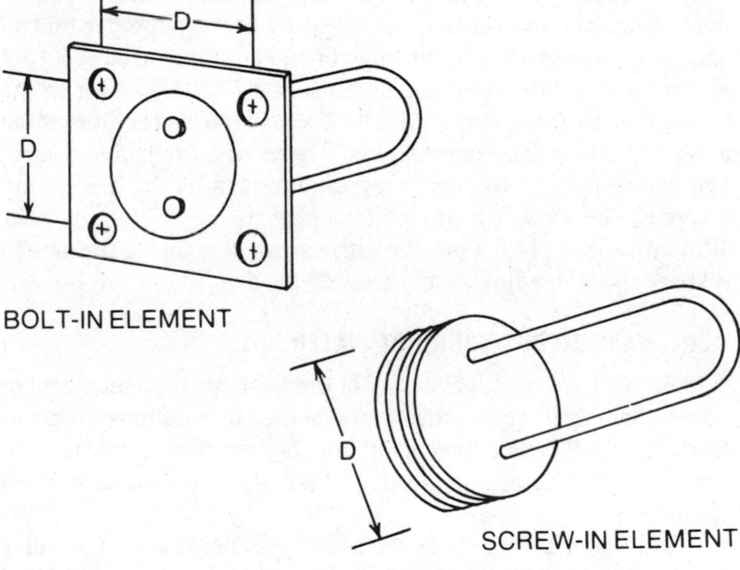

Fig. 14-7. Carefully note the mounting dimensions (D) of your heating element before buying a replacement. You will need to know the wattage of the element, which will be given on the nameplate of the water heater. Also, copy down the make and model number from the nameplate, just in case.

shut-off valve on top, you can close that instead of turning off the entire water supply into the house. Loosen the old element and be ready to shove the new element into the tank. As quickly as possible, remove the old element and replace it with the new one. Some water will run out the hole, but there will usually be enough vacuum in the tank so that not much water will run out.

SAVING WATER: SHOWERS VERSUS BATHS

Whether your family saves water and cuts hot water costs by taking showers instead of baths depends largely on the way you use the shower. You won't save anything by taking a 30-mile steaming hot shower. If, on the other hand, you use a low water-flow shower head and take 10-minute showers, you can save some money by switching from baths to showers.

A bath may use anywhere from 15 to 30 gallons of hot water. As a general estimate, a 2 × 5½-foot bathtub filled with 6 inches of water is about 40 gallons. Roughly half of that will be hot water. This means your bath probably requires roughly 20 gallons of hot water.

A 10-minute shower, on the other hand, requires roughly 10 to 15 gallons of hot water. This amount of water usage can be reduced even further if you replace the standard 6-10 gallon-per-minute shower head with a low water-flow shower head that used about 2-4 gallons per minute. You can also install a flow restrictor in the water line to the shower head to reduce the water flow to an acceptable 4 gallons per minute. These are available at most pumbing supply stores, and they can be installed by merely unscrewing the shower head and attaching the restrictor. Another alternative is to place a washer with a small hole inside the pipe to restrict the water flow to the shower head.

MORE WAYS TO CUT YOUR HOT WATER BILL

As we have mentioned, one of the best ways to cut your hot water costs is to reduce the water heater temperature to about 120°. This will be hot enough for most homes. You should use the lowest water temperature setting possible in washing dishes and clothes.

The water heater should be as close as possible to the water outlets that use the most hot water: bathroom, laundry room and kitchen. Reducing this distance cuts down on wasted hot water that cools off in the pipes between the water heater and the outlets. If you are installing a new water heater or are considering changing your plumbing, you might be wise to consider relocating your water heater nearer these rooms. At the very least, you should wrap these water lines with insulation to prevent heat loss from the water inside the pipes.

Repair any faucets that may be leaking. Usually all a leaky faucet needs is a 10-cent rubber gasket. A leaky faucet can waste thousands of gallons a year. That is money which is literally going down the drain! Even if the leak is on a cold water line, repairing the faucet will save many gallons of water that would boost your water bill.

15 Kitchen Appliances

Modern houses have many large appliances, including refrigerators, freezers, ranges and dishwashers. The list could go on and on. The number of modern appliances is increasing all the time as more items are developed for home use. Some of the newer appliances to come along in recent years are the microwave oven and trash compactor. In addition, more and more small electrical appliances are coming into use. The toaster oven, electric slow cooking pots and sandwich makers are among these items.

The number of appliances is not the only thing that is increasing. Most of them are getting larger, too! Compare the size of the refrigeratiors sold 20 years ago to the side of the refrigerators you find in appliance stores today. Today's appliances are built larger to hold more food, they have more features, and they use more energy.

Major kitchen appliances require regular maintenance, service and inspection to keep them in top operating condition. If they are not kept in good repair, they can waste large amounts of energy, adding quite a bit to the monthly utility bill.

Besides the savings that can be realized by keeping these appliances in top working order, you can also save money if you assess your everyday use of these appliances. There are a number of things you can do each time you use these appliances to make sure that you do not waste money.

In this chapter we outline several routine maintenance tips for the major appliances in your kitchen. Checking their operation and doing some simple maintenance once or twice a year will insure that your appliances are operating as efficiently as possible. We also have included a number of extremely simple suggestions for using these appliances that will save you energy money every day. Finally, this chapter includes things you will want to consider if you are buying a new kitchen appliance.

While the use of kitchen appliances is not the largest single item in your utility bill (your heating system uses much more energy), their use is nevertheless significant. By properly maintaining and using your appliances following the guidelines in this chapter you may be able to save up to $50 a year on your utility costs.

REFRIGERATORS AND FREEZERS

Refrigerators and freezers are usually among the most neglected appliances in the home, even though they may well be the most used. These appliances probably consume more energy than any other appliance you own, except for your water heater. The annual cost of operation for either a refrigerator or a freezer may be 50% greater than the cost of lighting in a typical home.

Since refrigerators and freezers do consume so much energy, it is important that they be kept in efficient operating condition. If not, they will waste a lot of your money that could be much better spent on something else.

One of the biggest energy robbers in a refrigerator or freezer are restricted coils that cannot transfer heat freely. When the coils are not clean, the efficiency of the unit plummets and it must operate longer to maintain the temperature of the food.

Inefficient heat transfer at the coils will occur at two places: the condenser coil outside the cooling compartment and the evaporator coil inside the cooling compartment. In the case of the evaporator coil, inefficient heat transfer occurs because of the buildup of frost on the coil. This frost prevents the evaporator from absorbing heat inside the refrigerator.

In the case of the condenser coil, inefficient heat transfer can occur because the condenser coil has become dirty. This reduces the ability of the coil to disperse heat removed by the evaporator.

DEFROSTING

Frost buildup on the evaporator is a very large source of wasted electricity in a refrigerator or freezer (Fig. 15-1). Frost on the evaporator acts as an insulator, shielding the cold evaporator

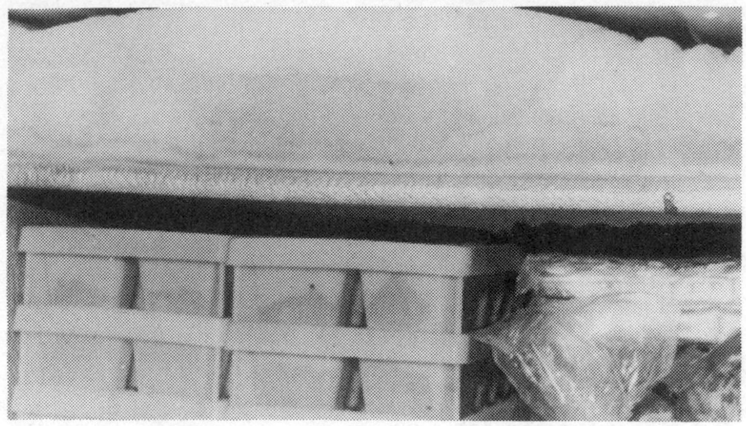

Fig. 15-1. When frost builds up on an evaporator this badly, the efficiency of the unit is greatly reduced. Frost and ice should never be allowed to build up more than a half inch.

coils from the air flow. This, of course, is very undesirable because the unit runs longer to remove the same amount of heat from the cooling compartment.

Older refrigerators and freezers, many of which are still in use today, require manual defrosting. This is a job that no homeowner likes. It is frequently put off until so much frost builds up in the unit that its efficiency is reduced considerably. This is no wonder because it can seem like a thankless task. All the food must be removed from the unit. The unit is turned off until the frost and ice cna be removed from the coil. Then the homeowner puts the food back in the unit and starts it again so frost can start building up once more! Like it or not, it is a task that must be done. For efficient operation, manual defrost refrigerators and freezers should be defrosted when the frost is ¼-inch thick. Half an inch of frost is the limit.

Frost Free Units

The manual defrosting has been eliminated with the newer, so-called "frost free" refrigerators and freezers. These units are not at all frost free in the strictest sense of the words. Frost still builds up on the evaporator coil, but these units have a panel to hide the frost. An automatic time clock periodically turns the cooling unit off and turns on heater strips to melt the frost. The heater stays on just a short time—only long enough to melt the frost and ice that have formed on the evaporator. Another type of automatic defrosting system utilizes hot vapor inside the refrigeration system to melt the ice from the evaporator.

The melted ice drains into a pan, usually located under the condenser at the bottom of the refrigerator or freezer. This water evaporates from the pan and removes some of the heat from the condenser. It increases the efficiency of the refrigerator because the condenser is kept cooler.

Some Problems

Although frost-free units take care of the messy and time consuming job of defrosting for you, they do cost more to purchase than manual defrost units. Their operating costs are roughly 50% higher than manual defrost models. In a typical home, this additional operating cost will amount to roughly $20 per year. But this figure can vary widely according to the size and model of your refrigerator or freezer, your electricity costs, and how careful you are about preventing frost buildup.

You may be unaware that some automatic defrosting refrigerators require you to defrost the freezer compartment manually. These are known as partial automatic defrost models. If you intend to purchase an automatic defrost model, you should check this out before buying.

As we mentioned, the frost free units have a drain which takes the melted ice from the coils and deposits it in a pan. If this drain becomes clogged, the water may run into the lower compartment. If the freezer compartment is located on the bottom of the refrigerator/freezer, this water will freeze inside the compartment and will have to be removed by manual defrosting methods. When you defrost any refrigerator, never use a sharp object to remove the ice. If you puncture a refrigerant tube, you may be in for some large repair bills.

Sometimes the controls on automatic defrosting units will malfunction. If a control malfunctions, the heater strips will not turn on and frost will build up on the evaporator, restricting air flow around the evaporator coils. If the timer mechanism that controls the defrost cycle malfunctions, the heater strips may not turn off. This will raise the temperature in the freezer compartment. If these problems occur, the controls will have to be replaced.

PREVENTING FROST BUILDUP

If you take steps to reduce the amount of frost that builds up in the first place, you will go a long way towards increasing the

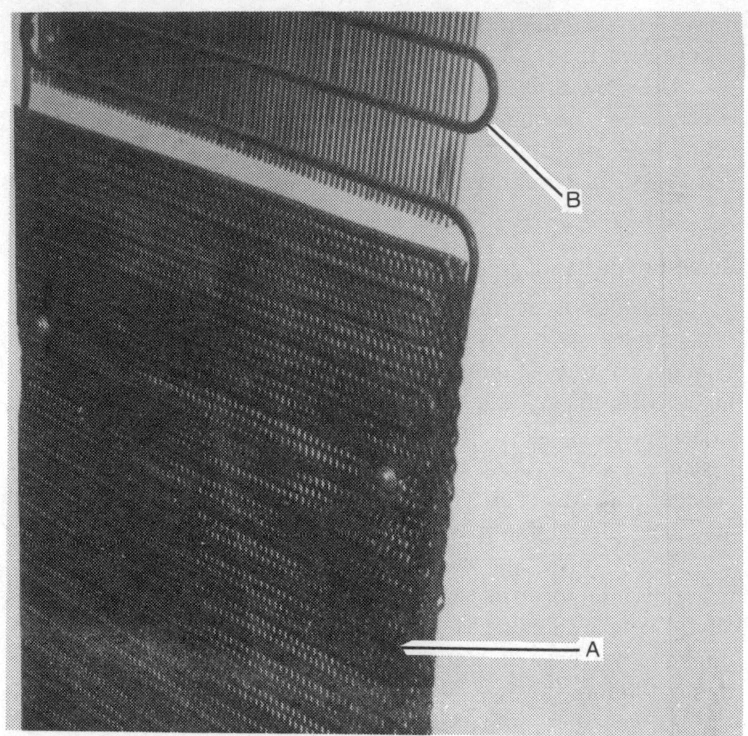

Fig. 15-2. The condenser (A) of this refrigerator is mounted on the back of the unit. This type of condenser is called a static condenser. The oil cooler (B) helps cool the lubricating oil circulated in the compressor. Vacuum the condenser coils several times a year to remove lint and dust, since this will keep the refrigeration unti operating at peak efficiency.

efficiency of your refrigerator or freezer. Manual defrosting can be done less often and with less difficulty, and automatic defrosting cycles will be shorter.

Frost buildup increases when you hold the unit's door open for long periods of time. This not only allows frost to reduce the efficiency of the unit, but it also lets the cold air out of the refrigerator or freezer. The warm air that rushes in must be cooled. A defective or torn door gasket and a door that is not forming a good seal can do the same thing. Placing hot food inside the unit increases frost buildup and forces it to remove the excess heat. Always allow hot foods to cool before placing them in your refrigerator or freezer.

Cover liquids stored in your refrigerator. This prevents the refrigerator air from drawing moisture and building up frost. Frost also will build up more quickly if the temperature control is set too cold.

CONDENSER

The parts of a refrigerator and freezer are basically the same as those of an air conditioner (discussed in Chapter 10). Refrigerators and freezers have a *condenser*, an *evaporator*, a *compressor* and *refrigerant*.

The condenser of a refrigerator may be found in several places. It may be attached to the back of the refrigerator as shown in Fig. 15-2.

Many of the newer refrigerators and freezers, however, have the condenser placed under the back wall of the unit (Fig. 15-3). Since the condenser releases heat that is removed from the air in the unit, there must be good air circulation around the condenser coils for it to do its job. The refrigerator will operate inefficiently if it is surrounded by cabinets so that air circulation to the condenser is blocked. The unit will also operate inefficiently if the condenser is clogged with dirt to block air flow and to insulate the condenser coil from the air flow.

Air Circulation

If a refrigerator has a condenser at the back of the unit and the refrigerator or freezer is built into a wall of cabinets, there can be

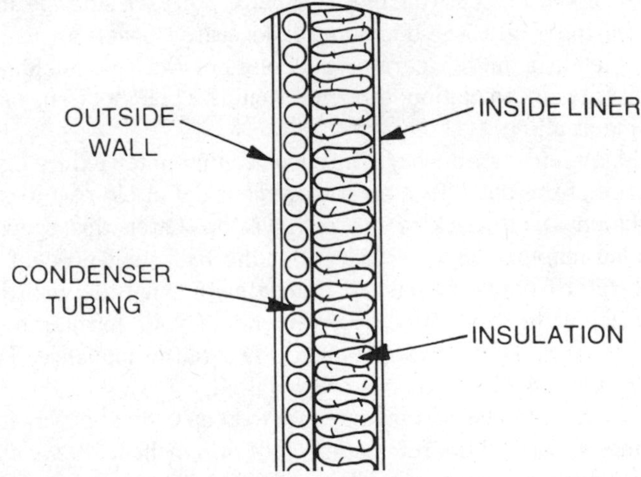

Fig. 15-3. This cross section of a regrigerator shows that the condenser can be located inside the outer wall. When the unit is running, the outside walls of the refrigerator will become warmer to the touch.

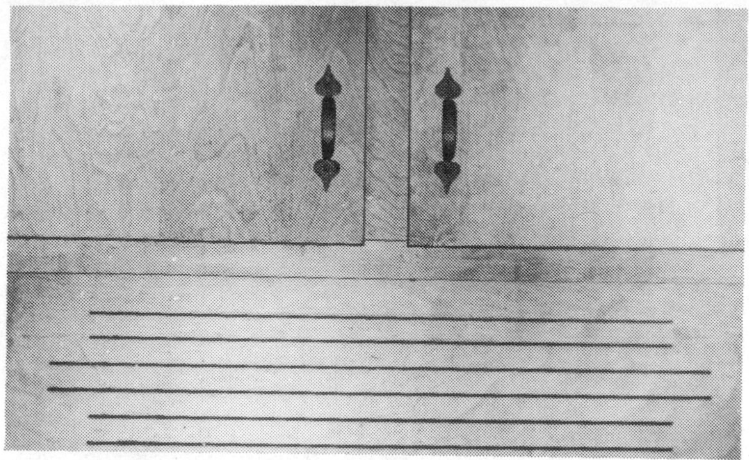

Fig. 15-4. If cabinets must be built around the refrigerator, use slotted panels to permit air circulation around the unit. Even with the slots, however, these are still not as good as uncovered air spaces around the refrigerator.

problems in supplying adequate air circulation to remove the heat from the condenser (Fig. 15-4). The condenser must have good air flow over it to allow the heat energy to escape. If the condenser area is closed off, the condenser will not be able to rid itself of the heat. The refrigerator's cooling capacity and efficiency will decrease quite a bit. On most refrigerators, there should be an air space of about 2 inches (the more the better) on each side and at the back and top (Fig. 15-5). If molding or decorative panels are used to cover the top of the refrigerator, cut holes or slots in the molding to permit free air circulation, though it would be best not to use such molding at all.

Many refrigerators have the condenser mounted externally on the back of the unit. Such as arrangement definitely requires air circulation at the back of the refrigerator. Often this space is provided automatically by spacers at the back that prevent the refrigerator from being pushed completely against the wall. If in doubt about the ventilation requirements of your refrigerator or freezer, check the instructions that came with the appliance. They should tell you what spacings are required.

The best kitchen arrangement is to keep cabinets away from the sides and top of the refrigerator by 4 or 5 inches. Do not close the gaps with any sort or trim. This will allow the air to move freely around the refrigerator, so there should be no problems with removing the heat from the condenser. If air flow is restricted through the condenser, heat will not be removed from the coil. The efficiency of the unit will drop and the unit may stop working completely.

Cleaning the Condenser

Many refrigerators and freezers have the condenser coil located in a frame on the back of the unit. An advantage of this system is that no fan is required to circulate air through the condenser, since the normal heating of the condenser produces convection air currents that quietly carry away the heat energy. However, the same air currents also bring with them the dust and lint that settle on the floor. This dust gradually accumulates on the condenser, restricting the flow of air and interfering with the transfer of heat energy between the coils and the surrounding air. Since the operating efficiency of the refrigeration unit goes down as the condenser coils become hotter, it is to your advantage to vacuum off the accumulated dust at least twice a year. This type of regular maintenance can easily save you over a dollar a year on your electric bill.

Some refrigerators and freezers have the condenser located in a compartment at the bottom of the unit. A condenser for a unit like this is shown in Fig. 15-6. This unit has a fan behind the condenser to help remove the heat. The fan and condenser coil must be free of dirt to get maximum performance.

A condenser on the back a refrigerator or freezer also collects dirt and lint, which must be removed. Often towels, paper, and

Fig. 15-5. Several inches of free air space on all sides of the refrigerator will give the best heat dissipation from the condenser. Most refrigerators and upright freezers require air spaces at the back and top, permitting air to enter from the grill at the bottom and flow up and back and out the top.

other objects fall behind the unit onto the condenser and restrict the air flow. Clean the condenser with compressed air or a vacuum cleaner. Hang a light on the back side of the condenser coil. If you cannot see the light shining through coil fins, you know the condenser really needs to be cleaned. Do not use a knife, screwdriver, or other sharp tools to clean the coil because you might damage the tubing inside the fins. Compressed air or water are best. If you use water, however, be careful not to let any drip or splash on the motor or any of the electrical connections.

ELECTRIC MOTORS

Condenser fan motors on forced-air refrigerators and freezers are small, but they have a big job to do. They move a lot of air through the condenser to remove heat, and when the fan blades and motor get dirty, the unit's efficiency can really be reduced. As air movement decreases, the fan motor gets hotter, and this can also cause the compressor motor to overheat and draw more current. When motors start to overheat, the motor bearings often tighten up, making the motors very hard to start. Electric motors draw a lot of current trying to start—even when they are in top shape. If the bearings are binding, this can really waste a lot of current, and may prevent the motor from starting.

Heat from the motors is dissipated through their outer housings. Sometimes the housings are constructed with fins on them to help get rid of the heat. But if these cases become dirty, oily, or covered with trash, the heat cannot be removed as easily. If the situation gets bad enough, heat will build up inside the motor, and the motor can burn out.

Such problems can be prevented by regular cleaning and inspection. Use a cleaning solvent that will evaporate quickly. For example, do not use fuel oil to clean the casings because fuel oil does not evaporate well, and it tends to collect dirt. Inspect the motor bearings—turn the shaft on the fan motor to see if any of the motor bearings are tight. If the shaft will not turn smoothly, you should remove the motor and clean it. It may be that the bearings just need a good cleaning, but if they are damaged, they should be replaces. (See the sections on cleaning fan motors in Chapter 8 and Chapter 11.)

WIRING AND EXTENSION CORDS

A freezer or refrigerator needs a lot of current when the motor is first starting up—usually three or four times as much as when it's

Fig. 15-6. The coil (A) of the forced air condenser has a fan (B) that pulls air through the condenser and blows it over the compressor (C).

running normally. Since the motor usually starts quickly, the surge of current does not last long enough to blow any fuses or open any circuit breakers. Since most kitchens have several 15 or 20 ampere circuits, there is rarely any problem with the usual assortment of appliances there. But problems may occur when two or more large appliances—toasters, grills, irons, toaster ovens, microwave ovens, etc.—are plugged into the same circuit.

The most important rule for refrigerators and freezers is this. Never plug two refrigerators or freezers into the same outlet unless you are absolutely positive that the circuit can handle both appliances. The danger here is that both units may try to start up at the same time. If the combined starting current is too great, the fuse or breaker may open. By the time you detect that something is wrong, it may be too late to save any of the food from spoiling.

Extension cords are frequently used with refrigerators and freezers because too many outlets are not located in convenient places. Since most appliances rarely have power cords longer than 5 or 6 feet, an extension cord is needed to make the connection. But extension cords are usually too small for the typical current draw of most large appliances. The majority of inexpensive extension cords are made of 16-gauge wire, which is simply too small for most appliances. (The larger the gauge number, the thinner the wire.) Even 14-gauge wire is too small for some appliances, especially if you must use more than a 10-foot cord. So if you find you must use an extension cord, use 14-gauge wire for short lengths and 12-gauge wire for anything longer than about 10 feet.

When extension cords are too small for the application, some power will be dissipated in the cord. The energy lost in this way heats up the power cord and, in extreme cases, may melt the insulation and even start electrical fires. What is not so obvious, though, is that the power loss also lowers the voltage reaching the appliance at the other end of the extension cord. The lower voltage is bad in two ways, since it both lowers the operating efficiency of the unit and increases the amount of current required for its operation. The lower efficiency means that your electric bill will be higher than it ought to be. But the increased current draw increases the possiblility of a fuse or circuit breaker opening, and it also indicates that the motor will have to work harder and longer to start up. The moral here is that it is foolish to risk losing all that stored food by skimping on the price of an extension cord.

Most appliances now have three-pronged plugs, with the third prong used for safely grounding the appliance to prevent accidental shock. If you need an extension cord for your appliance, buy one with the extra ground wire, or at least be sure to run an extra ground wire from the appliance to a suitable ground on the receptacle or a water pipe. Without this ground connection, you will be defeating a very important safety feature that was included for your benefit. Kitchens and basements can be very dangerous from the standpoint of electrical shocks because there are so many metal or wet surfaces around. Touching an unsafe appliance with one hand while touching a sink or some other grounded surface with the other can give you a lethal shock.

DOOR GASKETS

Refrigerators and freezers have *door gaskets* to seal the door so outside air does not enter the unit when the door is closed. These soft rubber gaskets are supposed to seal the door opening when the door is closed. If they do not seal well, your unit will waste energy with the cold air that escapes. Also, the warm air that replaces it will increase the build up of frost on the evaporator which further wastes energy.

You can easily check the seal on your door gasket by placing a piece of paper between the gasket and the door opening. With the door closed, pull the slip of paper toward you. If the gasket is sealing properly, there will be a drag on the paper as you pull it. You should make this test around the entire door opening.

If the door gasket is worn, cracked or not sealing properly, it will have to be replaced. Before you remove the old door gasket, you must first obtain a new one from a supply company or from your dealer. You also can order a new gasket from the manufacturer, but this may take longer to arrive. Jot down the unit's make, model number and serial number. Make a note of its type (i.e., side-by-side, two-door or single door).

Once you have the replacement gasket in hand, remove the door from the unit. If you have been planning to defrost the unit, this would be a good time to do it. Place the door on a flat surface and remove the screws or clips that hold the door gasket and inner liner in place (Figs. 15-7 and 15-8). The door's inner liner will come free, and the gasket can be removed.

Place the new gasket over the inner liner, lining up the screw holes. Be sure the gasket is placed tightly against the inner liner;

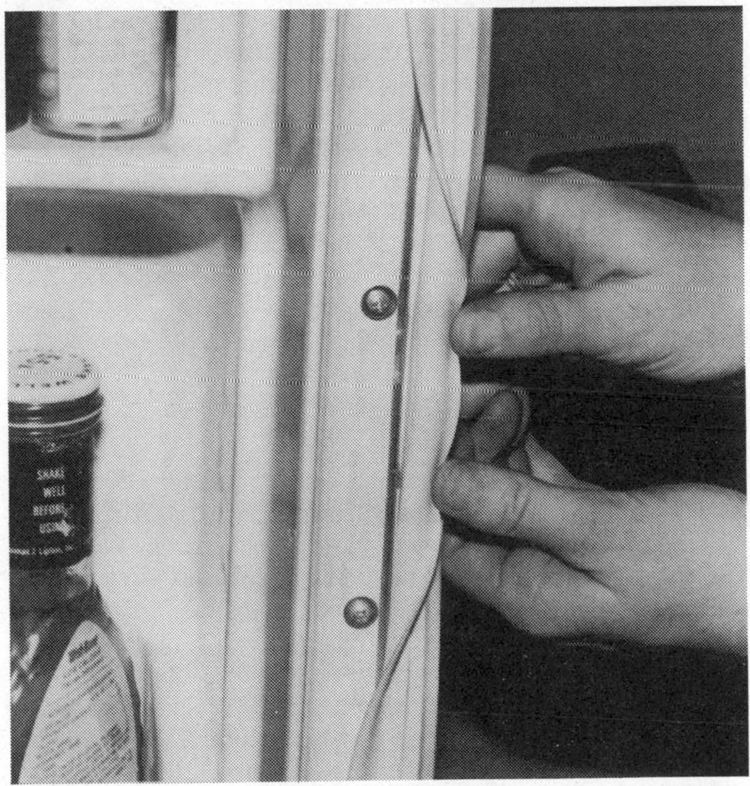

Fig. 15-7. If the door gasket does not fit properly or is cracked, replace it. The gasket can be removed by taking out the screws along the inside of the gasket.

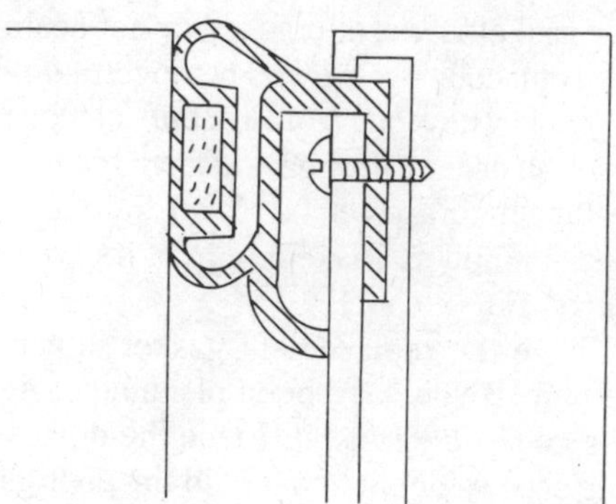

Fig. 15-8. This diagram shows a cross-section of how a door gasket is attached.

then replace the liner on the door. Tighten the corners first; making sure everything fits well and that the liner is flat against the door. You must be sure you do not overtighten one corner, which may cause the other corners to buckle. Once the gasket is in place without any warps or buckles, replace the door on the refrigerator or freezer. Check to be sure the gasket touches the cabinet surface tightly in all places.

Sometimes the door will not close properly after a new gasket has been installed. This usually happens when the new gasket binds on the side of the door with the hinges so that the door will not stay closed. If this happens, recheck the screws on that side holding the liner and gasket in place. Be sure they are tight. You may have to unscrew the door's hinges and place shims under them to move the door out from the cabinet on the hinged side. These shims can be made from light cardboard.

PURCHASING A REFRIGERATOR OR FREEZER

For a number of reasons, purchasing a refrigerator or freezer is not the simple task it once was. There are a myriad of sizes and styles, as well as a wide array of features that are now available. The energy crunch has brought a rush by manufacturers to produce units that can be advertised as "energy saving."

If your are purchasing a refrigerator or freezer, there are a few common sense considerations. If you are thinking of purchasing a freezer, a profitable inquiry is whether you need the unit at all. It costs about $50 to $75 a year to operate a standard-sized freezer. You should ask yourself whether that expense will be offset by savings you will realize by being able to stock up on meats and frozen goods that are on sale.

After deciding you do want to purchase a new refrigerator or freezer, carefully consider the size of the unit you want to purchase. There are many smaller-sized models available that may be large enough for your intended use. You are only wasting money—both in purchase prices and in operating costs—if you purchase a unit larger than you will need. Tables 15-1, 15-2 and 15-3 compare general operating costs for refrigerators, refrigerator-freezers and freezers.

Consider purchasing a manual defrost or a partial automatic defrost model. As we mentioned earlier in this chapter, automatic defrost models cost about 50% more to operate than do manual defrost models. See Tables 15-2 and 15-3.

In recent years, some manufacturers have increased the amount and quality of the insulation in their units. The better the insulation, the less it will cost to operate the unit (all other factors being equal). This better insulation will add a few dollars to the purchase price, however.

A chest type freezer is less expensive to operate than an upright freezer the same size. A side-by-side refrigerator/freezer usually will cost more to operate than a conventional refrigerator/freezer.

One feature often billed as an energy saver in advertisements is the outside in-door ice cube dispenser on refrigerators. This

Table 15-1. Total refrigerated Volume and Cost of Energy Ranges for Refrigerators (courtesy of Association of Home Appliance Manufacturers).

RANGES TO TOTAL REFRIGERATED VOLUME IN CUBIC FEET	RANGES OF COST OF ENERGY IN DOLLARS PER MONTH AT A RATE OF 4 CENTS PER KILOWATT-HOUR	
	Maximum	**Minimum**
Less than 3.5	1.10	1.90
1.5 to & including 4.5	1.10	2.70
2.5 to & including 5.5	1.10	2.70
3.5 to & including 6.5	1.40	2.70
4.5 to & including 7.5	1.40	2.20
5.5 to & including 8.5	1.40	2.20
6.5 to & including 9.5	1.60	1.90
7.5 to & including 10.5	1.80	2.40
8.5 to & including 11.5	1.80	2.40
9.5 to & including 12.5	1.80	2.40
10.5 to & including 13.5	1.80	2.40
11.5 to & including 14.5	1.70	2.90
12.5 to & including 15.5	1.70	2.90
13.5 and over	1.70	2.90

Table 15-2. Total refrigerated Volume and Cost of Energy Ranges for Combination Refrigerator-Freezers (courtesy of Association of Home Appliance Manufacturers).

RANGES OF TOTAL REFRIGERATED VOLUME IN CUBIC FEET	RANGES OF COST OF ENERGY IN DOLLARS PER MONTH AT A RATE OF 4 CENTS PER KILOWATT-HOUR FOR MODELS WITH			
	Partial Automatic Defrost		Automatic Defrost	
	Minimum		Minimum	Maximum
Less than 11.5	2.40	2.40	—	—
9.5 to & including 12.5	1.90	4.20	4.60	4.60
10.5 to & including 13.5	1.90	4.40	4.60	5.30
11.5 to & including 14.5	1.90	4.40	3.50	5.80
12.5 to & including 15.5	2.00	4.40	3.50	6.30
13.5 to & including 16.5	2.00	4.10	3.40	6.30
14.5 to & including 17.5	2.00	3.80	3.40	6.80
15.5 to & including 18.5	2.00	3.20	3.40	6.80
16.5 to & including 19.5	3.20	3.20	3.60	8.20
17.5 to & including 20.5			3.60	8.20
18.5 to & including 21.5			4.00	8.20
19.5 to & including 22.5			4.60	7.60
20.5 to & including 23.5			4.60	7.60
21.5 to & including 24.5			4.90	7.20
22.5 to & including 25.5			4.90	8.50
23.5 to & including 26.5			5.50	8.50
24.5 to & including 27.5			6.20	8.50
25.5 to & including 28.5			6.80	7.70
26.5 to & including 29.5			7.40	7.40
27.5 to & including 30.5			7.40	7.40
28.5 and over			—	—

device may indeed save you some money if your family is constantly opening the refrigerator to get ice cubes. Otherwise, it may add enough to the purchase price of the refrigerator that you could never recover that extra cost in energy savings.

Before purchasing a refrigerator or freezer, you should take a careful look at the different styles, models and features available. Carefully scrutinize your family's use of the appliance before deciding what size, style and features you should purchase.

ENERGY EFFICIENCY RATIO

Before buying any new appliance, you should take a look at its *energy efficiency ratio* (EER). This is a single number, usually carried to one decimal place, that is stamped on the appliance's nameplate or presented on an attached tag of many new appliances.

The EER is a rating of the appliance's efficiency and gives you a quick guide to comparing the operating costs of appliances. The higher the efficiency of the applicance, the higher the EER number will be and the lower your operating costs will be.

You must be careful, however. You cannot compare apples and oranges. The EER tells you the unit's *efficiency*, not its operating costs. Thus, do not assume that because a 14 cubic foot refrigerator/freezer has an EER of 8.7 and a 12 cubic foot refrigerator (with no freezer) has an EER of 8.5, that the larger refrigerator/freezer is cheaper to operate. The 8.7 EER on the refrigerator/freezer means that unit uses electricity more efficiently than does the smaller refrigerator. But the smaller refrigerator likely uses much less electricity overall, so it would be cheapter to operate.

Likewise, you cannot automatically compare operating costs of different sizes of refrigerators or freezers by merely examining the EER figure.

What the EER does tell you is how many BTU the unit will cool for its wattage rating. The equation to determine a unit's EER is:

Table 15-3. Total Refrigerated Volume and Cost of Energy Ranges for Freezers.

RANGES OF TOTAL REFRIGERATED VOLUME IN CUBIC FEET	RANGES OF COST OF ENERGY IN DOLLARS PER MONTH AT A RATE OF 4 CENTS PER KILOWATT-HOUR FOR MODELS WITH			
	Manual Defrost		Automatic Defrost	
	Minimum	Maximum	Minimum	Maximum
Less than 6.5	1.50	2.80	—	—
4.5 to & including 7.5	1.50	2.80	—	—
5.5 to & including 8.5	1.50	2.8U	—	—
6.5 to & including 9.5	1.50	3.10	—	—
7.5 to & including 10.5	2.60	3.10	—	—
8.5 to & including 11.5	2.80	3.10	—	—
9.5 to & including 12.5	2.80	4.40	—	—
10.5 to & including 13.5	2.40	4.40	5.10	5.10
11.5 to & including 14.5	2.40	4.40	5.10	5.10
12.5 to & including 15.5	2.40	4.30	4.00	6.40
13.5 to & including 16.5	2.70	5.40	4,00	6.80
14.5 to & including 17.5	2.70	5.40	4.00	6.80
15.5 to & including 18.5	3.00	5.40	4.60	6.80
16.5 to & including 19.5	3.00	5.00	4.60	6.80
17.5 to & including 20.5	3.20	5.00	5.70	7.10
18.5 to & including 21.5	3.20	5.00	5.70	7.10
19.5 to & including 22.5	3.30	4.90	6.00	8.00
20.5 to & including 23.5	3.30	5.50	8.00	8.00
21.5 to & including 24.5	4.20	5.50	8.00	8.00
22.5 to & including 25.5	4.20	5.60	—	—
23.5 to & including 26.5	4.60	5.60	—	—
24.5 to & including 27.5	4.60	5.60	—	—
25.5 to & including 28.5	4.60	6.40	—	—
26.5 to & including 29.5	4.80	6.40	—	—
27.5 to & including 30.5	6.40	6.40	9.80	9.80
28.5 and over	6.80	6.80	9.80	9.80

$$\frac{\text{BTU rating}}{\text{Size of unit in watts}} = \text{EER}$$

Thus, for units of the same BTU capacity, a higher EER means lower operating costs. In the previous example, the 14 cubic foot refrigerator/freezer would have a BTU capacity much larger than the smaller refrigerator. Thus, it would naturally have a higher overall operating cost, even though it used electricity more *efficiently*. The larger unit would simply use much larger amounts of electricity.

An EER ratio of 10 is considered excellent. An EER of 6 is considered poor.

EFFICIENT USE OF YOUR REFRIGERATOR AND FREEZER

Each time the door to your unit is opened, it costs you money. The cold air inside the refrigerator or freezer spills out into the room, and warm air rushes in to replace it. This warm air, of course, must be reheated and the air entering the refrigerator must be cooked. Try to reduce the number of times you open the refrigerator door, and never leave it standing open. Let hot dishes cool before placing them inside the unit.

Do not overload your freezer by placing a large amount of unfrozen food inside it at one time. If you to have to suddenly freeze a lot of food, space the items throughout the freezer and try to avoid placing them right at the top. Leave space around the items so air can circulate. If you place too much thawed food inside the freezer at one time, you can strain the compressor motor. Also, the food may spoil if the freezer cannot freeze it fast enough.

If you leave your home on a vacation, turn the refrigerator off, if possible. When you turn off the unit, remove all food and leave the door open a few inches.

SETTING THE THERMOSTAT

Your refrigerator or freezer has a thermostat that is easily adjusted to set the inside temperature of the unit. Not many units, however, have a thermostat that indicates the real temperature on the dial. Instead, the dial is simply marked off in numbers, say from 1 to 10. In order to obtan the desired temperature setting, you must resort to a trial-and-error method, using a reliable thermometer and a little patience.

It pays to get the refrigerator or freezer at the proper temperature. The colder you set the temperature, the more it will cost to operate. But running the unit at its coldest setting rarely has any effect on how long the food will keep; below a certain temperature, you're just wasting money. Normally, setting of 40°F is cold enough for a refrigerator compartment, and freezers perform well at temperatures between 0°F and 10°F. Higher temperatures than these might save money, but they would not preserve the food as long.

You can check and set your unit with an ordinary thermometer, although the thermometer should be accurate to within a few degrees. If you doubt the accuracy of the thermometer, fill a pitcher about half full of ice cubes, add water to the top, and use the thermometer to stir the contents of the pitcher. After about five minues, the thermometer should read 32°; if it does not, remember the error and apply it to your other measurements. For example, if the thermometer read 35°F instead of 32°F, your thermometer is going to read about 3 degrees high for all your measurements. For the refrigerator compartment to be at 40°F with this thermometer, you would have to adjust the thermostat until the thermometer indicated 3 degrees more than 40°F, or about 43°F. A few degrees one way or the other is not going to make much difference in most cases, but you certainly do not want anything in the refrigerator compartment to freeze.

Check your freezer or refrigerator by placing the thermometer on a shelf that is in the middle of the compartment and not resting on any packages of food. The thermometer will normally indicate the correct temperature of the air in the compartment after it has been in place about 15 minutes. Keep in mind, however, that a freezer or refrigerator may have to operate for several hours after it is first turned on before the temperatures inside will stabilize. So the best approach is to quickly check the reading on the thermometer at half-hour intervals until you are satisfied that the inside temperature is holding steady. Then adjust the thermostat up or down a little if any change is required.

Some food products have recommended storage temperatures that may differ slightly from the temperatures we have given. If your needs are different, use the methods just described to set the temperature of the compartment to the desired storage temperature. For example, if you wanted to use an old freezer chest to store beverages, you would most likely want to set it at a temperature of 40°F or so.

The thermostats in refrigerators and freezers eventually wear out, although most will outlast the useful life of the unit. To be on the safe side, though, you might want to keep a small thermometer inside the refrigerator or freezer so you can see the temperature at a glance whenever you open the door. A temperature variation of 5 degrees or more is possible fi you have kept the door open for a long time, or if you have just placed a lot of warm packages into the compartment. But the temperature should be back to normal within just a few hours after any such disturbance. Any unexplainable change in temperature should be investigated immediately.

WISE USE OF STOVES AND OVENS

Food preparation techniques have changed dramatically in recent years. More frozen foods and commercially prepared foods are being used than ever before. More families have speciality appliances that are often used in place of the traditional stoves and ovens. At the same time that advanced technology has made microwave ovens commonplace in American homes, a back to the basics ethic has increased the use of wood for cooking and heating.

Even with these dramatic changes in the way we cook, the standby for years—the *cooking range*—remains the most important cooking appliances. It also is the one that consumes the most energy. Correct operation of the range is important not only because it saves energy in the preparation of food. Also, cooking produces a lot of heat that ends up in the kitchen and increases the cooling load on the air conditioner during the summer.

You should assess your use of the stove and oven and attempt to get the most out of it for the energy dollars you spend. You may discover that alternative methods of cooking, such as using small speciality appliances to cook single meals or using a microwave oven to prepare some foods, will save you money. If the range is properly cleaned and located within the kitchen, you will also save money.

TYPES OF RANGES

Gas and electricity are the two fuels used in almost all cooking ranges. Gas ranges, like gas furnaces, may operate with natural gas, propane or another similar bottled gas. Although some users express a strong preferance for either gas ranges or electric ranges, generally, cost of operation is the factor that determines which type is purchased. In most areas, natural gas ranges are significantly cheaper to operate than electric ranges. Before you decide to purchase and install a gas range, be sure you can obtain the required gas connection for your home. In some areas of critical natural gas shortages, this may not be possible. Propane also is generally less expensive to use than electricity for cooking, but this depends on the prices of propane and electricity in your area.

Most gas ranges have a continuously burning pilot light. When the user turns the burners on, the pilot light lights the burners. With the recent concern for saving energy brought on by the energy shortage, however, most gas stove manufacturers are offering pilotless electronic ignition systems on their gas ranges. These devices ignite the gas only when the user turns the dial, and they can save about $10 a year on operating expenses. These systems add about $30 to $50 to the initial cost of your range, so it may take about five years for you to get your money back. If you intend to keep your range for several years, an electronic ignition system would be worth the money.

Some gas ranges have no automatic lighting system—neither an electronic ignition or a pilot light. These ranges must be manually lit by turning on the gas and then lighting the burner with a match.

AUTOMATIC CLEANING OVENS

Although automatic cleaning ovens often use more energy than conventional manual cleaning ovens and cost more to purchase, they offer a big advantage to the use in that they almost eliminate the messy chore of cleaning the oven. There are two basic types of automatic cleaning ovens: the self-cleaning oven and the continuous cleaning oven.

Self-Cleaning Ovens

The self-cleaning oven decomposes the residue that collects inside the oven with controlled high temperatures of up to 1,000°. When the user wishes to clean the oven, he sets the oven on the proper setting. The oven does the rest. This process takes about 2-3 hours. When the oven has finished cleaning, the user wipes the ash residue from the walls of the oven.

This type of oven can cost more to purchase than the continuous cleaning oven. The high temperatures necessary to activate the cleaning action consume extra electricity. These drawbacks may be offset, however, because the ovens usually contain extra insulation that can lower everyday operating costs of baking.

Continuous Cleaning Ovens

The walls of the continuous cleaning oven are coated with a chemical material that removes residue at normal oven temperatures. These ovens offer an advantage over self-cleaning ovens in that they do not have to operate at high temperatures to achieve the cleaning action. This saves energy. But you must follow the manufacturer's directions carefully if you choose to manually clean these ovens, as is sometimes necessary. Some chemical agents will damage the chemical coating and render the cleaning action useless.

MICROWAVE COOKERY

Microwave ovens offer an energy saving advantage over traditional ovens in that they use only a fraction of the energy required to cook by ordinary methods. These ovens operate by producing electronic waves that are absorbed by the food. The waves act upon the food in such a way that the food's molecules speed up, which creates friction and heat within the food itself. The air surrounding the food stays entirely cool, which means that these units create no additional heat gain for the air conditioner during the summer.

Although microwave ovens do save energy, their initial cost is high enough that their expense cannot be recovered in energy savings alone. And microwave ovens are at best auxiliary cooking devices, so they cannot be used as a replacement for your conventional oven.

The primary advantage to microwave ovens is that they can save a great deal of time in cooking. They are a real convenience because foods cook and heat much faster than in a conventional oven.

From the standpoint of energy conservation, if you have a microwave oven or are planning to purchase one on the basis of its increased convenience, you should try to use the oven to its full energy saving capabilities. It can be used to entirely cook many foods; with some dishes you may want to partially cook them in your microwave oven and finish cooking and browning them in your conventional oven.

OTHER COOLING CONSIDERATIONS

If you are partially heating your home with a wood stove, you may want to try your hand at some old-fashioned cooking with wood. If you do, you will save energy in the process. Dishes that are normally prepared by boiling on your gas or electric stove can be just as easily boiled on most wood stoves. When the food has boiled and you want it to simmar, you can raise it a few inches above the stove's surface with metal or other inflammable blocks placed between the stove and the bottom of the pan. Never use wood blocks for this purpose!

Your range should be located in your kitchen in a position where it is out of the direction of cold drafts during the winter. It should not be near a door, where cold air coming inside will cool the food. Similarly, the range should be located away from a refrigerator or freezer.

If you have a vent fan in your kitchen, you can reduce the cooling load on your air conditioner if you turn the fan on briefly after cooking is finished. This will remove the hot air in the kitchen produced by the stove and oven. The fan should be on only enough to remove excess heat, however. Otherwise, you will be sending air-conditioned air out the exhaust and will waste energy.

During the winter, the exhaust fan should only be used as necessary to remove cooking odors. You should keep the reflectors underneath your stove burners bright and clean. This helps reflect heat upward toward the pan on the burner.

ENERGY EFFICIENT COOKING

Each time you open your oven door to look at the food inside, about 25% of the heat in the oven escapes. If it's during the summer, this heat escaping into the living area must be cooled with your air conditioner. Whenever possible, keep that oven door closed!

If you have a self-cleaning oven, you will save energy on the cleaning cycle if you set it to clean immediately after you have finished baking, when the oven is still warm. This saves you the expense of warming the oven the first 350° or so on the cleaning cycle.

You should preheat your oven only for dishes that especially require it. Most dishes do not. Baking breads and cakes, however, does require preheating.

Try to cook as many dishes as possible in your oven at the same time. Space the dishes out inside the oven to allow good air circulation and even heating. If your range has two ovens, use the smaller oven whenever possible.

Flat-bottomed pans provide better contact with cooking surfaces and provide more even heating, especially on electric stoves. Do not use a burner larger than the pan you are cooking with. On a gas stove, do not turn the flame up so that it extends beyond the bottom of the pan.

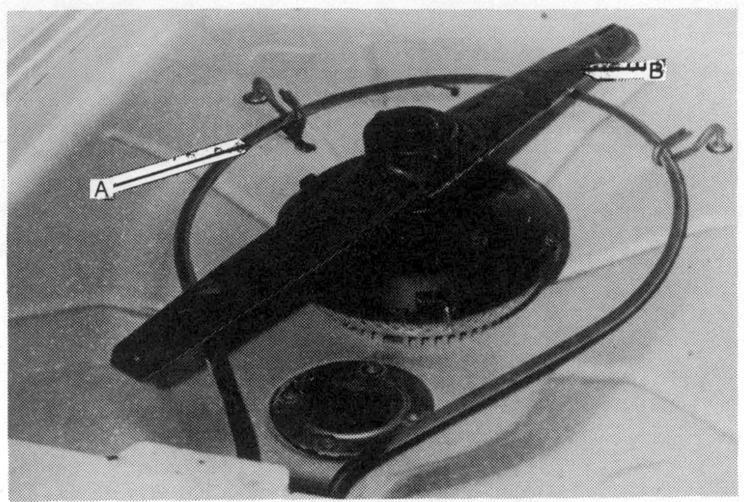

Fig. 15-9. The heating element (A) heats the water and dries the dishes. The spinner blade (B) sprays water around inside the dishwasher compartment to dislodge food particles and distribute soapy wash water and clean rinse water. A cap screw at the center of the blade holds the blade in place.

Food cooks faster and with less heat in covered pans. Water, especially, should be boiled in covered pans to save energy. Use the least amount of water necessary to cook the dish. There is no need to use energy boiling water you do not need.

DISHWASHERS

Dishwasher manufacturers, like manufacturers of other major appliances, are offering energy saving options on their newer models. The primary energy saving feature is a switch that shuts off the dishwasher after the wash and rinse cycles are completed. This eliminates the heat-drying cycle. To dry the dishes, the homeowner merely opens the door and allows the dishes inside to air dry.

You can easily accomplish the same result on your dishwasher, even if it does not have this quick shut-off feature. When the wash and rinse cycles finish and the drying cycle begins, stop the machine and open the door to let the dishes air dry.

You'll also save money if you only run your dishwasher when you have a full load of dishes—once a day for most families. If you rinse your dishes befoire placing them inside the dishwasher, you should always use cold water to cut hot water costs.

Hot Water Consumption

Although it is commonly thought that a dishwasher consumes more energy than washing dishes by hand, studies show that in some instances this is not the case. A dishwasher uses about 10 to 15 gallons of water to wash a full load of dishes, which is usually dishes from two to three meals. Maytag reports studies showing that washing dishes by hand consumes an average of 9-14 gallons of hot water for dishes from each meal. That's 18-28 gallons of hot water to wash dishes from two meals.

Your actual hot water use in hand washing dishes will depend almost entirely on your washing and rinsing techniques. If you rinse dishes in constantly running warm water, your hot water consumption in washing dishes by hand will be very large.

Operation and Maintenance

Most dishwashers use only hot water to wash and rinse the dishes. Since the hot water supplied to the dishwasher is rarely hot enough to sterilize the dishes, a heating element is included to heat the water to about 180°F. A water pump located in the bottom of

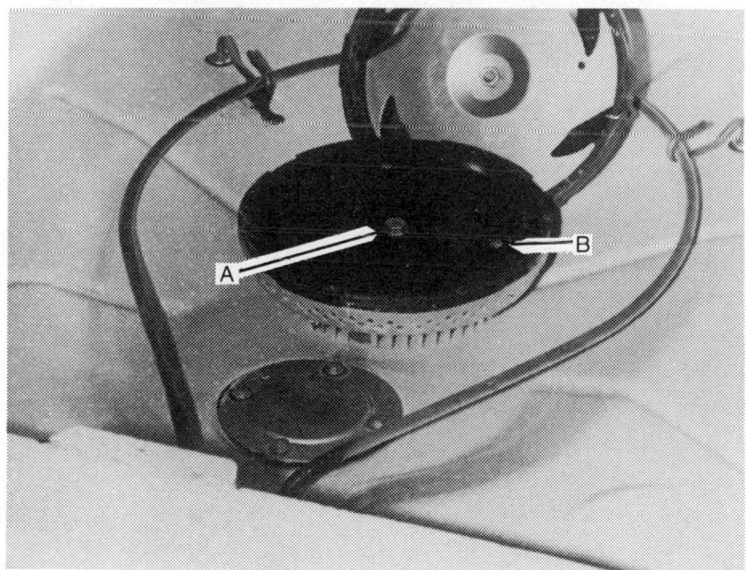

Fig. 15-10. With the spinner blade removed, you can see the water pump (A) and food screen (B). The pump provides the water pressure needed to spray a hard stream of water out of the nozzles on the spinner blade, and it also pumps used water out of the dishwasher. Because the food screen is under the pump, it does not usually have to be removed.

the dishwasher chamber (Fig. 15-10) provides a high-pressure spray of water to spin the blade and remove the water after each rinse and wash cycle. After the dishes are clean, the heating element comes on to help dry the dishes.

A food screen is located under the pump blade. This screen catches any food particles that might clog the pump or stop up the lines. If food particles fill this screen, the pump will not be able to pump enough water to clean the dishes. If the drain the drain is stopped up the motor may overheat.

If the water level is not set correctly the dishwasher may not fill with enough water to make the spinner turn and spray water over the dishes. Since dishwashers vary greatly in construction, read the instruction manual for your dishwasher and set the water level accordingly.

To use your dishwasher economically, be sure to always run a full load of dishes. Running only half a load will waste water and electricity. Install a drain hose sized according to the instructions for the dishwasher, and check it periodically to be sure there are no restrictions.

Laundry Appliances: Washers and Driers

16

We often take everyday appliances for granted, not giving much thought to the amount of energy they consume. But inefficient or improper operation in even the simplest appliance can waste energy, and that costs you money. For example, you washer uses both hot water and electricity when it operates. A clogged water line, a poorly operating motor, or using a full tub of water to wash a partial load of clothes will make it the washer use more energy than it should.

Driers may be powered by either gas or electricity. In either case, they consume quite a bit of energy in drying your clothes. The motors and heating components of a drier are much the same as found in gas or electric furnaces, so they are fairly easy to repair. There are also a number of simple steps you can take in your everyday laundry operation to help insure that you are getting the most benefit from the energy consumed by your drier.

Neither washers nor driers consumes large amounts of energy when compared to the amount of energy consumed in heating and cooling your home. Nevertheless, their use does add to your energy bill, especially if you have a large family and wash a lot of clothes. Therefore, it makes sense to maintain these appliances properly and to periodically assess your operation of them to be sure you are getting the lowest possible energy consumption.

In this chapter we show you how to check your washer and drier for proper operation. We explain how to clean the water lines and filters and how to make simple energy saving repairs. We also

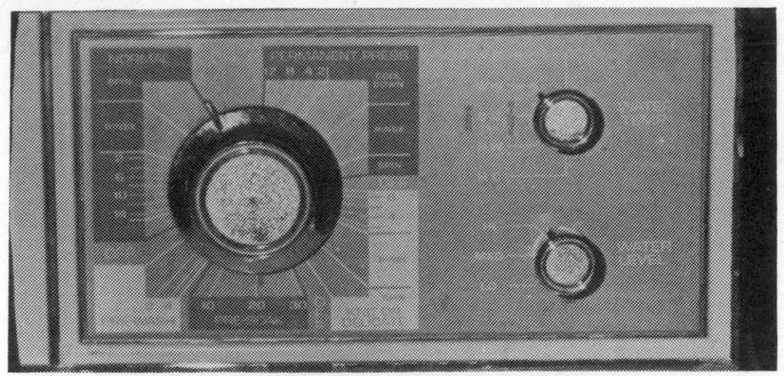

Fig. 16-1. Modern washing machines offer an incredible number of wash and rinse cycles for different fabrics. While these are judged by many as an important convenience—if not a necessity—for modern fabric blends, using them indiscriminately will waste money. You can wash clothes economically if you use the coolest water temperature you can for washing and rinsing each type of fabric.

discuss several energy saving tips that will be useful in your daily laundry operations for cutting energy consumption.

ENERGY SAVING TIPS FOR WASHERS

The largest cost in operating your clothes washer is the cost of heating the water. The motor actually consumes very little electricity. Thus, some of the energy saving tips we discussed in the earlier chapter on reducing hot water costs are directly applicable to reducing the cost of washer operation.

Notice that when you reduce the temperature of the water in your water heater, you will directly affect the temperature of the water in your clothes washer. Since clothes washers have controls that mix factory set amounts of hot and cold water for the different water temperatures, the temperature of water entering the washer for setting such as "hot" and "warm" will now be a bit cooler than it was before you reduced your water heater temperature. You should take this into account in selecting the water temperature on your clothes washer. Watch the washer's performance as you lower the water heater setting. If you find the clothes washed on the "warm" setting are not getting as clean as you would like, you may want to consider washing some of those loads on the "hot" setting.

Before doing that, consider other possible alternatives. Changing detergents might be in order, as we will discuss a bit later in this chapter. Perhaps you are overloading the washer so that the clothes will not clean properly. Presoaking or applying detergent directly on heavily soiled areas may eliminate any problems.

Most modern clothes washers have a variety of controls that allow the homeowner to select just the right water temperature, water level and wash cycle for the load of laundry being cleaned (Fig. 16-1). You can select any desired water temperature for the wash and for the rinse cycles. You can choose the correct type of wash cycle for the particular fabric you are washing, whether it be cotton, permanent press or delicate.

A big energy saver is the water level control that allows you to select the amount of water needed to wash a particular load of clothes. This control lets you wash a small load without completely filling the washer's tub with water that isn't needed.

If you have a washer with such a variety of controls, you should take full advantage of them to cut your laundry costs. If you are considering the purchase of a new washer, you should definitely think seriously about purchasing one that gives you a wide variety of settings and cycles to save energy.

Hot or Cold Water?

The largest cost in operating a clothes washer is in the expense for heating the water. You should consider ways to reduce the amount of hot water you use in your laundry. This may require you to change your traditional laundry practices a bit.

It is true that, all other things being equal, hot water washing will get clothes cleaner than warm or cold water. But some fabrics and colors will be damaged by washing in hot water. For most laundry applications, hot water is simply not needed. You will save money any time you can reduce your hot water consumption in your laundry by using "warm" or "cold" water settings. In many cases, you can get satisfactory results with cold water if you switch to cold

Table 16-1. General Wash Water Temperature Recommendations (courtesy of Maytag Company).

HOT	WARM	COLD
White cottons White underwear Diapers Heavily soiled or white PP & man-made fibers Heavily soiled items of any color	Normally soiled PP & man-made fibers Delicates (unless bright colors) Blends of natural & man-made fibers Normally soiled colored loads	Dark colors Bright colors Washable woolens Lightly soiled items

water detergents and pretreat soiled areas. By the same token, many times you can pretreat heavily soiled areas and get satisfactory results by washing even white garmets in warm water instead of the usual hot water. Table 16-1 provides a general guide you can use to determine general wash temperatures.

Substantial savings will be realized if you can adjust your laundry procedures so taht you are washing clothes in warm water that you used to wash in hot water. Also, wash clothes in cold water that you used to wash in warm water for still more savings.

This is not to say that cold water washing is not without its limitations. Hot water washing may be required, even wtih bright colors, in order to remove greasy soils or stains. But using bleaches and pretreatments can compensate for the lower cleaning ability of cold water.

If the water temperature in the washing machine is below 60°, you will get hardly any cleaning results. The Maytag Company reports that the chemical action of detergents practically ceases in water below that temperature. You therefore should check the temperature of the cold water entering your washing machine. Compensate accordingly with the water temperature setting if you find it is too cold to render the detergent effective. Note that the temperature of the cold water may vary with the season of the year. Most granulated detergents will not dissolve well in cool water, and this also reduces the cleaning effectiveness of the detergent. Therefore, a liquid laundry detergent or predissolved granular one is recommended for cooler temperatures.

While there may be advantages in some cases to using warm water to wash, there are no advantages in using a warm or hot rinse. Rinsing is basically a dilution process—not a washing process—so the chemical action of the residual detergent is of no concern. Maytag reports that a *cold water rinse is just as effective as a warm one*. You should use a cold water rinse for every load. Besides, most of the fabrics washed in the average homeowner's laundry are permanent press and manmade fabrics that should be rinsed in cold water anyway to reduce wrinkling.

Selecting a cold water rinse instead of a warm one will save about 10 gallons of hot water per load. If you wash eight to 10 loads of laundry a week, that can present a substantial savings in your hot water costs. Selecting a warm wash instead of a hot wash will save a similar amount.

Many older washer models, and some new ones, do not allow the homeowner to select a cold rinse temperature with all wash temperatures. The capability to use a cold rinse with any wash temperature is a feature you should look for if you are selecting a new washer.

Other Laundry Procedures

As we have already mentioned, you should always attempt to wash an entire load of clothes at once. Make sure the washer is filled with clothes so you do not run a full load of water to wash only a partial load of clothes. If your washer has a water level selector, you can wash a partial load by reducing the water level to "medium" or to "low."

When filling your clothes washer, be sure the washload consists of compatible fabrics and colors or you will likely be disappointed in the washing results. If you have a water level selector, you should wash two separate small loads of incompatible garments at a lower water level instead of washing one large load.

Be sure your washer is not overloaded. Packing too many clothes into the machine will not only render the cleaning action ineffective, but it also puts a strain on the motor that can eventually damage the machine. It also costs more to operate an overloaded motor.

Do not select a slow spin when washing absorbent items. The faster regular spin will remove more of the water from the garments and reduce drying time.

If you have an automatic drier, wash permanent press clothes on the regular cycle instead of the permanent press cycle to save water. This eliminates the "cool down" cycle and saves you a full tub of water on each load. If you use a cold rinse, this will provide sufficient protection against wrinkles, especially when used with an automatic dryer.

Other Water and Energy Saving Features

A washing machine feature that has become quite popular in the Southwest during recent water shortages is the wash water saver, which saves wash water for reuse on subsequent loads. Naturally, this feature can also save you energy money as well as water, because you save the cost of heating that reused water.

Washing machines with this feature are used in conjunction with a tub into which the water is discharged after the wash cycle is completed. After the first load is finished rinsing and spinning, a second load of clothes is added to the machine. The water is pumped from the tub back into the machine to wash the second load.

When using a washer with this feature, begin your laundry by washing white or lightly soiled clothes. In subsequent loads, wash garments that are more heavily soiled. You also can begin by washing the first load in hot water or warm water and progressing in subsequent loads to garments you would wash in cooler water. In subsequent loads you should add about one-half the amount of detergent normally used. In using this wash water saver, be sure to follow the manufacturer's directions.

WASHING MACHINE MAINTENANCE

Restrictions in the incoming water lines to the washing machine can interfere with the water temperature and waste hot water. If the cold water line is restricted, you will get mostly hot water when you set the water temperature setting for "warm." This, of course, is a needless waste of hot water and can even cause fabric damage to some garments.

There are two hoses that connect to the back of the washer to bring water into the washing machine. One hose brings in hot water, and the other brings in cold water. Many of these hoses have tiny screens in the water line to filter out any large mineral deposits that may be in the water. Such deposits can clog the screeens and restrict the water flow.

Unscrew the water hoses from their connections, making sure you know which hose goes on which connection so you can put them back. Usually each water line will have two small filter screens. One screen is at the faucet end of the rubber hose. The other screen is recessed in the line connecting to the back of the machine. Remove any blockages in these filter screens.

The possibility of a blocked filter screen should always be checked out before you make any decision that your water heater's thermostat must be raised due to poor laundry performance. As we have mentioned, lowering the temperature of your hot water at the water heater will mean you are washing with slightly cooler water than you used before the change. Most families will not even notice any difference in their laundry results.

Consider, on the other hand, what would happen if your hot water line were blocked due to a clogged filter. You would not be getting the amount of hot water into the machine that you should. This blockage might not make a significant difference at higher water heater temperatures because the water would still be warm enough to give you good results. But this may not be the case at lower temperatures, so you might be prompted to increase the hot water temperature at the water heater. It would be a needless waste of energy to adjust upward the thermostat on your water

Fig. 16-2. This is the motor assembly of the washing machine. Keep the motor (A) clean and check the V-belt (B) for cracks and tension. The gear box (C) contains its own oil reservoir and will rarely require lubrication unless it develops a leak. Blow out the accumulation of dust once a year when you check the motor and belts. Some motors have lubrication holes for adding oil, and a few drops of SAE 10 oil should be added each year. The V-belt should deflect about ½ inch when you press against it with your hand. Tighten the belt if necessary, but do not overtighten it, since this is hard on the motor bearings and will soon wear out the belt. Some washers have a spring-tensioned pulley to apply the right amount of tension on the V-belt, so the belt may deflect several inches as you press it.

heater to compensate for a clogged hot water line, so you should check out this possibility.

Check the motor of your washing machine about once a year (Fig. 16-2). Look for loose or cracked V-belts. Clean and oil the motor. Look for loose or defective electrical wiring. Oil puddles indicate the gear box is leaking; the leak should be located and stopped and the oil supply replensihed with the recommended oil.

If the drain hose is clogged or is too small, the motor will become strained trying to pump the water out. The motor may be overloaded and thus burn itself out. Periodically check the drain hose coming from the washer pump and keep it free of lint and dirt.

ENERGY SAVING TIPS FOR DRYERS

Your clothes drier uses either gas or electricity to provide the heat necessary to dry your clothes. The motor that turns the drum is powered by electricity. Most of the cost in operating the drier comes from the energy consumed in heating the air to dry clothes.

Electric driers use a heating element to warm the air drawn through the drier. Gas driers burn natural gas and use a heat exchanger, operating on the same principle as the heat exchanger for gas furnaces, to warm the air flowing through the drier. The cost of operation is about the same for both types. Most new driers sold today are electric models, although gas driers are still popular in many urban areas where natural gas lines are available.

If you are considering the purchase of a new drier, there are a number of features you can look for to cut your operating costs. For a gas drier, you will save about 25% of the annual operating costs if the drier is equipped with an electric ignition instead of the traditional pilot light. The pilot light, of course, must burn continuously even when the drier is not operating. Over the course of a year, this will add several dollars to your gas bill. The electric ignition, on the other hand, eliminates the constantly burning pilot light and uses gas only when the drier is turned on.

Drier Controls

There are a number of controls available on driers that not only give you the capability of saving energy, but also improve the drying results. A temperature control allows you to select the correct heat temperature for the garments and the type of fabric you are using. Many fabrics are prone to wrinkling when dried at high temperatures. The temperature control allows you to reduce both wrinkling and the amount of heat used at the same time.

Some driers have a cool-down period at the final five minutes or so of the drying cycle that turns off the heat while the clothes are still tumbling in the drier. The feature also helps prevent wrinkling of permanent press and synthetic fabrics. It conserves heat energy because it allows the drier to make use of all available heat before the drum stops.

Other controls establish the amount of time the drier will run. Some of the more sophisticated controls automatically stop the drier when the clothes are fully dried to prevent wrinkling and wasting heat by overdrying.

The basic drier control is a simple timer that allows the homeowner to select the amount of time the drier should run before it shuts off. With practice and skillful timer use, the homeowner can avoid overdrying and wasted heat energy. But if the user guesses wrong on the amount of time it will take to dry a particular load, it is quite easy to waste energy by excessive drying time.

With automatic shut-off drier controls the user can select the amount of dryness desired, and the drier will shut off automatically when the proper dryness is achieved. These controls sense the temperature of the exhausted air of the drier or the amount of moisture in the clothes and turn the drier off accordingly. Some have a signal that sounds when the load is dry.

When properly used these controls can prevent overdrying

and its accompanying waste of energy. Most of the guesswork needed in a timer control is eliminated.

Lint Filter

Since the lint filer of the drier should be cleaned often to prevent restricting the air flow through the drier, you should attempt to purchase a drier that allows easy access to the filter. On some models this filter is housed in a simple, easy to remove panel just inside the door. Thus, cleaning the filter before each drying load is an extremely easy chore.

Some manufacturers have redesigned their driers in recent years to increase the drum capacity and to maximize air flow. You should consider these products, examine product literature and compare prices before selecting a new drier.

EFFICIENT USE OF YOUR DRIER

You should avoid overdrying garments because this wastes energy and may harm fabrics or colors. If your drier has only a timer control and no automatic shut-off, you should attempt to check your clothes every few minutes as they approach the end of the drying cycle. Remove them promptly as they become dry. For garments you will iron, remove them slightly damp. This will make them easier to iron. The heat from the iron will evaporate the remainder of the moisture.

Dry loads consecutively whenever possible. The heat that remains in the drum will be used in the next load of clothes. This will save having to reheat the air at the beginning of the drying cycle.

When temperature controls are available, use the regular setting for normal or heavy loads. For heat sensitive fabrics and colors, use a lower temperature setting.

Do not overload the drier. This restricts the air flow through the unit and increases drying time, as well as the likelihood of wrinkling. Overloading also increases the strain on the drier motor and may damage the unit.

Your drier has a screen that removes the lint from the air flow to prevent lint buildup on the clothes inside the drum. If this filter becomes clogged with lint—and it certainly will after only a few loads—the air flow into the drier is severly restricted. This wastes much of the heat produced by the heating element.

Check the lint filter before drying each load. Clean it if there is a substantial accumulation. It is a good idea to clean this lint filter before each load.

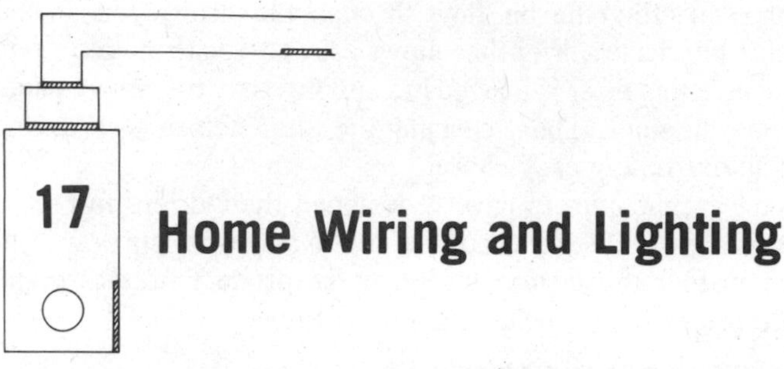

17 Home Wiring and Lighting

The wiring and lighting in a house is an important factor in the amount of electrical energy wasted. Over the years, the number of electrical appliances and light fixtures in the home has greatly increased. But while the original wiring in a home may have been adequate 10 or 20 years ago, the old circuits are probably not up to handling the additional load placed on them today. The old circuits may not be arranged well for the most efficient usage of modern-day appliances. You may need new outlets and circuits to handle your new appliances. Or you may need new lighting fixtures and light switches for added convenience or to save you an extra trip across the room to turn them on and off. Or perhaps you need some extra heat in a room where the problem can be easily solved by adding a baseboard heater. Whatever your particular needs, they will probably require some extra wiring.

WIRE SIZES

When you consider any rewiring job, such as adding electrical outlets, lights and switches, or baseboard heat, you should be sure you get the right size wire to carry the current you will draw from the circuit. For example, a 1000-watt toaster on a stnadard 120-volt residential electrical service will draw a current of 1000/120 = 8.3 amperes. Major appliances and baseboard heaters are supplied with ampere ratings to help you determine the wire size needed. Table 17-1 shows the current-carrying capacities of different wire sizes. Number 12 and 14 wire sizes are used for most electrical circuits in the home.

Table 17-1. Current Capacity of Standard Wire Sizes With Plastic Insulation.

WIRE GAUGE	AMPERES
18	5
16	10
14	15
12	20
10	30
8	40
6	65
4	85
2	100
0	125
00	145
000	200
0000	230
250	250

It is important with new electrical installations to be sure the wires are large enough to carry the current because starting out too small can only lead to trouble. Remember that you may later want to add more appliances to the circuits; it is unlikely that you will want to remove any.

If a heater or appliances does not have an ampere rating, you can find the approximate ampere rating by dividing the wattage of the unit by the voltage supplied by the household circuit. For example, a 1500-watt baseboard heater on a 240-volt circuit will draw $1500/240 = 6.25$ amperes.

As electrical appliances such as dishwashers, electric mixers, toasters and electric ranges are added to electrical circuits, the existing wiring may become inadequate to handle the extra load. When too much current is drawn through a wire, two things happen: the wire will overheat and a voltage drop will occur at the outlet end of the wire. When a wire overheats, it can cause a fire inside the walls. When a voltage drop occurs, the efficiency and output of your electrical appliances is reduced. Electric heaters produce less heat, lamps go dim, and electric motors have difficulty starting.

The efficiency of appliances with electric motors (freezers, room air conditioners, refrigerators, etc.) is greatly reduced because the voltage drop prevents the motors from receiving enough voltage to power them as they should be. Electric motors also draw a great deal of current when they are starting. When the circuit wire is too small, the motors have difficulty reaching their operating speed. This may cause the motor to kick on and off, operating erratically and wasting power. A compressor motor on a large refrigerator, for instance, will draw about 12 to 15 amperes when the motor is starting. If the room lights dim noticeably when an electric motor starts on a circuit, you know something is wrong. Circuit wires may be too small, there may be loose connections in the wiring, or there may not be enough power coming into the house from the electrical service lines. In any case, voltage drop is excessive when service becomes noticeably affected.

The homeowner may also find there have been so many electrical appliances added to his home that his present level of electric service is no longer adquate. The breaker box, incoming service lines, or inside wiring may have to be changed. This usually is the case when there is an extreme voltage drop in the circuits.

We recommend that you contact two or three reputable builders, electrical contractors, or representatives from your electric utility to get specific advice on electrical wiring unless you are knowledgeable in the field. These people can supply advice on local building codes, specific wire sizes, and designs of electrical circuits to fit specific needs.

LIGHT SWITCHES

One thing we all give a great deal of lip service to when we discuss ways to conserve energy is turning off lights when they are not in use. But if you are in one end of a 20-foot long living room and you leave to go into the kitchen, how likely are you to walk across the living room to turn out the light? Unless you are more consciencious about energy conservation than most people, you will leave the light on. On the other hand, if there is a switch to turn off the light at the kitchen at the kitchen doorway as well as at the living room entrance, you will turn off the light.

Three-way switches make it possible for you to put switches for a light at two locations. Combinations of three-way and four-way switches make it possible to put light switches at as many locations as you want. Figure 17-1 shows how one or more switches are wired to a light fixture.

Three-way switches (Fig. 17-2) are most often used at the opposite ends of hallways and large rooms. We recommend three-way switches be used in any room with two doorways, so a person passing through the room can turn on the light at one entrance when entering the room, and he can turn it off at the second when leaving. Thus, three-way switches can save you both electrical energy and walking energy.

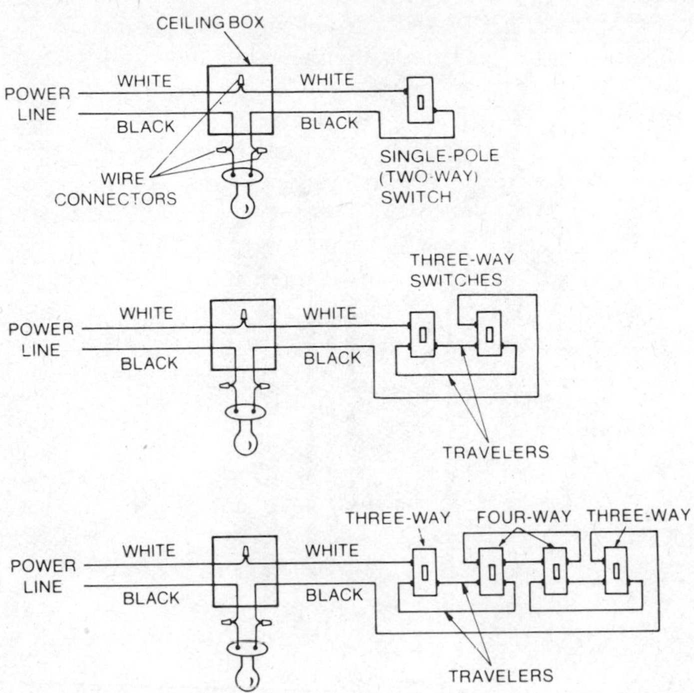

Fig. 17-1. A single-pole or two-way switch is used when only one switch is to be used to control a light. When two switches are required, three-way switches (having three terminals) are used; the two end terminals of one are wired to the next using a two-conductor wire called a traveler. When three or more switches are needed to control the same light, the traveler wires running between the three-way switches are interrupted to insert one or more four-way switches. Four-way switches have four terminals, two at each end, so that the traveler wires come into one end of the switch and leave at the center.

A light with two switches will have two three-way switches wired into the circuit. To change the lights to operate with two switches instead of with one switch, a second switch and switch box will have to be installed, and the original single-pole switch will have to be replaced with a three-way switch. Replace the original two-wire electrical cable with three-wire cable so you will have three conductor wires running to the lights. Number 14 wire is usually used for electric light applications unless a large number of lights on the same circuit makes the current draw more than 15 amperes.

The easiest way to replace the old two-wire cable is to attach the new three-wire cable to the old wire at the switch opening in the wall. Pull the old wire from the attic above. As the old wire

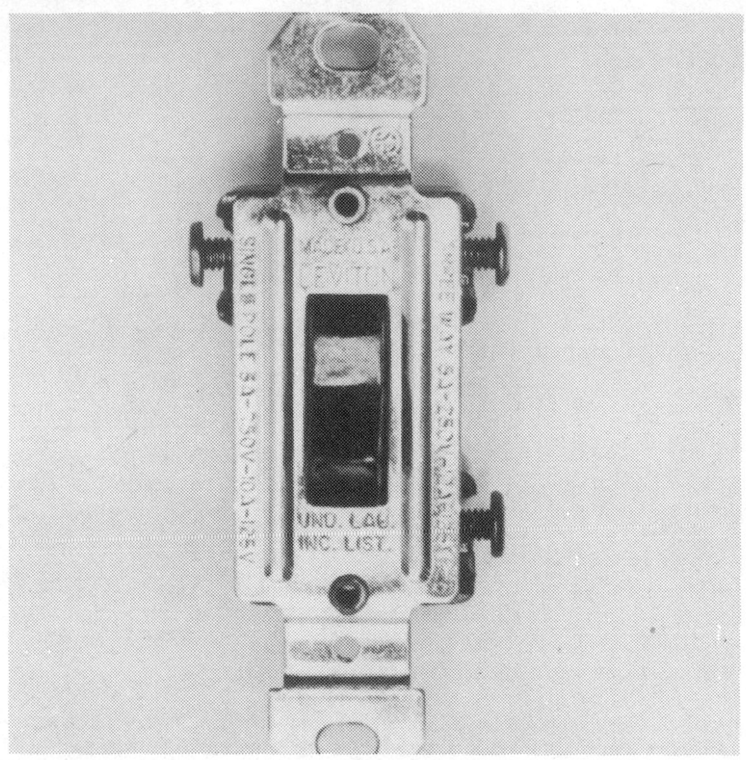

Fig. 17-2. A three-way switch has three terminals. The hot wire connects to the single terminal (A), either as it comes from the hot side of the power line or as it goes to the hot side of the light fixture. the two terminals (B) opposite each other at one end of the switch connect to the traveler wires that run from one switch to the next. When more than two siitches are needed to control a ligth, a three-way switch must be used at the beginning and end of the string of switches; four-way switches with four terminals are connected between the three-way switches.

comes out it will pull the new wire up the wall. The new wire is then run through the plate at the top of the studs that goes to the ceiling box.

To install a switch at a new location, first locate a wall stud where you want the switch placed. Cut a hole in the wall next to the stud for the switch box to fit into. From the attic, drill a hole in the plate at the top of the studs to feed the electrical cable down into the wall.

If a room has three doors or more, the light can be wired to be turned off at any door. Figure 17-1 shows how a light can be wired to turn *off* or *on* at any of four locations using two three-way switches and one four-way switch.

When both three- and four-way switches are to be installed in a circuit, the circuit must start and end with a three-way switch, as shown in the diagrams. Any number of four-way switches can be used to give you as many switches as you want, but the first and last switches in the series must be three-way switches. To wire in the four-way switches, you must have four wires connecting to the switch, so you will need to run two two-wire cables to the switch, one bringing power from the previous switch and the other carrying power to the next.

All electrical switch boxes should be connected to the ground wire in the electrical cable to prevent electrical shock. The ground wire is connected to a ground terminal in the fuse box, which goes to a rod driven into the ground. Never use this bare grounded wire as a conductor wire to run power to a light or to a switch. Three-wire cable will have three insulated conductor wires and a bare grounded wire. The bare ground wire is not to be connected to a power supply in any way.

When making connections on the lights and switches be sure all connections are made tightly. Most switch and light connections use solderless connectors that join the wires with a fastener or a screw. Make sure these connections are tight.

WIRING FOR ELECTRIC HEAT

If you are considering replacing your present furnace with an electric furnace, you must be sure that the electrical service to the furnace is correct, or you will not get the efficiency or performance you want. The first thing to do is notify the utility company of the proposed change. Usually the utility company's pole transformer will have to be changed (no cost to you) and probably your breaker box and entrance wires will have to be replaced with larger sizes. A 200-ampere breaker box will usually supply the homeowner with enough capacity and circuits to operate an electric furnace.

There are two types of electric furnaces. The first type has the entire furnace on one electric circuit. This furnace must have a large cable brining electricity to it, and the cable must be large enough to handle the amperage draw of all four heating elements in the furnace. The second type of electrical furnace has one circuit going to the furnace for each two heating elements in the furnace. The wires for this furnace can be smaller than for the first type. In either case, however the wires going to the electric furnace must be large enough to handle the current the furnace will use.

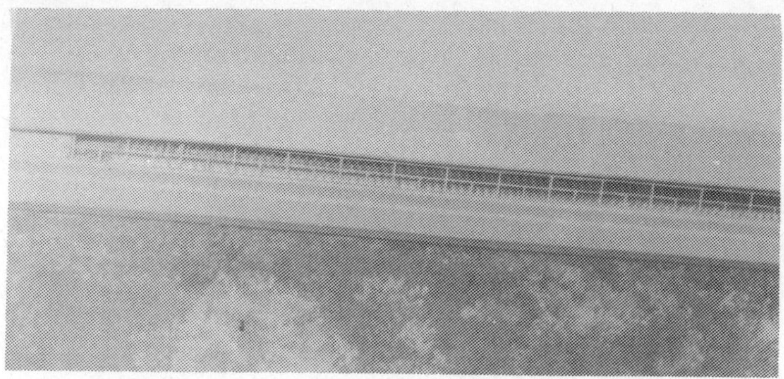

Fig. 17-3. The baseboard heater is a resistance heating element that mounts along the wall edge of the floor in a room. The heater has no fan; hot air is circulated by natural convection air currents.

INSTALLING BASEBOARD HEATERS

Supplemental electrical heat, such as baseboard heaters and portable electrical heaters, can save energy and money for the homeowner because they can be used to warm up only the room that needs heat. If the kitchen area of a house is the room used most during the day, supplemental electric heat can be used in the kitchen to bring the temperature in the kitchen to a comfortable level. This lets you set the furnace thermostat at a lower temperature, which saves money by not heating rooms that aren't being used very much. At night the supplemental heat can be turned on in the bedrooms where it is needed, and turned off in the other areas of the house where it is not needed.

There are several different types of electrical heating units for this application, but they all work on the principle of electrical resistance. Heat energy is formed as electricity flows through the heating element, which resists the flow of electricity. The electrical energy is thus converted into heat energy.

For complete portability, small electric heaters are available that will plug into an ordinary 120-volt wall outlet. Most of these heaters have thermostats, and some have fans to help circulate the air. Such units have the advantage of being very easy to move around, but to some pople they are unattractive and seem to get in the way. Unless you get a large unit, you may find it takes more than one unit to heat a room. Often, these heaters consume so much current that they must be connected to different electrical circuits. But two separate circuits may not be available in one room. Some of these heaters draw 12 to 15 amperes, enough to overload a circuit if another appliance is operating on the same circuit. A more permanent type of electric resistance heater is a baseboard heater, shown in Fig. 17-3. These units range in size from 500 watts to 2500 watts. Each room in the house has its own heater and the heaters in that room are wired to a separate circuit. Any number of heaters can be wired in the same circuit as long as the amperage draw is not high enough to overload the circuit wiring and circuit breaker. For example, a 2000-watt baseboard heater for 240V will draw 8.3 amperes, so two such heaters could be used in a 20-ampere circuit.

Baseboard heaters are available in 120-volt and 240-volt sizes. A circuit is run from the breaker box to the thermostat and heater, as in Figs. 17-4, 17-5, and 17-6.

Baseboard heaters can be used for supplementary heat, or they can be the only source of heat in a room or an entire house. Figure the heat load for each room and install a heater sized accordingly. If the baseboard heater is the only source of heat for the room, and the room is well insulated, figure about 1½ watts per square foot of floor area. A 10 × 12 foot room, for instance, would require an 1800-watt baseboard heater. If two-thirds of the heat needed to heat the room will be supplied by the furnace, use about a 750-watt heater. (These figures are for an area with a 0°F winter design temperature.)

Unlike conventional heating systems, baseboard heat does not have a fan to circulate the air in the room—air circulation is by

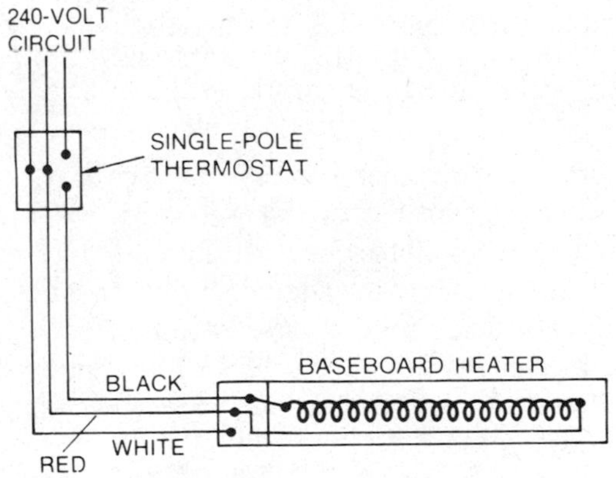

Fig. 17-4. A baseboard heater is wired through a thermostat. The heater is installed along a wall at the floor. The thermostat ahsould be installed on an inside wall so it is not affected by outside temperatures. The heater should not be installed under or near wood furniture.

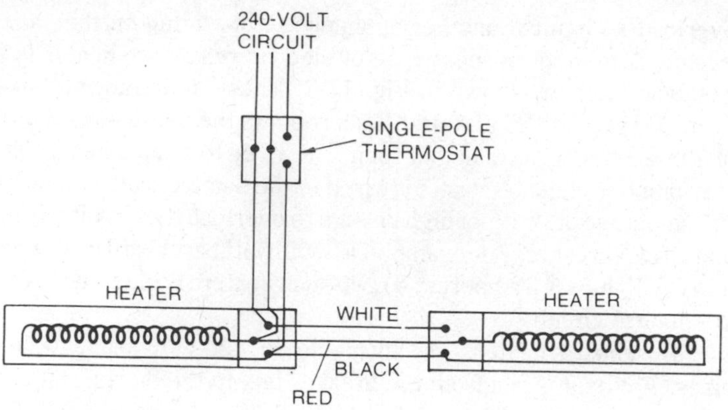

Fig. 17-5. Two heaters may be connected to one single-pole thermostat. The sum of the ampere ratings of the two heaters must be less than the capacity of the thermostat wire and circuit breaker. Two 2000-watt heaters ona 240-volt circuit would draw a total of 16. 7 amperes. These could be connected with three-wire number 12 cable on a 20-ampere circuit breaker.

natural convection air currents. But the baseboard heater does have a thermostat so you can set the room temperature for whatever you like (Fig. 17-7).

There are two types of thermostats used with baseboard heaters: single pole and double pole. The single-pole thermostat is used for installations using one or two heaters that pull a total of less than 20 amperes (Fig. 17-4 and 17-5). The double-ple thermostat can be used with these installations also, but the dobule-pole thermostat is also used when two large heaters are connected on two different circuits (Fig. 17-6). Some types of baseboard heaters have thermostats installed on the heater cases, so with these heaters you are saved the trouble of wiring a thermostat into the wall.

Be sure to use wires large enough to carry the current it takes to operate a baseboard heater. Since you will have to run extra circuits when you install baseboard heaters, be sure your breaker box has space available so the additional circuits can be connected. If you will be addding several baseboard heaters and relying on them heavily to heat your home, check with the utility company to be sure the electrical service into your house can handle the additional load.

INSULATING AROUND ELECTRIC WIRES

Infiltration air can enter a house through the holes that you have bored for the electrical wires. After electrical wires have

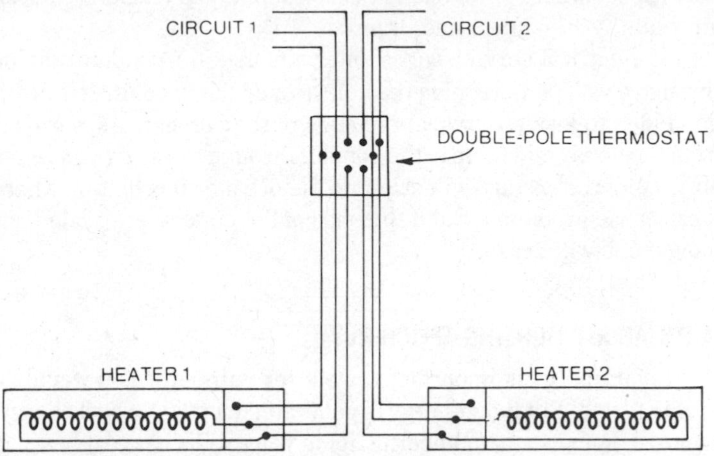

Fig. 17-6. These two large baseboard heaters are wired on different circuits, but they are on the same double-pole thermostat, so one thermostat controls both heaters.

been run through these holes, fill the holes with fiberglass insulation or with caulking material to prevent air flow through the hole.

Holes that are bored through the plate at the top of the studs in the attic should also be filled to stop air flow. Likewise, holes into the basement or unheated garage should be filled. It is especially important to fill any holes going to the outside, even holes in the

Fig. 17-7. Each baseboard heater is controlled by a thermostat located on the wall or on the heater cabinet. If a wall thermostat is used, install it on an inside wall where there is good air circulation.

crawl space where pipes enter. Seal off seams and cracks around all air vents, water lines, and drains.

If electrical service wires enter a house in a conduit running through a wall or plate, plug the hole around the conduit. It is also a good idea to insulate or seal the ends of the conduit. As warm air from the house moves up in the conduit through the attic, where the air is colder, moisture will drip into the breaker box below, where it can cause problems. But if the ends of the conduit are sealed, air movement will cease.

FACTS ABOUT LIGHTING EFFICIENCY

Light energy is important to you, for without it you wouldn't be able to see. But light energy is generated from electrical energy in most homes, so the number of lights you use has a great bearing on the size of your electric bill. What few people realize, however, is that not all lights are created equal, so to speak. That is, some lights give off much more light energy than others, even though they consume the same amount of electricity. For example, did you know that two 60-watt bulbs actually give off less light than a single 100-watt bulb? Or that one 40-watt fluorescent bulb produces almost as much light as two 100-watt incandescents? As you can see, your choice of lighting fixtures and bulbs can have a very significant effect on your electric bill.

Table 17-2 gives the light output of various lamps. The unit of light energy is the *lumen*—the more lumens a lamp produces, the more light you will have. But the number of lumens is only one side of the story. Lamps are powered by electricity, so what you are most interested in is the number of watts required to produce the desired amount of light. A measure of the efficiency of a light source is the ratio of lumens to watts. Table 17-2 shows that small incandescent lamps are less efficient sources of light than larger lamps. But note also that fluorescent lamps are much more efficient than incandescent lamps. In fact, a 40-watt fluroescent bulb gives off more than seven times as much light as a 40-watt incandescent.

Use Fewer Bulbs to Save Money

The fad these days in lighting fixtures is to use several low-wattage bulbs instead of one or two larger bulbs. Admittedly, this may make some lighting fixtures more attractive than others, but the fact still remains that they do not use electricity as efficiently. For example, suppose you have a ceiling fixture with four 40-watt

Table 17-2. Energy Efficiency of Various Lamps.

WATTS	LUMENS	LIFE (HOURS)	(LUMENSWATT)
Incandescent Lamps			
40	435	1500	10.9
60	840	1000	14.0
75	1140	750	15.2
100	1710	750	17.1
150	2740	750	18.3
200	3940	750	19.7
Three-Way Incandescent Lamps			
50-100-150	560-1630-2190	1200	11.2-16.3-14.6
50-200-250	550-3560-4110	1200	11.0-17.8-16.4
100-200-300	1290-3440-4730	1200	12.9-17.2-15.8
Fluorescent Lamps (Cool White)			
15 (T8)	870	7500	58.0
15 (T12)	770	7500	51.3
20	1220	7500	61.0
22 (Circline)	950	7500	43.2
30	2340	15000	78.0
32 (Circline)	1750	7500	54.7
40	3120	15000	78.0
75	6200	12000	82.7

bulbs. At 4 cents per kilowatt-hour, this fixture will use up to $18.69 of electricity per year if it is on for 8 hours a day. You could, on the other hand, take out the 40-watt bulbs and use just two 60-watt bulbs. The lighting fixture would give off the same amount of light, but it would cost only $14.02 per year to operate—a savings of $4.67.

An additional savings comes about as you replace the bulbs that burn out during the year. With the fixture being on 8 hours a day, this amounts to just under 3000 hours a year. Now, 40-watt bulbs have an average life of 1500 hours, compared to the 60-watt bulbs, which last only 1000 hours. But don't let this fool you! If you use 40-watt bulbs, you would have to replace all four bulbs twice each year, so you would have to buy eight bulbs. But if you used 60-watt bulbs, even though you would have to replace them three times during the year, you would still only have to buy a total of six bulbs, and that would save you the price of two bulbs each year. Using one 100-watt bulb to replace four-40 watt bulbs would save you $7.01 and the price of four bulbs per year. Your savings would be even greater if you burned the lights longer each day.

Lamp Life

The life expectancy of any bulb is shortened a little each time you turn it on. In an incandescent bulb, the initial surge of current presents quite a shock to the filament inside. If you stop to think about it, you will note that most bulbs seem to burn out just as you flip the switch to turn them on. When manufacturers calculate the average life of a bulb, they have to estimate how often the bulb will be turned on during its lifetime. If the bulb was only turned on once, and left on, the bulb would probably burn several times as long. On the other hand, if you turn the lights on and off dozens of times each day, the life expectancy of the bulbs will be shortened greatly.

It is claimed—and rightly so—that it doesn't pay to turn off the lights in a room if you are planning to be gone for less than about five minutes. This claim has often been denied in newspaper columns by people who don't understand much about lamps. The truth to the claim lies not in the tiny amount of extra electricity that is consumed during the surge when the bulb is turned on, but in the extent to which the life expectancy of the bulb is reduced. If you figure what the bulb would cost to replace, and weigh that against the small amount of electricity it would consume by being left on a few extra minutes, you will find that the cost of turning on the bulb is roughly equal to the cost of electricity it uses in five minutes. In other words, if you turn a bulb off for less than five minutes, you will save some electricity, but in the long run you will lose more money by having to replace the bulb sooner. This is one instance in which you can actually save money by wasting a little energy. How about the so-called long-life bulbs? These bulbs are claimed to last several times as long as regular bulbs. Indeed, they do last longer, but they don't give off as much light. (The lumen output is printed on the package the bulb comes in, so you can check it yourself.) These bulbs last longer because the filaments do not get as hot, and this means they do not give off as much light compared to regular bulbs. And to make things worse, manufacturers charge much more for these long-life bulbs. Thus, in the long run, the long-life bulb is no bargain. Still, if you need a long-lasting bulb in such hard-to-reach places as stairwells, you could buy a 130-volt bulb instead of the regular 120-volt type. A 130-volt bulb gives off about 15% less light energy when operated at 120V, but it would last over tiwce as long and cost about the same as a standard 120-volt bulb.

You will have noted in Table 17-2 that fluorescent bulbs last considerably longer than incandescent types. The life expectancy of these bulbs is usually calculated for industrial users who turn on the lights in the morning and don't turn them off again until night. Fluorescent bulbs also suffer from the shock of turning them on. They have filaments (called *cathodes*) at each end of the bulb to help the flow of current through the bulb. These filaments are heated just a little—they don't produce much light. Nevertheless, each time the bulb is turned on, the filaments are damaged a little, reducing the life of the bulb. In the home, though, the extremely long life of these bulbs (typically several years) hardly makes it worth the effort to take special measures to extend their life.

Fluorescent Lights

Factories, offices, and stores use fluorescent lighting for one reason—to save money! Although fluorescent fixtures typically cost two or three times as much as comparable incandescent fixtures, the savings in electricity will normally pay for the difference in less than two years. From then on fluorescent lighting costs far less than incandescent lighting. You can use the same justification for using them in your home too.

So why aren't more fluorescent fixtures used in the home? In part, the answer is simply ignorance. But there are also personal objections, such as not liking the "cold" white light they give off, or perhaps it's the box-like shapes of the fixtures.

The light produced by a fluorescent bulb is determined primarily by the mixture of phosphors used to coat the inside of the bulb. The most common phosphpor mixture is called *cool white* (CW), and this is the type used in most factories, offices, and stores. Colored phosphors, such as red, blue, yellow, and green, are used in many advertising signs. Other special phosphor mixes are used to make bulbs for growing plants indoors, and these bulbs produce a light that is similar to true sunlight. The point is that you don't have to be satisfied with cool white if you don't liek it, if it makes your home feel like an office building.

Incandescent lamps give off a light that is somewhat yellowish in color. Putting a CW fluorescent bulb in the same room with an incandescent just accentuates this difference. Many people find the clash objectionable. They may tolerate CW bulbs in their kitchen or bathrooms, but they don't want them in their living rooms. However, you can buy *warm white* (WW) bulbs from most electrical supply stores, and these bulbs give off a yellowish light that is very similar in color to incandescent light. You will rarely find WW bulbs in department and discount stores—they seem to be unaware of their existence, though most other people are too.

Manufacturers also make fluorescent lights using what they call *deluxe* phosphor mixtures. Regular phosphors suffer from the fact that they do not produce a balanced spectrum of light energy. That is, they produce a lot of light energy containing blues and greens, but they are lacking in reds and oranges. The odd thing about light is that you don't have to have all colors present to make "white" light; you just need a sampling of colors blended in the right proportions. So manufacturers have created *cool white deluxe* (CWX) and *warm white deluxe* (WWX) bulbs that balance the color spectrum by adding more reds and oranges. The CWX bulb still produces a light that "looks" just as white as a regular CW bulb, but if you hold a bright red cloth under the two lights, you will immediately see the difference. The red cloth will look drab and dull under the XW bulb, but it will be truly bright under the CWX bulb. The WWX bulb produces even more reds and oranges, giving the bulb a slightly pinkish appearance when side by side with a CW bulb. The "warm" light produced by the WWX bulb makes it attractive for use in the living areas of the home. Sad to say, deluxe phosphors are even harder to find in stores.

The "boxy" appearance of fluorescent fixtures is a harder problem to overcome. By far the most economical size bulb to buy is the four-foot 40-watt type since this is the size used by the millions in offices and stores everywhere. Lighting fixtures using these bulbs are also quite inexpensive compared to other sizes. Most fixtures contain one, two, or four bulbs; the most common being the two-light "rapid-start" fixture. Two-light fixtures are now coming in an increasing number of styles suitable for the living areas of the home. You could buy a traditional white enamel fixture for a kitchen, utility room, or other work area, or you can pain the trim in any color you desire. Today you can also buy prepainted fixtures, in bright colors, and fixtures with wood-grain trim. Office supply stores often carry a much larger selection of good-looking fluorescent fixtures than you will find in most department stores. Most fixtures have plastic covers to diffuse the light; acrylic covers are more desirable than polystyrene because they don't yellow or crack with age. Fluorescent fixtures cost more to make, so you must expect to pay more than similar incandescent fixtures. Just remember, though, that fluorescent fixtures use less electricity and will pay for themselves in a short time.

To illustrate the savings that can be obtained with a fluorescent fixture, consider a kitchen where the light will be on for a good part of the day. For a moderately large kitchen with a dining area, an incandescent fixture having four 75-watt bulbs would be needed to provide a good working light. Assuming that the lights are on for 8 hours each day and electricity costs 4 cents per kilowatt-hour, this incandescent fixture would cost $35.04 per year to operate, plus the cost of 16 bulbs, which would bring the total cost to about $43 per year. On the other hand, a twin-light rapid-start fixture containing two 40-watt fluorescent bulbs would require only about 95 watts to run. (The fixture's ballast transformer and lamp filaments would require about 15 watts.) The fixture would produce 37% more light, but it would use only $11.10 of electricity during the year. The bulbs, costing only about $3 for both, would last for several years before they needed replacing, so their cost would average less then $1 per year. In this case, the cost difference amounts to about $31 per year—it wouldn't cost much more than that to buy a good quality fixture. Thus, after the first year, the fixture would have almost paid for itself, and from then on you'd be *saving* $31 a year.

Lights Produce Heat Energy

Lights use electrical energy to make light, but most of the electrical energy goes into making heat. The light energy that is produced in the lamp strikes objects in the room and is eventually converted into heat energy. So in the end, you could say that all of the electrical energy used in lighting fixtures winds up as heat energy. In the winter this is good because it helps to heat your home. If you have electric heat,it doesn't cost you any more either. Electricity is electricity; it doesn't matter whether you heat your home with electric baseboard heaters or light bulbs—it costs the same either way. If you have oil or gas heat that costs less then electric heat, you can at least console yourself with the fact that the lights are helping to heat your home, although somewhat more expensively.

In the summer, however, it costs money to remove heat energy with air conditioning. In this case, you don't need the extra heat energy contributed by the lights in your house. For each watt of lighting power, you are generating about 3.4 BTU of heat energy that your air conditioner must remove. A 100-watt bulb thus creates 340 BTU of heat energy. Each lamp in your home adds its heat energy, running up your electric bill as it lights your house—and as it *heats* your house. In fact, all of your electric appliances produce heat energy that must be removed by your air conditioner.

Of course, you can't stumble around in your house with all the lights turned off. You need lights to see what you're doing. You need lights to read, to work, to play, even to watch television in order to cut down on the glare. The trick, though, is to use lights effectively so you don't waste electricity. This calls for a little planning and common sense. You need to have lamps positioned in the right places. You need to have light switches in convenient locations. But most of all, you need to have the right amount of light for the type of work or recreation you're doing. Light levels that are too low will strain your eyes, and too much light simply wastes electricity.

ESTIMATING YOUR LIGHTING REQUIREMENTS

The unit of illumination is the*foot.candle*, which originated as the amount of light falling on a surface placed one foot away from a lighted candle. In recent years this unit has been replaced by the *cnadela*, but most literature still uses the foot-candle. A light bulb produces light energy that is measured in lumens. If one lumen of this light energy falls on one square foot of surface, the surface is said to have an illumination level of one foot-candle.

Stores, factories, and office buildings typically have illumination levels of 100 foot-candles or more, and this has drawn much driticism lately because it is more light than necessary. Table 17-3 lists the typical amount of light that you need in various rooms for performing different tasks. The number of light bulbs you need to achieve these general lighting levels varies with the type of fixture you use and the coloring of the walls, floors, draperies and furniture in the room. A ballpark figure for the number of light bulbs you need in an average room can be found from the formula

$$\text{number of bulbs} = \frac{2 \times \text{foot-candle} \times \text{floor area}}{\text{lumens per bulb}}$$

For example, in a 12- by 15-foot living room, the floor area would be 180 square feet. From Table 17-3, the desired illumination level is 20 foot-candles. If 100-watt incandescent bulbs are used, each bulb would emit 1710 lumens. The number of bulbs required in this case would then be

$$\frac{2 \times 20 \times 180}{1710} = 4.2 \text{ bulbs}$$

So you would need approximately four 100-watt bulbs. Depending upon the type of fixture, the placement of the lamps in the room, and room colors, you might need more or less light, but at least you have a good starting point. If the bulbs were covered with a lamp

Table 17-3. Recommended Lighting Levels.

LOCATION OR TASK	FOOT-CANDLES	LOCATION OR TASK	FOOT-CANDLES
bathroom, general area	5	kitchen, work area	40
bathroom, at mirror	40	living room, general area	20
bedroom, general area	5	office, service area	10
bedroom, at mirror	20	office, file work	30
church, auditorium	10	office, close visual work	50
classroom	30	reading, short periods	20
closet	20	reading, long periods	40
dining room	5	sewing, light fabrics	40
garage, storage area	10	sewing, dark fabrics	120
garage, work area	50	stairway	10
hallway or corridor	5	utility room	10
ironing	100	writing	20
kitchen, general area	10		

shade, and the floors and furniture were medium to dark colors, you might need two or three times as many bulbs to achieve a satisfactory lighting level. Light colors will increase the lighting level by reflecting and bouncing light around the room; dark colors will absorb light.

If you are going to work close to the lamp, you will not be interested in the general level of light in the room. For example, you may be using a floor lamp or desk lamp for reading or sewing. The light level obtained directly from a bare light bulb is obtained from the formula

$$\text{foot-candles} = \frac{\text{lumens per bulb}}{12 \times \text{distance squared}}$$

For example, if you were reading a newspaper located 3 feet from a 100 watt bulb (1710 lumens), the light level would be

$$\frac{1710}{12 \times 3 \times 3} = 15.8 \text{ foot-candles}$$

Normally, the lamp would have a shade that would help direct the light, so the amount of light falling on the newspaper would be increased to about 20 or 30 foot-canldes.

Note that the amount of light striking a surface decreases as the *square* of the distance; that is, the distance times itself. This means that when you move twice as far away from a source of light, you will receive only one-fourth as much light. Similarly, if you were only half as far away, you would receive four times as much light. To put this fact to work for you, consider a 30-inch-high table standing below a flush-mounted ceiling fixutre in a room with an 8-foot ceiling. In this common situation, the light level on the table top will be about twice as much as at floor level without the table.

18 Homeowner's Energy Tax Credit & Other Conservation Incentives

When Congress passed the National Energy Act in late 1978, it included a plan to allow homeowners to reduce their income tax bills when they install qualifying energy saving items. This plan is called the *Residential Energy Tax Credit*, and it presently includes energy saving expenditures made from April 20, 1977 until 1986. Under the tax credit, a portion of the cost of qualifying energy saving items directly reduces your individual income tax bill on Form 1040.

The tax credit is available if you install items such as a set-back thermostat, an electronic ignition system to replace a gas pilot light on your furnace, or a more efficient furnace burner system. The credit is not available for expenditures such as wood heating systems, heat pumps or replacement furnaces. Items that qualify for the credit are discussed in detail later in this chapter.

HOW THE CREDIT WORKS

Under the new residential energy credits, 15 to 30% of the cost of qualifying energy saving items may be used to decrease your income tax bill. Thus, when you take account of the income tax savings, the actual cost of the energy saving item is substantially reduced.

The tax credit that applies to the types of items we have covered in this book is a 15% tax credit. For every $1 you spend on qualifying energy saving items, you can reduce your income tax bill by 15 cents. That's a direct reduction—or credit—of your income tax bill of 15 cents per dollar spent, no matter what your tax bracket is. The tax *credit* is different than a *deduction*, so you get the credit even though you do not itemize your deductions.

There is a second energy tax credit. This is a higher credit of 30% of the cost of "renewable energy source" items such as solar energy, geothermal energy or widn energy items. Since we have not discussed these types of devices in this book, we will not dwell on the 30% energy tax credit here. But if you are considering installing any of these "renewable energy source" items, you should check with your tax preparer to get the details on this credit. It can be a substantial savings.

Two thousand dollars is the maximum amount of expenditures eligible for the 15% credit. Thus, your maximum tax credit is $300. This limit applies for the time you own your home. If you spent $500 and took a $75 tax credit this year, you may claim a maximum credit of $225 during the following years.

You might think of the tax credit limit as a sort of "bank." You are given a beginning balance of $300 in tax credits available for $2000 in expenditures. Year by year, as you take an energy tax credit on your income tax, you reduce your balance in the "bank" by the amount of credit you have declared.

You can declare the entire $300 tax credit limit in one year if you make $2000 in qualifying expenditures. Or you can stretch the $300 "balance" out over several years. If you move into a new home, you start fresh with a new $300 limit.

To figure the amount of your credit, you simply take the cost of the qualifying item, add in the cost of labor for installation (if you did not install the item yourself), and multiply the total cost by 15%. This is the amount of your tax credit.

For example, suppose you install an automatic set-back thermostat this year. Assume the cost of the thermostat is $75, and the cost of installation is $35. Your tax credit would be:

$$\$75 + \$35 = \$110 \textit{ total cost}$$
$$\$110 \times .15 = \$16.50 \textit{ tax credit}$$

Thus, your tax credit on this item is $16.50, which is added to your tax credit for any other qualifying purchases for this year. If you had no other expenditures, your income tax bill would be reduced by the amount of the credit, $16.50.

SOME BASIC RULES

In order to qualify for the energy tax credit, there are a number of rules you must meet. First, the energy saving items must be installed on your *principal* residence. Thus, installations on vacation homes do not qualify.

The items must be new. The purchase and installation of used items does not qualify.

If your total tax credits in a year are less than $10, you will not be eligible to claim any credit at all for that year. Therefore, if you are considering making several small energy saving purchases, you might want to group several of them together to be purchased in the same year to put you above the $10 minimum.

The item must have an expected life of at least three years to qualify for the tax credit. You may claim the tax credit only in the year in which the qualifying item was *installed*, not when purchased.

The home on which the item is installed must have been completed—or at least "substantially completed" according to Congress—before April 20, 1977. You should save all receipts, canceled checks and records of your expenditures to justify your claim of the tax credit in case of an audit.

If you were eligible for a tax redit but did not declare it in prior years, you cannot aggregate those expenditures with the current year and take the credit on this year's tax return. However, you may be able to file an amended return for those earlier years. If you believe you were eligible in prior years for a tax credit that you did not declare, check with your tax preparer.

ITEMS THAT QUALIFY

The Residential Energy Tax Credit plan that passed Congress in 1978 lists a number of items that qualify for the 15% tax credit. It is likely that in the future additional items will be added to this list, so some of the items that do not qualify for the credit as of this writing may qualify in time. Also, future Internal Revenue Service (IRS) regulations may specify certain models of items that qualify for the credit. As of this writing, no such regulations have been issued.

If you are considering installing an energy conserving item, it would be a good idea to contact your tax preparer or local IRS information office to determine if the item you are considering is covered under the tax credit. Qualifying and non-qualifying items may change rapidly, so you should check to be sure.

Under the tax credit plan, these items are listed as items that qualify for the 15% tax credit:

—Meters that display the cost of energy usage.

—Automatic flue dampers. These are devices installed in the furnace flue that automatically close the flue when the furnace is off.

—Electrical or mechanical ignition systems that replace the pilot light in a gas heating system.

—Oil or gas furnace replacement burners that increase combustion efficiency and reduce the amount of fuel consumed.

—Furnace duct or water pipe insulation.

—Automatic set-back thermostats that include a clock mechanism to automatically lower the temperature in the home.

There are a number of other items that also qualify for the tax credit such as insulation, storm windows, etc., but they are not connected with the subject matter of this book and will not be covered here.

These items do not qualify for the energy tax credit as of this writing: replacement furnaces or boilers, heat pumps, wood burning stoves or furnaces and the cost of annual furnace tuneups.

However, as we noted earlier, there are a number of regulations soon to be issued that may change the picture. Some of the items that do not now qualify may qualify by the time you install them. If you are considering expenditures on any of the above items, contact your tax preparer or your local IRS information office. You may be pleasantly surprised.

STATE AND LOCAL GOVERNMENT ENERGY INCENTIVES

As of this writing, the Energy Tax Credit is the most important federal incentive plan for energy conservation available to homeowners. However, many states have taken a keen interest in residential energy conservaton and have enacted plans of their own to encourage it. The plans vary widely from state to state, but most include tax breaks of some type for expenditures on qualifying items. Some states provide reductions of state income taxes. In others, no sales taxes are applied to purchases of qualifying items. In still others, property tax abatements or reductions are available. The best way to find out what incentives are available in your area is to contact your state's energy office.

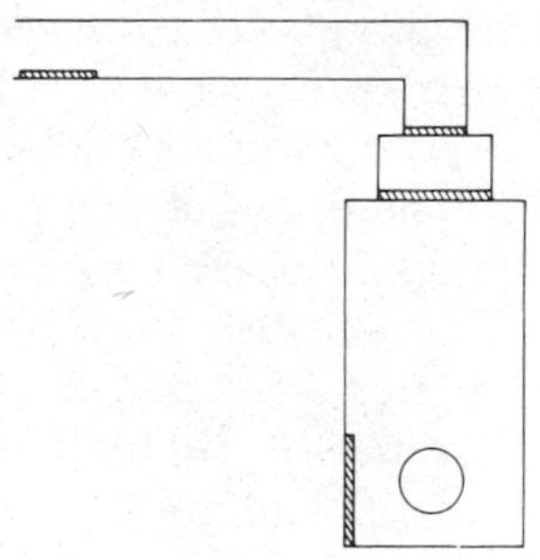

Glossary

air conditioner—A mechanical device used to cool the air in a closed space.

allen screw—A screw with a recessed hex-shaped head.

alternating current—The electric current used in homes and shops. The flow of current reverses every 120th of a second. One complete cycle of alternating current takes one 60th of a second.

ammeter—A meter used to measure the flow of electric current.

amperage—The flow of electricity is measured in amperes.

amperes—Also called amps. The unit of measurement for electric current.

automatic defrost—A feature found on most newer refrigerators and freezers in which ice and frost are removed from the evaporator coil automatically.

barometer—An instrument that measures atmospheric pressure.

bearing—A device used to reduce the friction of a rotating or moving part. Normally used around a rotating shaft.

bellhousing—The end housings of an electric motor that hold the bearings.

bimetal strip—A strip made with two different metals on each side of the strip, which is used to sense temperature. As the temperature changes, a bimetal strip will bend, opening or closing electrical contacts.

boiling point—The temperature at which a liquid evaporates to become a gas. Water boils at 212°F, or 100°C. A refrigerant might have a boiling point of —35°F.

breaker—See *circuit breaker*.

British thermal unit (BTU)—A measurement of heat energy. The amount of heat energy required to raise the temperature of one pound of water one degree Farenheit. Furnaces and air conditioners are sized in British thermal units.

BTU—British thermal unit.

burner—The part of a furnace where the fuel burns.

butane—A fuel used in gas furnaces.

capacitor—A device for storing an electric charge. Often used in starting and running electric motors.

capacitor-start motor—An electric motor that uses a capacitor to supply the additional torque to start the motor. The capacitor is taken out of the circuit (electrically) when the motor gets up to running speed.

carbon buildup—The smut and burned fuel particles left behind as a fuel burns. After a time, these particles collect and lower the performance of a fuel-burning device.

Celsius—A temperature scale used mostly for scientific calculations. The metric temperature scale. Water freezes at 0°C and boils at 100°C.

centrigrade—The celsius temperature scale.

charge—The amount of refrigerant in a refrigeration system. Also the amount of electricity stored.

circuit breaker—The protective device that opens an electrical circuit when too much current flows through the circuit.

closed-cell insulation—Plastic foam insulation that is constructed with millions of tiny cells fused together. The cells form individual dead-air spaces that reduce the transfer of heat energy.

closed circuit—An electrical circuit in which electricity can flow. All necessary connections are made and the circuit is not broken.

coil—A part of a heating or cooling system constructed with tubing in layers.

compound gauge—An instrument that measures both positive and negative pressure.

compressor—The unit in a refrigeration system that forces the refrigerant through the system.

condensate—Moisture that forms when warm air comes in contact with a cool surface.

condensation—Water that forms from water vapor in the air. When the temperature of the air drops, some of the water vapor in the air will change into water.

condense—The process of a gas, such as water vapor, changing into a liquid, such as water.

condenser—The part of the refrigeration system that releases heat energy into the outside air. The refrigerant enters the condenser as a gas and is put under pressure to return it to a liquid state. During the condensing process, heat energy is given off.

condenser fan—The fan that forces air over the condenser to help remove heat.

conduction—A method of heat transfer. Heat is transferred when a warm object touches a cool object. Ther term also refers to the passage of electrical current.

conductivity—The ability of a substance to transfer electricity or heat energy.

conductor—A substance that transfers heat or electricity easily.

convection—A method of heat transfer. Moving air picks up heat from nearby objects and transfers it to cool objects.

cooling load—Also called heat gain. The amount of heat energy that enters a structure during the cooling season.

current—Electricity flow.

damper—A device to control air flow.

dead-air space—A space in which air is not circulating.

defrost—To remove frost accumulation from evaporator coils.

defrost timer—A device on an automatic-defrost refrigerator that turns the refrigeration unit *off* and the heating strips *on* to defrost the unit.

degree day—A measure that expresses the average temperature difference relative to 65°F during a 24-hour day. If a certain day has an average temperature of 30°F, the degree days would be 35. Degree days are used to calculate heating and cooling loads and building requirements.

dehumidifier—A device that removes moisture from an enclosed area.

density—The weight of a substance per unit of volume. Measures the consistency of the substance.

design temperature—The hottest or coldest temperature in an area. Used for sizing heating and air conditioning systems.

dew point—The temperature where the water vapor in the air begins to condense. The dew point of a given sample of air will depend on the amount of moisture in that air.

dichlorodifluromethane—A refrigerant often known as R-12. Boiling point is—22°F at atmospheric pressure.

direct current—Electrical flow of current in one direciton only.

draft gauge—An instrument to measure air movement.

dry-bulb temperature—The temperature of an area not accounting for the effects of humidity and evaporation. The dry-bulb temperature is measured with an ordinary thermometer.

duct—A tube that takes air from the furnace or air conditioner into the living area of the house.

effective temperature—The total effect on the comfort of the human body of air movement, humidity, and temperature.

electron—A tiny part of an atom that carries a negative charge. Moving electrons transfer electricity.

electrostatic air filter—An air filter that removes dust and pollen from the air by using highly charged electric plates.

evaporation—The process of a liquid changing to a gas. Water changing into water vapor is an example of evaporation.

evaporative condenser—Water evaporation is used to cool the condenser and remove heat.

evaporator—The part of the refrigeration system where heat is absorbed. Refrigerant enters the evaporator as a liquid and evaporates, absorbing heat in the process.

evaporator fan—The fan that blows air over the evaporator.

expansion valve—The part of the refrigeration system that meters the refrigerant into the evaporator and allows the refrigerant to expand.

Fahrenheit—The temperature scale in common usage in the United States. Water freezes at 32°F and boils at 212°F.

filter—A device that removes dirt and dust particles from the air or from a fluid.

float valve—A valve opened and closed by a float. The float stays on top of the fluid in a basin, and the float valve controls the level of the fluid.

flue—A tube that allows gases formed during the burning process to escape.

freeze-up—The buildup of ice and frost on the refrigeration coil stops the air flow through the coil and renders the refrigeration system useless.

freezing—The changing of a liquid into a solid. For example, water freezes to form ice.

freezing point—The temperature at which a liquid becomes a solid. Water freezes at 32°F, or 0°C.

Freon—A DuPont Trademark for a group of refrigerants such as Freon 12 and Freon 22.

frost-free refrigerator—A refrigerator that has panels to hide the frost buildup on the evaporator coil and an automatic defrost cycle to remove the frost.

fuel—A substance that is consumed to generate energy.

fuel oil—A petroleum oil burned to produce heat energy.

fuse—A protective device containing a soft metal strip that melts to open the electrical circuit when too much current flows through the circuit.

gauge—An instrument that measures pressure. Compound gauges measure pressures above and below atmospheric pressure. High-pressure gauges measure positive pressures up to about 500 pounds per square inch (psi). Low-pressure gauges measure to about 50 psi, and vacuum gauges measure negative pressures. Gauges measure relative to atmospheric pressure. At atmospheric pressure (about 15 psi) a pressure gauge measures 0.

gas—The vapor state of a substance, such as methane (natural gas), propane, or butane. Sometimes used when referring to refrigerants or gasoline.

gasket—A flexible material that forms a leakproof seal when put between two contacting surfaces. Often used for sealing refrigerator and freezer doors.

gas valve—A device that controls the flow of gas in a gas furrnace.

ground—An electrical terminal or connection, such as a water pipe, metal housing, or case, that is at earth potential.

ground wire—An electrical wire connected from the frame of a unit to the electrical system ground. The system ground is attached to the earth. The purpose of the ground wire is to prevent shock if the unit has a short.

heat exchanger—Also called a heat chamber. The part of the furnace that houses the burners or the heating elements. Air is warmed as it passes through the heat exchanger.

heat gain—The amount of heat energy that enters the house from outside sources. Usually used in reference to summer cooling, but additional heat from outside sources during the winter is also heat gain. Often called cooling load.

heat leakage—The loss of heat.

heat load—Also called heat loss. The amount of heat lost through the structure of a building. Heat loads are measured in BTU per hour.

heat loss—see *heat load*.

heat pump—A reversible refrigeration unit that is able to both heat and cool. The condenser and evaporator coils reverse during the winter to transfer heat energy inside.

heat transfer—The movement of heat energy.

heat value—The amount of heat energy per unit supplied by a particular fuel.

horsepower—A unit of power sometimes used to measure the size of an air conditioner. One horsepower is roughly 8000 BTU of cooling capacity, depending on efficiency.

humidifier—A device that adds moisture to the air.

humidstat—A control that senses the humidity of the air and operates the humidifier.

humidity—The percentage of water vapor in the air.

infiltration air—Air that comes into a house unintentionally through cracks and openings in the structure.

insulating glass—Windows with two panes of glass sealed together in one sash. The extra air space between the panes reduces the heat flow through the window area.

insulation—Material that does not readily conduct heat energy.

jamp—The top and sides of a door or window frame that make contact with the door or the sash.

joists—The parallel framing boards that support the floor and ceiling. The joists run horizontally.

junction box—A box where electrical connections and splices are made.

K factor—A number indicating the amount of heat energy that will pass through a material. Also called the conductivity factor.
kilowatt—1000 watts. A unit of electrical power.

lath—Strips of building material, usually wood, attached to a wall to act as a nailing base. Used also as a plaster base.
limit control—A switch that interrupts or turns off electrical circuits when temperature limits are reached.
loose fill insulation—Insulation that is bought in a sack and poured into place.
LPG—Liquidified petroleum gas. Used as a heating fuel.

manifold—The part of the gas furnace that carries gas from the valve to the burners.
masonry wall—A wall constructed with stone, brick, concrete, or tile.
melting point—The temperature at which a solid substance begins to melt and form a liquid. Ice begins to melt into water at 32°F.
metric system—The scientific decimal system of measurement. Metric units include grams (weight), liters (volume), and meters (length).
mineral wool—A material used to make insulation, including loose fill insulation and insulation batting.
monochlorodifluoromethane—A refrigerant better known as R-22.

Natural gas—Methane, a heating fuel used in gas furnaces.

oil, fuel—A fuel used in oil-burning furnaces.
ohm—The unit of electrical resistance.
ohmmeter—An instrument that measures the resistance (in ohms) of a circuit. Also used to check for continuity in the circuit.
open circuit—An electrical circuit that does not have continuity, a broken connection.
orifice—The opening in the gas manifold or the oil burner nozzle that sprays the fuel into he burners. Also called a nozzle or jet.
overload—A condition in which too much electricity flows through an electrical circuit or device.

overload protector—A device that opens a circuit when too much current flows. Fuses and circuit breakers are common overload protectors.

parallel circuit—The most common way to wire a house. Each electrical load is wired in a parallel with the other loads in the circuit. When a circuit is wired in parallel, any load in the circuit can come on without the other loads being on.

particle board—A wood-like panel formed by pressing together wood shavings and wood particles.

parting stop—The part of the window assembly that separates the top and bottom sashes.

pilot light—The flame of a gas furnace that stays lit. The pilot light ignites the burners when the thermostat calls for heat.

plenum chamber—The chamber that connects the furnace to the duct system.

polystryrene—A closed-cell, plastic foam insulation with a high thermal resistance.

pressure regulator—A device that automatically maintains a given pressure in a refrigeration system.

propane—A fuel used in gas furnaces.

R-12—Refrigerant 12, dichlorodifluoromethane.

R-22—Refrigerant 22, Monochlorodifluoromethane.

radiation—A method of heat transfer. Infrared rays warm an object without contact from objects or air.

receptacle—An electrical outlet where a person plugs in appliances to connect them to a source of electricity.

refrigerant—The substance used in a refrigeration system to absorb and release heat energy. The refrigerant fills the tubes of the refrigeration system.

refrigerant charge—The amount of refrigerant contained in the system.

register—The cover at the end of the furnace duct. Grills and louvers in the register control the air flow.

relative humidity—The amount of water vapor in the air compared to the amount of water vapor that the air is capable of holding. Air at 50% relative humidity holds half as much water vapor as it is capable of holding.

relay—An electrical device used to control another circuit. A relay is often activated by a low-voltage circuit, and it then controls a higher voltage circuit such as a fan motor.

resistance, electrical—The difficulty with which electricity flows through a given material. Measured in ohms.

resistance heating—A method of generating heat energy from electrical energy. As electricity flows through a resistance, heat is produced. Baseboard heaters are one example of resistance heat.

resistance, thermal—The difficulty with which heat energy flows through a given material. The reciprocal of conductivity.

return air duct—The furnace duct that brings air from the living area to the furnace so it can be reheated.

R factor—The resistance of a material or an entire wall to the flow of heat. Insulation is rated in R values to show its resistance to heat flow.

rotor—The turning part of an electric motor.

rough opening—The opening in the framing of a house where windows and doors will later be installed.

sash—The frame holding the glass in a window.

saturation—The condition when a substance can hold no more moisture. Air is saturated at 100% relative humidity.

semiconductor—A material that will allow electricity to flow, but not as well as a conductor. Frequently used in resistance heating applications, such as baseboard heat or electric heaters.

series—A method of wiring electrical loads where the electricity must go through one load before it can go to the next one. When several loads are wired in series, all loads must be turned on before any will come on.

service valve—A device attached to the refrigeration system to check pressure in the system and to add refrigerant to the system.

shaded-pole motor—An ac motor that does not have separate windings for starting. Usually used as a fan motor. Speeds can be changed on the motor by changing the motor leads.

sheathing—The boards that cover the framing of a structure on the walls and roof.

short circuit—A circuit that does not follow the intended path. A common example is a loose wire touching a case or housing to cause a short circuit.

short cycling—A condition in which a heating or refrigeration system continually starts and stops after brief periods.

single-phase motor—An electric motor with start windings and run windings.

solar heat—Heat from the sun.

solar load—The number of BTU added to the cooling load of the structure by the sun.

split-phase motor—An electrical motor with start windings and run windings. The start windings are taken out of the circuit when the motor reaches its running speed.

squirrel cage fan—A fan with many fan blades parallel to the axis of the fan.

stack control—The device in an oil furnace that turns the burner off if the burner does not light.

starting relay—An electrical switch that connects and disconnects the electrical motor start windings.

start winding—The electric motor windings used when the motor is starting. The winding is disconnected when the motor gets up to running speed.

stator—The stationary section of an electric motor, usually containing the windings and iron pole pieces.

stoker—A mechanical device that feeds coal to a furnace.

studs—The parallel vertical boards that form the wall supports of a structure.

subfloor—The boards laid on top of the floor joists. The subfloor is between the finished floor and the floor joists.

suction line—The tube carrying refrigerant from the evaporator to the compressor. A low side line.

sweating—The formation of moisture droplets on a cold surface when it comes in contact with warmer air.

temperature, design—The hottest or cold temperature in an area. Used for sizing heating and air conditioning systems.

temperature difference—The difference in temperature between the inside and the outside of a home.

termite shield—A metal covering placed on a foundation wall to prevent termites from entering the house framing.

therm—A unit sometimes used for selling natural gas. One therm equals 100,000 BTU.

thermocouple—The device that senses the heat from the pilot light of a gas furnace and causes the gas valve to shut off if the pilot light goes out.

thermometer—An instrument used to measure temperatures.

thermostat—A device that controls a heating or cooling device by sensing the temperature of the surrounding air.

threshold—A wood, metal, or vinyl device that fills the space at the bottom of a door.

ton of refrigeration—Refrigeration equipment is sometimes measured in tons of refrigeration. One ton equals 12,000 BTU per hour.

transformer—An electric device that increases or decreases the voltage in a circuit, or which provides isolation between two circuits.

travelers—The wires in a three-way switch that run between the two such switches.

U factor—A number indicating the amount of heat that will pass through a wall. The U factor is a composite of the K factors of the individual materials in the wall.

vacuum—An area where the pressure is less than atmospheric pressure.

valve—A device that controls the flow of fluids and gases.

valve, expansion—A control in a refrigeration system that restricts the flow of refrigerant between the high-pressure evaporator side of the expansion valve and the low-pressure condenser side.

vapor—A substance in a gaseous state.

vapor barrier—A material that prevents moisture from passing through or condensing on the walls of a structure.

V-belt—A flexible drive belt with sides that slope together.

ventilation air—Air brought into a structure intentionally to circulate with the air in that structure.

volt—The unit of measure of electric force. The voltage in the circuit is what makes the current flow.

voltage drop—The condition existing when there is a drop of voltage in electrical lines.

voltmeter—An instrument that measures the voltage in an electrical circuit.

water-cooled condenser—A condenser that is cooled with water instead of air.

watt—The unit of electrical power found by multiplying the voltage times the amperes. Sometimes used to size baseboard heaters: 1 watt-hour equals 3413 BTU/hr.

wet-bulb temperature—The temperature of an area measured with a thermometer that has a wet cloth wrapped around the bulb. The evaporation of the water from the cloth measures the combined effects of humidity and temperature in the area.

weather stripping—Strips of material designed to be installed around doors and windows to stop the flow of air.

weep hole—The hole in the bottom edge of a storm window that allows moisture to drain from the enclosed space.

Appendix

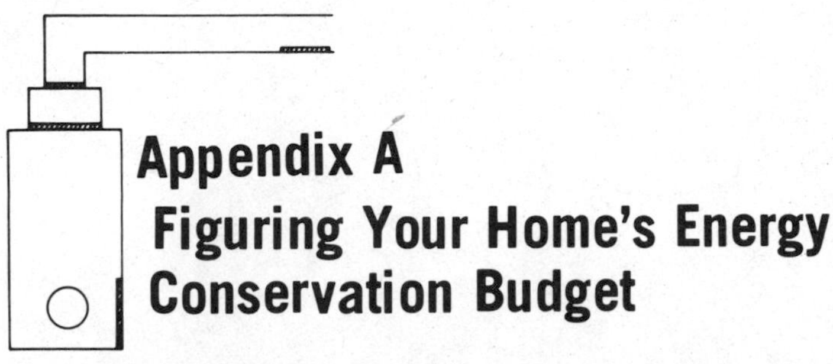

Appendix A
Figuring Your Home's Energy Conservation Budget

The following material is reprinted with permission from the U.S. Department of Commerce and National Bureau of Standards booklet, *Making the Most of Your Energy Dollars in Home Heating and Cooling*.

To find the "best combination" of energy conservation measures for your climate and fuel prices, use the tables on the following pages. This best combination gives you the largest, long run net savings on your heating and cooling costs for your investment. By comparing this best combination with what already exists in your house, you can figure out how much more needs to be added to bring your house up to the recommended levels.

The recommended improvements apply to most houses to the extent they can be installed without structurally modifying the house. Recommended improvements are based on sample costs given in Table A-9.

WORKSHEET INFORMATION

Follow the steps outlined below and fill in the information for your house on Worksheet A of Table A-1. We have filled in the information for a typical house located in Indianapolis, Indiana.

Locate your city on the heating zone map below (Fig A-1). (Our house is located in heating zone III.)

Locate your city on the cooling zone map below (Fig. A-2). (Our cooling zone is B).

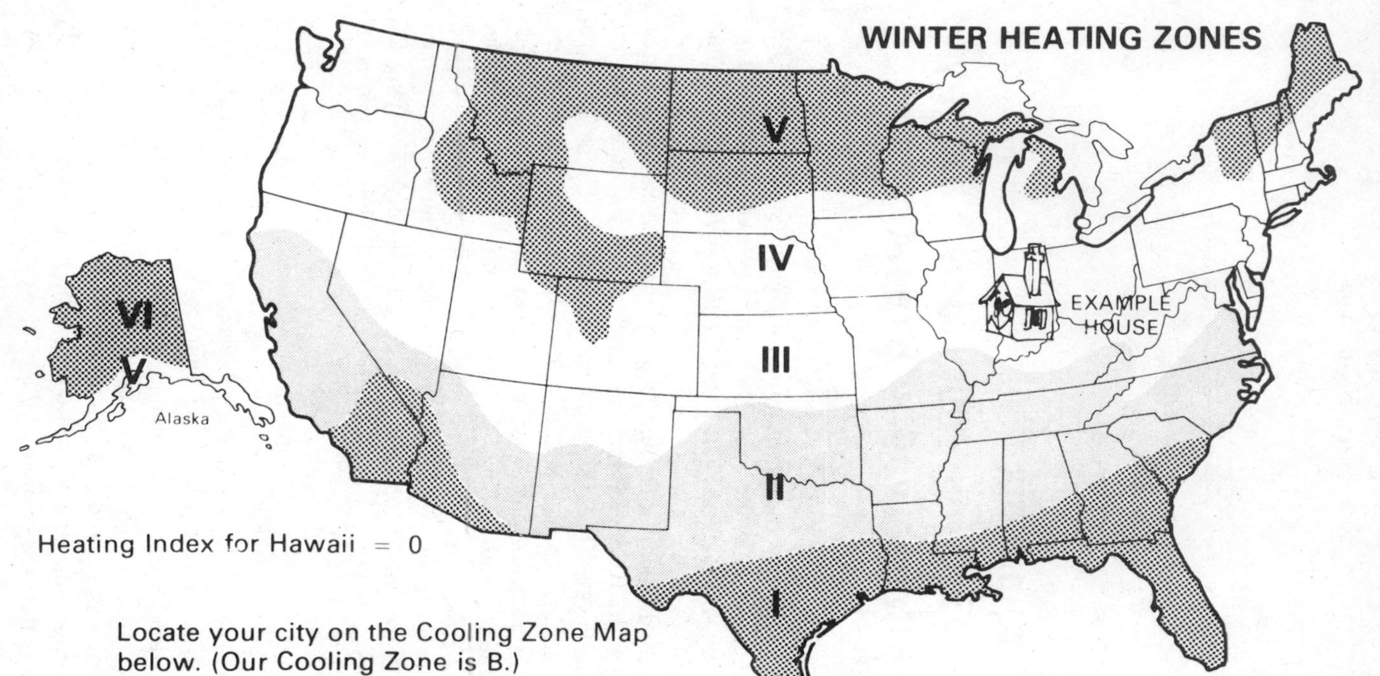

Fig. A-1. Find your city on this heating zone map.

Table A-1. Information in Worksheet A.

	EXAMPLE:	**YOUR CALCULATIONS:**
Climate:		
Heating Zone	III	
Cooling Zone	B	
Fuel Costs:		
Heating Energy	Oil	
Cost per Unit	34¢/gal.	
Cooling Energy	Electric	
Cost per Unit	4¢/KWH	
Indexes:		
Heating	20	
Cooling (Attic)	5	
Cooling (Wall)	2	
Heating + Cooling (Attic)	25	
Heating + Cooling (Wall)	22	

	BEST COMBINATION (Example)		BEST COMBINATION (Your Calculations)
Attic Insulation (Batt)	R-30 (10 inches)	FROM TABLE 4	
Duct Insulation (in attics)	R-16 (4 inches)	FROM TABLE 4	
Insulation Under Floors	R-19 (6 inches)	FROM TABLE 5	
Storm Doors	optional	FROM TABLE 5	
Wall Insulation (blown-in)	full-wall R-14 (3½ inches)	FROM TABLE 6	
Duct Insulation (in unheated crawl spaces, etc.)	R-16 (4 inches)	FROM TABLE 6	
Storm Windows (minimum size)	9 sq. ft.	FROM TABLE 6	
Weather strip and caulk windows and door frames	all		

Our house currently uses fuel oil at a cost of 34 cents a gallon to heat. It uses electricity a 4 cents a kilowatt hour to cool. Obtain your unit heating and cooling costs from the utility companies as follows. Tell your company how many therms (for gas) or kilowatt hours (for electricity) you use in a typical winter month and summer month (if you have air conditioning). The number of therms or kilowatt hours is on your monthly fuel bill. Ask for the cost of the last therm or kilowatt hour used, including all taxes, surcharges and fuel adjustments. For oil heating, the unit fuel cost is simply your average cost per gallon plus taxes, surcharges and fuel adjustments.

Locate your heating index from Table A-2 by finding the number at the intersection of your heating zone row and heating

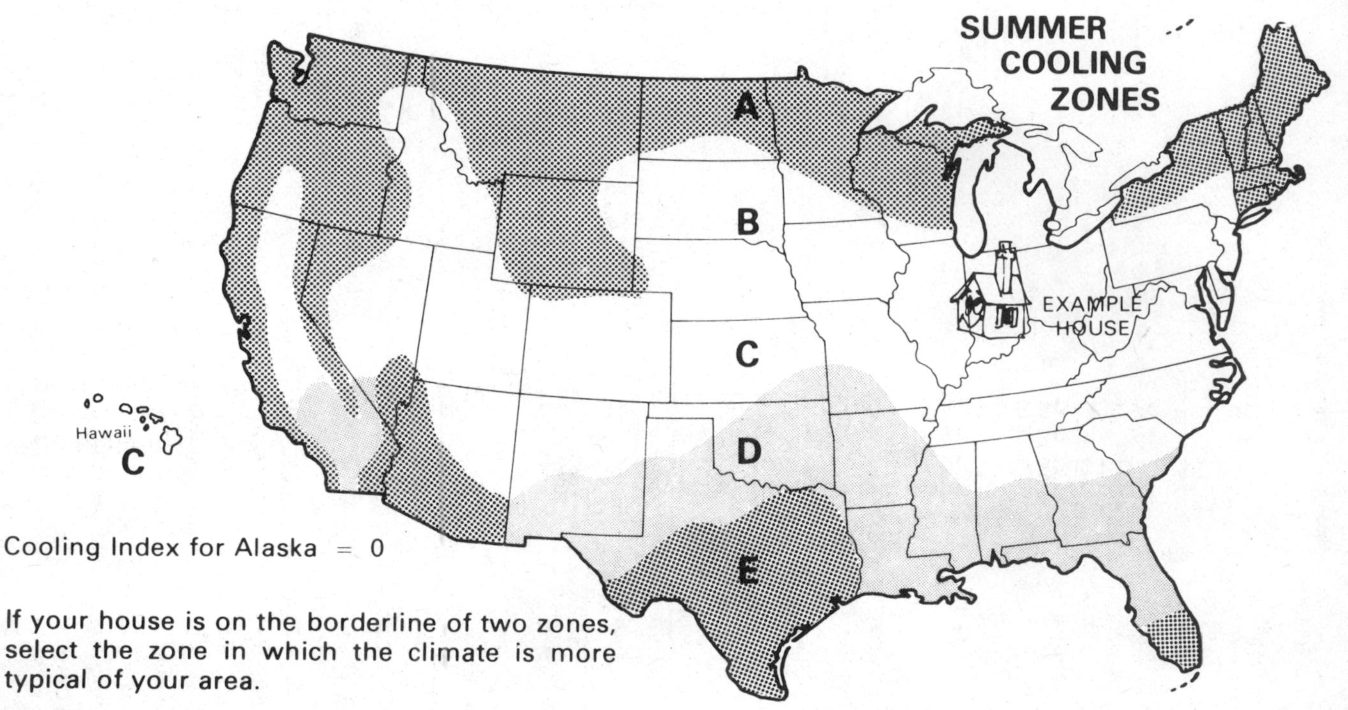

Cooling Index for Alaska = 0

If your house is on the borderline of two zones, select the zone in which the climate is more typical of your area.

Fig. A-2. Find your city on this cooling zone map.

Table A-2. Heating Index.

Type of fuel:	Cost per unit*									
Gas (therm)	9¢	12¢	15¢	18¢	24¢	30¢	36¢	54¢	72¢	90¢
Oil (gallon)	13¢	17¢	21¢	25¢	34¢	42¢	50¢	75¢	$1.00	$1.25
Electric (kWh)				1¢	1.3¢	1.6¢	2¢	3¢	4¢	5¢
Heat pump (kWh)	0.9¢	1.1¢	1.5¢	1.8¢	2.3¢	2.9¢	3.5¢	5.3¢	7¢	8.8¢
HEATING ZONE I	2	2	3	3	4	5	6	9	12	15
HEATING ZONE II	5	6	8	9	12	15	18	27	36	45
HEATING ZONE III	8	10	13	15	20	25	30	45	60	75
HEATING ZONE IV	11	14	18	21	28	35	42	63	84	105
HEATING ZONE V	14	18	23	27	36	45	54	81	108	135
HEATING ZONE VI	22	28	36	42	56	70	84	126	168	210

Table A-3. Cooling Index for Attics.

Type of air conditioner:		Cost per unit*						
Gas (therm)		9¢	12¢	15¢	18¢	24¢	30¢	36¢
Electric (kWh)		1.5¢	2¢	2.5¢	3¢	4¢	5¢	6¢
COOLING ZONE	A	0	0	0	0	0	0	0
	B	2	2	3	4	5	6	7
	C	3	5	6	7	9	11	13
	D	5	6	8	9	12	15	18
	E	7	9	11	14	18	23	27

fuel cost column (to the nearest cost shown). (Our house has a heating index of 20.)

If your house is air conditioned, or you plan to add air conditioning, find your cooling indexes. If your house is not air conditioned and it is not planned, you cooling indexes are zero.

Note: In Tables A-2 through A-4, if your fuel costs fall midway between two fuel costs listed, you can interpolate. For example, if our fuel oil costs were 38 cents a gallon, our Heating Index would be 22.5.

Locate your cooling Index for attics from Table A-3 by finding your cooling zone and cooling cost to the nearest cost shown. (Our house has a cooling index for attics of 5.)

Locate your cooling index for walls from Table A-4 by finding your cooling zone and cooling cost to the nearest cost shown in the table. (Our house has a cooling index for walls of 2.)

Find the sum of your heating index and cooling index for attics. (Our sum is 25.)

Find the sum of your heating index and cooling index for walls. (Our sum is 22.)

Table A-4. Cooling Index for Walls.

Type of air conditioner:		Cost per unit*						
Gas (therm)		9¢	12¢	15¢	18¢	24¢	30¢	36¢
Electric (kWh)		1.5¢	2¢	2.5¢	3¢	4¢	5¢	6¢
COOLING ZONE	A	0	0	0	0	0	0	0
	B	1	1	2	2	2	3	4
	C	2	2	3	4	5	6	7
	D	3	3	4	5	7	8	10
	E	4	5	6	8	10	13	15

Table A-5. Attic Floor Insulation and Attic Duct Insulation.

INDEX	ATTIC INSULATION	Approximate Thickness			DUCT INSULATION*	
Heating Index Plus Cooling Index for Attics	R-Value	Mineral Fiber Batt/Blanket	Mineral Fiber Loose-Fill**	Cellulose Loose-Fill**	R-Value	Approximate Thickness
1-3	R-0	0"	0"	0"	R-8	2"
4-9	R-11	4"	4-6"	2- 4"	R-8	2"
10-15	R-19	6"	8-10"	4- 6"	R-8	2"
16-27	R-30***	10"	13-15"	7- 9"	R-16	4"
28-35	R-33	11"	14-16"	8-10"	R-16	4"
36-45	R-38	12"	17-19"	9-11"	R-24	6"
46-60	R-44	14"	19-21"	11-13"	R-24	6"
61-85	R-49	16"	22-24"	12-14"	R-32	8"
86-105	R-57	18"	25-27"	14-16"	R-32	8"
106-130	R-60	19"	27-29"	15-17"	R-32	8"
131—	R-66	21"	29-31"	17-19"	R-40	10"

* Use Heating Index only if ducts are not used for air conditioning. ** High levels of loose-fill insulation may not be feasible in many attics. ***Assumes that joists are covered; otherwise use R-22.

Energy savings result from decreasing the heat flow through the exterior shell of the building. The resistance, or "R," value of insulation is the measure of its ability to decrease heat flow. Two different kinds of insulation may have the same thickness, but the one with the higher R value will perform better. For that reason, our recommendations are listed in terms of R values with the approximate corresponding thickness. R values for different thicknesses of insulation are generally made available by the manufacturers.

Find the resistance value of insulation recommended for your attic and around attic ducts from Table A-5. (For our house the recommended resistance value is R-30 for attic floors and R-16 for ducts.)

Find the recommended level of insulation for floors over unheated areas from Table A-6. (Our house should have R-19.) Using Table A-6, check to see whether storm doors are economical for your home. Storm doors listed as optional may be economical if the doorway is heavily used during the heating season.

Find the recommended level of insulation for your walls and ducts in unheated areas from Table A-7. (Our house should have full-wall insulation if none existed previously and R-16 insulation around ducts.) Table A-7 also shows the minimum economical storm window size in square feet for triple-track storm windows. (Our house should have storm windows on all windows 9 square feet in size or larger where storm windows can be used.)

Regardless of where you live or your cost of energy, it is almost always economical to install weatherstripping on the inside around doors and windows where possible and to caulk on the outside around doors and window frames—if you do it yourself. This is especially true for windows and doors which have noticeable drafts.

Table A-6. Insulation Under Floors and Storm Doors.

INDEX	INSULATION UNDER FLOORS*		STORM DOORS
Heating Index Only	R-Value	Mineral Fiber Batt Thickness	
0-7	0**	0"**	None
8-15	11**	4"**	None
16-30	19	6"	Optional
31-65	22	7"	Optional
66—	22	7"	On all doors

* If your furnace and hot water heater are located in an otherwise unheated basement, cut your Heating Index in half to find the level of floor insulation.

**In Zone I and II R-11 insulation is usually economical under floors over open crawlspaces and over garages; in Zone I insulation is not usually economical if crawlspace is closed off.

Table A-7. Wall Insulation, Duct Insulation and Storm Windows.

INDEX Heating Index Plus Cooling Index for Walls	WALL INSULATION (blown-in)	INSULATION AROUND DUCTS IN CRAWLSPACES AND IN OTHER UNHEATED AREAS (EXCEPT ATTICS)* Resistance and Approximate Thickness	STORM WINDOWS (Triple-Track) Minimum Economical Window Size
0-10	None	R-8 (2")	none
11-12	Full-Wall Insulation Approximately R-14	R-8 (2")	20 sq. ft.
13-15		R-8 (2")	15 sq. ft.
16-19		R-16(4")	12 sq. ft.
20-28		R-16(4")	9 sq. ft.
29-35		R-16(4")	6 sq. ft.
36-45		R-24(6")	4 sq. ft.
46-65		R-24(6")	All windows**
66—		R-32(8")	All windows**

* Use Heating Index only if ducts are not used for air conditioning. **Windows too small for triple-track windows can be fitted with one-piece windows.

Table A-8. Information in Worksheet B.

WORKSHEET B

OUR EXAMPLE:

ATTIC INSULATION

1. Attic area (sq. ft.)	1200	
2. Recommended level	R-30 (10")	
3. Existing level	R-11 (4")	
4. Add	R-19 (6")	
5. Cost/sq. ft.	$.25	
6. Total cost (1 × 5)		$300

WALL INSULATION (BLOWN-IN)

1. Wall area (sq. ft.)	900	
2. Recommended level	full-wall	
3. Existing level	some	
4. Add	0	
5. Cost/sq. ft.	$.60	
6. Total cost (1 × 5)		0

FLOOR INSULATION

1. Floor area (sq. ft.)	1200	
2. Recommended level	R-19 (6")	
3. Existing level	0"	
4. Add	R-19 (6")	
5. Cost/sq. ft.	$.30	
6. Total cost (1 × 5)		$360

DUCT INSULATION (ATTIC)

1. Length (ft.)	30'	
2. Perimeter (ft.)	2'	
3. Area (1 × 2 × 1.5)*	90 sq. ft.	
4. Recommended level	R-16 (4")	
5. Existing level	R-8 (2")	
6. Add	R-8 (2")	
7. Cost/sq. ft.	$.30	
8. Total cost (3 × 7)		$27

YOUR ESTIMATES:

ATTIC INSULATION

1. Attic area (sq. ft.)	____	
2. Recommended level	____	
3. Existing level	____	
4. Add	____	
5. Cost/sq. ft.	____	
6. Total cost (1 × 5)		____

WALL INSULATION (BLOWN-IN)

1. Wall area (sq. ft.)	____	
2. Recommended level	____	
3. Existing level	____	
4. Add	____	
5. Cost/sq. ft.	____	
6. Total cost (1 × 5)		____

FLOOR INSULATION

1. Floor area (sq. ft.)	____	
2. Recommended level	____	
3. Existing level	____	
4. Add	____	
5. Cost/sq. ft.	____	
6. Total cost (1 × 5)		____

DUCT INSULATION (ATTIC)

1. Length (ft.)	____	
2. Perimeter (ft.)	____	
3. Area (1 × 2 × 1.5)*	____	
4. Recommended level	____	
5. Existing level	____	
6. Add	____	
7. Cost/sq. ft.	____	
8. Total cost (3 × 7)		____

DUCT INSULATION (OTHER AREAS)

1. Length (ft.) 30'
2. Perimeter (ft.) 2'
3. Area (1 · 2 · 1.5)* 90 sq. ft.
4. Recommended level R-16 (4")
5. Existing level 0"
6. Add R-16 (4")
7. Cost sq. ft. $.50
8. Total cost (3 · 7) $45

STORM WINDOWS (over 9 sq. ft.)

size (sq. ft.)	number	cost each	sub-total
20	2	$35	$70
15	4	30	120
12	3	30	90
9	2	30	60

Total cost $340

STORM DOORS

1. Doors Needed 1 (Optional)
2. Cost per door $75
3. Total cost $75

WEATHER STRIPPING (MATERIALS ONLY)

1. Linear feet 200
2. Cost per foot $.10
3. Total cost $20

CAULKING (MATERIALS ONLY)

1. Variable costs $20-50
2. Estimated cost $33

Total cost of all improvements $1200

DUCT INSULATION (OTHER AREAS)

1. Length (ft.) ______
2. Perimeter (ft.) ______
3. Area (1×2×1.5)* ______
4. Recommended level ______
5. Existing level ______
6. Add ______
7. Cost/sq. ft. ______
8. Total cost (3×7) ______

STORM WINDOWS

size (sq. ft.)	number	cost each	sub-total

Total cost ______

STORM DOORS

1. Doors needed ______
2. Cost per door ______
3. Total cost ______

WEATHER STRIPPING (MATERIALS ONLY)

1. Linear feet ______
2. Cost per foot ______
3. Total cost ______

CAULKING (MATERIALS ONLY)

1. Variable costs ______
2. Estimated cost ______

Total cost of all improvements ______

*1.5 is an adjustment factor for increased width of insulation needed to fit around duct.

are substantially less than ours, you will want to go beyond the recommended level.

Similarly, if R-30 insulation in the attic costs 65 cents per square foot instead of our 39 cents price, the index number of 25 for attic insulation would be adjusted to

$$\frac{25 \times 39c}{65c} = 15$$

From Table A-5 we find that R-19 insulation is now recommended instead of R-30. In other words, if your costs are substantially greater than ours, you may want to use a little less than the recommended level.

YOUR DIVIDENDS GROW

You may not have thought about energy conservation this way, but investing in these improvements is better than most alternative low-risk, long-term investments you can make. When you invest in energy conservation improvements, you immediately begin to earn dividends in the form of reduced utility bills. These dividends not only pay off your investment, but they pay "interest" as well. And unlike dividends from many other investments, these are not subject to income taxes.

At current fuel prices, the recommended improvements will pay for themselves many times over during the life of the house. The energy conservation improvements for a house similar to our example house in Zone III B will pay for themselves in seven to nine years—and even more quickly if the improvements are installed by the homeowner. If the index numbers were higher, the improvements are installed by the homeowner. If the index numbers were higher, the improvements also would pay off more quickly. For example, with a heating index of 50, instead of 20, the recommended improvements (R-44 attic insulation, full-wall insulation, R-22 floor insulation, R-24 duct insulation, and storm windows on all suitable windows) would take only three to four years to pay back for this same house. Similarly, the more poorly insulated the house is to begin with, the shorter the payback period.

On the other hand, if the heating index number were less than 20 or if the house were better insulated to begin with, the payback period would be a little longer.

More important than the payback period are net savings. In our example house, R-19 insulation in the attic would cost less and pay back faster than the recommended R-30. But the long run net

You now know your best combination of energy conservation improvements. Of course, the size of your investment depends on your existing insulation and the size of your house.

In addition, some of the recommended improvements in this booklet are not appropriate for all houses. For instance, insulation cannot be added under floors in houses built on concrete slabs. In such cases, the other recommended improvements should still be added to the extent indicated in this booklet. Similarly, R-30 insulation may be recommended for your attic although only R-19 mat fit at the eaves or in areas where the attic is floored. In this case, you should still put R-30 insulation wherever it fits.

Use Worksheet B in Table A-8 and Table A-9 (or your own cost information) to calculate how much you need to add to reach your best combination and how much this will cost. We have provided this information on Worksheet B in Table A-8 for our example house. Our house only has R-11 attic insulation, some wall insulation, and R-8 attic duct insulation to begin with. To reach our best combination, the improvements would cost about $1200.

If you find that the costs of any of the improvements to your house are substantially different from the sample costs in Table A-9, you can easily compensate for the difference.

Take the index number appropriate for the improvement in question, multiply this by our sample cost, and divide the result by your cost. This will give you an adjusted index number with which you can find the best level of investment for that particular improvement.

$$\frac{\text{Original Index} \times \text{Our Cost}}{\text{Your Cost}} = \text{Adjusted Index}$$

EXAMPLE

For our example house, we might find that we can get good quality storm windows for $20 apiece instaed of our $30 estimate. Our index number for storm windows was 22. Our new adjusted index number for storm windows would be:

$$\frac{22 \times \$30}{\$20} = 33$$

Using our adjusted index number of 33 we find that storm windows are economical on all windows 6 square feet in size or larger, instead of 9 square feet in size. In other words, if your costs

Table A-9. Sample Improvement Costs.

These sample costs were used in estimating the best combination of energy conservation improvements for the various climates and fuel prices covered in this booklet. They include an allowance for commercial installation, except in the case of weather stripping and caulking which is considered to be a do-it-yourself project. While these costs are typical of 1975 prices, there may be considerable variation among specific materials, geographic locations, and suppliers. It usually is worth your time to obtain several estimates for materials and installation before making any purchase. Many of these items can be purchased at substantial discounts if you watch the advertised sales. Considerable savings may be made by installing these yourself, where possible.

ATTIC INSULATION
(ALL MATERIALS)

Installed cost per square foot of attic:

R-11 = 15¢ R-44 = 57¢
R-19 = 25¢ R-49 = 64¢
R-22 = 29¢ R-57 = 74¢
R-30 = 39¢ R-60 = 78¢
R-33 = 43¢ R-66 = 86¢

FLOOR INSULATION
(MINERAL FIBER BATT)

Installed cost:

R-11 = 20¢
R-19 = 30¢
R-22 = 34¢

WALL INSULATION
(ALL MATERIALS)

Installed cost = 60¢ per square foot of net wall area*

DUCT INSULATION
(MINERAL FIBER BLANKET)

Installed cost per square foot of material:

R-8	= 30¢	R-32	= 90¢
R-16	= 50¢	R-40	= $1.10
R-24	= 70¢		

STORM WINDOWS
(TRIPLE-TRACK, CUSTOM-MADE AND INSTALLED**)

Up to 100 united inches (height + width)	= $30.00
Greater than 100 united inches	= $30.00 + $.60 per united inch greater than 100″

STORM DOORS
(CUSTOM-FITTED AND INSTALLED**)

All sizes = $75.00

WEATHER STRIPPING AND CAULKING

Prices vary according to material used. Use the most durable materials available.

* Price includes allowance for painting inside surface of exterior walls with water vapor-resistant paint.

**Prices may be considerably less for stock sizes, homeowner-installed.

savings are greater with R-30 because each additional resistance unit—up to the recommended level—pays back more than it costs. The best combinations shown in this booklet have varying payback periods, but they always yield the *greatest net savings* over the long run.

Even though utility bills rise as energy prices increase, the rise will be much less than it would have been without increased insulation. In fact, you might think of energy insulation. In fact, you might think of energy conservation improvements as a hedge against inflation. (Are you beating inflation with your after-tax dividends from other investments?)

Even if you don't plan to live in your house long enough to reap the full return on your investment in the form of lowered utility bills, it will probably still pay to invest in energy conservation improvements now. Because of higher energy prices, a well-insulated house is likely to sell more quickly and at a higher price than a poorly insulated house that costs a lot to heat and cool. Show your low fuel bills to prospective buyers. They will find the small increase in monthly mortgage payments will be more than offset by monthly fuel bill savings, possibly bringing the cost of living in the house within their reach. The increased value of the house alone might cover the cost to you of making the investments in energy conservation improvements.

CAN YOU AFFORD YOUR INVESTMENTS?

You may have found that the amount of money needed to finance the best combination of energy conservation improvements is more than you can pay for all at once. If this is the case, you might consider taking a low-cost, long-term home improvement loan.

Whether it is to your advantage to borrow money depends to some extent on the existing condition of your house. A house that is poorly insulated compared to the levels recommended in this booklet requires a greater investment in energy conservation than a house which is close to these recommended levels. However, the poorly insulated house will yield much greater savings on fuel bills after the improvements are made. This means that your investment will generally pay back fast enough to cover the monthly payments on a long-term home improvement loan. Once the loan is paid off, the additional savings are free and clear!

If you feel you just can't afford to invest in the best combination of energy conservation improvements for your house, you can still make the most of a limited energy conservation budget. Keep

Table A-10. Some Insulation Facts.

	LESS COSTLY COMBINATION	BEST COMBINATION
Attic insulation (batts)	R-19	R-30
Duct insulation (attics)	R-8	R-16
Floor insulation	R-11	R-19
Storm doors	none	optional
Wall insulation (blown-in)	full-wall	full-wall
Duct insulation (other areas)	R-8	R-16
Storm windows (minimum size)	12 square feet	9 square feet

in mind the idea of a "balanced" combination—not spending too much on one improvement in relation to the other improvements.

To find this less costly, but still balanced, combination of improvements, decrease each of the index numbers you used in Tables A-5 through A-7 by the same percentage, say 20%. Use the new index numbers to find a new combination of improvements in these tables. Keep reducing your index numbers by the same percentage increments until you reach a balanced combination you can afford.

In the example house, we used index numbers of 25 in Table A-5, 20 in Table A-6 and 22 in Table A-7. Reducing these by 40 percent, for instance, gives us new index numbers of 15, 12, and 13, respectively. Using these numbers gives us the following balanced combination in Table A-10.

Based on our existing level of insulation, this new combination would cost about $750, compared to $1200 for the best combination. If this is still more than we can afford, we might reduce our index numbers by 50% or even 80%.

On the other hand, if you think that you will eventually add all the recommended improvements in your best combination, but that it will take a year or two to get them all in, it is usually best to start with those which provide the first level of protection—such as insulation in places where none exists, storm windows, and weather stripping and caulking, where you have poorly fitting windows and doors. Add the others as you can afford them.

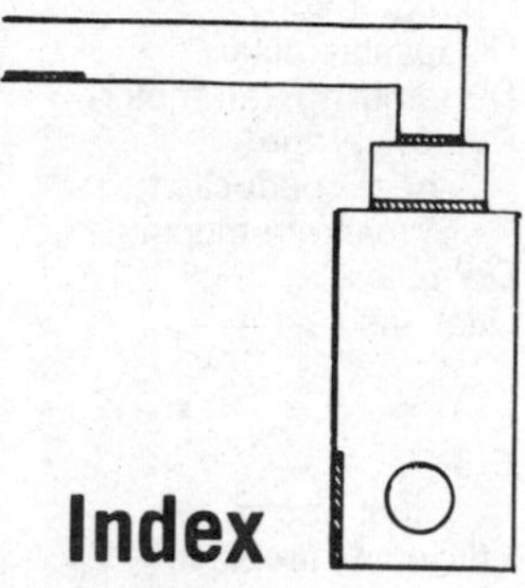

Index

Z